Page deliberately le\

Instructors,
what if you could...
...get your students to *actually* read the text?
...focus on what you do best: teaching.
...set up your course in minutes?
"Student performance after implementing Vantage is incredible...."
—Karen Deeming
Instructor, Merced College
Choose to use this textbook on the Vantage learning platform
See why you'll love Vantage at
collegepublishing.sagepub.com/vantage
Sage Vantage
engage. learn. soar.
Sage Vantage is not available for purchase outside of the United States.
Gargiulo, An Introduction to Young Children With Delays and Disabilities 6e, 9781071859216

An Introduction to Young Children With Delays and Disabilities

Sixth Edition

This book is dedicated with deep appreciation and much love to my family. Thank you for your continual support, encouragement, and understanding during this writing process. You give purpose and meaning to my life and remain, as always, my inspiration to help others and advocate for those who are the least among us.

RMG

This book is dedicated to my mother, GrandBetty, an ever-present role model who encouraged and supported me throughout my career. It was through her guidance that I learned the importance of deep and abiding relationships within the family and community. To GrandBetty, I say thank you and hope that I pass her strong convictions and influence on to my dear daughter, AK. With much love to my family and colleagues,

JLK

As a global academic publisher, Sage is driven by the belief that research and education are critical in shaping society. Our mission is building bridges to knowledge—supporting the development of ideas into scholarship that is certified, taught, and applied in the real world.

Sage's founder, Sara Miller McCune, transferred control of the company to an independent trust, which guarantees our independence indefinitely. This enables us to support an equitable academic future over the long term by building lasting relationships, championing diverse perspectives, and co-creating social and behavioral science resources that transform teaching and learning.

An Introduction to Young Children With Delays and Disabilities

Birth Through Age Eight

Sixth Edition

Richard M. Gargiulo

University of Alabama at Birmingham

Jennifer L. Kilgo

University of Alabama at Birmingham

Sage

FOR INFORMATION:

2455 Teller Road
Thousand Oaks, California 91320
E-mail: order@sagepub.com

1 Oliver's Yard
55 City Road
London, EC1Y 1SP
United Kingdom

Unit No. 323-333, Third Floor, F-Block
International Trade Tower
Nehru Place, New Delhi – 110 019
India

18 Cross Street #10-10/11/12
China Square Central
Singapore 048423

Printed in the United States of America

Library of Congress Cataloging-in-Publication Data

Names: Gargiulo, Richard M., author. | Kilgo, Jennifer Lynn, author.

Title: An introduction to young children with delays and disabilities : birth through age eight / Richard M. Gargiulo, University of Alabama at Birmingham, Jennifer L. Kilgo, University of Alabama at Birmingham.

Other titles: Introduction to young children with special needs

Description: Sixth edition. | Thousand Oaks, California : SAGE Publications, Inc, [2025] | Includes bibliographical references and index.

Identifiers: LCCN 2024030620 (print) | LCCN 2024030621 (ebook) | ISBN 9781071859216 (paperback) | ISBN 9781071859186 (epub)

Subjects: LCSH: Children with disabilities—Education (Early childhood) | Early childhood special education.

Classification: LCC LC4019.3 .G27 2025 (print) | LCC LC4019.3 (ebook) | DDC 371.9—dc23/eng/20240705

LC record available at https://lccn.loc.gov/2024030620

LC ebook record available at https://lccn.loc.gov/2024030621

Acquisitions Editor: Leah Fargotstein

Content Development Editor: Kenzie Offley

Production Editor: Veronica Stapleton Hooper

Copy Editor: Diana Breti

Typesetter: diacriTech

Cover Designer: Candice Harman

Cover Artist: Fran Bostick

Marketing Manager: Victoria Velasquez

This book is printed on acid-free paper.

24 25 26 27 28 10 9 8 7 6 5 4 3 2 1

BRIEF CONTENTS

DETAILED CONTENTS

Instructors,
what if your students...
...truly enjoyed their reading?
...were better prepared for class?
...felt invested in their learning?
"Interactive, engaging, and simple to use."
—Alyssa Salazar, Student
University of North Texas
Choose to use this textbook on the Vantage learning platform
See why you'll love Vantage at
collegepublishing.sagepub.com/vantage
Sage Vantage
engage. learn. soar.
Sage Vantage is not available for purchase outside of the United States.
Gargiulo, An Introduction to Young Children With Delays and Disabilities 6e, 9781071859

PREFACE

As the title indicates, *An Introduction to Young Children With Delays and Disabilities: Birth Through Age Eight* offers a foundation for professionals who will serve young children with delays and disabilities, from birth through eight years old, and their families. As early intervention/early childhood special education (EI/ECSE) has evolved over the past fifty years, it is increasingly apparent that a comprehensive book is needed to present an overview of this field, which provides services to infants, toddlers, preschoolers, and early primary children with delays and disabilities and their families.

As professors at a university with a program in EI/ECSE, we have experienced the need for a textbook to afford a strong foundation for the multifaceted components of the EI/ECSE field. Some introductory special education texts focus exclusively on infants and toddlers, some on preschoolers, and some on children from birth through age five. Others address children from birth through age twenty-one, with limited emphasis placed on the early years. Because the field of early childhood is recognized by the Division for Early Childhood (DEC) of the Council for Exceptional Children (CEC) and the National Association for the Education of Young Children (NAEYC) as including children from birth through age eight, this book is designed to specifically emphasize children in this age range and their families.

We acknowledge that the early years of a child's life constitute the most critical period of development. Early interventionists/early childhood special educators, general early childhood educators, related services personnel (e.g., physical therapists, occupational therapists, and speech–language pathologists), and other professionals who work with young children must understand that what happens during the earliest years of a child's life significantly impacts later development and learning. A growing number of young children, however, encounter less than optimal situations and circumstances during the early years. Conditions such as congenital disabilities; environmental factors such as poverty, trauma, abuse and neglect; and cultural and linguistic backgrounds often place some children at risk for future delays and disabilities. Early intervention and early childhood special education services were established based on supporting evidence that the earlier children receive services, the better their outcomes. In addition, early intervention and early childhood special education services were developed based on evidence that families who receive services earlier are better equipped to provide support for their children and advocate for them later in life.

As we have described, the focus of this book is on infants and young children from birth through age eight, some of whom have been identified as having disabilities, others who have developmental delays, and still others who are at risk for developmental issues due to exposure to adverse genetic, biological, or environmental conditions. These children with delays and disabilities are members of families, programs, schools, teams, communities, and society. They have the right to appropriate services, beginning with early intervention and early childhood special education designed to meet their individual needs and prepare them for the future. Hopefully, this textbook will provide the foundation for comprehensive, appropriate services for young children with delays and disabilities and their families within the context of their natural environments and communities.

ORGANIZATIONAL FEATURES AND TERMINOLOGY

There are four major parts to this book. Part I, *Perspectives, Policies, and Practices of Early Childhood Special Education*, provides a foundation to frame the field of early intervention/early childhood special education. Part I introduces the field as well as its legal and historical bases. This part examines the multifaceted influences that have shaped the field of early intervention and early childhood special education in addition to service delivery options for educating young children with delays and disabilities.

Part II, Assessment and Planning for Young Children With Delays and Disabilities, includes two chapters that address the processes involved in assessment, planning, and curriculum. Part III, Organization and Intervention for Young Children With Delays and Disabilities, is composed of three chapters that focus on designing, adapting, and organizing the learning environment and implementing instructional programs for young children with delays and disabilities. Part IV, Contemporary Issues and Challenges in Early Childhood Special Education, discusses the issues and challenges that exist in the field today, as well as future directions.

We recognize that words matter. Therefore, throughout this text, we use "person first" language, which means that we discuss *children with disabilities* rather than *disabled children*. By placing the noun before the adjective, we hope the reader realizes that the emphasis is correctly on the humanity and dignity of the child, rather than solely on their disability. This shift in language aims to promote inclusivity, respect, and empowerment for individuals with disabilities. In all cases, however, it is essential to use the terminology preferred by the person with a disability and their family.

The term *special needs* is discouraged in discussions about individuals with delays and disabilities because it can be seen as overly generalizing and potentially stigmatizing, as it suggests that individuals with delays and disabilities have needs that are fundamentally different from those without disabilities. Additionally, it can be perceived as patronizing, implying that individuals with disabilities are somehow less capable or independent. Instead, the preference is to use more person-centered language that emphasizes the individual, rather than their disability.

KEY FEATURES OF THE TEXT

This edition has several unique features described below.

- **Vignettes** about three young children and their families help to illustrate how theory is translated to practice in the field of early intervention/early childhood special education.
- The **Making Connections** feature throughout the text highlights the three young children of different ages and their families in the vignettes and provides insight into the services required to meet the unique needs of each child and family.
- Each chapter includes contemporary information, topics, evidence-based practices, and research services for young children with delays and disabilities and their families. This includes suggestions for incorporating assistive technology in the learning environments of young children.
- EI/ECSE Standards are identified and discussed in individual chapters.
- DEC Recommended Practices are identified and discussed in individual chapters with examples provided.
- A glossary of key terms in Spanish is located after the English glossary.

Readers of this text will encounter certain recurring themes that reflect our professional beliefs and values about programs and services for young children with delays and disabilities and their families. These themes, along with certain basic premises, provide the theoretical and philosophical foundations for this book. The following list depicts those orientations that we consider requisites for delivering high-quality services. We value, support, and encourage the following:

- Services in natural and inclusive environments
- Family-centered services
- Authentic assessment
- Evidence-based decision making

- A blended approach to curriculum to foster inclusion
- Cultural and linguistic awareness, sensitivity, and responsiveness
- Responsive intervention and embedded instruction
- Inclusive practices
- Collaboration and teaming
- A transdisciplinary service delivery model
- Comprehensive services for young children with delays and disabilities and their families

NEW TO THIS EDITION

As described previously, the sixth edition of this textbook has undergone significant modifications. This edition is filled with updated information, photos, vignettes, examples, reflections, applications, references, and resources. Also addressed in this edition of the textbook are the latest developments in and influences on the field of early intervention and early childhood special education including legislative and philosophical influences as well as evidence-based practices.

A notable new addition to this book is the ground-breaking *Initial Practice-Based Professional Preparation Standards for Early Interventionists/Early Childhood Special Educators* developed by DEC and CEC in 2020 (referred to as the EI/ECSE Standards). The EI/ECSE Standards represent the first stand-alone standards to specifically focus on the preparation and professional development of early interventionists and early childhood special educators to work with young children ages birth through eight with delays and disabilities and their families. The EI/ECSE standards are grounded in current evidence-based practices in EI/ECSE and also reflect professional and family wisdom and values. The book highlights how the EI/ECSE Standards provide teacher preparation and professional development programs with an increased opportunity for growth and collaboration to impact quality inclusive services for young children. The EI/ECSE Standards cover a wide range of content, including (a) Child Development and Early Learning; (b) Partnering with Families; (c) Collaboration and Teaming; (d) Assessment Processes; (e) Application of Curriculum Frameworks in the Planning of Meaningful Learning Experience; (f) Using Responsive and Reciprocal Interactions, Interventions, and Instruction; (g) Professionalism and Ethical Practices; (h) Field Experiences and Clinical Practices. The full set of EI/ECSE Standards and components along with supporting explanations and knowledge bases for each standard are in Appendix A.

Also emphasized throughout this text are the DEC Recommended Practices. The DEC Recommended Practices build on the Developmentally Appropriate Practice (DAP) guidelines of the NAEYC. The DEC Recommended Practices were developed based on an extensive review of the research in the field that spanned across the literature of multiple disciplines and were designed to bridge the gap between research and practice. The revised DEC Recommended Practices are divided into eight strands that focus on components of early intervention and education (leadership, assessment, environment, family, instruction, interaction, teaming and collaboration, and transition). The revised practices offer guidance to professionals and families on specific strategies to promote the development and support the learning outcomes of young children with delays and disabilities. The DEC Recommended Practices have been infused throughout this book and addressed specifically in each chapter with examples provided. A brief overview of the updates to the chapters follows.

Chapter 1, "Foundations of Early Childhood Special Education," has been reorganized to provide a more comprehensive overview of early intervention/education. The chapter includes updated references and new and revised tables and figures. After reviewing this chapter, the reader will have a clear understanding of the basis for the field of early intervention and early childhood special education.

Chapter 2, "The Context of Early Childhood Special Education," has been restructured in the same way as Chapter 1. Legislative information has been added with new and extensive coverage of current legislation and the impact on young children with delays and disabilities. New content has been added on early primary students, six through eight years of age.

Chapter 3, "Family-Centered Approach to Early Childhood Special Education," has been modified to reflect the changes that have occurred in society that have had an impact on the characteristics of the American family. Greater emphasis is placed on family-centered services and how families must be supported as contributing members of the team according to their individual preferences. Cultural responsiveness to young children and their families representing diverse cultural, structural, and socioeconomic backgrounds is emphasized throughout this chapter.

Chapter 4, "Delivering Services to Young Children With Delays and Disabilities," has been restructured, and we have imposed a conceptually sound presentation of content. Updated coverage of an individualized family service plan (IFSP), an individualized education program (IEP), and Section 504 accommodation plans are included in addition to various ways to engage cooperative teaching. (See Appendices D and E and the accompanying website for examples of an IFSP and IEP.)

Chapter 5, "Assessment of Young Children With Delays and Disabilities," addresses assessment in a more comprehensive, coordinated manner as suggested by current recommended practices in the field of early intervention and early childhood special education. Chapter 5 has expanded coverage of authentic, team-based, and culturally responsive assessment practices. The emphasis is on the coordination of all phases of the assessment process from screening to eligibility to program planning and progress monitoring.

Chapter 6, "Curriculum for Young Children With Delays and Disabilities," has been updated and substantially reorganized to address current practices in the field related to appropriate curriculum development. General early childhood education content and practices serve as the foundation for curriculum development, and early childhood special education recommended practices are added based on the individual needs of young children with delays and disabilities. Increased coverage in this chapter includes a holistic and eclectic approach to curriculum development and implementation for young children with delays and disabilities in inclusive settings.

Chapter 7, "Designing Learning Environments for Young Children With Delays and Disabilities," has been reorganized to focus on infants and toddlers, preschoolers, and early primary age children. The content is reorganized and is now more conceptually sound and includes web-based resources, examples, and guidelines to broaden the readers' understanding of ways in which the environment can be organized to foster learning for young children with delays and disabilities.

Chapter 8, "Adapting Learning Environments for Young Children With Delays and Disabilities," has been expanded to provide broader coverage of organization and intervention for young children with delays and disabilities. A process for determining evidence-based recommended practices also is addressed in this chapter.

Chapter 9, "Intervention and Instructional Strategies for Supporting Young Children With Delays and Disabilities," provides a more in-depth focus on how intervention and instruction should be delivered for the birth through eight-year-old population based on evidence-based practices. Increased coverage of early primary students with delays and disabilities is a highlight of this chapter.

Chapter 10, "Emerging Issues and Contemporary Challenges in Early Childhood Special Education," has been structured to accurately reflect some of the most important issues in the field today including response to intervention (RTI), universal design for learning (UDL), assistive technology, cultural and linguistic diversity, and poverty. Current references and resources are included in this chapter, as well as future directions in early intervention/early childhood special education.

ACKNOWLEDGMENTS

The development of a comprehensive textbook requires a collaborative effort, and the sixth edition of this book is no exception. We gratefully acknowledge the contributions of Dr. Jenna Weglarz-Ward (Chapter 9). Her expertise and professionalism significantly enhanced the quality of this project. We extend our gratitude to A. K. Bruton for her meticulous and thorough editing of this manuscript. Her expert work has elevated the quality of this textbook. We are deeply appreciative of the family members, professionals, and colleagues who provided input throughout the book. We extend our heartfelt thanks to the RISE Center of the University of Alabama for participating in this project wholeheartedly. From filming content to participating in interviews, your contributions were amazing. Our deep appreciation is offered to our entire team for their involvement in the sixth edition of our textbook. Their continuous support, influence, and enthusiasm were instrumental in bringing this work to fruition.

Appreciation also is extended to the team at SAGE Publications who believed in the vitality of this textbook and offered us the opportunity to write a sixth edition. We offer our heartfelt gratitude to our editor, Leah Fargotstein, for her support, visionary ideas, and continuing commitment to ensuring that *An Introduction toYoung Children With Delays and Disabilities* is a market leader. To the other professionals at SAGE Publications, including Kenzie Offley, content development editor; and Veronica Stapleton Hooper, production editor, we deeply appreciate your dedication, hard work, sense of humor, and commitment to this project. Writing a textbook of this scope requires the efforts of many people at many different levels, and we are indebted to all of those who worked on this project along the way.

Finally, we are indebted to our reviewers. These professionals provided invaluable input and helpful suggestions. Their thoughtful commentary and insights definitely helped to shape the direction of this edition.

Regina M. Adesanya
New Jersey City University
Consuela N. Amos
Reach University
Beverly Argus Calvo
The University of Texas at El Paso
Kimberly Cassidy
Shawnee State University
Inna N. Dolzhenko
Chicago State University
Charolette Ellington
University of Tennessee at Chattanooga
Helane Folske-Starlin
Peru State College
Patricia R. Huskin
Texas A&M University, Kingsville
Kai Kaisser
Saddleback College
Samantha Murray
Roosevelt University
Anne M. Ryan Beigel
St. Petersburg College
Kathleen Sheriff

Stephen F. Austin State University
Vanessa Tucker
Pacific Lutheran University

In addition to the reviewers, we would like to acknowledge the work of our cover artist, Fran Bostick. The title of her artwork is "Colorful Circle of Friends" and depicts that we are all different shapes, colors, and sizes and have different personalities, strengths, and abilities. But together we make up a beautiful community of friends that begins at an early age. Our friends are all different, but each brings something unique to the circle. Our relationships and connections within our "Colorful Circle of Friends" make us better, more well-rounded, and more caring individuals. Our friendships and relationships leave handprints on our hearts. Thank you, Fran Bostick, for your perfect and valuable contribution to this textbook.

Our sincere thanks are extended to all who have generously contributed their time and resources to this project. As a result, we have a product of which we are extremely proud, one that we believe will make a significant contribution to the field of early intervention and early childhood special education.

ABOUT THE AUTHORS

RICHARD M. GARGIULO

I have always desired to be an educator. I guess I am a rarity in that I never changed my undergraduate major or left the field of education. My undergraduate education began at Hiram Scott College in Scottsbluff, Nebraska. Three years later, I was teaching fourth graders in the Milwaukee public schools while working toward my master's degree in intellectual disability at the University of Wisconsin–Milwaukee. At the conclusion of my first year of teaching, I was asked to teach a class of young children with intellectual disability. I jumped at the opportunity and for the next three years essentially became an early childhood special educator. It was at this point in my career that I decided to earn my doctorate. I resigned my teaching position and moved to Madison, where I pursued a PhD in the areas of human learning, child development, and behavioral disabilities. Upon receiving my degree, I accepted a faculty position in the Department of Special Education at Bowling Green State University (Ohio), where for the next eight years I was a teacher educator. In 1982, I moved to Birmingham, Alabama, and joined the faculty of the University of Alabama at Birmingham (UAB), where, until my retirement, I served as a professor in the Department of Curriculum and Instruction. In November 2014, I was awarded professor emeritus status by the board of trustees of the University of Alabama system.

I have enjoyed a rich and rewarding professional career spanning more than four decades. During the course of this journey, I have had the privilege of twice serving as president of the Alabama Federation, Council for Exceptional Children (CEC); serving as president of the Division of International Special Education and Services (DISES), CEC; and serving as president of the Division on Autism and Developmental Disabilities (DADD), CEC. I mostly served as the Southeast representative to the board of directors of DADD. I have lectured abroad extensively and was a Fulbright Scholar to the Czech Republic in 1991. In 2007, I was invited to serve as a Distinguished Visiting Professor at Charles University in Prague, Czech Republic.

Teaching has always been my passion. In 1999, I was fortunate to receive UAB's President's Award for Excellence in Teaching. In 2007, I received the Jasper Harvey Award from the Alabama Federation of CEC in recognition of being named the outstanding special education teacher educator in the state.

With a background in both educational psychology and special education, my research has appeared in a wide variety of professional journals including *ChildDevelopment, Journal of Educational Research, Journal of Learning Disabilities, American Journal of Mental Deficiency, Childhood Education, Journal of VisualImpairment and Blindness, British Journal of Developmental Psychology, Journal ofSpecial Education, Early Childhood Education Journal, International Journal of ClinicalNeuropsychology,* and *InternationalJournal of Special Education*, among a host of others.

In addition to the present text, I have authored or coauthored more than ten books, several enjoying multiple editions, ranging in topics from counseling parents of children with disabilities to child abuse, early childhood education, teaching in inclusive classrooms, and, most recently, instructional strategies for students with intellectual disability.

JENNIFER L. KILGO

Personal experience and unforeseen opportunities led me to a career in early intervention and early childhood special education (EI/ECSE). When I was a young child, my sibling was born with multiple medical complications and died shortly after birth. This tragic event sparked my interest in early childhood disabilities and set me on a path toward a career in EI/ECSE. While I was studying psychology as an undergraduate, Congress passed Public Law 94-142, the Education for All Handicapped Children Act, which provided services for children with developmental delays and disabilities. This legislation opened new opportunities for me and solidified my passion for improving opportunities for infants and young children with delays and disabilities, as well as their families. I have pursued this passion in higher education.

Currently, I am a professor of early intervention/early childhood special education at the University of Alabama at Birmingham (UAB). I hold a BS in psychology from Auburn University; teacher certification in general early childhood education; an MA in special education and certification in administration from UAB; and a doctoral degree in EI/ECSE from the University of Alabama (Tuscaloosa). Prior to my appointment to the faculty at UAB, I taught at Virginia Commonwealth University and the University of Hawaii. As a professor at UAB, I enjoy interprofessional teaching of graduate students representing a variety of disciplines (e.g., ECSE, physical therapy, occupational therapy) who are learning to collaboratively provide team-based services to young children with delays and disabilities and their families.

My involvement in EI/ECSE has extended for many years. Before becoming a higher education faculty member, I provided direct services to young children with delays and disabilities and their families in various community agencies and school settings. Also, I worked as a teacher at an EI/ECSE program at the University of Alabama, the RISE Center. My experience with young children and their families has informed my ability to teach others, as well as my interest in various scholarly activities.

My involvement at the state and national/international levels in service, scholarship, and personnel preparation activities has been a highlight of my career. For example, my leadership positions have included serving as the president of the Division for Early Childhood (DEC) of the Council for Exceptional Children (CEC). Additionally, I have been a member of the editorial review board for leading national journals, served as the principal investigator of numerous federally funded grants, and delivered presentations at conferences throughout the country. My research has focused on teamwork and interprofessional education. Through a series of federally funded grants spanning more than 25 years at UAB, my work has focused on teaming and collaboration as professionals representing multiple disciplines learn to work as members of transdisciplinary teams in early intervention and early childhood special education throughout the community. Collaboration with community partners is central to the success of my career.

The recognition and accolades I have been fortunate to receive have primarily highlighted my dedication to teaching and my collaborative endeavors. In 2013, I received the honor of being designated a University Professor by the UAB Board of Trustees. The criteria for this appointment includes "numerous achievements and extensive recognition in the individual's chosen professional field, and academic competence to enable her to undertake cross-departmental, cross-disciplinary activities in research and teaching and community service." I also was presented with the Sam Brown Bridge Builder Award for my collaborative efforts with multiple disciplines at UAB and within the community. In 2020, I received the Ingalls Award for Lifetime Achievement in Teaching Excellence at UAB. Being acknowledged by my students and colleagues has held significant value for me throughout my rewarding career. I aspire to have made meaningful contributions to interprofessional education within higher education and to have played a role in enhancing services for infants and young children with delays and disabilities, as well as their families.

PART I

PERSPECTIVES, POLICIES, AND PRACTICES OF EARLY CHILDHOOD SPECIAL EDUCATION

iStock.com/kali9

1 FOUNDATIONS OF EARLY CHILDHOOD SPECIAL EDUCATION

LEARNING OBJECTIVES

After reading this chapter, you will be able to

1.1 Describe the theories and philosophies of historical figures and their contributions to the development of the fields of general early childhood education and early intervention/early childhood special education (EI/ECSE).

1.2 Discuss the evolution of educational opportunities for children with delays and disabilities.

1.3 Explain the concept of compensatory education.

EI/ECSE Professional Standards

The content of this chapter aligns with the following EI/ECSE Standard:

Standard 1. Child Development and Early Learning

Candidates understand the impact of different theories and philosophies of early learning and development on assessment, curriculum, instruction, and intervention decisions. Candidates apply knowledge of normative developmental sequences and variations, individual differences within and across the range of abilities, including developmental delays and disabilities, and other direct and indirect contextual features that support or constrain children's development and learning. These contextual factors as well as social, cultural, and linguistic diversity are considered when facilitating meaningful learning experiences and individualizing intervention and instruction across contexts.

Authors' Note: As you read this chapter and other chapters, you will find information related to EI/ECSE Standard 1, Child Development and Learning. Appendix A contains a complete list of the EI/ECSE Standards and accompanying components.

Early childhood, as described in this text, refers to the period from birth through age eight. In educational terms, this includes early intervention, early childhood special education, and early primary special education. The individuals who require these services represent an especially heterogeneous group of young children. The children vary in their chronological age and cultural, linguistic, ethnic, and socioeconomic backgrounds, as well as in the types and severity of their delays and disabilities. Thus, early childhood special education professionals encounter young children with a wide range of physical, cognitive, communication, health, and social abilities, strengths, and needs (Allen & Cowdery, 2022; Cook et al., 2020; Kilgo, 2006).

As emphasized in EI/ECSE Standard 1, the need for ECSE professionals to consider children's social, cultural, and linguistic diversity is of critical importance when facilitating meaningful learning experiences and individualizing intervention and instruction across contexts (Guralnick, 2017; Shonkoff & Richter, 2013). Therefore, this textbook is designed to help practitioners provide appropriate and effective early intervention/education programs for infants and young children with delays and disabilities and their families who are receiving early intervention and early childhood special education services in a variety of settings.

THE ORIGINS OF EARLY CHILDHOOD SPECIAL EDUCATION

In the past five decades, there has been a significant increase in awareness, services, and opportunities for young children with delays and disabilities. EI/ECSE Standard 1stresses the importance of professionals understanding the influence of various theories and philosophies on the field (Odom, 2016). Also important to consider is the impact of legislative initiatives, litigation, public policy, and the efforts of advocacy groups, which have helped to focus attention on young children with delays and disabilities and their families. As a field of study, early childhood special education is relatively young but has rapidly emerged and has been influenced by different theories and philosophies of early learning and development (Dunst, 2007; Peterson, 1987).

The foundation for appropriate learning experiences for young children with delays and disabilities is built on three related fields. The origins of early childhood special education can be traced to trends and developments in general early childhood education, special education for school-age students, and compensatory programs such as Head Start (Hanson & Lynch, 1995; Peterson, 1987). In each of their unique ways, all these movements have played imperative roles in the evolution of early childhood special education. Therefore, it is vital to consider the field of early intervention and early childhood special education as a hybrid field built upon the evolving recommended practices of general early childhood and special education, plus the research evidence from empirical investigations documenting the success of compensatory education programs (Peterson, 1987). Figure 1.1 shows this threefold foundation of the field.

General early childhood education has an extensive history rich with tradition. It is important to remember that the value of children and their education reflects the social, political, and economic conditions of particular time periods (Harkness et al., 2013). The efforts of past religious leaders, reformers, educational theorists, and philosopher helped to shape contemporary thinking about the education of young children. The work of these individuals also has introduced many of the concepts and practices used with young children with developmental delays and disabilities and those children

FIGURE 1.1 ■ The Foundations of Early Childhood Special Education

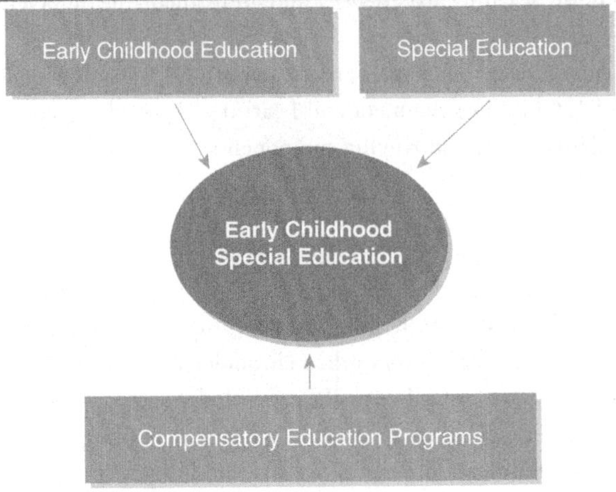

at risk for future delays and disabilities. What follows is a description of the influence of important early contributors to general early childhood education.

Early Contributors

Although he was an important historical religious leader, Martin Luther (1483–1546) also is remembered for advocating for the importance of literacy and widespread, mandatory education. He was a resolved believer in publicly supported schools for all children, including girls. Luther's legacy includes his visionary idea that family participation is a critical component of a child's education.

Another early religious leader and educational theorist was Jan Ámos Comenius (a.k.a. Komenský; 1592–1670). He was a firm believer in universal education, which ideally should begin in the early years due to the plasticity or malleability of the child's behavior. In *The Great Didactic* (1657), Comenius summarizes his view that young children are capable of easily being molded and shaped. Schooling in the first six years of life must begin at home at the mother's knee ("School of the Mother's Knee") and progress throughout an individual's lifetime. Comenius also advocated that all children, including those with delays and disabilities, should receive an education (Gargiulo & Černá, 1992).

Comenius believed that young children learn best by being actively involved in the learning process.

Petr Bonek / Alamy Stock Photo

Many modern-day practices, as well as the contributions of later theorists such as Montessori and Piaget, can be found in Comenius's early ideas about children's learning and development. As an example, Comenius realized the importance of a child's preparedness for an activity. He also emphasized that children learn best through active involvement in the learning process. Additionally, Comenius placed great weight on sensory experiences and the utilization of concrete examples.

John Locke (1632–1704) was a seventeenth-century English philosopher and physician who also influenced thinking about young children. The concept that children are born very much like a blank slate (**tabula rasa**) is attributed to Locke. All that children learn, therefore, is a direct product of experiences, activities, and sensations rather than intrinsic characteristics. Locke was a firm advocate of an environmental point of view. What a child becomes is a consequence or result of the type and quality of experiences to which they are exposed.

Locke's belief in the dominance of the environment is echoed in the behavioral theories of B. F. Skinner and other modern theorists as well as today's compensatory education programs directed at remedying the concerns of a disadvantaged environment. Early learning and school experiences for children at risk, such as the popular Head Start program, is a prime example. Because Locke also emphasized the importance of sensory experiences, his theorizing influenced Montessori's view on the significance of sensory training in early education.

One social theorist and philosopher who had a substantial influence on education was Jean-Jacques Rousseau (1712–1778). Through his writings—in particular, *Emile* (1762)—Rousseau explained his views on child-rearing and education. His ideas, which were radical for his time, included a natural approach to the education of young children. Rousseau urged a laissez-faire approach, one void of limitations and interference, which would allow the natural unfolding of a child's abilities. Childhood was viewed as a distinct and special time during which children grew or "flowered" according to innate timetables. Rousseau stressed the significance of early education. He also believed that schools should be based on the interests of the child (Graves et al., 1996).

Educational historians typically esteem Rousseau as the dividing line between the past and present periods of education. He significantly influenced future reformers and thinkers such as Pestalozzi, Fröbel, and Montessori, all of whom have contributed to modern early childhood practices.

According to Rousseau, children develop according to innate timetables.

Heritage Images / Contributor via Getty Images

Pioneers in Early Childhood Education

Johann Heinrich Pestalozzi (1746–1827), a Swiss educator, is credited with establishing early childhood education as a distinct discipline. Like Rousseau, Pestalozzi believed in the value of education through nature and following the child's natural development. He also promoted developing school experiences focused on the interests of the student. Pestalozzi understood, however, that learning does not occur simply through a child's initiative and experimental behavior; adult guidance is essential. Teachers, therefore, need to create "object" lessons to balance the child's self-guided experiences. Due to Pestalozzi's belief in the importance of sensory experiences, instructional lessons amalgamated manipulative activities like counting, measuring, feeling, and touching concrete objects (Lawton, 1988).

Three additional ideas differentiate Pestalozzi's contributions to the field of early childhood education. First, Pestalozzi stressed the education of the whole child; second, he was a firm believer in involving parents in a child's early education; and, finally, he saw the value of multiage grouping whereby older students could assist in teaching younger learners.

Social reformer and entrepreneur Robert Owen (1771–1858) is recognized for launching an infant school in 1816. Influenced by the theorizing of Rousseau and Pestalozzi, Owen was worried about the living and working conditions of the children and their parents who worked in textile mills. As the manager of a mill in New Lanark, Scotland, Owen was able to introduce his reform ideas. Very young children were forbidden from working at all, and the working hours of older children were restricted. Perhaps more significant, however, was the formation of a school for children between the ages of three and ten. He believed early education was critical to the development of a child's character and behavior. The early years were the most opportune time to influence a young child's development. By controlling and manipulating environmental conditions, Owen, like other Utopians, sought to build a better society. Education was seen as a medium for social change.

Owen believed that early education was crucial to the development of a child's character and behavior.

Hulton Archive / Freelance Photographer via Getty Images

Owen's infant school was noted for its emphasis on the development of basic academics as well as creative experiences such as dance and music. This pioneer of early childhood education did not believe in forcing children to learn and was opposed to punishment, emphasizing shared respect between teacher and child. His ideas were enormously popular, and more than fifty infant schools were established by the late 1820s throughout Scotland, Ireland, and England. Several schools flourished in urban areas of the United States, yet their influence had lessened by the mid-1830s.

Owen's infant schools served as a harbinger of kindergartens. They were also seen as a way of immunizing children living in poverty from the harms of nineteenth-century urban living. This social reformer was idealistic; he recognized the vital relationship between education and societal developments. Owen trusted, as did other reformers of that time, that poverty could be forever eradicated by instructing and socializing young children from poor families.

Fröbel is considered to be the "father of the kindergarten."
Bildagentur-online / Contributor via Getty Images

Graves and his colleagues (1996) describe Friedrich Wilhelm Fröbel[1] (1782–1852) as the one individual who perhaps had the highest impact on the field of early childhood education. A student of Pestalozzi and a teacher in one of his schools, Fröbel was a strong advocate for the education of young children. He translated his beliefs into a system for teaching young children in addition to developing a curriculum, complete with methodology. His efforts earned him the well-deserved title "Father of the Kindergarten."

Also encouraged by the writings of Rousseau and Comenius, Fröbel conceived an educational theory ("Law of Universal Unity") partly based on their thoughts as well as his personal experiences and religious views. His fundamental idea was principally religious in nature and emphasized a unity of all living things—a oneness of humans, nature, and God. His concept of unity led Fröbel to advocate that education should be based on collaboration rather than competition. Like Comenius and Pestalozzi, he also considered progress as a process of unfolding. Children's learning should, therefore, follow this natural development. The role of the teacher (and parent) was to identify this process and provide activities to help the child learn whenever they were ready (Morrison, 2012).

Fröbel used the garden to symbolize early childhood education. Like a flower blooming from a bud, children would grow naturally according to their own laws of development. A kindergarten education, therefore, should follow the nature of the child's development. Play, a child's natural activity, was the foundation of learning (Spodek et al., 1991).

Fröbel founded the first kindergarten (German for "children's garden") in 1837 near Blankenburg, Germany. This early program enrolled young children between the ages of one and seven. Structured play was an important component of the curriculum. Unlike many of his contemporaries, Fröbel saw the educational value and benefit of play. Play is the work of the child. Because he believed that education was knowledge being transmitted by symbols, Fröbel developed a set of materials and activities that would aid the children in their play activities as well as teach the concept of unity among nature, God, and humankind. Education was to begin with the concrete and move to the abstract.

Fröbel presented his students with "gifts" and "occupations" rich in symbolism. In his curriculum, **gifts** were manipulative activities to assist in learning color, shape, size, counting, and other educational tasks. Wooden blocks, cylinders, and cubes; balls of colored yarn; geometric shapes; and natural objects, such as beans and pebbles, are all examples of some of the learning tools used.

Occupations were arts-and-crafts-type activities designed to develop eye–hand coordination and fine motor skills. Illustrations of these activities include bead-stringing, embroidering, paper folding,

[1] Information on Friedrick Fröbel, John Dewey, Maria Montessori, and Jean Piaget is adapted from *Young Children: An Introduction to Early Childhood* by S. Graves, R. Gargiulo, and L. Sluder, St. Paul, MN: West, 1996.

cutting with scissors, and weaving. Fröbel's curriculum also used games, songs, dance, rhymes, and finger play. Other components of his curriculum were nature study, language, and arithmetic in addition to developing the habits of cleanliness, courtesy, and punctuality.

According to Fröbel, teachers were to be designers of activities and experiences utilizing the child's innate curiosity. They were also responsible for directing and guiding their students toward becoming contributing members of society (Morrison, 2012). This role of the teacher as a facilitator of children's learning would later be echoed in the work of Montessori and Piaget.

Influential Leaders of the Twentieth Century

The educational ideas espoused by John Dewey, Maria Montessori, and Jean Piaget, along with his contemporary, Russian theorist Lev Vygotsky, have significantly influenced the field of general early childhood education. Many of the practices that are common in today's classrooms originated with the work of these four individuals.

John Dewey

The influence of John Dewey (1859–1952) can be traced to the early days of the twentieth century when conflicting points of view about young children and kindergarten experiences began to transpire. Some individuals professed a strong allegiance to Fröbel's principles and practices. Other professionals, known as Progressives, saw little value in adhering to Fröbel's symbolism. Instead, they embraced the developing child study movement with its focus on empirical study. Because of the work of G. Stanley Hall, the father of the child study movement, formal observations and a scientific basis for understanding young children replaced speculation, philosophic idealism, and religious and social values as the means for guiding the education of young children. Observations of young children led to new ideas about kindergarten practices and what should be considered of educational value for children.

Dewey founded a school of thought known as Progressivism.

Bettmann / Contributor via Getty Images

Dewey, a student of Hall, was one of the first Americans to significantly impact educational theory as well as practice. He is generally regarded as the founder of a school of thought known as **Progressivism**. This approach with its emphasis on the child and their interests, was counter to the then prevalent theme of teacher-directed, subject-oriented curriculum. According to Dewey, learning flowed from the interests of the child instead of from activities chosen by the instructor. Dewey, who taught at both the University of Chicago and Teachers College, Columbia University, coined the terms *child-centered curriculum* and *child-centered schools* (Morrison et al., 2022). Consistent with Dewey's beliefs, the purpose of schools was to prepare the student for the realities of today's world, not just to prepare for the future. In his famous work, *My Pedagogic Creed,* this philosopher emphasized that learning occurs through real-life experiences and that education is best described as a process for living. He also stressed the concept of social responsibility. Basic to his philosophy was the idea that children should be equipped to function effectively as citizens in a democratic society.

Traditionally, children learned predetermined subject matter via rote memory under the strict guidance of the teacher, who was in complete control of the learning environment. In Dewey's classroom, however, children were socially active, engaged in physical activities, and discovering how objects worked. They were continually afforded opportunities for inquiry, discovery, and experimentation. Daily living activities such as carpentry and cooking could also be found in a Dewey-designed classroom (Morrison et al., 2022).

Dewey (1916) advocated for the child's interaction with the total environment. He believed that intellectual skills emerged from a child's own activity and play. He further rejected Fröbel's approach to symbolic education.

Some have unfairly criticized Dewey as only responding to the whims of the child; this was a false accusation. Dewey did not abandon the teaching of subject matter or basic skills. He was merely opposed to imposing knowledge on children. Instead, he favored using the child's interests as the origin of subject matter instruction. Thus, curriculum could not be fixed or established in advance. According to Dewey, educators are to guide learning activities, observe and monitor, and offer encouragement and assistance as needed. They are not to control their students.

Although Dewey's impact has lessened, his contributions to early childhood education in America and other countries are still evident. Many so-called traditional early childhood classrooms today have their philosophical roots in Dewey's progressive education movement.

Maria Montessori

In examining the roots of modern early childhood special education, the work of Maria Montessori (1870–1952) stands out. Her contributions to the field of general early childhood education are significant. A feminist, she became the first female to earn a medical degree in Italy. (Montessori also held a PhD in anthropology.) She began working as a physician in a psychiatric clinic at the University of Rome. It was in this hospital setting that she came into frequent contact with "idiot children," or individuals with intellectual disability. At the turn of the century, intellectual disability was, unfortunately, often viewed as indistinguishable from mental illness. A careful observation of these children led her to conclude that educational intervention would be a more effective strategy than medical treatment. She began to develop her theories for working with these children. In doing so, she was following an historical tradition upon which the early foundation of special education is built—the physician turned educator. Dr. Montessori was influenced by the writings of Pestalozzi, Rousseau, and Fröbel and the work of Édouard Séguin, a French physician who pioneered an effective educational approach for children with intellectual disability. She concluded that intelligence is not static or fixed but can be influenced by the child's experiences. Montessori developed an innovative, activity-based sensory education model involving teaching, or **didactic materials**. She was eminently successful.

Montessori believed that children learn best by direct sensory experiences.

Pictorial Press Ltd / Alamy Stock Photo

Montessori believed that children learn best by direct sensory experience. She was further convinced that children have a natural tendency to explore and understand their world. Like Fröbel, she envisioned child development as a process of unfolding; however, environmental influences also have a critical role. Education in the early years is crucial to the child's later development. Montessori also thought children progress through **sensitive periods**, or stages of development early in life when they are able, due to their curiosity, to learn particular skills or behaviors more easily. This concept is very similar to the idea of a child's readiness for an activity.

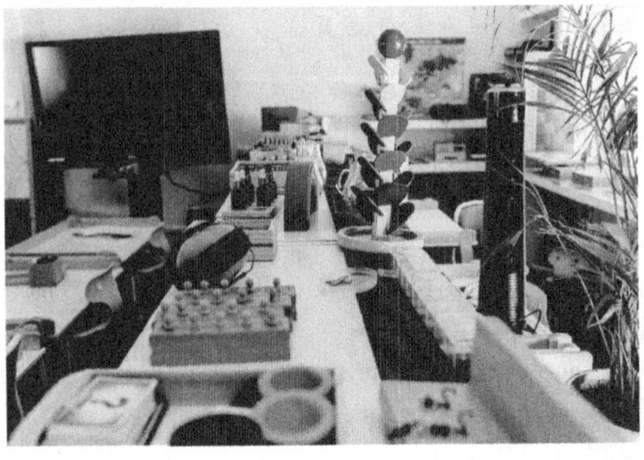

Montessori classrooms are characterized by their attractive learning materials and equipment.

iStock.com/CorbalanStudio

To promote the children's learning, Montessori constructed an orderly or **prepared environment** with specially designed tasks and materials. Much like Fröbel's gifts, these materials included items such as wooden rods, cylinders, and cubes of varying sizes; sets of sandpaper tablets arranged according to the degree of smoothness; and musical bells of different pitches (see Table 1.1). Dr. Montessori's program also emphasized three growth periods—practical life experiences, sensory education, and academic education. Each of these components was considered to be essential in developing the child's independence, responsibility, self-reliance, and productivity.

TABLE 1.1 ■ Examples of Montessori's Sensory Materials

Material	Purpose	How It Is Used by Children
Wooden cylinders	Visual discrimination (Size)	Ten wooden cylinders varying in diameter, height, or variations of both dimensions. Child removes cylinders from wooden holder, mixes them up, and replaces in correct location.
Pink tower	Visual discrimination (Dimension)	Ten wooden cubes painted pink. Child is required to build a tower. Each cube is successively smaller, varying from ten to one centimeter. Repeats activity.
Green rods	Visual discrimination (Length)	Ten wooden pieces identical in size and color but varying in length. After scattering rods, child arranges them according to gradations in length—largest to smallest.
Material swatches	Sense of feel	Matches identical pieces of brightly colored fabric (e.g., fine vs. coarse linen, cottons, and woolens). Initially performs task without blindfold.
Sound cylinders	Auditory discrimination	Double set of cylinders containing natural materials such as pebbles or rice. Child shakes cylinder and matches first according to similarity of sound and then according to loudness.
Tonal bells	Auditory discrimination	Two sets of eight metal bells, alike in appearance but varying in tone. Child strikes the bells with a wooden hammer and matches the bells on the basis of their sound; first according to corresponding sounds and then according to the musical scale.

Source: Adapted from R. Orem (Ed.), *A Montessori Handbook: Dr. Montessori's Own Handbook* (New York, NY: Putnam's Sons, 1966).

Practical life experiences focused on personal hygiene, self-care, physical education, and responsibility for the environment. Examples of this last activity include tasks such as sweeping, dusting, or raking leaves while utilizing child-size equipment. Sensory education was very important in Montessori's education scheme. She designed a wide variety of teaching materials aimed at developing the children's various senses. Her didactic materials are noteworthy for two reasons. They were self-correcting—that is, there was only one correct way to use them. Thus, the materials could be used independently by the children to help them become self-motivated students. The sensory training equipment was also graded in difficulty—from easiest to the most challenging and from concrete to abstract. Her sensory training materials and procedures reflected her educational belief that cognitive ability results from sensory development. The final stage, academic instruction, introduced the child to reading, writing, and arithmetic in the sensitive period, ages two to six. Various concrete and sensory teaching materials were used in the lessons of this last stage (Montessori, 1965).

Montessori's classrooms were distinguished by their attractive and child-size materials and equipment. The furniture was movable, and the beautifully crafted materials were very attractive—appealing to the child's senses. Teaching materials were displayed on low shelves in an organized manner to encourage the children's independent use. Children worked at their own pace, selecting learning materials of their choice; however, they had to complete one assignment before starting another. Dr. Montessori fully believed in allowing children to do things for themselves. She was convinced that children are capable of teaching themselves through interaction with a carefully planned learning environment. She identified this concept as **auto-education**.

Teachers in Montessori classrooms are facilitators and observers of children's activities. By using skillfully crafted lessons, the teacher (or *directress* in Montessori terminology) slowly and carefully demonstrates concepts to the children. Ideas are presented to the children in small, sequential steps and build on previous experiences that form the basis for the next level of skill development. Teachers foster the development of independence in young children. A Montessori-designed classroom typically is focused on individual children's activities rather than group work.

Many of Montessori's beliefs and concepts are directly applicable to young children with disabilities, including the following:

- *The use of mixed-age groupings.* The mixed-age groupings found within a Montessori classroom are conducive to a successful inclusion experience. Mixed-age groupings necessitate a wide range of materials within each classroom to meet the individual needs of children rather than the average need of the group.
- *Individualization within the context of a supportive classroom community.* The individualized curriculum in Montessori classrooms is compatible with the individualization required for children with disabilities. Work in a Montessori classroom is introduced to children according to individual readiness rather than chronological age.
- *An emphasis on functionality within the Montessori environment.* Real objects are used rather than toy replications whenever possible (e.g., children cut bread with a real knife, sweep up crumbs on the floor with a real broom, and dry wet tables with cloths.) In a Montessori classroom, the goal is to prepare children for life. Special education also focuses on the development of functional skills.
- *The development of independence and the ability to make choices.* Montessori classrooms help all children make choices and become independent learners in various ways; for example, children may choose any material for which they have had a lesson given by the teacher. This development of independence is especially appropriate for children with delays and disabilities.
- *The development of organized work patterns in children.* One objective of the practical life area and the beginning point for every young child is the development of organized work habits. Children with delays and disabilities who need to learn to be organized in their work habits and their use of time often benefit from this emphasis.
- *The classic Montessori demonstration.* Demonstrations themselves have value for learners who experience disabilities. A demonstration uses a minimum of language selected specifically for its relevance to the activity and emphasizes an orderly progression from the beginning to the end of the task.
- *An emphasis on repetition.* Children with delays and disabilities typically require lots of practice and make progress in small increments.
- *Materials with a built-in control of error.* Materials that have a built-in control of error benefit all children. Because errors are obvious, children notice and correct them without the help of a teacher.

- *Academic materials that provide a concrete representation of the abstract.* Montessori classrooms offer a wide range of concrete materials that children can learn from as a regular part of the curriculum. For children with disabilities, the use of concrete materials is critical to promote real learning.
- *Sensory materials that develop and organize incoming sensory perceptions.* Sensory materials can develop and refine each sense in isolation. A child who cannot see will benefit enormously from materials that train and refine the sense of touch, hearing, and smell, for example. (Morrison, 2009, p. 148; North American Montessori Center, 2016)

Jean Piaget

Jean Piaget (1896–1980) is one of the major contributors to the understanding of how children think. He is considered by many to be the premiere expert on the development of knowledge in children and young adults.

Piaget studied in Paris, where he had the opportunity to work with Théodore Simon, who in conjunction with Alfred Binet was constructing the first test for assessing children's intelligence. While standardizing the children's responses to test questions, Piaget became extremely interested in the incorrect answers given by the children. His careful observations led him to notice that they gave similar wrong answers. He also discovered that the children made different types of errors at different ages. This paved the way for Piaget to investigate the thinking process that led to incorrect responses.

According to Piaget's (1963, 1970) point of view, children's mode of thinking is qualitatively and fundamentally different from that of adults. He also believed that children's thought processes are modified as they grow and mature. Because Piaget's ideas about intellectual development are complex, only his basic concepts will be presented.

Piaget is widely recognized for his ideas on the development of the intellect.

Patrick Grehan/Corbis Historical/Getty Images

First, it is important to understand Piaget's (1963, 1970) view of intelligence. He was concerned with *how* knowledge is acquired. Piaget avoids stating a precise definition of intelligence; instead, he attempts to describe it in general terms. Piaget speaks of intelligence as an instance of biological adaptation. He also looks at intelligence as a balance or equilibrium between an individual's cognitive structures and the environment. His focus is on what people *do* as they interact with their environment. Knowledge of reality must be discovered and constructed—it results from a child's actions within, and reactions to, their world. It is also important to note that Piaget is not concerned with individual differences in intelligence (Ginsburg & Opper, 1969).

Piaget's (1970) theory rests on the contributions of maturational and environmental influences. Maturation establishes a sequence of cognitive stages controlled by heredity. The environment contributes to the child's experiences, which dictate how the child develops. Thinking is a process of interaction between the child and the environment. An individual's capacity to learn, according to Piaget, is derived from experiences. He viewed children as active learners and initiators of learning (Cook et al., 2020). Children are self-motivated in the construction of their own knowledge, which occurs through activity.

One consequence of interaction with the environment is that the person soon develops organizing structures or schema. These schema, or mental concepts, become a basis from which later cognitive structures are established. Piaget developed three concepts that he believed individuals use to organize their personal experiences into a blueprint for thinking. He referred to these adaptive processes as assimilation, accommodation, and equilibration.

Assimilation occurs when the child is able to integrate new experiences and information into existing schemes—that is, what the child already knows. Children will view new situations in light of previous experiences in their world. As an illustration, when a toddler first encounters a pony, they will most likely call it a dog or similar animal, something the toddler is already familiar with.

Accommodation is Piaget's second process, which involves modifying existing cognitive structures so that new data can be utilized effectively. Current thought patterns and behaviors are changed to fit new situations. Accommodation involves a change in understanding. For example, two-year-old Victoria visits Santa Claus at the mall. Later that day, she is shopping with her mother and sees an elderly gentleman with a long white beard whom she calls Santa Claus. Victoria's mother corrects her daughter's mistake by saying that the man is old. When Victoria next meets a man with a white beard, she asks, "Are you Santa Claus, or are you just old?" Victoria has demonstrated accommodation—she changed her knowledge base.

Assimilation and accommodation are involved in the final process of equilibration. Here an attempt is made to achieve a balance or equilibrium between assimilation and accommodation. Piaget believed that all activity involves both processes. The interaction between assimilation and accommodation leads to adaptation, a process of adjusting to new situations. **Equilibration** is the tendency to reach a balance, which accounts for the formation of knowledge. Intellectual growth, according to Piaget, is achieved through the interplay of these three processes.

Four stages of cognitive development were identified by Piaget. He believed that children pass through these stages in an orderly, sequential fashion. Each stage is a prerequisite for the next one. The ages identified in Table 1.2 are only rough estimates of when a child enters each stage. Children progress at their own rate, which is influenced by their experiences and existing cognitive structures, in addition to their maturation.

TABLE 1.2 ■ Piaget's Stages of Cognitive Development

Approximate Age	Stage	Distinguishing Characteristics
Birth to 1.5–2 years of age	Sensorimotor	• Knowledge constructed through sensory perception and motor activity • Thought limited to action schemes • Beginning to develop object permanence
2–7 years of age	Preoperational	• Emergence of language, symbolic thinking • Intuitive rather than logical schemes • Egocentric in thought and action
7–11 years of age	Concrete operations	• Beginning of logical, systematic thinking; limited, however, to concrete operations • Diminished egocentrism • Understands reversibility and laws of conversation
12 years of age to adulthood	Formal operations	• Abstract and logical thought present • Capable of solving hypothetical problems • Deductive thinking and scientific reasoning is possible • Evidences concern about social issues, political causes

Lev Vygotsky

Russian psychologist Lev Semyonovich Vygotsky (1896–1934) was a contemporary of Piaget and another influential contributor to present understanding of how children learn and develop.

Vygotsky emphasized the importance of social interaction.
Heritage Images / Hulton Archive/Getty Images

A brilliant young man (he was literate in eight languages), Vygotsky entered Moscow University in 1914, where he studied law, one of the few vocations open to a Jew in tsarist Russia. Upon graduation in 1917, he returned to the city of Gomel, where he had spent most of his youth, and taught in several local institutions. The massive changes brought about by the Russian Revolution provided Vygotsky with the opportunity to teach at Gomel's Teacher's College. It was here that he became attracted to the fields of psychology and education, where his lack of formal training as a psychologist proved to be a distinct advantage. It allowed Vygotsky to view the field of psychology as an outsider, someone with fresh perspectives and creative ideas about child development (Berk & Winsler, 1995). A visionary thinker, Vygotsky significantly shaped contemporary theories and beliefs about children's language, play, cognition, and social development.

In his book, *Mind in Society,* Vygotsky (1978) argue that people—children in particular—are the products of their social and cultural environments. Children's development is significantly influenced by their social and cultural worlds and the individuals they encounter such as parents, teachers, and peers. Social experiences were very important to Vygotsky because he believed that higher-order cognitive processes, such as language and cognition, necessitate social interaction. What begins in a social context is eventually internalized psychologically. In his writings, Vygotsky emphasized the link between the social and psychological worlds of the young child. Learning and development occur via social interaction and engagement.

Learning awakens a variety of developmental processes that are able to operate only when the child is interacting with people in his environment and in collaboration with his peers. Once these processes are internalized, they become part of the child's independent developmental achievement. (Vygotsky, 1978, p. 90)

Vygotsky (1978, 1986) believed that social interaction not only fosters intellectual development but also is vital to the development of social competence. Vygotsky's emphasis on the reciprocity of social relationships, however, is contrary to the theorizing of Piaget. Recall that Piaget saw children as active yet solitary and independent discoverers of knowledge.

Perhaps the best-known Vygotskian concept is the **zone of proximal development (ZPD)**. Simply described, it is a hypothetical region defined by Vygotsky (1978) as "the distance between the actual developmental level as determined by independent problem solving and the level of potential development as determined through problem solving under adult guidance or in collaboration with more capable peers" (p. 86). The ZPD exists between what a child can presently accomplish independently and what the child is capable of doing within a supportive environment. Support is typically viewed as coming from more mature thinkers like adults and competent peers, although, according to Hills (1992), it may be derived from materials and equipment. The ZPD is actually created, Tudge (1992) writes, through social interaction. It is the arena or "magic middle" (Berger, 2020) in which learning and cognitive development occur. Figure 1.2 portrays Vygotsky's concept of ZPD.

Scaffolding is an idea related to Vygotsky's notion of a ZPD. It refers to the assistance given to a child by adults and peers that allows the individual to function independently and construct new concepts. Social interaction and collaboration with others typically provide infants and young children with opportunities for scaffolding. One of the primary goals of scaffolding is to keep children working on tasks that are in their ZPD. This goal is generally obtained by providing the minimum amount of assistance necessary and then further reducing this support as the child's own competence grows (Berk & Winsler, 1995). Within this context, the teacher's or caregiver's role is one of promoting and facilitating children's learning.

As can be seen, collaboration and social interaction are key tenets in Vygotsky's sociocultural approach to understanding children's learning and development. For Vygotsky, learning leads to

FIGURE 1.2 ■ Vygotsky's Zone of Proximal Development

development rather than following it. Learning is not itself development; rather, structured learning experiences play a major role giving impetus to developmental processes that would be difficult to separate from learning (Tudge, 1992). According to Vygotsky, development and learning are neither identical nor separate processes; instead, they are interrelated and integrative functions. This perspective sees developmental change as arising from a child's active engagement in a social environment with a mature partner. Growth occurs, therefore, within this ZPD. His approach to education could accurately be described as one of assisted discovery, also known as guided practice or assisted performance (Berk & Winsler, 1995).

Vygotsky also spoke on the issue of children with delays and disabilities. In fact, he enjoyed the title "Father of Soviet Defectology," which loosely translates to mean special education. Vygotsky (1993) emphasized that the principles that govern the learning and development of children without disabilities also apply to children with delays and disabilities. He was firmly convinced that the optimal development of young children with disabilities rested on fully integrating them into their social environment while ensuring that instruction occurs within their ZPD (Berk & Winsler, 1995). Children with learning difficulties should be educated, according to Vygotsky, in the same fashion as their peers without disabilities.

One of the major difficulties encountered by children with delays and disabilities is how their limitations impact their interaction with, and participation in, their social environment and not the disability itself. A child's disability often results in restricted interactions with adults and peers, and this contributes to the creation of a secondary—yet more debilitating—social deficit. Potentially more harmful than the primary disability, Vygotsky believed that these cultural limitations are more amenable to intervention than the original disorder is.

Several contemporary practices in early childhood special education can be traced to Vygotsky's theory. His conceptualizations suggest that young children with delays and disabilities should be included as much as possible in environments designed for typically developing learners. As an early advocate of the concept of inclusion, Vygotsky believed that a segregated placement results in a different social climate, thus restricting children's interactions and collaborative opportunities and thereby limiting cognitive development. Furthermore, educators should focus on children's strengths and abilities rather than their needs. What a child can do (with or without assistance) is more important than what they cannot do. Finally, a child's learning (social) environment should be rich with opportunities for scaffolding, which is seen as assisting in development of higher-order cognitive processes.

Vygotsky's contributions to children's learning and development were not limited to children with disabilities. Many well-known instructional strategies are grounded in his theories. Teachers who engage in cooperative learning activities, peer tutoring, guided practice, and reciprocal teaching and incorporate mixed-age groupings or a whole-language approach can thank Vygotsky.

A Concluding Thought

This brief examination of the historical roots of general early childhood education offers two conclusions. First, efforts on behalf of young children were and are frequently constrained by the political and social realities of the times. Second, much of what is often considered new or innovative has been written about and tried before. Present services for young children with disabilities have been influenced significantly by the history of education for young children. As an illustration, many contemporary programs for young children with delays and disabilities emphasize parent involvement, a child-centered curriculum, and interventions based on practical applications of child development theory. These programs also recognize that early experiences impact later social, emotional, and intellectual competency (Meisels & Shonkoff, 2000).

Table 1.3 presents a brief summary of the contributions of key individuals to the development of the field of early childhood education. Attention will now be given to the contributions emerging from the second parent field—special education.

TABLE 1.3 ■ Key Contributors to the Development of Early Childhood Education

Sixteenth Century	
Martin Luther	Strong believer in publicly supported schools. Advocate of universal, compulsory education.
Seventeenth and Eighteenth Century	
Jan Ámos Comenius (Komenský)	Advanced the notion of lifelong education, beginning in the early years. Realized the importance of a child's readiness for an activity. Stressed student's active participation in the learning process.
John Locke	Believed that children are similar to a blank tablet (tabula rasa). Environmental influences strongly impact a child's development. Sensory training is a critical aspect of learning.
Jean-Jacques Rousseau	Emphasized the importance of early education, which should be natural and allow for the unfolding of a child's abilities. School should focus on the interests of children.
Johann Heinrich Pestalozzi	Advocated education through nature and following the child's natural development. Early champion of the whole child and involving parents in the education process. Promoter of sensory education.
Nineteenth Century	
Robert Owen	Theorized that the early years were important in developing a child's character and behavior. Linked social change and education. His infant school served as a forerunner of kindergartens.
Friedrich Wilhelm Fröbel	Established the first kindergarten. Believed in the educational value and benefit of play. Considered development as a natural process of unfolding that provides the foundation for children's learning.
Twentieth Century	
John Dewey	Founder of the school of thought known as Progressivism. Argued that learning flows from the interests of the child rather than from activities chosen by the teacher. Coined the phrases child-centered curriculum and child-centered schools. Viewed education as a process for living; stressed social responsibility.
Maria Montessori	Believed that children learn best by direct sensory experience; was also convinced that there are sensitive periods for learning. Designed learning materials that were self-correcting, were graded in difficulty, and allowed for independent use. Classroom experiences were individualized to meet the needs of each child.

(Continued)

TABLE 1.3 ■ Key Contributors to the Development of Early Childhood Education (*Continued*)

Jean Piaget	Developed a stage theory of cognitive development. Cognitive growth emerges from a child's interaction with and adaptation to their physical environment. Children are self-motivated in the construction of their own knowledge, which occurs through activity and discovery.
Lev Semyonovich Vygotsky	Russian psychologist who theorized that children's development is significantly influenced by their social and cultural environments and the child's interactions with individuals therein. Saw learning and development as interrelated and integrative functions. Originator of the concept of a zone of proximal development (ZPD).

THE DEVELOPMENT OF SPECIAL EDUCATION: HISTORICAL PERSPECTIVES ON CHILDREN WITH DELAYS AND DISABILITIES

The history of special education provides a second point of departure for examining the evolution of early childhood special education. Society has chosen to deal with such individuals in a variety of ways. Often, programs and practices for individuals with delays and disabilities reflect the prevailing social climate, in addition to people's ideas and attitudes about disability. A change in attitude is often a precursor to a change in the delivery of services. The foundation of societal attitude in the United States can be traced to the efforts and philosophies of various Europeans. The attention will now turn to the historical contributions of these individuals with vision and courage.

People and Ideas

Current educational theories, principles, and practices are the product of pioneering thinkers, advocates, and humanitarians. These dedicated reformers were catalysts for change. Historians typically trace the roots of special education to the late 1700s and early 1800s. This is where the following brief examination of early leaders in the field begins.

One of the earliest documented attempts at providing special education involved the efforts of Jean Marc Gaspard Itard (1775–1838) to educate Victor, the so-called wild boy of Aveyron. A French physician and expert on hearing impairment, Itard endeavored in 1799 to "civilize" and teach Victor through a sensory training program and what today would be known as operant procedures. Because this adolescent failed to fully develop language after years of instruction and only mastered basic social and self-help skills, Itard considered his efforts a failure. Yet Itard demonstrated that learning is possible even for an individual described by other professionals as a hopeless and incurable idiot. The title "Father of Special Education" is bestowed on Itard because of his groundbreaking work more than two hundred years ago.

Another important pioneer was Itard's student, Édouard Séguin (1812–1880), who designed instructional programs for children his contemporaries thought to be incapable of learning. He believed in the importance of sensorimotor activities as an aid to learning. Séguin's methodology was based on a comprehensive assessment of a young child's strengths and needs coupled with an intervention plan of sensorimotor exercises prescribed to remediate specific disabilities. Seguin also emphasized the critical importance of early education. He is considered one of the first early interventionists. His theorizing also provided the foundation for Montessori's later work with the urban poor and children with intellectual disability.

The work of Itard, Séguin, and other innovators of their time helped to establish a foundation for much of the work done in special education today. Table 1.4 summarizes the work of European and American pioneers whose ideas have significantly influenced special education in the United States.

TABLE 1.4 ■ Pioneering Contributors to the Development of Special Education

Contributors	Their Ideas
Jacob Rodrigues Péreire (1715–1780)	Introduced the idea that persons who were deaf could be taught to communicate. Developed an early form of sign language. Provided inspiration and encouragement for the work of Itard and Séguin.
Philippe Pinel (1745–1826)	A reform-minded French physician who was concerned with the humanitarian treatment of individuals with mental illness. Strongly influenced the later work of Itard.
Jean Marc Gaspard Itard (1775–1838)	A French doctor who secured lasting fame due to his systematic efforts to educate an adolescent thought to be severely intellectually disabled. Recognized the importance of sensory stimulation.
Thomas Gallaudet (1787–1851)	Taught children with hearing impairments to communicate via a system of manual signs and symbols. Established the first institution for individuals with deafness in the United States.
Samuel Gridley Howe (1801–1876)	An American physician and educator accorded international fame due to his success in teaching individuals with visual and hearing impairments. Founded the first residential facility for the blind and was instrumental in inaugurating institutional care for children with intellectual disability.
Dorothea Lynde Dix (1802–1887)	A contemporary of Howe, Dix was one of the first Americans to champion better and more humane treatment of people with mental illness. Instigated the establishment of several institutions for individuals with mental disorders.
Louis Braille (1809–1852)	A French educator, who himself was blind, who developed a tactile system of reading and writing for people who were blind. His system, based on a code of six embossed dots, is still used today. Today this standardized code is known as Unified English Braille.
Édouard Séguin (1812–1880)	A student of Itard, Séguin was a French physician responsible for developing teaching methods for children with intellectual disability. His training program emphasized sensorimotor activities. After immigrating to the United States, he helped found the organization that was a forerunner of the American Association on Intellectual and Developmental Disabilities.
Francis Galton (1822–1911)	Scientist concerned with individual differences. As a result of studying eminent persons, he believed that genius is solely the result of heredity. Those with superior abilities are born, not made.
Alfred Binet (1857–1911)	A French psychologist, Binet authored the first developmental assessment scale capable of quantifying intelligence. Also originated the concept of mental age with his colleague Théodore Simon.
Lewis Terman (1877–1956)	An American educator and psychologist who revised Binet's original assessment instrument. The result was the publication of the Stanford-Binet Intelligence Scales. Terman developed the notion of intelligence quotient (IQ). Also famous for lifelong study of gifted individuals. Credited as being the grandfather of gifted education.

The Establishment of Institutions

Taking their cues from the Europeans, other American reformers such as Boston physician and humanitarian Samuel Gridley Howe (1801–1876) spearheaded the establishment of residential programs. A successful teacher of students who were both deaf and blind, Howe was instrumental in establishing the New England Asylum for the Blind (later the Perkins School) in the early 1830s. Almost two decades later, he played a major role in founding an experimental residential school for children with intellectual disability, the Massachusetts School for Idiotic and Feebleminded Youth. This facility was the first institution in the United States for individuals with intellectual disability. Now known as the Fernald Developmental Center in honor of its third superintendent, the center closed its doors in November 2014.

Residential schools for children with disabilities received additional impetus due to the untiring and vigorous efforts of social activist Dorothea Lynde Dix (1802–1887). A retired teacher, Dix was very influential in helping to establish several state institutions for people believed to be mentally ill, a group of individuals she felt to be grossly underserved and largely mistreated.

By the conclusion of the nineteenth century, residential institutions for persons with disabilities were a well-established part of the American social fabric. Initially established to offer training and some form of education in a protective lifelong environment, these institutions gradually deteriorated, for a variety of reasons, in the early decades of the twentieth century. The mission of the institutions changed from training to one of custodial care and isolation. The early optimism of special education was replaced by prejudice, unproven scientific views, and fear that helped to convert institutions into gloomy warehouses for the forgotten and neglected (Gargiulo & Bouck, 2021).

Special Education in Public Schools

It was not until the latter part of the nineteenth century that special education began to appear in the public schools. In fact, in 1898, Alexander Graham Bell (1847–1922), a teacher of children who were deaf, advocated that public schools begin serving individuals with disabilities. Services for students with disabilities began slowly and served only a small minority of those who needed them. The first public school class was organized in Boston in 1869 to serve children who were deaf. Children with intellectual disability first attended public schools about three decades later when a class was established in Providence, Rhode Island. The Chicago public schools inaugurated a class for children with physical impairments in 1899, quickly followed by one for children who were blind in 1900 (Gargiulo & Bouck, 2021). By the mid-1920s, well over half of the largest cities in America provided some type of special education services. The establishment of these programs was seen as an indication of the progressive status of the school district. Still, these earliest ventures mainly served children with mild disabilities; individuals with severe or multiple impairments were either kept at home or sent to institutions.

Institutions at one time were common across the United States.

iStock.com/BDphoto

Meisels and Shonkoff (2000) assert that the economic depression of the 1930s and the ensuing world war led to the decline of further expansion of special education programs in public schools; instead, greater reliance was placed on institutionalization. The residential facilities, however, were already overcrowded and provided educationally limited experiences. The postwar years saw an increase in the recognition of the needs of Americans with disabilities. Impetus for the shift of societal attitude resulted from two related factors—the large number of people deemed unfit for military service and the large number of war veterans who returned home with disabilities.

With the Second World War behind the nation, the stage was set for the rapid expansion of special education. This growth has been described as a virtual explosion of services occurring at both the state and federal levels. Litigation at all levels, legislative activities, increased fiscal resources, and federal leadership, in addition to social and political activism and advocacy, are some of the factors that helped fuel the movement and revitalize special education (Gargiulo & Bouck, 2021). Significant benefits for children with disabilities resulted from these efforts. For example, in 1948, approximately 12 percent of children with disabilities were receiving an education appropriate for their needs (Ballard et al., 1982), yet from 1947 to 1972, the number of students enrolled in special education programs increased an astonishing 716 percent as compared to an 82 percent increase in total public school enrollment (Dunn, 1973).

The last decades of the twentieth century also witnessed a flurry of activity on behalf of children with delays and disabilities. Evidence of this trend includes the 1975 landmark legislation PL 94–142; the Individuals with Disabilities Education Act (IDEA; originally known as the Education for All Handicapped Children Act); and its 1986 amendments, PL 99–457; together they constitute one of the most comprehensive statutes affecting infants, toddlers, and preschoolers with delays and disabilities and their families. The growth of services for preschoolers with delays and disabilities, programs for infants and toddlers, the transition initiative, and calls for inclusion of students with disabilities (discussed in Chapter 4) are additional indications of a changing attitude and expansion of opportunities for children and youth with disabilities.

COMPENSATORY EDUCATION PROGRAMS

The compensatory education movement of the 1960s also played a major role in the development of early childhood special education. As the name implies, this effort was designed to compensate for or ameliorate the environmental conditions and early learning experiences of children living in poverty. Such children were thought to be disadvantaged or "culturally deprived" (a popular term in the 1960s). The goal of compensatory education programs was to assist these children "by providing educational and environmental experiences that might better prepare them for the school experience" (Gearhart et al., 1993, p. 385). The compensatory education movement had its foundation in the idealism and heightened social consciousness that typified America more than five decades ago. It was also aided by the convergence of three distinct social issues: President Kennedy's interest in the field of intellectual disability, President Johnson's declaration of a War on Poverty, and the emerging civil rights movement (Meisels & Shonkoff, 2000).

In addition to sociological reasons, the compensatory education movement was aided by solid theoretical arguments. The cogent and persuasive writings of J. McVicker Hunt (1961) and fellow scholar Benjamin Bloom (1964) raised serious questions about the assumption of fixed or static intelligence. The malleability of intelligence and the importance of the early years for intellectual development were recognized by scientists and policymakers alike. Thus, the powerful contribution of early and enriched experiences on later development laid the cornerstone for programs like Head Start. It also set the stage for the concept of early intervention. It was thought that the deleterious effects of poverty could be remediated by early and intensive programming. The emphasis of preschool programs shifted from custodial caregiving to programming for specific developmental gains (Thurman & Widerstrom, 1990).

Representative Compensatory Programs

Project Head Start

Project Head Start came into existence as a result of the 1964 Economic Opportunity Act. Federally sponsored, Head Start was a critical component of a larger national agenda referred to as the War on Poverty. As the first nationwide compensatory education program, Head Start was conceived as an early intervention effort aimed at reducing the potential for school failure in disadvantaged young children from low socioeconomic communities. Initiated in the summer of 1965 as an eight-week pilot program, Project Head Start served approximately 560,000 four- and five-year-olds in more than 2,500 communities. In 2019, more than 873,000 preschoolers from low-income families received services. Since its inception more than five decades ago, Head Start has served more than 37 million children and their families (Head Start Program Facts, 2019).

According to Zigler and Valentine (1979), the first volley on the War on Poverty was constructed around three fundamental ideas:

1. Compensatory experiences initiated in the preschool years would result in successful adjustment to school and enhanced academic performance.
2. Early intellectual growth and development is directly dependent upon the quality of care and type of experiences to which young children are exposed.
3. Socioeconomically impoverished environments include biological, environmental, and other risk factors, which can adversely affect chances of school success and impede intellectual growth.

Head Start was envisioned to be a comprehensive, multidimensional intervention effort aimed at the very roots of poverty in communities across America. It represented a coordinated federal effort at comprehensive intervention in the lives of young children (Zigler & Valentine, 1979). Head Start was unique in its emphasis on the total development of the young child and on strengthening the family unit, as well as in its comprehensive nature of the services provided. The goals of the Head Start effort included increasing the child's physical, social, and emotional development; developing the child's intellectual skills and readiness for school; and improving the health of the child by providing medical, dental, social, and psychological services. Head Start was also unusual not only in its intent—to bring about a change for the child, their family, and the community—but also for its use of a multidisciplinary intervention model wherein the importance of seeing the whole child was recognized (Brain, 1979).

Parents played an unprecedented role in the Head Start program. Parents' involvement and their meaningful participation were considered vitally important. They had a key voice in the local decision-making process in addition to opportunities for employment in the program or for volunteering their expertise. The inclusion of training programs for low-income adults and the establishment of a career development ladder for employees and volunteers also distinguished the Head Start program.

It is important to remember that Head Start was not specifically directed at children with disabilities, although many of the young children served would today be identified as an at-risk population. The enactment of PL 92–424 in 1972 did require, however, that the project reserve no less than 10 percent of its enrollment for children with disabilities.

Fortunately, thanks to changes in federal regulations regarding Head Start, this program is now able to play a larger role in the lives of young children with disabilities. In January 1993, new rules for providing services to preschoolers with disabilities enrolled in Head Start were published in the *Federal Register*. Some of the many changes guiding Head Start agencies are the following requirements:

- A model designed to locate and serve young children with disabilities and their parents
- The development of an individualized education program (IEP) for each child determined to be disabled
- Quicker screening of children suspected of needing special education services
- Revised evaluation procedures for determining who might be eligible for special education and related services
- The establishment of a disability services coordinator who would be responsible for overseeing the delivery of services to preschoolers with disabilities (Head Start Program Final Rule, 1993)

These goals are to be met through a detailed and comprehensive disabilities service plan, which outlines the strategies for meeting the needs of children with delays and disabilities and their families. Among the several provisions are standards that call for the assurance that young children with disabilities will be included in the full range of activities and services provided to other children; a component that addresses the transitioning from infant and toddler programs into Head Start, as well as exiting

Head Start to the next placement; and a provision stipulating that eligible children will be provided a special education with related services designed to meet their unique needs. Recent statistics indicate that 13 percent of individuals, or approximately 113,500 children, enrolled in Head Start have an identified disability (Head Start Program Facts, 2019). By way of comparison, only 10.4 percent of infants, toddlers, and preschoolers were served via IDEA during the 2019–2020 school year (U.S. Department of Education, 2022).

In December 2007, Head Start was reauthorized through 2012 via the enactment of PL 110–134, the Improving Head Start for School Readiness Act of 2007 (also simply called the Head Start Act). The legislation was designed to help greater numbers of children from low-income families and those whose families are unhomed begin kindergarten ready to succeed. Emphasis was also placed on ensuring that educators working in Head Start programs are well prepared with at least 50 percent of these teachers possessing a baccalaureate degree in early childhood education or related area by 2013. Yearly professional development activities are also required of all full-time Head Start teachers. Additionally, individuals providing direct services to children and families in Early Head Start programs were mandated to possess a Child Development Associate (CDA) credential by 2010. Lastly, Head Start programs are to incorporate research-based early childhood curricula that support children's emerging literacy skills and vocabulary development.

One consequence of the passage of PL 110–134 in 2007 was the development of new Head Start performance guidelines that define standards and minimum requirements for Head Start programs. Almost ten years in the making, these standards represent the first revision since the original standards were promulgated in 1975. These revisions, published on September 1, 2016, affect both Head Start and Early Head Start programs. The goal of these efforts is to promote effective teaching and learning via a comprehensive and rigorous curriculum that is developmentally appropriate and aids in school readiness. Some of the other provisions call for the phase-in of all-day, year-round schooling in an effort to better prepare children for kindergarten. Additionally, individualized professional development activities aimed at improving teacher skills and competencies were set forth while the new rules also strengthen Head Start's commitment to children with disabilities, children in foster care, families experiencing homelessness, and bilingual children. Finally, these new guidelines retain parents' role as key decision makers in program governance (Administration for Children and Families, 2017).

Head Start is considered to be a visionary program model. The framers of the project had the foresight to insist on comprehensive services, meaningful parent involvement, and a multidisciplinary approach to intervention. Many of these aspects can be found in contemporary programs and legislation. Head Start also served as a forerunner of other compensatory initiatives, which will now be examined.

Project Follow-Through

Project Follow-Through was developed in 1967 in response to controversy surrounding the effectiveness of the Head Start efforts. Some educational research data suggested that the cognitive gains of the Head Start experiment were not maintained once the children enrolled in elementary school (Cicerelli et al., 1969). Professionals quickly realized that a short-term intervention program was ineffective in inoculating young children against the deleterious effects of poverty. Follow-Through was introduced in an effort to continue the gains developed in Head Start. A new model was designed, which extended the Head Start concept to include children enrolled in kindergarten through the third grade. Like its predecessor, Project Follow-Through was comprehensive in its scope of services while maintaining the Head Start emphasis on creating change in the home and community. Unfortunately, a congressional funding crisis precipitated a retooling of the project's original goals and objectives. According to Peterson's (1987) analysis, the focus shifted from a service operation very much like Head Start to an educational experiment dedicated to assessing the effectiveness of various approaches aimed at increasing the educational attainment of young disadvantaged and at-risk children. Rather than offering a single model of early childhood education for low-income children, Project Follow-Through studied a variety of approaches and strategies, realizing that a singular model would not meet the needs of all children. Local public schools were free to adopt the program model that they believed best met the unique needs of their communities.

Home Start

In 1972, another program variation, Home Start, was created. Simply stated, this program took the education component typically found in Head Start centers into a child's home. The focus of Home Start was low-income parents and their preschool-aged children. Efforts were aimed at providing educational stimulation to the children in addition to developing and enhancing the parenting skills of adults. This task was accomplished through the utilization of home visitors who were skilled and trained residents of the community.

Early Head Start

Early Head Start emerged from a growing recognition among service providers, researchers, policymakers, and politicians of the need to extend the Head Start model downward to the birth-to-three age group. This awareness of the need for comprehensive, intensive, and year-round services for very young children resulted in Early Head Start (Halpern, 2000; Meisels & Shonkoff, 2000). The 1994 reauthorization of Head Start (PL 103–252) created Early Head Start, a program focusing on low-income families with infants and toddlers as well as on women who are pregnant. The mission of this program, which began in 1995, is to

- promote healthy pregnancy outcomes;
- enhance children's physical, social, emotional, and cognitive development;
- enable parents to be better caregivers and teachers to their children; and
- help parents meet their goals, including economic independence.

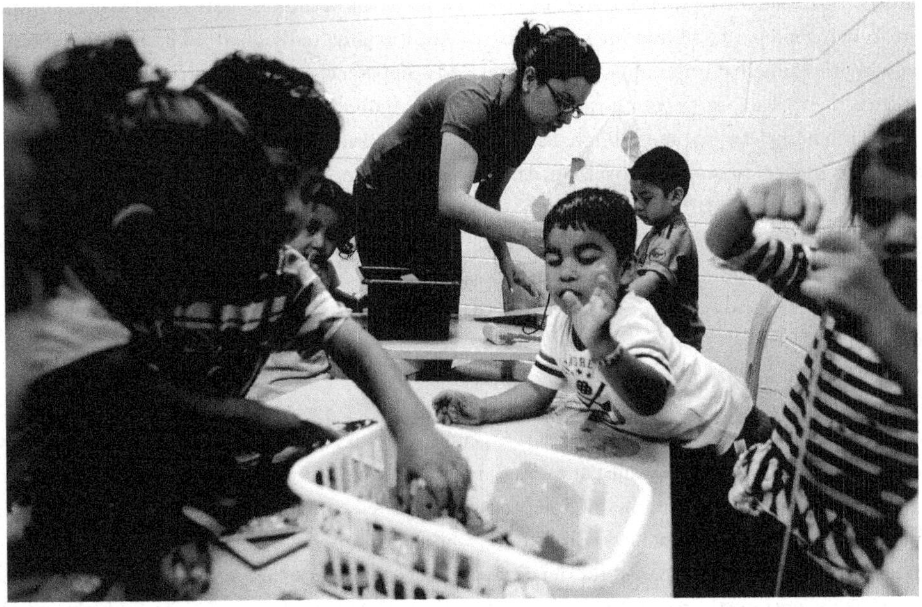

Head Start was the first nationwide compensatory education program.

Chicago Tribune/Tribune News Service/Getty Images

Early Head Start incorporates a "four corner strategy," which embodies child, family, community, and staff development. Services provided through this program include high-quality early education and care both in and out of the home; home visits; child care; parent education; comprehensive health services including services before, during, and after pregnancy; nutrition information; and peer support groups for parents. Early Head Start recently served more than 216,000 infants and toddlers (65 percent of the children are either one or two years old). Slightly more than 200,000 families also received a wide range of health, educational, and social services. Additionally, approximately 15,000 pregnant women were served by Early Head Start programs (Office of Head Start, 2019).

Research Activities

In addition to involvement and action by the federal government, individual scientists and researchers have been concerned about the damaging consequences of poverty on young children and their families. Two representative intervention projects are the Carolina Abecedarian Project and the Perry Preschool Project. Both of these programs focus on improving the cognitive skills of young children, thereby increasing their chances for later scholastic success.

The Carolina Abecedarian Project attempted to modify environmental forces impinging upon the intellectual development of young children living in poverty. Designed in 1972 as a longitudinal experiment, Craig Ramey and his colleagues (Ramey & Campbell, 1977, 1984; Ramey & Smith, 1977) found that children enrolled in a center-based preschool intervention program who were exposed to intensive and stimulating early learning experiences achieved higher IQ scores when compared to matched age-mates who did not participate in the project. A follow-up of participants found that, at age twelve and fifteen, children exposed to early intervention continued to outperform control subjects on standardized measures of intellectual development and academic achievement. Additionally, these individuals had significantly fewer grade retentions and special education placements (Campbell & Ramey, 1994, 1995). As young adults, these individuals scored higher on measures of intellectual and academic achievement and were more likely to attend a four-year college (Campbell et al., 2002). The Carolina program clearly demonstrates, as noted earlier, the plasticity of intelligence and the positive effects of early environmental intervention.

The second illustration is the Perry Preschool Project in Ypsilanti, Michigan. This program is one of the best examples of the long-term educational benefit of early childhood experiences. The Perry Preschool Project was designed as a longitudinal study to measure the effects of a quality preschool education on children living in poverty. Based on the work of Jean Piaget, it strongly emphasized cognitive development. More than 120 disadvantaged children were followed from age three until late adolescence. The results of the investigation can be summarized as follows:

> Results to age 19 indicate long-lasting beneficial effects of preschool education in improving cognitive performance during early childhood; in improving scholastic placement and achievement during the school years; in decreasing delinquency and crime, the use of welfare assistance, and the incidence of teenage pregnancy; and in increasing high school graduation rates and the frequency of enrollment in postsecondary programs and employment. (Berrueta-Clement et al., 1984, p. 1)

Additional longitudinal follow-up (Schweinhart et al., 1993; Schweinhart et al., 2005) demonstrated that, in comparison to a control group, individuals in their mid-twenties and at age forty who participated in this project as preschoolers had higher incomes, were more likely to own a home, had significantly fewer arrests, and had less involvement with community social service agencies.

Likewise, other investigators (Bakken et al., 2017; Campbell et al., 2012; Reynolds & Temple, 2005; Temple & Reynolds, 2007) also report long-term positive outcomes for children from economically disadvantaged backgrounds who participated in high-quality early education intervention programs.

Despite the methodological difficulties inherent in conducting early intervention research in a scientifically rigorous fashion, this research evidence unequivocally illustrates that early intervention generates positive academic outcomes and significantly improves the quality of participants' later lives. Most early childhood special educators fully agree with Guralnick's (2005) observation that "the early years may well constitute a unique window of opportunity to alter children's' developmental trajectories" (p. 314).

A Concluding Thought

It is safe to conclude that, generally speaking, compensatory education programs do benefit young children who are at risk of not succeeding in school. The optimism exhibited by the early supporters of various intervention initiatives has been tempered, however, by a host of political, financial, and other factors. Reality has reminded educators, policymakers, and researchers that there are no quick or magical solutions to complex social problems like poverty. Yet it is important not to be overly pessimistic; education does remain an important vehicle for successfully altering the outcomes of young children and their families.

SUMMARY

Although early childhood special education is a relatively young field, the forces that have helped to shape its identity have a rich and distinguished history. Drawing upon the work of early educational theorists and writers such as Piaget, Vygotsky, Montessori, Dewey, and others, early childhood special education has evolved into a distinct field with its own identity and theoretical underpinnings. Yet it is interesting to note that many of the current practices in early childhood special education (e.g., individualized instruction, family-centered services) and the values to which the field of early childhood special education subscribes are not especially contemporary. Perhaps there is truth to the maxim that "The past is prologue." Three distinct fields—general early childhood education, special education, and compensatory education—have contributed, in their own ways, to the emergence of a wide array of programs and services for young children with delays and disabilities and their families. Professionals representing multiple disciplines recognize how extremely important the early years of a child's life are for later social, emotional, and cognitive growth and development (Dunst, 2007; Harkness et al., 2013).

Today the field of early childhood special education is perhaps best conceptualized as a synthesis of various theories, principles, and practices that have evolved from each of its parent fields (Peterson, 1987). Early childhood special education is a field that continues to evolve and is in a strong position to successfully build on the accomplishments and achievements of the past.

KEY TERMS

Accommodation
Assimilation
Auto-education
Compensatory education
Didactic materials
Early Head Start
Early intervention
Early childhood special education
Equilibration
Gifts
Home Start
Occupations
Prepared environment
Progressivism
Project Follow-Through
Project Head Start
Scaffolding
Schema
Sensitive periods
Tabula rasa
Zone of proximal development (ZPD)

CHECK YOUR UNDERSTANDING

1. Various religious leaders, philosophers, and educational theorists played major roles in the development of early childhood education. List five of them and their contributions found in contemporary early childhood programs.
2. Describe the "gifts" and "occupations" of Fröbel's children's garden.
3. Explain Dewey's ideas about educating young children.
4. Identify the major elements of Montessori's approach to teaching young children.
5. How did Piaget believe intelligence develops?
6. Describe Vygotsky's concept of zone of proximal development (ZPD).
7. Why would Vygotsky be considered an early advocate of integration?

8. What role did Europeans play in the development of special education in the United States?
9. Describe the three parent fields that have influenced the field of early childhood special education.
10. Define the term *compensatory education.*
11. What is the purpose of Project Head Start and Early Head Start?
12. List five significant events that have helped to shape the field of early childhood special education.

REFLECTION AND APPLICATION

1. What evidence do you see of Dewey, Piaget, and Vygotsky in today's early childhood education settings? What are the strengths of each philosophy? Compare and contrast the three philosophies.
2. In what ways do you see contemporary educators building on the work of earlier philosophers? How does each of the philosophers mentioned in this chapter describe curriculum? What are their fundamental ideas about how children learn?
3. What influence does the environment have on infants, toddlers, and young children in today's society? What did Dewey say about the environment and its impact on teaching and learning? What did Piaget and Vygotsky say about the environment and early childhood learning?
4. How has the development of compensatory programs such as Head Start helped to strengthen today's young children and families experiencing poverty? In what ways can early childhood special education programs make compensatory programs available to their children and families? Provide examples.

iStock.com/FatCamera

2 THE CONTEXT OF EARLY CHILDHOOD SPECIAL EDUCATION

LEARNING OBJECTIVES

After reading this chapter, you will be able to

2.1 Define the terms *disability, handicap, developmental delay*, and *at risk*.

2.2 Discuss how judicial decisions and legislative enactments have benefited young children with delays and disabilities.

2.3 Summarize the major provisions contained in both PL 94–142 and PL 99–457.

2.4 Identify at least four benefits of early intervention/early childhood special education for young children with delays and disabilities.

2.5 Explain the concept of ecology and its importance to the field of early intervention/early childhood special education.

Early intervention/early childhood special education (EI/ECSE) is a unique and specialized field that focuses on providing services and supports to young children with delays and disabilities, ages birth through eight years, and their families. Although EI/ECSE is a relatively young field that draws upon the long history, rich legacy, and contributions of general early childhood education, special education, and compensatory education, it is a distinct field with its own identity and purpose (Bricker et al., 2020; McLean et al., 2016). To fully appreciate the EI/ECSE discipline, several elements that are basic to the understanding of its development should be explored. These elements help provide a firm foundation for the later examination of programs and services for young children with delays and disabilities and their families. Attention will be focused on key terminology, the impact of litigation and legislation on the growth of the field, the prevalence of young children with delays and disabilities, the research evidence on the efficacy of early intervention and early childhood special education, and the validity of an ecological approach for examining the world of young children with delays and disabilities.

DEFINITIONS AND TERMINOLOGY

Early childhood professionals serve a wide range of individuals. An increasing number of these young children have developmental delays and disabilities and others are at risk for future educational difficulties. What do these terms mean? Is a disability synonymous with a handicap? What is a developmental delay? What factors jeopardize a child's future educational success? Unfortunately, clear-cut answers to these basic questions are sometimes difficult to achieve. Confusion and misinterpretation are not unusual, even among EI/ECSE professionals. Hence, the following descriptions are an attempt to clarify key terminology and provide a common foundation for understanding the terminology associated with infants, toddlers, preschoolers, and early primary students with delays and disabilities.

Exceptional Children

The field of special education often identifies the children they serve as **exceptional children**. This inclusive term generally refers to individuals who are neurodivergent and differ from societal or community standards of normalcy. These children will, therefore, require educational services customized to their strengths and needs. Some exceptionalities are obvious and easy to identify while others are less obvious, such as a child who is deaf. The term *exceptional children* encompasses children who are intellectually talented and may greatly benefit from their exceptionality in the educational process, while in other situations an exceptionality may prove to be a significant issue.

Professionals must not lose sight, however, of the fact that a child with any type of delay or disability is first and foremost a child—an individual who is more like their typically developing peers than they are different. The fact that a child is identified with a delay or disability should never prevent professionals from realizing just how similar the individual is to their peers in many other ways.

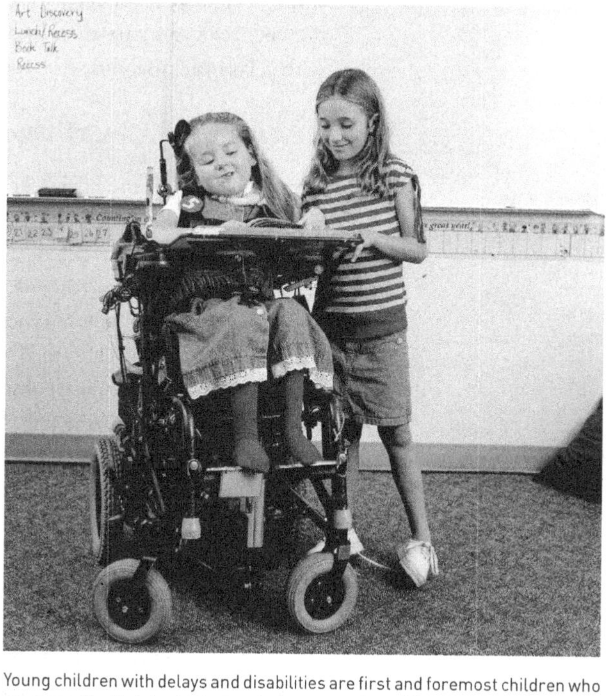

Young children with delays and disabilities are first and foremost children who are more like their typically developing peers than different.

Rebecca Emery / Stockbyte/via Getty Images

Disability *and* Handicap

All too often, professionals, as well as the general public, use the terms *disability* and *handicap* interchangeably. These terms, however, have distinct meanings and are not synonymous. When professionals talk about a **disability**, they are referring to the inability of an individual to do something in a certain way. A disability may be thought of as an incapacity to perform in a similar way as other children due to impairments in sensory, physical, cognitive, and other areas of functioning. A **handicap**, on the other hand, refers to the problems that children with a disability encounter as they attempt to function and interact in their environment. Mandy, for example, has cerebral palsy. This is a disability. If her disability prohibits her from becoming a professional ice skater, then Mandy is considered to have a handicap. Stephen, a four-year-old who is legally blind (a disability), would have a handicap if his preschool teacher inadvertently used a promethean board while explaining a cooking activity. A disability may or may not be a handicap depending upon the specific circumstances. For instance, a six-year-old child who wears ankle-foot orthoses (AFOs) or leg braces, might have difficulty walking upstairs; however, in the classroom art center, his creativity and talents are easily demonstrated. Today, professionals rarely use the term *handicap* and then only when explaining the consequences or impact imposed on a young child by their disability. Gargiulo and Bouck (2021) urge educators to separate the disability from the handicap.

Early Intervention and Early Childhood Special Education

Continuing the discussion on terminology, it is important to clarify the terms *early intervention* and *early childhood special education*. EI/ECSE services have been explicitly defined in the United States by the Individuals with Disabilities Education Act (IDEA; Turnbull et al., 2004). Generally, *early intervention* refers to the delivery of a coordinated and comprehensive set of specialized supports and services to infants and toddlers (from birth through age two) with a developmental delay or disability and their families. The term *early intervention* can be found specifically in Part C of IDEA (to be discussed later in this chapter). Describing the nature of early intervention is not an easy task. Early intervention can be characterized according to the type of service provided (physical therapy, vision services), location of service (home, childcare center), and service provider (early childhood special educator, occupational therapist, nurse), to mention just some of the critical features of this concept (Bricker et al., 2020; McWilliam, 2016).

The goal of early intervention is multifold. One purpose is to minimize the impact or effect of a disability or delay, while another goal is to prevent future learning and developmental difficulties in children (Long, 2019; McWilliam, 2016). An additional purpose is to provide families with individualized support and services (Kilgo, 2022). Accordingly, early intervention is an opportunity to enhance and maximize the potential of young children as well as their families.

The term *early childhood special education* is an umbrella term used for services for birth through eight-year-olds with delays and disabilities. Also, it used specifically when talking about the provision of customized services uniquely crafted to meet the individual needs of young children from three through eight years of age with delays and disabilities. It is important to note that special education does not refer to a particular location but rather a system of supports and services for young children with delays and disabilities (Gargiulo & Bouck, 2021).

Developmental Delay *and* At Risk

Because of the adverse effects of early labeling, recommended practice suggests that young children with delays and disabilities be identified as eligible for services as either developmentally delayed or, in some instances, at risk. These terms, in fact, are incorporated in PL 99–457. This significant enactment requires that local schools provide comprehensive services to children from ages three to five with delays and disabilities. The children, however, do *not* have to be identified with a disability label. The 1991 amendments (PL 102–119) to IDEA allow states to use a generic category like "children with disabilities." According to one national survey (Danaher, 2011), nine states utilize a noncategorical description exclusively when classifying preschoolers with delays and disabilities. These generic labels include "preschool child [student] with a disability" (Colorado, New Jersey, New York); "preschool special needs" (West Virginia); and "noncategorical early childhood" (Texas). Many professionals believe that the use of a categorical disability label for most young children is of questionable value, unfairly stigmatizes young children, and creates a self-fulfilling prophecy (Danaher, 2011; Division for Early Childhood, 2009). A noncategorical approach to serving young children with delays and disabilities is, therefore, perfectly acceptable as well as legal. Many early childhood special education programs offer services without categorizing children on the basis of a disability. Thus, instead of a categorical approach, programs serving young children with delays and disabilities frequently use the broad term *developmental delay*.

As a result of the passage of PL 105–17, it is now permissible, at the discretion of the state and local education agency, to use the term *developmental delay* for children ages three through nine. The most recent reauthorization of IDEA, PL 108–446, reiterated the appropriateness of this term for children ages three to nine (or any subset of this group). Forty-two states use the term *developmental delay* or a similar variation (e.g., *significant developmental delay*) when describing these children (Danaher, 2011).

Developmental Delay

Congress realized that establishing a national definition of **developmental delay** would be an almost insurmountable task and, therefore, left the responsibility of developing a satisfactory definition to the individual states. One consequence of this action is the tremendous diversity of criteria found in the various meanings of this term. Many states incorporate a quantitative approach when determining which children meet the developmentally delayed eligibility criteria (Danaher, 2011; Early Childhood Technical Assistance Center, 2022). Typical of this strategy is a reliance on data derived from various assessment instruments. Two common criteria for a developmental delay are

- a delay expressed in terms of standard deviations (SD) below the mean on a norm-referenced assessment (Georgia, Indiana: 2 SD in one developmental area or 1.5 SD in two areas[1]), and
- a delay expressed in terms of a difference between a child's chronological age and actual performance level (Alaska: 50 percent or greater delay in one or more developmental areas, West Virginia: 25 percent delay in one or more developmental areas).

Table 2.1 lists examples of criteria used by the states when quantifying a developmental delay. Obviously, there is no one correct way to define this concept. Each approach has its advantages and disadvantages. In fact, some states allow for the use of a qualitative determination when considering whether or not a child has a developmental delay. Texas is one example while Puerto Rico permits the use of informed clinical opinions of members of a multidisciplinary team.

A qualitative determination is allowed due to the lack of valid and reliable dependent measures appropriate for young children. The predictive validity of these assessment instruments is also suspect. As a result, the regulations accompanying IDEA require that informed clinical opinion be included as part of eligibility determination (Shackelford, 2006; Smiley et al., 2022).

There are several advantages to using the term *developmental delay.* First, because it suggests a developmental status rather than a category, it is anticipated that placement of young children in developmentally appropriate classrooms will be more likely. Second, it is hoped that this concept will lead to services being matched to the needs and abilities of the child rather than having services decided by a categorical label. Third, professionals believe that the utilization of this term is likely to encourage inclusive models of service delivery instead of services being primarily driven by a disability label. Finally, the use of this term prevents the possibility of misidentifying a young child when the etiology or cause of the child's delay is not clearly evident (Division for Early Childhood, 2009).

At Risk

When professionals refer to children being **at risk**, they are speaking of children "who have not been formally identified as having a disability, but who may be developing conditions that will limit their success in school or lead to disabilities. This can be the result of exposure to adverse genetic, biological, or environmental factors" (Spodek & Saracho, 1994a, p. 16). This definition parallels an earlier description of risk factors identified by Kopp (1983). She defines risk as "a wide range of biological and

[1] Developmental areas include physical, communication, cognitive, social or emotional, and adaptive.

TABLE 2.1 ■ Representative Examples of Definitions of Developmental Delay

State	Criteria
Arkansas	25% or greater delay in one or more developmental areas
Florida	1.5 SD below the mean in two or more areas or 2 SD below the mean in one or more developmental areas
Michigan	20% or 1 SD below the mean in one or more developmental areas
Nebraska	2 SD below the mean in one developmental area or 1.3 SD below the mean in two or more developmental areas
New Hampshire	33% delay in one or more developmental areas; or atypical behavior
Tennessee	25% delay in two developmental areas or a 40% delay in one area
Utah	1.5 SD at or below the mean, or at or below the 7th percentile in one or more areas of development on approved instrument
Virginia	At least 25% below chronological or adjusted age in one or more areas of development or atypical development (even in the absence of 25% delay)

Source: Adapted from National Early Childhood Technical Assistance Center. (2022). *State and Jurisdictional Eligibility Definitions.* Chapel Hill, NC: University of North Carolina, FPG Child Development Institute.

Note: SD = standard deviation below the mean on a norm-referenced assessment instrument.

Areas refers to physical, communication, cognitive, social or emotional, and adaptive areas of development.

environmental conditions that are associated with increased probability for cognitive, social, affective, and physical problems" (p. 1081).

In both of these definitions, exposure to adverse circumstances *may* lead to later problems in development and learning, but it is not a guarantee that developmental problems will occur. Risk factors only set the stage or heighten the probability that differences will arise. Many young children are subject to a wide variety of risks, yet they never evidence developmental problems. Table 2.2 presents some of the common factors and conditions that may place a child at risk.

Professionals typically classify risk factors into two (Lipkin & Schertz, 2008) or three (Shackelford, 2006) at-risk categories. Shackelford's work is but one example of a model that is widely accepted today. This tripartite classification scheme includes established, biological, and environmental risk categories. These categories are not mutually exclusive and frequently overlap. In some instances, a young child identified as being biologically at risk due to prematurity may also be at risk due to environmental factors like severe poverty. As a result of this "double vulnerability," the probability for future delays and learning difficulties dramatically increases.

Established Risk

Children with a diagnosed medical disorder of known etiology and predictable prognosis or outcome are considered to manifest an **established risk**. Illustrations of such conditions would include children born with cerebral palsy, Down syndrome, spina bifida, an inborn error of metabolism such as PKU (phenylketonuria), or severe sensory impairments. Young children identified with an established risk condition must be served if the state receives IDEA Part C monies.

Biological Risk

Included in this category are children with a history of pre-, peri-, and postnatal conditions and developmental events that heighten the potential for later atypical or aberrant development. **Biological risk** factors include conditions or complications such as premature births, infants with low birth weights, maternal diabetes, rubella (German measles), anoxia, bacterial infections like meningitis, and HIV (human immunodeficiency virus) infection.

TABLE 2.2 ■ Representative Factors Placing Young Children at Risk for Developmental Delays

Maternal alcohol and drug abuse
Children born to teenage mothers or women over age 40
Home environment lacking adequate stimulation
Maternal diabetes, hypertension, or toxemia
Exposure to rubella
Chronic poverty
Primary caregiver is developmentally disabled
Infections such as encephalitis and meningitis
Oxygen deprivation
Child abuse and neglect
Accidents and head trauma
Inadequate maternal and infant nutrition
Genetic disorders such as Down syndrome, phenylketonuria, and galactosemia
Family history of congenital abnormalities
Exposure to radiation
Prematurity
Rh incompatibility
Low birth weight
Ingestion of poisons and toxic substances by child
Prolonged or unusual delivery

Note: Factors are not ranked in order of potential influence.

Environmental Risk

Environmentally at-risk children are biologically typical, but their life experiences and/or environmental conditions are so limiting or threatening that the likelihood of delayed development exists. Extreme poverty, child abuse, absence of adequate shelter and medical care, parental substance abuse, and limited opportunities for nurturance and social stimulation are all examples of potential **environmental risk** factors. This risk category, as well as children who are biologically at risk, results in discretionary services. States may elect to provide early intervention if they wish to, but they are not mandated to serve infants and toddlers who are biologically or environmentally at risk.

Given the magnitude of factors that may place a child at risk for developing disabilities, the value of prevention and early intervention cannot be underestimated. Of course, prevention is better than remediation.

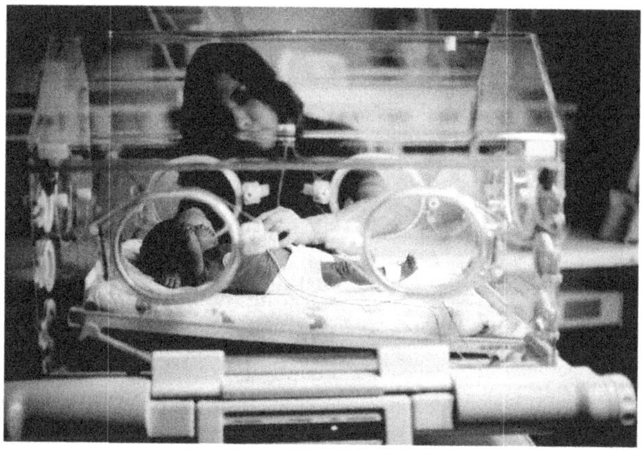

Some young children may be at risk for future difficulties in learning and development due to biological risk factors.

rubberball/Brand X Pictures/via Getty Images

Federal Definition of Disability

As previously noted, early childhood special educators serve a variety of young children with delays and disabilities, but who are these children? The federal government, in IDEA (PL 108–446), defines a student with a disability according to the thirteen distinct categories listed in Table 2.3. The government's interpretation of these labels is presented in Appendix C. Individual states frequently use these federal guidelines to construct their own standards and policies as to who is eligible to receive early intervention and special education services.

TABLE 2.3 ■ Federal Classification of Disabilities

Autism	Orthopedic impairment
Deaf-blindness	Other health impairments
Developmental delay*	Speech or language impairment
Emotional disturbance	Specific learning disability
Hearing impairment	Traumatic brain injury
Intellectual disability**	Visual impairment
Multiple disabilities	

Note: *Defined according to individual state guidelines.

**Formerly known as mental retardation. Federal legislation (PL 111–256) changed this designation on October 5, 2010.

The term *children with delays and disabilities* is used to describe the infants, toddlers, preschoolers, and early primary students (birth through age eight) who are the focus of this textbook. Early childhood special educators should consider the similarities between children with delays and disabilities and their typically developing peers, not differences. Attention also should be focused on the children's strengths and abilities, not their delays and disabilities.

LITIGATION AND LEGISLATION AFFECTING CHILDREN WITH DELAYS AND DISABILITIES

Early childhood special education is an evolving discipline. In addition to drawing upon its three parent fields (general early childhood education, special education, and compensatory education), judicial action has played a key role in the growth of the field. Litigation initiated by parents and special interest groups has helped pave the way in securing numerous rights for children with disabilities and their families. Since the 1960s and early 1970s, a plethora of state and federal court decisions have continually shaped and defined a wide range of issues that impact contemporary special education policies and procedures. The U.S. Supreme Court has ruled on a number of cases involving special education. These cases have resulted in decisions that have addressed issues regarding special education programming, such as the provision of a free appropriate public education, related services, discipline, and procedural issues (Yell & Bateman, 2020; Zirkel & Yell, 2024). Table 2.4 summarizes some of the landmark cases affecting the field of special education. Many of the judicial remedies emanating from these lawsuits form the cornerstones of both federal and state legislative enactments focusing on children with delays and disabilities. Furthermore, many accepted practices in today's special education programs, such as nondiscriminatory assessments and due process procedures, have their roots in various court decisions.

Key Federal Legislation

Federal legislative intervention in the lives of persons with disabilities is of relatively recent origin. Prior to the late 1950s and early 1960s, little federal attention was devoted to citizens with disabilities. When legislation was enacted, it primarily assisted specific groups of individuals such as those who were visually impaired or had an intellectual disability. The last sixty years, however, have witnessed a flurry of federal legislative activity, which has aided the growth of special education and provided educational benefits and other opportunities and rights to children and adults with disabilities.

TABLE 2.4 ■ A Synopsis of Selected Court Cases Influencing Special Education

Case	Year	Issue	Judicial Decision
Brown v. Board of Education	1954	Educational segregation	Segregation of students by race ruled unconstitutional. Children are being deprived of equal educational opportunity. Effectively ended "separate but equal" schools for white and black students. Used as a precedent for arguing that children with disabilities cannot be excluded from a public education.
Hobson v. Hansen	1967	Classifying students	Grouping or "tracking" of students on the basis of standardized tests, which were found to be biased, held to be unconstitutional. Tracking systems discriminated against poor and minority children. Equal protection clause of Fourteenth Amendment violated.
Diana v. State Board of Education	1970	Class placement	Linguistically different students must be tested in their primary language as well as in English. Students cannot be placed in special education classes on the basis of tests that are culturally biased. Test items were to be revised so as to reflect students' cultures. Group-administered IQ tests cannot be utilized for placement of children in programs for students with intellectual disability.
Pennsylvania Association for Retarded Children v. Commonwealth of Pennsylvania	1972	Right to education	State must guarantee a free public education to all children with intellectual disability, ages 6–21, regardless of degree of impairment or associated disabilities. Students were to be placed in the most inclusive environment. Definition of *education* expanded. Case established the right of parents to participate in educational decisions affecting their children.
Mills v. Board of Education of the District of Columbia	1972	Right to education	Extended the *Pennsylvania* decision to include all children with disabilities. Specifically established the constitutional right of children with disabilities to a public education regardless of their functional level. Presumed absence of fiscal resources is not a valid reason for failing to provide appropriate educational services to students with disabilities. Due process procedures established to protect the rights of the child.
Larry P. v. Riles	1972, 1979	Class placement	A landmark case parallel to the *Diana* suit. African American students could not be placed in classes for the educable mentally retarded (EMR)* solely on the basis of intellectual assessments found to be culturally and racially biased. The court instructed school officials to develop assessments that would not discriminate against minority children. The failure to comply with this order resulted in a 1979 ruling, which completely prohibited the use of IQ tests for identifying African American students for placement in EMR classes. Ruling applies only to the state of California.
Jose P. v. Ambach	1979	Timelines and delivery of services	A far-reaching class action lawsuit that restructured the delivery of special education services in New York City public schools. Judgment established (1) school-based support teams to conduct evaluations and provide services; (2) stringent timelines for completing evaluations and placement; (3) due process procedures; (4) guidelines for nondiscriminatory evaluation; (5) detailed monitoring procedures; and (6) accessibility of school facilities.

(Continued)

TABLE 2.4 ■ A Synopsis of Selected Court Cases Influencing Special Education (*Continued*)

Case	Year	Issue	Judicial Decision
Armstrong v. Kline	1979	Extended school year	States' refusal to pay for schooling more than 180 days for students with severe disabilities is a violation of their rights to an appropriate education as found in PL 94–142. The court moved that some children with disabilities will regress significantly during summer recess and have longer recoupment periods; thus, they are denied an appropriate education if not provided with a year-round education.
Tatro v. State of Texas	1980	Related services	A U.S. Supreme Court decision, which held that catheterization qualified as a related service under PL 94–142. Catheterization not considered an exempted medical procedure as it could be performed by a health care aide or school nurse. Court further stipulated that only those services that allow a student to benefit from a special education qualify as related services.
Board of Education v. Rowley	1982	Appropriate education	First U.S. Supreme Court interpretation of PL 94–142. Court addressed the issue of what constitutes an "appropriate" education for a student who was deaf but making satisfactory academic progress. Supreme Court ruled that an appropriate education does not necessarily mean an education that will allow for the maximum possible achievement; rather, students must be given a reasonable opportunity to learn. Parents' request for a sign language interpreter, therefore, was denied. An appropriate education is not synonymous with an optimal educational experience.
Honig v. Doe	1988	Exclusion from school	Children with disabilities whose behavior is a direct result of their disability cannot be expelled from school due to misbehavior. If behavior leading to expulsion is not a consequence of the disability, children may be expelled. Short-term suspension from school not interpreted as a change in child's individualized education program (IEP).
Daniel R. R. v. State Board of Education	1989	Class placement	A Fifth Circuit Court of Appeals decision that held that a segregated class was an appropriate placement for a student with Down syndrome. Preference for inclusive placement viewed as secondary to the need for an appropriate education. Court established a two-prong test for determining compliance with the least restrictive environment (LRE) mandate for students with severe disabilities. First, it must be determined whether a student can make satisfactory progress and achieve educational benefit in a general education classroom through curriculum modification and supplementary aids and services. Second, it must be determined whether the student has been included to the maximum extent appropriate. Successful compliance with both parts fulfills a school's obligation under federal law. Ruling affects LRE cases in Louisiana, Texas, and Mississippi, but has become a benchmark decision for other jurisdictions as well.
Oberti v. Board of Education of the Borough of Clementon School District	1992	Least restrictive environment	Placement in a general education classroom with the use of supplementary aids and services must be offered to a student with disabilities prior to considering more segregated placements. A child cannot be excluded from a general education classroom solely because curriculum, services, or other practices would require modification. A decision to exclude a learner from the general education classroom necessitates justification and documentation. Clear judicial preference for educational inclusion established.

Case	Year	Issue	Judicial Decision
Agostini v. Felton	1997	Provision of services	A U.S. Supreme Court decision that reversed a long-standing ruling banning the delivery of publicly funded educational services to students enrolled in private schools. Interpreted to mean special educators can now provide services to children in parochial schools.
Cedar Rapids Community School District v. Garret F.	1999	Related services	A U.S. Supreme Court decision that expanded and clarified the concept of related services. This case affirmed that intensive and continuous school health care services necessary for a student to attend school, and which are not performed by a physician, qualify as related services.
Arlington Central School District Board of Education v. Murphy	2006	Recovery of fees	The issue in this U.S. Supreme Court case is whether parents are able to recover the professional fees of an educational consultant (advocate) who provided services during legal proceedings. The Court ruled that parents are not entitled to reimbursement for the cost of experts because only attorneys' fees are addressed in IDEA.
Winkelman v. Parma City School District	2007	Parental rights	One of the more significant Supreme Court rulings. The Court, by unanimous vote, affirmed the right of parents to represent their children in IDEA-related court cases. Ruling seen as an expansion of parental involvement and the definition of a free appropriate public education. Decision also interpreted to mean that IDEA conveys enforceable rights to parents as well as their children.
Forest Grove School District v. T. A.	2009	Tuition reimbursement	A Supreme Court decision involving tuition reimbursement for a student with learning disabilities and attention deficit hyperactivity disorder as well as depression who was never declared eligible for special education and never received services from the school district. Parents removed the child from the school and unilaterally enrolled the child in a private school. Subsequently they sought reimbursement from the school district for expenses. In a 6–3 decision, the Court found that IDEA authorizes reimbursement for private special education when a public school fails to provide a free appropriate education and the private school placement is appropriate, regardless of whether the student previously received special education services.
Fry v. Napoleon Community Schools	2017	IDEA exhaustion doctrine	A suit filed on behalf of a young girl with a severe form of cerebral palsy who used a service animal. Because the school provided the student with a personal aide in accordance with her IEP, the school district refused to allow her the use of her service dog. The girl's parents sought relief under the Americans with Disabilities Act Amendments Act of 2008 (ADAAA) and Section 504 of the Rehabilitation Act rather than IDEA, which required the parents to exhaust all administrative remedies (e.g., due process hearing) prior to suing under the ADAAA and 504. As this was a disability discrimination issue and the adequacy of the student's educational services were not in question, the Court ruled unanimously that because the parents were not seeking relief under the free appropriate public education clause of IDEA, the exhaustion requirement of IDEA was not applicable.

(Continued)

TABLE 2.4 ■ A Synopsis of Selected Court Cases Influencing Special Education (*Continued*)

Case	Year	Issue	Judicial Decision
Endrew F. v. Douglas County School District	2017	Educational benefit	A far-reaching Supreme Court decision involving an eight-year-old boy with autism. The child's parents removed him from public school and enrolled him in a private school due to an IEP, which they believed did not provide sufficient academic and social progress. The school district refused the parents' request for tuition reimbursement. Although the lower courts agreed with the school district, the parents appealed to the Supreme Court. The Court found, in a unanimous decision, that an IEP must provide more than *de minimis* or minimal educational benefit. It stated that an IEP must be "appropriately ambitious" considering a student's circumstances and every student must be given the opportunity to meet challenging objectives.
Perez v. Sturgis Public Schools	2023	Exhausting disputes under IDEA and ADA	This case involved a student who was deaf alleging that the school system failed to provide him with a qualified sign-language interpreter and misconstrued his academic progress to his parents. The Supreme Court's unanimous decision was that families of students with disabilities do not need to exhaust administrative remedies under IDEA before seeking compensatory damages under the ADA.

Source: Adapted from R. Gargiulo and E. Bouck, *Special Education in Contemporary Society*, 7th ed. (Thousand Oaks, CA: Sage, 2021), pp. 41–42.

Note: *Considered appropriate terminology during this time period.

Due to the multitude of the public laws (PL) affecting special education, discussion will be reserved for landmark legislation. The following examines seven significant pieces of legislation that have dramatically affected the educational opportunities of infants, toddlers, preschool children, and school-age children with delays and disabilities. The initial review will focus on PL 94–142, the Individuals with

Today, education for children with delays and disabilities is a right, not a privilege.

AP Photo/David Zalubowski

Disabilities Education Act (IDEA) or, as it was previously called, the Education for All Handicapped Children Act. This change came about due to the enactment on October 30, 1990, of PL 101–476. Provisions contained in this legislation will be reviewed later.

Public Law 94–142

The Individuals with Disabilities Education Act is viewed as a "Bill of Rights" for children with exceptionalities and their families. It is considered by many individuals to be one of the, if not *the,* most important piece of federal legislation ever enacted on behalf of children with disabilities. Some advocacy groups consider this enactment as a vital first step in securing the constitutional rights of citizens with disabilities (Allen & Cowdery, 2022). The intent of this bill was

> to ensure that all handicapped children have available to them . . . a free, appropriate public education which emphasizes special education and related services designed to meet their unique needs, to ensure that the rights of handicapped children and their parents or guardians are protected, to assist States and localities to provide for the education of all handicapped children and to assess and ensure the effectiveness of efforts to educate handicapped children. (Section 601 (c))

In addition to these four purposes, there are six major components incorporated in this legislation:

1. *The right to a free appropriate public education (FAPE)—all* children, regardless of the severity of the disability, must be provided an education appropriate to their unique needs at no cost to the parent(s)/guardian(s). Included in this feature is the concept of related services, which requires that children receive, for example, as necessary, occupational and physical therapy, as well as speech therapy, among other services.
2. *The principle of least restrictive environment (LRE)*—children with exceptionalities are to be educated, to the maximum extent appropriate, with typical students. Placements must be consistent with the student's educational needs.
3. *An individualized education program (IEP)*—this document, developed in conjunction with the parent(s)/guardian(s), is an individually tailored statement describing an educational plan for each learner with exceptionalities. The IEP is required to address (a) present level of academic functioning; (b) annual goals and accompanying instructional objectives; (c) educational services to be provided; (d) the degree to which the student will be able to participate in general education programs; (e) plans for initiating services and length of service delivery; and (f) an annual evaluation procedure specifying objective criteria to determine whether instructional objectives are being met.
4. *Procedural due process*—IDEA affords parent(s)/guardian(s) several safeguards as it pertains to their child's education. Briefly, parent(s)/guardian(s) have the right to examine all records; to obtain an independent evaluation; to receive written notification (in parent's native language) of proposed changes to their child's educational classification or placement; and to an impartial hearing whenever disagreements occur regarding educational plans for their son/daughter.
5. *Nondiscriminatory assessment*—prior to placement, a child must be evaluated in all areas of suspected disability by tests that are neither culturally nor linguistically biased. Students are to receive several types of assessments; a single evaluation procedure is not permitted.
6. *Parental participation*—PL 94–142 mandates parental involvement to the degree they desire. Sometimes referred to as the "Parent's Law," this legislation requires that parents participate in the decision-making process that affects their child's education. IDEA regulations currently allow assistance to parents as part of a preschooler's IEP if such assistance is necessary for the child to benefit from special education. Parental training (e.g., coaching) activities are also permissible as a related service.

Congress mandated by September 1, 1980, a free appropriate public education for all eligible children ages three through twenty-one. The law, however, did *not* require services to preschool children with disabilities. An exception was contained in the legislative language:

> except that, with respect to handicapped children aged three to five and eighteen to twenty-one, inclusive, the requirements . . . shall not be applied . . . if such requirements would be inconsistent with state law or practice, or the order of any court, respecting public education within such age groups within the state. (Section 612 (2) (B))

Because many states were not providing preschool services to typically developing children, an education for young children with delays and disabilities, in most instances, was not mandated. Although this legislation fails to require educational services for young children, it clearly focused attention on the preschool population and recognized the value of early education.

PL 94–142 did, however, contain benefits for children under school age. The enactment offered small financial grants (Preschool Incentive Grants) to the individual states as an incentive to serve young children with delays and disabilities. It also carried a mandate for schools to identify and evaluate children from birth through age twenty-one suspected of evidencing a disability. Finally, PL 94–142 moved from a census count to a child count, or the actual number of young children being served. The intent of this feature was to encourage the states to locate and serve young children with delays and disabilities.

Public Law 99–457

In October 1986, Congress passed one of the most comprehensive pieces of legislation affecting young children with delays and disabilities and their families—PL 99–457. This law, which was originally known as the Education of the Handicapped Act Amendments of 1986, changed both the scope and the intent of services provided to preschoolers with delays and disabilities in addition to formulating a national policy for infants and toddlers with or at risk for delays and disabilities.

Farran (2000) believes that one of the assumptions behind the enactment of PL 99–457 was that early intervention is cost-effective, a way of lowering future costs of special education. This rationale is vastly different from the thinking behind the passage of PL 94–142, which was rooted in the civil rights movement and saw an education for children with disabilities as a constitutional right. Thus, PL 99–457 was enacted primarily as a prevention measure.

PL 99–457 contains several parts. The discussion that follows is primarily on Part B, the preschool provision, as well as Part C (formerly known as Part H), the section that allows for services to be provided to infants and toddlers with delays and disabilities.

As noted earlier, IDEA contains language that gave states the opportunity, through financial incentives, to provide an education and related services to preschool children with disabilities. This was a permissive or voluntary element of the act, not a mandated requirement. Trohanis (1989) reported congressional data that revealed that less than 80 percent, or 260,000 of the estimated 330,000 exceptional children ages three to five, were being served. An estimated 70,000 preschoolers were, therefore, unserved. Koppelman (1986) found that 31 states and territories did not require special education services for preschoolers with delays and disabilities. PL 99–457 was enacted to remedy this situation.

Simply stated, Part B is a downward extension of PL 94–142, including all rights and protections. It requires that as of the 1991–1992 school year, *all* preschoolers with disabilities, ages three to five inclusive, are to receive a free appropriate public education. This element of the law is a mandated requirement. States will lose significant amounts of federal preschool funding if they fail to comply. The goal of this legislation was finally accomplished in the 1992–1993 school year, when all states had mandates in place establishing a free appropriate public education for all children ages three through five with disabilities. In fact, five states (Iowa, Maryland, Michigan, Minnesota, and Nebraska) have chosen to mandate services from birth, while Virginia begins a FAPE at age two (Lazara et al., 2010). Table 2.5 shows the year that each state mandated a free appropriate public education for children with disabilities.

TABLE 2.5 ■ School Year in Which States Mandated a Free Appropriate Public Education for Preschoolers With Disabilities

Year	State
1973–1974	Illinois
	Michigan*
	Wisconsin
1974–1975	Alaska
	Texas
1975–1976	Iowa*
	Virginia**
1976–1977	Massachusetts
	Rhode Island
	South Dakota
1977–1978	Louisiana
	New Hampshire
1978–1979	Maryland*
1979–1980	Nebraska
1980–1981	Hawaii
1983–1984	District of Columbia
	New Jersey
1985–1986	North Dakota
	Washington
1986–1987	Minnesota*
1988–1989	Utah
1989–1990	Idaho
1990–1991	Montana
	Nevada
	Wyoming
1991–1992	Alabama
	Arizona
	Arkansas
	California
	Colorado
	Connecticut
	Delaware
	Florida
	Georgia
	Indiana
	Kansas

(Continued)

TABLE 2.5 ■ School Year in Which States Mandated a Free Appropriate Public Education for Preschoolers With Disabilities (*Continued*)

Year	State
	Kentucky
	Maine
	Mississippi
	Missouri
	New Mexico
	New York
	North Carolina
	Ohio
	Oklahoma
	Pennsylvania
	South Carolina
	Tennessee
	Vermont
	West Virginia
1992–1993	Oregon

Source: Adapted from A. Lazara, J. Danaher, R. Kraus, S. Goode, C. Hipps, and C. Festa (Eds.), *Section 619 Profile* (17th ed.), 2010. Chapel Hill: University of North Carolina, FPG Child Development Institute, National Early Childhood Technical Assistance Center.

Note: *Eligible for services beginning at birth.

**Eligible for services beginning at age two.

Other provisions of the earlier legislation remain the same, such as an education in the least restrictive environment (LRE), IEPs, due process safeguards, and confidentiality of records. Family services are also recognized as being vitally important; thus, family counseling and training are allowable as a related service. Depending on the needs of the child, service delivery models can either be home-based or center-based, full-time or part-time. As noted earlier, states are not required to report to the U.S. Department of Education the number of children served according to a disability category. Thus, preschoolers do not have to be identified with a specific disability, such as intellectual disability.

All states were required to modify their state plans and policies to ensure compliance with the law. Funding for serving preschool children also has increased dramatically.

Part C of PL 99–457 created the Handicapped Infants and Toddlers Program, a new provision aimed at children from birth through age two with developmental delays and disabilities. This component of the legislation is voluntary; states are not compelled to comply. Part C of this statute creates a discretionary program that assists states in implementing a statewide, comprehensive, coordinated, multidisciplinary, interagency program of services for very young children with developmental difficulties and their families. Each state that chose to participate was required to provide early intervention to children who evidence a physical or mental condition that has a high probability of resulting in a delay such as cerebral palsy or Down syndrome. At their discretion, states may also offer services to children who are medically or environmentally at risk for future delays. As of September 30, 1994, all states had plans in place for the full implementation of Part C (U.S. Department of Education, 1997).

The enactment of PL 99–457 reflects a major shift in thinking regarding public policy and service provision for infants and toddlers at risk for or with delays and disabilities (Harbin et al., 2000; McWilliam, 2016). This paradigm shift is reflected in Table 2.6, which illustrates pre and post-IDEA service delivery.

TABLE 2.6 ■ Changes in Service Delivery for Infants and Toddlers Resulting From the Passage of Public Law 99-457 (IDEA)

Area	Pre-IDEA Services	Post-IDEA Services
Entitlement	Served only some of the eligible children	Serve all children
Eligibility	Served only children with disabilities and waited until children evidenced measurable delays	Serve children with diagnosed conditions regardless of whether measurable delays are present May serve at-risk children in order to prevent developmental delay
Early identification	Waited until children came to program	Find children as early as possible
Service array	Confined services to what program offered	Provide an array of services across programs
System	Provide separate, autonomous programs	Provide comprehensive, coordinated, interagency system of services
Focus	Child-centered	Family-centered
Individualization	Offered a package of services	Offer individualized services
Inclusion	Established segregated, self-contained programs	Establish inclusive programs and use of community resources
Disciplines	Disciplines worked autonomously	Disciplines work together to integrate all services (interdisciplinary, transdisciplinary)
Therapies	Provided separate and sometimes insufficient therapies	Provide sufficient integrated therapies
Procedural safeguards	Families had no recourse for complaints	Procedural safeguards in place
Transition	Unplanned traumatic transitions	Planned transition from infant and toddler program to preschool program
Funding	Single primary funding source	Coordinate and use all possible funding sources

Source: G. Harbin, R. McWilliam, and J. Gallagher, "Services for Young Children With Disabilities and Their Families." In J. Shonkoff and S. Meisels (Eds.), *Handbook of Early Childhood Intervention*, 2nd ed. (Cambridge, England: Cambridge University Press, 2000), p. 388.

There are several features of this law that are worthy of examination. Under this act and its accompanying amendments, infants and toddlers are eligible for services if they meet the following conditions:

- They are experiencing developmental delays in one or more of the following areas: cognitive development, physical development, communication development, social or emotional development, or adaptive development.
- They have a physical or mental condition that has a high probability of resulting in a delay (e.g., cerebral palsy, Down syndrome).
- At the state's discretion, they are medically or environmentally at risk for substantial delay if early intervention is not provided.

Eligible children and their families must receive a multidisciplinary assessment conducted by qualified professionals and a written individualized family service plan (IFSP). Similar to the IEP, the IFSP is designed as a guide to the delivery of services to infants, toddlers, and their families. Developed by a multidisciplinary team, the IFSP, as promulgated in PL 99–457, must contain these components:

- A statement of the infant's or toddler's present levels of physical development, cognitive development, communication development, social or emotional development, and adaptive development
- A statement of the family's resources, priorities, and concerns
- A statement of major outcomes expected to be achieved for the infant or toddler and the family
- A statement of specific early intervention services necessary to meet the unique needs of the infant or toddler and the family
- The projected dates for initiation of services and the anticipated duration of such services
- The name of the service coordinator
- A description of the natural environments in which early intervention services will be provided
- The steps supporting the transition of the toddler with a disability to services provided under Part B (preschool)

Unlike an IEP, the focus of the IFSP is on the family rather than the individual child exclusively, thereby resulting in a comprehensive and multidisciplinary plan addressing the needs of the family as well as those of the infant or toddler. Parents are viewed as full-fledged partners with professionals. Their participation ensures that services occur within the context of the family unit and meet the unique needs of the child and their caregivers. This goal is clearly reflected in the IFSP statement, which addresses the issue of the "family's resources, priorities, and concerns." It is imperative for professionals to remember that while families may have a variety of needs (e.g., informational, management, support), they also have strengths and resources that must not be overlooked. Recommended practice dictates that services should be individualized and responsive to the goals and preferences of the parents (caregivers) while supporting their role as primary decision maker (Division for Early Childhood, 2014; Kilgo, 2022).

A final noteworthy aspect of Part C of IDEA is the concept of service coordination. A service coordinator originally was a professional selected from the discipline closest to the child's primary problem—for example, a speech–language pathologist for toddlers with delayed language or a physical therapist for a young child with cerebral palsy. PL 102–119 not only changed the terminology from *case management* to *service coordination* and from *case manager* to the less clinical term *service coordinator*, but it also broadened the category of service coordinator to *any* qualified professional who is best able to

An individualized family service plan is developed by a multidisciplinary team.

Reza Estakhrian/Iconica/Getty Images

assist the family. Typically, the service coordinator's roles are to function as an advocate for the family, to ensure the coordination of early intervention services, to monitor the implementation of the IFSP, to assist in transition planning, and to foster family empowerment, among other duties. It is important to remember that the activities and responsibilities of the service coordinator are determined in conjunction with the child's family and are always individualized (Kemp, 2003).

An IFSP must be reviewed every six months (or sooner if necessary) to assess its continual appropriateness. The infant or toddler is required by law to be reevaluated annually. Regulations further stipulate that an IFSP must be developed within forty-five days after a referral is made for a child to receive services.

PL 99–457 is the culmination of many years of dedicated effort by both parents and professionals from various disciplines and agencies. It represents an opportunity to intervene and effect meaningful change in the lives of the nation's youngest and most vulnerable children.

Public Law 101–476

Arguably, one of the most important changes contained in this legislation was the renaming of PL 94–142 to the Individuals with Disabilities Education Act. The word *children* was replaced with the term *individuals*, and *handicapped* became *with disabilities*. This latter phrase also signifies a change in attitude to a more appropriate people-first point of view because it is recognized that an individual's disability is but one aspect of their personhood.

PL 101–476 also expanded the scope of the related services provision by adding two services—social work and rehabilitation counseling. A final element of this legislation was the identification of autism and traumatic brain injury as distinct disability categories. Previously, these disabilities had been subsumed under other disability labels.

Public Law 102–119

In 1991, IDEA was amended again by PL 102–119, the Individuals with Disabilities Education Act Amendments. As noted earlier, PL 102–119 permits states to use a noncategorical label when identifying preschoolers with delays and disabilities. Amendments to Part C require that early intervention services are to be in "natural environments" with typically developing age-mates as appropriate for each child. Transition policies and procedures are to be established so that infants and toddlers receiving early intervention services can move smoothly, if eligible, to preschool special education services. States also are allowed to use an IFSP as a guide for services for children ages three through five as long as IEP requirements are met.

Additionally, states were permitted to use Part C monies for preschoolers with disabilities. Likewise, these amendments allow for the use of Part B funds to serve infants and toddlers with delays and disabilities. Finally, the amount of funds allocated by Congress increased from $1,000 to $1,500 per child.

Public Law 105–17

IDEA was reauthorized once again via the Individuals with Disabilities Education Act Amendments of 1997. This bill was signed into law by President Bill Clinton on June 4, 1997. PL 105–17 restructures IDEA into four parts, revises some definitions, and revamps several key components ranging from funding to disciplining students with disabilities to how IEPs are to be developed. Highlights of this major retooling are as follows:

- Students with disabilities who bring weapons to school, possess or use illegal drugs, or pose a serious threat of injury to other children or themselves may be removed from their current placement and placed in an interim alternative educational setting as determined by the IEP team, but for no more than forty-five days, after a due process hearing has been conducted. Students who are suspended or expelled are still entitled to receive a free appropriate public education as addressed in their IEP.
- Students with disabilities who exhibit less serious infractions of school conduct may be disciplined in ways similar to children without disabilities (including a change in placement),

provided that the misbehavior was not a manifestation of the student's disability. Additionally, either before taking disciplinary action, but no later than ten days after, the IEP team must conduct a functional behavioral assessment and develop (or implement) a behavior intervention plan.

- IEPs are required to state how students with disabilities will be involved with, and progress in, the general education curriculum. Other provisions stipulate that general educators will become part of the IEP team; short-term instructional objectives will no longer be required, but rather, the emphasis will be on measurable annual goals; and lastly, the assistive technology needs of each learner must be considered by the IEP team.
- Orientation and mobility services for children with visual impairments are now included in the definition of related services.
- The present mandate of comprehensive triennial reevaluations of children with disabilities is lifted if school authorities and the student's parents agree that this process is unnecessary.
- A new section on mediation requires states to offer mediation services to help resolve disputes as an alternative to using more costly and lengthy due process hearings. Parental participation is voluntary, and parents still retain their right to a due process hearing.
- The eligibility category of *developmental delay* may be used for describing children ages three through nine. The use of this term is at the discretion of the state and local education agency.
- Initial evaluations and reevaluations are not restricted to the use of formal, standardized tests. A variety of assessment tools and strategies must be utilized in an effort to gather relevant, functional, and developmental information. Curriculum-based tests, portfolio reviews, parental input, and the observations of teachers and related service providers may be considered in determining whether or not the student is eligible for services and in developing the content of the IEP. A student may not be considered eligible for a special education if their educational difficulties are primarily the result of limited proficiency in English or lack of adequate instruction in math and/or reading.
- A new mechanism for distributing federal monies occurs once the appropriations reach a threshold of $4.9 billion. Upon attaining this level, states and local school systems will receive additional funding based upon 85 percent of the population of children ages three to twenty-one and 15 percent of the number of children ages three through twenty-one who live in poverty. This switch to a census-based formula rather than an enrollment-driven formula was due to a concern that some schools were overidentifying students with disabilities in order to receive additional funding. No state would receive less than the amount of support it received in the year prior to the activation of this new scheme.
- The reauthorization of IDEA requires schools to establish performance goals for students with disabilities in an effort to assess their academic progress. Additionally, these children are to be included in state and district-wide assessment programs or given alternative assessments that meet their unique needs.
- Early intervention services must be "family-directed," and to the extent appropriate, these services are to be provided in noninstitutional settings such as the young child's home or child care environment.
- Child Find requirements are extended to children with disabilities who are enrolled in private schools, including students attending parochial schools. A special education and related services may be provided on the premises of a private school (including parochial) to the extent permissible by law.
- IFSP requirements are modified to include a statement justifying the extent, if any, that early intervention services are not provided in the natural environment.

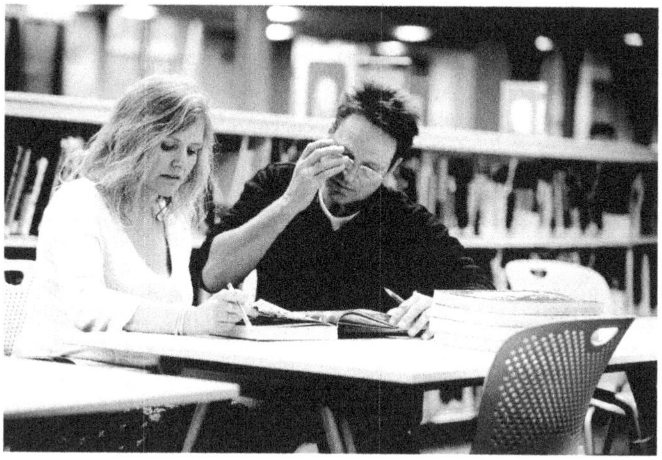

Legislation requires that general educators be included as IEP team members.
iStock/track5

Public Law 108–446

The most recent amendments to IDEA are incorporated in PL 108–446, the Individuals with Disabilities Education Improvement Act of 2004. This historic piece of legislation is commonly referred to as IDEA 2004. One of the goals of IDEA 2004 was to align this law with the No Child Left Behind Act (PL 107–110) enacted in 2001. The focus of PL 107–110 was to improve the academic performance of *all* students in reading and math (with science eventually being added) by the year 2014. Particular attention is paid to the achievement of students with disabilities, children from low-income families, English learners, and individuals from racial and ethnic minority groups. The No Child Left Behind Act further requires that teachers are to be highly qualified professionals and that they incorporate scientifically validated practices in their instructional programs (Gargiulo & Metcalf, 2023).

The following summary[2] represents some of the significant issues contained in PL 108–446.

Individualized Education Program (IEP) Process

- Short-term objectives and benchmarks are no longer required except for those students who are evaluated via alternate assessments aligned to alternate achievement standards.
- Assessment of the progress that a student is making toward meeting annual goals, which must be written in measurable terms, is still required. Reference, however, to the current requirement of reporting to the "extent to which progress is sufficient to enable the child to achieve goals by the end of the year" is eliminated. IEPs will now need to describe how the individual's progress toward achieving annual goals will be measured and when these progress reports will be made.
- PL 108–446 also requires that the IEP address the student's "academic and functional performance" instead of the previously used term "educational performance." This modification of terminology more closely aligns IDEA with the No Child Left Behind Act.

Identifying Students With Specific Learning Disabilities

Although young children are rarely identified with a learning disability, under IDEA '97, when identifying an individual for a possible learning disability, educators typically looked to see if the student exhibited a severe discrepancy between achievement and intellectual ability. IDEA 2004 modified this discrepancy provision.

---

[2] Information adapted from *Teaching in Today's Inclusive Classrooms* (4th ed.) by R. Gargiulo and D. Metcalf, Boston, MA: Cengage Learning, 2023.

School districts will now be able, if they so choose, to use a process that determines if the student responds to empirically validated, scientifically based interventions, a procedure known as response to intervention (treatment). Under these guidelines, rather than comparing IQ with performance on standardized achievement tests, general education teachers can offer intensive programs of instructional interventions. If the child fails to make adequate progress, a learning disability is assumed to be present, and additional assessment is warranted.

Discipline

- PL 108–446 stipulates that when a student is removed from their current educational setting, the child is to continue to receive those services that enable them to participate in the general education curriculum and to ensure progress toward meeting IEP goals.
- IDEA '97 allowed school authorities to unilaterally remove a student to an interim alternative setting (IASE) for up to forty-five days for offenses involving weapons or drugs. IDEA 2004 now permits school officials to remove any student (including those with and without disabilities) to an IASE for up to forty-five days for inflicting "serious bodily injury."
- Removal to an IASE will now be for forty-five *school* days rather than forty-five calendar days.
- Behavior resulting in disciplinary action still requires a manifestation review; however, language requiring the IEP team to consider whether the student's disability impaired their ability to control their behavior or comprehend the consequences of their actions has been eliminated. IEP teams will now only need to ask two questions:
    1. Did the disability cause or have a direct and substantial relationship to the offense?
    2. Was the violation a direct result of the school's failure to implement the IEP?
- IDEA 2004 modifies the "stay put" provision enacted during the appeals process. When either the school district (local education agency) or parent requests an appeal of the manifestation determination or placement decision, the student is to remain in the current IASE until a decision is rendered by the hearing officer or until the time for violation concludes. A hearing must be held within twenty school days of the date of the appeal.

Due Process

- Parents will encounter a two-year statute of limitations for filing a due process complaint from the time they knew or should have known that a violation occurred. Alleged violations might involve identification, assessment, or placement issues or the failure to provide an appropriate education.
- A mandatory "resolution session" is now required prior to proceeding with a due process hearing. (The parents or school district may waive this requirement and directly proceed to mediation.) School districts must convene a meeting with the parents and the IEP team members within fifteen days of receiving a due process complaint. If the complaint is not satisfactorily resolved within thirty days of the filing date, the due process hearing may proceed.

Eligibility of Students

- School districts will be required to determine the eligibility of a student to receive a special education and the educational needs of the child within a sixty-day time frame. (This provision does not apply if the state has already established a timeline for accomplishing this task.) The sixty-day rule commences upon receipt of parental permission for evaluation.
- Reevaluation of eligibility for special education may not occur more than once per year (unless agreed to by the school district and parent); and it must occur at least every three years unless the parent and school district agree that such a reevaluation is unnecessary.
- IDEA 2004 modifies the provision pertaining to native language and preferred mode of communication. New language in the bill requires that evaluations are to be "provided and administered in the language and form most likely to yield accurate information on what the child knows and can do academically, developmentally, and functionally, unless it is not feasible to do so or administer."

Assessment Participation

- PL 108–446 requires that *all* students participate in all state and district-wide assessments (including those required under the No Child Left Behind Act) with accommodations or alternate assessments, if necessary, as stipulated in the child's IEP. States are permitted to assess up to 1 percent of students (generally those students with significant cognitive deficits) with alternate assessments aligned with alternate achievement standards. IDEA 2004 further requires that assessments adhere to the principles of universal design when feasible.

Services for Infants and Toddlers With Delays and Disabilities

- Early intervention services are to be based upon peer-reviewed research.
- Individualized family service plans (IFSPs) are to include measurable outcomes for pre-literacy and language skills.
- IDEA 2004 permits states to provide early intervention services from age three until the child enters kindergarten.

  IDEA 2004 maintains the use of the label *developmental delay* for children from three to nine years of age.

Table 2.7 shows the unique components of Part C for infants and toddlers and provides a comparison of the provisions of Part C and Part B of IDEA.

TABLE 2.7 ■ Comparison of IDEA Part C Early Intervention and Part B Special Education

Components	Part C Early Intervention	Part B Special Education
Ages Served	Birth to third birthday	Ages three to twenty-one
Purpose	To provide extra help for infants and toddlers with delays and disabilities to learn the skills that usually develop in the first three years as well as services for the family to enhance their ability of their child	To provide individualized services and instruction to meet the unique needs of the child along with any related services (e.g., physical and occupational therapy) for the child to participate in the general education curriculum to the greatest extent possible
Individualized Plans	Individualized Family Service Plan (IFSP)	Individualized Education Program (IEP)
Focus Areas	Developmental needs of child, family focus, coaching model	Educational needs, child-specific
Responsible Agency	Lead agency designated by each state	State Department of Education, Local Educational Agency (LEA)
Location of Services	Services provided in the natural environment or settings that are typical for children without disabilities (e.g., home, childcare center, or other community settings)	Services are provided in the Least Restrictive Environment (LRE). To the maximum extent appropriate for the student, schools must educate students with disabilities in the general education classroom with appropriate aids and services along with their nondisabled peers in the school they would attend if they did not have a disability.
Family Involvement	Participate on all teams making decisions about the child's services. Recipient of services designed to improve the family's ability to meet the needs of their child.	Encouraged to participate on all teams making decisions about services for their child.

Section 504 of the Rehabilitation Act of 1973[3]

The six pieces of legislation just examined are representative special education laws. PL 93–112, the Rehabilitation Act of 1973, however, is a *civil rights* law. Section 504 of this enactment is the first public law specifically aimed at protecting children and adults against discrimination due to a disability. It said that no individual can be excluded, solely because of their disability, from participating in or benefiting from any program or activity receiving federal financial assistance, which includes schools (Yell, 2019). Unlike IDEA, this act employs a functional rather than a categorical model for determining a disability. According to this law, an individual is eligible for services if they

- have a physical or mental impairment that substantially limits one or more major life activities;
- have a record of such impairment; or
- are regarded as having such an impairment by others.

"Major life activities" are broadly defined and include, for example, walking, seeing, hearing, working, and learning.

To fulfill the requirements of Section 504, schools must make "reasonable accommodations" for students with disabilities so that they can participate in educational programs provided to other students. Reasonable accommodations might include modifications of the general education program, the assignment of an aide, a behavior plan, or the provision of special study areas (Smith, 2002; Smith & Patton, 2007). Students may also receive related services such as occupational or physical therapy if they are receiving a special education through IDEA.

Because the protections afforded by this law are broad, an individual who is ineligible for a special education under IDEA *may* qualify for special assistance or accommodations under Section 504. A second grader with attention deficit hyperactivity disorder (ADHD) or a preschooler with severe allergies, for example, might be eligible for services via Section 504. All students who are eligible for a special education and related services under IDEA are also eligible for accommodations under Section 504; the converse, however, is *not* true.

Federal law requires that schools make reasonable accommodations for students with disabilities.

iStock/FatCamera

Similar to IDEA, there is a mandate contained within Section 504 to educate children with disabilities with their typically developing peers to the maximum extent possible. Additionally, schools are required to develop an accommodation plan (commonly called a "504 plan") customized to meet the unique needs of the individual. This document should include a statement of the student's strengths and a list of necessary accommodations, and the individual(s) responsible for ensuring implementation. The purpose of this plan is to enable the student to receive a free appropriate public education (Smith, 2002). A closer examination of 504 plans with greater detail is in Chapter 4.

---

[3] Information adapted from *Special Education in Contemporary Society* (7th ed.) by R. Gargiulo and E. Bouck, Thousand Oaks, CA: Sage, 2021.

PREVALENCE OF YOUNG CHILDREN WITH DELAYS AND DISABILITIES

The number of young children with delays and disabilities receiving services has increased dramatically over the past several years. This growth has been spurred by litigation, legislative enactments (especially IDEA and its amendments), and a greater awareness of the benefits of early intervention, among other factors.

Infants and Toddlers

Recent data provided by the U.S. Department of Education (2022b) reveal that more than 427,000 infants and toddlers from birth through age two were receiving early intervention during the 2019–2020 school year. This statistic represents 3.7 percent of the entire birth through age two population. Over the past several years, the number of infants and toddlers receiving early intervention services has steadily increased.

Figure 2.1 illustrates this growth pattern. This trend reflects a 128 percent increase in the number of very young children served over the past twenty-one years. This growth pattern is most likely due to greater public awareness, successful Child Find efforts, and program expansion.

FIGURE 2.1 ■ Number of Infants and Toddlers Served Under the Individuals with Disabilities Education Act in Representative Years

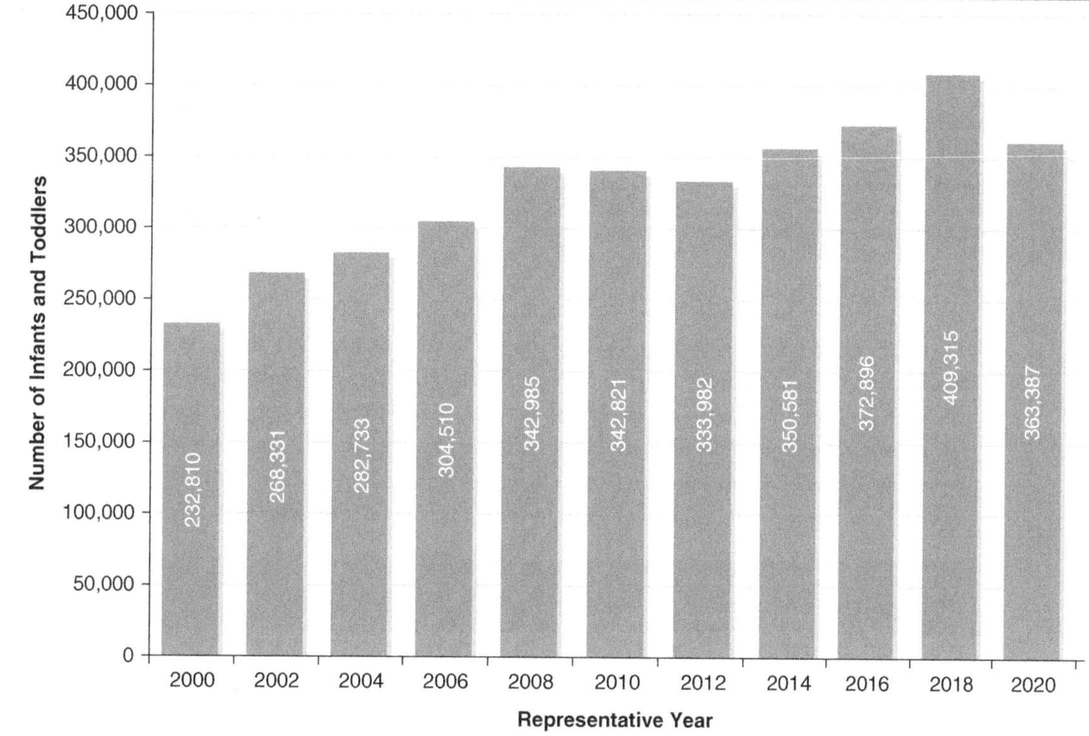

Source: U.S. Department of Education. (2006). *Twenty-sixth Annual Report to Congress on the Implementation of the Individuals with Disabilities Education Act, 2004* (Vol. 1). Washington, DC: Author; U.S. Department of Education. (2021). *Forty-second Annual Report to Congress on the Implementation of the Individuals with Disabilities Education Act, 2020.* Washington, DC: Author.

Preschoolers

Data from the U.S. Department of Education (2022b) reveal that approximately 806,000 preschoolers ages three to five were served during the 2019–2020 school year under Part B of IDEA. This figure represents approximately 6.7 percent of the population of three- to five-year-old children in the United States. Table 2.8 reflects a 41 percent increase in the number of preschoolers receiving a special education over the past twenty-one years.

TABLE 2.8 ■ Number of Preschoolers Served Under the Individuals with Disabilities Education Act in Representative Years

Year	Number of Preschoolers
1998	573,637
2000	599,678
2002	679,420
2004	701,949
2006	714,384
2008	709,004
2010	735,245
2012	750, 131
2014	753,697
2016	759, 801
2018	815,010
2019	806,319

Source: U.S. Department of Education. (2012). *Thirty-first Annual Report to Congress on the Implementation of the Individuals with Disabilities Education Act, 2009.* Washington, DC: Author; U.S. Department of Education. (2020). *Forty-first Annual Report to Congress on the Implementation of the Individuals with Disabilities Education Act, 2019.* Washington, DC: Author; U.S. Department of Education. (2021). *Forty-second Annual Report to Congress on the Implementation of the Individuals with Disabilities Education Act, 2020.* Washington, DC: Author.

Note: Table based on data from the fifty states, District of Columbia, Puerto Rico, Bureau of Indian Affairs schools, and four outlying areas. The forty-second annual report also includes data from the three freely associated states of Micronesia, the Republic of Palau, and the Republic of the Marshall Islands.

Early Primary Students

Children ages six, seven, and eight who are receiving special education services are sometimes recognized under the category of developmental delay,[4] while in other instances, a categorical disability label is used. The U.S. Department of Education (2022a) reports that 164,073 children ages six through eight were eligible for services under the developmental delay category during the 2019–2020 school year. This figure represents approximately 12 percent of the more than 1.38 million students in this age range receiving a special education. Table 2.9 portrays the number of early primary students with a specific disability.

TABLE 2.9 ■ Number of Early Primary Students Receiving Special Education Services in the 2019–2020 School Year

Disability Category	Six Years Old	Seven Years Old	Eight Years Old
Autism	52,773	59,586	59,598
Deaf-Blindness	*	114	*
Developmental Delay	70,743	56,463	36,867
Emotional Disturbance	6,030	11,556	17,340
Hearing Impairment	3,927	4,734	5,109
Intellectual Disability	9,825	15,039	20,676
Multiple Disabilities	5,130	6,249	7,521

[4] IDEA permits the use of the term *developmental delay* for children ages three to nine.

Disability Category	Six Years Old	Seven Years Old	Eight Years Old
Orthopedic Impairment	2,274	2,598	2,457
Other Health Impairment	29,559	48,366	68,118
Specific Learning Disability	17,046	59,259	124,623
Speech or Language Impairment	204,492	202,488	170,655
Traumatic Brain Injury	717	918	1,308
Visual Impairment	1,389	1,569	1,776
Total	403,995	468,939	516,138

Source: U.S. Department of Education. (2020). *ED Facts Data Warehouse: IDEA Part B Child Count and Educational Environments Collection.* Available at https://www2.ed.gov/programs/osepidea/618-data/index.html

Note: *Data unavailable due to small number of students.

THE IMPORTANCE OF EARLY INTERVENTION/ EARLY CHILDHOOD SPECIAL EDUCATION

Is early intervention/early childhood special education effective? Does it benefit young children with delays and disabilities and their families? Unfortunately, these are not simple questions, and their answers are equally, if not more, complex. It is perhaps best to respond to these queries by saying, "It depends." The reason for vagueness is that the initial inquiries only lead to additional questions. For instance, what constitutes intervention? How early is early? Are short-term or long-term benefits considered? Who are the children referred to—infants and toddlers, young children who are environmentally at risk, children with suspected developmental delays, or preschoolers and early primary students with documented disabilities like Down syndrome or cerebral palsy? Obviously, the population served can affect the answer to the question.

Our initial concerns notwithstanding, our primary questions can be answered in the affirmative. *Quality* early intervention/early childhood special education programs *do* make a difference in the lives of young children with delays and disabilities and their families (McLean et al., 2016). Guralnick (1998), in fact, considers early intervention to be "the centerpiece of our nation's efforts on behalf of vulnerable children and their families" (p. 337).

Next is a review the reasoning for the position that early intervention/early childhood special education is effective. First, it is important to establish an understanding of what intervention is. Historically speaking, Fallen and Umansky (1985) describe early intervention as the process of intruding upon the lives of young children with disabilities and their families for the purpose of altering the direction and consequences of a disability or delayed development. These experts state that "the action required is individual, but it encompasses any modification or addition of services, strategies, techniques, or materials required to maximize the child's potential" (p. 160). Likewise, another early viewpoint comes from Peterson (1987), who believes that the purpose of intervention for young children with delays and disabilities is to

1. minimize the effects of a handicapping [disabling] condition upon a child's growth and development and maximize opportunities to engage in the normal activities of early childhood;
2. prevent, if possible, at-risk conditions or early developmental irregularities from developing into more serious problems that become deviant to the extent that they are labeled as handicapping [disabling]; [and]
3. prevent the development of secondary handicaps [disabilities] as a result of interference from a primary disability. (pp. 72–73)

More recently, Hallahan et al. (2009), in synthesizing the thinking of educators and researchers, echo these early perspectives. These writers offer the following rationale for early intervention:

- A child's early learning provides the foundation for later learning, so the sooner a special education program or intervention is begun, the further the child is likely to go in learning more complex skills.
- Early intervention is likely to provide support for the child and family that will help prevent the child from developing additional problems or disabilities.
- Early intervention can help families adjust to having a child with disabilities; give parents the skills they need to handle the child effectively at home; and help families find the additional support services they may need such as counseling, medical assistance, or financial aid. (p. 69)

Thus, the aim of early intervention/early childhood special education is to affect positively the overall development of the child's social, emotional, physical, and intellectual well-being. This whole-child approach is important because these aspects are interrelated and dependent on each other (Zigler, 1990).

Over the years, educators and social scientists (Boyd et al., 2016; Bricker et al., 2020; Howard et al., 2014; Long, 2019; Odom, 2016; Raver, 2009; Shonkoff & Meisels, 2000) have identified a variety of reasons why early intervention/early childhood special education is important for young children at risk for or with delays and disabilities (see Table 2.10). Many of these reasons are derived from research evidence, theoretical arguments, expert opinion, and societal values. Frequently identified themes include the following:

- A belief that early environmental stimulation can positively facilitate subsequent development and readiness for learning.
- A sensitive or critical periods hypothesis, which suggests that intervening during key periods in a child's life is vitally important if the child is to acquire more complex skills and competencies later on (Allen & Cowdery, 2022; Gallagher et al., 2023). The exclusivity of this notion, however, has been challenged by some professionals who advocate that the early years of a child's life are *not* the only crucial period of development; in fact, development continues across the life span (Shonkoff & Phillips, 2000; Sousa, 2022; Zero to Three, 2014). Similarly, Ramey and Ramey (1998) argue that there is no compelling evidence to support the belief of an absolute critical period of development such that interventions introduced after a certain age are ineffective. Yet research does suggest that earlier enrollment in intervention programs produces the greatest benefit, implying that it is a matter of developmental timing (Bruder, 2010; Garcia et al., 2016; Hardman et al., 2017; National Early Childhood Technical Assistance Center, 2011a; Reynolds & Temple, 2005).
- The intensity of these early intervention efforts can also substantially influence outcome effectiveness (Guralnick & Conlon, 2007; McCormick et al., 2006).
- An assumption that early intervention can minimize the impact of particular disabling conditions or risks (Bailey et al., 2005; Long, 2019) like the effect of a severe hearing loss on the development of speech and language and possibly prevent or attenuate the occurrence of secondary disabilities.
- The proposition that intervention programs can ameliorate learning deficits and problems frequently attributed to certain risk factors such as environmental conditions (Lipkin & Schertz, 2008).
- Benefits that accrue to families of young children at risk for or with delays and disabilities. These children frequently present many new challenges and additional responsibilities for caregivers and can potentially impact the entire family constellation. Early intervention/early

childhood special education professionals can assist families by providing factual information, support, resources, and specific training or coaching as requested (Bailey et al., 2005). A further role for professionals is to establish meaningful partnerships with families guided by the principles of enablement and empowerment (Bruder, 2010; Dunst et al., 1988; Turnbull et al., 2022).

- Benefits that extend beyond the child and their family to society at large. Early intervention is cost-effective. The effectiveness has been documented in terms of dollars saved and the reduced need for special education services at an older age (Guralnick, 2004; Odom, 2016; Schweinhart et al., 2005; Temple & Reynolds, 2007).

TABLE 2.10 ■ Why Intervene Early?

Neural circuits, which create the foundation for learning, behavior, and health, are most flexible or "plastic" during the first three years of life. Over time, they become increasingly difficult to change.
Persistent "toxic" stress, such as extreme poverty, abuse and neglect, or severe maternal depression, can damage the developing brain, leading to lifelong problems in learning, behavior, and physical and mental health.
The brain is strengthened by positive early experiences, especially stable relationships with caring and responsive adults, safe and supportive environments, and nutrition.
Early social/emotional development and physical health provide the foundation upon which cognitive and language skills develop.
High-quality early intervention services can change a child's developmental trajectory and improve outcomes for children, families, and communities.
Intervention is likely to be more effective and less costly when it is provided earlier in life than later.

Source: Adapted from National Early Childhood Technical Assistance Center. (2011a). *The Importance of Early Intervention for Infants and Toddlers and Their Families.* Chapel Hill, NC: University of North Carolina, FPG Child Development Institute.

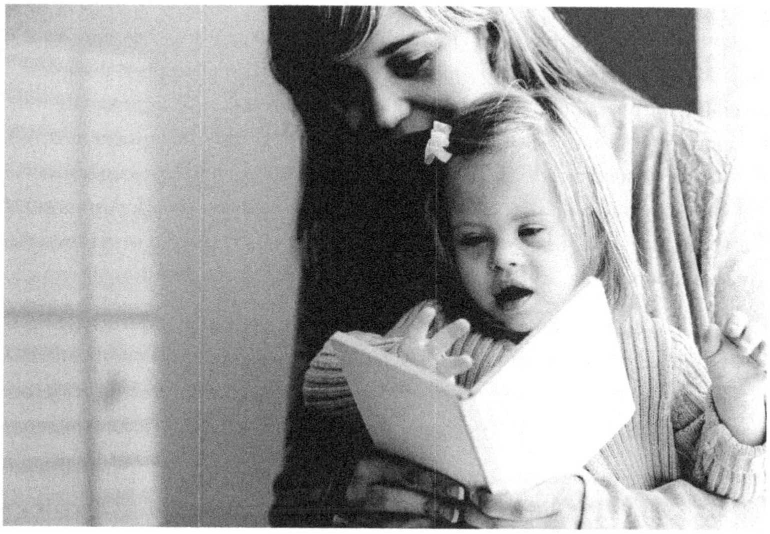

Early intervention/early childhood special education has been shown to positively impact the lives of young children with delays and disabilities.

iStock.com/kali9

In summary, early intervention/childhood special education for children with disabilities has definite advantages for society, the family, and, of course, the child. Early childhood special education can make a significant difference in the quality of life for young children with delays and disabilities and their families. In fact, early intervention as a strategy to prevent later problems has almost become conventional wisdom (Kamerman, 2000). Researchers have consistently demonstrated that well-designed early intervention programs produce modest positive outcomes according to their intended purpose (Garcia et al., 2016; Guralnick & Conlon, 2007; Long, 2019; National Early Childhood Technical Assistance Center, 2011b; Ramey & Ramey, 1998; Zigler, 2000). Thus, Ramey and Ramey's (1998) persuasive argument that "early intervention can improve the course of early human development" (p. 118) is widely accepted. Equally meaningful and significant are the conclusions reached by Shonkoff and Phillips (2000), who found that high-quality, well-designed early intervention programs "have been shown to influence the development trajectories of children whose life course is threatened by socioeconomic disadvantage, family disruption, and diagnosed disabilities" (p. 11).

Representative Research Evidence on the Effectiveness of Early Intervention/Early Childhood Special Education

Over the past several decades, there have been numerous investigations examining the effectiveness of early intervention/early childhood special education with young children who are at risk for or have delays and disabilities. Many reviews, commentaries, and summaries of these efforts have been published (Boyd et al., 2016; Bruder, 2010; Bruder et al., 2020; Farran, 1990, 2000; Guralnick, 1997; Shonkoff & Phillips, 2000; White et al., 1986). As might be expected, the analyses revealed, for a variety of reasons, contradictory findings. As a whole, however, the reports indicate positive outcomes for early intervention, especially when a distinction is made between statistical significance and clinical significance. A group of children who learn to accomplish specific self-care skills, like eating independently, might not evidence statistical significance due to small sample size, but this accomplishment is important for young children with delays and disabilities and their families (Bailey & Wolery, 1992). Although the research evidence does provide qualified support for the effectiveness of early intervention, several investigators and authors comment on the difficulty of conducting methodologically sound experiments (Bowe, 2007; Farran, 1990; Guralnick, 1988, 1991, 1998). Potential problems in interpreting the research literature lie with the appropriateness of the dependent measures; the absence of control groups; small sample sizes; improper sampling procedures; inappropriate statistical techniques; inadequate documentation of the treatment; the validity of the assessment instruments; and the variability within specific subject populations. Odom (1988) suggests that some of the research difficulties are due to the fact that early childhood special education is an applied discipline and focused on answering pragmatic questions; researchers, therefore, have less control over variables in natural settings than in laboratory environments. Despite the shortcomings and the vulnerability of the research efforts, positive conclusions about the efficacy of early intervention/education can be drawn. Guralnick (1998), for instance, emphatically states that "comprehensive early intervention programs for children at-risk and for those with established disabilities reveal a consistent pattern of effectiveness" (p. 323). More recently, this expert in the field of early intervention/education noted that

> the thoughtful implementation of systematic, comprehensive, experientially based early intervention programs . . . will enhance the development of young children already exhibiting intellectual delays (of known or unknown etiology) both by altering their developmental trajectories and by preventing secondary complications from occurring. (Guralnick, 2005, p. 314)

What follows is a review some of the research evidence related to the effectiveness of early intervention/education. Described first is the classic but methodologically controversial study conducted by Skeels and Dye (1939), which significantly influenced the then current thinking about intelligence. These investigators reported an experiment where thirteen children under three years of age were removed from an orphanage and placed in an institution for individuals with intellectual disability, where they received a great deal of care and attention from female residents who acted as surrogate mothers. A control group of twelve children remained at the overcrowded orphanage and were not exposed to individual stimulation or training. Intellectual assessments were conducted at the time of transfer. When the children were reevaluated eighteen to thirty-six months later, significant differences were observed between the experimental and control subjects. The thirteen children placed on the ward with the young women with intellectual disability demonstrated an average gain in IQ scores of 27.5 points, while the initially higher-IQ-scoring control children showed a loss of 26.2 points. Each of the children who transferred to the more enriched environment showed an increase in measured intelligence, while all except one of the controls suffered a loss; ten children had a decrease in IQ score between 18 and 45 points.

Research into the effectiveness of early intervention/education has a long and sometimes controversial history.
iStock / FatCamera

Perhaps the most significant finding of this investigation is the long-term follow-up of the subjects into adulthood. Even as adults, the differences between the two samples are significant. Skeels (1966) reports that members of the treatment group maintained their gains and all were self-supporting. Their median grade-level attainment was greater than twelfth grade, whereas the children who remained at the orphanage had a median educational attainment of less than third grade. Differences in occupational achievement were also noted, with the experimental subjects enjoying greater career accomplishment while the controls remained wards of the state or largely worked as unskilled laborers.

Although the methodology of the Skeels and Dye (1939) investigation has been criticized, the study did demonstrate that environmental conditions affect development as well as point out that the deleterious experiences of early childhood can be reversed. The work of Skeels and Dye, as Bailey and Wolery (1992) note, "remains as one of the few truly longitudinal studies of intervention effectiveness" (p. 6).

Another pioneering study is the work of Kirk (1958), who investigated the effects of preschool experiences on the mental and social development of children ages three to six with intellectual disability. Eighty-one children with IQ scores ranging from 45 to 80 either were assigned to an intervention group or served as control subjects. Two experimental groups were established containing children who lived in the community or resided in an institution. The control subjects also lived either at home or in a residential environment. Both intervention groups who were exposed to two years of preschool experiences demonstrated significant gains on measures of intellectual and social functioning as compared to young children without the benefit of intervention. The performance of the control children decreased. Follow-up indicated that the experimental subjects retained their advantage until age eight. However, some of the community-based control subjects did catch up to the experimental children after one year of school.

Kirk's research, as well as the efforts of Skeels and Dye (1939), attests to the malleability of early development in addition to providing strong evidence of the effectiveness of early intervention. As noted elsewhere in this text, in the 1960s the social conscience of America was awakened. The nation became cognizant of the devastating effects of poverty and other social ills on the lives of young children and their families. One consequence of this heightened social awareness was the establishment of preschool intervention programs for poor children, or, in contemporary terms, children who are environmentally at risk. The lasting effects of some of these projects were evaluated by the Consortium for Longitudinal Studies. Lazar and his colleagues (Lazar & Darlington, 1979; Lazar et al., 1982) issued two major reports summarizing the results of twelve comprehensive follow-up studies of children enrolled in cognitively oriented preschools established in the 1960s. None of the projects focused specifically on children with delays and disabilities, although several selected participants on the basis of low IQ scores (range 50–85). Using original data from each program, Lazar found that environmentally at-risk enrollees had higher achievement and intelligence test scores as compared to children who did not have the benefit of preschool intervention. Their analysis also revealed that early intervention experiences significantly reduced the number of young children placed in special education and retained in their current grade. In comparison to control groups, preschool graduates had more positive attitudes toward school and furnished more achievement-oriented responses in follow-up interviews. Lazar and his coworkers concluded that, overall, the projects produced lasting positive outcomes and were cost-effective when compared to later remediation efforts or special class placement. Table 2.11, derived from a composite of empirical investigations, summarizes some of the short- and long-term benefits that result from participating in a well-run preschool program.

TABLE 2.11 ■ Beneficial Outcomes of High-Quality Preschool Programs
Enhanced scholastic achievement
Less grade retention
Higher IQ scores
Decreased likelihood of receiving special education services
More positive attitudes toward school and learning
Greater likelihood of graduating from high school
Less likelihood of accessing public assistance
Greater possibility of securing meaningful employment

The efficacy of early intervention has also been examined with children manifesting an established risk. One population that has received considerable attention is young children with Down syndrome. An example is the work of Guralnick and Bricker (1987). Using stringent criteria for inclusion, these investigators evaluated the outcomes of eleven projects. They concluded, based on the substantial number of "first generation" studies reviewed, that the documented decline in cognitive ability with advancing chronological age typically found in children with Down syndrome can be significantly reduced, prevented, and, to some extent, reversed as a result of early intervention. This significant outcome is consistent across a wide variety of programs incorporating diverse experimental designs.

The issue of maintenance of cognitive gains, however, is not clear-cut, due to limited information and contradictory findings. Equally difficult to answer is the question of when the best time is to begin early intervention. The research evidence is, once again, contradictory. Both of these issues await more extensive and systematic research that is skillfully designed to answer these questions. Despite these shortcomings, empirical investigations strongly speak to the positive benefits of early intervention with children with Down syndrome.

Another illustration of the efficacy of early intervention is the highly visible work of Casto and Mastropieri (1986). These investigators used a comprehensive statistical integration approach known as meta-analysis. In this method, all available research (both published and unpublished) incorporating a range of experimental designs is evaluated in an attempt to detect global statistical patterns, which yield an "effect size" reported as standard deviations (SD). Seventy-four studies of early intervention efforts of heterogeneous groups of children were analyzed. Criteria for inclusion were minimal. Overall, the meta-analysis outcomes supported the efficacy of early intervention. Modest gains were observed in children's test scores—typically standardized intelligence tests or other cognitive assessments. Cognitive measures yielded a mean effect size of .85 SD. When other dependent measures were included, such as motor and language assessments, the effect size was reduced to .68 SD. This means that the typically developing child with delays and disabilities in an early intervention program scored .68 of a standard deviation higher than a counterpart who was not receiving early services.

Casto and Mastropieri (1986) also reported that early intervention programs that are longer in duration and more intense usually demonstrate greater effectiveness. Two intriguing and controversial findings emerged, however, both of which were contrary to conventional wisdom and challenged two widely held beliefs of the field. First, Casto and Mastropieri found no support for the belief that the earlier the intervention commences ("earlier is better"), the greater its effectiveness. Second, their meta-analyses suggested that greater parental participation does not necessarily lead to enhanced program effectiveness.

As might be expected, professional reaction to these summary statements was swift and intense (Dunst & Snyder, 1986; Strain & Smith, 1986). Critics of the Casto and Mastropieri (1986) meta-analyses assailed the conclusions, claiming that the analysis was methodologically ("apples and oranges approach") and conceptually flawed. It must be remembered, however, that this investigation was based on an enormously heterogeneous group of children incorporating different intervention methods and procedures as well as employing diverse outcome measures. It would be prudent, therefore, to draw only limited conclusions.

A subsequent and better controlled meta-analysis using a subset of the original database focusing exclusively on children younger than three years of age yielded different and more positive results (Shonkoff & Hauser-Cram, 1987). This more selective analysis revealed that young children with mild disabilities had better outcomes with earlier enrollment, and higher levels of parent involvement were associated with greater child progress and performance.

A final example is Guralnick's (1997) extensive examination of "second generation" research studies involving children at risk and children with a broad spectrum of established risks. This review examined the efficacy of early intervention and the variables that impede or enhance its effectiveness, such as child characteristics (type and severity of disability), family characteristics, and program features (curriculum, parent–child interventions, social support). Some of the conclusions gleaned from this work support the following generalizations—the outcomes of intervention are positive, albeit modest; the sheer number of deleterious variables affecting development may be more significant than any one factor; and finally, careful consideration should be given to ecological factors affecting child–caregiver and child–family relationships.

Despite the chronic problems in conducting efficacy evaluations, most believe that early intervention/education does make a difference in the lives of young children with delays and disabilities. It would appear that the field of early childhood special education has moved beyond the global question of whether early intervention works to more precise avenues of inquiry: for whom, under what conditions, and toward what outcomes (Guralnick, 1988). Bailey (2000) emphasized that the debate will no longer be whether to provide early intervention, "but rather how much and what kind of intervention are children and families entitled to" (p. 74). A major task confronting the field will be to identify which early intervention programs work best and what elements are clearly essential to achieve maximum benefit (Boyd et al., 2016; Zigler, 2000).

Early intervention/education research is not static, but rather an ongoing process. It can help guide researchers, policymakers, and educators in their quest to develop new models, programs, and services that benefit infants, toddlers, preschoolers, and early primary children with delays and disabilities and their families.

AN ECOLOGICAL PERSPECTIVE ON YOUNG CHILDREN WITH DELAYS AND DISABILITIES AND THEIR FAMILIES

A long-standing approach in early childhood special education is to view children as part of a larger social scheme wherein they influence, and are influenced by, various environments. This context, referred to as ecology, looks at the interrelationships and interactions of individuals within the environment. The primary advocate of this ecological model is Urie Bronfenbrenner (1977, 1979, 1992). From this ecological perspective, Bronfenbrenner attempts to understand the relationship between the immediate environments in which a young child develops and the larger context of those settings. A developing child, therefore, can be viewed not in isolation but rather as part of a larger social system. As described throughout this text, it is impossible to discuss children without also describing the context in which they develop and interact—their families and communities. As an illustration, early childhood professionals must have an appreciation for the child's total environment—home, school, community, and the larger society, in addition to the individuals encountered therein—parents, siblings, classmates, playmates, and therapists, among other people. Spodek and Saracho (1994b) support this viewpoint. They write that

> the influence of the classroom on the young child, many educators believe, cannot be separated from the influence of the family or from the context in which both the classroom and family exist. Home, school, community, and culture are all linked to each other. (p. 80)

As noted, the foundation of this viewpoint emerges from the theorizing of Bronfenbrenner (1977), who defines the ecology of human development as

> the scientific study of the progressive, mutual accommodation, throughout the life span, between a growing human organism and the changing immediate environments in which it lives, as this process is affected by relations obtaining within and between these immediate settings, as well as the larger social contexts, both formal and informal, in which the settings are embedded. (p. 514)

Widely accepted is his "unorthodox" belief (Bronfenbrenner, 1979) that development is grounded in the context in which it occurs. Basic to this notion is the idea that the contexts in which a person develops are nested, one inside the other, similar to a set of *matryoshka,* or Russian nesting dolls.

Bronfenbrenner identified four environments in which people develop:

- Microsystems are those immediate environments in which an individual develops.
- Mesosystems are identified as the relationships between various microsystems.
- Exosystems are social structures that have an influence on the development of the individual; however, the person does not have a direct role in the social system.
- Macrosystems are the ideological, cultural, and institutional contexts in which the preceding systems are embedded.

These nested relationships, as they relate to young children with delays and disabilities and their families, are portrayed in Figure 2.2. This ecological context provides us with a framework for understanding the world of young children (Hemmeter & Golden, 2014; Odom, 2016) and has led to the contemporary practice of viewing families as systems embedded within other systems. The *microsystem* looks at relationships within the crucial setting of the child's family in addition to the environments typically encountered by young children—child care centers, homes of relatives or friends, and, in certain circumstances, institutional settings like hospitals. The second layer, or *mesosystem,* relates to the relationships, at a particular point in a child's life, between caregiver and teacher or physician as well as the interaction of one professional with another. The *exosystem* takes into consideration the various social structures that impact family functioning. Early intervention programs as well as health/social service agencies are typical representatives of this third setting. The final context is the *macrosystem* and includes societal values and attitudes toward individuals with disabilities, in addition to legislative enactments and judicial remedies, which in turn affect the lives of young children and their families. IDEA is a powerful example of a macrosystem in action.

FIGURE 2.2 ■ The Ecology of Human Development

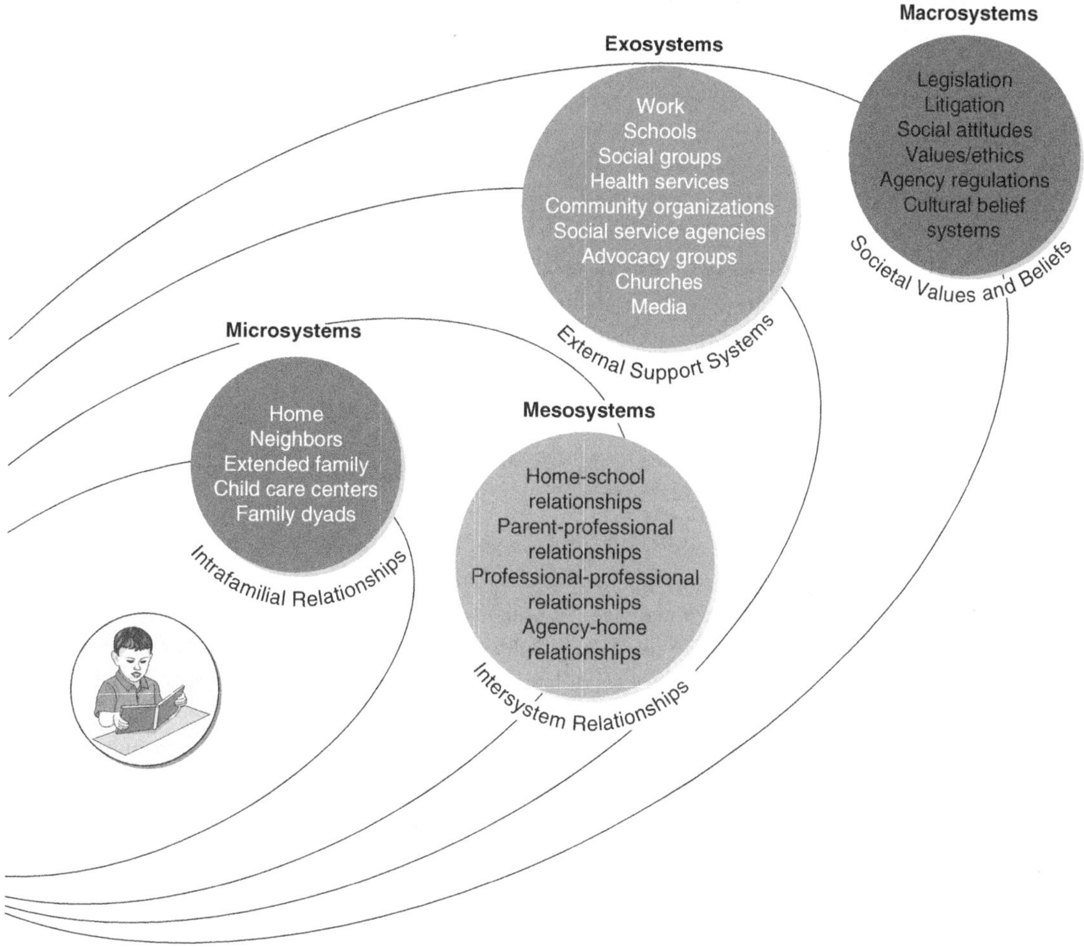

Source: Adapted from D. Bailey and M. Wolery, Teaching Infants and Preschoolers with Disabilities, 2nd ed. (Upper Saddle River, NJ: Pearson Education, 1992), p. 66.

Of course, the impact of time and history on the spheres of influence surrounding the developing child must also be considered. Bronfenbrenner and Morris (1998) refer to the interaction and influence of historical time on the four systems supporting the child as the chronosystem.

Gallagher et al. (2023) embrace a concept very similar to Bronfenbrenner's ecological model. These writers also believe it is vital for early childhood professionals to consider the familial and social context encountered by children with disabilities. The child is seen as being at the center of successive layers of influence, with the family being the primary and frequently most influential context. Other orbits include the peer group (which may include typical children and those with disabilities), schools, and society itself (see Figure 2.2). Like Bailey et al., (1986) in addition to Odom and Wolery (2003), Gallagher and his colleagues (2023) view the child with delays and disabilities in dynamic and complex interaction with many layers of environmental forces.

Recommended practices in early childhood special education rely heavily on the importance of the child's family (Council for Exceptional Children, 2022; Division for Early Childhood, 2014; Dunst & Espe-Sherwindt, 2016; Kilgo, 2022). According to Kirk et al. (2015):

> The trend toward early intervention (before the age of 5) increases the importance of the family. Much of the intervention with young children is directed toward changing the

> family environment and preparing the parent(s) or caregivers to care for and teach children with disabilities. At the very least, intervention tries to support constructive parent-child interactions. (p. 17)

The value of the emphasis on families can be seen in the Head Start commitment to meaningful parent (caregiver) involvement and participation. It also is clearly evident in IDEA and its accompanying amendments.

Successful program planning and intervention, therefore, must take into consideration the fact that the child is part of a system that interacts reciprocally within their environment. Bronfenbrenner (1979) observes that accomplishment of a specific task or activity "may depend no less on how he [the child] is taught than on the existence and nature of the ties between the school and home" (p. 3). Vincent et al., (1990) also note that "a change in the child is dependent not just on professional skills or the child's disability, but also upon complex interrelationships among family values, intra and extra-family supports, and the extent to which service is offered, match what families need and want" (p. 186).

The message is clear. Quality programs for young children with delays and disabilities demand that professionals see the child within the context of their family, their cultural background, and the family's interrelationships and interactions with other, larger social systems (Dunst & Espe-Sherwindt, 2016; Rogoff et al., 2017; Spicer, 2010).

SUMMARY

Early childhood special educators serve a wide variety of young children in a diversity of settings. It is imperative, therefore, that early childhood special education professionals have a clear understanding of how children from birth through age eight qualify for special education services. Of equal, if not greater, importance is the belief that young children with delays and disabilities are more like their typically developing peers than they are different. Early childhood special educators should focus on the strengths and abilities of each child.

The growth of early childhood special education as a discipline has been aided by judicial action and federal legislation. In several instances, principles addressed in various judicial proceedings have found their way into both state and national legislation. Many contemporary special education policies, practices, and procedures are derived from court decisions of the 1960s and 1970s. Likewise, the rights, opportunities, and benefits presently available for young children with delays and disabilities and their families are the result of federal legislative activity.

A question typically encountered by early interventionists and early childhood special educators is "Is EI/ECSE effective? Does it really make a difference in the lives of young children?" Perhaps the best way to answer this difficult query is to say, "It depends." One of the issues is the documented difficulty in conducting a methodologically sound investigation. In spite of this shortcoming, there is a very strong rationale for EI/ECSE, and the efficacy of these efforts has been substantially demonstrated.

The number of young children receiving early childhood special education services has grown dramatically in the past several years. This growth is partially the result of litigation, legislation, and the benefits attributed to EI/ECSE. In the 2019–2020 school year, more than 1.23 million young children from birth through age five were receiving some type of EI/ECSE services.

Contemporary thinking in early childhood special education strongly suggests the validity of viewing children as part of a larger social system, wherein they influence and are influenced by various environments. Children and their families need to be understood in the context in which they develop and interact. There is a reciprocal relationship among the various layers of environmental forces. This ecological perspective encourages early childhood professionals to consider the child's total environment and the key individuals encountered within these several interrelated spheres of influence.

KEY TERMS

At risk
Biological risk
Chronosystem
Developmental delay

Disability
Ecology
Environmental risk
Established risk
Exceptional children
Exosystems
Handicap
Individualized education program (IEP)
Individualized family service plan (IFSP)
Least restrictive environment (LRE)
Macrosystems
Mesosystems
Meta-analysis
Microsystems
No Child Left Behind Act

CHECK YOUR UNDERSTANDING

1. What is the difference between a disability and a handicap? Why is it preferable to use the term *disability* rather than *handicap?*
2. List the advantages of using the developmental delay category in early childhood special education.
3. What is meant by the terms *special education* and *related services?*
4. Identify the significance of the following court cases:
   a. *Pennsylvania Association for Retarded Children v. Commonwealth of Pennsylvania*
   b. *Mills v. Board of Education of the District of Columbia*
   c. *Larry P. v. Riles*
   d. *Board of Education v. Rowley*
5. List the major provisions of PL 94–142 and PL 99–457.
6. What is an individualized family service plan (IFSP)?
7. What is the role of a service coordinator in providing services for children from birth to three years old and their families?
8. Identify at least four benefits of early intervention/early childhood special education for young children at risk for or with delays and disabilities.
9. What general conclusions can be drawn from the efficacy research on early intervention/ education?
10. According to Bronfenbrenner, how should early childhood special educators view young children and their families?

REFLECTION AND APPLICATION

1. Trace the evolution of education law for children with delays and disabilities. How have early childhood special educators become better prepared to meet the needs of young children with delays and disabilities as result of legislative activity?
2. How has the role of families changed over the years? What evidence do you see that families and caregivers are involved in the early intervention/early education of their children?
3. How has the development of the IFSP/IEP process improved services for young children with delays and disabilities? What types of information can an early childhood special educator contribute to an IFSP/IEP meeting? How are the IFSP and the IEP similar? Different?
4. In what ways do you see the philosophy of Bronfenbrenner being incorporated in early intervention or early childhood special education services? Do you agree with Bronfenbrenner's ideas?
5. Conduct a mock IFSP/IEP meeting and write a script that leads to developing a well-written IFSP or IEP. Be sure to include the family as a key partner in this process.

MAKING CONNECTIONS

In order to help understand programs and services for young children with disabilities, three children are introduced: Maria Ramirez, T. J. Browning, and Cheryl Chinn. We will be exploring the educational needs of Maria, T. J., and Cheryl over the next several chapters. By getting to know these children, you will develop a better understanding of the diversity of services required for young children with delays.

Maria Ramirez

Bubbly, outgoing, and *affectionate with a constant smile* are some of the terms Maria's interventionists use when describing her. This thirty-month-old with Down syndrome is the youngest child of Bruce and Catherine Ramirez. Mr. Ramirez is an executive with a local bank. Maria's mother is employed as an intensive care nurse at the regional hospital. Her two older brothers enjoy their role as protectors of their little sister. The Ramirez family lives in an affluent section of a small town approximately fifty miles from a large Midwestern city.

A service coordinator comes to Maria's home one morning a week to provide assistance with the achievement of her individualized family service plan (IFSP) outcome statements. Due to her parents' work schedules and other commitments, Maria's grandparents provide child care and are prepared to work with her. Maria's entire family is committed to maximizing her potential.

Team members have recommended that Maria transition to an inclusive community-based program in order to receive Part B services. Although the family understands that with the approach of her third birthday, a change in service delivery is necessary, they are reluctant to agree to this recommendation. Maria's parents and grandparents have several concerns. Among their fears are issues of working with a new set of professionals, the length of her day, transportation to and from school, and Maria's interaction with typically developing peers.

Thomas Jefferson (T. J.) Browning

T. J. is a rambunctious little boy who just celebrated his fourth birthday two months ago. He lives with his mother and a twelve-year-old stepbrother, Willy. His mom has been separated from his dad for fourteen months. The family lives in a large apartment complex for citizens with incomes at or below the poverty level. There are few playmates his own age in the complex. T. J. does not have a close relationship with his older brother; his mom has suspicions that Willy may be involved with a neighborhood gang.

T. J. has been attending the Epps Head Start Center for the past fifteen months. In the center, T. J. has few friends. The staff observe that he has a short attention span, is easily distracted, and is overly aggressive. T. J. frequently uses his large size to get what he wants from the other children. Although well-coordinated, he has delays in fine motor skills, and his teachers suspect some cognitive deficits. T. J. receives speech therapy twice a week from a speech–language pathologist, which is provided in the classroom. The director of the Epps Center and her staff are concerned about his readiness to attend kindergarten in the fall.

T. J.'s mother is a concerned parent who wants her son to be successful in school. Her job as a waitress limits her participation in center activities and prevents her from attending meetings and class field trips.

Cheryl Chinn

Cheryl is a petite first grader attending an elementary school located in a large metropolitan area. She is the youngest of four children. Her father is a senior project manager for a multinational corporation. Cheryl's mom, Elizabeth, does not work outside of the home.

Cheryl was an unplanned pregnancy. Elizabeth was forty-one years old when Cheryl was born. Cheryl was born at thirty weeks gestational age and weighed slightly more than four pounds at birth. The first ten days of Cheryl's life were spent in a neonatal intensive care unit. Developmental milestones were accomplished about six months later than normal. Other than recurring episodes of otitis media, the first few years of her life were unremarkable.

Cheryl was enrolled in a preschool program when she turned three. She attended this program three days a week for two years. Due to a late-summer birthday, her parents considered delaying her entrance to kindergarten. She started kindergarten, however, with the other children from her neighborhood. Difficulty in following directions and instructions and with task completion, a short attention span, and social immaturity were soon observed. Cheryl required a "learning buddy" (peer helper) for her academic work. Because school officials were opposed to grade retention, Cheryl was promoted to first grade.

Many of the problems that Cheryl encountered in kindergarten were magnified in first grade. Shortly before a referral for special education services was to be made, Cheryl's pediatrician diagnosed her with attention deficit hyperactivity disorder (ADHD). Cheryl's teacher believes that a 504 accommodation plan would help Cheryl with her impulsivity, distractibility, and short attention span. The use of a peer helper was also continued.

Cheryl's parents are very involved in her education and fully support the development of a 504 accommodation plan. They were reluctant, however, to have their daughter referred for special education and possibly eligible for services under the developmental delay category, especially since two of her older brothers are receiving services for children with gifts and talents.

SDI Productions/E+/via Getty Images

3 FAMILY-CENTERED SERVICES IN EARLY CHILDHOOD SPECIAL EDUCATION

LEARNING OBJECTIVES

After reading this chapter, you will be able to

3.1 Describe how relationships among families and professionals in early childhood special education have changed over the years.

3.2 Describe the influences contributing to the emergence of a family-centered orientation in early childhood special education.

3.3 Explain family systems theory and provide examples of each element of this model.

3.4 Describe the benefits of family-centered services and capacity-building practices to support families in early childhood special education.

3.5 Discuss the importance of strong family-professional reciprocal partnerships in early childhood special education.

3.6 Describe the key components of family-professional collaboration, as well as strategies to foster positive interactions among families and professionals.

EI/ECSE Professional Standards

The content of this chapter aligns with the following professional EI/ECSE Standard:

Standard 2. Partnering with Families

Candidates use their knowledge of family-centered practices and family systems theory to develop and maintain reciprocal partnerships with families. They apply family capacity-building practices as they support families to make informed decisions and advocate for their young children. They engage families in opportunities that build on their existing strengths, reflect current goals, and foster family competence and confidence to support their children's development and learning.

DEC Recommended Practices

The content of this chapter also aligns with the following DEC Recommended Practices:

Family

- F1. Practitioners build trusting and respectful partnerships with the family through interactions that are sensitive and responsive to cultural, linguistic, and socioeconomic diversity.
- F2. Practitioners provide the family with up-to-date, comprehensive, and unbiased information in a way that the family can understand and use to make informed choices and decisions.
- F3. Practitioners are responsive to the family's concerns, priorities, and changing life circumstances.
- F4. Practitioners and the family work together to create outcomes or goals, develop individualized plans, and implement practices that address the family's priorities and concerns and the child's strengths and needs.
- F5. Practitioners support family functioning, promote family confidence and competence, and strengthen family–child relationships by acting in ways that recognize and build on family strengths and capacities.
- F6. Practitioners engage the family in opportunities that support and strengthen parenting knowledge and skills and parenting competence and confidence in ways that are flexible, individualized, and tailored to the family's preferences.
- F7. Practitioners work with the family to identify, access, and use formal and informal resources and supports to achieve family-identified outcomes or goals.
- F8. Practitioners provide the family of a young child who has or is at risk for developmental delay/disability, and who is a dual language learner, with information about the benefits of learning in multiple languages for the child's growth and development.
- F9. Practitioners help families know and understand their rights.
- F10. Practitioners inform families about leadership and advocacy skill-building opportunities and encourage those who are interested to participate.

Authors' Note: As you read this chapter, you will find the standards and recommended practices discussed throughout. See Appendix A for a complete list of the EI/ECSE Standards and Appendix B for a complete list of the DEC Recommended Practices.

In the field of EI/ECSE, professionals involved in the education and care of young children with delays and disabilities and their families increasingly have embraced the importance of focusing on and partnering with families. A family is a child's consistent or primary caregivers who have responsibility for their well-being and development and who are partners in the child's intervention and education. This may represent a variety of individuals, such as the child's biological, adoptive, or foster parents; legal guardians; grandparents or other relatives; and other individuals within their primary support network (DEC, 2020; Mapp & Kuttner, 2013; Turnbull et al., 2022). In today's American families, it is only realistic to define families more generally. The definition of **family** used in this chapter refers to a group of people who regard themselves as family, may be related by blood or circumstance, and rely upon one another to carry out functions that families typically perform—for example, daily care, affection, and/or financial support. Families often vary in their composition and how they function. As an illustration, when a young child was asked to draw a picture of his family, he drew a picture of himself and his grandmother by his bed and explained his drawing by saying, "A family is having someone to tuck you in bed at night."

Also emphasized throughout this book and in EI/ECSE Standard 2. Partnering with Families, one of the most important responsibilities of early childhood special educators is the development of effective reciprocal relationships with families, which should be nurtured and maintained. There is general recognition and understanding that families are the child's first and most important teachers as they learn about themselves and the world, requiring a commonsensical approach in which professionals view families as full-fledged partners. This type of true collaboration requires shared trust and equality in the relationship. Like any relationship, family-professional partnerships take time and effort to sustain.

A common belief among early childhood special education professionals today is that a family-centered perspective should influence all aspects of services and include assessment, team meetings, program planning and implementation, intervention activities, service coordination, and transition. Thus, early childhood professionals representing multiple disciplines must embrace a family-centered approach, provide support to families, and appropriately address the needs of families with diverse cultures and backgrounds. Findings from research have provided evidence to support the belief that family-centered practices have positive outcomes for young children with delays and disabilities and their families (Bruder, 2010; Division for Early Childhood, 2014; Dunst & Espe-Sherwindt, 2016; Keilty, 2016; Tomeny et al., 2021; Trivette & Banerjee, 2015). These factors, among others, have led to the strong emphasis on and establishment of family-centered practices in the field of early childhood special education.

This changing view of families' participation in their children's early childhood special education services has emerged over the last several decades. A variety of research studies, program models, and literature reviews and analyses have provided evidence to support the mutual benefits of such **collaboration** among families and professionals who work together with mutual respect and cooperation to reach shared outcomes and goals (Blue-Banning et al., 2004; Division for Early Childhood, 2014, 2022; Dunst & Espe-Sherwindt, 2016; Trivette & Banerjee, 2015). Thus, the roles of family members have transformed to a marked degree over the years, and the rationale for building effective partnerships between families and professionals is more compelling than in the past (Aldridge et al., 2016; Kilgo, 2022). Further, a dramatic increase has occurred in awareness, opportunities, services, and supports for families of young children with delays and disabilities. In this chapter, we will examine these and other factors related to family-centered early childhood special education services.

HISTORICAL AND LEGAL PERSPECTIVES

We acknowledge that the family is the fundamental social institution and the foundation of our society. Further, we recognize that the family is the primary context in which young children, with or without delays and disabilities, are socialized and exposed to the beliefs and values of their culture. Therefore, it is impossible to overemphasize the impact of the ongoing interactions that occur among young children within routine family environments and the potential progress that can take place in the early years (Bronfenbrenner & Morris, 2006). Families play a critical role in facilitating and supporting young children's development, and it is the responsibility of professionals to support families in understanding the significance of their role. Thus, the importance of strong collaborative relationships among professionals and families in early childhood special education, as well as general early childhood education, cannot be overemphasized (Kilgo, 2022).

All involved in the education and care of young children with delays and disabilities should be invested in building on the progress that has been made over the years in the provision of family-centered services and the connection to current recommended practices. Family involvement in programs for children with delays and disabilities is not a new concept. In fact, it is an evolving process that has transpired over many years.

The family movement gained increased attention in the 1960s in the United States. Many factors contributed to the emergence of the emphasis placed on families in the 1960s and 1970s, among them political, social, economic, and educational issues and events. Political movements, such as the civil rights and women's movements; advocacy efforts; and legislative actions led to the current emphasis that is placed on the provision of high-quality programs for young children with delays and disabilities and their families. Influences also have come from the fields of general early childhood education, early childhood special education, and compensatory education (e.g., Head Start), as well as professional organizations. Professional organizations such as the Division for Early Childhood (DEC; 2014), the National Association for the Education of Young Children (NAEYC; 2022), and others have established recommendations, standards, and policies regarding families. These documents stress that the benefits of family-professional collaboration early in children's lives extend far beyond the early intervention, preschool, and early primary years.

Table 3.1 provides a chronology of the family movement in special education with significant events, outcomes, and examples. Families of young children with delays and disabilities in the twenty-first century remain as an instrumental force in moving the field of early childhood special education forward. Many parents are involved in professional and parent organizations and often assist other families (e.g., parent-to-parent support). Additionally, families are involved in advocacy efforts and have a strong voice in supporting legislation and services for their children and other children and families (Kilgo, 2022).

TABLE 3.1 ■ Family Movement Progression and Accomplishments

Timeline	Significant Events and Accomplishments of the Family Movement	Examples
1950s	Parents organized services for children with disabilities in their local communities, established national organizations, and initiated political and advocacy efforts.	Schools opened for children with disabilities, and national organizations formed for parents of children with disabilities.
1975	The passage of P.L. 94–142, the Education for All Handicapped Children Act.	Parents' roles formalized in the educational process for school-aged children with delays and disabilities.
1980s	There was an increased grassroots movement for parent-to-parent support groups.	Parent-to-parent support groups were established for families of children of various age ranges and types of disabilities.
1983	Legislation was passed that established Parent Training and Information Centers on the national level.	National centers provided training, information, and assistance for families of children with disabilities throughout the country.
1986	The passage of P.L. 99–457 mandated that families should be the focus of services for children from birth through age three.	Individual Family Service Plans (IFSPs) were required, which center on families as the focus of services.
1990s	Advocacy movements facilitated by families grew in number, momentum, and influence.	Advocacy efforts grew in the areas of early childhood, inclusion, transition, and self-advocacy.

(Continued)

TABLE 3.1 ■ Family Movement Progression and Accomplishments (*Continued*)

Timeline	Significant Events and Accomplishments of the Family Movement	Examples
1997	Amendments were made to the Individuals with Disabilities Education Act (IDEA) that placed greater emphasis on the involvement of parents in all aspects of service, including families of children from birth through age three in early intervention.	Parent involvement was required to a greater degree in the special education processes (e.g., eligibility, placement, and planning) for their children with delays and disabilities. Families of newborns to three-year-olds were included as integral partners in early intervention processes.
2004	The passage of P.L. 108–446, the Individuals with Disabilities Education Improvement Act, emphasized to a greater degree the critical role of families.	Families were given written notification of their rights and responsibilities annually, as the law required, rather than only when they first receive services.

Source: J. Kilgo, Our Proud Heritage: The evolution of family-centered services in early childhood special education. *Young Children, 77*(4), 2022 p. 86.

Changes in American Family Characteristics

As professionals attempt to provide appropriate services and support to families, the changes that have occurred in the characteristics and composition of families over the last several decades are important to recognize. As we know, the conventional nuclear family is a family group consisting of, most commonly, a father and mother and their children. The traditional American family was once defined as (a) two parents (a male and a female), who were married to each other and always had been; (b) two or more children from the parents' union; (c) two sets of grandparents, living within fifty miles; (d) the mother working in the home and caring for the children; and (e) the father working outside the home and interacting with the children in the evenings and on weekends. This description of the family is much like the television sitcom *Leave It to Beaver*, which was based on the lives of the Cleaver family—a traditional American family of the 1950s. Of course, no longer is it valid to think of a typical family in the twenty-first century as a mom who is a full-time homemaker and a working dad along with their children who are all living together (Aldridge et al., 2016). This traditional view of the nuclear family has changed over the years and will continue to change. In fact, a limited number of families in the United States currently fit the traditional description. This is due to the changes in the characteristics of families with young children in America in recent years.

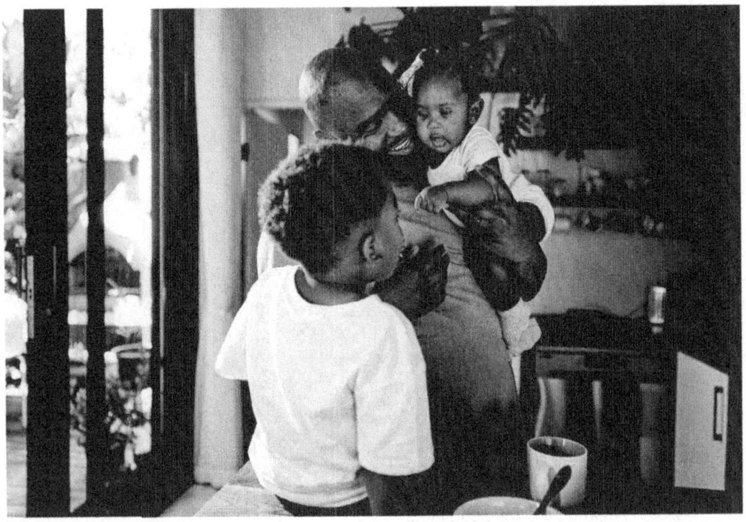

Few traditional nuclear families exist in American society today.

iStock.com/pixdeluxe

A number of changes have occurred in American families that reflect broader societal shifts (e.g., economic challenges, cultural diversity) and have had a significant impact on the experiences and needs of young children and families. Because of these changes and the numerous societal issues having an impact on families, fewer traditional families exist in American society today. What follows is a description of some of the changes that have occurred in American families since the 1950s that have significant implications for early intervention/education and the support and resources families need to thrive.

Family structure. The structure and composition of families with young children has become more diverse. There are increasing numbers of families with same-sex parents, multiracial families, and single-parent households. Also, there are countless family configurations including teen parents, families with adopted children, families with foster children, grandparents raising grandchildren, blended families, and other structures in addition to traditional mother/father roles.

Cultural diversity. American families have become more culturally diverse. In addition to race, ethnicity, and language, there are other influences on a family's cultural identity, such as religion, gender, age, structure, geographic location, and socioeconomic status.

Economic challenges. The cost of living and raising children has increased, leading to financial stress for many families. Many families, especially low-income families, face economic challenges such as job loss, wage stagnation, and high levels of debt.

Child care needs. More families are relying on two incomes and now have both parents working outside the home. With an increase in the number of mothers working outside the home, there is an increased need for child care.

Also represented today is the **hybrid family**, which Aldridge et al. (2016) describe as a family that redefined itself and produced something new and different from the origins that created it. An example of a hybrid family is one in which each parent has a different ethnic and religious background. Rather than implementing the cultural and religious practices of one parent or the other, the family chooses to practice a blend of both cultures and a religion that is different in many respects from either parent's family of origin. The parents have created a hybrid family that is different from either family of origin. Because of the changes that have occurred in families, early childhood professionals often face many unique challenges and opportunities related to the diversity of young children and their families in the twenty-first century (Aldridge et al., 2015, 2016; Aldridge et al., 2011; Barrera et al., 2003).

The family structures and backgrounds of children are diverse, which calls for an individualized approach to effectively serve each child and family.

Jeff Greenberg/Universal Images Group/via Getty Images

The diverse characteristics of families require an individualized approach in establishing family-professional relationships. Each family configuration and background adds to the complexity of interactions among families and professionals and the need for individualization. Early childhood special educators must consider multiple factors when working with various family structures and backgrounds, as well as the impact of these distinctions on family-professional relationships (Hanson & Espinosa, 2016). The DEC (2014) emphasizes that professionals must build trusting and respectful relationships with families, which means that they must be sensitive to the unique cultural, linguistic, and socioeconomic characteristics of the families they serve [DEC Recommended Practices F1].

As family characteristics continue to change, early childhood professionals must determine the most effective methods to provide support and services to families and individualize them to meet their needs (Aldridge et al., 2016; Kilgo, 2022; Kilgo & Aldridge, 2011).

FAMILY RESPONSES TO YOUNG CHILDREN WITH DELAYS AND DISABILITIES

Vital for early childhood special educators to consider is the impact that having children with delays and disabilities may have on families. When a child with a delay or disability becomes a member of the family, whether through birth, adoption, or later onset of the disability, the ecology of the family is transformed, and often the entire family must adjust. Each parent or family member may respond to a child's delay or disability in their own way, requiring an individualized approach to each family and/or family member. In the same way that early childhood personnel understand that all children are unique individuals, they also must recognize that families are distinctive entities. Responses and feelings may be dramatically different from one family to another and from one family member to another. Early childhood personnel, therefore, usually encounter a wide variety of behaviors and emotional responses on the part of parents and other family members.

Many years ago, some professionals conceptualized families based on a "stage theory" model of parental adjustment in response to having a child with a delay or disability. In recent years, however, this theory has been strongly criticized (Ferguson, 2002; Gallagher et al., 2003; Seligman & Darling, 2007). The way in which this model evolved is surprising in that it began with a study that was designed to assess parents' perceptions, feelings, and attachments to their children with delays and disabilities (Drotar et al., 1975). Based on the findings of this study, Drotar et al. developed a linear "stage theory" model of parental adjustment that followed a progression of acceptance beginning with shock and moving through denial and anger to a point of reorganization and acceptance. According to this model, parents are ready to cope with the responsibilities of their children with delays and disabilities once they have moved through the various stages of acceptance and have dealt with guilt accompanying having a child with a delay or disability.

Later in the 1980s, stage theories were contested by researchers who rejected the idea of families, all of whom are unique, going through the same specific stages of acceptance. Further, they disagreed with the idea of family reaction being judged and classified according to this continuum. In fact, some researchers suggested that the stage theory of acceptance of a child's disability is a disservice to families and is an oversimplification of a complex process that families experience (Blacher & Hatton, 2001; Gallagher et al., 2003).

The field of early intervention and childhood special education today acknowledges that families may react differently to having a child with a delay or disability based on a myriad of characteristics, resources, and supports that are unique to the individual family. Researchers recognize that a variety of factors can interact to influence a family's response and subsequent adjustment to a child with a delay or disability, which can include personal characteristics of family members, family structure, patterns of family interactions, health and safety factors, cultural background, and others. Stress factors or needs associated with delays and disabilities also can affect family functioning and partnerships between professionals and families. For example, professionals who work with four-year-old T. J. must carefully consider the influences of his brother's behavior and suspected gang activities, the neighborhood in which the family lives, his parents' separation, and other family dynamics. From a more optimistic perspective, certain family characteristics could be considered as positives, such as having a large extended family or a family with effective coping skills or strong religious faith, which may mitigate many of the stresses associated with a child with a delay or disability (Turnbull et al., 2022).

The needs of parents and other family members reflect not only their ability to cope but also the child's developmental needs. For example, the challenges addressed by the professionals who initially share the news of a child's disability with a family may be very different from those of the professionals who help families deal with the fears associated with the child's transition into preschool or kindergarten. Another example is that the needs of families of children with various types of disabilities, such as autism or complex medical disabilities, may be different from the needs of the families of children with speech delays and visual impairments. Professionals must tailor their interactions and provide support according to the distinct and ever-changing needs of families.

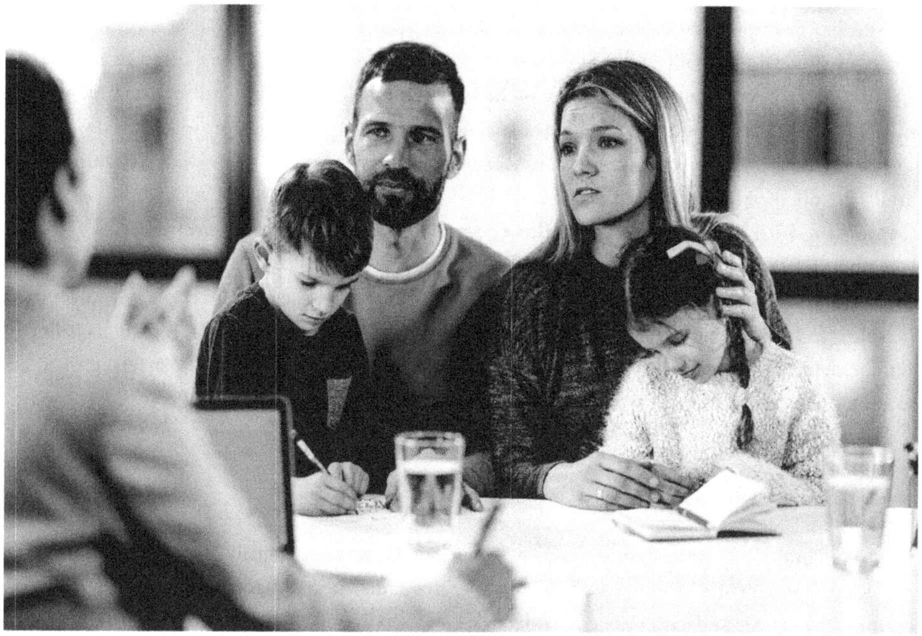

Professionals should provide support based on the individual and changing needs of each family.
iStock.com/skynesher

As Allen and Cowdery (2022) recounted, often families of young children with significant delays and disabilities and/or medically complex conditions face difficult issues, such as the following:

- Exorbitant expenses and financial burdens associated with medical treatment, surgery, and/or child care, as well as other needs such as special foods, equipment, or transportation
- Frightening, often recurring crises, such as when a child experiences seizures or faces life-threatening situations
- Continuous demands, often both day and night, to provide routine but difficult caregiving tasks (e.g., feeding, suctioning, monitoring)
- Constant fatigue, lack of sleep, and little or no time to meet the needs of other family members or to participate in recreational or leisure activities
- Difficulty locating qualified child care and respite care for children with delays and disabilities, which can interfere with the parents' abilities to fulfill work responsibilities, participate in social activities, and so on
- Reaction of siblings who may feel the child with a delay or disability requires *all* the family's attention and resources that results in jealousy or resentment
- Marital relationship stress arising from finances, fatigue, and lack of time to devote to the marital relationship

Of course, many families manage the increased demands and adapt well to the challenges they face, particularly when they have sufficient support. The responses of families, however, can differ and alter over time. Many families report the positive impact of a member with a delay or disability and successful adaptation. For example, Janice Fialka, who is the parent of an adult with a disability and advocate, explained her husband's reaction when asked if he was "in denial" about his son's disability. He stated categorically that he was not "in denial" but was "in hope" instead, which indicates an optimistic approach to his son's disability. Susan Weisman Lee, an early childhood special education teacher and the parent of a daughter with Rett syndrome, emphasized her daughter's positive qualities and encourages professionals to assume competence and acknowledge families' hopes and dreams for their children. Another example focuses on a sibling's positive response to his sister's disability. Jordan Spieth, a successful professional golfer who has a sister with a neurological disability, often explains that his sister, Ellie, is the best person in his family, is the funniest family member, and adds so much joy to his family. He credits her membership in their family with providing him with perspective on what is most important in life. Professionals have much to learn from the experiences, stories, and recommendations of family members of children with delays and disabilities.

In working with each family, early childhood special educators must attempt to achieve a balance between being optimistic and realistic about the future of each child. Children's strengths should be stressed, along with their needs. Families should be supported as they analyze, plan, and prepare for their child's future. As one mother stressed, "What families need most from professionals is hope and encouragement. They should try to support the family's hopes and dreams. We often need to adjust them a bit, but we need support from professionals to achieve them."

FAMILY SYSTEMS THEORY

The fundamental belief underlying family systems theory is that a family is an interactional system with unique characteristics and needs. A family operates as an interconnected and interdependent unit; therefore, occurrences and experiences that have an impact on one family member also affect the other family members or the entire family unit. Each family member may have their own set of needs that may or may not be congruent with the needs of other family members or with the needs of the family overall. Because of the relationship that exists among family members, professionals must consider the entire family unit as the possible focus of their attention. As explained earlier, professionals should apply family systems theory by individualizing their relationship with each family, just as they customize their work with each child with a delay or disability (Hanson & Lynch, 2013; Turnbull et al., 2022).

Family systems theory was adapted many years ago by Turnbull et al. (1984) to focus specifically on families of young children with delays and disabilities and is a theory that is used widely today in the field of special education (Turnbull et al., 2022). The family systems conceptual framework includes the following four key elements, which are interrelated.

1. *Family characteristics* are the attributes of a family, such as cultural identity and lived experiences.
2. *Family interactions* refer to the relationships among family members or subsystems, including parents, partners, siblings, and extended family members.
3. *Family functions* are the needs and interests of family members that are influenced or met by the family, including affection, self-esteem, spirituality, economics, daily care, socialization, recreation, and education.
4. *Family life cycle* refers to all the changes, such as developmental stages and transitions, that affect families and influence family resources, interactions, and functions.

Figure 3.1 offers an illustration of the components of the family systems framework. What follows is a discussion of each component.

Family Characteristics

The first element of family systems theory is family characteristics, which are the dimensions that make each family unique (e.g., family size and form, cultural background, geographic location). Additionally, each family member's health status (both physical and mental), distinct coping style, and the nature of the child's disability are considered personal characteristics. One final characteristic is the specific

FIGURE 3.1 ■ Family Systems Conceptual Framework

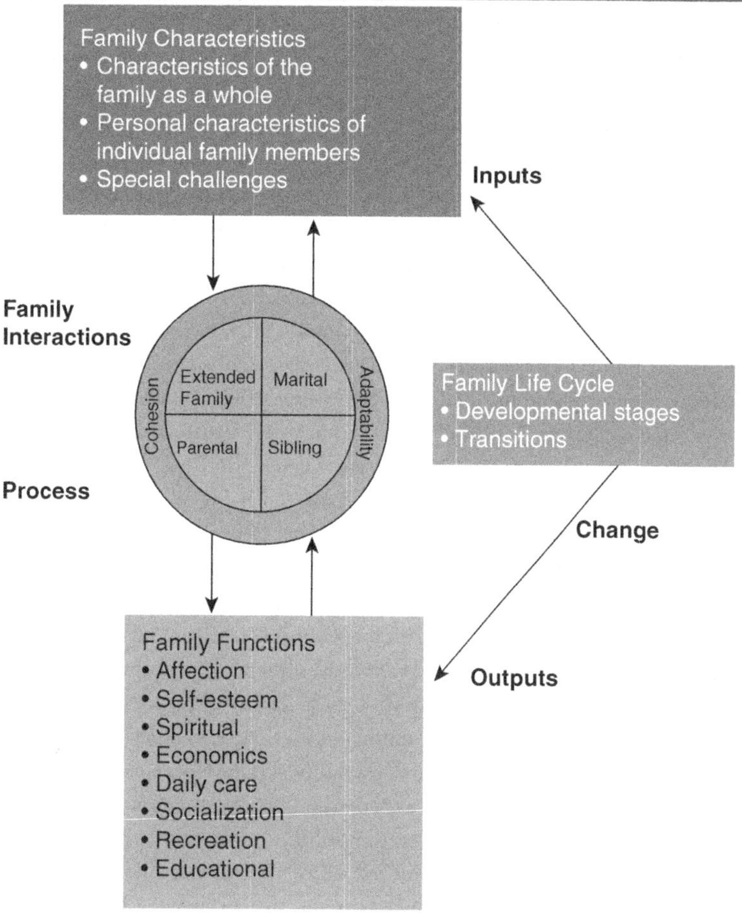

Source: Adapted from A. Turnbull, R. Turnbull, G. Francis, M. Burke, K. Kyzar, S. Haines, T. Gershwin, K. Shepherd, N. Holdren, & G. Singer, *Families and professionals: Trusting partnerships in general and special education* (8th ed.) (Pearson, 2022), p. 82.

challenges that families may face, such as poverty, substance abuse, and parents who themselves have disabilities. Together, these variables constitute each family's unique identity and influence interactional patterns among the members while also determining how the family responds to the child's disability (McCormick et al., 2008). It is easy to understand how a large family with numerous children living below the poverty level in a rural geographic location might adapt differently than a wealthy suburban family with only one child. In both examples, the families may be effective in their adaptation to a child with a delay or disability; however, their responses, needs, and adaptive strategies may be very different.

Family Interactions

The second component of the family systems framework is family interactions, which are the interactions that occur among and between the various family subsystems or subgroups (Hanson & Lynch, 2013). These subsystems typically include the following:

- Partner (e.g., husband-wife)
- Parental (e.g., parent-child)
- Sibling (e.g., child-child)
- Extended family (e.g., nuclear family, friends, neighbors, larger community including professionals) (Turnbull et al., 2022)

How a particular family interacts depends, in part, on the degree of cohesion and adaptability in interactions. These two elements of family interaction influence the quality of interactions and can only be interpreted within the context of the family's cultural background.

Cohesion that occurs among family members is a type of emotional bonding that holds them together. It indicates the degree of freedom and independence experienced by each member of the family unit. Cohesion occurs along a continuum of behavior ranging from enmeshment to detachment. Highly enmeshed families are overly cohesive, which can impede the development of independence in individual family members. Families who are highly enmeshed are viewed as being overly protective and having weak boundaries between the subsystems. Conversely, inflexible subsystem boundaries characterize disengaged families—believed to have a low degree of cohesion. In this situation, families are portrayed as being underinvolved, and the child with a delay or disability may experience a lack of support (Hanson & Lynch, 2013). Ideally, well-functioning families attain a balance in cohesiveness, which means that the limitations between systems are clearly defined and family members feel a close bonding as well as a sense of autonomy (Seligman & Darling, 2007; Turnbull et al., 2022).

Adaptability refers to the family's ability to alter its power structure, role relationships, and rules in response to crises, stressful events, or transitions occurring over the lifespan. Like cohesiveness, adaptability occurs along a continuum from rigidity to chaos and is influenced by each family's cultural background and other family characteristics and experiences. When a stressful event occurs, some families operate more rigidly and answer according to prearranged roles and responsibilities, often seeming incapable of acclimating to the demands of the new situation. According to Seligman and Darling (2007), this type of behavior puts a family at risk for becoming isolated and disengaged. When a child with a delay or disability becomes a member of a family, some form of accommodation or adjustment often is required. Yet, in a family with a strict, defined hierarchy of power, the child care needs more than likely become the responsibility of the mother, with little assistance provided by other family members. Conversely, some families have low adaptability and have been characterized as chaotic due to the continuous change and instability they experience. In many situations, there is no family leader, and the few existing rules are frequently changed, resulting in substantial confusion, particularly for young children who need parental and family reliability and predictability. Most well-functioning families, however, appear to maintain a balance between the extremes of high and low adaptability (Nichols, 2014; Taibbi, 2015).

Each family has unique characteristics that determine how the family responds to a child's delay or disability.

David McNew/Getty Images News/via Getty Images

Family Functions

The third element of the family systems framework is family functions, which refer to the interrelated activities that are essential in fulfilling the individual and collective needs of families. These areas as described by Turnbull et al. (2022), with examples of each, are as follows:

1. *Affection*—emotional commitments and display of affection
2. *Self-esteem*—personal identity and self-worth, recognition of positive contributions
3. *Spirituality*—needs related to church, religion, or God
4. *Economics*—production and utilization of family income
5. *Daily care*—day-to-day survival needs such as food, shelter, and healthcare
6. *Socialization*—developing social skills, establishing interpersonal relationships
7. *Recreation*—leisure time and play activities for both family and individuals
8. *Education*—involvement in educational activities and career choices

Turnbull et al. (2022) classified these nonprioritized functions as "outputs" and emphasized that it is impossible to discuss family functions without considering the other three main components of the family systems framework. Although these tasks and activities (e.g., economics, daily care, recreation) are shared in all families, they are likely to be affected by a child with a delay or disability. For example, there may be less time and resources for recreation due to the increased cost and time required in addressing the needs of a child with a disability such as cerebral palsy or autism. A concern of most parents today, particularly for those employed outside the home, is not having enough time to carry out family functions and meet all the needs of the family. This concern is often magnified for parents of children with delays and disabilities.

The "Where Will I Find the Time" excerpt provides the words of Helen Featherstone, who authored a book many years ago, *A Difference in the Family: Life With a Disabled Child* (1980). As the mother of a son named Jody who had significant disabilities and was unable to walk or talk, Featherstone described the struggles she faced each day as she grappled with having insufficient time to complete all tasks required of her. In this passage, she wrote about an occupational therapist asking her to add a fifteen-minute regimen to her day-to-day routine, which she simply could not do due to not having the time. Featherstone illustrated the importance of professionals being sensitive to the tremendous demands placed on families of children with delays and disabilities that are in addition to the many other tasks involved in family functioning. This book had a tremendous impact on the way in which many professionals perceived the complexities and demands placed on families of children with delays and disabilities.

Where Will I Find the Time?

I remember the day when the occupational therapist at Jody's school called with some suggestions from a visiting nurse. Jody has a seizure problem, which is controlled with the drug Dilantin. Dilantin can cause the gums to grow over the teeth; the nurse had noticed this overgrowth, and recommended innocently enough, that [his] teeth be brushed four times a day, for 5 minutes, with an electric toothbrush. The school suggested that they could do this once on school days, and that I should try to do it the other three times a day; this new demand appalled me; Jody is blind, cerebral palsied, and retarded. We do his physical therapy daily and work with him on sounds and communication. We feed him each meal on our laps, bottle him, bathe him, dry him, put him in a body cast to sleep, launder his bed linens daily, and go through a variety of routines designed to minimize his miseries and enhance his joys and his development. (All this in addition to trying to care for and enjoy our other young children and making time for each other and our careers.) Now you tell me that I should spend 15 minutes every day on something that Jody will hate, an activity that will not help him to walk or even defecate, but one that is directed at the health of his gums. This activity is not for a finite time, but forever. It is not guaranteed to help, but "It can't hurt." And it won't make the overgrowth go away but may retard it. Well, it's too much. Where is that 15 minutes going to come from? What am I supposed to give up? Taking the kids to the park? Reading a bedtime story to my eldest? Washing the breakfast dishes? Sorting the laundry? Grading students' papers? Sleeping? Because there is not time in my life that hasn't been spoken for, and for every 15-minute activity that is added one must be taken away.

Source: Excerpt from H. Featherstone, *A Difference in the Family* (Basic Books, New York, NY, 1980), p. 76.

In most cases, families have modified priorities for each family function based on their situation. In one family with limited financial and community resources, for example, meeting the daily needs of food and shelter is of greatest importance, while for another family with abundant financial and community resources, the emphasis may be on their needs in such areas as education or recreation and leisure. One can easily appreciate why members of a family living in poverty may place greater emphasis on meeting their needs for food and shelter. A teenage single mother may focus on completing high school, as well as spending time with friends or dating. Berry and Hardman (2008) noted that some families, particularly those with restricted resources, may require aid in several areas while others may need support in only a few areas. The amount of support families request from professionals also will differ depending upon other specific family circumstances.

Family Life Cycle

Family life cycle is the final element of the family systems theory framework. This factor of the theory refers to developmental changes that occur in families over time. Most of these changes are foreseeable, such as a child beginning kindergarten or graduating; however, they can be nondevelopmental or unexpected, such as the untimely death of a family member, divorce, or marriage within a family; loss of employment; or the unplanned birth of a child. These changes alter the structure of the family and, in turn, impact relationships, functions, and interactions. Researchers have classified as few as six to as many as twenty-four developmental stages that may occur in families (Hanson & Lynch, 2013; McGoldrick et al., 2015). Regardless of the number of stages, each stage brings change, supplementary demands, and new stressors. How the family individually and collectively answers to these situations dictates, in part, the way in which the family typically functions.

The movement from one stage to another and the accompanying adjustment period is considered to be a transition. Transitions can be taxing events for families, but particularly for families of young children with delays and disabilities. For many families, transition is a time of challenges and uncertainty as to what the next stage holds for the child and family as well. For instance, when a child starts preschool or a preschooler moves to kindergarten, this transition can cause heightened anxiety and substantial stress. Transition plans are composed as part of the individualized family service plan (IFSP) for children from birth to three years old and as part of the individualized education program (IEP) for three through eight year olds to prepare for the changes and to foster smooth transitions and successful adjustments for children and families.

According to the family systems theory, life cycle functions are exceedingly age related. As a family moves through the lifespan, the focus may shift when the family encounters new situations (Seligman & Darling, 2007). Turnbull et al. (2022) discussed four major life cycle stages and the associated issues that the family members of a child with a delay or disability may confront along their journey. The lifespan of a family characteristically includes the stages of the early childhood years, the school-age years, adolescence, and adulthood (McGoldrick et al., 2015). Possible developmental concerns that a child with a delay or disability may present to their family during the early childhood years (birth through age eight) are presented in Table 3.2. Professionals must keep in mind, however, that the way in which a family adapts to various stages throughout the lifespan is highly personal. Not all families successfully negotiate changes that occur across the life cycle without assistance, both formal and informal, from professionals and the community. It is important to remember that families of children with delays and disabilities may encounter stressors at distinct points in time, and a family's behavior may sometimes seem extreme; however, most families eventually achieve a healthy balance.

TABLE 3.2 ■ Potential Family Lifespan Issues in the Early Years

Stage	Potential Issues
Early Childhood (Birth–Age 3)	Obtaining an accurate diagnosis Informing family members and others of diagnosis Seeking to understand the diagnosis Establishing routines to carry out family functions Locating services Learn about the early intervention system Participating in IFSP meetings Preparing for transition to new preschool services
Preschool (Ages 3–5)	Transitioning to new services or school Facing issues associated with acceptance of the child's delay or disability Participating in the first IEP meetings Making placement and service decisions Worries associated with going to preschool (e.g., acceptance, inclusion)
School Age (Ages 5–8)	Adjusting emotionally to educational implications Clarifying issues of inclusion and making placement and service decisions Participating in the IEP meetings Adjusting to the expectations of early primary school Locating information and community resources Arranging for extracurricular activities

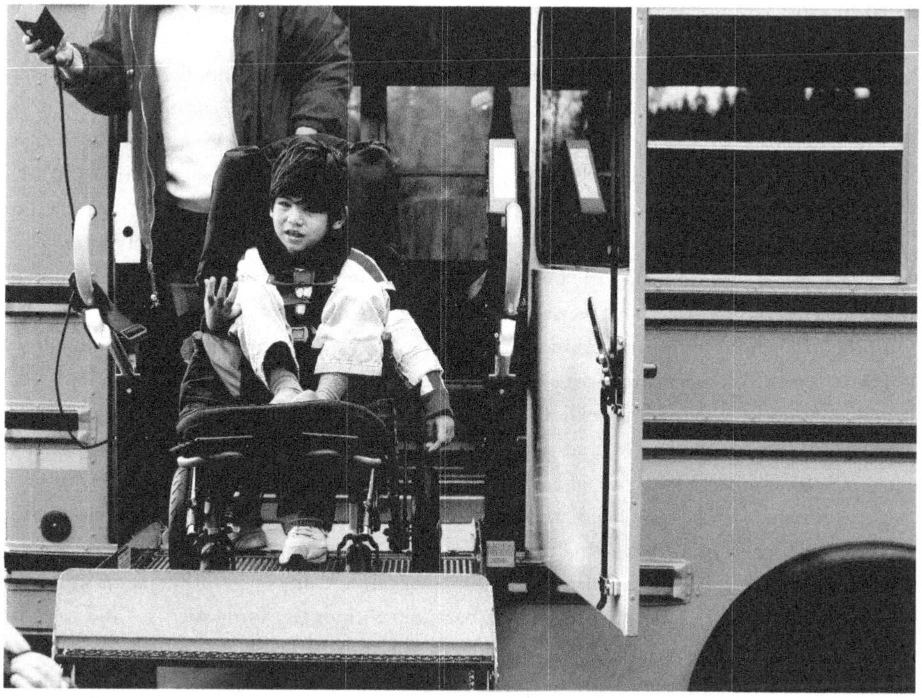

Without appropriate planning, transitions (e.g., when a child leaves preschool and begins kindergarten) can cause increased stress for the family.

iStock.com/jarenwicklund

Understanding the family as a social and emotional unit rooted within other units and networks enables early childhood special educators to understand the complex nature of families and work with them in more efficient ways. Applying this view permits professionals to comprehend that events and changes in one unit may directly and indirectly impact the behavior of individuals in other social units. A systems perspective deems events within and between social units as supportive to the extent that they have positive influences on family functioning. Each family member is viewed as a system and as a part of many other systems, such as the early intervention program, school, community, and society (Guralnick, 2011; Odom, 2016).

As described in Chapter 2, an ecological perspective highlights that power is derived from the nature and structure of human relationships within environmental contexts (Bronfenbrenner, 1979). For example, an infant's need to develop trust is realized within the primary relationship system of the family. This need also may be strongly shaped by other social systems, such as the neighborhood or a child care program (Guralnick, 2011; Odom, 2016).

Internally, as discussed earlier, the family system has basic functions that provide a broad framework through which a range of roles and tasks are carried out. These functions change in response to developmental shifts in the family itself, as well as individual family member shifts (e.g., job loss, illness). The structure of the family system and any changes in the structure (e.g., new family member, death of a family member) may have an influence on all other elements.

Applications of Family Systems Theory

Knowledge and application of the family systems theory framework is helpful in early childhood special education. Based on this model, the family is viewed as an interactional system with unique and changing characteristics, strengths, and needs which evolve across the lifespan (Odom, 2016). Professionals can apply family systems theory in their interactions with families in early intervention, preschool, school, and beyond.

In early intervention (EI), an important component of the successful provision of family-centered services for infants and toddlers (birth to three) is service coordination, which is mandated by Part C of the Individuals with Disabilities Education Act (IDEA). Service coordination is an ongoing process designed to assist families as they access services and assure their rights to services. To accomplish this, service coordinators have roles on the early intervention team to support families in navigating the early intervention system and other community resources (Early Childhood Technical Assistance Center, n.d.). Service coordination can be provided by professionals representing a variety of disciplines (e.g., education, social work, and therapists) and the qualifications vary widely across the nation. However, the common purpose of service coordinators is to maintain the primary relationship directly with the family while personnel from other disciplines provide support to the family through the service coordinator. Service coordination has been described as the linchpin of early intervention because of the critical role it plays in laying the foundation for applying family systems theory and providing family-centered services throughout the early childhood years and beyond.

To provide optimal support to families, a strengths-based approach also is recommended that concentrates on the inherent strengths of children and families. Thus, professionals view children and their families as resourceful, resilient, and self-determined (Green et al., 2004). Rather than focusing on the needs, challenges, and stressors each family encounters, it is important to remain attentive to the family's strengths and resources. Early childhood special education professionals must work with families to recognize and develop their individual strengths and assets as they receive services for their children (DEC, 2014). Examples of one family's strengths included support from extended family for child care, flexible employment, friendships with other parents of children with delays and disabilities, and living in an urban area with outstanding medical and early intervention and school-based services.

In the family systems theory framework, the development of individuals and families is a dynamic process of person-environment relationships. Therefore, the behavior of a child, a family, or a child and family is viewed as a part of a set of interconnected "systems" that powerfully impact one another. By comprehending experiences and activities of families and assessing the influences on the families, professionals can work with them to design strategies to promote well-being in the family system. For example, if Maria's service coordinator appreciates and builds upon the close relationship Maria's brothers have with their thirty-month-old sister, the brothers can be encouraged to participate in some of the learning activities and strategies designed to be used at home, which will benefit Maria.

MAKING CONNECTIONS

FIGURE 3.2 ■ Eco-Map for Maria Ramirez and Family

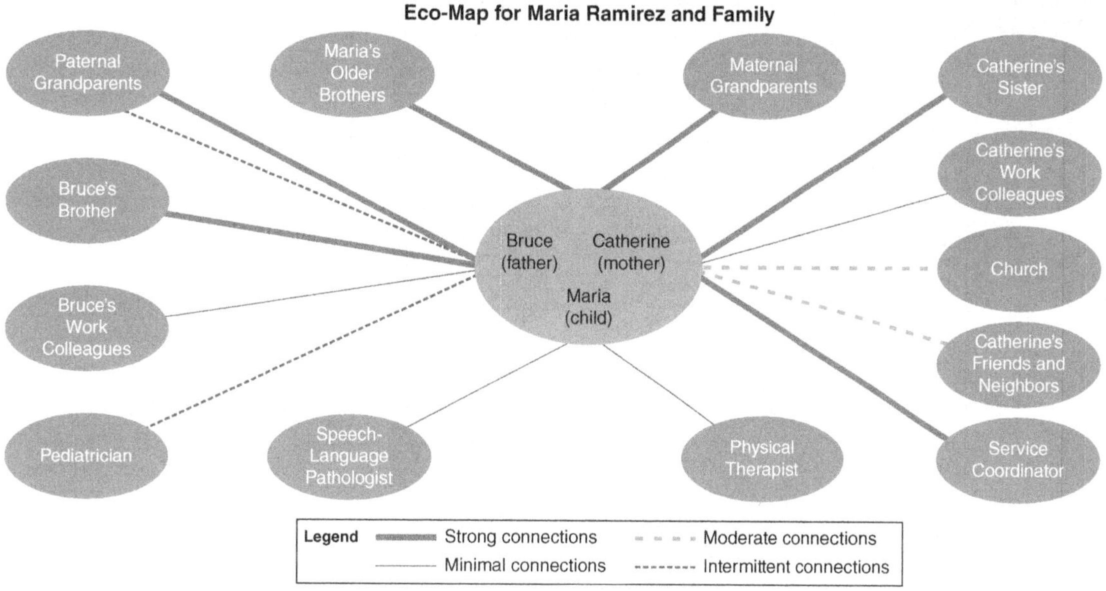

The Making Connections feature delivers an example of an eco-map developed with Maria's family to acquire more knowledge about the family structure, assess needed services, and establish a connection with the Ramirez family. For example, the service coordinator who works with thirty-month-old Maria must consider that Maria's interactions with her brothers, grandparents, friends from her affluent neighborhood, and therapists who visit weekly, as well as other significant people and experiences in her life, will have a profound influence on Maria.

A number of strategies and protocols are used in early childhood special education that are based on applications of family systems theory. Many early childhood special education teams have found eco-maps, or family maps, to be useful in determining important information such as family structure, strengths, and resources. According to McCormick et al. (2008), eco-maps were "originally developed as a visual representation of the family system at the beginning of intervention" (p. 18). Developing an eco-map requires specific steps that include identifying (a) informal family supports, (b) strengths and relationships, and (c) formal family supports. The eco-map can be used to link the IFSP or IEP outcomes/goals to support services for children and families and to review formal and informal family resources.

An important concept that is integral to the understanding of family systems theory and the application of family-centered practices is empowerment, which has been used for many years by persons in various helping professions. Most professionals agree that it is much more precise to describe the concept of family empowerment as a route rather than an end state. Family empowerment is a progression through which individuals increase their ability to impact those people and organizations that affect their lives, as well as the lives of their children and others they care about. Empowered individuals or families seek control over their lives and strive to get what they need for themselves and their families (Levine, 2013; Trivette & Dunst, 2004). It is within the family ecology that children and parents cultivate their sense of power as they access and utilize needed resources, make decisions and solve problems, and interact effectively with others in the social exchange process to obtain the needed resources.

Early childhood special education personnel must keep in mind that the concept of empowerment is dynamic, interactive, and process oriented (Levine, 2013; Nichols, 2014; Taibbi, 2015). Those who accept the empowerment paradigm share the notion that all families have strengths. Professionals are in a strategic position to promote positive, empowering communications with families by providing quality programs for young children, involving parents in partnerships, and supporting families in all aspects of early childhood special education services.

Parents often obtain support from early childhood special education professionals as they access needed services and resources for their children.

Mark Boster/Los Angeles Times/via Getty Images

One of the most imperative functions of empowerment is to afford skills that endorse self-sufficiency. Empowerment may grow through a family's changes in self-perception, increased self-confidence, ability to set goals, acquisition of skills to attain goals, and the opportunity for supported practice. In most cases, empowerment means promoting access to resources, competence, confidence, and self-efficacy (Dunst et al., 2014; Hanson & Espinosa, 2016; Hanson & Lynch, 2013). Relationships between professionals and families can be fostered through family empowerment because families develop trust in them, and professionals perceive families as part of an equal, reciprocal partnership. Families, with the support of professionals as needed, take actions to solve problems and get what they need for their children and other family members (Turnbull et al., 2022).

A FAMILY-CENTERED APPROACH

A family-centered perspective should be evident in all aspects of early childhood services. Early childhood programs all over the country have incorporated a family-centered philosophy that is the foundation of early childhood special education (Kilgo, 2022). As described previously, this family philosophy in early childhood special education has changed over time. Dunst et al. (1991) traced the history of the role of professionals in working with families of young children with delays and disabilities.

The first model defined by Dunst et al. (1991) is a professional-centered activity whereby the professional was the solitary source and distributor of knowledge. Families were considered dysfunctional and incapable of resolving their own problems. The family-allied model came next—families served as teachers of their children, implementing family interventions arranged by the professionals. This perspective gradually was replaced by a family-focused emphasis. Professionals at this stage regarded families in a more optimistic light but, unfortunately, often misinterpreted family practices as being nice to families and doing what they wanted, which dominated the complexities of family life and the role of family-centered practices in "supporting and strengthening meaningful changes in child, parent, and family functioning" (Dunst & Espe-Sherwindt, 2016, p. 38). Families were seen as capable of collaborating with professionals; however, most professionals still assumed that families needed their assistance.

In a family-centered model, the family is the center of the service delivery system. As such, services are planned around families based on their individual needs. This approach is consumer-driven, which means professionals are working at the direction of the family. Other terms that have been used in recent years include *family-driven* and *family-directed*. Regardless of the term used, early childhood special education professionals today believe that families are the primary decision makers and units to provide support and assistance as desired in fulfilling their goals for their children.

Using the view of the family as a system, the ecological perspective, and the empowerment paradigm, professionals are acknowledging and responding to families as strong, unique, and able to identify their own concerns, priorities, and resources, which will change over time based on each family's life circumstances [DEC Recommended Practices F3]. The concept of **family-centered practices** in this context indicates specific techniques and procedures of working with families. Family-centered practices support and build on family strengths and capacities and strive to enhance family skills, confidence, competence, and family-child relationships [DEC Recommended Practices F5]. Families are not mere recipients of services but are active partners in preparing and applying service delivery processes (Kilgo & Raver, 2009; Kilgo, 2022; Woods et al., 2011).

As Maria's mother noted, "When Maria was six months old, she still couldn't sit up and didn't smile, make sounds, and play like her brothers did. My pediatrician connected me with an early intervention program, and now Maria is receiving services that really help her. She is making lots of progress, and we are learning what we can do to help her. We now know that we weren't doing anything wrong. Maria just doesn't do things as quickly as other children her age. But now she is making progress, and we have lots of support."

Early childhood special educators and other professionals who work with families of young children with delays and disabilities must carefully consider the following underlying premises of a family-centered approach. First, there is the recognition that families are all different. They differ in their concerns, resources, priorities, and other areas; therefore, an individualized approach to working with families must be used to address each family's specific needs [DEC Recommended Practices F3, F4]. Each family's unique characteristics and goals must be respected. Second, families should be partners with professionals in planning, service provision, and decision making related to issues such as the child's placement and the family's level of involvement in early childhood special education services. This relationship must include valuing and supporting the equality within the partnership, building on the family's strengths and desires, and promoting parents' confidence and competency to support their child's development and learning [DEC Recommended Practices F5, F6]. Finally, families must be regarded as the ultimate teachers and decision makers for their children. They are the constant in the lives of young children and the key focus of family-centered services (Division for Early Childhood, 2014; Keilty, 2016; Trivette & Banerjee, 2015).

A family-centered approach focuses on the strengths and priorities of families as they make informed choices and decisions about their children's current and future services.

Jett Loe/The Las Cruces Sun-News via AP

The DEC (2014) Recommended Practices define the three themes of a family-centered approach in early childhood special education:

> 1. *Family-centered practices*: Practices that treat families with dignity and respect; are individualized, flexible, and responsive to each family's unique circumstances; provide family members complete and unbiased information to make informed decisions; and involve family members in acting on choices to strengthen child, parent, and family functioning.
> 2. *Family capacity-building practices*: Practices that include the participatory opportunities and experiences afforded to families to strengthen existing parenting knowledge and skills and promote the development of new parenting abilities that enhance parenting self-efficacy beliefs and practices.
> 3. *Family and professional collaboration*: Practices that build relationships between families and professionals who work together to achieve mutually agreed upon outcomes and goals that promote family competencies and support the development of the child. (p. 10)

The DEC Recommended Practices (DEC, 2014; Trivette & Dunst, 2005) explain the parameters of family-centered practices, which offer the foundation for high-quality services for young children with delays and disabilities and their families. A long-standing belief held by professionals in the field of early childhood special education is that families need both informal and formal resources and supports to have the knowledge and skills, as well as the physical and psychological energy and time, to engage in child-rearing responsibilities and parenting activities that promote their children's development. As described in EI/ECSE Standard 2: Partnering with Families, family-centered practices potentially have child-, parent-, and family-strengthening and competency-enhancing and capacity-building results. These family capacity-building practices afford participatory opportunities to families that can strengthen their existing parenting knowledge and skills and promote the development of new abilities that enhance parenting self-efficacy beliefs and practices. Of course, these experiences are guided by each family's individual strengths and needs, as well as their priorities, goals, and preferences (DEC, 2014).

To be most effective, early childhood special education personnel must hold a set of values that place families at the center of the service delivery process and as the directors of services for their children. This marks a dramatic shift from past practices when professionals concentrated solely on the child and devised interventions based on what they thought was best the child with little or no input from the family. Professionals have replaced the role of expert with the role of partner in a relationship where they assist families. The focus is on the strengths and capabilities of families, with families making fully informed decisions regarding services for their children. This aligns with the DEC Recommended Practices that emphasize the importance of practitioners providing families with current and complete information that is impartial and comprehensible, which families can use to make informed choices and decisions about their children [DEC Recommended Practices F2]. As one person described, "We've come a long way from trying to get all families involved in their children's education in the same manner. Today families are at the center of services and make the decisions about their children's education. We provide support to them as they deem appropriate."

According to the DEC Recommended Practices, the intent of family-centered practices is to (a) promote families' participation in decision making related to their child (e.g., assessment, program planning, intervention); (b) lead to the development of a service plan (e.g., outcomes or goals for the family and child and the services and supports to achieve them); and/or (c) support families in achieving the outcomes or goals they hold for their child and the other family members (Division for Early Childhood, 2014). Families and professionals must collaborate to create personalized plans (e.g., an IFSP or IEP) for each child and family in which their anticipated results and goals are included and practices are applied that address the families' priorities and concerns and the children's strengths and needs [DEC Recommended Practices F4]. One father stressed, "My child's team helped us consider our child's strengths and needs, although they were unlike what we expected, and build upon them.

They made us realize that what we thought and wanted mattered. We felt like the team supported what was important to us."

Researchers have suggested for many years that a family-centered approach usually results in benefits to both the child and the family (Dunst & Espe-Sherwindt, 2016). Trivette and Dunst (2005) provided research evidence that social support has positive effects on family well-being. Figure 3.3 contains a model they used to demonstrate the direct and indirect influences of social support on personal and family well-being, parent-child interactions, and child behavior and development. According to this model, "social support and resources directly influence the health and well-being of parents; both support and health/well-being influence parenting styles; and support, well-being, and parenting styles directly and indirectly influence child behavior and development" (p. 108). Through this model, it is easy to recognize the far-reaching impact of family-centered practices on both children and families and the importance of utilizing such an approach. Benefits of a family-centered approach may include the following: (a) child functioning; (b) family competence and skills, confidence, and emotional well-being; (c) families' view of service effectiveness and sense of control over their child's care; (d) problem-solving ability; (e) capacity of families to care for their child; (f) cost-effectiveness; and (g) family empowerment. Evidence of the effectiveness of a family-centered approach has encouraged programs throughout the country to embrace family-centered practices (Crnic et al., 2017; Division for Early Childhood, 2014; Kilgo, 2022; Sandall et al., 2005; Trivette & Banerjee, 2015).

FIGURE 3.3 ■ Model of the Direct and Indirect Influences of Social Support and Intrafamily Factors on Families

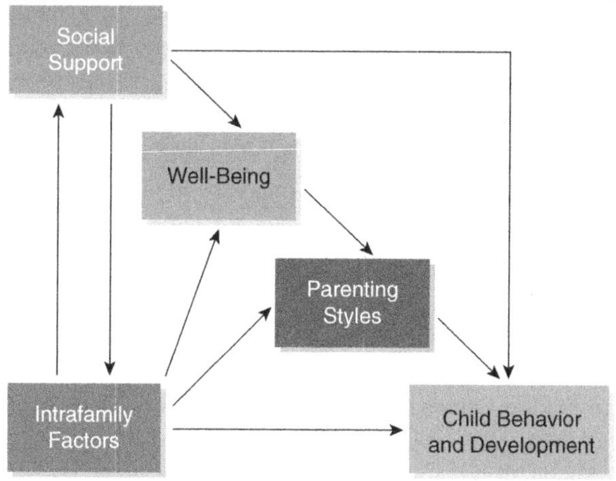

Source: Adapted from C. Trivette and C. Dunst (2005). "DEC Recommended Practices: Family-Based Practices." In S. Sandall, M. Hemmeter, B. Smith, and M. McLean (Eds.), *DEC Recommended Practices: A Comprehensive Guide for Practical Application in Early Intervention/Early Childhood Special Education,* (Division for Early Childhood, 2005). p. 108.

FAMILY-PROFESSIONAL COLLABORATION AND PARTNERSHIPS

Early childhood special educators must apply their knowledge of family systems theory and family-centered practices to develop and maintain reciprocal partnerships with families, as described in EI/ECSE Standard 2: Partnering with Families. The rationale for the development of collaborative partnerships between families and professionals has been emphasized in early childhood special education for many years (Summers et al., 2005). The rationale includes the following: (a) family members spend more time with their child with a delay or disability than anyone else, (b) families have more information about the child than anyone else, (c) how families function will determine what types of intervention and services will work for them, and (d) families have the ultimate control over the services provided for their children and themselves.

As one early interventionist described, "We've changed dramatically over the years. We've moved from trying to figure out how we can involve parents and provide training in areas that professionals think are important to how we can provide support to parents in areas that they consider important to their child and family." Because there is a difference between the meaning of family involvement and family engagement or collaboration, it is important for early childhood special educators to understand and respond to the differences. Family involvement means that parents are doing what is suggested or expected by the program or school (e.g., parent-teacher conferences, open houses, classroom visits, fundraising activities). However, family/parent engagement or collaboration is quite different and means working together with early childhood professionals to create a successful learning environment for the child and support for the family.

No matter how concerned and capable professionals are, or how devoted parents are to their children, each cannot accomplish alone what they can achieve by working together. The groundwork for building positive relationships between professionals and families must contain a mutual understanding of their roles in supporting children's development and learning. This method of mutual understanding can permit both parties to empathize and ascertain ways to support one another in their roles. The early years are not only a foundational period for young children, but also a critical and challenging time for families. Families often need and welcome support as they face the numerous challenges of family life during the early years of the life of a young child with a developmental delay or disability (Keilty, 2016).

Essential principles have been identified for professionals to follow in order to establish collaborative relationships with families and professionals within home, program, school, and community settings (e.g., communication, respect, trust, commitment, equality, and advocacy). Professionals should learn as much as possible about each child and family to maximize the possibilities of the child's success. Initial experiences and interactions of children, families, and professionals in early childhood special education programs should be compassionate and optimistic. Early childhood special educators who are reassuring to families are much more likely to construct a positive relationship with them. Like any relationship, family-professional partnerships take time and effort to maintain (Woods et al., 2011). The professional's responsibility is to find ways to cultivate partnerships with family members because young children with delays and disabilities are the ultimate recipients of these partnerships. An understanding of each family from a systems standpoint will provide insight to help professionals approach families as partners in the early development and education of their young children. This type of true collaboration necessitates shared trust and equality in the relationship.

DEC (2014) indicates that during the early childhood years, practitioners apply skills in family-professional collaboration as they inform families of their rights and support them in the comprehension of these rights and the development of leadership and advocacy [DEC Recommended Practices F9, F10]. Parents often need to employ these advocacy skills across the lifespan as they seek services for their children. In addition, professionals support families in identifying and accessing formal and informal resources within their communities [DEC Recommended Practices F7].

Jill Cunningham, a nursing faculty member at a university and the parent of a teen-age daughter (LeaAnna) with a rare chromosome disorder and complex healthcare needs, explained the significance of family-professional collaboration and the extensive support she received from early intervention personnel as she promoted preschool services in her neighborhood school. During this process, Jill's in-laws, parents, and extended family offered widespread support through afterschool care, as well as emotional and social support. This afforded time for Jill's career to flourish and provided time for her to advocate for additional services for LeaAnna and other children in the community. Individuals and groups from their community (neighborhood, church, and work) have been supportive as well. With their support, Jill has provided leadership in the creation of an exemplary summer camp program for children with multifaceted healthcare needs and other disabilities. This family's experiences demonstrate the use of formal and informal resources and extensive advocacy efforts.

CENTRAL COMPONENTS OF FAMILY-PROFESSIONAL COLLABORATION

As demonstrated throughout this chapter, families and professionals collaborate on multiple levels to address the needs of young children with delays and disabilities. Effective family-professional collaboration is the foundation of early childhood special education. Key components of family-professional collaboration include (a) culturally responsive practices, (b) effective communication, (c) information exchange and support, (d) home visits, and (e) meetings and conferences. What follows is a description of each of these components with suggested strategies for fostering successful partnerships with families.

Culturally Responsive Practices

One of the most critical influences on the relationships that develop among families and professionals is how professionals respond to the culture of the family. **Culture** refers to the values and beliefs that provide the foundation for how individuals perceive, interpret, and behave within their family, community, and world. Culture is the blend of thoughts, feelings, attitudes, beliefs, values, and behavior patterns that are shared by ethnic, racial, religious, or social groups. Thus, a family's culture establishes how the family members think, perceive, believe, and behave (Gollnick & Chinn, 2017; Hanson & Espinosa, 2016). Culture is especially applicable to relationships between families and professionals because culture includes many diverse factors that shape one's sense of group identity, including geographic location, income status, gender, sexual orientation, language, disability status, value of education, and occupation. It is the basis within which individuals, families, or groups understand their experiences and progress their visions of how they want to live their lives (Hanson & Espinosa, 2016; Hanson & Lynch, 2013).

Cultural responsiveness is a multifaceted concept encompassing the mindfulness, acknowledgment, and acceptance of each family's culture and cultural values. Cultural responsiveness necessitates professionals to observe each family as an individual unit that is impacted by, but not defined by, its culture (DEC, 2022). As such, professionals must prevent **stereotyping**, which transpires if assumptions are made that all individuals within a cultural group share the same viewpoints or react in a predetermined manner. Such expectations are often mistaken and limit the ability to understand and develop relationships with families (Aldridge & Goldman, 2007; Lynch & Hanson, 2011; Matuszny et al., 2007).

As we explore the influence of culture on family-professional relationships in early childhood special education, it is important to consider the following components that may have a direct or indirect consequence on the relationship between professionals and families:

- *Religion* and the beliefs and customs associated with religion are likely to influence such things as the holidays families celebrate and associated activities (e.g., holiday events, schedules, traditions, and practices). The religious beliefs of families are likely to influence their attitude toward delays and disabilities, health and illness, medical care, diet, belief in and reliance on a higher power, and willingness to accept help from outside the family.
- *Language* influences all aspects of communication with families if they do not speak English or are unable to read in English (or any other language). For children who are dual language learners, practitioners provide families with information about the benefits of their children learning in multiple languages and the effect this can have on their growth and development [DEC Recommended Practices F8].
- *Race*, which may influence the likelihood of families experiencing discrimination if they are members of the non-majority culture, may foster skepticism about trusting others of a different race and accepting help from them.
- *Ethnicity* may have an impact on families' feelings of belonging or perceptions of themselves as outsiders in early childhood special education programs.
- *Gender* may influence beliefs about the roles that various family members assume in caretaking and advocating for their children, as well as interacting with professionals.
- *Age* of the family members can influence their life experiences—for example, teenage mothers who have parental responsibilities or grandparents who are raising their grandchildren.

- *Geography* often creates certain opportunities and barriers to family-professional partnerships; for example, differences exist in rural settings where families live long distances from an early intervention or early childhood special education program without public transportation and inner-city settings where families must alter their lifestyles if violence and crime are issues.
- *Income* or socioeconomic status may influence the resources available to families and the extent to which their housing, medical care, and nutrition are adequate to meet the needs of young children with delays and disabilities.

Early childhood personnel must recognize that culture often shapes families' attitudes not only concerning their child's disability, but also their child-rearing practices, choice of goals and outcomes, and view of professionals. We also must appreciate that culture is not a fixed concept. In fact, there is considerable variation within cultural groups that can change over time. Further, the influence of culture can vary from family to family even when families have similar cultural backgrounds. As defined earlier, many hybrid families and cultures are assisted in early childhood special education today (Aldridge et al., 2016); therefore, early childhood special education practitioners may encounter challenges, as well as opportunities, related to cultural diversity. Family-professional relationship building should be modified and accomplished in ways that are responsive to each family's cultural background and linguistic and social diversity [DEC Recommended Practices F1].

We are not suggesting that professionals must know everything about the culture of families they serve in early childhood special education. What we recommend, however, is that professionals should gain an understanding of each family's cultural beliefs and values as they relate to their children and their goals or outcomes (Hains et al., 2005). After gaining general information about a family's culture, more specific knowledge can be gleaned by talking to the family, asking for clarification, and seeking family members' assistance in understanding information about their cultural beliefs and practices and the implications for services to be offered. The following is an example from Kilgo and Aldridge (2009) of what could be expressed to a family of Sikh faith to gain clarification about their child's eating goal: "I read that people who practice the Sikh faith believe that all of life is sacred and that playing with food such as eggs is not appropriate. Is that true of your family? Because eating solid foods is a goal for your child, please tell us what we should know to assist with this" (p. 4). In this example, the early childhood special educator is asking the family for more information about their beliefs that would have an impact on their child's goals related to eating.

In some instances, when professionals and families have differing cultural beliefs and practices, these can serve as barriers to the development of their relationships (Kalyanpur & Harry, 2012). The significance of professionals understanding differences between their own viewpoints and those of families representing diverse cultural backgrounds cannot be overemphasized. To do this, each professional also must explore their own background, beliefs, and values. In doing so, the practitioner will increase their capability of comprehending the individual perspectives that are unique to each family and how they differ from the professional's own circumstance and set of beliefs. Professionals who do not recognize values and beliefs of families are more likely to make prejudiced and inaccurate judgments that may weaken their relationships with families.

Professionals sometimes work with a **cultural mediator** who is from a family's culture within the community if available. A cultural mediator serves as a link between the program or school and the family as the professionals seek to learn more about the cultural background of the family (e.g., beliefs about disability, communication or interaction style, and child-rearing practices; Allen & Cowdery, 2022). By sharing information with the program or school, families can more fully contribute to the educational process for their child. Professionals must recognize, however, that diverse family backgrounds, structures, parenting styles, and other factors will influence each family's interactions and level of involvement. Getting to know families allows early childhood special educators to understand the family dynamics, cultural differences, and individual preferences.

Families can more fully participate in the educational process for their children when they develop meaningful relationships with early childhood special educators and therapists.

TODD SUMLIN/MCT/Newscom

Collaboration among families and professionals when cultural differences and/or conflicts occur requires respect, trust, and cooperation (Hanson & Espinosa, 2016; Lynch & Hanson, 2011). The professional's obligation is comprehending, appreciating, and responding to differences to positive ways, which usually has a positive bearing on efficient collaboration among families and professionals. To efficiently assist children and families representing diverse cultural backgrounds, we recommend the following strategies:

- Professionals should use multiple resources to become more culturally competent. For example, they should participate in ongoing staff development and learn from families, other professionals, policymakers, and members of the cultural communities served by the program.
- Professionals should learn as much as possible about the cultural backgrounds of the families with whom they work.
- Professionals must understand that there are many hybrid families and cultures; they should avoid stereotypes and overgeneralizations.
- When professionals meet with the families, they should let them know that they are prepared and ready to learn from them about their culture, beliefs, and traditions.
- Professionals should ask appropriate questions and listen to what the families tell them; they should be open to learning about and appreciating each family.
- Based on what is learned from families, professionals should adapt practices as needed to ensure they respect and include the values, beliefs, and customs of families.

Effective Communication

One of the most significant elements in relationships between families and professionals in early childhood special education is communication that is effective. As we know, professionals and families now have increased access to and use of technology, which has changed the way in which they interact and communicate. Simply stated, **communication** is a process used by two or more individuals to send and receive messages, and it is dynamic and ever-changing. Regardless of the mode of communication, professionals and families must maintain an open, straightforward relationship based on trust, which of course depends on successful communication (Turnbull et al., 2022; Whitbread et al., 2007). Thus, communication skills rank among the most necessary of all the skills possessed by early childhood personnel. In this section, we discuss the importance of communication, as well as skills and strategies to foster effective communication and collaboration among professionals and families to expand learning and support children's development. Many forms of communication are used during interactions among families and professionals, both nonverbal and verbal.

Verbal communication strategies, which include acute listening and observation skills, are obligatory for efficient family-professional relationships. These strategies and skills can be practiced and refined over time as early childhood personnel have discussions with families. Early childhood special educators should never underestimate the importance of communication and the power of their words in their relationships with families. Feature 3.1 includes what parents perceive as some of the most helpful comments made to them by professionals.

FEATURE 3.1 THE MOST IMPORTANT COMMENTS PROFESSIONALS HAVE MADE TO PARENTS

- "We value your input."
- "Tell us about James. What does he like to do? What makes him happy?"
- "What is your vision for Lauren? Where do you see her next year or in five or ten years?"
- "We will follow your lead."
- "You are the expert on your child."
- "We will work on this together. I'll be right here beside you."
- "I support your goals. Now how can I help?"
- "We're working on it" (rather than saying the child cannot do something or does not have a skill).
- "What a great idea."
- "How should we work on this?"
- "What do you think we should do next?"
- "We have so much to learn from you."
- "You have contagious optimism."
- "I support your dreams for Alyssa."
- "I am assuming competence in your child."

Although not everyone has perfected their communication skills, it is imperative to note that verbal and nonverbal communication abilities and strategies can be learned and improved with practice. Early childhood special education personnel are encouraged to methodically exercise verbal and nonverbal communication skills so that they become unprompted and natural. Turnbull et al. (2010) and Winton et al. (2010) offered extensive information about communication to form cooperative relationships among professionals and families in the CONNECT Modules.

Nonverbal communication is any communication other than spoken or written words and involves body language that expresses information. Body language incorporates facial expressions, eye contact, posture, voice tone and tempo, physical proximity, and gestures. Desirable facial expressions, for example, may include direct eye contact, warmth and concern shown in facial expressions, and appropriately mixed and dynamic facial expressions. However, it is vital to note that every culture has its individual way of displaying nonverbal behaviors. In some Asian cultures—for example, Japan—direct eye contact can be considered inappropriate or impolite (Lynch & Hanson, 2011). Less eye contact may indicate politeness. Table 3.3 provides examples of desirable nonverbal communication skills, which should be customized based on families' cultural inclinations. Nonverbal behaviors to avoid include checking time frequently, looking at the ground, excessive movement, a fake smile, excessive blinking, and others. These nonverbal behaviors may indicate disinterest, irritation, or not listening.

The way early childhood special educators use responsive communication strategies in their interactions with families plays a central role in fostering positive relationships.

iStock.com/Steve Debenport

TABLE 3.3 ■ Nonverbal Communication Strategies
Comfortable Setting
A warm, comfortable setting that puts families at ease
Facial Expressions
Appropriate eye contact (respecting cultural preferences)
Warm, pleasant, encouraging facial expressions
Varied, animated facial expressions (with smiles when appropriate)
Posture and Gestures
Appropriate gestures (meaning may vary according to culture)
Relaxed, comfortable physical posture
Absence of repetitive movements (e.g., tapping fingers, shaking foot)
Affirmative movements such as nodding head in agreement (as appropriate)
Voice
Can be heard clearly, but not too loud
Warmth in voice tone with natural speech tempo
Physical Proximity
Three to five feet between speakers whether seated in chairs, on sofa, or on floor (respecting cultural preferences for personal space)

The way in which professionals communicate with and support families plays an imperative role in fostering positive parent-professional communication (Banks et al., 2003). Therefore, professionals are encouraged to use communication strategies based on each family's unique characteristics, needs, and preferences. For example, specific strategies may be needed when families have cultural or linguistic differences. Depending on the family's cultural practices or primary language, altered support may be compulsory to help with communication. Early childhood special educators must understand the importance and value of effective communication in parent-professional collaboration.

Professionals should show respect for the family's knowledge and understanding of their child and convey a feeling of acceptance of the information families can offer. Further, personnel should create opportunities for parents and other family members to provide this type of meaningful information. For professionals to understand families' concerns, priorities, and vision for their child, gaining input from families of the utmost importance. Early childhood special educators often must probe to solicit families' perspectives. In addition, they must try to confirm the perceptions of the family's intent and meaning. Through interactive listening and observation, attempts can be made to understand what families are saying, what they are feeling, and what they want for their child. Acknowledgment of the family's concerns, priorities, and vision and a willingness to follow the family's lead will help to establish the trust necessary for an ongoing working relationship.

Another important factor to consider is that most families have no previous experience with developmental delays and disabilities. This may be their first exposure to the terminology that is used in the early intervention or early childhood special education process. Their conceptualization of such terms as *eligibility, developmental delay*, or *disability* may be different from that of professionals; therefore, the terminology used should be made clear to families. Further, clear everyday language should be used when possible, and technical terms, professional jargon, and acronyms (e.g., IEP, IFSP, PT, OT, SLP) should be kept to a minimum. Common acronyms should be used only when families clearly understand their meaning.

In addition, it is critical for the professional to communicate clearly about the policies and practices of the program. Professionals are advised to supply families with information before they enter the program and appraise it on an constant and as-needed basis. Parents and other family members need to be informed about various facets of the program such as the assessment process, related services, health and safety requirements, daily schedules, home visits, and other program features. Having sufficient information about the program obligations helps to lay a positive groundwork for a successful partnership.

Information Exchange and Support

Professionals should respect each family's right to choose how communication will occur and their level and style of participation in early childhood special education services. Modes of communication can be both formal and informal in early intervention/early childhood special education. Formal methods may include program, classroom, or home visits, individual parent meetings, group parent meetings, newsletters, and communication notebooks. The use of technology, such as smartphones and social media, has become widespread in families with young children. Therefore, other methods of communication may be utilized, such as phone calls, text messages, e-mails, webpages, or social media. Usually, multiple methods of correspondence between families and professionals are available. The following are some logical recommendations for providing continuing support and communication exchanges with families. Because families have individual communication needs, styles, and preferences, early childhood special educators should

- Ask families their preferred method for ongoing communication (e.g., e-mails, text messages, phone calls, meetings).
- Let families know they value their communication with them and treat every incoming or outgoing message as important.
- When communicating via phone call or text message, always ask first if it is a good time for the family to communicate or if there is a more convenient time.
- Personalize conversations by addressing the family members by name and begin by saying something positive about the child and/or family.

- Provide opportunities for families to ask questions (If professionals are unable to address a family's question, then they should let the family know they received the message and will get back in touch shortly.).
- Be knowledgeable of resources to share with families and have linkages with others in the community who may provide additional information
- Return calls, e-mails, and other communication from families as promptly as possible.
- Summarize what is communicated and indicate the next steps when appropriate.
- Always follow up on what was agreed upon to demonstrate trustworthiness and dependability.

As in any relationship, successful communication between families and professionals involves a clear understanding and knowledge of the anticipations, requirements, and responsibilities of each party in the relationship. Communication must be frequent, consistent, and beneficial to be effective. Sharing information that is not useful to families or communicating too irregularly will do little to assist the achievement of families' goals/outcomes for their child. Irrespective of the method of communication or when it happens, early childhood special educators must be keen to listen and seek to understand the families' points of view.

Early childhood special educators must support families to make informed decisions and advocate for their young children, which is highlighted in EI/ECSE Standard 2: Partnering with Families. They must recognize that families are the best advocates for their children, which is augmented when professionals keep families informed and afford them with reassurance, support, and positivity, which must be organized, comprehensible, and well-matched to each family's needs (Kaczmarek, 2007; Trivette & Dunst, 2005). A variety of techniques can be used when discussing a child's abilities and performance with families. Early childhood special educators must engage families in opportunities that build on their existing strengths, reflect current goals, and foster family competence and confidence to support their children's development and learning. Respect, concern, and a sincere desire to collaborate in all aspects of services must be demonstrated. Early childhood special educators should regularly share updates on their child's progress and any changes in their educational plan. Families that are supported and have the knowledge they need are more likely to respond to early childhood special education services in a significant way.

To meet each family's individualized needs and priorities, early childhood special educators should be acquainted with the various resources that are available and should share that information with families so they can support their child's development and well-being. Further, professionals must offer multiple options for how information is disseminated to families, such as through online resources, other parents, and community resources.

In addition to the support available from early childhood special educators, many families can profit from the support and advice of other families that also have children with delays and disabilities (Hanson & Lynch, 2013). A family may establish a relationship with another family, or families may become members of parent-to-parent organizations that are founded at the local, state, or national level. Many of these organizations have websites, social media platforms, listservs, chat rooms, blogs, and discussion boards. Networking with other families provides opportunities for families to problem-solve concerning various subjects and produces opportunities for enrichment and learning from one another as well. There are numerous organizations available to provide support, information, and resources for families, as shown in Feature 3.2.

FEATURE 3.2 REPRESENTATIVE WEB RESOURCES FOR FAMILY INFORMATION

PACER Center: http://www.pacer.org

The PACER Center is a national parent information resource for families of individuals with disabilities, ranging from birth to young adulthood. The PACER Center has publications, training, and other resources, including education and other services, that parents may need as they make decisions for their children with disabilities across the lifespan.

Center for Parent Information and Resources (CPIR): http://www.parentcenterhub.org

The CPIR is the central "Hub" of information and products created for the network of Parent Centers serving families of children with disabilities. The CPIR's intent is to create products and services that increase Parent Centers' knowledge and capacity in specific domains. The materials available on the CPIR Hub were created and archived for Parent Centers throughout the country to be used to provide support and services to the families they serve.

Family Voices: http://www.familyvoices.org

This is a national organization of comprised of families and friends of children and youth with special health care needs and disabilities. The purpose is to link family organizations across the country that provide support at all levels to improve health care services and policies.

IRIS Center: https://iris.peabody.vanderbilt.edu/module/fam/

The IRIS Center's module addresses the importance of engaging families of children with disabilities in the educational process. Some of the key factors that affect families are highlighted, as well as suggestions for involving families and developing relationships among parents and professionals.

Home-Based Services

Home-based services are delivered in the natural environment by professionals who make **home visits** to address the development and learning of the child and support the family, which requires coordinated planning and collaboration among families and professionals. Home-based service delivery is a crucial component of early intervention services for children from birth to three years old with delays and disabilities because the home is the usual setting in which infants and toddlers receive early intervention services (McWilliam, 2012; Roggman et al., 2016). Home-based services also are provided for some preschoolers and children with multifaceted health care needs or other types of disabilities. Home-based services have copious benefits for both young children and families, and they allow parent-professional relationships to progress on a more casual and individual level. According to many researchers, families involved in home-based services cultivate more positive relationships with professionals with whom they work, learn valuable information and strategies, and are more likely to follow through on suggested activities as recognized in the IFSP (Hanson & Lynch, 1995; McWilliam, 2012, 2016).

As McWilliam (1999) noted, "The child does not learn from home visits—the family does" (p. 24). Families can point out specific areas of need and learn how to support their child's development and learning in the natural environment on an continuing basis. Supporting families in the natural environment offers ideal carryover and generalization because they have the chance to practice skills with their children in daily routines and activities (Akamoglu & Dinnebeil, 2017; Woods et al., 2011). With thoughtful planning, adaptable application, and recurrent examining, home visiting can be a highly successful service delivery model with numerous advantages for families and professionals (Brady et al., 2004; McWilliam, 2012, 2016).

Important to remember is that the goal of home visits is to offer families the skills and supports essential to meeting their priorities, outcomes, or goals identified in the IFSP or IEP. Therefore, it is more likely for the families to experience satisfaction if the expectations of the home visit are clear. Meticulous planning must occur so that each family understands and is comfortable with the process. The following are examples of decisions to be made preceding the home visit so that the family will know what to anticipate:

- How long will each visit last?
- What will be the agenda and format of the visit?
- Which family members will participate actively in the session?
- How will progress be monitored and family satisfaction determined?

Because home visits require professionals to enter a family's home, special attention should be given to honor the family's confidentiality and preferences regarding the logistics of the meeting (e.g., time of day, location). Families should be offered choices in scheduling that are opportune and changeable. In some cases, families may not want home visits to occur because they may feel that having practitioners in their home is intrusive. In such instances, other arrangements can be made for services to be provided in other locations (e.g., child care center, playground, park).

When home visits occur, there are numerous practical factors to consider. When traveling in the community and entering homes, safety is an important concern and, therefore, professionals should follow basic safety precautions. Many resources are available that supply procedures to follow when conducting home visits. The following provides a summary of practical suggestions that home visitors should follow.

- Schedule visits at times that are convenient for each family member at times that are best for the child (e.g., before or after naptime), and when identified routine activities usually occur (e.g., dressing, mealtime, playtime)
- Always arrive and leave on time to home visits; cancel visits only when absolutely necessary
- Dress appropriately and comfortably to allow for interaction with children
- Greet and interact with all family members (e.g., siblings, extended family)
- Be aware of any family customs (e.g., leaving shoes at the door)
- Be informal but not too casual; practice professional behavior even though it is a home environment
- Respond with sensitivity to offers of food and beverages
- Expect distractions in the home environment (e.g., phone calls, visitors, unexpected occurrences); be flexible if there is an interruption of what is planned
- Be prepared with resources, materials, and activity plans; prepare activities for siblings if needed
- Make sure that families participate in the home visit to the extent they desire (sometimes this will be one parent, or it may include both parents)
- Use items and toys found within the home; demonstrate intervention strategies using these items to encourage follow-up by families
- Encourage parents to interact with their child while supporting the parents and modeling strategies as needed
- Share thoughts and suggestions about strategies that are used and provide feedback; explain why certain strategies are used over others
- Agree with families on strategies they can use between home visits
- Consider safety issues; alter the visit if you feel unsafe
- Before going on home visits, always leave a schedule and location of visits with a colleague or supervisor
- Observe and document progress during each home visit and discuss your perceptions with families
- Solicit feedback from the family regarding progress and satisfaction
- Allow time to interact with family members regarding family outcomes, discuss questions and concerns, and exchange information
- At the conclusion of the visit, summarize what was discussed and accomplished, discuss next steps, and schedule a time for the next home visit

By planning properly and following these recommendations, home visits can be individualized and an effective way to provide services.

Home-based services have multiple benefits as young children are able to learn and practice skills in daily routines and activities in the natural environment.

iStock.com/NoSystem images

The Making Connections feature offers an example of the process that is followed during a home visit with the Ramirez family. A family interview was used to gain feedback from members of Maria's family about their experiences with early intervention services and the information and support they were afforded.

MAKING CONNECTIONS

HOME VISIT WITH MARIA'S FAMILY

Based on the information presented in the vignette about Maria, the following is an example of the format for a home visit with the Ramirez family.

Arrival and greeting. The service coordinator (who is an early childhood special educator) is greeted by Maria's mother, Catherine, and Maria's grandparents. They exchange greetings and general information (e.g., important events that have occurred, what has been happening since the last home visit).

Information exchange and review. The service coordinator and Maria's family review and discuss the prior visit, the strategies or interventions that have been used, and the progress that has been made toward achieving the desired outcomes. Maria's mother explains that she is pleased with the strategies being used and comments on the progress Maria has made in several areas. The service coordinator observes Maria to review and reassess the appropriateness and success of the interventions and strategies considering her progress.

Development of new goals/outcomes and modification of strategies. Based on the review of the prior goals/outcomes and family priorities, strategies or techniques can be modified. This phase may include an examination of family routines to determine how and when strategies will be used.

Coaching. Through coaching, the professional(s) work with the child's family to explain why certain strategies are selected and how to integrate them into the daily routines that will help them make progress toward achieving their goals. Demonstrating, modeling, and practicing the new strategies can be helpful, with encouragement and specific feedback provided to the family. Time should be allowed for extensive discussions and questions by both the professional(s) and the parent or other family members. During this phase of the meeting, the home visitor should remain sensitive to the individual needs of the family and the circumstances in the home.

Closure. At the end of the home visit, the service coordinator summarizes the session to ensure mutual understanding of what has been accomplished and decisions that have been made. Mrs. Ramirez asks several questions to make sure that she understands all that has been planned. The service provider provides a record of the visit using pictures and instructions for the strategies for follow-up and seeks input from Mrs. Ramirez regarding how well the session went and the progress being made by Maria. They agree that the next home visit will take place the following week at the same time.

Meetings and Conferences

Early childhood special education programs and schools offer a range of important activities for coordinated preparation such as individual or group meetings. In each of these activities, of course, communication is vital. A recurrent way of communicating with families is through individual meetings. These meetings can occur in a variety of settings, use an assortment of formats, and occur for various reasons. When possible, meetings should be conducted in settings where families feel comfortable and are treated as appreciated members of the team.

Successful meetings with families necessitate advanced arrangements. Families should be contacted prior to the meeting to discuss the purpose, what is to be accomplished, and the procedure that will be followed during the meeting. The timespan of meetings should be established in advance. Feedback should be solicited from families concerning the particular topics they wish to examine. Further, families should be confident of the privacy of the information communicated during meetings.

At the beginning, the purpose of the meeting should be reexamined, the amount of time allocated should be reaffirmed, and again, discretion should be emphasized. During the meeting, professionals should share any knowledge they have about the problems or issues and ask for any information or feedback from family members. The considerations should remain dedicated to the designated issues or subjects, and information should be amalgamated throughout the meeting. Regardless of the issue or topic, families' input should be sought and used to ascertain main concerns and to construct a plan to address these priorities. Any meeting should close with a summary and agreement regarding the next steps. When possible, meetings or conversations should conclude on an optimistic and uplifting note.

An example of one of the key methods in which families can be active participants in the program planning process is through the participating in the development of the IFSP or IEP, which is centered on their concerns and priorities for their child [DEC Recommended Practices F3, F4]. The intent of the IFSP or IEP is to offer more accountability and to increase the level of family participation. Recall from preceding chapters that IFSPs are written for children from birth to three years old and IEPs for children aged three and older. More thorough information about these personalized plans can be found in Chapter 4.

As explained previously, a specific obligation of Part C of the Individuals with Disabilities Education Improvement Act of 2004 (IDEA) is to improve the capability of families to aid in meeting each child's delays and disabilities. Much of the literature regarding the IFSP consists of recommended practices intended to guide the development of the IFSP and the distribution of services.

Like the IFSP, the IEP process affords an opportunity for families and professionals to share information and concerns about the child. Both the family and professionals can profit from positive partnerships. This process can also support the family in better understanding the program in which the child is enrolled, which in turn may enhance the self-assurance of the parents in the method in which they view the program and staff. Another benefit of the IEP is that it is meeting the anticipated goal of providing information about the child's progress. Effective use of IFSPs and IEPs can be a remarkable help to the early childhood special educators in supplying appropriate services and educational programs to young children with disabilities and their families.

Regardless of the type of meeting that takes place between families and professionals, strategies are necessary to facilitate coordinated planning and communication during meetings. Early childhood special educators should choose times wisely for meetings and attempt to plan times that are jointly agreeable. Some programs provide child care and support with transportation. Being adaptable in planning to meet families' needs establishes to families that the professionals are dedicated to involving them. Table 3.4 provides a checklist to follow when planning meetings with families.

TABLE 3.4 ■ Considerations When Planning Meetings With Families

Planning and Notifying Family
Notify parents (and other family members, when appropriate) of the reason for the meeting in an understandable and nonthreatening manner.
Follow up written notification with an e-mail or call to be certain that family members know the reason for the meeting, answer questions, and find out whether assistance with child care or transportation is needed.
Consider the family's preferences when planning the time and location of the meeting.
Discuss with family members whether they would like to have professionals from specific disciplines or other individuals participate in the meeting.
Tell the family what they might do to prepare for the meeting in advance.
If the family is linguistically diverse, make arrangements for native-speaking individuals or interpreters, if needed.
Developing the Agenda
Make sure that the agenda includes topics the family has indicated as important.
Create an agenda that is flexible enough to accommodate last-minute additions.
Ensure that the agenda allows adequate time for discussion with family members.
Determine whether family members are comfortable with a written agenda or would prefer that a more informal approach be used.
Preparing the Environment
Determine whether the family prefers to hold the meeting in a setting other than the program or school, such as the family's home, a coffee shop, or the community library.
Plan to meet in a private, comfortable, well-lighted room that has limited distractions.
Gather all necessary materials and supplies (e.g., paper, pens, written materials, beverages, tissues) available for all participants.
Make sure that the furniture is arranged in a manner that reflects equality (e.g., avoid having the teacher or other professionals sitting behind a desk or at the head of the table).
Provide information to the participants so that they are able to locate and access the building, parking lot, and meeting room.

Source: Adapted from A. Turnbull, H. Turnbull, E. Erwin, L. Soodak, and K. Shogren, *Families, Professionals, and Exceptionality: Positive Outcomes Through Partnerships and Trust* (7th ed.). (Pearson Education, 2015), p. 210.

Proper preparation and trustworthiness will guarantee that ongoing communication and information exchange is personalized for each family, which can be a vital factor in providing family-centered services. Trust, consistency, and dependability increase the probability of an effective relationship developing. If professionals agree to assume specific responsibilities or gather information for the family, they must always follow through. Accountability demonstrates to the family that the family can depend on them, which helps to build a trusting relationship. This can be accomplished most effectively when professionals are approachable, respectful, and empathetic. These recommendations for working with families are intended to facilitate the development of a beneficial and meaningful relationship among families and professionals (Gargiulo & Bouck, 2021). By adopting these strategies, professionals can establish positive and effective relationships with families and support the success of their children with delays and disabilities.

SUMMARY

A family-centered approach explicitly acknowledges the families of young children as a central focus of early childhood special education services and the primary decision makers in the service delivery process. A specific requirement of IDEA is to enhance the capacity of families to meet the needs of their children with delays and disabilities. Professionals are encouraged to make changes in policy and practices to move families to the forefront of the service delivery system.

As has been shown throughout this chapter, a family-centered viewpoint is the foundation of recommended practice in early childhood special education. Rather than requiring families to adjust to ECSE programs' policies and needs, recommended practice suggests that programs must adjust services according to families' concerns, priorities, and resources. Families are seen as full partners in early intervention and early childhood special education programs.

A family-centered approach is founded on a family systems model. That is, young children with delays and disabilities are regarded as part of their family system, which in turn is viewed as part of a larger network of informal and formal systems. What happens to one member of the family often impacts all members, and each family member has their own needs and abilities. Thus, professionals must formulate an approach for each family served to engage the family members and support their knowledge, skills, and priorities that is customized, adaptable, and personalized to the family's preferences. To accomplish this, they require a thorough understanding of how families work and the influence that the birth of a child with a delay or disability, or the diagnosis of a child's disability, may have on how families adjust and function. Further, professionals must know how to collaborate with families and other professionals to successfully meet the needs of young children with delays and disabilities.

The idea of strong relationships between families and professionals who work with young children with delays and disabilities has abundant benefits. However, many changes have occurred over the years in families, laws, and relations between professionals and families. These variations contribute to a complicated challenge for personnel in offering appropriate learning experiences and services for young children and their families. Therefore, it has become increasingly vital for early childhood special educators to remember the concerns, priorities, and resources of families and to view each family as an individualized system with many interacting forces.

The relationship between parents and professionals can have a strong impact on a child's learning.
iStock.com/SDI Productions

The following are some basic understandings in the establishment of effective family-professional partnerships:

- The relationship early childhood special educators develop with a family has a powerful effect on the child's learning.
- All families deserve to be valued, respected, understood, and appreciated.

- An open, trusting relationship between family members and professionals is essential to successful early childhood special education services. This relationship develops over time.
- Early childhood special educators should start where the families are, listening to their points of view, reflecting on what they communicate, and clarifying their thoughts and feelings.
- Families can provide valuable information and often have answers or solutions that the early childhood special educator and other team members did not consider—that is the beauty of partnerships.

KEY TERMS

Adaptability
Coaching
Cohesion
Collaboration
Communication
Culture
Cultural mediator
Cultural responsiveness
Ecological perspective
Eco-map
Empowerment
Family
Family and professional collaboration
Family capacity-building practices
Family-centered practices
Family characteristics
Family function
Family interactions
Family life cycle
Family systems theory
Home visits
Hybrid family
Nonverbal communication
Nuclear family
Service coordination
Stereotyping
Strengths-based approach
Verbal communication

CHECK YOUR UNDERSTANDING

1. How have relationships among families and professionals in early childhood special education changed over the years? What circumstances have influenced this process?
2. Describe the possible reactions of a family to a child with a delay or disability.
3. What is the rationale for using a family systems theory model?
4. Identify the four key elements of a family systems theory model. Explain the characteristics of each of these elements.
5. What kinds of influences have contributed to an emergence of a family-centered approach in programs for young children with delays and disabilities?
6. Discuss reasons why an effective family-professional relationship is critical to successful programs for young children with delays and disabilities.
7. Discuss key components of family-professional collaboration and strategies to ensure successful implementation of each component: (a) culturally responsiveness practices, (b) effective communication, (d) home visits, (e) meetings and conferences, and (f) information exchange and support.

REFLECTION AND APPLICATION

1. Identify a family interaction that you have experienced and discuss how the family systems theory could be applied and used to understand the family system and enhance your interactions with the family.

2. Observe in an early childhood special education setting (early intervention, preschool, or early primary). What evidence is there that families are a key part of the program's mission? How do they work in partnership with families? What types of services are being provided to the families?
3. What specific roles do the families play on the team in meeting the needs of Maria, T. J., and Cheryl? How can the early childhood special educator provide support to families in the roles they assume?
4. In the development and implementation of an IFSP or an IEP, explain how the early childhood special educator can provide support to the families.
5. Observe a home visit or interview a professional who conducts home visits. Describe the benefits of home visiting for families and professionals.
6. Observe a meeting between parents and professionals. Describe the beneficial aspects of the meeting, as well as recommendations to foster improved parent-professional collaboration.

SolStock/E+/via Getty Images

4 DELIVERING SERVICES TO YOUNG CHILDREN WITH DELAYS AND DISABILITIES

LEARNING OBJECTIVES

After reading this chapter, you will be able to

4.1 Explain five benefits of providing services to young children with delays and disabilities in inclusive settings.

4.2 Identify the advantages and disadvantages of center- or school-based and home-based service delivery models for young children with delays and disabilities.

4.3 Explain the differences between multi-, inter-, and transdisciplinary team models and explain the advantages of a transdisciplinary model.

4.4 Describe the various collaborative teaching models.

4.5 List and describe the required components of an individualized family service plan (IFSP) and an individualized education program (IEP).

4.6 Outline the steps needed to ensure effective transitions for young children and their families.

EI/ECSE Professional Standards

In addition to other EI/ECSE Standards discussed in previous chapters and throughout the text, the content of this chapter aligns with the following standard regarding the important role teaming and collaboration play in all aspects of EI/ECSE:

Standard 3. Collaboration and Teaming

Candidates apply models, skills, and processes of teaming when collaborating and communicating with families and professionals, using culturally and linguistically responsive and affirming practices. In partnership with families and other professionals, candidates develop and implement individualized plans and successful transitions that occur across the age span. Candidates use a variety of collaborative strategies while working with and supporting other adults.

DEC Recommended Practices

The content of this chapter aligns with the following Division for Early Childhood (DEC) Recommended Practices:

Environment

- E1. Practitioners provide services and supports in natural and inclusive environments during daily routines and activities to promote the child's access to and participation in learning experiences.
- E3. Practitioners work with family and other adults to modify and adapt the physical, social, and temporal environments to promote each child's access to and participation in learning experiences.

Family

- F3. Practitioners are responsive to the family's concerns, priorities, and changing life circumstances.
- F4. Practitioners and the family work together to create outcomes or goals, develop individualized plans, and implement practices that address the family's priorities and concerns and the child's strengths and needs.
- F5. Practitioners support family functioning, promote family confidence and competence, and strengthen family–child relationships by acting in ways that recognize and build on family strengths and capacities.
- F9. Practitioners help families know and understand their rights.

Teaming and Collaboration

- TC1. Practitioners representing multiple disciplines and families work together as a team to plan and implement supports and services to meet the unique needs of each child and family.

- TC2. Practitioners and families work together as a team to systematically and regularly exchange expertise, knowledge, and information to build team capacity and jointly solve problems, plan, and implement interventions.
- TC3. Practitioners use communication and group facilitation strategies to enhance team functioning and interpersonal relationships with and among team members.
- TC4. Team members assist each other to discover and access community-based services and other informal and formal resources to meet family-identified child or family needs.
- TC5. Practitioners and families may collaborate with each other to identify one practitioner from the team who serves as the primary liaison between the family and other team members based on child and family priorities and needs.

Transition

- TR1. Practitioners in sending and receiving programs exchange information before, during, and after transition about practices most likely to support the child's successful adjustment and positive outcomes.
- TR2. Practitioners use a variety of planned strategies with the child and family before, during, and after transition to support successful adjustment and positive outcomes for both the child and family.

Authors' Note: As you read this chapter, you will find EI/ECSE Standard 3 and other standards along with the aforementioned DEC Recommended Practices discussed throughout. See Appendix A for a complete list of the EI/ECSE Standards and Appendix B for a complete list of the DEC Recommended Practices.

The overarching goal of early intervention and early childhood special education efforts is to provide young children with delays and disabilities and their families with the best possible beginning. As a field, EI/ECSE has been driven by the recognition of the importance of providing services to young children with delays and disabilities "as early and comprehensively as possible in the least restrictive setting" (Carta et al., 1991, p. 4). The major professional organization for the field of EI/ECSE, the Division for Early Childhood (DEC) of the Council for Exceptional Children (CEC), developed the DEC Priority Issues Agenda that called for EI/ECSE to achieve high-quality inclusion for all young children with delays and disabilities (DEC, 2020).

A focus of this chapter is how to provide appropriate services in the natural environment. The literature strongly suggests that services provided in inclusive settings, rather than segregated settings, are in keeping with contemporary recommended practices (Bruder, 2010a; Cook et al., 2020; Deiner, 2013; DEC, 2014; Noonan & McCormick, 2014; Winton, 2016). An ongoing challenge to early childhood special education professionals, as Carta and colleagues (1991) noted, is to develop delivery systems that provide high-quality services in inclusive environments. This leads to the second focus area, which also provides a framework for this chapter: how to best design services for young children with delays and disabilities in a manner that is responsive to the individual strengths and abilities of each child and their family's goals and priorities.

As described in EI/ECSE Standard 3: Collaboration and Teaming, this chapter will examine the variety of placement options or models available for providing services, as well as the importance of teaming and collaboration. Teamwork, with families as central members of the team process, is necessary if programs are to effectively function and meet the needs of young children with delays and disabilities and their families (Kilgo, 2006, 2022; Kilgo et al., 2019). Road maps for delivering services—that is, individualized family service plans (IFSPs), individualized education programs (IEPs), and Section 504 accommodation plans—will be examined. Finally, the importance of carefully planned transitions will be discussed.

Services for young children with delays and disabilities are provided in inclusive learning environments.

E.D. Torial / Alamy Stock Photo

INCLUSIVE LEARNING ENVIRONMENTS

With the advent of the Individuals with Disabilities Education Act (IDEA) and its reauthorizations, along with support from the Americans with Disabilities Act (PL 101–336), options for delivering services to infants, toddlers, preschoolers, and early primary students with delays and disabilities have dramatically changed. Services for infants and toddlers are required to be provided in natural environments. This provision is generally interpreted to mean those settings that are typical or natural for the young child's peers without delays and disabilities and includes a wide variety of community placements (Guralnick, 2023). Services for preschoolers and students in the early primary grades with delays and disabilities are under the jurisdiction of the public schools, who are mandated to serve these children according to the provisions of IDEA—including providing services in the least restrictive environment (LRE; Winton, 2016; see also Chapter 2). Although there is support for providing services in the natural environment, they must be appropriate to the needs of the child and in concert with the goals, values, and priorities of the child's family.

Most communities have a variety of options to provide services for young children with delays and disabilities in inclusive settings. The idea of providing services to young children with delays and disabilities in natural settings is not new. Early childhood special educators have been challenged by this issue for many years. Many professionals and families have long advocated for the provision of services in natural environments that include both children with and without disabilities. Unfortunately, one of the problems with the implementation of this principle has been the absence, in some communities, of appropriate placements or settings for infants, toddlers, and preschoolers with delays and disabilities (Downing, 2008; Howard et al., 2014; Winton, 2016). To fully appreciate contemporary practice, it is important to review its conceptual evolution and understand key terminology.

The 1970s saw the establishment of a strong foundation for merging early childhood programs that integrated young children with and without disabilities (Guralnick, 1994). The decade of the 1980s, according to Guralnick (1990), witnessed the repeated demonstration that inclusive early childhood programs could effectively be implemented. The challenge facing professionals in the 1990s was to construct program models that would allow for services to be delivered in nonspecialized or natural settings (Carta et al., 1991). Fortunately, today, the most common programs for infants, toddlers, preschoolers, and early primary students with delays and disabilities are those that are primarily designed for children without disabilities. Across the United States, there is a strong emphasis on the provision of services for children with delays and disabilities as early as possible in the most natural environment (Bruder, 2010a; Guralnick, 2023; Hardman et al., 2017; McLean et al., 2016; Noonan & McCormick, 2014; Winton, 2016).

Bricker (1978), more than forty years ago, and Guralnick (2023) more recently, identified social–ethical, legal–legislative, and psychological–educational arguments supporting the educational inclusion of young children with delays and disabilities. These arguments have been reinforced by an expanding research knowledge base, judicial decisions, and legislative enactments (U.S. Department of Health and Human Services & U.S. Department of Education, 2015). Today, many professionals and families alike appreciate the benefits and opportunities that have accrued to young children with and without disabilities and their families. They are the result of many years of arduous effort. Still, despite these gains, there are some professionals (and families, too) who believe that not enough has been done in advocating for the inclusion of all children with delays and disabilities in all aspects of society—but especially in educational programs.

Inclusion

The term *inclusion* is defined as the social and instructional integration of children with delays and disabilities in educational programs whose primary purpose is to serve individuals without disabilities. At one time, *mainstreaming* was the common or popular word for describing the practice of educating children with disabilities, including preschoolers and early primary students, in natural learning environments. The concept of inclusion has been woven into the fabric of American education for more than forty years. Despite significant barriers and obstacles to implementing inclusive services, many successful programs have been established across the United States partly due to the Americans with Disabilities Act and Section 504 of the Rehabilitation Act of 1973. These programs include Head Start, university child development centers, cooperative preschools, and family child care settings, among other options, collectively suggesting that an inclusive education may occur across multiple types of early childhood programs (Love & Horn, 2021).

The least restrictive environment is individually determined for each child.

iStock/Wavebreakmedia

Fortunately, because of litigation and legislation, families no longer have to prove that their child with a delay or disability should be included; rather, early childhood programs and schools must justify their position to exclude and justify that they have made a good faith effort at inclusion or present strong evidence that an inclusionary setting is unsatisfactory (Yell, 2019). IDEA 2004 currently supports this thinking.

The key to understanding inclusion is that it must provide children with an appropriate education based on the individual needs of each child. The framers of IDEA never envisioned that inclusion would be interpreted to mean that *all* young children with delays and disabilities must be placed in inclusive classrooms; to do so would mean abandoning the idea of determining what is the most appropriate placement for a particular child. IDEA clearly stipulates that, to the maximum extent appropriate, children with disabilities are to be educated with their peers without disabilities. For some young children, an inclusive setting, even with supplementary aids and services, might be an inappropriate placement due to the child's unique characteristics. A least restrictive environment does *not* automatically mean placement with peers without disabilities. Early childhood special educators must make the distinction between the concepts of appropriateness and restrictiveness (Gargiulo & Bouck, 2021).

Yet it is important to remember that just because a young child with a delay or disability receives services in a natural setting, such as a child care center or a Head Start classroom, it does not mean that they will be provided with an appropriate education. Families and professionals alike must carefully evaluate the setting into which a child is placed. Simply placing a young child with a delay or disability in an early childhood program serving children without disabilities does not guarantee that the specific and unique needs of the child with a delay or disability will be fulfilled. It requires extensive collaboration among practitioners representing multiple disciplines, families, agencies, and service providers (Bricker et al., 2022; Cook et al., 2020; Dillon et al., 2021).

Least Restrictive Environment

The terms *inclusion* and *least restrictive environment (LRE)*, though closely linked, should not be used interchangeably. Their meanings are educationally distinct. *Inclusion* refers to the integration of children with delays and disabilities into natural settings or general education classrooms. *LRE*, on the other hand, is a legal term interpreted to mean that young children with delays and disabilities are to be educated in settings as close as possible to a general education environment. Inclusion is but one means of fulfilling the LRE requirement. IDEA does not require inclusion in every instance. The goal of the LRE principle is to prevent the unwarranted segregation of students with disabilities from their peers without disabilities. An LRE is not a particular place but rather a relative concept. It is perhaps best thought of as the most enabling environment for the individual (Mercer et al., 2011).

The determination of the LRE is individually defined for each child. It is based on the student's educational needs—not their disability. The LRE mandate applies equally to preschoolers and the school-age population. The provision for educating young children with delays and disabilities as much as possible with children without disabilities also requires that service delivery options be available. A continuum of educational placements has been devised to meet the LRE requirements. Figure 4.1 portrays an example of one possible option.

FIGURE 4.1 ■ A Continuum of Service Delivery Options

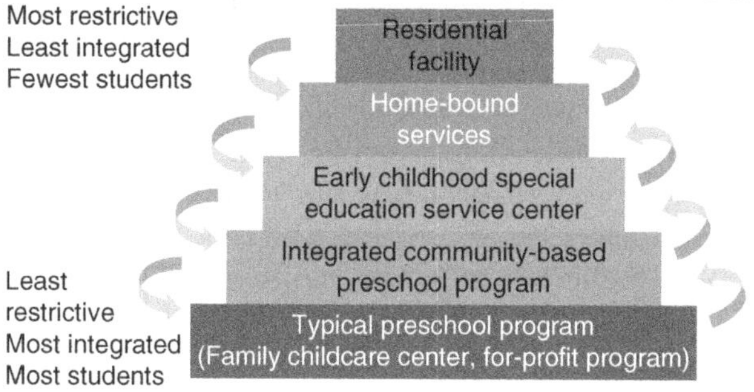

The continuum illustrated in Figure 4.1 reflects varying degrees of restrictiveness, which refers to the amount of opportunity to associate with learners without disabilities. Being placed only with children with delays and disabilities is considered most restrictive, while placement with individuals who are not disabled is viewed as least restrictive. Ascending the continuum, the environments provide fewer and fewer possibilities for interaction with peers without disabilities—hence, greater restrictiveness. Although involvement with students without disabilities is highly desirable, it must be balanced by the requirement of providing an education appropriate to the unique needs of the child (Gargiulo & Metcalf, 2023). Each situation must be individually assessed and decided on a case-by-case basis. Furthermore, educational placements are meant to be fluid. As the needs of the child change, so can the setting in which they receive services (Gargiulo & Bouck, 2021).

The idea of a continuum of service delivery options allows for, in limited situations, the removal of a child from inclusive environments if it is in the best educational interest of the student. Segregation, though not desirable, might be necessary in some situations to provide an appropriate education (Yell, 2019).

As an example, Bricker (1995) explains that placement in more restrictive setting may be the placement of choice if it increases the child's chances for future placement in a general education program. Judicially speaking, the courts have allowed, under certain circumstances, more restrictive placements for students with disabilities (Yell, 2019). Yet it is recognized in the field of early childhood special education that maximum inclusion with peers without disabilities is highly desirable and should be the goal.

When correctly instituted, inclusion is characterized by its virtual invisibility. Children with delays and disabilities, regardless of the type or severity of their disability, are fully included in the learning environments they would normally attend if they did not have a disability. "They are seen," Gargiulo and Bouck (2021) write, "as full-fledged members of, not merely visitors to, the general education classroom" (p. 68). See Table 4.1 for representative key features of some inclusion models. Early childhood special educators can provide individualized services in educational settings while working collaboratively with their general education colleagues. This partnership optimizes social and learning opportunities and outcomes for children both with and without disabilities, and it would occur within the LRE.

TABLE 4.1 ■ Representative Elements of Inclusion Models for Young Children With Disabilities

"Home School" Attendance. Defined as the local program or school the child would attend if they did not have a delay or disability.

Natural Proportion at the Site. The percentage of children with delays and disabilities enrolled in a particular school is in proportion to the percentage of students with disabilities in the entire school district; in general education classes, this would mean approximately two to three students with disabilities.

Zero Rejection. All students are accepted at their local program or school; children are not screened out or grouped separately because of their type of delay or disability.

Age-/Grade-Appropriate Placement. Inclusion calls for serving children with delays and disabilities in general education settings according to their chronological age rather than according to the child's academic ability.

Source: W. Sailor, M. Gerry, and W. Wilson, "Policy Implications for Emergent Full Inclusion Models for the Education of Students with Disabilities," in W. Wang, H. Wolberg, and M. Reynolds (Eds.), *Handbook of Special Education*, Vol. 4 (New York, NY: Pergamon Press, 1991). pp. 175–193; S. Stainback and W. Stainback, "Schools as Inclusive Communities," in W. Stainback and S. Stainback (Eds.), *Controversial Issues Confronting Special Education: Divergent Perspectives* (Boston, MA: Allyn & Bacon, 1992), pp. 29–43.

The concept of LRE, however, is not an all-or-nothing proposition. Only if a full continuum of settings is available can one reasonably ensure that an appropriate placement will be made.

Most professionals believe that *some* children with delays and disabilities may require more intensive services if they are to achieve educational progress (Salend, 2016; Yell, 2019; Yell, Crockett et al., 2017; Yell, Katsiyannis et al., 2017; Zigmond, 2007). Of course, simply placing children in a special education setting does not automatically mean that they will receive the specialized instruction needed. Likewise, placement in a general education classroom does not guarantee that students will receive an appropriate education (Heward et al., 2022). Regardless of where a child receives services, the learning experience must be as meaningful and effective as possible. More important than *where* the instruction is provided is *how* the instruction is delivered and *what* is being taught. According to Zigmond (2003), "place is not what makes special education 'special' or effective. Effective teaching strategies and an individualized approach are the more critical ingredients in special education and neither of these is associated solely with one particular environment" (p. 198).

Hallahan et al. (2009) also emphasize that IDEA, as presently interpreted, gives parents the right to choose which environment they, not the professionals, believe is most appropriate and least restrictive for delivering services to their child. The notion of making decisions based on the individual needs of the child is fundamental to the foundation of special education.

Services for young children with delays and disabilities should be provided in inclusive settings.

Tony Anderson/DigitalVision/via Getty Images

DEC has a long history of advocating for inclusion. Inclusion has implications for serving young children with delays and disabilities and is advocated for very young children with disabilities. For example, in a position paper crafted by Sexton et al. (1993), the Association for Childhood Education International (ACEI) affirmed its support for inclusion of infants and toddlers with disabilities. ACEI believes that the very youngest of children with delays and disabilities should be served in settings designed for their same-age peers without disabilities. A single inclusive system of care, intervention, and education is considered best practice for all children and their families. It is also seen as a quality indicator of early intervention and early childhood special education (Bruder, 2010a; Winton, 2016).

The DEC Recommended Practices statement E1 emphasizes that to promote children's access to and participation in learning, their experiences, services, and supports should be provided by practitioners in natural and inclusive environments (DEC, 2014). Table 4.2 illustrates DEC's position on inclusion (DEC/NAEYC, 2009).

TABLE 4.2 ■ The Division for Early Childhood Position Statement on Inclusion

A Joint Position Statement of the Division for Early Childhood (DEC) and the National Association for the Education of Young Children (NAEYC)

April 2009

Today an ever-increasing number of infants and young children with and without disabilities play, develop, and learn together in a variety of places—homes, early childhood programs, neighborhoods, and other community-based settings. The notion that young children with disabilities and their families are full members of the community reflects societal values about promoting opportunities for development and learning, and a sense of belonging for every child. It also reflects a reaction against previous educational practices of separating and isolating children with disabilities. Over time, in combination with certain regulations and protections under the law, these values and societal views regarding children birth to 8 with disabilities and their families have come to be known as early childhood inclusion. The most far-reaching effect of federal legislation on inclusion enacted over the past three decades has been to fundamentally change the way in which early childhood services ideally can be organized and delivered. However, because inclusion takes many different forms and implementation is influenced by a wide variety of factors, questions persist about the precise meaning of inclusion and its implications for policy, practice, and potential outcomes for children and families.

The lack of a shared national definition has contributed to misunderstandings about inclusion. DEC and NAEYC recognize that having a common understanding of what inclusion means is fundamentally important for determining what types of practices and supports are necessary to achieve high quality inclusion. This DEC/NAEYC joint position statement offers a definition of early childhood inclusion. The definition was designed not as a litmus test for determining whether a program can be considered inclusive, but rather, as a blueprint for identifying the key components of high-quality inclusive programs.

Definition of Early Childhood Inclusion

Early childhood inclusion embodies the values, policies, and practices that support the right of every infant and young child and their family, regardless of ability, to participate in a broad range of activities and contexts as full members of families, communities, and society. The desired results of inclusive experiences for children with and without disabilities and their families include a sense of belonging and membership, positive social relationships and friendships, and development and learning to reach their full potential. The defining features of inclusion that can be used to identify high quality early childhood programs and services are access, participation, and supports.

Note: Full statement available at www.decdocs.org/position-statement-inclusion

Source: DEC/NAEYC. (2009). *Early childhood inclusion: A joint position statement of the Division for Early Childhood (DEC) and the National Association for the Education of Young Children (NAEYC).* Chapel Hill: The University of North Carolina, FPG Child Development Institute.

Services for infants and toddlers with delays and disabilities are often provided in their homes or child care settings.

MoMo Productions/Stone/via Getty Images

SERVICE DELIVERY MODELS

There are a variety of service delivery options for providing services to young children with delays and disabilities and their families. These arrangements are usually referred to as service delivery approaches—where intervention or education is provided. The location of service delivery is frequently dependent on the age of the child (infant vs. preschooler), geographical considerations (rural vs. urban), child characteristics (severity and type of disability), and community resources as well as child/family goals and objectives (Graves et al., 1996; McWilliam, 2016). Additionally, the philosophy and beliefs of the agency, program, or school regarding the inclusion of children with delays and disabilities with their peers without disabilities may also influence where intervention/education is rendered.

As noted earlier in this chapter, contemporary practices strongly support the notion that intervention and other services for infants and toddlers with delays and disabilities should occur in natural environments—that is, those locations viewed as typical for children of similar chronological age without disabilities. These locations might include child care settings, the child's home, or a neighborhood play group. Places viewed as restrictive or "unnatural" include, for example, hospitals, clinics, or therapists' offices. This preference for services in natural environment parallels the concept of LRE or inclusive settings for infants and toddlers, preschoolers, and school-age students with disabilities. The location where intervention is provided should not be viewed as more important than the services, supports, and activities available to the child and their family. Location, though important, should not take precedence over meeting the needs of the infant or toddler (Howard et al., 2014).

Traditionally, programs for young children with delays and disabilities are identified as home-based, center-based, or school-based services. Most professionals agree with this conventional classification service delivery scheme. Yet it should be remembered that there is no single, accepted standard regarding where young children with delays and disabilities should be served. Furthermore, the decision as to where services are provided primarily resides with the child's family. They should be the primary decision makers. Noonan and McCormick (2014) suggest that the location of services should also reflect the "family's cultural values, the intensity of services that the child needs, and geographical accessibility for the family" (p. 11).

Even though there is no one best model, recommended practice guidelines for the delivery of early intervention and special education services have been formulated. Regardless of where services are provided, McDonnell and Hardman (1988) suggest that programs include the following dimensions:

- *Inclusive placements*—systematic contact with peers without disabilities
- *Comprehensive*—full range of services available
- *Normalized*—age-appropriate skills and intervention strategies; instruction across a variety of settings
- *Adaptable*—flexible procedures meeting individual needs of the child
- *Peer and family referenced*—parents perceived as full partners; curriculum geared toward child, family, peers, and community (that is, an ecological approach)
- *Outcome-based*—developing skills with present and future usefulness

These suggestions hold true today. In fact, current recommendations based on empirical evidence and recommend practice (DEC, 2014; Howard et al., 2014; Winton, 2016) strongly suggest that services for young children with delays and disabilities should be provided in inclusive settings along with appropriate and individualized supports [DEC Recommended Practices E3]. A child who receives services in an inclusive environment is afforded opportunities to develop more advanced social, linguistic, and cognitive skills that will aid in achieving success in integrated learning communities.

Important to keep in mind is that the practices identified by McDonnell and Hardman (1988), DEC Recommend Practices (2014), and others are simply recommended indicators of quality. As such, they should be used as guidelines for early childhood special education programs. The needs of individual children with delays and disabilities and their families dictate where, how, and what services are provided.

Home-Based Services

For some young children, especially infants and toddlers, the most appropriate location for providing services is often in their homes. Here, interventions can individually be provided by the primary caregiver in the child's most natural environment. The primary caregiver, typically a parent, works cooperatively with various professionals on implementing specific intervention strategies. These strategies should reflect recommended practices that are evidence-based (Boyd et al., 2016; Cook et al., 2020). Service providers make regular and frequent visits to the home to work directly with the child, to assist and support the parent and other family members, and to monitor the child's progress. Forming meaningful partnerships with parents and families is crucial to the success of home-based services (McWilliam, 2016). Although service providers are primarily concerned with advancing the developmental status of the child, they are also concerned with enhancing the well-being and competency of the family (Dunst & Espe-Sherwindt, 2016).

The DEC (2014) of the Council for Exceptional Children has developed a set of recommended practice guidelines for early intervention and early childhood special education programs. The recommendations that are appropriate for home-based services include the following four examples:

1. Interventions should be embedded in naturally occurring daily activities such as snack and mealtime, bathing, play activities, or bedtime.
2. Interventions address family members' identified priorities and preferences.
3. Interventions include all family members who desire to participate.
4. Professionals and family members work collaboratively to achieve family-identified outcomes.

Delivering services in the child's home has multiple advantages. The primary advantage is that services are provided in a setting that is familiar to the child and by the child's first and primary teacher—their parent. Parents also can intervene on an ongoing basis as behaviors naturally occur. Furthermore, skills learned in a child's natural environment are easier to maintain. Finally, disruption to the child's and family's routines is frequently minimized. With home-based services, costs may be less, transportation is not a concern, and services are responsive to family needs. The potential for family involvement with the interventions is also greater, and ongoing support can be provided to the family (Dunst & Espe-Sherwindt, 2016) [DEC Recommended Practices F5]. This model is especially appropriate for children living in rural or sparsely populated communities, and as noted earlier, home-based services are appropriate for infants and toddlers. Eighty-nine percent of infants and toddlers receiving early intervention are provided these services in their home (U.S. Department of Education, 2022).

In some cases, there are certain disadvantages to home-based services. A commonly noted drawback is the commitment required by, and the responsibilities placed upon, the family. Not all parents have the time or want to assume this role. Providing intervention in a child's home also requires that professionals demonstrate culturally and linguistically responsive and affirming practices according to the values, beliefs, and customs of each family (Hanson, 2011; Hanson & Espinosa, 2016; Hanson & Lynch, 2013). Furthermore, in some situations, the implementation of this model may be challenged due to family circumstances such as a single-parent household, poverty, and other risk factors. Opportunities for social interaction with other children are sometimes absent in home-based services. Finally, a considerable amount of professionals' time is usually spent traveling from one home to another.

Center- or School-Based Programs

As the name implies, center- or school-based programs are located away from the child's home. Settings may be churches or synagogues, child care centers, preschools, public schools, Head Start centers, or other accessible locations. Center- or school-based programs are common settings for preschoolers with delays and disabilities. Children are typically transported to the site where they receive services from professionals representing a variety of disciplines such as physical and occupational therapists or speech–language pathologists. The primary direct service provider for preschoolers with delays and disabilities, however, is usually the child's early childhood special education teacher. Center- or school-based programs typically stress the acquisition of developmental, social, cognitive, and self-care skills necessary for success in elementary school (Allen & Cowdery, 2022; Hooper & Umansky, 2014).

Children usually attend a program for several hours each day. Some young children with delays and disabilities participate in daily programs, while others attend only two or three times a week. Recommended practice guidelines published by DEC (2014) for center- or school-based learning environments include the following representative examples:

- Classrooms are safe and clean environments, barrier free, and physically accessible for all children.
- Toys, learning materials, and activities are appropriate to the age and developmental needs of the children.
- Environments stimulate children's interactions and choice making while promoting high levels of engagement with peers and adults.
- Curriculum is consistent with developmentally appropriate practices and based on principles of child development.
- Professionals communicate with their colleagues and family members on a regular basis.

Center- or school-based programs provide opportunities for families to be central members of the team. Professionals consider the collaboration with and participation by parents and other family members to be necessary and beneficial. Parental involvement often increases the effectiveness of the interventions. According to Heward et al. (2022), "virtually all effective programs for young children with disabilities recognize the critical need to involve parents" (p. 433).

Center- or school-based service delivery models have several advantages, such as

- The development of social skills plus opportunities for social interaction between children with and without disabilities
- Access to comprehensive services from specialists representing many different disciplines
- Availability of specialized equipment and materials
- Enhanced efficiency of staff time
- Family involvement and the chance to develop social networks with other families
- Exposure to experiences and the development of skills that will aid in the transition to kindergarten or the next program

Center- or school-based programs are not without limitations and drawbacks. Disadvantages can include the following:

- The cost of transportation to and from the program (considered a related service according to IDEA)
- Extended periods of travel time to and from the program

- The expense of maintaining the facility and its equipment
- In comparison to home-based services, the possibility of limited opportunity for establishing meaningful working partnerships with parents

In some situations, administrators of center- or school-based programs are also confronted with the difficult task of providing services within a normalizing environment as mandated by IDEA. Unfortunately, too few public schools provide preschool programs for children without disabilities; therefore, creative and alternative ways for serving young children with delays and disabilities are being developed. A growing number of early childhood programs are including children with delays and disabilities and are meeting their individualized needs by utilizing itinerant teachers and therapists or consultants for the delivery of specialized services (Sadler, 2003). Recent data provided by the U.S. Department of Education (2022) reveal that almost 65 percent of three-, four-, and five-year-old children with disabilities are being served in a typical early childhood program—a trend that is anticipated to continue and increase.

Where services are delivered does not define the quality or the effectiveness of an intervention program. A recommended approach suggests that a range of options be made available so that parents may choose the service delivery option that best fits their needs and those of their son or daughter. Most early childhood special education professionals believe that what is most important is matching the services to the needs of the child while reflecting the priorities, needs, and values of the family. What is an appropriate program for one family may be inappropriate for another. Meyen (1996) believes that "the optimal model for service delivery depends on family and child characteristics and needs, intensity of services, and geographic characteristics of the service area" (p. 171). Cook and her colleagues (2020) agree with this argument. They, too, believe that no one location is best for all children and their families. They also emphasize that any setting for delivering services must be culturally responsive to the values and child-rearing practices of the family.

PROFESSIONAL TEAMING AND COLLABORATION

The idea of professionals working together in a cooperative manner has been part of the fabric of special education for over forty years. Since the implementation of PL 94–142, attention has been focused on how professionals from a variety of disciplines can work collaboratively in the planning and delivering of services to young children with delays and disabilities and their families. In fact, the concept of collaboration is an integral part of the philosophical foundation of IDEA. It should be apparent that no one discipline, agency, or professional possesses all the resources or clinical skills needed to devise appropriate interventions or construct appropriate educational plans for young children with disabilities, many of whom have complex needs. Furthermore, collaboration can be the vehicle by which services are provided in an integrated rather than fragmented fashion. Effective collaboration requires a high degree of cooperation and mutual respect among service providers (Gargiulo & Metcalf, 2023).

Professionals representing a variety of disciplines are involved in delivering services to children with delays and disabilities. Professionals typically involved in the assessment and delivery of services to young children with delays and disabilities include early childhood special educators, physical therapists (Kennedy & Effgen, 2016), occupational therapists (Wakeford, 2016), and speech–language pathologists (Crais & Woods, 2016), in addition to a host of other professionals [DEC Recommended Practices TC1].

Teams differ not only in their composition but also according to their structure and function. Three types of team organizations are typically utilized in delivering services: multidisciplinary, interdisciplinary, and transdisciplinary teams. These approaches are all interrelated and represent a historical evolution of teamwork (Bruder, 2010a; Kilgo et al., 2017, 2019; Noonan & McCormick, 2014). This evolutionary process can be portrayed as concentric circles, with each model retaining some of the attributes of its predecessor (Gargiulo & Bouck, 2021). Figure 4.2 illustrates these various configurations.

FIGURE 4.2 ■ Multidisciplinary, Interdisciplinary, and Transdisciplinary Team Models

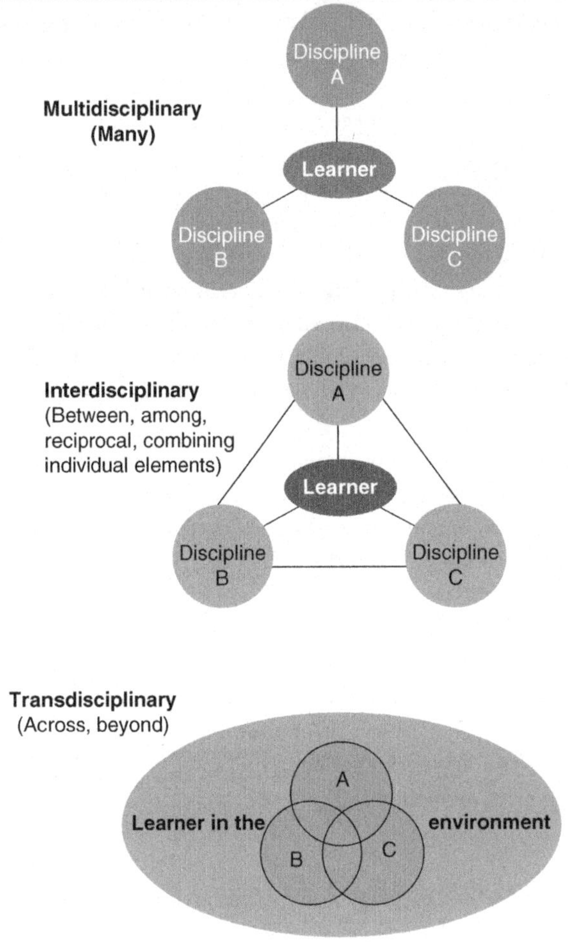

Source: M. Giangreco, J. York, and B. Rainforth, "Providing Related Services to Learners with Severe Handicaps in Educational Settings: Pursuing the Least Restrictive Option," *Pediatric Physical Therapy, 1*(2), p. 57. Copyright © 1989, Wolters Kluwer Health. Reprinted by permission.

Multidisciplinary

The idea of a **multidisciplinary team** can be found in PL 94–142 and its subsequent reauthorizations. This approach, whose origins are grounded on a medical model, utilizes the expertise of professionals from several disciplines, each of whom performs assessments and other tasks (e.g., report writing, goal setting) independent of the others. Each individual contributes autonomously according to their own specialty area with minimal coordination or collaboration across discipline areas (Gargiulo & Metcalf, 2023). A multidisciplinary model is characterized as a patchwork quilt whereby different, and sometimes contrasting, information is integrated but not necessarily with a unified outcome (Friend, 2021). Because information to the parents flows from several sources, parents often encounter difficulty synthesizing all the data and recommendations from the various experts. The multidisciplinary model is not considered to be family-friendly or represent recommended practice.

Interdisciplinary

With an **interdisciplinary team**, members perform their evaluations independently; however, program development and recommendations are the result of information sharing, joint planning, and mutual decision making. Coordination and collaboration exist among the team members, leading to an integrated plan of services. Direct services, however, such as physical therapy, are usually provided in isolation from one another. Families typically meet with the team or its representative; for the infant or toddler with delays and disabilities, this role is fulfilled by the service coordinator.

In addition to the potential for professional turf protection among team members, Noonan and McCormick (2014) call attention to another possible flaw with this model. They observe that information generally flows in one direction—from the various professionals involved in the assessment to the service provider. There is no mechanism in this model for the provider to give feedback as to the appropriateness of the intervention recommendations; for example, are they practical, functional, and meeting the needs of the child and the family?

Transdisciplinary

The **transdisciplinary team** approach to providing services builds upon the strengths of the interdisciplinary model. It is distinguished, however, by two additional and related features: role sharing and a primary therapist. Professionals in the various disciplines conduct their initial evaluations; yet they relinquish their roles (role release) as service providers by teaching their skills to other team members, one of whom will serve as the primary service provider and family liaison based on child and family priorities and needs [DEC Recommended Practices TC5]. For young children with delays and disabilities, this role is usually filled by an early interventionist, an early childhood special educator, or a therapist depending on the needs of the child. This individual relies heavily on the support and consultation provided by their professional peers. Discipline-specific interventions are still available, although they occur less frequently (Gargiulo & Metcalf, 2023).

"The primary purpose of this approach," according to Bruder (1994), "is to pool and integrate the expertise of team members so that more efficient and comprehensive assessment and intervention services may be provided" (p. 61). The aim of the transdisciplinary model is to avoid compartmentalization and fragmentation of services. It attempts to provide a more coordinated and unified or holistic approach to assessment and service delivery; team members function as a unit. Professionals from various backgrounds teach, learn, and work together to accomplish a common set of goals for the child and their family (Bruder, 2010b; Friend, 2021; Kilgo, 2006; Kilgo et al., 2017, 2019). Individuals who implement this approach, however, need to be cautious that they work effectively as a team member, do not overstep the boundaries of their professional competency and expertise, and engage in joint planning and decision making with practitioners from other disciplines.

Professionals work collaboratively when planning services for young children with delays and disabilities.

iStock/track5

A transdisciplinary service delivery model includes families as full members of the team who are central to the decision-making process as they systematically share information and expertise to jointly plan, problem solve, and implement intervention [DEC Recommended Practices TC2]. This model is currently viewed as a recommended practice in early intervention and early childhood special education (Bruder, 2010a; DEC, 2014; Kilgo, 2022; Kilgo et al., 2017, 2019).

"A transdisciplinary model," according to Davis et al. (1998), "lends itself to integrated therapeutic services in the natural environment" (p. 57). This approach is recommended over a pullout model whereby children are removed from a setting to receive various therapeutic services. Because young children learn best through interactions and experiences that occur in their natural environment (DEC, 2014), integrated therapies that incorporate the child's typical routines and natural activities result in increased skill acquisition (Bruder, 1994, 2010b; McWilliam, 2016).

The transdisciplinary model is equally appropriate for infants, toddlers, preschoolers, and early primary students with delays and disabilities due to its emphasis on family-centered services, cross-disciplinary collaboration, and effective communication [DEC Recommended Practices TC3]. It is also recommended as the vehicle for ensuring mutual decision making and effective inclusionary practices (Bruder, 2001, 2010a; Kilgo, 2006; Kilgo et al., 2017, 2019). When using a transdisciplinary model, team members assist each other to identify and access community services and resources (both formal and informal) to meet child and family needs [DEC Recommended Practices TC4].

Figure 4.3 highlights, in hierarchical fashion, some of the characteristics of each team model discussed, while Table 4.3 compares various components of each teaming model.

FIGURE 4.3 ■ Characteristics of Team Models

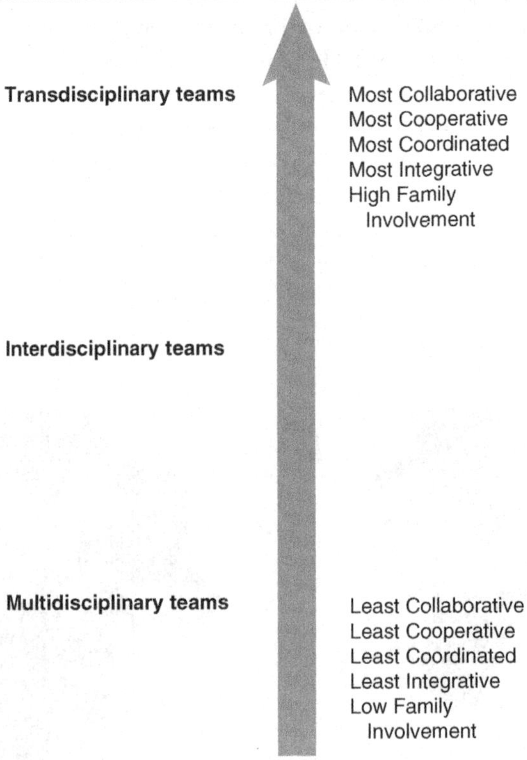

In conclusion, there is a professional appreciation for the importance of integrating interventions across developmental domains through interdisciplinary collaboration. Professional teaming is the key to delivering services in a judicious fashion. Through teaming, families and professionals are linked together as program partners (Kilgo, 2022).

TABLE 4.3 ■ A Comparison of Multi-, Inter-, and Transdisciplinary Team Models

	Multidisciplinary	Interdisciplinary	Transdisciplinary
Assessment	Separate assessments by team members	Separate assessments by team members	Team members and families conduct a comprehensive developmental assessment together
Family participation	Families meet with individual team members	Families meet with team or team representative	Families are full, active, and participating members of the team
IFSP/IEP development	Team members develop plans for their discipline	Team members share their separate plans with one another	Team members and the parents develop a service plan based on family priorities, needs, and resources
IFSP/IEP responsibility	Team members are responsible for implementing their section of the plan	Team members are responsible for sharing information with one another, as well as implementing their section of the plan	Team members are responsible and accountable for how the primary service provider implements the plan
IFSP/IEP implementation	Team members implement the part of the service plan related to their discipline	Team members implement their section of the plan and incorporate other sections, where possible	A primary service provider is assigned to implement the plan with the family
Communication style	Informal lines	Periodic case-specific team meetings	Regular team meetings where continuous transfer of information, knowledge, and skills occurs among team members
Guiding philosophy	Team members recognize the importance of contributions from other disciplines	Team members are willing and able to develop, share, and be responsible for providing services that are a part of the total service plan	Team members make a commitment to teach, learn, and work together across discipline boundaries to implement a unified service plan

Source: Adapted from G. Woodruff and M. McGonigel, Early intervention team approaches: The transdisciplinary model. In J. Jordan, J. Gallagher, P. Hutinger, and M. Karnes (Eds.), *Early Childhood Special Education: Birth to Three*, (Reston, VA: Council for Exceptional Children, 1998), p. 166. Reprinted by permission.

COLLABORATIVE TEACHING[1]

In addition to the teaming models just examined, cooperative teaching, also known as **collaborative teaching**, is another example of collaborative efforts. It is not unusual to find general educators working in concert with early childhood special educators to provide inclusive services. Cooperative teaching is an increasingly common service delivery approach for expanding instructional options for young children with disabilities in inclusive preschool programs and early primary grades. With this strategy, general education teachers and early childhood special educators work together in a collaborative and

[1] Information adapted from *Teaching in Today's Inclusive Classrooms* (4th ed.) by R. Gargiulo and D. Metcalf, Boston, MA: Cengage Learning, 2023.

cooperative manner, with each professional sharing in the planning and delivery of instruction to a heterogeneous group of children.

Villa et al. (2013) define **cooperative teaching**, also commonly referred to as co-teaching, as follows: "Co-teaching is two or more people [educators] sharing responsibility for teaching all students assigned to a classroom. It involves the distribution of responsibility among people [teachers] for planning, differentiating instruction, and monitoring progress for a classroom of students" (p. 4).

Likewise, Friend (2021) views cooperative teaching as a special form of teaming, a service delivery option whereby substantive instruction is jointly provided by one or more professionals to a diverse group of students within inclusive learning environments.

Cooperative teaching is a service delivery approach based on collaboration. It is an instructional model that fosters shared responsibility for coordinating and delivering instruction to a group of children with unique learning needs. Essentially, cooperative teaching is about a true partnership and parity in the instructional process.

The aim of cooperative/collaborative teaching is to create options for learning and to provide support to *all* learners in the general education classroom by combining the content expertise of the general educator with the instructional accommodation talents of the early childhood special educator (Cook et al., 2017; Little & Dieker, 2009; Murawski, 2015; Scruggs & Mastropieri, 2017; Scruggs et al., 2007). Cooperative teaching can be implemented in several different ways, as there are multiple versions of this instructional strategy. These arrangements, as identified by Friend (2021) and Murawski (2015), typically occur for set periods of time each day or only on certain days of the week. Some of the more common instructional models for cooperative teaching are depicted in Figure 4.4.

FIGURE 4.4 ■ Cooperative/Collaborative Teaching Arrangements

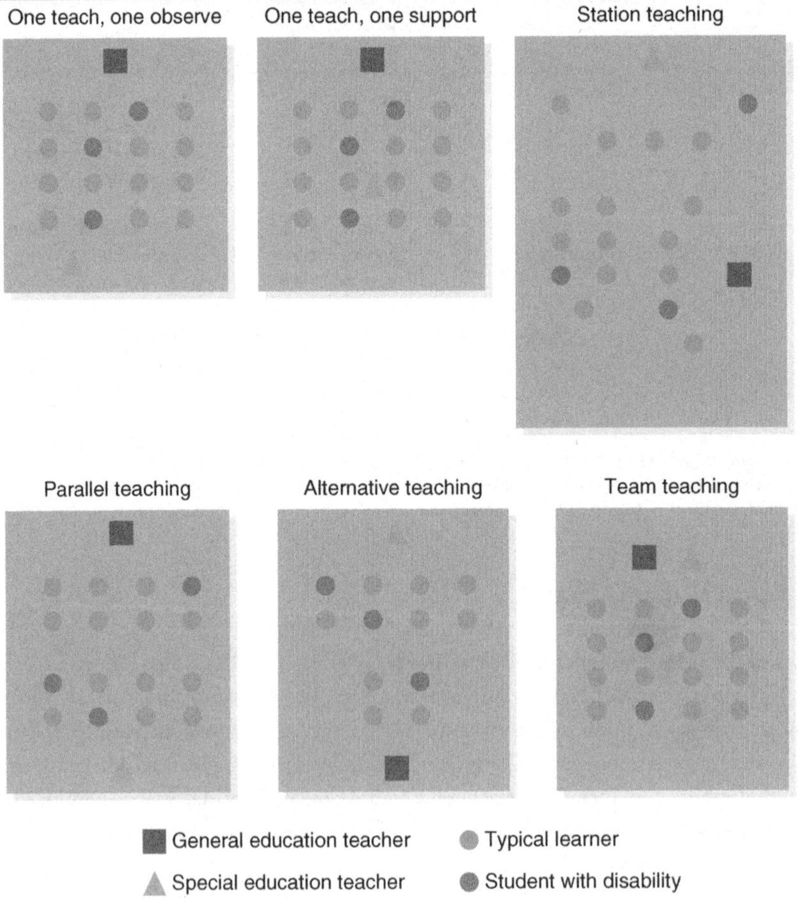

Source: Adapted from M. Friend, *Interactions: Collaboration Skills for Professionals*, 9th ed. (Hoboken, NJ: Pearson Education, 2021), p. 172.

The particular strategy chosen often depends on the needs and characteristics of the children, curricular demands, amount of professional experience, and teacher preference, as well as such practical matters as the amount of space available. Many educators use a variety of arrangements depending upon their specific circumstances. Next is a brief description some of the more common cooperative or collaborative teaching options.

One Teach, One Observe

In this version of cooperative teaching, one teacher presents the instruction to the entire class while the second educator circulates gathering information (data) on a specific child, a small group of students, or targeted behaviors across the whole class such as productive use of center time. Although this model requires a minimal amount of joint planning, it is very important that teachers periodically exchange roles to avoid one professional being perceived by children, and possibly parents, as the "assistant teacher."

One Teach, One Support

Both individuals are present, but one teacher takes the instructional lead while the other quietly provides support and assistance to the children. It is important that one professional (usually the early childhood special educator) is not always expected to function as the assistant; rotating roles can help to alleviate this potential problem. It is also recommended that this model be used sparingly or as one of several approaches to prevent students from becoming overly dependent on additional assistance as well as to avoid jeopardizing the credibility of one of the teachers.

Station Teaching

In this type of cooperative teaching, the lesson is divided into two or more segments and presented in different locations in the classroom. One teacher presents one portion of the lesson while the other teacher provides a different portion. Then the groups rotate, and the teachers repeat their information to new groups of children. Depending on the class, a third station can be established where students work independently or with a learning buddy to review material. Station teaching has been shown to be effective at all grade levels, and it affords both teachers the opportunity to instruct all of the children, albeit on different content.

Cooperative teaching is a service delivery approach based on collaboration.

iStock/kali9

Parallel Teaching

This instructional arrangement decreases the teacher–student ratio. Instruction is planned jointly but is delivered by each teacher to one-half of a heterogeneous group of children. Coordination of efforts is crucial. This format lends itself to drill-and-practice activities rather than initial instruction or projects that require close teacher supervision. As with station teaching, noise and activity levels may pose problems.

Alternative Teaching

Some children benefit from small-group instruction; alternative teaching meets that need. With this model, one teacher provides instruction to a heterogeneous group of learners while the other teacher interacts with a small group of children. Although commonly used for remediation purposes, alternative teaching is equally appropriate for enrichment as well as preteaching activities and in-depth study. Teachers need to be cautious, however, that children with delays and disabilities are not exclusively and routinely assigned to the small group; all members of the class should participate periodically in the functions of the smaller group.

Team/Co-Teaching

In this type of cooperative teaching, which is the most collaborative of the six models, both teachers equally share the instructional activities for the entire class. Each teacher, for example, may take turns leading a discussion about eating healthily, or one teacher may talk about the parts of speech while the co-teacher gives several examples illustrating this concept. Students view each teacher, therefore, as having equal status. This form of cooperative teaching, sometimes called interactive teaching (Walther-Thomas et al., 2000), requires a significant amount of professional trust and a high level of commitment. Compatibility of teaching styles is another key component for successful teaming.

Advantages and disadvantages of cooperative/collaborative teaching options are summarized in Table 4.4.

TABLE 4.4 ■ Advantages and Disadvantages of Representative Cooperative/Collaborative Teaching Arrangements

Instructional model	Advantages	Disadvantages
Team teaching (whole class)	• Provides systematic observation/data collection • Promotes role/content sharing • Facilitates individual assistance • Models appropriate academic, social, and help-seeking behaviors • Teaches question asking • Provides clarification (e.g., concepts, rules, vocabulary)	• May be job sharing, not learning enriching • Requires considerable planning • Requires modeling and role-playing skills • Becomes easy to "typecast" specialist with this role
Station teaching (small group)	• Provides active learning format • Increases small-group attention • Encourages cooperation and independence • Allows strategic grouping • Increases response rate	• Requires considerable planning and preparation • Increases noise level • Requires group and independent work skills • Is difficult to monitor
Parallel teaching (small group)	• Provides effective review format • Encourages student responses • Reduces student–teacher ratio for group instruction or review	• Hard to achieve equal depth of content coverage • May be difficult to coordinate • Requires monitoring of partner pacing • Increases noise level • Encourages some teacher–student competition
Alternative teaching (large group, small group)	• Facilitates enrichment opportunities • Offers absent students catch-up times • Keeps individuals and class on pace • Offers time to develop missing skills	• May select same low-achieving students for help • Creates segregated learning environments • Is difficult to coordinate • May single out students

Source: Adapted from C. Walther-Thomas, L. Korinek, V. McLaughlin, and B. Williams, *Collaboration for Inclusive Education* (Needham Heights, MA: Allyn & Bacon, 2000), p. 190. Reprinted by permission.

DELIVERING INDIVIDUALIZED SERVICES

Effective programs for infants, toddlers, preschoolers, and early primary students with delays and disabilities require that professionals and families work together as a team. EI/ECSE Standard 3 emphasizes the importance of EI/ECSE practitioners having skills to effectively collaborate with families and other professionals in developing and implementing individualized plans. Perhaps nowhere else is this linkage more crucial than in the development of an individualized family service plan (IFSP), an individualized education program (IEP), or a 504 accommodation plan. By mandate of federal law, each young child identified as being eligible for special education services is required to have an individualized program plan for specially designed instruction that addresses the unique needs of the child and their family. The design and delivery of customized services and instruction is guided by one of these documents.

Individualized Family Service Plan

Recall from Chapter 2 that an IFSP is the blueprint behind the delivery of early intervention services to infants and toddlers who are at risk for or have a disability or developmental delay. Although IFSPs primarily focus on children younger than age three, changes in thinking now allow them to be used with preschoolers who require a special education. In an effort to minimize the differences between early intervention and preschool special education services, the federal government has encouraged states to establish "seamless systems" designed to serve children from birth through age five (Stowe & Turnbull, 2001). As a result of this policy decision, states now have the authority to use IFSPs for preschoolers with delays and disabilities until the child's sixth birthday. States are reminded that when a free appropriate public education is provided by an IFSP, the Part B rights and protections still apply.

The shift in policy is partly derived from a belief that similarities in service delivery for children from birth through age five are greater than the differences. Additionally, the needs of children are generally best met with a single system of service. Although there are several exchangeable features of IEPs (which are discussed below) and IFSPs, a few distinguishable components stand out; for example, the IEP is silent regarding the issue of service coordination and transition planning for young children. Another difference is the IFSP acknowledgment of the family as the focal point of services in contrast to the emphasis in the IEP on the individual child and their educational needs.

The IFSP is developed by a team consisting of professionals and the child's parents, who are the key members of the team. Additionally, parents may invite other family members, as well as an advocate, to participate. Typically, the service coordinator who has been working with this family, those professionals involved in the assessment of the child, and the service providers constitute the remainder of the group charged with the responsibility of writing the IFSP.

An IFSP is to be developed within a reasonable period of time. The U.S. Department of Education interprets this requirement to mean within forty-five days of referral. The following required components are the result of the enactment of PL 108–446:

- A statement of the infant's or toddler's present levels of physical development, cognitive development, communication development, social or emotional development, and adaptive development based on objective criteria
- A statement of the family's resources, priorities, and concerns
- A statement of measurable results or outcomes expected to be achieved for the infant or toddler and the family, including preliteracy and language skills, as developmentally appropriate for the child, and the criteria, procedures, and timelines used to assess progress toward achieving the results or outcomes
- A statement of early specific intervention services, based on peer-reviewed research, necessary to meet the unique needs of the infant or toddler and the family, including the frequency, intensity, and method of delivering services (see Table 4.5 for a list of representative early intervention services)

- A statement of the natural environments in which early intervention services shall be provided or justification if services are not provided in said environment
- The projected dates for initiation of services and the anticipated duration of such services
- The identification of the service coordinator
- The steps supporting the transition of the toddler with a disability to preschool or other appropriate services at age three

The IFSP, which is to be reviewed at least every six months, is intentionally designed to preserve the family's role of primary caregiver. Well-constructed IFSPs fully support the family and encourage its active and meaningful involvement. (See Appendix D for an IFSP completed for Maria Ramirez and her family.) This thinking is in keeping with an empowerment model, which views families as capable (with occasional assistance) of helping themselves (Turnbull et al., 2022). This point of view allows parents to retain their decision-making role, establish goals, and assess their needs, among other functions. It is also in keeping with an ecological perspective that argues that one cannot consider a child without considering the various systems and spheres of influence that provide support—in this instance, the infant's or toddler's family and community (Hanson & Lynch, 2013).

TABLE 4.5 ■ Representative Early Intervention Services Available to Infants and Toddlers and Their Families

Assistive technology devices and services
Audiology
Family training and counseling
Health services
Medical services (only for diagnosis and evaluation)
Music therapy
Nursing services
Nutrition services
Occupational therapy
Physical therapy
Psychological services
Service coordination
Social work services
Special education
Speech-language pathology
Transportation services
Vision services

A number of features of the IFSP reflect a family focus. One feature in particular, however, stands out: the assessment of the family's concerns, priorities, and resources [DEC Recommended Practices F3]. Although IDEA encourages early intervention programs to gather this information, family assessment is to be a voluntary activity on the part of the families. Although a personal interview with key family members is one way to gather information, there are questions among professionals about the most appropriate strategies to use for obtaining information about the family (Noonan & McCormick, 2014). Furthermore, any information obtained must be gathered in a culturally sensitive fashion and reflect the family members' perception of their concerns, priorities, and resources.

Bruder (2001, 2010a) and others (Howard et al., 2014; Turnbull et al., 2022) urge professionals to carefully listen to what families have to say so that they may better understand what is important for the family. Service providers are encouraged to appreciate the concerns and understand the priorities of the family from the family's perspective. As emphasized earlier, families need to be the primary decision makers about what is best for them and their children. Service providers are expected to form partnerships with families that are fashioned around mutual trust and respect and support the natural caregiving role of families (Cook et al., 2020). The role of early childhood special educators is to support families in their efforts.

Information obtained from the family and data about the infant's or toddler's developmental status are used to generate outcome statements or goals for the child and their family. Practitioners have increasingly emphasized real-life or authentic outcomes for infants and toddlers (as well as preschoolers) with delays and disabilities (Johnson et al., 2015). These goals are reflected in the IFSP's required outcome statements. Recommended practice suggests that these statements focus on the concerns and priorities of the family. These outcomes may be specific to the child or the family. Families must know and understand their rights; therefore, practitioners often help families know and understand their rights, which may be identified on the IFSP as a family outcome [DEC Recommended Practices F9].

Parents play a critical role in developing their child's IFSP.

iStock.com/vm

Individualized Education Program

The IEP is part of an overall strategy designed to deliver needed services appropriate to the individual preschooler (and older students). By the time the IEP stage is reached, the appropriate permissions have been gathered, assessments have been conducted, and an eligibility determination has been made. Now the IEP must be developed, followed by placement in the most appropriate and least restrictive setting with reviews occurring at least annually. (Parents may request a review prior to the annual review.) A complete reevaluation of the child's eligibility for special education must occur every three years. PL 105–17 waives this stipulation, however, if both parents and school officials agree that such a review is unnecessary.

Bateman and Linden (2012) make a very important point about *when* the IEP is developed. They explain that IEPs are often written at the wrong time. Legally, the IEP is to be developed within thirty days following the evaluation and determination of the child's disability but *before* a placement recommendation is formulated. Placement in the LRE is based on a completed IEP, not the other way around (see Figure 4.5). A commonly noted abuse is developing the IEP based on available placements or simple administrative convenience. Although professionals frequently follow this procedure, it is illegal. What often happens is that children are fit into programs rather than planning programs to meet the needs of the students. The IEP is not to be limited by placement options or the availability of services.

FIGURE 4.5 ■ Correct Route for IEP Placement Decision Making

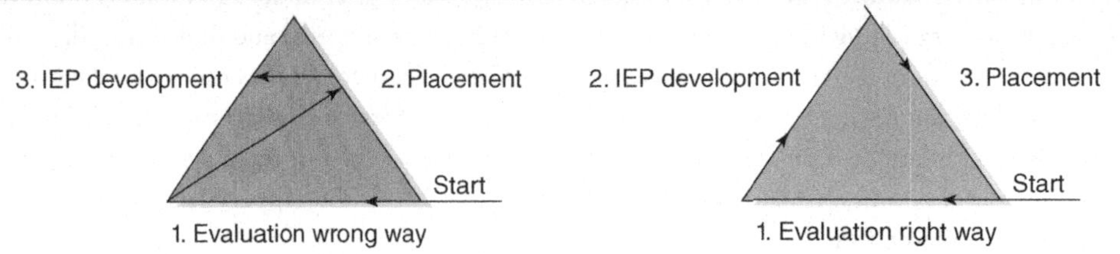

Source: Adapted from B. Bateman and M. Linden, *Better IEPs: How to Develop Legally Correct and Educationally Useful Programs*, 5th ed. (Verona, WI: Attainment Company, 2012), p. 74. Reprinted by permission.

A benchmark of early childhood special education is individualization. Instead of fitting the child into the program (curriculum), a curriculum is tailored that meets the individual needs of the student. One of the cornerstones of constructing appropriate curricula for young children with delays and disabilities is the IEP. Based upon a multidisciplinary educational evaluation of the child's strengths and needs, an individualized plan of learning activities and goals is prescribed. It is perhaps best to envision the IEP as a management tool or planning vehicle that ensures that children with delays and disabilities receive an individualized education appropriate to their unique needs. According to Gargiulo and Bouck (2021), the IEP "stipulates *who* will be involved in providing a special education, *what* services will be offered, *where* they will be delivered, and for *how long*. In addition, an IEP gauges *how successfully* goals have been met" (p. 60).

Like the IFSP, IEPs are written by a team. At a minimum, participation must include one or both parents/guardians; the child's teachers (including an early childhood special educator and at least one general education teacher); an individual capable of interpreting evaluation results; and a representative from the school district. When appropriate, the student (unlikely due to their age) and other professionals whose expertise is desired may participate at the discretion of the parent or school.

Parents have a legal right to meaningfully participate in this planning and decision-making process; they serve as the child's advocates. Although IDEA mandates a collaborative role for parents, it does not stipulate the degree or extent of parental participation. The parents choose the extent to which they wish to be involved. They alone define their role on the team. Professionals must respect the parents' right to choose their level of involvement and participation.

The role of the general educator and early childhood special education teacher is crucial in the IEP development process; these professionals are usually ultimately responsible for implementing the team's decisions. Contemporary thinking suggests that both the special educator and early childhood teacher should equally be viewed as the child's teacher. Their role in developing the IEP is complementary and mutually supporting.

Table 4.6 illustrates the required content of an IEP according to IDEA 2004. In addition, federal regulations require that the IEP team consider the following factors when developing a child's IEP:

- If a child's behavior impedes their learning or that of classmates, allow them the use of proactive behavioral supports.
- For a student with limited English proficiency, consider the language needs of the child as those needs relate to the IEP.
- For a child who is blind or visually impaired, provide for instruction in Braille and the use of Braille unless the IEP team determines that instruction in Braille or the use of Braille is inappropriate.
- For a child who is deaf or hard of hearing, consider the child's language or communication needs, including their preferred mode of communication.
- Evaluate the need for assistive technology devices and services.

IFSPs and IEPs are developed by parents and other team members.
iStock.com/huePhotography

TABLE 4.6 ■ Elements of a Meaningful IEP for Young Children With Delays and Disabilities

Current performance. A statement of the child's present levels of educational and functional performance, including how student's disability affects their involvement and progress in the general education curriculum, or for preschoolers, how the disability affects participation in age-appropriate activities
Goals. A statement of measurable annual goals (both functional and academic) that addresses the student's involvement and progress in the general education curriculum as well as the student's other education needs; short-term objectives or benchmarks are required for children who take alternate assessments aligned to alternate achievement standards
Special education and related services. A statement of special education, related services, and supplementary aids and services (based on peer-reviewed research) to be provided, including program modifications or supports necessary for the student to advance toward attainment of annual goals; to be involved and progress in the general education curriculum, extracurricular, and nonacademic activities; and to be educated and participate in activities with other children both with and without disabilities
Participation with typically developing students. An explanation of the extent, if any, to which the student will not participate in the general education classroom
Participation in state and district-wide assessments. A statement of any individual modifications needed for the student to participate in state or district-wide assessment; if student will not participate, a statement of why the assessment is inappropriate and how the child will be assessed
Dates and places. Projected date for initiation of services; expected location, duration, and frequency of such services
Measuring progress. A statement of how progress toward annual goals will be measured and how student's parents (guardians) will be regularly informed of such progress

Source: R. Gargiulo and E. Bouck, *Special Education in Contemporary Society,* 7th ed. (Thousand Oaks, CA: Sage, 2021), p. 60. Reprinted by permission.

Unfortunately, the preceding elements do not contain any provision for family goals and services as found in an IFSP. Yet there is no rationale for excluding this component. In fact, it could reasonably be argued that this element is equally as important for preschool children and early primary students with delays and disabilities and their families as it is for infants and toddlers. DEC (2014) also suggests that services for young children with delays and disabilities should be family based, reflecting family priorities [DEC Recommended Practices F4]. Although rarely used, one possible remedy for this situation would be to use an IFSP (as permitted by state law) instead of an IEP until the child's sixth birthday. For a comparison of the required components of an IEP and IFSP, see Table 4.7.

TABLE 4.7 ■ Comparable Components of an IEP and an IFSP

Individualized Education Program	Individualized Family Service Plan
A statement of child's present levels of academic achievement and functional performance, including involvement and progress in the general education curriculum; for preschool children, how the disability affects participation in age-appropriate activities	A statement of the infant's or toddler's present levels of physical, cognitive, communication, social/emotional, and adaptive development
No comparable feature	A statement of the family's resources, priorities, and concerns
A statement of measurable annual goals, including benchmarks or short-term instructional objectives, for children who take alternate assessments aligned to alternate achievement standards	A statement of measurable results or outcomes expected to be achieved for the infant or toddler and the family
A statement indicating progress toward annual goals and a mechanism for regularly informing parents/guardians of such progress	Criteria, procedures, and timelines used to determine the degree to which progress toward achieving the outcomes or results is being made
A statement of specific special education and related services and supplementary aids and services, based on peer-reviewed research, to be provided and any program modifications	A statement of specific early intervention services, based on peer-reviewed research, necessary to meet the unique needs of the infant or toddler and the family
An explanation of the extent to which the child will not participate in general education programs	A statement of the natural environments in which early intervention services will appropriately be provided, or justification if not provided
Modifications needed to participate in state or district-wide assessments	No comparable feature
The projected date for initiation of services and the anticipated duration, frequency, and location of services	The projected date for initiation of services and the anticipated duration of services
No comparable feature	The name of the service coordinator
At age 16, a statement of transition services needed, including courses of study in addition to measurable postsecondary goals	The steps to be taken to support the child's transition to other services at age 3

Source: Adapted from Individuals with Disabilities Education Improvement Act of 2004, Title 20 U.S. Code (U.S.C.) 1400 *et seq*, Part B Section 614 (d) (1) (A), and Part C Section 636 (d).

The IEP serves as the basis for constructing a tailor-made plan of services for each child with a developmental delay or disability who requires a special education. IEPs are not written, however, to be so detailed or complete that they serve as the entire instructional agenda, nor are they intended to prescribe curriculum (Gargiulo & Bouck, 2021). IEP goals are designed, according to Cook et al. (2020), "to target particular developmental lags or to teach specific skills. The intent is to focus attention and teaching on critical areas of need" (p. 105). These goals, listed by priority, form the foundation from which daily instructional plans can be developed within developmental domains. Typical areas might include speech and language, fine/gross motor skills, social development, and cognitive activities, along with self-care or adaptive skills.

Based on the child's present level of educational and functional performance, goals are developed that represent reasonable estimates of the child's progress. Goal setting is a complex process, and it sometimes can be difficult to project future accomplishments for young children. Priorities for determining measurable annual goals are formulated based on critical needs—what the child needs to meaningfully participate in present and future environments. Educational goals for preschoolers or early primary students with delays and disabilities should reflect skills that are relevant to everyday functioning, focus on authentic or real-life situations, and occur within naturally existing activities and routines. Recent thinking suggests that goals should be crafted so the student can make progress, considering their educational needs, and also provide an opportunity to meet challenging and ambitious annual goals (Yell & Bateman, 2020).

Practitioners no longer teach skills in isolation; rather, goals are developed that are relevant to the daily activities and routines of the child and their family. These statements need to be practical and functional, reflecting authentic situations that occur in the natural environment. Contemporary thinking encourages service providers to structure learning opportunities that emphasize the acquisition of competence in natural settings. According to Notari-Syverson and Shuster (1995), five components are necessary for meaningful goals:

1. *Functionality*—skills necessary for independently interacting within the daily environment
2. *Generality*—general vs. specific skills that are adaptable to meet the individual needs of the child
3. *Ease of integration*—skills that can be used in a variety of natural environments such as the home, classroom, or playground
4. *Measurability*—skills that must be capable of being measured such as their frequency or duration
5. *Hierarchical relationship*—complex skills that need to be logically sequenced, building upon earlier behaviors

Table 4.8 provides a checklist for determining whether or not goal statements fulfill the preceding criteria.

TABLE 4.8 ■ Checklist for Writing IFSP and IEP Goals for Young Children With Delays and Disabilities

Functionality	
1. Will the skill increase the child's ability to interact with people and objects within the daily environment?	
The child needs to perform the skill in all or most of environments in which they interact.	
Skill:	Places object into container.
Opportunities:	Home—Places sweater in drawer, cookie in paper bag.
	School—Places lunch box in cubbyhole, trash in trash bin.
	Community—Places milk carton in grocery cart, rocks and soil in flower pot.
2. Will the skill have to be performed by someone else if the child cannot do it?	
The skill is a behavior or event that is critical for completion of daily routines.	
Skill:	Looks for objects in usual location.
Opportunities:	Finds coat on coat rack, gets food from cupboard.
Generality	
3. Does the skill represent a general concept or class of responses?	
The skill emphasizes a generic process, rather than a particular instance.	
Skill:	Fits objects into defined spaces.
Opportunities:	Puts mail in mailbox, places crayons in box, puts utensils into sorter.
4. Can the skill be adapted or modified for a variety of disabling conditions?	
The child's sensory impairment should interfere as little as possible with the performance.	
Skill:	Correctly activates simple toy.
Opportunities:	Motor impairments—Activates light, easy-to-move toys (balls, rocking horse, toys on wheels, roly-poly toys).
	Visual impairments—Activates large, bright, noise-making toys (bells, drums).

(Continued)

TABLE 4.8 ■ Checklist for Writing IFSP and IEP Goals for Young Children With Delays and Disabilities *(Continued)*

5. Can the skill be generalized across a variety of settings, materials, and/or people?	
The child can perform the skill with interesting materials and in meaningful situations.	
Skill:	Manipulates two small objects simultaneously.
Opportunities:	Home—Builds with small interlocking blocks, threads lace on shoes.
	School—Sharpens pencil with pencil sharpener.
	Community—Takes coins out of small wallet.
Instructional Content	
6. Can the skill be taught in a way that reflects the manner in which the skill will be used in the daily environments?	
The skill can occur in a naturalistic manner.	
Skill:	Uses object to obtain another object.
Opportunities:	Uses fork to obtain food, broom to rake toy; steps on stool to reach toy on shelf.
7. Can the skill be elicited easily by the teacher/parent within the classroom/home activities?	
The skill can be initiated easily by the child as a part of daily routines.	
Skill:	Stacks objects.
Opportunities:	Stacks books, cups/plates, wooden logs.
Measurability	
8. Can the skill be seen and/or heard?	
Different observers must be able to identify the same behavior.	
Measurable skill:	Gains attention and refers to object, person, and/or event.
Nonmeasurable skill:	Experiences a sense of self-importance.
9. Can the skill be directly counted (by frequency, duration, distant measures)?	
The skill represents a well-defined behavior or activity.	
Measurable skill:	Grasps pea-sized object.
Nonmeasurable skill:	Has mobility in all fingers.
10. Does the skill contain or lend itself to determination of performance criteria?	
The extent and/or degree of accuracy of the skill can be evaluated.	
Measurable skill:	Follows one-step directions with contextual cues.
Nonmeasurable skill:	Will increase receptive language skills.
Hierarchical Relation Between Long-Range Goal and Short-Term Objective	
11. Is the short-term objective a developmental subskill or step thought to be critical to the achievement of the long-range goal?	
Appropriate:	Short-term objective—Releases object with each hand.
	Long-range goal—Places and releases object balanced on top of another object.
Inappropriate:	The short-term objective is a restatement of the same skill as the long-range goal with the addition of an instructional prompt. The short-term objective is not conceptually or functionally related to the long-range goal.

Source: Adapted from A. Notari-Syverson and S. Shuster, 1995, "Putting Real-Life Skills into IEP/IFSPs for Infants and Young Children," *Teaching Exceptional Children, 27*(2), p. 31. Reprinted by permission.

Goal statements are intentionally broad. Their intent is to provide long-range direction to a child's educational program and not to define exact instructional tasks.

The business of guiding instruction is the role filled by short-term objectives, which are typically one to three months in duration. These statements, written after goals have been crafted, describe the sequential steps the child will take to meet the intent of the goal statement(s). IDEA 2004 only requires objectives, however, for school-age students who take alternate assessments aligned to alternate achievement standards—typically individuals with very severe disabilities. Instructional objectives are usually written by the child's teacher.

Criteria for effective short-term objectives, commonly called benchmarks, include three components: a description of the behavior using observable and measurable terminology; a statement of conditions under which the behavior will be exhibited; and finally, a standard or performance criterion for assessing the adequacy of the student's accomplishment (Yell, 2019). Writing meaningful instructional objectives is not an easy task. Teachers are sometimes confused about what constitutes a useful objective. Deiner (2013) believes that high-quality objectives should be functional, measurable, generalizable, and easily integrated into daily routines, as well as being conceptually related to the goal statements. These indicators of quality are equally appropriate for developing IEPs and IFSPs.

In conclusion, the quality of an IEP largely depends on having well-written and appropriate goals that address the unique needs of the child. The IEP should be viewed as a "living" or dynamic document, guiding the delivery of special education services to young children with delays and disabilities. It is not something to be filed away and forgotten until the end of the academic year approaches. IEPs are the vehicle for ensuring that a specially designed educational program is provided. (See Appendix E for a typical IEP developed for four-year-old T. J. Browning.)

Section 504 Accommodation Plan[2]

Recall from Chapter 2 that Section 504 of the Rehabilitation Act of 1973 (PL 93–112) is a civil rights law designed to prohibit discrimination against individuals with disabilities. The intent of this legislation, according to Smith (2002), is to create equal opportunities for persons with disabilities or, in the words of Miller and Newbill (2006), "to level the playing field for students facing life challenges" (p. 13). Far-reaching in its intent and coverage, this law holds great significance for educators. Section 504 provides, among other things, that students with disabilities (who are otherwise qualified) must have equal access to programs, activities, and services that are available to children without disabilities. This includes, for example, field trips, extracurricular activities, and academic courses (with appropriate accommodations) in addition to physical accessibility. Interestingly, because this law is an antidiscrimination statute, federal funds are not available to help schools meet the various requirements of Section 504. As this law pertains to education, PL 93–112 requires schools adhere to the following provisions:

- Annually identify and locate all children with disabilities who are unserved.
- Provide a "free, appropriate public education" to each student with a disability, regardless of the nature or severity of the disability. This means providing general or special education and related aids and services designed to meet the individual educational needs of persons with disabilities as adequately as the needs of nondisabled persons are met.
- Ensure that each student with disabilities is educated with nondisabled students to the maximum extent appropriate.
- Establish nondiscriminatory evaluation and placement procedures to avoid the inappropriate education that may result from the misclassification or misplacement of students.

[2] Information adapted from *Teaching in Today's Inclusive Classrooms* (4th ed.) by R. Gargiulo and D. Metcalf, Boston: MA: Cengage Learning, 2023.

- Establish procedural safeguards to enable parents and guardians to participate meaningfully in decisions regarding the evaluation and placement of their children.
- Afford children with disabilities an equal opportunity to participate in nonacademic and extracurricular services and activities. (Office for Civil Rights, 1989, p. 8)

Who Is Protected by Section 504? Although 504 protections are afforded to persons with disabilities across their lifespan, the focus here is on school-age individuals, particularly early primary students. As noted in Chapter 2, all students eligible for services under IDEA are also protected by Section 504. The converse of this statement is not true, however. Some examples of young children eligible for services under Section 504 include

- A student referred for special education services but who does not qualify under IDEA
- Individuals who are no longer eligible for services under IDEA or who transition out of a special education program
- Victims of abuse and neglect
- Children with health needs, such as diabetes, asthma, severe allergies, hemophilia, or communicable diseases
- An individual with a low IQ but who is not considered to have an intellectual disability

Obviously, due to the broader scope of the definition of a disability incorporated in Section 504, significantly greater numbers of students are eligible to receive a free, appropriate public education via Section 504 than would be afforded services under IDEA.

Accommodation Plans. Once a student has been found eligible for Section 504 services, an accommodation plan must be developed. **Section 504 accommodation plans** should be simple, inexpensive, and easy to use. Most accommodations will occur in the general education classroom. It is important to note that special educators are not liable for Section 504 accommodations; this responsibility belongs to general education teachers. Designed for an individual student, these plans should include the information necessary to enable the individual to have equal access to educational and extracurricular activities while also providing an equal opportunity to be successful (Smith, 2002). Many of the accommodations are common sense and will vary depending on the needs of the learner. Examples include

- Preferential seating
- Extended test time
- Rest periods during the school day
- Recorded lessons
- Virtual learning options
- Modified attendance policies
- Oral testing options
- Peer notetaker
- Outlines and study guides
- Textbooks kept at home

Accommodation plans do not have mandated components like IEPs do. The format of these plans will, therefore, greatly vary. At a minimum, this document should identify the child's strengths and needs, the type of accommodation required, the individual(s) responsible for implementation, and team members. See the accompanying Making Connections feature for an example of a 504 plan completed for Cheryl Chinn.

TRANSITION

Change is inevitable in the lives of young children with delays and disabilities and their families. Each year, thousands of young children move from one type of early childhood program to another. The most common reason for this transition is the age of the child (Allen & Cowdery, 2022). When this movement occurs, it generally affects the children, their caregivers, and service providers. Change also brings with it the potential of stress due to the disruption of patterns of behavior and fearfulness of new situations and environments. Yet a typical dimension in the lives of infants, toddlers, preschoolers, and early primary students with delays and disabilities and their families is change, or transition, to new service programs.

Transition is succinctly defined as the process of moving from one type of placement to another (see Chapter 3). Bruder (2010b) characterizes transition as an outcome-oriented process consisting of a series of well-planned steps that move a child from one program or service delivery model to another. Examples of transition can range from moving from a hospital neonatal intensive care unit to home-based services, from an early intervention program to a community-based inclusive preschool program, or from a Head Start program to kindergarten. A transition can also occur within a particular program and is exemplified when a child begins working with a new teacher or is placed in a different classroom. Regardless of the type of transition that occurs, key elements of this process include planning, coordination, cooperation, and follow-up [DEC Recommended Practices TR1, TR2].

One of the main goals of early intervention and early childhood special education programs is successful transition. If accomplished, it presents to the children and their families opportunities for continued growth and development with a seamless movement from one program to the next. Poorly orchestrated transitions, however, may lead to stress, anxiety, frustration, and confusion (Noonan & McCormick, 2014).

Transitions may occur at any time during the early childhood years. They can be characterized as either vertical or horizontal transitions (Bruder, 2010b; Winter, 2007). A vertical transition occurs across settings within the same time frame. For example, for preschoolers with disabilities, it occurs upon entering a preschool special education program and exiting from it. Young children may enter from day care, from early intervention programs, or from being at home, and they leave to be placed in kindergartens or other appropriate educational settings. A horizontal transition refers to the provision of multiple services typically offered by different providers and delivered at different locations. For instance, a four-year-old boy with Down syndrome might attend an inclusive preschool program in the mornings and an after-care facility in the afternoon while receiving physical therapy once a week at his therapist's office.

Inherent in the concept of transition is allegiance to the philosophy of normalization. An attempt is usually made to place a child in a program less restrictive than the preceding one. The goal should always be to serve the child in the most natural and inclusive setting (Noonan & McCormick, 2014).

MAKING CONNECTIONS

SECTION 504 ACCOMMODATION PLAN

Review Date: At the end of the six-week grading period.

General Strengths: Cheryl has above-average intellectual ability. Although socially immature, she is popular with her classmates. Discipline is generally not a problem. Supportive and concerned parents.

General Weaknesses: Cheryl exhibits attention deficit hyperactivity disorder (ADHD). She has difficulty concentrating (except for brief periods of time) and is easily distracted. Classroom assignments and homework are frequently not completed. Recent evidence of growing frustration and loss of self-esteem.

Specific Accommodations

Accommodation #1

Class: All classes

Accommodation(s): Worksheets will be modified so less material is presented on each page. Allow extra time for completion if necessary.

Person Responsible for Implementation: Mrs. Newman

Accommodation #2

Class: All classes

Accommodation(s): Cheryl will be given access to a study carrel when working on classroom assignments or taking tests.

Person Responsible for Implementation: Mrs. Newman

Accommodation #3

Class: All classes

Accommodation(s): Cheryl will record daily homework activities in assignment notepad. Teacher will check for accuracy, and parents will sign notepad and return it to school.

Person Responsible for Implementation: Mrs. Newman

Accommodation #4

Class: All classes

Accommodation(s): Cheryl will receive praise and recognition for task completion and appropriate behavior. Teacher to provide immediate feedback whenever possible.

Person Responsible for Implementation: Mrs. Newman

General Comments: Weekly progress reports to parents via telephone or email.

Name: Cheryl Chinn	**Birthdate:** August 1, 2015
School: Tuggle Elementary	**Grade:** First
Teacher: Jane Newman	**Date:** November 14, 2022

Accommodation Plan Team Members:

Name	Team Member's Signature	Position/Title
Ms. Elizabeth Chinn	Elizabeth Chinn	Parent/Guardian
Mr. Robert Johnson	Robert Johnson	Assistant Principal/504 Coordinator
Ms. Nancy Washington	Nancy Washington	School Counselor
Mr. Samuel Oden	Samuel Oden	Resource Teacher
Ms. Jane Newman	Jane Newman	General Educator

Copies: Parent

Classroom Teacher(s)

Cumulative File

Other: ______________________________

Source: Form adapted from T. Smith and J. Patton, *Section 504 and Public Schools*, 2nd ed. (Austin, TX: Pro-Ed, 2007), p. 46.

One of the primary objectives of transition planning is to enable the child to be as successful as possible in future environments (Howard et al., 2014). In concert with this aim, EI/ECSE Standard 3 emphasizes the importance of EI/ECSE practitioners having skills to effectively collaborate with families and other professionals in planning and implementing successful transitions that occur across the lifespan to ensure continuity of services.

The need for effective transitioning is clearly articulated in IDEA and its accompanying rules and regulations, with specific details about this issue. Part C, which focuses on infants and toddlers, specifies that the IFSP must include a transition plan that outlines the procedures to be undertaken as infants and toddlers move from early intervention to preschool special education programs. Language in Part B, the preschool grant program, also emphasizes the importance of carefully planned transitions. Yet there is no legislative mandate for transition planning as students move from preschool special education programs to kindergarten. Continuity of services, however, is of paramount importance for both the child and their family.

When a transition occurs, it impacts more than the toddler or preschooler. As explained previously, change affects families and professionals as well. Transition is a crucial time for all involved. Bronfenbrenner (1977, 1993) supports this idea and contends that transitions produce "ripple effects" within systems. Like a pebble being dropped in a pond, when a young child moves from an infant program to a preschool program or from a preschool special education program to a kindergarten, this change in ecology disturbs the existing ecological structure. Obviously, the child's microsystem is changed. Families will establish new family–professional relationships; thus, the mesosystem is also modified. Furthermore, involvement with a variety of new and different agencies (ecosystems) is possible, and encounters with different regulations, rulings, and even values (macrosystem) are likely. Professionals must be sensitive to how families react to these changes. The more existing behavior patterns and routines are disrupted, the greater the likelihood that stress and anxiety will develop. One remedy for this problem is careful and skillful preparation for transitioning. A smooth transition relies on proactive and comprehensive planning. Preparation, by necessity, involves the child, family, and service providers.

Child Involvement

A critical component of successful transition is the preparation of the child. A smooth transition depends, in a large part, on the child demonstrating the skills and behaviors required in the new environment. This information is usually gathered by future environment surveys, which describe behaviors needed in the receiving program. Generally, there should be a match between the skills in the child's repertoire and the requirements and expectations of the new placement. This typically requires an assessment of the individual's strengths and needs and subsequent instruction in the essential social, behavioral, and academic requirements of the new environment. Identifying and teaching critical skills and routines will enable the child to participate with greater independence and success in the new setting. Knowing what skills are expected in the new learning environment also facilitates the transition process (Downing, 2008).

Noonan and McCormick (2014) note that early childhood educators generally do not consider skills associated with academic readiness as crucial as those associated with independence such as

Planning is crucial for successful transitions.

Cultura RM Exclusive/Hybrid Images/Image Source/via Getty Images following directions, adhering to classroom rules and routines, and participating in group activities. It is important to remember, however, that in any discussion, essential skills and behaviors are seen as optimal goals, *not* prerequisites for placement in a new setting (Allen & Cowdery, 2022). A child's failure to demonstrate specific skills should not prohibit movement to a new placement. Rather, it is a starting point for identifying needed adaptations, supports, and initial intervention targets and for preparing the child for a successful transition experience (Downing, 2008; Noonan & McCormick, 2014).

Family Involvement

The family of a young child with delays and disabilities plays a vital role in the transition process. Recall that in Chapter 2, the importance of professionals viewing the child within the context of the family and the family in interaction with larger social systems is emphasized. A transition from an early intervention program to a community-based inclusive preschool provides a good example. An effective transition requires that professionals not only prepare the child but also fully involve and prepare the family for this change (see the Making Connections feature). A change in programs can be especially stressful for families—routines and schedules are altered, new relationships are established, and old ones are relinquished. Attendance at meetings is often necessary as well as helpful in establishing new goals and expectations for the child. An active role in the decision-making process and meaningful involvement can minimize the adverse effects of change. Families must be integrally involved in the transition planning. Professionals must view the child's family as an equal member of the transition team (DEC, 2014).

Although families have much to offer professionals, as well as much to gain by their involvement in the transition process, professionals must be sensitive to the needs, priorities, and expectations of the individual family. Each family has its own preferred level of involvement. Professionals need to ascertain what the optimal level of involvement is for each family. Teachers and other service providers should not assume that all families want to be involved in the transition process, nor are all families prepared for the responsibility (Allen & Cowdery, 2022).

Professionals (Bruder, 2010b; Cook et al., 2020; Deiner, 2013) point out that family members will often require support and information to actively participate in the transition process. Successful transitions require adherence to essential collaborative practices, such as cooperation, communication, and comprehensive planning with families.

Professional Involvement

The third component of this tripartite strategy for ensuring smooth transitions requires the involvement of a variety of service providers. Professionals from the program the child is exiting (sending program), as well as providers from the program the child is entering (receiving program), must be involved. Team members will most likely include, for example, general and special educators, administrators, physical and occupational therapists, speech–language pathologists, service coordinators, and a host of other professionals involved in providing services to the child with delays and disabilities and their family. It is very important that professionals from both the sending and receiving programs work together and understand one another's goals and procedures (Noonan & McCormick, 2014). Cooperative and collaborative planning between groups will help to facilitate a smooth transition. Formal program/agency policies and procedures will also aid in the transition process. Joint involvement is important due to the number of logistical and programmatic issues that need to be addressed. These concerns include the identification of program exit criteria, coordination responsibilities, transfer of records, and discussion of placement options. Figure 4.6 provides a flowchart/checklist of transition activities necessary for facilitating effective transitions.

FIGURE 4.6 ■ Flowchart/Checklist of Transition Steps

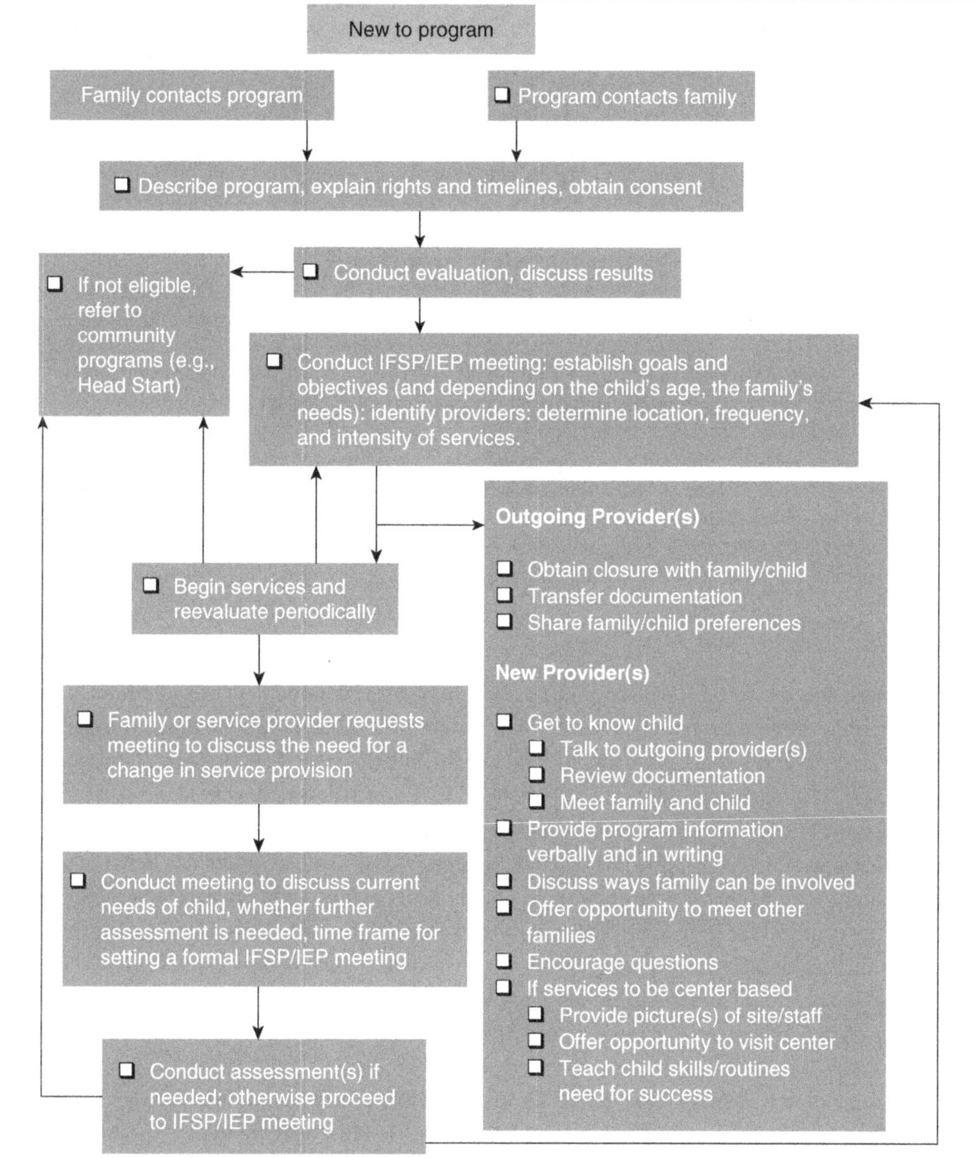

Source: B. Hussey and H. Bernstein, Transitions and Service Coordination in Early Childhood and Early Childhood Special Education, in *The Program Administrator's Guide to Early Childhood Special Education*, J. Taylor, J. McGowan, and T. Linder (Eds.), (Baltimore, MD: Paul H. Brookes, 2009), p. 178. Reprinted by permission.

MAKING CONNECTIONS

FAMILY PARTICIPATION IN TRANSITION PLANNING

With the approach of Maria Ramirez's third birthday, her early intervention team members have recommended to Mr. and Mrs. Ramirez that Maria transition from her home-based services to an inclusive, community-based program to begin receiving Part B services. Her parents and grandparents are very reluctant to agree to this recommendation. They have expressed their concerns to their service coordinator. Among their worries are working with a whole new staff, the length of Maria's school day, her involvement with typical playmates, her social readiness, transportation difficulties, and other potential problems.

The following suggestions illustrate specific activities that may assist Mr. and Mrs. Ramirez in understanding the transition process, in addition to diminishing their anxieties about their daughter's success in a new setting. Remember, successful transitions depend, in part, on being sensitive to the needs and concerns of the parents.

- The service coordinator schedules a meeting with Maria's parents (and grandparents if desired) to discuss their preferences, explain the transition process and rationale, review legal rights, and ascertain the parents' need for support.
- The service coordinator arranges for Maria and Mr. and Mrs. Ramirez (and grandparents) to visit the facility. An opportunity is provided for Maria's parents to meet staff, teachers, and related service providers. Maria visits her classroom and meets other children and staff.
- As desired by Maria's parents, the service coordinator arranges a meeting with parents of other children enrolled in the class and/or provides Mr. and Mrs. Ramirez with appropriate written materials.
- At least ninety days prior to Maria's third birthday, her service coordinator, her parents, other early intervention team members, and professionals from the program jointly develop a transition plan.
- With her parents' permission, the service coordinator arranges for program staff to observe Maria's therapy sessions to ensure continuity of service and to answer her parents' questions.
- The service coordinator arranges for Maria to visit her classroom on several different occasions. Maria's parents (and grandparents) are provided an opportunity to qualitatively assess the impact of attendance on their daughter.

Although effective transition policies are seen as crucial to the development of a coordinated system of transitioning children from one service delivery system to another, families frequently perceive the process as stressful and anxiety producing (Harbin et al., 2000; Malone & Gallagher, 2009; Mahurin-Smith, 2022). Having strong relationships with EI/ECSE practitioners, however, can help alleviate uncertainty and create more favorable outcomes for families (Mahurin-Smith, 2022).

Whenever possible, service providers should attempt to minimize the differences between sending and receiving environments. A transition should be skillfully planned and gradual rather than abrupt and commence anywhere from six to twelve months before the toddler or preschooler exits their current program. Children in transition need time to adjust to the demands and expectations of their new setting. Noonan and McCormick (1993) offer recommendations that can help facilitate the movement from one program to another—in this example a kindergarten:

1. *Visits or field trips to the "new" school.* Ideally such visits would include lunch in the cafeteria, some time for play on the playground, and participation in a few activities.
2. *Reading stories about the fun of new adventures and new friends.* Read or tell stories about new experiences.
3. *Helping the children create a scrapbook about kindergarten.* Each child's scrapbook could include photos taken during the field trip, as well as pictures of kindergarten activities created by the child.
4. *Role playing "going to the new school."* In the course of role-play sessions, encourage the children to express their feelings about the new experiences.
5. *Inviting kindergarten teachers to visit the preschool class.* Try to arrange for each receiving kindergarten teacher to visit the preschool class. The goal is for the kindergarten teachers to get to know the children in settings that are familiar to the children.

These steps provide an excellent illustration of the type of activities T. J. Browning's teachers could use to facilitate his movement from the Epps Head Start Center to kindergarten (see Appendix E and "Making Connections" in Chapter 2).

Steps for Planning Effective Transitions

Smooth transitions do not just happen; they demand extensive preparation on the part of everyone involved. Successful transitions require adherence to a series of well-planned steps. Utilizing the following strategies and recommendations can help to minimize the disruption of services; reduce stress for children, families, and service providers; and ensure that movement from one program to another progresses as smoothly as possible. The intent of transition planning is to maximize children's chances for success in their future environment.

Noonan and McCormick (2014) state that transitions involve three distinct phases: preparation, implementation, and follow-up. Each of these elements is evident in Table 4.9. These steps are appropriate when planning transitions from an early intervention program to a preschool program or from a preschool special education placement to a kindergarten.

TABLE 4.9 ■ Steps in Planning Transitions

1. Form a transition team that includes parents, current program staff, and staff of the most likely receiving programs.
2. Schedule meetings—the first meeting will be to develop an initial written plan; the later meetings will consider specific transition tasks.
3. Identify possible receiving settings.
4. Identify basic transition tasks—what will be necessary to implement the transition?
5. Agree on assignments—specifically, who will perform each of the different transition tasks?
6. Establish timelines, including the referral date and dates for preplacement activities.
7. Decide communication procedures, including transfer of records and other information.
8. Agree on preplacement activities such as
   a. Parent visits to potential receiving environments
   b. Information sharing between teaching staff in sending and receiving agencies
   c. Observations in the receiving setting to determine needed adaptations
   d. Arrangements for whatever family support will be provided
   e. Therapy and other special services
   f. f. Future consultative interactions
9. Plan for follow-up activities—should be planned and carried out between the family and the agencies involved.
10. Place the child after needed environmental adaptations have been completed.
11. Provide consultation and therapy services.
12. Follow up and evaluate.

Source: M. Noonan and L. McCormick, *Early Intervention in Natural Environments* (Pacific Grove, CA: Brooks/Cole, 1993), p. 359.

Effective transition planning, however, does not terminate upon a child's entry into the receiving program; rather, it is an ongoing process. Transition team members should continue to serve as resources for the family and each other even after the child transitions.

For additional information on transition planning, early childhood professionals should consult the website of the National Early Childhood Transition Center, www.hdi.uky.edu/nectc/NECTC/home.aspx.

SUMMARY

One subject that has sparked considerable conversation among professionals is the inclusion of young children with delays and disabilities. Important to keep in mind is that there is no one ideal placement option capable of meeting the needs of *all* learners. A myriad of research, policies, and recommended practices, however, support inclusion in terms of positive outcomes for young children with and without disabilities, as well as broader benefits for families and communities (Grisham-Brown & Hemmeter, 2017; Guralnick, 2023).

Young children with delays and disabilities receive services in a variety of locations. Traditionally, these settings have been identified as home-based or center- or school-based, yet no one service delivery approach is necessarily superior to another. The delivery of services must be tailored to the individual needs of the infant, toddler, preschooler, or early primary student and their family. The field is presently experiencing a thrust toward more inclusive environments for young children with delays and disabilities. The challenge is to develop models that allow for delivery of comprehensive services in the most inclusive setting.

Young children with delays and disabilities typically receive services from a several different professionals. The idea of professionals from various disciplines working together as a team is a well-established aspect of early intervention and early childhood special education. No one discipline, agency, or professional possesses all of the skills or resources needed to develop appropriate educational experiences for infants, toddlers, preschoolers, and early primary students with disabilities. Professionals need to work together, usually forming teams. Three common team structures typically encountered by young children with delays and disabilities and their families are multidisciplinary, interdisciplinary, and transdisciplinary models. Each model has its own unique features and serves a specific function. Teaming and professional collaboration is invaluable. It serves as the foundation for delivering services in a judicious fashion.

Cooperative/collaborative teaching, in its multiple forms, is an important type of professional teaming. It is a service delivery approach based on collaboration whose purpose is to create options for learning and offer support to *all* children in the general education classroom.

States have been encouraged to develop seamless systems for providing services to children with delays and disabilities from birth through age eight. One consequence of this shift in government policy is that individualized family service plans (IFSPs) can be used to guide the delivery of services to preschoolers with disabilities as well as to infants and toddlers. This is a commendable effort at providing continuity and minimizing the disruption of services to young children with delays and disabilities and their families.

The IFSP is the driving force behind the delivery of services to infants and toddlers who are at risk for or have delays and disabilities. The IFSP acknowledges the child's family as the focal point of services. This focus is clearly evident in the required statement of the family's resources, priorities, and concerns. A well-developed IFSP encourages the parents' full and meaningful involvement while supporting their role as primary decision makers for their son or daughter.

An individualized education program, more commonly referred to as an IEP, is the vehicle that ensures that preschoolers and school-age students with delays and disabilities receive an individualized education appropriate to their unique needs. Written by a team, it is the basis for constructing a customized plan of instruction. At the heart of an IEP are well-written goals. An IEP is not developed solely for compliance purposes; rather, it is a dynamic document and the primary tool for providing a specially designed educational program.

Section 504 accommodation plans are frequently developed for students who have learning needs but are not eligible for a special education under IDEA. Developed by general educators, these plans are designed to ensure that these individuals have equal access to programs, services, and activities that are available to students without disabilities.

Movement or transitioning from one type of placement to another is an important element of early intervention and early childhood special education programs. Successful transitions are enabling experiences for both the child and the family. The intent is to provide continuity of services. Smooth transitions require comprehensive planning and collaboration in addition to ongoing communication among all parties involved. The preparation for transitioning must involve the child and their family as well as both current and new service providers.

KEY TERMS

Center- or school-based programs
Collaborative teaching
Cooperative teaching
Home-based services
Inclusion
Interdisciplinary team
Multidisciplinary team
Natural environments
Section 504
Section 504 accommodation plan
Transdisciplinary team

CHECK YOUR UNDERSTANDING

1. What are natural environments for young children with delays and disabilities from birth through age eight?
2. Describe the evolution of the movement toward inclusion.
3. Provide a rationale for inclusion in early intervention and early childhood special education. Provide support for your answer.
4. Identify some of the advantages and disadvantages of center-/school-based and home-based service delivery models.
5. What are the similarities and differences between multidisciplinary, interdisciplinary, and transdisciplinary team models?
6. Why is a transdisciplinary approach to providing services currently viewed as recommended practice?
7. Describe cooperative teaching. What are the advantages and disadvantages of this instructional option?
8. What is the rationale for using IFSPs for young children with delays and disabilities?
9. List the required components of an IFSP.
10. Identify at least five types of early intervention services available to infants/toddlers and their families.
11. What are the reasons for including families in the development of an IFSP?
12. What is the purpose of an IEP?
13. How does an IEP differ from an IFSP?
14. Describe the function of a Section 504 accommodation plan.
15. What roles do the child, parents, and service providers play in the transition process?
16. List five outcomes or goals of the transition process.

REFLECTION AND APPLICATION

1. Compare and contrast home-based and center- or school-based programs as appropriate service delivery models for young children with delays and disabilities. How can the quality of related support services be ensured in each model?
2. Examine each of the three teaming models discussed in this chapter. What is the role of the family in each model? How might the role of the family be strengthened in each model?

3. Visit early childhood facilities and public schools in your area that engage in collaborative teaching. What form of cooperative teaching did you observe? How do the teachers feel about this form of teaming? What do they see as the advantages and disadvantages of each approach?

4. Locate a preschooler with a disability who attends an inclusive center/school-based program. Talk to the child's teacher and family to determine what they see as the advantages and disadvantages of this setting. What do the parents desire for their child's future environment? Develop a transition plan that will effectively prepare them for this new placement.

PART

II

ASSESSMENT AND PLANNING FOR YOUNG CHILDREN WITH DELAYS AND DISABILITIES

© iStock.com/DGLimages

5 ASSESSMENT OF YOUNG CHILDREN WITH DELAYS AND DISABILITIES

LEARNING OBJECTIVES

After reading this chapter, you will be able to

5.1 Explain the primary objectives of assessment in early childhood special education for children from birth through age eight.

5.2 Describe recommended practices for conducting appropriate assessments of young children with delays and disabilities.

5.3 Describe four methods that can be used to collect assessment information for young children with delays and disabilities.

5.4 Differentiate between assessment for determining eligibility and assessment for individual program planning and implementation in early childhood special education.

5.5 Explain the importance of opportunities for family involvement and the emphasis placed on family preferences and priorities in the program planning and implementation process.

5.6 Explain the importance of progress monitoring and evaluation in programs serving young children with delays and disabilities and their families

EI/ECSE Professional Standards

The content of this chapter aligns with the following EI/ECSE Standard:

Standard 4. Assessment Processes

Candidates know and understand the purposes of assessment in relation to ethical and legal considerations. Scholars choose developmentally, linguistically, and culturally appropriate tools and methods that are responsive to the characteristics of the young child, family, and program. Using evidence-based practices, scholars develop or select as well as administer informal measures, and select and administer formal measures in partnership with families and other professionals. They analyze, interpret, document, and share assessment information using a strength-based approach with families and other professionals for eligibility determination, outcome/goal development, planning instruction and intervention, monitoring progress, and reporting.

DEC Recommended Practices

The contents of this chapter align with the following Division for Early Childhood (DEC) Recommended Practices:

Assessment

- A1. Practitioners work with the family to identify family preferences for assessment processes.
- A2. Practitioners work as a team with the family and other professionals to gather assessment information.
- A3. Practitioners use assessment materials and strategies that are appropriate for the child's age and level of development and accommodate the child's sensory, physical, communication, cultural, linguistic, social, and emotional characteristics.
- A4. Practitioners conduct assessments that include all areas of development and behavior to learn about the child's strengths, needs, preferences, and interests.
- A5. Practitioners conduct assessments in the child's dominant language and in additional languages if the child is learning more than one language.
- A6. Practitioners use a variety of methods, including observation and interviews, to gather assessment information from multiple sources, including the child's family and other significant individuals in the child's life.
- A7. Practitioners obtain information about the child's skills in daily activities, routines, and environments such as home, center, and community.

- A8. Practitioners use clinical reasoning in addition to assessment results to identify the child's current levels of functioning and to determine the child's eligibility.
- A9. Practitioners implement systematic ongoing assessment to identify learning targets, plan activities, and monitor the child's progress to revise instruction as needed.
- A10. Practitioners use assessment tools with sufficient sensitivity to detect child progress, especially for the child with significant support needs.
- A11. Practitioners report assessment results so that they are understandable and useful to families.

Authors' Note: As you read this chapter, you will find the EI/ECSE Standards and DEC Recommended Practices discussed throughout. See Appendix A for a complete list of the EI/ECSE Standards and Appendix B for a complete list of the DEC Recommended Practices.

The availability of a comprehensive assessment process for young children with delays and disabilities is an essential element of high-quality early intervention (EI) and early childhood special education (ECSE) services for children from birth through age eight. To apply recommended assessment practices, early childhood professionals must consider the purposes of assessment, guidelines for conducting appropriate assessments, and strategies for linking initial assessment with program planning, implementation, and progress monitoring (Pretti-Krontczak et al., 2023). In this chapter, we provide an overview of the objectives and characteristics of assessment in early childhood special education, discuss recommended assessment practices, and outline the processes used to conduct assessments for the purposes of screening, eligibility determination, program planning and implementation, and progress monitoring. These assessment processes are designed to meet the Individuals with Disabilities Education Act (IDEA) regulations, as well as provide children with optimal learning experiences.

OVERVIEW OF ASSESSMENT IN EARLY CHILDHOOD SPECIAL EDUCATION

First, we focus on the definition of assessment to appreciate the extensiveness of the entire assessment process. We note that *assessment* is a broad term, as illustrated in the definitions that follow. McLean et al. (2014) provided a simple definition explaining that assessment is the process of gathering information for decision making. This definition suggests that assessment is a dynamic, ongoing process allowing for various decisions to be made about children with delays and disabilities. This also indicates that assessment is a systematic, collaborative process for gaining information from a range of sources (e.g., observations, interviews, portfolios, assessment instruments) to be used in making decisions about each child's characteristics, needs, and progress, and whether professionals should alter intervention and instructional strategies (Pretti-Krontczak et al., 2023). The Division for Early Childhood (2014) emphasizes the importance of utilizing an array of ongoing methods to gather data from multiple sources, which includes the family and other significant individuals (e.g., child care providers), not only to identify and plan learning targets but also to monitor each child's improvement and revise instruction as needed [DEC Recommended Practices A6, A9]. McConnell and Rahn (2016) supported this dynamic view of assessment and defined assessment as "the systematic collection and evaluation of information to determine what if anything to do differently" (p. 90).

Assessment information is gathered in a variety of ways to determine and document the progress each child is making.

Next, the origin of the word *assessment* is considered, which can be traced to the Latin word *assidere* meaning "to sit beside." Assessment in early childhood special education is designed to be an experience through which professionals and families work together and exchange information to advance a child's growth, development, and learning (Division for Early Childhood, 2007, 2014). Therefore, assessment in early childhood should be *assidere* viewed as a fact-finding and problem-solving procedure shared by families and professionals.

Figure 5.1 illustrates the components of the assessment process in early childhood special education, which are examined in the sections that follow. Collaboration with families, multiple disciplines, and agencies is a recommended practice in the field of early intervention and early childhood special education, as well as required by federal legislation for young children with delays and disabilities (Bricker, Felimban et al., 2022). As can be seen in Figure 5.1., collaboration is necessary throughout each step of the assessment process.

FIGURE 5.1 ■ Components of a Collaborative Assessment Process in Early Childhood Special Education Leading to Goals and Outcomes

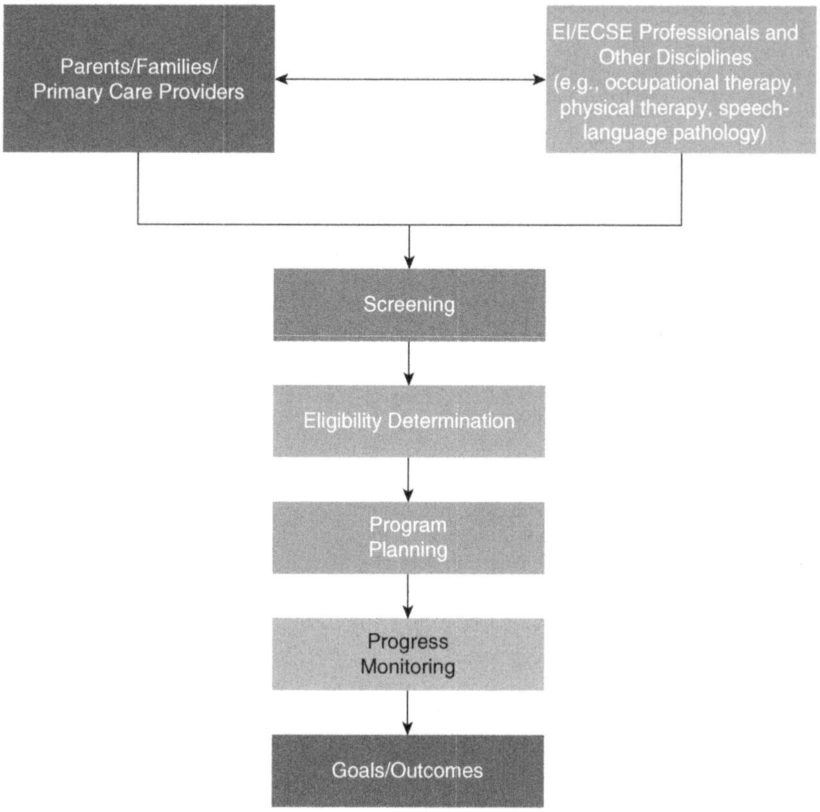

Source: Adapted from D. Bricker, *Assessment, Evaluation, and Programming System (AEPS®) for Infants and Children*, 2nd ed., Vol. 1 (Paul H. Brookes, 2002), p. 19.

Assessment Objectives in Early Childhood Special Education

According to EI/ECSE Standard 4. Assessment Processes, candidates must understand the purposes of assessment to make informed decisions and select appropriate tools and methods to meet the unique characteristics of each young child, family, and program. Assessment information is gathered to be used in making a decision in one or more of the following four areas:

1. Screening
2. Eligibility

3. Individual program planning and implementation
4. Progress monitoring and program evaluation

As noted by McCormick (1997), "assessment, planning, intervention, and evaluation are overlapping activities" (p. 223). Various forms of assessment may occur concurrently on different levels for various reasons. The different assessment objectives or purposes demand the use of assessment instruments and procedures by qualified professionals representing multiple disciplines (e.g., early childhood special educator, physical therapist, occupational therapist, psychometrist, speech-language pathologist).

Types of Assessment in Early Childhood Special Education

Because early childhood is a unique period of development, appropriate assessment instruments and procedures are designed specifically for young children. Typical assessment procedures in early childhood special education include norm-referenced tests, criterion- or curriculum-based instruments, observations, interviews, and other measures. Because there are many purposes of assessment, instruments designed for one purpose are in most cases inappropriate to use for a purpose other than that for which they were intended (Kritikos et al., 2012; McLean et al., 2014). The assessment instruments and procedures that are selected depend on several factors, such as the reason for the assessment, state and program guidelines, professional preferences, and family preferences. In addition to standardized tests, informal assessment measures are recommended that are less rigid and more precise to the context in which they are used. Table 5.1 provides example of assessment instruments and procedures frequently used in early childhood special education.

TABLE 5.1 ■ Assessment Instruments and Procedures in Early Childhood Special Education

Type	Description
Developmental Assessment	Assess children's developmental skills and abilities, such as cognitive, language, motor, and social-emotional development.
Diagnostic Test	Diagnose specific disabilities, delays, and conditions, such as autism, intellectual disabilities, or learning disabilities.
Achievement Test	Assess children's academic skills, such as reading, writing, and mathematics.
Behavioral and Emotional Assessment	Assess children's behaviors and emotions, including problem behaviors, emotional regulation, and social skills.
Adaptive Skills Assessment	Assess children's daily living skills, such as self-care, communication, and independence.
Functional Behavioral Assessment	Assess the specific behaviors that are impacting a child's functioning in the home or school environment.
Parent/Caregiver Report	Gather information from parents or caregivers about a child's development and behavior, including strengths and challenges.
Observation	Observe children in different settings, such as in the classroom or at home, to gather information about their behaviors, skills, and needs.

Assessment Instruments

Depending on the purpose of the assessment, specific types of tests are appropriate (Andersson, 2004; Kritikos et al., 2012). Assessment instruments are planning tools to learn from in order to determine the next steps. Of the assessment procedures used with young children, formal testing is the method most frequently used during the initial phases of assessment (e.g., screening, eligibility determination). During formal testing, standardized tests are administered; however, tests have many limitations. In fact, many professionals have advised against the overreliance on tests and describe them as predetermined collections of questions or tasks for which predetermined types of responses are sought to determine a score. In other words, a standardized test is one by which an individual child's performance, or a child's behavior that is demonstrated while putting specific skills into action, is interpreted in relation to the performance of a group of peers of the same age group who have previously taken the same test, or a "norming" group. We recognize that the behavior or performance of young children is inconstant; therefore, it is challenging to compare young children based on a single test.

Norm-referenced tests provide data about how a child is developing in relation to a larger group of children of the same age. They provide a score that is relative to the scores of other children in a particular group—that is, the source of the norms (Cohen & Spenciner, 2020). Norm-referenced measures have certain benefits; they compare young children to other children of the same age for eligibility purposes, report reliability and validity information, and usually can be overseen in a short period. A drawback of no-referenced assessment measures, particularly for children with delays and disabilities, is that the administration of norm-referenced tests usually takes place in unfamiliar settings (e.g., clinic, testing room) rather than the natural environment (e.g., home, classroom, playground, park). Another issue is the lack of useful evidence that norm-referenced tests provide for determining functional, appropriate results. Further, norm-referenced measures often are prejudiced against children with delays and disabilities and children from culturally or linguistically diverse backgrounds (Nagel et al., 2020). Bias is defined as any quality that unfairly discriminates against a child based on gender, socioeconomic status, or cultural or linguistic background (Losardo & Notari-Syverson, 2011).

Professionals and parents work collaboratively to gather assessment information.
iStock.com/PeopleImages

Norm-referenced tests for children from birth through age five result in quantitative scores, often reported as developmental age scores (e.g., the average age at which 50 percent of the normative sample achieved a particular raw score) and percentile ranks (e.g., the percentage of the same-aged population that performed at or below a given score). The developmental age for children with delays and disabilities usually will vary from their chronological age contingent on the effects of each child's delay or disability. For early primary–level students aged five through eight norm-referenced tests provide standard scores, percentile ranks, and grade-level equivalents in assorted subject areas (e.g., reading, math, science; Sattler, 2020). This permits early childhood special educators to compare a child's performance to performances of other children of a similar age.

Criterion-referenced assessments are used to regulate whether a child's performance meets conventional criteria or a certain level of mastery within various developmental domains (e.g., cognitive, motor, self-care) or subject areas (e.g., math, literacy). Numerical scores represent the proportion of the domain or subject area a child has mastered. Specific advantages of criterion-referenced instruments are that they offer a continuum of skills linked to the curriculum that can be beneficial for program planning and implementation and observing individual child progress. Criterion-referenced processes may be administered in the natural environment, and they allow professionals to adjust items so that children can demonstrate their skills and competence. Limitations of criterion-referenced instruments are that they are time consuming to administer and may include items that are inappropriate for some children. Criterion-referenced measures may be biased against children with delays and disabilities, as well as children representing culturally or linguistically diverse backgrounds.

Curriculum-based assessments are similar to criterion-referenced assessments; however, curriculum-referenced instruments are utilized to interpret a child's performance in regard to specific curriculum content. In most cases, curriculum-based assessment instruments are most pertinent for program planning and implementation purposes (Cohen & Spenciner, 2020; Sattler, 2020). They are used to classify a child's entry point in an educational program, as well as modify instruction.

Although a thorough description of the psychometric aspects of assessment instruments is beyond the scope of this chapter, it is imperative for these concepts to be understood by those who are responsible for the selection of certain assessment instruments for any phase of the assessment process. Reliability and validity are two of the psychometric concepts to be considered. Reliability refers to the consistency or dependability of an assessment instrument over time and across observers. In other words, does the test measure what it is supposed to measure in a dependable manner?

If T. J. were tested on two different occasions within a short time, would his performance and score on the test be similar each time? If so, the tester could assume with some confidence that the results were reliable or free of inaccuracy. Also, if two different examiners who independently tested T. J. should obtain similar test results, or if several children were given the same test and received different scores, the tester would want to know that the variability in the scores was due to the differences in their abilities. The examiner needs to feel confident that the test is consistently measuring what it is intended to measure. Reliability is important for generalizing about children's learning and development. Reliability is represented by a figure between .00 and 1.0, with values closer to 1.0 providing evidence of better reliability (Kritikos et al., 2012).

Observation of a child's performance during everyday learning activities provides valuable information during the assessment process.

Photofusion Picture Library/Alamy Stock Photo

Another important psychometric property of an assessment instrument is validity or the extent to which an assessment instrument measures what it was designed to measure. For example, if T. J. was given a test to measure his pragmatic language, the test items should represent a comprehensive range of pragmatic skills (e.g., turn-taking, greeting others, requesting). Validity is represented by a figure between .00 and 1.0, such that values closer to 1.0 indicate better validity. Several different types of validity should be of concern to early childhood special educators, as well as professionals representing other disciplines. The first is content validity, which refers to how well the test represents the content it purports to measure.

A second type of validity is instructional validity. This is the degree to which the information gained from an assessment instrument would be suitable in planning intervention programs for young children with delays and disabilities. A third type of validity, construct validity, focuses on the degree to which a test addresses the constructs on which it was based. A fourth type of test validity is concurrent validity. This type of validity is concerned with how well a test connects with other accepted measures of performance administered close in time to the first. Finally, predictive validity focuses on the extent to which a test relates to some future measure of performance. When early childhood professionals are choosing an assessment measure, attention should be focused on the reliability and validity information reported in the manuals of the assessment instruments (Sattler, 2020).

Authentic Assessment

Authentic assessment is based on the premise that the behavior of young children must be observed in natural settings during real-life situations. Authentic assessment is the systematic recording of developmental observations over time about the naturally occurring behaviors and functional competencies of young children in daily routines by familiar and knowledgeable caregivers in the child's life. It represents the process of observing, recording, collecting, and otherwise documenting what children do and how they do it for the purpose of making educational or intervention decisions. Authentic assessment is sometimes referred to as naturalistic, play-based, and performance-based assessment. Information can be gathered through a variety of processes and structured to provide a comprehensive overview of a child's performance on meaningful tasks in real-life situations over time (Cohen & Spenciner, 2020; Division for Early Childhood, 2007; Losardo & Notari-Syverson, 2011; Pretti-Frontczak et al., 2023). Authentic assessment is employed easily in home-based programs for infants and toddlers or inclusive classrooms for preschool and early primary children, as well as other natural environments.

Observational assessment is an example of the way in which authentic information can be gathered. Observational assessment is a process of gathering recordings of children's behavior in real-life situations and familiar settings. Assessment methods often include systematic observations of the interactions between children and their families, primary caregivers, or peers. Several different assessment instruments or strategies can be used to configure observations and measure information that is gathered such as checklists, rating scales, and structured observations (Division for Early Childhood, 2007, 2014) [DEC Recommended Practices A7].

Play-based assessment is an example of an observational procedure used frequently in early childhood education for infants, toddlers, and preschoolers. According to Losardo and Notari-Syverson (2011), "the context of play provides a comprehensive, integrated view of a child's interaction with people and objects within a meaningful context" (p. 80). During play, children spontaneously and genuinely display knowledge, skills, and behaviors. Play-based assessment offers a nonthreatening method to collect information about the level of progress of young children in a play situation, which allows them to demonstrate behaviors that they usually exhibit in natural settings.

An interview is an assessment technique in which questions are asked by the investigator to gain information from the interviewee. In early intervention and early childhood special education, interviews can be conversations among the assessor(s) and families or caregivers, teachers, siblings, or the child and are used to gather information about the areas on which to focus during the assessment process, specific information about the child (e.g., how a child responds to various situations), the family preferences or desires, daily routines, functional skills, or other types of information that may be relevant to the assessment process (McWilliam, 2010). Because interviews take place with a particular purpose in mind, it is important to have some structure to ensure that the intended goal(s) are accomplished. Although they may require some structure (e.g., preliminary preparation, introduction, inventory/questions, summary, closure), interviews should be adaptable enough for everyone to feel comfortable with the process (Turnbull et al., 2022).

Recent assessment trends suggest a need for an increased focus on the *process* of assessment rather than just the *product* with a greater emphasis on informal processes (Division for Early Childhood, 2014; Neisworth & Bagnato, 2005; Pretti-Krontczak et al., 2023). A recommended informal process is an **arena assessment**, which is based on a transdisciplinary model with professionals representing multiple disciplines along with the child's family participating in the assessment. Arena assessments have been reported as effective for use with infants, toddlers, and preschoolers and are frequently used by those serving these populations.

As you may recall from the previous chapters, transdisciplinary teams plan and provide services within and across discipline boundaries to provide services. Figure 5.2 illustrates how professionals from several disciplines participate in an arena assessment along with the child and family members, who frequently are seated in a circle around the child. The team jointly collects information about specific developmental areas, as well as the interrelatedness of these areas within the child. One or more of the team members and parent/family members interact(s) with the child while others observe, record information, and score test protocols. Using an arena assessment process, professionals from various disciplines with input from the family complete a complete and cohesive assessment report.

FIGURE 5.2 ■ Example of Arena Assessment Conducted With a Young Child

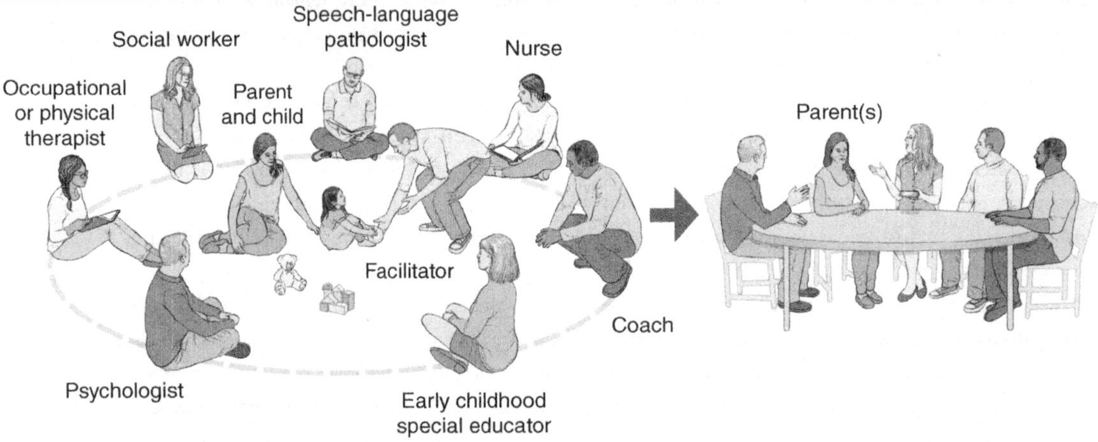

Source: Adapted from C. Garland, M. McGonigel, A. Frank, and D. Buck, The Transdisciplinary Model of Service Delivery, (Child Developmental Resources, 1989); and G. Woodruff and C. Hanson, Project KAI Training Packet. Unpublished manuscript. (Funded by the U.S. Department of Education, Office of Special Education Programs. Handicapped Children's Early Childhood Program, 1987).

GUIDELINES IN THE ASSESSMENT OF YOUNG CHILDREN WITH DELAYS AND DISABILITIES

Driven by many years of experience and research showing the limitations of traditional, single-dimensional assessment procedures, recommended practices have emerged (Division for Early Childhood, 2007, 2014; McConnell & Rahn, 2016; Neisworth & Bagnato, 2005). There is growing unanimity that assessment should be considered a process, not a single procedure. Most experts in the field of early childhood special education acknowledge that assessment is a process that involves systematic observation and analysis.

Because assessment in early childhood special education involves numerous disciplines, this necessitates a blending of assessment models and an understanding of different methods and terminology used by professionals representing various disciplines so that the information is useful to all members of the team. All assessment information must be compiled, including information from families, to make important decisions about the child's need for services, individually targeted skills, and methods to be used in providing support to the child and family (Kritikos et al., 2012). Table 5.2 displays the recommended assessment characteristics and processes examined throughout this chapter.

TABLE 5.2 ■ Examples of Assessment Characteristics in Early Childhood Special Education

Characteristics	Examples
Team-based	Assessments are conducted by a team, with equal status afforded to the family and professionals representing multiple disciplines.
Family-centered	Family is involved in all aspects of the assessment process based on each family's preferences.
Multidimensional	Assessment information is collected in a number of child domains and behaviors (as appropriate) to provide a holistic and comprehensive view of each child.
Multimethod	Assessment information is collected using a variety of formats and techniques, such as direct testing, observation, and interviews.
Multisource	Assessment information is collected from a several sources that are knowledgeable about the child, including families, caregivers, and professionals.
Multicontext	Assessment occurs in multiple environmental contexts, including the home, school, child care, or other relevant natural environments.
Culturally and linguistically appropriate	Assessment respects and is responsive to the unique cultural and linguistic background of each child and family.
Strength-based	Assessment procedures are designed to identify strengths, concerns, resources, needs, and priorities for intervention planning; emphasis is placed on assessing resources, strengths, and concerns, rather than deficits.
Ongoing and collaborative	The collection of assessment information is an ongoing, collaborative process among families and professionals representing multiple disciplines.

Recommended Assessment Practices and Standards

Practices and standards for the assessment of young children with delays and disabilities have been established through legislation, literature, and professional organizations such as the Division for Early Childhood (2007, 2014). The assessment of young children requires a careful subjective and objective appraisal of a child's performance in natural learning environments. Thus, professionals representing multiple disciplines, as well as the child's family, are involved in the assessment process to collect holistic, authentic information. Additionally, EI/ECSE Standard 4. Assessment Processes emphasizes that professionals analyze, interpret, document, and share assessment information using a strengths-based approach in all aspects of the assessment process.

Assessment is a process requiring a collaborative effort among families and professionals that occurs on an ongoing basis.

Angela Hampton Picture Library/Alamy Stock Photo

Team Process

As explained previously, the Individuals with Disabilities Education Improvement Act of 2004 requires a multidisciplinary team to be involved in the assessment of young children. A multidisciplinary team refers to the involvement of two or more professionals representing different disciplines in early childhood special education activities (e.g., early childhood special educators, physical and occupational therapists, speech–language pathologists; Kilgo & Aldridge, 2011). Transdisciplinary teams, the type of team model often used and suggested in early intervention and early childhood special education, are made up of family members and professionals representing a variety of disciplines who address specific assessment questions. For example, children with sensory impairments (e.g., auditory or visual) or children with developmental needs (e.g., communication delays, movement issues) necessitate professionals on the team to have expertise in those areas (e.g., vision specialist, speech–language pathologist, physical therapist, occupational therapist).

The DEC Recommended Practices (Division for Early Childhood, 2014) emphasize a team approach in which professionals work with family members and other team members from a range of disciplines throughout the assessment process. Families are encouraged to indicate their assessment preferences and be involved in gathering assessment information [DEC Recommended Practices A1, A2]. For example, members of the family may indicate the best time of day for the assessment to occur and how they would like to participate. Prior to a play-based assessment that is scheduled following the child's morning nap, the speech–language pathologist and early childhood special educator may work with the mother or other caregiver in determining the child's interests and favorite toys and routines. The mother or caregiver may elect to observe and assist as needed during the assessment.

Multiple Assessment Domains

The Division for Early Childhood (2014) recommends that the assessment of young children should cover all areas of development and behavior to gain a holistic and comprehensive estimate of their abilities, needs, and preferences [DEC Recommended Practices A4]. Further, the DEC indicates that early childhood assessment materials and strategies must be appropriate for infants and preschoolers, match their ages, and accommodate for their individual characteristics and developmental levels across all domains [DEC Recommended Practices A3]. This may be interpreted to mean that materials and activities should be carefully selected to match children's chronological age so that the materials and activities focused on during the assessment process are consistent with those of their peers without disabilities. However, this also means that the selected materials and strategies should meet the unique needs and abilities of each child.

Cultural Considerations

Young children who possibly will be eligible to receive early intervention or early childhood special education services are characterized by their diversity along many dimensions, including culture, ethnicity, language, geographic location, family structure, socioeconomic status, and others (Hanson & Espinosa, 2016; Lynch & Hanson, 2011). There are many possible issues related to cultural bias in assessment instruments and processes; thus, those administering assessments must try for accurate and suitable assessments of children from diverse backgrounds, which entails attention to each child's cultural background and experience.

Professionals have struggled for many years with how to use proper, impartial assessments of young children that do not punish them based on their cultural background or experience. A **culturally biased assessment** is one that measures only skills and abilities valued by the dominant Western culture. Thus, those children from nondominant or non-Western cultures are placed at a disadvantage. Problematic situations often exist when conventional, standardized assessment measures are used that are culturally biased. An example of likely bias can be found in a commonly used screening instrument that contains a test item that asks four- to six-year-old children to indicate "what a shoe is made of" with the acceptable response being "leather." A child whose familiarity with shoes is limited to tennis shoes, sandals, or flip-flops would not be given credit for providing the right answer if they responded "rubber," "cloth," or "plastic." This item would be missed due to the child's unfamiliarity with leather shoes and would suggest that items on this test are culturally biased for this child.

As we have emphasized, it is vital that the child's and family's cultural and linguistic backgrounds are considered in the assessment process to limit bias and foster communication and collaboration among the family and professionals (Division for Early Childhood, 2007; Lynch & Hanson, 2011). In designing the process, the team must use the most effective strategies for accumulating information centered on each child's and family's unique background, primary language(s), and cultural expectations (Hanson & Espinosa, 2016). The Division for Early Childhood (2014) recommends that assessments must be conducted in the child's dominant language with additional languages addressed as well if the child is acquiring other languages [DEC Recommended Practices A5]. Another consideration is that the child-rearing practices or patterns of adult-child interaction may be different in a child's culture, which may have a confounding influence in the assessment process.

Cook et al. (2020) recommended the following methods to accomplish a culturally impartial assessment: (a) use multiple assessment techniques within naturalistic settings, involving the families as significant partners in the process; (b) examine test items and materials to be certain they are not biased against children or families of various cultural backgrounds; (c) examine test manuals to determine whether the group to which the child is being compared is culturally compatible; (d) provide directions in the child's native language; and (e) use a transdisciplinary (or multidisciplinary) process so that multiple professionals, along with the family, can contribute. Lynch and Hanson (2011) proposed several practical ideas for aggregating information about young children from diverse cultural and linguistic backgrounds and offered specific suggestions for conducting observations of children and interviews with families.

Professionals must pay careful attention to the uniqueness of each child's background and experience to avoid cultural bias during the assessment process.

Zak Waters/Alamy Stock Photo

ASSESSMENT PURPOSES AND PROCESSES IN EARLY CHILDHOOD SPECIAL EDUCATION

The remaining section of this chapter is focused on specific purposes of each type of assessment in early intervention and early childhood special education. The types of assessment are discussed in the order of screening, eligibility, program planning and implementation, and progress monitoring and evaluation. Table 5.3 provides a definition of each type of assessment and displays the kind of information collected, the types of decisions made, and the time at which the information is gathered.

TABLE 5.3 ■ Description of the Types of Assessment in Early Childhood Special Education

Type of Assessment	Information Gathered	Decision(s) Usually Made	Occurs When
Screening			
A procedure designed to identify children in need of referral for more in-depth assessment.	Potential for developmental disability or delay; vision; hearing; health and physical disabilities.	Should the child be referred for more in-depth assessment?	Prior to entry into a program.
Eligibility			
A comprehensive diagnostic process to determine whether a child meets the criteria to be eligible for early intervention or early childhood special education services.	Comprehensive diagnostic information that is standardized, norm-referenced, and comparative.	Is the child eligible for services as specified in the state's criteria for eligibility (0–3, 3–5, K–3)?	Prior to entry into a program.
Individualized Program Planning and Implementation			
A procedure used to identify desired outcomes or goals for the IFSP or IEP and how to design instruction.	Evidence of the child's skills and behaviors; family preferences and priorities; family resources and strengths; settings in which the child spends time and the demands of those settings.	What routines, activities, materials, and equipment; style(s) of learning; and adult and peer interactions may work best?	Ongoing process; intensively at the beginning of a program year, during the first several weeks of entry in a program; during and immediately after any major changes in a child's life.
Progress Monitoring and Evaluation			
A process of collecting information about a child's progress toward outcomes, the family's satisfaction with services, and the program's effectiveness.	Evidence of the child's skills and behaviors compared to those skills at entry into the program; family satisfaction and indication of priorities having been met; the child's ability to be successful in the setting they spend time in.	Effectiveness of programming for an individual child or group of children; changes in a child's skill and behaviors; family's satisfaction; program's overall effectiveness	Ongoing basis to determine whether intervention is effective and outcomes have been achieved; at the end of a program year; or when determined by administrative policy and funding sources.

Source: Adapted from M. Davis, J. Kilgo, and M. McCormick. *Young Children with Special Needs: A Developmentally Appropriate Approach* (Pro-Ed, 1998), p. 73. Adapted with permission.

Assessment teams must consider the purpose of each assessment and gather initial information at the beginning of the process. The following are some general considerations, which will differ depending on the purpose of the assessment.

- What is the purpose of this assessment, or why is it being conducted (e.g., screening, eligibility, program planning and implementation, progress monitoring, program evaluation)?
- What are the characteristics of the child (e.g., age, physical abilities, communication skills, temperament, delay or disability)?
- Who will take the lead or coordinate the assessment (e.g., early childhood special educator, physical therapist, speech–language pathologist)?
- Where will the assessment sessions take place (e.g., home, child care program, classroom, playground)?
- Who will be involved in the assessment (e.g., parents, other family members, early childhood special educator, related service professionals), and what roles will these individuals assume (e.g., facilitator, observer, assessor)?
- When will the assessment sessions take place (e.g., in the morning, after child's nap)?
- How will the assessment be conducted (e.g., formal testing, observation, interview)?
- What areas of development or content will be assessed? Will all integrated developmental domains or content areas be the focus of the assessment?
- What assessment instrument(s) will be used (e.g., formal test, observational checklist, play-based measure, family interview)?
- How will the assessment area(s) be set up (e.g., amount of space needed, equipment or materials needed)?
- What skills or behaviors are important to the child's family, and what are the family's priorities (e.g., walking, talking, social skills, eating, toileting, literacy)?
- What skills or behaviors are important to the child in their environment (e.g., communicating, toileting, turn-taking, following directions)?
- What adaptations are necessary for the child to display optimal skills (e.g., use of an alternative communication system, adaptive seating, assistive technology)?

A plan can be devised regarding how the assessment process will be executed for each child and family according to the answers to these questions and the family's preferences. The assessment plan may address one or more purposes of assessment examined in the sections that follow.

Screening Young Children

Assessment information can be gathered to decide whether concealed problems require further assessment. The screening process originates immediately following birth. Routine examinations of infants serve as a means of foreseeing abnormalities. One of the first screenings experienced by infants and their families is the administration of the **Apgar Scale** (Apgar & James, 1962). Infants are screened at one-minute and five-minute intervals following their birth in the following areas: (a) heart rate, (b) respiration, (c) reflex response, (d) muscle tone, and (e) color (see Table 5.4).

For newborns, the five-minute Apgar has been an accurate predictor of future developmental progress (Batshaw et al., 2019). A low Apgar score may show that further medical assistance is needed or that a referral should be made for a more in-depth assessment. Blood and urine tests are additional routine procedures used to detect metabolic disorders, such as a **PKU screening** to detect phenylketonuria (PKU).

TABLE 5.4 ■ The Apgar Scale

			1 min.	5 min.
Heart rate	Absent	0		
	Less than 100	(1)		
	100 to 140	(2)	1	2
Respiratory effort	Apneic	(0)		
	Shallow, irregular	(1)		
	Lusty cry and breathing	(2)	1	2
Reflex response	No response	(0)		
	Grimace	(1)		
	Cough or sneeze	(2)	1	2
Muscle tone	Flaccid	(0)		
	Some flexion of extremities	(1)		
	Flexion resisting extension	(2)	1	2
Color	Pale blue	(0)		
	Body pink, extremities blue	(1)		
	Pink all over	(2)	0	1
		TOTAL	4	9

Through early identification of PKU and appropriate intervention, which includes a restricted diet, many of the unfavorable outcomes associated with PKU, such as intellectual disability, can be avoided.

In early childhood special education, screening is an assessment procedure intended to decide, from within a large population of children, those who need to be referred for further assessment in one or more areas of development (Losardo & Notari-Syverson, 2011). Referrals for screenings usually are made by professionals from various disciplines who encounter young children whom they suspect have delays and disabilities.

IDEA requires active identification, evaluation, and eligibility determination for both Part C (0-3) and Part B of the law. Part B mandates that school districts must identify and evaluate all children with delays and disabilities aged three to twenty-one. The regulation draws specific attention to children with disabilities in traditionally marginalized groups. Part C requires a "comprehensive child find system." Part C is required to be consistent with Part B but also to include in its child find efforts all other major primary referral sources (i.e., hospitals, physicians, parents, social services, LEA, schools). Public awareness is a part of the Part C child find procedures.

According to this federal legislation, each state must establish a Child Find system of locating children who may have delays and disabilities, which makes them eligible for early childhood special education services. Child Find necessitates community and interagency teamwork with professionals from a variety of disciplines and agencies (e.g., Head Start, education, social services, public health) working together through this process. Child Find teams are responsible for directing public awareness campaigns to notify the community so that referrals for screening will be made. Advertisements often are disseminated through the local media, grocery stores, shopping malls, or other places frequented by families of young children. Professionals who often make referrals are from high-risk nurseries, health clinics, pediatricians' offices, community programs, or schools. Because of extensive Child Find efforts, families, other caregivers, and members of the community also make referrals (IDEA Child Find Project, 2004).

Screenings can be accomplished by using a variety of procedures, including specific instruments or checklists, observations of the child, and parent/family interviews. Screening involves a brief analysis to determine whether a child's skills are satisfactory or whether there are inconsistencies from typical expectations that demand further assessment. A screening procedure may last anywhere from five to fifteen minutes. Although the Child Find process varies from state to state, many states offer screenings for preschoolers before entering kindergarten. In some states, screening is compulsory before children enter kindergarten. The purpose is to identify children with potential developmental, vision, and/or hearing concerns, and so on. As stated earlier, the outcomes of screening establish whether children have the potential for a developmental delay or disability and should be referred for a comprehensive evaluation to determine whether they are eligible for services (IDEA Child Find Project, 2004).

A screening instrument should be chosen based on specific criteria. Accuracy, for example, is imperative for several reasons. Some children who need services may be overlooked and are, therefore, not referred if a screening instrument is not accurate. Sometimes children who do not need services are referred for further assessment, and, thus, over-referral also is a problem when a tool is not accurate. A screening instrument's rate of under- and over-referral is linked to its sensitivity and specificity. Table 5.5 contains sample instruments that are often utilized for screening purposes.

Sensitivity refers to a screening instrument's ability to identify children who need additional assessment. The less sensitive a screening instrument is, the greater the number of under-referrals or false negatives there will be from the results (see Table 5.6). A false negative designates a child who needs special services but was not referred because of the screening. Specificity denotes the capacity of a screening procedure to correctly rule out children who should not be classified.

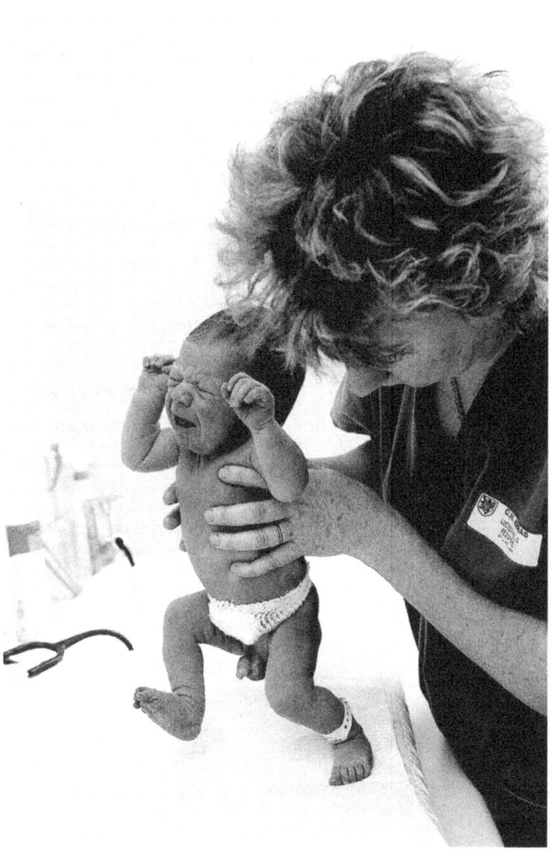

The screening process begins immediately after birth through examinations of newborns, using such measures as the Apgar Scale.

BSIP/UIG/via Getty Images

TABLE 5.5 ■ Selected Screening Instruments Used in Early Childhood Special Education

Instrument	Age Range	Domains/Content Areas	Publisher
Ages and Stages Questionnaires, 3rd ed. (ASQ-3)	1–66 months	Communication, gross motor, fine motor, problem-solving, personal-social	Paul H. Brookes
Battelle Developmental Inventory, 3rd ed. (BDI-3)	Birth–7 years, 11 months	Personal, social, adaptive, motor, communication, cognition	Riverside Publishing Company
Developmental Indicators for the Assessment of Learning, 4th ed. (DIAL-4)	2–6 years	Motor concepts, language, behavioral	Pearson Education
Denver Developmental Screening Test, 2nd ed. (DDST-II)	Birth–6 years	Personal-social, fine motor, adaptive, language, gross motor	Denver Developmental Materials Inc.
Brigance Early Childhood Screens III	0–3 years, 3–5 years, Grades K–1	Physical, language, academic/cognitive, self-help, social-emotional skills	Curriculum Associates

TABLE 5.6 ■ Potential Outcomes for Screening

	Referred for Evaluation	Not Referred for Evaluation
Eligible for special services	Sensitivity (accurate referral)	False negative (under-referral)
Not eligible for special services	False positive (over-referral)	Specificity (accurate nonreferral)

In other words, a test that is precise will not refer children who do not need further assessment. Losses in specificity result in more over-referrals or false positives. A **false positive** designates a child who has been referred because of the screening but does not need special services. The levels of sensitivity and specificity measure the screening instrument's validity, which tells us the magnitude to which a test measures what it intends to measure. Great precaution should be taken when selecting screening instruments to guarantee that they are indeed valid and accurate. When an instrument is accurate, the likelihood of inappropriate referrals is reduced.

The simplicity of a screening instrument is another important criterion. The administration and scoring of instruments should be quick, easy, systematic, and usable by professionals from numerous disciplines. Ideally, a screening instrument should be economical to administer yet still be accurate. Another vital criterion of a screening instrument is that it should be comprehensive, focusing on several areas (e.g., educational, health, behavioral, and environmental concerns). However, it is vital that some assessment instruments are designed to look precisely at one area, such as language.

Another criterion is that screening assessment instruments should incorporate family feedback and contribution. Because of the wide range and variations in standard development and behavior during the early years, the screening process for infants and young children is often challenging. Parent involvement can relieve some of these challenges. Most screening instruments include observations, parent/family reports, or some combination of the two. A comprehensive screening process includes the accumulation of information about a wide scope of children's abilities, and, of course, parents/families have the most extensive information. A technique that has been used to collect information is a parent-completed screening questionnaire. Although parent-completed questionnaires offer essential developmental information, not all parents are willing or able to complete independent questionnaires. This is determined after evaluating each family's desire and ability, which may vary over time. See the accompanying Making Connections feature for an example of how T. J.'s mother progressively became more at ease with participation in the assessment process.

MAKING CONNECTIONS

T. J.'S MOTHER AND THE ASSESSMENT PROCESS

T. J.'s mother was initially hesitant to participate in the assessment process by completing questionnaires and answering all the questions about T. J.'s development. It was not because she didn't care about T. J.—that was not the case at all. She simply did not comprehend the usefulness of this information and how imperative her role was in the assessment process. Although she was unwilling at first to have T. J. participate in the screening and for him to be referred for a comprehensive assessment, she soon developed a relationship with the service providers, learned to trust them, and became more involved as a member of the team during the assessment process and beyond. As described in Chapter 3, trust is a vital part of the development of strong and successful parent–professional relationships.

DETERMINING ELIGIBILITY FOR EARLY CHILDHOOD SPECIAL EDUCATION SERVICES

After it is determined during the screening process that a young child needs additional screening, a thorough **eligibility** assessment ensues to determine whether infants, toddlers, preschoolers, and early primary-aged children do, in fact, meet the eligibility requirements for early intervention or early childhood special education services. This phase of the process is directed by a team of professionals representing multiple disciplines (e.g., special education, speech–language pathology, physical therapy, and others as determined by the individual characteristics of each child). A battery of assessment instruments verifies whether a child meets the eligibility criteria according to state and federal requirements of the Individuals with Disabilities Education Improvement Act of 2004.

Eligibility Criteria

Over the past several years, there have been discussions regarding eligibility criteria and categories for infants and toddlers, preschoolers, and early primary-level children with delays and disabilities to receive early intervention and special education services. Recall from Chapter 2, according to federal legislation, each state controls the eligibility criteria for infants and toddlers. The Division for Early Childhood (2014) encourages professionals to supplement assessment results with clinical reasoning in determining a child's functioning levels and eligibility for services [DEC Recommended Practices A8], which can help integrate the results of evaluations and direct observations in various settings. **Informed clinical opinion** refers to the use of professional judgment, based on experience and expertise, and family input to make recommendations for initial and continuing eligibility for EI/ECSE services and to plan services for those children whose developmental status and EI/ECSE needs may be difficult to assess with formal measures (Shackelford, 2022).

Through IDEA 1991, each state was offered the option of using a developmental delay eligibility category for preschoolers. In the absence of an identified disability, children can be determined to be eligible for receiving services based on the eligibility criteria determined within their state (e.g., 25 percent delay in one or more developmental domains). This decision obviously depends on state and local eligibility criteria that specify precisely how eligibility is determined in a certain program.

For early primary–level children, IDEA 1997 permitted the developmental delay eligibility category to be extended to age nine if states desire. However, states and localities still are obligated by IDEA and its amendments to cultivate definitions of developmental delay thoughtfully, so that the result will be eligibility procedures that are based on knowledge of young children with delays and disabilities and will guarantee appropriate services for them and their families. Children within the three- to nine-year-old age range may also qualify for special education services by meeting the criteria for an IDEA disability category, such as visual impairment, hearing impairment, or autism. This process was expounded upon in greater detail in Chapter 2.

Eligibility Procedures and Instruments

To decide whether young children meet the eligibility guidelines for early intervention or early childhood special education services, procedures must be utilized to determine whether a child's skills are significantly different from the skills of a large group of children whose development falls within the typical range. This determination traditionally has been made by comparing a child's performance to the anticipated performance of children of the same age; thus, the assessment instruments are managed in a specific way. For example, the same materials, directions, and scoring procedures are utilized each time a tool is administered. Although norm-referenced assessment instruments typically have been required as the primary means for decisions on eligibility, many leaders in the field of early childhood special education have proposed the use of curriculum-based measures for eligibility reasons (Bagnato, 2005; McLean, 2005). As stated previously, recommended practice recommends that no major decision about a child's eligibility should be made based *solely* on the results of a single test. Decisions regarding eligibility should be based on multiple assessment methods and processes.

A sample of the numerous instruments used for eligibility determination is included in Table 5.7. Many other instruments are available, depending on the age of the child, that allow professionals to evaluate strengths and needs in specific developmental domains (e.g., communication, social) and content areas (e.g., language literacy, mathematics). What these instruments have in common is that they all measure a child's skills and development as compared to those of a norm group of children who have previously been given the test. If a child's test scores fall significantly below the scores of the children in the norm group, the child may have a developmental delay or disability and be qualified for early childhood special education services.

The team of professionals and family should work together to determine a child's eligibility for services by reviewing the health and medical history, determining current level of functioning in major development areas, and assessing unique strengths and needs. Observations and other assessment procedures should be used to authenticate the findings from the assessment instruments. By collecting supplementary information from the child's family and other caregivers and observing the child's behavior in natural settings, examiners can make an informed decision about the presence of a developmental delay or disability and need for services.

TABLE 5.7 ■ Select Assessment Instruments for Determining the Developmental Status of Young Children

Name of Instrument	Age Range Addressed	Domains or Content Areas	Results
Battelle Developmental Inventory (3rd ed.), Riverside Publishing Company (BDI-3)	Birth–7 years, 11 months	Personal-social, adaptive, motor, communication, cognitive ability	Developmental levels in each domain
Bayley Scales of Infant Development (4th ed.), Pearson Assessment (Bayley-4)	16 days–42 months	Cognitive, language, motor, social-emotional, adaptive	Standardized scores for mental and motor development; descriptions of social-emotional and adaptive behavior
Carolina Curriculum for Infants and Toddlers With Special Needs (3rd ed.), Paul H. Brookes (CCITSN-3)	Birth–36 months	Personal-social, cognition, cognition-communication, communication, fine motor, gross motor	Status in each curriculum domain
Carolina Curriculum for Preschoolers With Special Needs (3rd ed.), Paul H. Brookes (CCPSN-3)	2–5 years	Personal-social, cognition, cognition-communication, communication, fine motor, gross motor	Status in each curriculum domain
Developmental Assessment of Young Children (2nd ed.), PRO-ED (DAYC-2)	Birth–5 years, 11 months	Cognition, communication, social-emotional development, adaptive behavior, physical development	Standard scores, percentile ranks, and age equivalents in each curriculum domain; general development quotient (GDQ)
Hawaii Early Learning Profile Strands (Birth to age 3 years), VORT Corporation	Birth–36 months	Regulatory/sensory, cognitive, language, gross motor, fine motor, social-emotional, self-help	Developmental age levels in each domain
Hawaii Early Learning Profile (2nd ed.), VORT Corporation (HELP 3–6)	3–6 years	Cognitive, language, gross motor, fine motor, social-emotional, self-help	Developmental age levels in each domain
Learning Accomplishment Profile-Diagnostic (3rd ed.), Kaplan Early Learning Company (LAP-D 3)	30–72 months	Fine motor, gross motor, cognition, language	Child's skill level in comparison to normative scores

Source: Adapted from J. Taylor, J. McGowan, and T. Linder, *The Program Administrator's Guide to Early Childhood Special Education: Leadership Development and Supervision* (Paul H. Brookes, 2009), p. 74.

Parents and other family members can add valuable information to the eligibility decision by participating in the assessment process in a variety of ways. Families can provide information informally through discussions with team members; they can complete questionnaires, checklists, or parent reports; and/or they can be present with their child during the assessment. Often, they can provide valued feedback on the skills or behaviors the child is displaying (e.g., whether this is a typical behavior, what other skills or abilities the child has demonstrated, and other supplemental information). (Steed et al., 2023).

Early childhood professionals are encouraged to be sensitive to families when discussing eligibility assessment information. Using a two-step process when initially informing families that a child requires early intervention or early childhood special education services is recommended. After sharing diagnostic, assessment, eligibility, or other information, professionals should give families time to comprehend and absorb the information. Family concerns must be dealt with prior to proceeding with matters such as intervention recommendations. These issues can be addressed in follow-up meetings according to the family's readiness.

Following are suggestions developed by Cohen and Spenciner (2020) for professionals sharing eligibility information with families:

- Provide family members with an opportunity to receive the assessment report in a one-to-one setting rather than during a large team meeting (e.g., parent–teacher meeting), which allows the family time to ask questions and reflect on the information prior to the larger, full-staff meeting.
- Be honest and straightforward regarding the delay or disability and eligibility for services.
- Be sensitive to families if they are not ready to hear details.
- Allow time for families to express their feelings.
- Be willing to say when you do not know the answer to questions.
- Offer to provide additional information and suggest additional resources.
- Be available to the family for further discussions.
- Of course, arrange to have a native-language interpreter available if families need assistance.

If a child meets the eligibility criteria and is determined eligible to receive early childhood special education services, the subsequent step in the process is conducting assessments for program planning and implementation.

ASSESSMENT FOR INDIVIDUAL PROGRAM PLANNING AND IMPLEMENTATION

The initial assessment procedures used to determine eligibility are distinctly different from the assessment procedures necessary for individual program planning and implementation. To plan effective, successful programs for young children with delays and disabilities, appropriate **program planning and implementation assessment** is required. The DEC Recommended Practices emphasize that early childhood special educators should work with the family in the assessment process, including gathering assessment information; identifying the child's strengths, needs, preferences, and interests; and communicating information that is understandable and respects cultural identity. A well-planned and ongoing process is needed that centers on the children's individual skill levels, strengths, needs, backgrounds, experiences, and interests, as well as the family's preferences and priorities. Ongoing assessment provides the foundation for constructing and maintaining personalized programs for young children with delays and disabilities. Table 5.8 displays the major differences in assessment for eligibility and assessment for individual program planning and implementation purposes

TABLE 5.8 ■ Comparison of Assessment for Eligibility and Program Planning in Early Childhood Special Education

Assessment for Eligibility	Assessment for Program Planning and Implementation
Compares a single child to a large group of children.	Identifies the child's current levels of developmental skills, behaviors, and knowledge.
Uses instruments, observations, and checklists with predetermined items or skills.	Determines the skills and behaviors necessary for a child to function in the settings where they spend time.
Determines whether a child's skills or behaviors fall below a specified cutoff level.	Determines the skills, behaviors, or knowledge that the child's family and primary caregivers have set as priorities for the child to learn.
Designed to differentiate children from one another.	Designed to determine the individual child's strengths, interests, and learning style.
Assessment instrument items do not necessarily have significance in the everyday lives of young children.	Assessment instrument items are usually criterion-based or curriculum-based or focus on functional skills that have importance in the everyday lives of young children.

Source: Adapted from M. Davis, J. Kilgo, and M. McCormick, *Young Children with Special Needs: A Developmentally Appropriate Approach* (PRO-ED, 1998), p. 81. Adapted with permission.

Of critical importance is the linkage between assessment and curriculum to ensure that program content is meeting the needs of all children and the concerns of their families (Neisworth & Bagnato, 2005). As described previously, in recent years, formal assessments have been found to be unsuitable for program planning and implementation, which has caused a shift away from the use of formal assessment measures toward the use of informal means of assessment (e.g., curriculum- or criterion-based instruments, observations, family reports, and play-based measures) with young children. These approaches are examined later in this chapter. Assessment procedures that are suitable for determining a child's eligibility for services (e.g., standardized, norm-referenced instruments) should not be used in isolation and should not be relied upon to plan instruction or interventions for young children with delays and disabilities (Bagnato, 2007; McLean, 2005; Neisworth & Bagnato, 2005).

To accurately assess the child's strengths and needs, assessment for individual program planning and implementation should concentrate on the whole child within the setting of the natural environment (e.g., home, child care, preschool, or school settings). Gathering information of this kind is vital to planning individualized programs and arranging appropriate interventions and supports for young children with delays and disabilities and their families.

Collecting Information for Individual Program Planning and Implementation

The purpose of assessment for program planning and implementation is to respond to several questions associated with each child's abilities, the desired child and family goals/outcomes, the types of services to be afforded, and the intervention strategies to be implemented. Assessment information is used not only to plan individualized instruction, but also to alter the instruction a child is receiving. Decisions must be made to establish (a) what to teach, (b) how to teach it, and (c) what expectations are realistic for each child.

Early childhood special educators utilize recommended practices for conducting assessments to be used in program planning and implementation by doing the following:

- Select assessment instruments and processes that are individualized and appropriate for each child and family
- Report assessment results in a manner that is both useful for planning program goals/outcomes and understandable and useful for families [DEC Recommended Practices A11]
- Rely on processes that capture the child's authentic behaviors in routine circumstances within the natural environment [DEC Recommended Practices A7]

Assessment information amassed for program planning and implementation purposes is used to foster an individualized family service plan (IFSP) or individualized education program (IEP) for each child and family. Recall from Chapter 2 that the IFSP and IEP are envisioned to be planning documents used to shape and influence the day-to-day provision of services to young children with developmental delays and disabilities. The IFSP is necessary for the provision of early intervention services for eligible infants and toddlers from birth to age three and their families. The IEP is used for special education services supplied to eligible children ages three and older. IFSPs and IEPs contain personalized outcomes or goals that can be determined by appraising the skills required for the child to participate in a variety of natural environments as just explained. This process allows information to be collected that has relevance to each child and family. When this method is utilized, the IFSP or IEP should be developed according to the family's routines (e.g., at home, at school, and in other environments) and priorities. Thus, outcomes and goals outlined in the IFSP or IEP should be developed to reflect the necessary skills the child will need to participate in natural environments and routines within those environments (Noonan & McCormick, 2014).

When managing assessments for program planning, the following five objectives should be accomplished for each child and family:

1. The identification of appropriate outcomes or goals
2. The identification of unique styles, strengths, and interests

3. The identification of parents' priorities and outcomes or goals

4. The development of a shared and integrated perspective among practitioners and family members regarding the child's and family's strengths, needs, and resources

5. The creation of a shared commitment to collaboratively establish and carry out activities to meet outcomes or goals

While accomplishing these objectives, the team members should be provided with the information necessary to make program planning and implementation decisions related to activities and strategies to meet the distinctive outcomes and goals of individual children and families.

Family Involvement in the Assessment Process

As emphasized throughout this chapter, parents and other family members can supply a plethora of information about the child, as well as information about the family, and this necessitates parent-professional collaboration (Hendricks & McCracken, 2009; Slade et al., 2018). Although addressing family concerns, priorities, and resources is not a novel concept in early intervention for children from birth to three years old, it has earned increased attention in recent years due to the importance of IFSPs for families with infants and toddlers and an greater emphasis on family-centered practices in all facets of services for preschoolers and early primary-level students with delays and disabilities. Thus, it is most imperative for family members to be encouraged to become operating members of their child's assessment team. If family members are ready and able to play an active role in the assessment process, their involvement will ensure the legitimacy of the established outcomes and goals.

To help ensure that the family has input into the evaluation, an "outcome-driven" assessment process is needed. By focusing on family-identified outcomes for the child as the starting point of the assessment, the family's vision for the child becomes the fundamental focus of the evaluation process (Turnbull et al., 2022). At what level does the family hope to see the child functioning in their skills and abilities (e.g., in the next six months, year, three years)? What are the family's priorities? For example, one family's top priority was for the child to communicate and feed herself, while another family wanted the child to be toilet trained and develop friendships with peers. Another family's top concerns were for their child to read and use assistive technology to communicate. Another question is what settings in which the family would like the child to participate. For example, does the family want the child to be in an inclusive kindergarten program? Family-identified outcomes are vital to determine as part of the assessment process.

An effective early childhood special educator recognizes the uniqueness of each family and realizes the importance of families having chances to provide feedback during the assessment process and serving as essential members of the team. Assessment information should be collected from families on an ongoing basis, should be an integral part of the planning process, and should be a collaborative effort; therefore, it is necessary for families to develop trust and be sure that the assessment process will maintain privacy and discretion.

A family-centered approach suggests that families participate in the assessment process at the level that is comfortable for them. Regardless of the degree to which the family members choose to participate in the assessment process, the way they contribute, or the format in which they offer information, family members' participation, and the information they offer serves an instrumental purpose in program planning (Slade et al., 2018). Turnbull et al. (2022) emphasized that families should be offered options for the way they participate in the assessment process. Families can provide input in areas such as the following:

- Collaborate with professionals in planning the assessment process (e.g., where, when, and how it will take place, who will be involved)
- Determine to what extent they want to be a part of the assessment process
- Provide information about their children's developmental history, play and interaction preferences, interests, and daily routines and schedule

- Provide information about the settings where their children spend time and the demands placed upon their children in those settings
- Report on their children's current skills, where and how those skills are used by the children, and under what circumstances the skills are exhibited
- Report on their children's strengths, abilities, and needs in multiple settings
- Share information about their children that will not be gained through traditional measures
- Share their priorities, resources, and concerns
- Share their vision for their children's future

Gathering information from families about their concerns, priorities, and resources is an important component of the assessment process. Information can be collected from families in several different ways—through interviews, observational methods, parent reports, instruments, and other measures—to determine their need for support, information, education, services, and so forth. Conversation, rather than formal family interviews, is recommended. Each family's preferences must be taken into consideration before information is collected. Some families may prefer to offer information in writing, such as a family needs survey or checklist. However, in most instances, informal assessment instruments and processes are preferable for most families.

Information is collected about children's individual strengths and needs in major developmental areas to determine their eligibility for services.

iStock.com/SDI Productions

Along with the various instruments available to recognize family concerns, priorities, and resources, some early childhood special education programs have established their own measures. Irrespective of the measures used, families should be encouraged to point out their concerns and resources and establish their priorities for their children and the family as a whole. Professionals should recognize that the range of concerns families may have is significant. Families of young children with delays and disabilities often feel overwhelmed and unsure of where to begin. Professionals can supply information to help them communicate their concerns and make judgements about their priorities. It is probable, however, that their concerns and priorities will adjust over time. Examples of potential family concerns include how their children's medical needs can be met or how their children will be treated when they begin preschool. Family priorities, for example, might be how to be educated more about the child's delay or disability or how to communicate effectively with the child. Family resources might include consistent transportation, relatives who live nearby, and community support. Examples of how this information is integrated into an IFSP can be seen in Appendix D.

Assessment in the Natural Environment

For assessment information to be practical, emphasis must be placed on the context in which children develop and the sway of the environment on skill attainment. It is essential that the environment(s) in which a child functions and the skills needed to be thriving in those environments are considered during the assessment process (Vanderheyden, 2005). Thus, assessments in the natural environment supply chances for children to utilize skills across multiple areas of development within the context of routines in the natural environment (e.g., home, center, community) [DEC Recommended Practices A7].

The burdens placed upon children by the circumstantial aspects of the natural environment can have a tremendous effect on their development and the skills or behaviors they display. For example, if T. J. lives in a neighborhood in which all the children learn to ride bicycles at an early age, then he may be enthused to learn to ride his bike at a young age as well. Or if a family lives in a warm environment and goes to the beach or pool on a frequent basis as a family activity, then the children may be likely to learn to swim or participate in water sports at an early age.

A naturalistic assessment evaluates the skills needed by a child to participate in their natural environment during the day. The specific natural environment, expectations, and levels of participation are defined by the child, the family and other primary caregivers, the community, and the family's culture. This kind of assessment is distinctly different from the kind of traditional child assessment in which the child's skills are observed and noted. McCormick (1997) explained the naturalistic assessment process, stressing that functional goals and objectives are to originate within the natural environment with a twofold purpose of this process:

1. To generate information about the social, educational, and functional activities and routines in natural environments where the child is to be an active and successful participant
2. To determine the resources and supports needed for the child to participate in and receive maximum benefits from activities and routines in the environments (p. 237)

The product of a naturalistic assessment provides more than the skill level at which a child is functioning; it provides a comprehensive understanding of the context and environmental expectations that are imperative for the child. For example, when a naturalistic assessment occurs for T. J. at a Head Start center, the observer notices that there are several times when the children are required to make transitions from one activity to another during the morning routine. Based on this observation, the team determined that these transitions are important requirements in the environment in which T. J. will be participating. With this information, the team conducting the assessment will know to focus on T. J.'s ability to make transitions like the ones that happen in his early childhood program.

The contexts, conditions, and expectations evaluated by naturalistic assessments help the team members in identifying the specific skills that should be examined during the assessment process. Furthermore, the assessment in the natural environment enables the assessment team to identify the skills vital to the child's success in their current settings. In other words, the result of the ecological assessment is a protocol, or assessment format, that can be utilized to decide the skill areas on which to concentrate and the specific skills to be observed during the assessment.

A naturalistic assessment views the family members and other primary caregivers as critical contributors to the assessment process. Family members and caregivers are comprised of parents, siblings, grandparents, child care providers, or other significant people in a child's life, such as neighbors. These individuals, in addition to teachers and other professionals, will determine which of the child's skills are important to focus on during the assessment. Conducting assessments of children within their natural environments requires

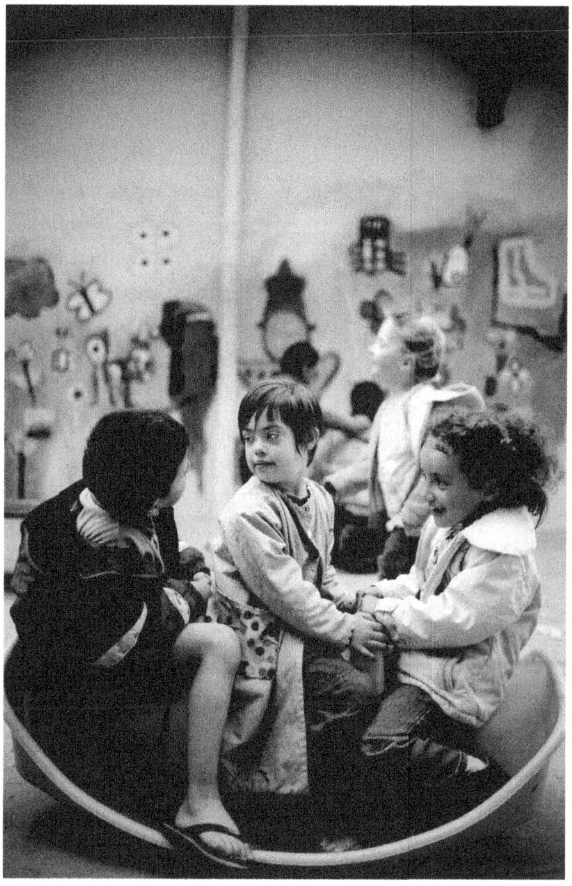

To get an accurate idea of a child's typically occurring behavior and abilities, assessment information should be collected in natural environments.

BSIP SA/Alamy Stock Photo

a step-by-step approach. By evaluating the environments in which children live and the expectations related to those surroundings, the skills to be focused upon can be better determined. Program planning and implementation can logically grow from the assessment information that is collected.

To determine whether a child has a **functional skill**, the assessment information should be gathered in the natural environment(s) where they use the skill. A functional skill is a basic skill that is required on an everyday basis (e.g., eating, toileting, requesting assistance, turn-taking) in the natural environment. If eating independently during mealtime is an important skill for a child to obtain, the assessment team will know to conduct some portion of the assessment during a meal, either at home, at school, or in another setting. An assessment in the natural environment results in a more precise and useful child assessment. The assessment team will recognize the skills to emphasize, the materials or activities the child favors, and the setting(s) in which to conduct the assessment. The results of a thorough assessment in the natural environment serve as a guide for the program planning and implementation phase of the assessment procedure.

Another type of assessment that is used to investigate the environmental variables contributing to and/or maintaining a challenging behavior is a **functional behavioral assessment**. This involves systematically identifying the challenging behavior, the events that precede this behavior (antecedents), and the events that maintain the behavior (consequences). This information is then used to identify, plan, implement, and support others to implement individual behavior support plans (Dunlap & Fox, 2011).

Methods and Procedures for Collecting Information

The DEC Recommended Practices (Division for Early Childhood, 2014) provide evidence-based standards to address and the methods and procedures to use when collecting useful assessment information for individual planning. The whole child should be the focus when planning programs for young children with delays and disabilities rather than segmenting students' abilities in the various developmental or content areas. In Maria's case, for example, she has a diagnosis of Down syndrome with delays in several developmental domains (e.g., communication, self-care, cognitive skills). To meet her multiple needs, program planning and implementation assessment should be holistic and speak to all areas of development, which are coordinated to accomplish most tasks.

Another recommended assessment practice suggested by Neisworth and Bagnato (2005) is that the assessment team should utilize only those measures that have high treatment validity (e.g., link assessment, individual program planning and implementation, progress evaluation). To certify that the entire process is connected, the selection of appropriate instruments and measures is of vital importance. Criterion- or curriculum-based instruments are recommended to establish a connection between assessments for program planning, implementation, and progress monitoring.

As explained previously, a criterion-based assessment instrument is one in which a child's response(s) is compared to a predetermined criterion or level of performance in an area of knowledge or skill, rather than to the response(s) of a group of children or normative group. Results are typically reported as levels of proficiency, such as an emerging skill or mastery of a skill. The criteria used to determine whether a child has obtained a skill often are flexible ones that can have distinctive interpretations for different settings. On curriculum-based measures, each assessment item coincides directly to a specific educational objective in the program's curriculum. Curriculum- and criterion-based measures provide a level of adaptability that is not available with standardized, norm-referenced instruments. Because the skills being assessed are within a natural context, represent certain skills that have been determined by the child's family and other team members to be valuable to their development, and are generally in a developmental sequence, they often can be very beneficial in program planning and implementation. On a cautionary note, it is essential to remember that many curriculum- or criterion-based instruments are drawn from items on standardized tests, thus diminishing their significance to the child's unique needs and to the necessary program planning to meet those needs. Curriculum-based measures do permit team members to determine how significant skills are within the context or environment in which they are utilized.

As shown in Table 5.7, there are several widely used, curriculum-based assessment instruments that afford a strong linkage to program planning and implementation. The Assessment, Evaluation, and Programming System (AEPS-3; Bricker, Dionne et al., 2022) is one example of a comprehensive instrument designed to use observational techniques to obtain assessment data within the context of the natural environment. The AEPS and other curriculum-based measures typically are multidomain instruments that subdivide major developmental milestones into reduced increments. For example, the AEPS subdivides fine motor skills into three strands—reach, grasp, and release—and functional use of fine motor skills. Each of the strands is further divided into goals and objectives that link the assessment process to the preparation of an educational plan to guide intervention.

MAKING CONNECTIONS

PROGRAM PLANNING FOR T. J.

The chart below displays characteristics of individual program planning and implementation assessment, an explanation of the procedures utilized, and examples of T. J.'s assessment process.

Characteristic	Procedure	Example
Assessment includes a variety of assessment measures administered in a variety of settings.	The assessment procedures include the curriculum-based measures, teacher-developed and informal tests, direct observation in natural settings (e.g., home, classroom), and interviews with those who know the child best.	The teacher uses developmental measures to assess T. J.'s communication, motor, and cognitive development. She devises testing situations to determine how he performs specific skills. She observes him during play sessions with peers to note his social interaction, play, and communication skills. She observes him at lunch and in the bathroom to identify his self-care skills. She interviews his parents, former teachers, and therapists to secure additional information.
Assessment results provide a detailed description of the child's skills, abilities, and interests.	The results include a description of (a) the child's developmental skills in all relevant areas, (b) what the child can and cannot do, and (c) the factors that influence the child's skills, abilities, and interests.	The teacher analyzes the results of the assessment activities, summarizes what T. J. can do in each area, and describes the factors that appear to influence his performance (e.g., favorite toys, peers, assistance needed with different tasks, interesting and motivating activities).
Assessment activities involve the child's parents and other family members.	The parents/family should receive information from professionals; observe assessment activities; provide information about the child's development, needs, and interests; gather new information; and validate the assessment results.	The teacher plans the assessment with the family. She asks the family members about how T. J. performs specific skills and spends his time, as well as their concerns and goals for him. She encourages them to observe during the assessment and asks them to gather information on skills at home. She reviews the results and asks them to confirm, modify, and qualify the findings.
Assessment activities are conducted by team members representing multiple disciplines.	Frequently, assessment information is needed from the following disciplines: speech–language pathology, physical therapy, health (e.g., nurses, physicians), nutrition, special education, and sometimes others.	The teacher coordinates the assessment activities of the team. Because of T. J.'s communication delays, a speech–language pathologist participates in the assessment process. An audiologist assesses his hearing, a physical therapist and an occupational therapist participate to determine and assess his motor skills, and the early childhood special educator assists the kindergarten teacher in determining his social and cognitive skills.
Assessment activities result in the identification of high-priority objectives.	Assessment activities identify more skills than possible to teach; therefore, the most critical skills are identified. All team members, including the family, are involved in this decision. Skills are selected if they are useful to the child, have long-term benefits, and/or are important to the family.	After the results have been analyzed, the team reviews the findings. They discuss the skills T. J. needs to learn that will be most useful, will result in long-term benefits, and are most important to his family. The most important skills are listed as goals on his IEP.

The items on the AEPS, as is usually true with curriculum-based measures, follow a typical developmental progression. The curriculum activities that parallel test items are aimed to teach skills related to the needs of the individual child. Another example of a curriculum-based instrument is the Carolina Curriculum (Johnson-Martin et al., 2004a; Johnson-Martin et al., 2004b), which offers developmental markers for assessing young children across developmental domains. The Carolina Curriculum also recommends altering test items for children with motor or sensory impairments. Another instrument, the Hawaii Early Learning Profile (HELP) (Parks, 2007; Teaford, 2010), affords developmental assessment and curriculum activities for home and preschool environments. For early primary–level students between the ages of five and eight, a variety of curriculum- and criterion-based assessment instruments are available in various content areas (e.g., language and literacy, mathematics, science, social studies).

Criterion- and curriculum-based assessment instruments are examples of measures that can be used to amass information for program and intervention planning and progress monitoring. Other methods include informal, teacher-made tests; play-based measures; observations; and interviews with family members or other primary care providers.

The supplementary Making Connections feature contains an explanation of the characteristics of assessments and examples of the various types of information that can be gathered to design and apply programs for young children with delays and disabilities. In individual program planning for T. J., the team could use a criterion-based instrument to measure his abilities in cognitive, communication, and motor development. They could formulate situations to regulate how T. J. presents skills in the context of the natural environment(s), such as riding a tricycle, eating a meal, and communicating with peers. More than likely, the team would also discern social interactions during a play situation with his peers.

Useful information is collected in the natural environment about a child's self-care skills such as eating independently.

Jim West/Alamy Stock Photo

PROGRESS MONITORING AND PROGRAM EVALUATION

The final purpose of assessment to be considered is **progress monitoring and program evaluation**. As previously described, the efficacy of early intervention and early childhood special education has received much attention during recent years with the outcome being an augmented awareness of the importance of continuing progress monitoring and evaluation as it relates to the development and growth of services for young children with delays and disabilities and their families. Progress monitoring of outcomes helps ensure uninterrupted feedback that is imperative to advise decision making about all aspects of early childhood special education services.

Early childhood programs must have a series of procedures for collecting and using data to monitor the effectiveness of program efforts. A comprehensive evaluation plan in early childhood special education services should exemplify the scope of the most essential components of intervention: the child, the family, and the program. Without this critical feedback regarding these interlocking components, early childhood special education services can never fully meet the desired outcomes for young children with disabilities and their families. Table 5.9 displays the questions, purposes, and procedures that are the focus of assessment conducted for program monitoring and evaluation.

TABLE 5.9 ■ Program Monitoring and Program Evaluation

Assessment Questions	Purposes	Procedures
Once intervention or instruction begins, is the child making progress?	To monitor the child's progress	Curriculum- or criterion-based assessments
Should the intervention or instruction be modified?	To understand the appropriate pace of intervention	Observations
Should the intervention or instruction be modified?	To understand what the child can do prior to and following intervention	Interviews Checklists Family reporting Portfolios Permanent products Journals
Has the child met the goals of the IFSP or IEP?	To determine whether the program was successful in meeting the child and family outcomes (IFSP) or child goals (IEP)	Curriculum- or criterion-based assessment measures
Has the child made progress?	To determine whether adjustments are needed	Observations
Has the program been successful for the child and family?	To determine whether the program was successful in meeting the child's IFSP or IEP outcomes or goals	Interviews Questionnaires
Does the child continue to need services?	To determine whether the child continues to need services	Family reports
Has the program achieved its goals?	To evaluate program effectiveness	Surveys Interviews

Source: Adapted from L. Cohen and L. Spenciner, *Assessment of Children and Youth with Special Needs*, 2nd ed. (Pearson Education), p. 309–310. Copyright © 2003. Adapted by permission of Pearson Education.

Assessment information must be collected over time to monitor the progress of individual children and the overall effectiveness of the program.

iStock.com/FatCamera

As recommended for many years, evaluation in early childhood programs must be multidimensional and comprehensive (Division for Early Childhood, 2014; Grisham-Brown & Hemmeter, 2017; Neisworth & Bagnato, 2005; Pretti-Krontczak et al., 2023; Sandall et al., 2019). For children receiving early childhood special education services, the measurement procedures should match the specific outcomes for which they are formulated. This typically includes information that reflects the children's attainment of targeted skills documented on the IFSPs or IEPs, state and/or program standards, and global outcomes. In addition, the outcomes of various family variables (e.g., family satisfaction, family outcomes) should be measured. Last, specific aspects of the overall program should be evaluated using the recommended practice standards promulgated by the major professional organizations, such as the Division for Early Childhood of the Council for Exceptional Children and the National Association for the Education of Young Children.

An ongoing evaluation plan is recommended that encompasses a schedule of data collection. This schedule includes initial program planning assessment, ongoing monitoring of IFSP and IEP outcomes or goals, family outcomes, evaluation of program effectiveness, and annual evaluation across all program participants. Ongoing examination of child outcomes affords the team realistic feedback about each child's progress. In addition, systematic data-based evaluations hold professionals accountable not only to themselves but to the children and families they serve. All measures should be conducted on a schedule that includes a **formative assessment**, which is led during program operation, and a **summative assessment**, which is done at the end of the year or at the conclusion of services. Formative assessment examines children's learning to improve the quality of teaching and overall learning rather than for evaluating the progress of individual children. These types of assessments usually occur at the beginning of the year and are ongoing. Summative assessments, on the other hand, review learning to gauge whether children have met general program outcomes and goals. Most standardized measures are comprehensive and are not designed to provide feedback during the learning process and, therefore, are conducted at the end of the program or school year.

Monitoring Child Progress and Outcomes

Accumulating individual, child-focused data can serve as a valuable monitoring tool to provide input about child outcomes and program efficacy. Results should be collected regularly and systematically and used in making intervention decisions. A variety of methods are recommended to ensure a collection of reliable, valid, and beneficial progress-monitoring data (Branscombe et al., 2014). Adequate time must be permitted to review and interpret the data to inform and alter practice. Such data may be collected through direct observation of child behaviors, permanent product samples (e.g., photos, writing samples, video recordings), continuing performance data collection, family reporting, and the use of curriculum- or criterion-based assessment measures (Grisham-Brown & Hemmeter, 2017; McAfee & Leong, 2011; Pretti-Krontczak et al., 2023).

Assessment tools must be used that have sufficient sensitivity to detect child progress, particularly for young children with significant support needs [DEC Recommended Practices A10]. Regardless of the methods selected, it is vital for data to be connected to children's goals and used to modify the intervention and program activities in accordance with changes in children's development and progress made toward accomplishing their goals (Hojnoski et al., 2009). Table 5.10 provides a description of some of the different methods or monitoring procedures that can be used.

The Making Connections features provide examples of how observational data are accumulated to observe T. J.'s and Maria's progress, which includes anecdotal recording, interval recording, and time sampling. By using the anecdotal recording format, for example, early childhood special educators can make notes about significant events concerning a child's behavior and activities or record observations of the child's physical or emotional state on a given day, which may be factual or an interpretive type of data. If the information recorded is a teacher's subjective interpretation, this should be well-defined in the written narrative. Anecdotal records may involve written notes on specific behaviors, including events that preceded and followed each behavior observed (e.g., skill development for a child in a

TABLE 5.10 ■ Examples of Methods to Monitor a Child's Progress

Monitoring Method	Description of Data Collection Procedure
Event or frequency count (number of times/how often)	Each occurrence of the target behavior is recorded, and at the end of the observation, the total number of times is counted to determine the frequency count. Best used with behaviors that are short in duration and have a clear beginning and end (e.g., positive behaviors, such as requests, social initiations, or participations) Uses some indicator, such as tally marks on a recording form.
Time sampling	Specific time intervals (e.g., 30 seconds, 2 minutes) are selected and used in observing and recording the target behavior. Sampling methods provide an approximation of the frequency of behavior as opposed to a precise recording of actual frequency.
Accuracy (How well a behavior is performed)	How accurately a behavior is performed. This could be the number or percent of items correct or it could be the number or percent of trials completed correctly.
Duration (How long a behavior lasts)	The elapsed time between onset and offset of the target behavior is recorded (each occurrence or total duration). Observer starts the stopwatch when the behavior begins and stops the watch when the behavior ends. Best used with behaviors with a clear beginning and end (e.g., length of time a child plays, participates, cries, or stays on task).
Latency (length of time to respond)	The elapsed time between the prompt of request for behavior and the performance of the target behavior is recorded. Observer starts the timer when the prompt or request is given and stops it when the behavior is initiated. Latency data can be summarized by each occurrence. Best used with behaviors that have a clear beginning and are signaled by some type of prompt (e.g., the time between the direction, prompt, or request and the child's response).

Source: Adapted from R. Hojnoski, K. Gischlar, and K. Missall, "Improving Child Outcomes with Data-Based Decision Making: Collecting Data," *Young Exceptional Children, 12*(3), p. 39. Copyright © 2009 Sage Publications, Inc. Reprinted by permission.

particular domain, what words a child used during specific activities, and in what situations a child engaged in spontaneous communication). Anecdotal records may include lengthier written narratives in some instances, explaining the sequence of events when children display certain behaviors (e.g., temper tantrum, seizure, accident involving the child). Anecdotal records usually focus on the content or style of the behavior or the circumstances in which the behavior occurred rather than the frequency or duration.

MAKING CONNECTIONS

MONITORING T. J.'S PROGRESS

T. J.'s teacher observed him in the classroom setting to monitor his progress on fine motor skills. Below are two examples of the data collection approaches she used, anecdotal recording and time sampling.

Example of Anecdotal Recording

Child's name: T. J.	Date: 1/24 Time: 9:20 a.m.
Observer's Name: J. K.	Location: Preschool Classroom

Anecdote

T. J. was playing with the small blocks. He was putting one block on top of another. He was having trouble balancing the blocks on top of each other. He tried to build a tower of three blocks. His teacher approached him, and he turned away. Just then, A. K., another child in the room, walked over to where T. J. was playing. T. J. picked up the blocks and started to take A. K.'s blocks. A. K. began to retrieve the blocks. Teacher noticed this incident and encouraged A. K. to move to another part of the room.

Comment

Need to find out why he was having difficulty balancing the blocks.

Why did T. J. turn away from his teacher? Need to observe T. J. in other settings.

Example of Time Sampling

Child's name: T. J.	Date: 3/24 Time: 11:10 a.m.
Observer's Name: J. K.	Location: Preschool Classroom

Time	Observation	Comment:
11:10	Watching block building	
11:12	Watching A. K. color	Switches hands
11:14	Writing name	
11:16	Moves to block area	
11:18	Playing with blocks	
11:20	Playing with blocks	Switches from right hand to left, right again
11:22	Playing with blocks	

MAKING CONNECTIONS

MONITORING MARIA'S PROGRESS

Maria's service coordinator developed a system to monitor her progress in toilet training and involvement in play activities. Below are illustrations of the data collection methods she used, time sampling and interval recording.

Example of Time Sampling

Name: Maria Date: 2/16/2024

Objective: Maria will urinate when placed on potty

Key: D = dry, W = wet, V = vocalized, P = placed on potty, + = urinated in potty, – = did not urinate in potty

Time (a.m.)	Monday	Tuesday	Wednesday	Thursday	Friday
8:00	D	D	D	D	D
8:30	W	W	P-	VP+	P+
9:00	D	D	W	D	D
9:30	D	D	D	D	D
10:00	D	VP-	D	D	D
10:30	VP-	D	D	VW	VP+
11:00	W	W	VP+	D	D
11:30	D	W	D	D	D

An Interval Record Using One-Minute Intervals

Behavior	Child	Total	Percentage	1	2	3	4	5	6	7	8	9	10
Requests help	Maria	9	90%	X	X	X	X	X	X	X	X	X	0

A suggested format to record and monitor children's progress over time is a portfolio assessment, a type of authentic assessment system widely used in early childhood education. A portfolio assessment is a means to provide a purposeful and complete overview of a child's accomplishments. More precisely, a portfolio is a systematic and organized record of children's work and behaviors that is gathered at fixed intervals that can be used for qualitative comparisons of their knowledge, skills, efforts, and progress over time.

The information that is collected via a portfolio assessment process meets several of the criteria necessary in program planning and progress monitoring. That is, it is amassed over time, it relies on many sources of information, it collects information from many different individuals about children's skills, and, most importantly, it collects skill information in the setting where the child has demonstrated the skill. The data is used to document progress made toward the accomplishment of each child's individual outcomes or goals.

As a purposeful collection of a child's work and progress, portfolios can be a record of teachers' and other team members' observations and notes about children's activities and behaviors, audio recordings of significant skills (e.g., verbal communication skills), video recordings of important skills (e.g., mobility), checklists of skills (e.g., vocabulary words used spontaneously), photographs of children's work or activities in which they have engaged, a wide array of the child's work (e.g., artwork, writing samples), summaries of observations, anecdotal records of specific events, information shared by families, and any other evidence of children's skills and progress (Kritikos et al., 2018). The information and materials that are included in a portfolio can be selected by any member of the team—the teacher, therapists, family, or even the child.

A portfolio may merely be a container for carrying documents such as a notebook or pizza box covered in contact paper, or it may be crafted using an electronic format (Losardo & Notari-Syverson, 2011). No rules dictate a portfolio's appearance; however, a portfolio should be well structured so that pertinent information and materials can be located with minimal effort. These collections are used as evidence to monitor the evolution of the child's skills, behavior, knowledge, and even their interests, attitudes, or personal reflections. Table 5.11 provides guidelines for developing and implementing a portfolio assessment process. Depending on the specific purpose, the portfolio can be divided into different sections according to IFSP or IEP goals, types of documents (e.g., photographs, drawings, anecdotal notes, test results, video or audio recordings), developmental or curriculum areas, sources of information (e.g., teachers, therapists, family), or context (e.g., classroom, home, community). The data in the portfolio should be properly labeled with explanatory caption statements and summaries about children's progress.

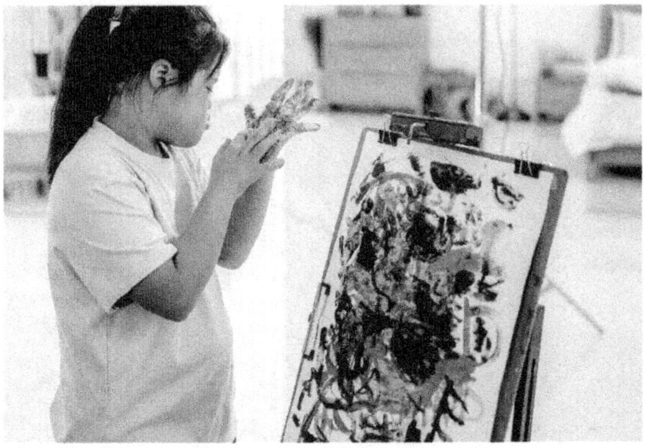

Examples of children's work can be used to document their progress.

athima tongloom/Movement/via Getty Images

TABLE 5.11 ■ Guidelines for Implementing Portfolio Assessment

- Start portfolios at the beginning of the year.
- Parents, caregivers, and other team members should identify in advance the purpose for the portfolio, as well as expectations for children's work.
- Children should be told the purpose of their portfolios.
- Establish types of documentation for each outcome or goal and criteria for evaluating work.
- Develop a plan for when and how data will be collected and by whom.
- Date all work promptly.
- Determine who will evaluate the portfolio.
- Identify ways to involve the child and the family in work selection and evaluation. When appropriate, teach children the skills needed to participate in this process.
- Portfolio contents should be representative of children's work, growth, and accomplishments.
- Explain to parents, caregivers, and children the reasons for selecting samples. If possible, allow children to participate in the selection process.
- Decide how to organize the portfolio to include
    - Content areas
    - IFSP or IEP goals
    - Themes
    - Chronological order of work
- Decide who will be responsible for the portfolio and where it will be stored.
- Establish clear, agreed-on guidelines to manage access to the portfolio and ensure confidentiality.
- Determine criteria for monitoring children's progress.
- Schedule quarterly conferences with children (when appropriate), family, teachers, and other team members to review the portfolio.
- At these meetings, discuss team member observations and documentation to check for subjectivity and bias.
- Frequent debriefings with other team members can help track the various types of documentation being gathered.
- Criteria for evaluating the portfolio may include
    - Quantity, quality, and diversity of items
    - Organization of the portfolio
    - Level of child involvement
    - Meaningfulness of caption statements
    - Quality of summary statements about growth and change

Source: Adapted from A. Losardo, and A. Notari-Syverson, *Alternative Approaches to Assessing Young Children*, 2nd ed. (Paul H. Brookes, 2011), p. 13. Reprinted by permission.

Family Input in the Monitoring Process

If collected properly, family input is an invaluable resource in monitoring child and family status within the larger context of determining program effectiveness. As IFSPs or IEPs are implemented, data should be collected from families regarding the appropriateness of the outcomes and goals, the success of the strategy in meeting the child's needs, and the family's worries and priorities. The IFSP or IEP should be modified based on the feedback provided by the family or upon the family's request. In addition to families having opportunities to evaluate the effectiveness of the IFSP or IEP, they should have many opportunities to provide input into the overall efficacy of the early intervention or early childhood special education program and the services they are receiving. Information can be gathered regarding their perceptions of the program staff, the policies and procedures, the team process, and other aspects of services.

Overall Program Effectiveness

Program evaluation is defined as an objective, systematic process for obtaining information concerning a program, or set of activities, that can be used for the following three purposes:

1. To ascertain a program's or school's ability to achieve the originally conceived and implemented goals;
2. To suggest modifications that may lead to improvement in quality and effectiveness; and
3. To allow well-informed decisions about the worth, merit, and level of support a program warrants.

For evaluation to be effective, it must be designed with a specific purpose in mind. Early childhood special education programs and schools must have well-developed purposes and evaluation plans prior to the start of services to increase the programs' ability to document outcomes. For example, frequently the emphasis is on measuring the success of the curriculum in meeting the goals of the school or program.

Early childhood special education programs and schools that serve young children with delays and disabilities and their families must consider many issues when designing evaluation plans. Many years ago, Bailey et al. (1996) posed questions to gain insight into the overall quality of a program, school, or classroom. These questions are still pertinent today in discerning overall program quality. Can the program, school, or classroom exhibit each of the following?

- The methods, materials, and overall service delivery represent recommended practices.
- The methods espoused in the overall philosophy are implemented accurately and consistently.
- It attempts to verify empirically the effectiveness of interventions or other individual program components for which recommended practices have yet to be verified.
- A system is in place for determining the relative adequacy of child progress and service delivery.
- It is moving toward the accomplishment of program outcomes and goals.
- The goals, methods, materials, and overall service delivery system are in accordance with the needs and values of the community and children and families it serves.

Assessment information must be collected over time to monitor the overall effectiveness of a program or school.

Spencer Grant/Science Source

These answers can provide a well-defined and realistic framework for understanding and monitoring the operations and efficacy of early intervention and early childhood special education programs.

SUMMARY

Assessment of young children with delays and disabilities is a comprehensive process with coordinated components rather than a single procedure. Assessments of young children are conducted to help early childhood special educators and other team members make informed, evaluative decisions at several levels. The type of decision to be made will determine the purpose of the assessment, as well as the assessment instruments to be used and the processes to be followed. Depending on the purpose of the assessment, the process can be formal and/or informal and can include testing, observations, interviews, portfolios, and other procedures.

Assessment is an ongoing process with a variety of purposes that can start with screening and continue with eligibility, program planning and implementation, and progress monitoring and evaluation. Screenings are conducted to detect children who may have a delay or disability. Through screenings, the determination is made whether children should have more in-depth assessment procedures. Eligibility assessments discern whether children meet the requirements of a given program or service. Program planning and implementation assessment is devised to collect information about the child's intervention and service needs. To determine the effectiveness of services and intervention, children's progress toward the fulfilment of their individual outcomes or goals, as well as family outcomes, must be carefully observed. Progress monitoring should be conducted recurrently and should take place in authentic, naturalistic settings. This will supply a record of children's progress and specify whether services and interventions should be amended. Furthermore, information must be accumulated regarding family satisfaction and overall program success.

Conducting appropriate assessments of young children has been the topic of discussion and debate for many years. Some of the main issues are (a) the limited number of assessment instruments appropriate for young children, (b) the nature and characteristics of young children and families, and (c) culturally biased assessments. Therefore, recommended assessment practices have noticeably changed over the last several years. Because of the limitations of standardized and formal assessment instruments, informal procedures are used more often with young children. Important to remember is that the key component of assessment is for early childhood special educators, in collaboration with families and other team members, to gain an accurate representation of the child's current abilities and behaviors in the context of the natural environment. As a team, they should use this assessment information to effectively determine eligibility, develop child- and family-centered outcomes and goals, plan for instruction and intervention, and monitor progress to document efficacy of programming.

KEY TERMS

Apgar Scale
Arena assessment
Assessment
Authentic assessment
Bias
Child Find
Concurrent validity
Construct validity
Content validity
Criterion-referenced assessments
Culturally biased assessment
Curriculum-based assessments
Developmental age score
Eligibility
False negative
False positive
Formative assessment
Functional behavior assessment
Functional skill
Informed clinical opinion
Instructional validity
Interviews
Norm-referenced tests
Observational assessment
Percentile ranks
Performance
PKU screening
Play-based assessment
Portfolio assessment
Predictive validity
Program evaluation
Program planning and implementation assessment
Progress monitoring and program evaluation
Protocol

Referral
Reliability
Screening
Sensitivity
Specificity
Standardized tests
Summative assessment
Tests
Validity

CHECK YOUR UNDERSTANDING

1. Provide a definition of assessment in early childhood special education.
2. Identify and describe the four purposes of assessment in early childhood special education.
3. Describe four types of assessment procedures commonly used in early childhood special education.
4. Discuss problems or issues associated with the assessment of young children and provide suggestions for addressing them.
5. Describe at least five recommended procedural guidelines for conducting appropriate assessments of young children.
6. Describe how professionals can ensure that assessment instruments and processes are culturally appropriate, sensitive, and responsive.
7. Differentiate between assessment conducted for screening purposes and assessment designed to determine eligibility for services.
8. Describe the difference between assessment to determine eligibility for services and assessment for program planning and implementation purposes.
9. Explain the importance of considering family preferences in the program planning and implementation process.
10. Describe strategies for including families in the assessment process and discuss the advantages of their participation in the assessment of young children.
11. Describe four different methods that can be used to collect assessment information about young children.
12. Provide a rationale for considering (as part of the assessment process) the environments or settings where children spend time and the demands placed on them in those environments. Explain why naturalistic assessment has many advantages over traditional assessment practices.
13. Explain how each of the following levels of evaluation should be addressed in the overall evaluation plan of an early childhood program in which children with delays and disabilities are served: (a) child level, (b) family level, and (c) program level.
14. Explain the importance of monitoring the progress of young children with delays and disabilities.

REFLECTION AND APPLICATION

1. Observe the assessment process in an early childhood special education setting. What was the purpose of the assessment? Who was involved in the process? Where did it take place? What was done to prepare the environment prior to the assessment? How was rapport established with the child and family prior to the assessment?
2. Discuss with an early childhood special educator their role in each component of the assessment process (e.g., screening, eligibility, program planning and implementation, and progress

monitoring). Compare and contrast the roles of early childhood special educators serving infants and toddlers, preschoolers, and early primary students.

3. Examine several assessment instruments used in early childhood special education. Compare and contrast the instruments in terms of purpose, age range, domains, cost, administration, psychometric properties, inclusion of the family, cultural and linguistic considerations, and usability of results for individualized program planning and implementation.

4. Review systems used to monitor progress within an early intervention, preschool, and early primary settings. How are they similar, and how do they differ? Interview an early childhood special educator for recommendations on how to monitor progress.

5. How could the families of Maria and T. J. be involved in the assessment process? What specific roles might the families play? How can early childhood special educators help support families in the roles they assume? Explain how the early childhood special educator could provide support to the families to encourage their involvement in assessment for program planning and implementation and progress monitoring.

iStock.com/FG Trade

6 CURRICULUM FOR YOUNG CHILDREN WITH DELAYS AND DISABILITIES

LEARNING OBJECTIVES

After reading this chapter, you will be able to

6.1 Provide a definition of curriculum in early childhood special education (ECSE).

6.2 Describe the interrelated developmental and content domains of curriculum.

6.3 Discuss the influence of various curriculum approaches on curriculum development for young children with delays and disabilities.

6.4 Provide examples of well-known curriculum programs with advantages and disadvantages of each and the applicability to young children with delays and disabilities.

6.5 Explain how curriculum has evolved in ECSE because of historical, legislative, and philosophical influences.

6.6 Explain a model for blending recommended practices from general ECE and ECSE.

6.7 Describe a framework for curriculum development for young children with delays and disabilities.

EI/ECSE Professional Standards

The content of this chapter aligns with the following EI/ECSE Standard:

Standard 5: Application of Curriculum Frameworks in the Planning and Facilitation of Meaningful Learning Experiences

Candidates collaborate with families and professionals to use evidenced-based, developmentally appropriate, and culturally responsive early childhood curriculum addressing developmental and content domains. Candidates use curriculum frameworks to create and support universally designed, high-quality learning experiences in natural and inclusive environments that provide each child and family with equitable access and opportunities for learning and growth.

DEC Recommended Practices

The content of this chapter aligns with the following Division for Early Childhood (DEC) Recommended Practices:

Environment

- E1. Practitioners provide services and supports in natural and inclusive environments during daily routines and activities to promote the child's access to and participation in learning experiences.
- E3. Practitioners work with family and other adults to modify and adapt the physical, social, and temporal environments to promote each child's access to and participation in learning experiences.

Teaming and Collaboration

- TC1. Practitioners representing multiple disciplines and families work together as a team to plan and implement supports and services to meet the unique needs of each child and family.

Authors' Note: As you read this chapter, you will find the EI/ECSE Standards and DEC Recommended Practices discussed throughout. See Appendix A for a complete list of the EI/ECSE Standards and Appendix B for a complete list of the DEC Recommended Practices.

In recent years, the fields of general early childhood education (ECE) and early childhood special education (ECSE) have placed increased attention on curriculum for young children. As described in EI/ECSE Standard 5, ECSE professionals must collaborate with other disciplines and families to develop evidence-based, developmentally appropriate, and culturally responsive early childhood curriculum. They must use curriculum frameworks that create learning experiences in natural and inclusive environments (Council for Exceptional Children [CEC] & Division for Early Childhood [DEC], 2020). This chapter provides a comprehensive curriculum framework and the process used to develop curriculum in programs serving young children with delays and disabilities.

This chapter begins with an overview of curriculum development for young children with delays and disabilities from birth through age eight. After we define curriculum and describe the developmental domains and content areas of curriculum, we provide a brief description that follows the historical, legal, and philosophical influences on curriculum. We also review the major theoretical perspectives that have shaped curriculum in early childhood special education, as well as well-known curriculum programs that are used in programs today. A discussion follows of recommended practices from general early childhood education and early childhood special education. Practices from both fields address the needs of young children in the age range of birth through age eight. Emphasis is on how these perspectives can be blended to create high-quality learning experiences that provide young children with delays and disabilities with equitable opportunities for learning in natural and inclusive environments.

A variety of curriculum models and programs are used in programs for young children with delays and disabilities.

Bob Ebbesen/Alamy Stock Photo

OVERVIEW OF CURRICULUM

Effective **curriculum** is one of several program features contributing to the efficacy of early childhood special education services for children with delays and disabilities (Boyd et al., 2016; Bruder, 1997). Many definitions of curriculum can be found in the early childhood literature. In the past, the term *curriculum* represented, at least to some, a purchased package of materials, objectives, and activities designed to guide instruction. This, of course, is an extremely limited view of curriculum. In this chapter, we move past this narrow view of curriculum and recognize the historical, legislative, and philosophical influences on curriculum development. We also emphasize the importance of each child's unique needs and interests, the environment, the family's priorities, the cultural context, and the desired goals and outcomes. **Outcomes** are defined as what is to be taught to young children with delays and disabilities (Carta & Kong, 2007).

Most professionals in general early childhood education today view curriculum in terms of a theoretical approach reflecting beliefs about what should be taught and in what order. NAEYC (2022) described curriculum as consisting of "developmentally appropriate and educationally significant goals and outcomes as well as all aspects of the environment, materials, play and learning experiences, and planned interactions that promote children's learning and attainment of the specified goals and outcomes" (p. 215). According to this definition, curriculum is the foundation for effective teaching in an early childhood setting. Not only does the content (what children are learning) but also the organization of the learning environment, routines, schedules, child-teacher interaction, and progress monitoring fall under the umbrella of curriculum. Copple and Bredekamp (1997) stated, "it (curriculum) provides the framework for developing a coherent set of learning experiences that enables children to reach identified goals" (p. 42).

In services for young children with delays and disabilities, this perspective must be coupled with their unique and individual abilities and needs, the environmental demands placed on them, and what will be crucial for them to be successful in their natural and inclusive environments. Many years ago, Dunst (1981) defined curriculum for young children with delays and disabilities as consisting of a series of carefully planned and designed activities, events, and experiences intentionally organized and implemented to reach specified objectives and goals, and which adhere and ascribe to a particular philosophical and theoretical position, and whose methods and modes of instruction and curriculum content are logically consistent with the perspective from which it has been derived (p. 9).

Similarly, the Division for Early Childhood (2007) of the Council for Exceptional Children provided a comprehensive definition of curriculum: "A complex idea containing multiple components including goals, content, pedagogy, and instructional practices . . . a comprehensive guide for instruction and day-to-day interactions with young children" (p. 3).

Related to these definitions and others, we believe that curriculum is comprehensive and provides the theoretical and philosophical foundation on which programming is based. Curriculum supplies a basis for the content to be taught and serves as the guide for all that occurs during instruction and interactions with young children (Bowe, 2008; Davis et al., 1998; Grisham-Brown & Hemmeter, 2017; Sandall et al., 2019). As McCormick (1997) suggested, it is easier to define curriculum in terms of what it is not rather than what it is. She stated that "curriculum is *not* a set of activities: It is *what* is to be learned" (p. 268). In this chapter, the primary focus is on child outcomes and *what* is to be learned by young children with delays and disabilities. Chapters that follow address the intervention and instructional methods to be used in providing support and teaching these young children from birth through age eight.

INTERRELATED DEVELOPMENTAL AND CONTENT DOMAINS OF CURRICULUM

Curriculum for young children, both with and without disabilities, centers on the whole child and highlights their development in all areas rather than on only one aspect of learning (Morrison et al., 2022). To thoroughly grasp curriculum in early childhood special education, it is beneficial to focus on the interrelated developmental curriculum domains. **Developmental domains** refer to specific areas of human growth and development. When considering the developmental domains in early childhood curriculum development, we focus primarily on the key skill areas: cognition, motor/physical, communication, social-emotional, and adaptive behavior. We also focus on **play**, which is another distinct developmental area that contributes to the basis for curriculum in early childhood. Play is a context for learning and characterized by activities with objects and people that capture a child's attention and interest. Through play, children's learning goals can be embedded in indoor and outdoor activities across environments (Barton & Wolery, 2008; Brown, 2009; Lifter et al., 2011). Figure 6.1 illustrates how the skills within various developmental domains are interrelated.

Other important aspects of early childhood curriculum development are the **content domains**, which commonly include the content areas of language arts, mathematics, science, art, music, and social studies. These are the knowledge and skill areas consisting of the information on which intervention and instruction are based and that children are expected to learn in academic programs and those promoting academic readiness. Standards from these areas help to provide curriculum content.

FIGURE 6.1 ■ Interrelationships of Skill Areas in the Curriculum

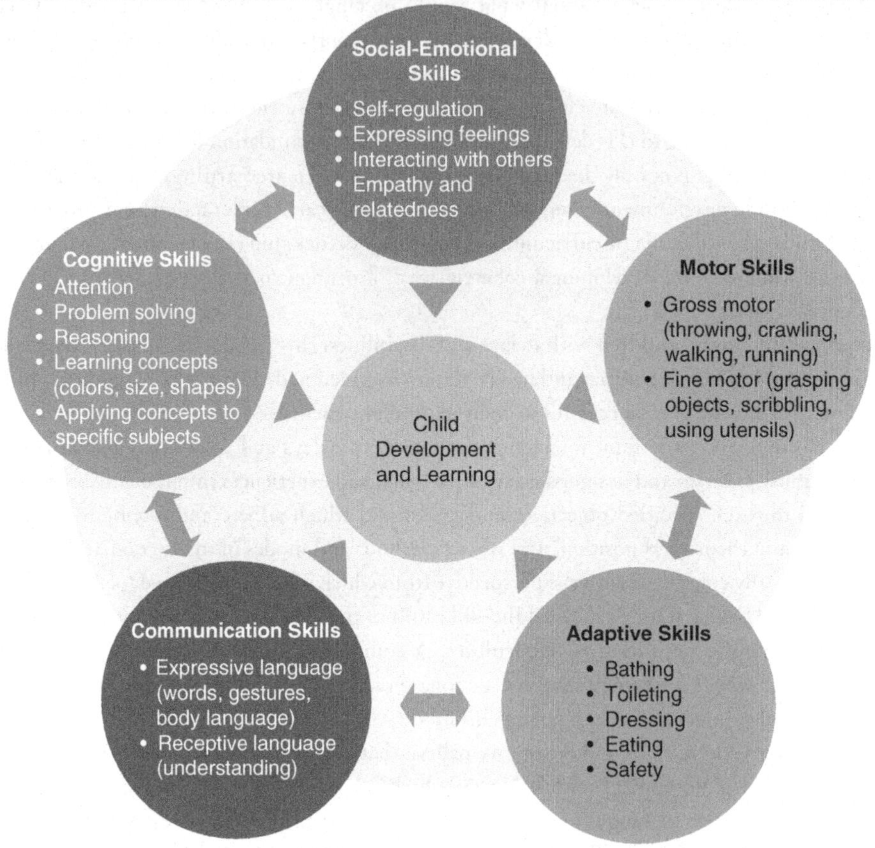

Play is an important component of the curriculum for young children.

Bob Ebbesen/Alamy Stock Photo

In curriculum development, the terms *scope* and *sequence* are used to explain what is to be taught and the order in which it is to be taught. Scope refers to the developmental skill areas (e.g., cognition, motor/physical, communication, adaptive, social-emotional) and content areas (e.g., literacy, math, science). Sequence is the order in which the content is taught (e.g., ages, stages, grade levels) and is often specified in a developmental progression—from easier to more challenging (Division for Early Childhood, 2007). The interconnected developmental domains and content areas of early childhood special education are described in the section that follows.

Cognitive Skills

Cognitive skills refer to a child's evolving mental and intellectual ability and comprise a skill area that significantly alters all other areas of development. A remarkable amount of progress is made in this area of development during the first two years of a child's life. An infant's initial cognitive behavior is predominantly reflexive and becomes more refined as they interact with the environment. Cognitive skills during this period include the concepts of object permanence, spatial relationships, imitation, means-end, causality, and object usage. Cognitive development occurs and is evidenced when children react to stimuli, integrate new information with existing knowledge and skills, and accomplish increasingly complex problem-solving tasks. In addition, cognitive skills include a child's capacity to predict occurrences, the use of short- and long-term memory, the ability to sequence activities, the ability to detect differences among objects and events, and the capacity to plan what one will do in the future.

During the preschool years, cognitive skills are developed through play and interaction with peers and the environment. Preschool cognitive skills tend to focus more on pre-academic skill areas, which involve literacy, math and science skills, letter recognition, counting, and sorting. Cognitive development during the early primary years speaks to more advanced pre-academic/academic skills. At this point, children's cognitive abilities have become more sophisticated as evidenced by their knowledge of concepts, ability to tell short stories in sequence, and quantitative abilities (Goswami, 2011; Morrison et al., 2022). Cognitive skills continue to become increasingly complex as pre-academic/academic skills develop in the early primary years.

Motor/Physical Skills

In the motor area, the skills are divided into gross and fine motor abilities. **Gross motor skills** are described as the physical ability to move and navigate the environment. Gross motor skills involve the movement and control of the large muscles used for such skills as rolling, sitting, crawling, standing, walking, throwing, and jumping, as well as overall body coordination, strength, balance, and agility. **Fine motor skills** refer to the ability to use small muscle groups such as those in the hands, feet, and face. Fine motor skills are utilized in reaching for, grasping, and releasing an object; building towers; cutting with scissors; writing; and using a keyboard. The progressive development of children's fine motor skills involves object manipulation, dexterity, and steady or fluid finger and hand use (Favazza & Siperstein, 2016).

Infants' motor skills are solely reflexive at birth. As the brain matures and the muscles strengthen, the ability of young children to regulate their movements and move about their environment progresses. Not only do most young children gain increased control of their movements, but they also gain increased coordination and complexity as their motor skills develop. They progress in general strength, flexibility, endurance, and eye-hand coordination. Between the ages of two and six, children typically learn to complete a variety of motor tasks with more refinement such as walking, balancing, running, and performing many fine motor tasks with more precision (e.g., cutting with scissors, buttoning, using writing implements). An eight-year-old who is experiencing typical development usually has mastered gross motor skills such as tumbling, roller-skating, bicycle riding without training wheels, and ball handling (e.g., throwing accurately). In the range of fine motor skill development, eight-year-olds who are experiencing typical development have refined their handwriting skills so that they can print most words, draw pictures with details, and appropriately use puzzle pieces, blocks, or other small objects.

Motor skill development is focused on both gross and fine motor areas with emphasis placed on the quality and accuracy of children's motor skills and how children use these skills in the context of their daily routines. Development of both gross and fine motor skills is important within itself, linked to other developmental areas, and necessary for children to become more adept in play and school activities, as well as self-care (Best et al., 2005; Favazza & Siperstein, 2016; Kilgo, 2014).

Communication Skills

In the domain of communication skills, there are three facets of development to consider: communication, language, and speech. Communication, introduced in Chapter 3, refers to the exchange of messages between a speaker and a listener. **Language** is the use of symbols (the letter sounds that are used in various combinations to form words), syntax (the rules that guide sentence structure), and grammar (the way sentences are constructed) when communicating with one another. **Speech** is the oral-motor action used to communicate. The communication skill domain speaks to both receptive and expressive language. **Receptive language** refers to the child's ability to understand and comprehend both verbal and nonverbal information. **Expressive language** is the capacity to communicate thoughts or feelings and may include vocalizations, words, gestures, and other behaviors used to relay information.

The most critical period for communication and language development is early in a child's life. The communication of infants is unintended in the beginning; however, by the age of three, most children have obtained all the major components of a system of communication. Language development has been hypothesized to develop through a series of stages that begin in infancy. When communication skills are delayed, the focus is on communicative intent, which means that attention is given to what a child is attempting to communicate using a variety of means (e.g., gestures, eye gaze, vocalizations; Bernstein & Levy, 2009). By the time most children without delays and disabilities enter school, in most cases they are using all the sentence forms produced by adults (Lane & Brown, 2016; Owens, 2010).

Social-Emotional Skills

Social-emotional skills refer to a range of behaviors linked to the development of social relationships (Brown et al., 2008). During infancy, the foundation is laid for the development of long-term social relationships with others. This domain involves how children react in social situations, interact with others, initiate communication, and respond to interactions initiated by others. When children interact with adults, they need skills such as how to participate in reciprocal interactions. When they interact with peers, young children need skills such as how to play cooperatively, share toys, or request a turn. Emotional skills are children's abilities to identify and communicate feelings, as well as their capacity to act on their emotions while respecting the rights of others. Skills in this area include how to regulate one's impulses or temper and how to resolve conflicts. As children age, their personalities are defined by their early childhood experiences.

To be proficient in social and emotional skills involves a range of cognitive, communication, and motor skills; therefore, there is an interrelationship between children's social skills and other skill areas. Social development from infancy through early childhood is natural, purposeful, and leads to children's social competence. The social competence of a preschooler entails that a child participates with peers in a variety of activities (e.g., play, greetings, group/circle time, snack/lunch) that involve multiple skills (e.g., requesting a turn, sharing, communicating needs or preferences, following rules). These skills continue developing in the early primary years and demands that social competence in the classroom is generalized in other contexts (e.g., home, playground) with a range of partners, materials, and situations (Joseph et al., 2016).

Adaptive Behavior

Adaptive behavior, or self-care skills, primarily center on the areas of eating and personal care (e.g., toileting, grooming, dressing). As children progress in the other skill areas (e.g., gross and fine motor), the skills from these areas become integrated so that children are able to execute self-care and adaptive skills at higher levels of independence. In early infancy, the adaptive skill or self-care areas that predominate are sleeping and eating. However, as children mature and spend greater amounts of time interacting with their environment, they attain greater independence in the areas of eating, dressing, and other capacities of personal care.

Eating skills usually progress from an infant's suck-swallow response to a toddler's finger feeding and cup drinking to a preschooler's independent feeding with suitable utensils. Toileting, washing hands, brushing teeth, and combing hair are examples of personal care skills, which also become more advanced as young children practice and gain more independence. Similarly, in most preschool children, dressing skills progress from cooperation in undressing and dressing to independent dressing skills.

By the time children reach kindergarten and the early primary grades, usually they can perform all or most of the basic adaptive or self-care skills with support provided on the more challenging tasks (e.g., manipulating buttons or snaps on jeans). Gradually, children increase their capability to function with greater independence across an array of tasks (e.g., selecting clothing, fastening seat belt) in diverse environments (e.g., home, school, community). Emphasis is placed on precision in performing more advanced adaptive skills, as well as at a greater level of speed and independence.

In this section, we provided a short overview of the interconnected developmental domains and content areas that are the heart of skill attainment within the curriculum for young children both with and without delays and disabilities. Through the early childhood period, development cannot be separated into isolated skill domains. This is because the developmental areas are interdependent and interact in complex ways. In fact, a direct functional relationship exists between changes in one area of development and those that occur in another area. When a young child learns to walk, for example, they are offered new experiences that will impact skill development in other areas (e.g., cognitive, social, and communication skill development).

Families should have opportunities to be involved as much as possible in the curriculum planning process for their children.

Paul Doyle/Alamy Stock Photo

Knowledge of each of the developmental and content domains and how they are interrelated is helpful to understand the child as a whole. Typical development is useful as a general guide and reference point to consider when determining each child's individual strengths, needs, and progress. However, it is vital to recall that the learning that happens in early childhood is episodic and uneven with great variability among children representing diverse cultural backgrounds, circumstances, and experiences (Hanson & Espinosa, 2016; Morrison et al. 2022; NAEYC, 2022). This is particularly true for those children with developmental delays and disabilities. To learn more about curriculum for young children with delays and disabilities, it is beneficial to consider theoretical influences on curriculum for young children, which are addressed in the section that follows.

THEORETICAL INFLUENCES ON CURRICULUM DEVELOPMENT

As explained previously, most professionals in early childhood concur that a critical component of any curriculum is the theoretical perspective on which it is based. Several theoretical perspectives have been highlighted in early childhood special education (Hanson & Lynch, 1995; Noonan & McCormick, 2014; Odom, 2016; Odom et al., 2009) as having shaped the curriculum development. The major curriculum influences include (a) developmental, (b) developmental-cognitive, (c) pre-academic/academic skills, and (d) functional perspectives. It is imperative to note that, in practice, most early childhood programs rely on a combination of theoretical approaches. That is, different parts of any one or more of the various theoretical perspectives are combined to match the needs of a given group of children, which is often referred to as an eclectic approach to curriculum development in early childhood. This is not shocking, however, because the field of early childhood special education has such a diverse background of historical, legislative, and theoretical influences.

Developmental Perspective

The most traditional early childhood curriculum model primarily reflect a developmental focus. A **developmental approach** is an example of a traditional curriculum model that is built on theories of typical child development (Morrison et al., 2022; Odom, 2016). The sequence of skills in this model incorporates the developmental areas described above, including physical, adaptive, social, and communication and language development, which are based on well-known child growth and maturation studies dating back many years (Gesell & Amatruda, 1947).

According to the developmental approach, children's development is genetically predetermined, suggesting that children who are experiencing typical development usually attain skills in a fairly expected sequence. For instance, in the gross motor area, children usually learn to roll over, sit, crawl, and stand before they learn to walk. Curriculum that is based on the developmental or maturational model contains a sequenced list of developmental milestones structured into a common set of domains with accompanying activities to progress skill development.

The skills in a developmental model are determined by and compared to the age-related norms of children who are undergoing typical development. Children's active interaction with the physical and social aspects of the environment is vital to the acquisition of more advanced developmental skills. Thus, children are reinforced as active participants in the learning process. Intervention and instructional approaches are structured to imitate activities engaged in by children without delays and disabilities (Morrison et al., 2022).

By utilizing a developmental model, it was originally supposed that teaching the same sequences of skills to young children with disabilities, although at a slower pace, would help them to conquer many of their developmental delays and disabilities. This perspective implies that curriculum outcomes for children with delays and disabilities should focus on the grasp of skills that follow a typical developmental sequence (Carta & Kong, 2007; Odom, 2016). The developmental focus in general early childhood curriculum may partly be due to the eligibility criteria for early childhood special education services that accentuate a discrepancy between a child's sequential age and developmental abilities.

Although a developmental focus is prevalent in early childhood programs today, it is important to recognize that such an approach has several limitations when designing curriculum for young children with delays and disabilities. A curriculum based on a linear model of development is challenging for children with disabilities because, instead of focusing on the actual skills needed to be effective in the natural environment, it tends to center on the skills that children need to develop compared to age-related norms of children without delays and disabilities (Carta & Kong, 2007; Odom, 2016; Rainforth et al., 1997). Further, children with delays and disabilities frequently do not follow a typical sequence in skill development. For example, a child with cerebral palsy may skip many communication and gross motor skills. Rather than using two or three words to make his needs known, the child may use a communication device to express them. Or rather than learning to walk independently, he may use a wheelchair to navigate his environment.

In addition, a developmental curriculum does not reference the natural environments in which a child participates and the expectations of those environments (Noonan & McCormick, 2014). For example, the skills required to participate successfully during group time at T. J.'s child care program (e.g., raising his hand to have a turn) would not be addressed in a developmental curriculum. Also, it is rare that individual differences and family preferences would be given appropriate consideration when using a developmental perspective in curriculum design.

Developmental-Cognitive Perspective

Another major influence on curriculum development for young children is the developmental-cognitive perspective. The **developmental-cognitive approach** is a theory-driven model that is based on the work of Piaget (Noonan & McCormick, 2014; Morrison et al., 2022). As discussed in Chapter 1, Piaget (1952) theorized that cognitive development occurs because of physiological growth and the child's interaction with the environment. The developmental-cognitive model is defined by the content that is covered and the instructional methods that are used. The content of the developmental-cognitive model is like that of the developmental model; however, the cognitive skill domain is highlighted. The cognitive domain includes skill sequences derived from Piaget's description of the various periods of intellectual development, such as the sensorimotor and preoperational periods (Piaget, 1952). The instructional approach used in a developmental-cognitive model, like the one used in a developmental or maturational approach, focuses on children's interaction with a stimulating, well-planned environment (Allen & Cowdery, 2022; Hanson & Lynch, 1995; Odom, 2016).

The criticisms of a developmental-cognitive model are like those of the developmental model. The main drawback is that children's functional skills are not addressed in this model. Functional skills, introduced in Chapter 5, are those skills that the child will use often in his natural environment (e.g., functional communication skills such as greeting others, requesting a turn, and indicating needs). It is simple to comprehend why functional skills are imperative to young children with disabilities. Because the developmental-cognitive model does not speak to functional skills, it has limited utility in designing curriculum for young children with delays and disabilities (Cook et al., 2020; Noonan & McCormick, 2014; Snell & Brown, 2011).

Pre-Academic/Academic Perspective

Closely related to the developmental and developmental-cognitive curriculum models is the basic pre-academic or academic skills perspective. The pre-academic/academic approach supposes that the development of children without disabilities is based on a core set of skills that are imparted to children during the preschool years, which commonly are referred to as pre-academics, and the early primary years, referred to as academics. This core group of skills includes literacy, math, and science.

There are numerous disadvantages in applying a pre-academic/academic approach to curriculum for young children with delays and disabilities. First, a pre-academic/academic curriculum is centered on the traditional subject areas of literacy, math, and science. Nonacademic skills that children with delays and disabilities need to attain, such as appropriate social skills (e.g., asking a friend to play with them, turn-taking behaviors) and adaptive skills (e.g., dressing, toileting, eating, safety), are not addressed. Second, pre-academic/ academic skills often are taught in isolation during separate periods of the day with specific materials and tasks. Yet, participation in most activities within the natural environment entails young children performing several different skills within the same activity (e.g., playing a board game usually requires fine motor, cognitive, communication, and social skills, as well as some basic academic skills such as reading or counting). Another concern is that children with delays and disabilities will be unable to generalize skills learned in seclusion to the functional context in which they are required in daily life. As one mother remarked, "My son learned to count to twenty and recognize coins, but he never learned to pay for his hamburger at McDonald's or buy snacks in a vending machine." The basic pre-academic/academic skills that are taught may be dissimilar to those required by young children with delays and disabilities to accomplish functional tasks in natural contexts (Snell & Brown, 2011). As an illustration, rather than just counting money out of context, children learn the skills essential to using money to buy items within their natural environment such as making choices and placing an order at McDonald's.

The curriculum for young children with delays and disabilities must be individually tailored to meet each child's unique needs.

E.D. Torial/Alamy Stock Photo

Functional Perspective

In recent years, many early childhood special educators have utilized a functional approach to developing curriculum for young children with delays and disabilities, especially when children have high intensity needs. Within this perspective, functional skills or behaviors that are beneficial for children to adapt to current or future environmental demands are identified and facilitated. Thus, skills having direct relevance to children are emphasized, such as interacting in a usual manner based on the demands of the environment and performing skills necessary for daily tasks such as dressing, eating, and many other functional skills performed in natural environments and inclusive settings (Carta & Kong, 2007; Owens, 2010; Snell & Brown, 2011).

Developmental age is of less significance than is children's proficiency in acquiring important age-appropriate skills. In most cases, functional skills geared toward daily living activities, rather than developmental or academic sequences, are the focus. In some cases, relevant skills are task-analyzed into a sequence of observable and measurable subskills. For example, a skill such as eating with a fork would be reduced to steps, beginning with picking up the fork, moving on to stabbing food with the fork, bringing the fork to the mouth, taking a bite, and finally, returning the fork to the plate.

A functional approach has multiple advantages over developmental and other theoretical approaches for children with delays and disabilities (Carta & Kong, 2007; Noonan & McCormick, 2014; Owens, 2010; Snell & Brown, 2011). First, the curriculum is based on practical and age-appropriate skills needed by children in a variety of natural environments within the community. Learning to execute these skills enables children to function more independently in various settings. When children with delays and disabilities perform in a competent manner, the expectations of others are raised. Another advantage of the functional curriculum approach is that many of the targeted skills are completed routinely by children without disabilities. When children with delays and disabilities learn many of the same day-to-day tasks accomplished by children without disabilities, the opportunities increase for them to be successfully included within the natural environment. Third, task analysis can be utilized as a method to identify specific responses to be taught, which facilitates individualization. A particular task may be dissected into any number of discrete steps based on the unique strengths and needs of the children (Snell & Brown, 2011).

A major shortcoming of the functional skills approach is that it lacks a well-defined organizational framework. Because there are no universal or generally accepted criteria for determining what skills are functional and relevant for children, the potential exists for idiosyncratic curriculum content that is particular to each child. Difficulty can arise when early childhood special educators try to address the unique skills that each and every child needs (Noonan & McCormick, 2014; Rainforth et al., 1997; Snell & Brown, 2011).

Multiple Curriculum Perspectives

This explanation of the various theoretical perspectives that have impacted curriculum development models is greatly oversimplified. Most early childhood special educators appreciate that the perspectives explained above are not necessarily mutually exclusive approaches. Hanson and Lynch (1995) professed that curriculum content frequently is based on developmental, cognitive, and/or functional theoretical approaches. Intervention or instructional approaches, however, are often derived from a behavioral approach, which is based on the learning principles of behaviorists (e.g., Skinner, Bijou, Baer). Behaviorism is one of the major classical theories that is the foundation of early childhood special education practices. From a behavioral point of view, importance should be placed on the activities in which a child participates within their environment and the skills that are necessary to engage in those activities in an age-appropriate way (Hanson & Lynch, 1995; Odom, 2016; Snell & Brown, 2011; Strain et al., 1992). Instructional procedures such as prompting, shaping, or reinforcing are used to facilitate skill acquisition, based on the progress that children make, adjustments are made in instructional activities (DEC, 2014; Janney & Snell, 2008). The major drawback with a behavioral approach is the degree of structure and precision required in the execution, which is more challenging to blend with the theoretical perspectives espoused in most general early childhood programs (Strain & Hemmeter, 1997).

There is seldom a strict adherence to any one curriculum perspective in early childhood programs, and, in fact, many would agree that an amalgamation of approaches may be most efficient for young children with delays and disabilities (Carta & Kong, 2007; Cook et al., 2020; Odom, 2016; Odom & Wolery, 2003). Many factors separate the various approaches to curriculum (Cook et al., 2020). Bailey (1997) identified that one of the primary features to classify curriculum approaches is the role of the early childhood special educator and other adults related to the child. Approaches that are directive or adult-centered accentuate the teacher preparing the curriculum activities, setting goals for children, and engaging in prearranged instructional activities. On the other hand, approaches considered to be responsive or child-centered accentuate the child as the initiator of interactions with the adult responding to the child's interests in a facilitative approach. Early childhood special educators must select a method to curriculum development that is suitable for individual children as well as the group of children being served. The viewpoints described above and the dichotomies that exist in defining characteristics of curriculum approaches (e.g., developmental vs. functional approaches to curriculum content; directive vs. responsive approaches to teaching) are the center of much discussion in the field of early childhood education.

In addition to endorsing to a particular theoretical perspective, curriculum can vary along an assortment of dimensions. Curriculum can accentuate one or more developmental domains or content areas. For example, the curriculum focus can be on broad-based, integrated constructs such as play (Linder, 2008), or curriculum can address multiple content areas (such as communication, social-emotional, cognitive, self-care, and motor skills). The target of curriculum can differ as well with the target being the child only, the family only, or both. This dimension can vary based on the focus of the intervention (e.g., direct intervention vs. relationship-oriented intervention), the age of the child, and other factors. Curriculum also can vary according to the contexts in which it is implemented, such as when directed toward the home, program, or school environment. The application of the curriculum can range from highly structured, teacher-directed learning episodes to more naturalistic activities (Cook et al., 2020; Noonan & McCormick, 2014). Further, these dimensions of curriculum are neither mutually exclusive nor comprehensive (Bruder, 1997; Sandall et al., 2019). As explained in this section, a variety of formal theoretical perspectives and approaches underlie curriculum in early childhood special education.

CURRICULUM MODELS FROM GENERAL EARLY CHILDHOOD EDUCATION

A **curriculum model** represents a conceptual framework and organizational structure, combining theory with practice, that designates what to teach and how to teach (Aloi, 2009; Morrison et al., 2022). Because early childhood special educators provide services to young children with delays and disabilities in a variety of settings, it is important to be familiar with the different curriculum programs used in early childhood programs today. High-quality early childhood programs necessitate a curriculum approach that is based on research and evidence-based practices demonstrating its effectiveness, as well as several other important features (please see Table 6.1). Curriculum programs may be altered in many ways to meet the needs of young children with delays and disabilities.

TABLE 6.1 ■ Curriculum Features in High-Quality Programs for Young Children With Delays and Disabilities

Founded on research and evidence-based practices
Responsive to families' outcomes/goals
Evidence of Developmentally Appropriate Practice
High value on play
Active learning involved
Integrated activities across domains and content areas
Outcomes/goals incorporated into daily activities

(Continued)

TABLE 6.1 ■ Curriculum Features in High-Quality Programs for Young Children With Delays and Disabilities (*Continued*)
Balance between teacher-directed and child-directed activities
Appropriate level of teacher support and guidance
Engaging interactions
Concrete materials and concepts
Authentic learning
Responsive environment
Learning activities relevant to children's lives
Easily adapted for young children with delays and disabilities
Meaningful involvement opportunities for families
Cultural and linguistic responsiveness
Progress monitoring

Theories of child development and learning provide the groundwork of curriculum programs; the differences in curriculum emphasis represent the distinctions of values about what is important for young children to learn, how children learn, and the way they should be instructed. Some of the well-known curriculum programs today are *The Creative Curriculum, Bank Street, HighScope, Montessori, Reggio Emilia*, and *Project Approach or Theme-Based.* Although these curricula vary in their core premises, the following are some of the most widely utilized programs available today. These programs were developed mainly for children experiencing typical development and must be enhanced with a variety of strategies to ensure that young children with delays and disabilities learn important skills in their early learning environments, which will be discussed later in this chapter.

The Creative Curriculum

The Creative Curriculum is aimed toward programs serving infants, toddlers (Dodge et al., 2006), and preschoolers (Dodge et al., 2010). Termed as an assessment and curriculum system that is inclusive of all children, *The Creative Curriculum* is used in many various types of early childhood programs throughout the United States, particularly Head Start (Dodge, 2004). Founded on research of how children learn, *The Creative Curriculum* supplies thorough guidance for early childhood educators by aiding them in understanding how to work with children of varying abilities. It intends to be an assessment and curriculum system that is inclusive of all children (Aloi, 2009). Specific indoor interest areas with high-quality materials (e.g., blocks, dramatic play, toys and games, art, library, discovery, sand and water, music and movement, cooking, and computers) are suggested in the curriculum. A parent component of *The Creative Curriculum* is also available with guides and resources to help early childhood educators build relationships with families.

Bank Street Curriculum

Another program is the *Bank Street Curriculum*, also known as the Developmental Interaction Approach, which is based on the theories of Piaget, Erikson, and Dewey, among others. In this model, the curriculum is adaptable within a planned framework encompassing developmentally appropriate knowledge and skills. The emphasis is on open education in which the classroom provides children with direct and rich interactions with a wide variety of materials, ideas, and people in their environment. Because the *Bank Street Curriculum* is a child-initiated and child-directed approach that aims for actively involving children in acquiring competence, children spend most of their time exploring, discovering, and engaging in hands-on activities.

The teacher's position within the *Bank Street Curriculum* is to serve as a guide and facilitator of learning by creating a constant, organized environment; providing a selection of materials; and generating opportunities for experiences from which children are to choose. Children participate actively, supported by adults who help to expand, elaborate on, and interpret the meaning of their experiences. Early childhood educators play a critical role in this approach, examining child behavior, child-adult interaction, and the social and physical environment of the classroom. Teachers anticipate opportunities to encourage cognitive development by creating a climate that encourages questioning, investigation, and children's growing understanding of patterns and relationships in the ideas and environment around them (Cufarro et al., 2005).

HighScope Curriculum

The *HighScope Curriculum* (Hohmann et al., 2008) is a renowned curriculum program based on Piagetian theory of child development. The *HighScope Curriculum* approach was developed by Weikart and his colleagues to be used with the Perry Preschool Project in the 1960s. The Perry Preschool Project, a longitudinal study to determine that early education could avoid future school failure in disadvantaged children, is now known as HighScope Educational Research Foundation (Goffin & Wilson, 2001; Hohmann & Weikart, 2002). A vital part of the *HighScope Curriculum* is the belief that young children should be actively involved in learning. The job of the teacher is to support learning as children choose materials and activities within the learning environment. The materials usually found in a *HighScope Curriculum* program are operated by children through a hands-on approach instead of a teacher-directed approach. Another key component of the *HighScope Curriculum* is that children are dynamic learners who learn best from activities they plan, carry out, and reflect upon, which is known in the *HighScope Curriculum* as the Plan-Do-Review process.

The five curriculum content areas that are the heart of the *HighScope Curriculum* include (a) approaches to learning; (b) language, literacy, and communication; (c) social and emotional development; (d) physical development, health, and well-being; and (e) arts and sciences (i.e., math, science and technology, social studies, and the arts). The curriculum framework of the *HighScope* is based on 58 developmental indicators, which were formerly referred to as key experiences and guide the teacher in supporting and extending the child's development and learning.

Montessori Curriculum

The *Montessori Curriculum* is founded on the work of Maria Montessori, described in detail in Chapter 1. The model is child directed, and the responsibility of the teacher is to serve as a guide who takes the lead from the children. In a Montessori classroom, children are actively engaged in the learning process within a well-prepared environment. Carefully designated and ordered materials are available that allow each child to decide whether they want to engage in an activity.

The materials are concrete, interesting, and usually self-correcting, which means that they can be utilized only one way, to prevent errors, promote mastery through repetition, and build confidence through competency (Goffin & Wilson, 2001; Morrison et al., 2022). The *Montessori Curriculum* focuses on five areas with interest centers in the classrooms: (a) practical life skills (e.g., self-care); (b) sensory awareness; (c) language arts; (d) mathematics and geometry; and (e) culture. Further, Montessori classrooms are made up of mixed age groups so that older children can serve as role models and teachers for the younger children.

Reggio Emilia Curriculum

The *Reggio Emilia Curriculum*, developed in the villages around Reggio Emilia, Italy, is a distinctive and groundbreaking approach in many ways. The *Reggio Emilia Curriculum* is defined as one that is emergent or builds on children's interests. It is a hands-on approach that is based on the theory that children learn best by doing and when they are interested in the topic. Thus, early childhood educators are encouraged to let the children's interests guide the curriculum as children use all their senses to learn through music, art, language, and movement (Cook et al., 2020).

The *Reggio Emilia Curriculum* is a dynamic approach. Projects are built on children's interests, with the teacher's role being that of a learner alongside the children as they work together to plan and carry out long-term projects. The learning environment also is considered a significant and necessary component of the learning process, with carefully organized space for small and large group projects, as well as common space for all children to learn together (e.g., dramatic play areas, worktables, discovery areas). Teachers use documentation, similar to portfolios, as a tool in the learning process. Proponents of *Reggio Emilia* resist the tendency to define the approach as a curriculum model because they believe the designation goes against the program's dynamic and emergent characteristics (Edwards et al., 1993; Goffin & Wilson, 2001).

Theme-Based or Project Approach

A *Theme-Based Approach*, commonly used with infants, toddlers, and preschoolers, centers on topics found in common events, culture, and the shared environment of young children. Early childhood educators often use themes based on topical areas that are pertinent and intriguing to young children (e.g., animals, transportation, community helpers, and special events that all the children have experienced, such as a trip to the local grocery store, bakery, or circus). An array of activities and learning experiences are constructed around a topical area or central idea.

Themes provide an exceptional way to incorporate curriculum, as well as unify topics, so that they are relevant to young children. Depending on the thematic units selected, curriculum activities can be designed to address multiple areas of development and children's special interests and needs. Several factors should be considered when thematic topics are designated (Davis et al., 1998; Kostelnik, 1991). The topic should

- be broad enough to address the wide range of abilities of the children;
- be generated based on the interests and experiences of the children;
- be selected based on the availability of resources and materials necessary;
- focus on the here and now, which means the topic should relate directly to children's real-life experiences and should build on what they know;
- represent a concept or topic for children to discover more about;
- integrate content and processes of learning; and
- allow for the integration of several content, subject, and/or skill areas.

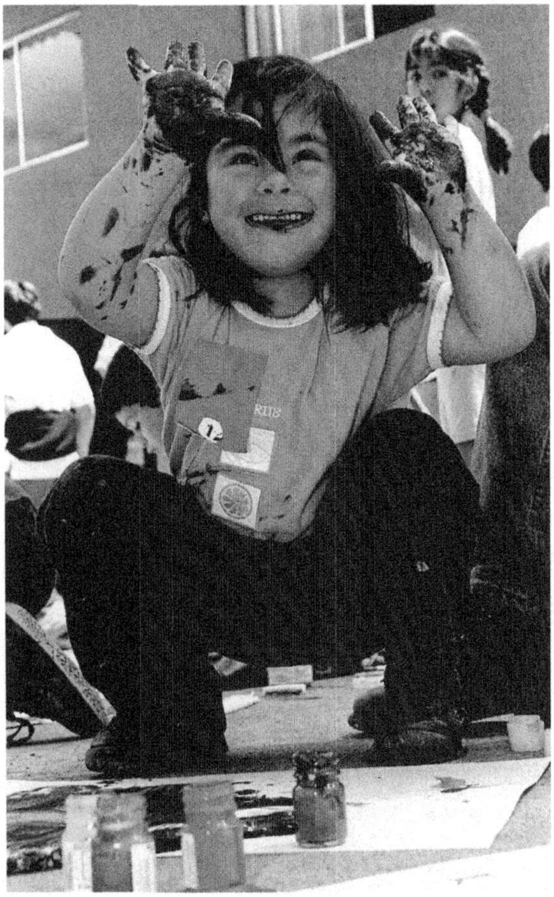

A Project-based Approach is used often in early childhood classrooms, which allows for individualized and group learning.

CRIS BOURONCLE/Staff/via Getty Images

An extension of the *Theme-Based Approach* is a *Project Approach*, which involves an in-depth investigation of a topic selected by the early childhood special educator, the general education teacher, and other adults based on the children's interest, curriculum, and availability of local resources (Helm & Beneke, 2003). Often, a "topic web" is then organized by the teacher as a structure to influence the project. Children engage in investigation by gathering information on the selected topic. Projects have a structure with a beginning, middle, and end, to help the teachers/adults organize the activities within the topic of study according to the development of the children's interests, individual goals, and progression. A *Project Approach* is often used during preschool and the early primary years and has been recounted to be effective with children in inclusive early childhood classrooms (Harte, 2010).

When a *Theme-Based* or *Project Approach* is used with early primary-level students, this process often is referred to as unit teaching. Teachers/adults integrate material from several subject areas to create one unified plan, which includes preassessment, integrated objectives, and evaluation of learning performance. Unit teaching focuses on group learning, is project oriented, and often is encouraging and motivating to students who have trouble engaging in academic learning (Harte, 2010; Jenkins, 2005).

Group projects or themes are used to engage children and promote skills from multiple domains.

Hill Street Studios/DigitalVision/via Getty Images

TABLE 6.2 ■ Advantages and Disadvantages of Curriculum Models and Their Applicability to Young Children With Delays and Disabilities

Curriculum Model	Advantages	Disadvantages
The Creative Curriculum	Children learn by doing; the environment plays an important role; integrates all areas of learning; includes assessment tool.	An expensive model that must be followed correctly; adults must be well trained in using the model.
Bank Street	Child-initiated and directed approach; teachers guide and facilitate learning; stimulating environment.	Requires well-prepared teachers who may not be available; interests of children with delays and disabilities may be overlooked; they may require more direction.
HighScope	Encourages creative exploration; emphasizes active learning; promotes socialization; establishes consistent routine, including the Plan-Do-Review process.	Teachers/adults may be unsure of their roles; there may not be enough teacher-directed activities for some learners; less structured environment.
Montessori	Emphasis on sensory learning; highly organized environment; carefully sequenced materials that are self-correcting; teachers require extensive training in the approach; active learning and independence are encouraged.	Materials designed to be used in only one way and to prevent errors; requires well-prepared teachers/adults, although few programs have them; limited opportunity for pretend play; majority of time spent in independent activities; children with delays and disabilities often need more direction and support; used infrequently with children with delays and disabilities.
Reggio Emilia	Teachers/adults use children's interests to guide the curriculum; long-term projects designed to stimulate children's curiosity; much attention placed on the organization of the environment; advocates that children learn by doing; encourages cooperation and collaboration among children and teacher; children with disabilities or "special rights" are welcomed.	Complex approach; requires well-prepared teachers/adults who may not be available; less exposure to this model in the United States; often difficult for teachers to allow children to make decisions about what to investigate; children with delays and disabilities may not be able to independently choose what to investigate.
Theme-Based or Project Approach	Integrates all areas of development and learning; helps children connect learning with things in the environment.	Preplanned activities or lessons on topics selected by teacher; often time-consuming to prepare thematic units; may be difficult to address the interests of all the children; lacks organizational structure.

Source: Adapted from J. Taylor, J. McGowan, and T. Linder, *The Program Administrator's Guide to Early Childhood Special Education* (Paul H. Brookes, 2009), p. 121.

As we have explained, several curriculum approaches exist in early childhood education programs in which children with delays and disabilities are included. There are advantages and disadvantages associated with each model. For the selected program described, Table 6.2 displays the advantages, disadvantages, and pertinence to young children with delays and disabilities.

The Making Connections feature includes a description of the array of curriculum approaches often used in early childhood programs serving young children with delays and disabilities. Early childhood special educators and other adults must be aware of recommended practices and stay current with changing curricular trends to determine fitting curriculum models and approaches for the children they serve. Further, they must be capable in determining how to supplement methods and strategies for young children with delays and disabilities to learn essential skills and experience success in their early learning environments.

MAKING CONNECTIONS

CURRICULUM PROGRAMS IN PROGRAMS FOR T. J. AND OTHER PRESCHOOLERS

T. J.'s early childhood special education teacher, Mrs. Harnish, works with young children with delays and disabilities in a variety of settings. T. J. is in a Head Start program where *The Creative Curriculum* is utilized. The other children on her caseload are served in programs that are based on multiple different curriculum models and approaches. One program implements a *Montessori Curriculum*, another employs the *Bank Street Curriculum*, another uses a *Theme-Based Approach*, and another program is centered primarily on a behavioral approach. It is easy to see why it is so imperative for Mrs. Harnish to be acquainted with the various curriculum models to meet the needs of the children who are served in various early childhood classrooms and is responsible for ensuring that T. J.'s individualized goals are addressed. She, along with the other team members, regulates the supplemental methods and strategies needed for T. J., as well as the other children, to succeed with their individual goals and to be as efficacious as possible within their learning environments.

HISTORICAL AND LEGISLATIVE INFLUENCES ON CURRICULUM

Curriculum for young children with delays and disabilities from birth through age eight is influenced by several complex factors including research, professional organizations, recommended practices, and legislation. In early childhood special education, the many varied approaches to curriculum for young children with delays and disabilities have developed from three different fields of education: general early childhood education, special education (e.g., for older children), and compensatory education (e.g., Head Start; Peterson, 1987). Each of these areas embodies a different point of view about young children and their development and learning. The field of general early childhood education, for example, emphasizes the young child's need to construct their own knowledge through active engagement with and exploration of the environment. On the other hand, special education stresses the use of remedial instruction and the provision of related services to facilitate skill acquisition (e.g., physical, occupational, or speech-language therapy). Compensatory education is founded on the perspective that early childhood special education can aid to minimize or alleviate the effects of environmental influences such as poverty and other risk factors.

Along with these influences, research in the field of child development has offered a chance to expand the focus of services for young children to include children's caregiving environments. The transactional view of child development (Sameroff & Chandler, 1975), which emerged many years ago, recommends that a child's developmental status differs as a function of the transactions between the child's biological characteristics and the environmental or contextual surroundings in which they live. The prominence placed on a child's relationship with their family and other primary caregivers has greatly influenced the development of early childhood curriculum. Another important influence on curriculum is the early learning standards that states have developed to designate the desired outcomes and content of early education.

The designation of recommended practice in curriculum development for young children with delays and disabilities has progressed over a period of years due to the different fields of education and federal legislation, particularly the Individuals with Disabilities Education Act (IDEA). In fact, the explicit requirements of the individualized family service plan (IFSP) and individualized education program (IEP) have changed the nature of curriculum. In most instances, a broad-based application of curriculum is used in early childhood special education. The IFSP and IEP outcomes/goals, which are pertinent to each child within the context of their home and community, are used to individualize the experiences of children with delays and disabilities (Cook et al., 2020; Noonan & McCormick, 2014).

Perhaps the most impactful influence has been the input from both the general early childhood education and early childhood special education fields related to the inclusion of young children with delays and disabilities (McLean et al., 2016). As described in Chapter 2, the inclusion of infants, toddlers, preschoolers, and early primary children with delays and disabilities in high-quality early childhood programs is a crucial goal of early intervention and early childhood special education. Furthermore, all young children with delays and disabilities should not only have access to high-quality inclusive settings, but they should also receive the individualized supports required to meet high expectations (Grisham-Brown & Hemmeter, 2017). The placement of children with delays and disabilities in high-quality inclusive programs does not ensure that they will reach high standards. As described in previous chapters, the 2004 amendments to IDEA command that all children, regardless of ability, have access to the general curriculum and can participate, as well as make progress, in the general curriculum.

To underscore how appropriate inclusion should occur, the Division for Early Childhood and the National Association for the Education of Young Children (2009) published a joint position statement that identified three vital features of inclusion—access, participation, and supports. This document underlined that it is imperative that young children with delays and disabilities are included in suitable programs and provided effective instruction to reach high standards. Further, the Division for Early Childhood (2014) stresses that practitioners must offer supports in natural or inclusive environments during daily routines and activities to promote children's access to and participation in learning experiences [DEC Recommended Practices E1, E3]. Professionals representing multiple disciplines and families must work as a team to plan and provide supports and services [DEC Recommended Practices TC1] to guarantee that children have the opportunities to reach high standards.

Ultimately, the goal is for all children, with and without disabilities, to receive effectual instruction and achieve established standards in early learning environments (Barton & Smith, 2015; Division for Early Childhood, 2014). The term **blended practices** is used in early childhood education and early childhood special education to denote the integration of knowledge about effective practices for teaching children with and without disabilities into a widespread approach to certify that all children in inclusive settings meet high standards (Grisham-Brown & Hemmeter, 2017). All aspects of an accessible curriculum (e.g., assessments, outcomes/goals, content, environment, instruction, interactions, materials, progress monitoring) invite active participation of all children regardless of ability, which is known as **universally designed curriculum (UDL)**. The use of daily routines and activities as the context for learning in a universally designed curriculum framework guarantees that standards and individually targeted skills are addressed in a manner that expands, modifies, or is integral to the activity in a meaningful way (Johnson et al., 2014). High-quality learning contexts that incorporate the principles of universal design serve as the basis for intervention and instructional planning for all children. For young children with delays and disabilities who need supplementary support, accommodations are provided to help ensure progress toward meeting their desired outcomes (Horn et al., 2016; Sandall et al., 2019).

In addition, response to intervention (RTI) has influenced curriculum in recent years. RTI is a framework to detect those children who might benefit from additional support and connect children's formative assessment information with specific teaching and intervention approaches within the curriculum. In Tier 1, universal interventions are those designed to provide a high-quality learning program for all children; in Tier 2, secondary interventions are embedded learning opportunities; and in Tier 3, tertiary interventions are instructional strategies to provide highly personalized and intensive support. Much work also has been done with school-age students (K–12) around multi-tiered systems of support (MTSS) in both academics and behavior (Freeman et al., 2015). This work has continued in early childhood and has influenced how to deliver instruction to all young children in natural and inclusive settings (Carta et al., 2016; DEC, 2021; Hemmeter et al., 2016; Pretti-Frontczak et al., 2023). MTSS involves consciously creating social interactions to help each child meet the criteria of academic success, cultural competence, and critical consciousness (Forman & Crystal, 2015). Both RTI and MTSS challenge norms (e.g., expectations regarding language, behavior, and social interactions) to be responsive to marginalized children and families and work towards greater equity for all learners.

Considering the multiple influences on curriculum, a suggested framework for curriculum development to which all children have equitable access and participation is presented later in this chapter. In the section that follows, we describe the influences on curriculum of guidelines and recommended practices from both general and special early childhood education.

RECOMMENDED PRACTICES AND GUIDELINES

As described previously, the designation of recommended practice in curriculum development for young children with delays and disabilities continues to evolve. When we think about curriculum that will optimize development for young children with delays and disabilities, it is important to look to all guidelines and standards that help to provide quality services to young children and their families. Within the two disciplines of general early childhood education and early childhood special education, professionals representing the major professional bodies have constructed documents that represent contemporary thought regarding practices that should be used in the education of young children, both with and without delays and disabilities. For general early childhood special education, the National Association for the Education of Young Children (NAEYC) has developed guidelines for appropriate practices and for early childhood special education, the Division for Early Childhood (DEC) of the Council for Exceptional Children (CEC) has provided recommended practices.

The question that emerges is how to reconcile the apparent pedagogical and philosophical differences between these two approaches. We believe that common ground must be established with the increased legislative and educational importance on including children with delays and disabilities in programs beside their peers without disabilities. To provide enough support for a blended approach to curriculum development and implementation in programs serving children with delays and disabilities, the recommended practices from early childhood education and early childhood special education must be explored.

General Early Childhood Education Practices

One of the most widely used descriptors of recommended practice in general early childhood curriculum is Developmentally Appropriate Practice (DAP). DAP is a set of guidelines established by the NAEYC to articulate appropriate practices for the early education of young children from birth through age eight. The idea of constructing a statement of DAP was inaugurated in 1987 as a vehicle for providing information to early childhood programs seeking accreditation through NAEYC (Bredekamp, 1987). The document also operated as a reactionary statement to the growing fears of the increasing emphasis on academic demands and the expectations encountered by young children in preschool and early primary programs (Carta et al., 1991; Udell et al., 1998).

Many professionals in the general early childhood community, as well as parents, were concerned that too many early childhood programs and classrooms were focusing on academic preparedness and not providing young children with sufficient opportunities to engage in play-based activities and other less structured activities that exemplify the early childhood period of development. As one mother explained, "Although I'm not a teacher, I know from experience that four-year-olds should not be expected to sit at a table and complete worksheets for an hour at a time! No one should be expected to do the same task for that long without getting bored and misbehaving." A long-standing fundamental premise of DAP is the belief that "early childhood programs should be tailored to meet the needs of children, rather than expecting children to adjust to the demands of a specific program" (Bredekamp, 1987, p. 1).

The DAP guidelines were developed to endorse high-quality programs for all children and their families. Some mistake DAP for a curriculum model; however, DAP does not meet the criteria to be considered a thoroughly developed curriculum model. Rather than being a curriculum model, DAP was designed to be used as a tool to help differentiate between appropriate and inappropriate practices to be used with young children regardless of the curriculum model employed in the programs they were attending (Kostelnik et al., 2010).

After a decade of extensive dissemination, the 1987 position statement became the most widely accepted guidelines for recommended practices in the field of general early childhood education. The DAP guidelines were conceived as a living document and not as educational dogma; they were hypothesized as a dynamic and evolving statement of recommended practices that were designed to be subject to change and amenable to revisions as thinking and recommended practices, which are essentially time-bound, changed. NAEYC published revised guidelines in 1997 titled *Developmentally Appropriate Practice in Early Childhood Programs: Serving Children From Birth Through Age 8* (Bredekamp & Copple, 1997), a third edition in 2009 (Copple & Bredekamp, 2009), and more recently a fourth edition (NAEYC, 2022).

The fourth edition of the DAP guidelines has been updated to address how to apply them in the evolving field of early childhood education with particular emphasis on equity for all children and cultural, social, and historical contexts of development. They consider children within their unique learning environments and as members of families and communities as well. Therefore, to be developmentally appropriate, early childhood practices must be culturally, linguistically, and ability appropriate for each individual child. They focus on young children as distinctive and valued individuals and recognize and build on their strengths and characteristics to foster their development and learning across all developmental domains and content areas (NAEYC, 2022).

To inform early childhood educators' decision making in the program planning process for young children, DAP requires them to have knowledge and understanding of how to apply these three core considerations:

1. *Commonality* in children's development and learning (birth through age eight);
2. *Individuality* reflecting each child's unique characteristics and experiences, within their families and communities, related to their development and learning; and
3. *Context* in which development and learning occur including specific social, cultural, linguistic, and historical contexts for each child, educator, and program.

These core areas of knowledge about each child are key to the concept of DAP, as well as the role of the child and teacher in the learning environment. When applying these core considerations to curriculum development, the goals underlying curriculum content and activities should reveal what is known about the commonality of child development and learning and, at the same time, should be responsive to the individual variations in development. Curriculum should consider individuality and be responsive to unique differences in children such as their interests, personalities, motivations, family language, and individual learning needs. Curriculum and learning experiences should be designed based on the social and cultural contexts in which children live. Further, curriculum should be culturally and linguistically responsive and affirming by empowering individuals intellectually, socially, emotionally, and politically by using cultural and historical referents to convey knowledge, impart skills, and change attitudes. Based on the DAP guidelines, Table 6.3 describes key factors and the role of the early childhood special educator in planning curriculum that is developmentally appropriate for children from birth through the primary grades (NAEYC, 2022).

TABLE 6.3 ■ Key Factors in Curriculum Planning From the DAP Guidelines

Key Factors in Curriculum Planning	Role of Early Childhood Educators
Important goals for young children's development and learning are identified and clearly articulated, including those that are culturally and linguistically responsive.	● Early childhood educators consider what children are expected to know, understand, and be able to do when they transition from the setting. ● Early childhood educators are thoroughly familiar with state early learning standards and other mandates. ● Early childhood educators establish and regularly update goals with input from all stakeholders, including families.
A comprehensive, effective curriculum is used that targets the identified goals across all developmental domains and subject areas.	● Early childhood educators familiarize themselves with the curriculum to consider in addressing goals. ● If published curriculum products are used, early childhood educators must ensure that they are developmentally, culturally, and linguistically responsive for the children served and provide flexibility to make adaptations to meet the children's specific interests and learning needs. ● If curriculum is developed by teachers, they must make certain it targets identified learning goals and early learning standards.
Early childhood educators use the curriculum framework to ensure there is attention to important learning goals and coherence of the overall experience for children.	● Early childhood educators are familiar with the skills in each domain and content area that are key for the children they are teaching. ● In planning and implementation, early childhood educators use the curriculum framework along with what they have learned about the children's knowledge, interests, progress, languages, and learning needs (based on their observation, documentation, and other assessment). ● In determining the sequence and learning pace, early childhood educators consider the learning progressions that children typically follow, including the usual sequences in which skills and concepts develop.
Early childhood educators make meaningful connections a priority in the learning experiences of each child.	● Early childhood educators plan curriculum experiences that integrate children's learning in all developmental and content domains. ● Early childhood educators plan experiences to build on the knowledge of each child, family, and community to provide culturally and linguistically responsive and sustaining learning experiences. ● Early childhood educators plan curriculum experiences that follow logical learning sequences and allow for depth, emphasis, and revisiting concepts as needed.
Early childhood educators collaborate with those teaching in the preceding and subsequent age groups or grade levels.	● Early childhood educators share information about children and work to increase continuity and coherence across ages and grades. ● Early childhood educators strive to implement curriculum that is consistent and coherent and based on the principles of DAP at each level (e.g., infants, toddlers, preschoolers, early primary-level children).
Early childhood educators have a planned and written for curriculum in place for all age groups.	● Although it will vary across the age span, early childhood educators plan curriculum that lays the foundation to promote each child's development and learning. ● Across the age span, early childhood educators implement curriculum that supports all domains of development and subject areas, as well as culturally and linguistically sustaining practices.

Early Childhood Special Education Recommended Practices

The field of early childhood special education did not have a set of guidelines like DAP until 1993, when the Division for Early Childhood of the Council for Exceptional Children published the first document to provide recommendations for programs serving young children with delays and disabilities and their families and indicators of quality in these programs (Division for Early Childhood Task Force on Recommended Practices, 1993). In 2000, 2005, and 2014, the Division for Early Childhood produced guidelines referred to as the *DEC Recommended Practices* (Division for Early Childhood, 2014; Sandall et al., 2005; Sandall et al., 2000) that synthesized the knowledge found in the scientific professional literature and the knowledge from experiences of parents, practitioners, and administrators about those practices that produced the best results for children. Further, and perhaps most important to this discussion, the guidelines contain many recommendations that have application to curriculum development and implementation. In designing early childhood curriculum for young children with delays and disabilities and their families, it is imperative to consider the premises underlying the DEC Recommended Practices and quality indicators that support the goals of early childhood special education.

The classroom environment is an integral component of the curriculum and sets the stage for learning.

Bob Ebbesen/Alamy Stock Photo

Premises underlying recommended practices for early childhood special education include but are not limited to the following:

- *Learning experiences should be family-centered.* This means that the curriculum must be responsive to families' goals, outcomes, and priorities for their children. As described in Chapter 3, a dramatic shift in advocated practices has occurred in early childhood special education over the years, from a child-oriented approach to a family-centered approach. Although federal legislation is largely credited with providing the rationale for basing services on the family, the law put into policy what had been an already burgeoning movement. Family participation is now guided by the goal of a partnership of equals being built between the family and the early childhood special education service system (a family-centered service delivery model) (Kilgo, 2022). The spirit of this family movement is founded on the belief that the families' visions for their children should provide the foundation for program planning (Kilgo & Aldridge, 2009) and that family preferences should play a vital role in determining the curriculum content and strategies. Thus, family input is encouraged and supported, and families' rights to make decisions about their children's experiences are encouraged and respected.
- *Learning experiences should be evidence-based.* Buysse et al. (2006) defined evidence-based practices as "a decision-making process that integrates the best available research evidence with family and professional wisdom and values" (p. 3). That is, specific strategies that

early childhood special education professionals use should have empirical support or be wisdom or value driven, which means they are supported by current wisdom or values held by professionals the field and the family (McLean et al., 2016; Snyder, 2006). This implies that early childhood special education professionals must continually examine their current practices and procedures to ensure their effectiveness (Reichow, 2016).

- *Learning experiences should be culturally and linguistically responsive.* Appropriate educational experiences should reflect the diverse values, backgrounds, and experiences of young children and families served within a program, acknowledging the individuality of children and families (Aldridge et al., 2016; Hanson & Espinosa, 2016; Kilgo & Aldridge, 2009). The cultural and linguistic backgrounds of the children and families should help to guide curriculum development.
- *Learning experiences should provide for input from professionals representing multiple disciplines.* Because children with disabilities often have a need for services such as physical therapy, speech-language therapy, occupational therapy, and/or other related services, there are often many different professionals who work with the child and family. Practices should reflect a team approach whereby all team members share information and expertise, communicate frequently, and participate in joint decision making (Aldridge et al., 2015; Kilgo & Aldridge, 2011). Input from the various disciplines should be integrated into the design of the curriculum.
- *Learning experiences should be developmentally, individually, and culturally appropriate.* The key to developing appropriate educational experiences (for any child) is to create a match between the unique, individual needs of the child and the curriculum (NAEYC, 2022). Making this match for children with delays and disabilities may require taking individualization to a higher level by paying attention to the physical and social environment, adapting or using specialized equipment and materials, and/or using specialized instructional strategies and techniques to support each child's development and learning (Sandall et al., 2016; DEC, 2014).
- *Learning experiences should be normalized.* The concept of normalization is defined as making available to all children "the patterns of life and conditions of everyday living which are as close as possible to the regular circumstances and ways of life of society" (Nirje, 1976, p. 231). Normalization is often narrowly interpreted to mean that children with delays and disabilities should be placed in inclusive environments. Although that is one application of normalization, placement within the natural environment or inclusive settings does not ensure that services are equitable and appropriate. When applied to young children with delays and disabilities, it includes examining several different aspects of each child's educational placement to include educational programming, intervention or instructional strategies, the physical and social environment, and family-centered practices.

Teachers and therapists collaborate in planning all aspects of the curriculum.

Bob Daemmrich/Alamy Stock Photo

The underlying premises of the DEC Recommended Practices assist the general goals of early educational experiences for young children with delays and disabilities (Division for Early Childhood, 2014; Sandall et al., 2005). By using the DEC Recommended Practices, potential benefits for participants in early childhood special education services are described as follows:

- *Families are supported in achieving their goals for their children.* Children with delays and disabilities may have complex needs that are better understood when professionals interact with families and learn about the priorities that parents have for their children (Division for Early Childhood, 2014). As the mother of a three-year-old with cerebral palsy told her child's teacher, "All I want is for my child to learn to walk." Thus, this mother's priority became the major focus of intervention. Although the child never actually learned to walk, he did learn to use an electronic wheelchair to get from place to place independently. If early childhood special educators do not have knowledge of the families' priorities, the likelihood of success will be diminished. It is critical for professionals to understand that families function as a system. Thus, they must develop rapport with families, have ongoing interactions with them, and support them in achieving the goals they have for their children (Turnbull et al., 2022).
- *Child engagement, independence, and mastery are supported.* Through the early childhood special education curriculum, each child's engagement with people, materials, and activities in their natural environment (e.g., home, child care, school) is supported, which enables him or her to master the demands associated with each of these environments (Grisham-Brown & Hemmeter, 2017). A mother of a four-year-old child who has Turner syndrome with accompanying delays in all developmental areas encouraged professionals to examine the routines and demands of the general early childhood program where her daughter was enrolled to determine the focus of intervention. For the child, Kathryn, to become more independent and to be successful in this setting, the focus of her program needed to be on what was expected of her within this setting. As stressed for many years, efforts should be made to "promote active engagement (participation), initiative (choice making, self-directed behavior), autonomy (individuality and self-sufficiency) and age-appropriate abilities in many normalized contexts and situations" for young children with disabilities (Wolery & Sainato, 1996, p. 53).
- *Development and learning are promoted in all areas.* Experiences for young children with delays and disabilities should be designed to promote progress in each of the key areas of development as described earlier in this chapter. Many activities in which young children participate require the integrated use of skills from various domains. For example, when Maria is participating in a snack time activity, she is using skills from several areas such as fine motor, communication, social, and adaptive skills. The development of young children with delays and disabilities is behind that of their peers without disabilities and, therefore, individual outcomes/goals are targeted for each child and instructional strategies are used that lead to rapid learning in order to help children with delays and disabilities make progress in achieving desired outcomes/goals (Wolery & Sainato, 1996; Sandall et al., 2005).
- *The development of social competence is supported.* Most would agree that social skills (e.g., developing relationships, getting along with peers, playing cooperatively) are among the most important skills for young children to learn (Brown et al., 2008). Young children with delays and disabilities reportedly engage in less sophisticated and less frequent social interactions than their peers without disabilities (Guralnick, 1990). Therefore, many children with delays and disabilities have difficulty developing these skills and must be taught to interact effectively and properly (Goldstein et al., 2001). As a result, one of the primary benefits of early childhood special education is that the social competence of young children with disabilities is further developed. As one mother noted, "My son needed to learn the social and behavioral expectations of the kindergarten classroom to be successfully included. His teacher didn't seem to mind that he couldn't write his name, but she did expect him to walk in a line with his classmates to the lunchroom and to stay in his seat during group time."

- *The generalized use of skills is emphasized.* Skill generalization is especially vital when teaching young children with delays and disabilities who have extreme difficulty in generalizing or applying the skills they learn to different situations, people, and materials (Drew et al., 1992). Bethany is a four-year-old with Down syndrome who learned to communicate at her preschool program by using sign language along with a few words. Her initial success in communicating at preschool was followed by the emphasis of her program expanding to her communication skills being used at home, in the after-school program, and in other environments. As Wolery and Sainato (1993) pointed out, "Early interventionists should not be satisfied if children learn new skills; they should only be satisfied if children use those skills when and wherever they are appropriate" (p. 54).
- *Children are provided with, and prepared for inclusive life experiences.* Because IDEA and its amendments reflect the normalization principle, which was discussed previously, services for young children with delays and disabilities should be provided to the greatest extent possible in settings that are as similar as possible to the typical settings in which children without disabilities play and learn (Cook et al., 2020). Therefore, a crucial purpose and potential benefit of early education for young children with delays and disabilities is to provide an appropriate curriculum, which should prepare them for inclusive life experiences. Learning environments for a two-year-old child may be a play group with other children in the neighborhood, a child care program, or a babysitter's home. Some examples of inclusive life experiences for T. J. could include going to church, attending birthday parties, or eating at McDonald's. The literature describes the benefits of placements in the natural environment or inclusive settings and suggests strategies for effective inclusive early childhood services (Guralnick, 2001; Sandall & Schwartz, 2008).
- *The emergence of future problems, delays, and disabilities may be prevented.* A final benefit of the early childhood special education curriculum is to prevent the development of additional problems in young children with delays and disabilities (Carta et al., 2016). For example, Audrey is a four-year-old with cerebral palsy who needs trunk support and, therefore, spends most of her day in a wheelchair or another adaptive seating device. Without the trunk support and continued physical therapy, Audrey probably will develop scoliosis (a curvature of the spine). Jimmy is a three-year-old with a visual impairment. As a result of his visual impairment, he does not receive the same visual stimulation as other children his age, does not move around to explore his environment, and exhibits few social initiations. Without encouragement and support to explore his surroundings and initiate interactions with others, Jimmy is likely to develop delays in related areas such as cognitive, social, and/or motor development. In each of these examples, the child has a primary disability that will lead to secondary problems unless provided with a curriculum that meets their individual needs, which includes modifications to the environment, materials, equipment, and instruction.

These principles and potential benefits undergird curriculum content and experiences for young children with delays and disabilities. Based on the DEC Recommended Practices, many strategies can be used by early childhood professionals who develop and implement appropriate curriculum for young children with delays and disabilities. The questions that emerge include the following: (a) Are the DAP guidelines appropriate for and do they meet the needs of young children with delays and disabilities? and (b) How can recommended practices from both NAEYC and DEC be blended to effectively meet the needs of children with differing abilities?

Applicability of DAP to Young Children With Delays and Disabilities

The increased regularity of young children with delays and disabilities receiving services alongside their peers without disabilities in inclusive environments has created a critical need to examine the standards that guide general early childhood education. Over the years, it has been deliberated in the literature regarding the applicability of NAEYC's Developmentally Appropriate Practice for young children with disabilities (Carta & Kong, 2007). Within the field of early childhood special education, most professionals agree that DAP lacks the degree of specificity needed for general early childhood educators to provide individualized approaches (Gregg, 2011).

Curriculum models emphasizing DAP are desirable but usually are insufficient without adaptations and instructional techniques that are individually personalized to meet the needs of children with delays and disabilities (Carta, 1994; Carta et al., 1991; Johnson, 1993; Sandall et al., 2005; Wolery & Bredekamp, 1994). As Wolery et al. (1992) emphasized, "a program based on the guidelines alone is not likely to be sufficient for many children with special needs" (p. 106). Carta and her colleagues (1991) also shared this viewpoint. Their analysis of DAP revealed the following needs as they pertained to young children with delays and disabilities:

- Programs serving young children with delays and disabilities must offer a range of services that vary in intensity based on the needs of the children.
- Assessment must be derived from many sources, be carried out across settings, and be frequent enough to monitor children's progress toward their individual goals, outcomes, and objectives.
- Programs serving young children with delays and disabilities must develop individualized intervention or teaching plans consisting of goals/outcomes and objectives/benchmarks that are based on a careful analysis of each child's strengths, needs, and interests, as well as the skills required for future school and other environments.
- Intervention and instructional methods and procedures for teaching young children with delays and disabilities should be effective, efficient, functional, and normalized.
- The intervention and instructional procedures employed by early childhood special educators and other adults should result in children's high levels of active involvement and participation in activities.
- Programs serving young children with delays and disabilities should focus on strengthening the abilities of families to nurture their children's development and to promote normalized community adaptation.
- Programs serving young children with delays and disabilities must be outcome-based, with specific criteria, procedures, and timelines to determine whether individual children progress toward stated outcomes.

Further, Carta and colleagues (1991) clearly acknowledged that DAP practices have much in common with the underlying principles of the field of early childhood special education; yet they provide several illustrations for each of their points where the DAP practices are considered insufficient for meeting the needs of young children with delays disabilities and their families. DAP practices do not go far enough as a vehicle for guiding the development of curriculum and the delivery of intervention or instruction to young children with delays and disabilities.

DAP has been and continues to be championed as an approach for working with *all* young children, including those with delays disabilities (Bredekamp, 1993a, 1993b; Bredekamp & Rosegrant, 1992; Copple & Bredekamp, 2009; Kostelnik et al., 2010; NAEYC, 2022). Current consensus is that the DAP practices do not conflict with the DEC Recommended Practices for children with delays and disabilities (Division for Early Childhood, 2014; Sandall et al., 2005). We concur that strategies and practices valued by professionals in early childhood special education are compatible with what is viewed as important for teaching children without delays and disabilities.

Over the years, leaders in the field of early childhood special education have noted that there are no areas of major incongruity in practices advocated by either general early childhood educators or early childhood special educators that avoid blending practices in serving all children (Grisham-Brown & Hemmeter, 2017; McLean & Odom, 1993). When differences emerge, they are differences of intensity or emphasis and not a suggestion of conflict. Differences are in the application and emphasis of certain guidelines within each field. In particular, these differences include (a) the role of the family and (b) the models of service delivery. As stressed earlier, current consensus is that DAP is a necessary condition for programs serving all young children, including those with delays and disabilities (Fox & Hanline, 1993; Gregg, 2011; Guralnick, 1993). However, leaders in the field of ECSE caution, as they have for many years, that although DAP curriculum approaches are necessary, they are insufficient to support the learning needs of young children with delays and disabilities. NAEYC's DAP guidelines have value for young children with disabilities; however, adaptations, modifications, and instruction must be tailored to each child's individual needs (Carta & Kong, 2007; DEC, 2014; Fox et al., 1994; Odom, 2016; Sandall et al., 2016).

We believe that the application of DAP is indeed appropriate for young children with delays and disabilities; however, we must consider gauging the appropriateness of suggested practices by how well they meet the needs of the individual child. Effective practices associated with the field of early childhood special education within the DAP framework neither prohibit nor inhibit their use. However, early childhood special education services that are exclusively constructed around DAP are likely to be inadequate for meeting the needs of many young children with disabilities (Grisham-Brown & Hemmeter, 2017). Our task as early childhood professionals (both ECE and ECSE) is "to identify the practices that are relevant for all children and to understand when, and under what conditions, differences and adaptations of practices are required" (Wolery & Bredekamp, 1994, p. 335). Curriculum that reflects the blended practices of both early childhood education and early childhood special education is likely to result in appropriate services for all children.

Blended Practices From Early Childhood Education and Early Childhood Special Education

As we have explained, much discussion has occurred across and within the general early childhood education and early childhood special education fields concerning the similarities and differences in the guidelines of NAEYC and DEC related to philosophical origins, language, and emphases within practices used with young children. Nonetheless, both the fields of early childhood education and early childhood special education have provided excellent guidelines that should be used when creating educational experiences for young children with delays and disabilities (DEC, 2014; Gregg, 2011; Grisham-Brown & Hemmeter, 2017; Sandall et al., 2005; NAEYC, 2022).

As stated previously, the emergent interest in blending practices from early childhood education and early childhood special education can be attributed largely to the inclusion movement and services for young children with delays and disabilities being provided in natural environments and inclusive settings (Odom, 2016). This movement has been spurred by public laws (e.g., the IDEA amendments and the Americans with Disabilities Act) and the belief that young children with disabilities should obtain services in settings they would be in if they did not have a delay or disability (Division for Early Childhood & National Association for the Education of Young Children, 2009; Gargiulo & Metcalf, 2023). As described in Chapter 4, the providing of services to children with delays and disabilities in natural and inclusive environments has had, and will continue to have, a tremendous impact on curriculum development.

We support the importance of collaboration between general early childhood education and early childhood special education practitioners. As Burton et al. (1992) highlighted years ago, working partnerships are required as the demand for services outstrips available resources in both fields. Collaboration among general early childhood education and early childhood special education is essential to the success of young children with delays and disabilities in inclusive settings. For DAP to serve as the groundwork for programs serving young children with delays and disabilities, several steps must be taken. First and foremost, early childhood education and early childhood special education professionals must have a certain understanding of what constitutes recommended practice in their respective fields. Moreover, they must understand the congruencies and distinctions between early childhood education and early childhood special education philosophies and practices, which will aid them in moving toward a model in which DAP is the foundation upon which appropriate programming for any child can be built. Finally, early childhood programs must incorporate early childhood special education practices into developmentally appropriate programs. The outcome should be motivating programs that meet the needs of *all* young children and their families.

A conceptual model developed at the Teaching Research Early Childhood Program at Western Oregon University views DAP as the foundation on which individualized programs are formed. Early childhood special education practices are added as needed for individual children. According to Udell et al. (1998), both DAP and early childhood special education practices can exist within the same setting. An adapted and updated version of their analysis illustrates a conceptual base for dealing with the issue of compounding recommended practice from early childhood special education and DAP. In Figure 6.2, a builder is shown who is trying to create a program or school by combining DAP and early childhood special education practices. Figure 6.3 shows how the builder reconciles this issue by having DAP serve as the foundation and early childhood special education practices as the material to finish the structure. Udell and his colleagues encourage professionals to recognize that the early childhood

FIGURE 6.2 ■ Builder With Two Sets of Materials: ECSE and DAP

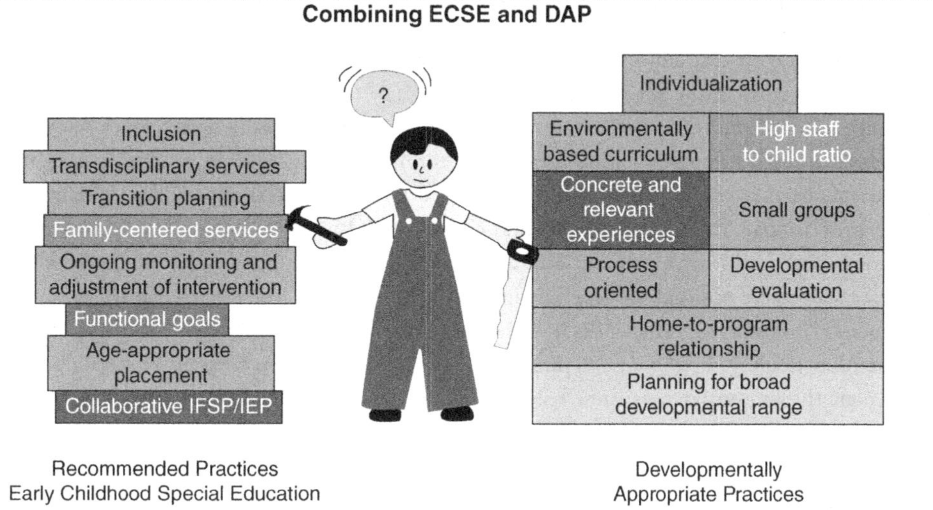

Source: Adapted from T. Udell, J. Peters, and T. Templeman, "From Philosophy to Practice in Inclusive Early Childhood Programs," *Teaching Exceptional Children, 30*(3), p. 48–49. Copyright © 1998 Council for Exceptional Children (CEC). Reprinted by permission.

FIGURE 6.3 ■ DAP + ECSE

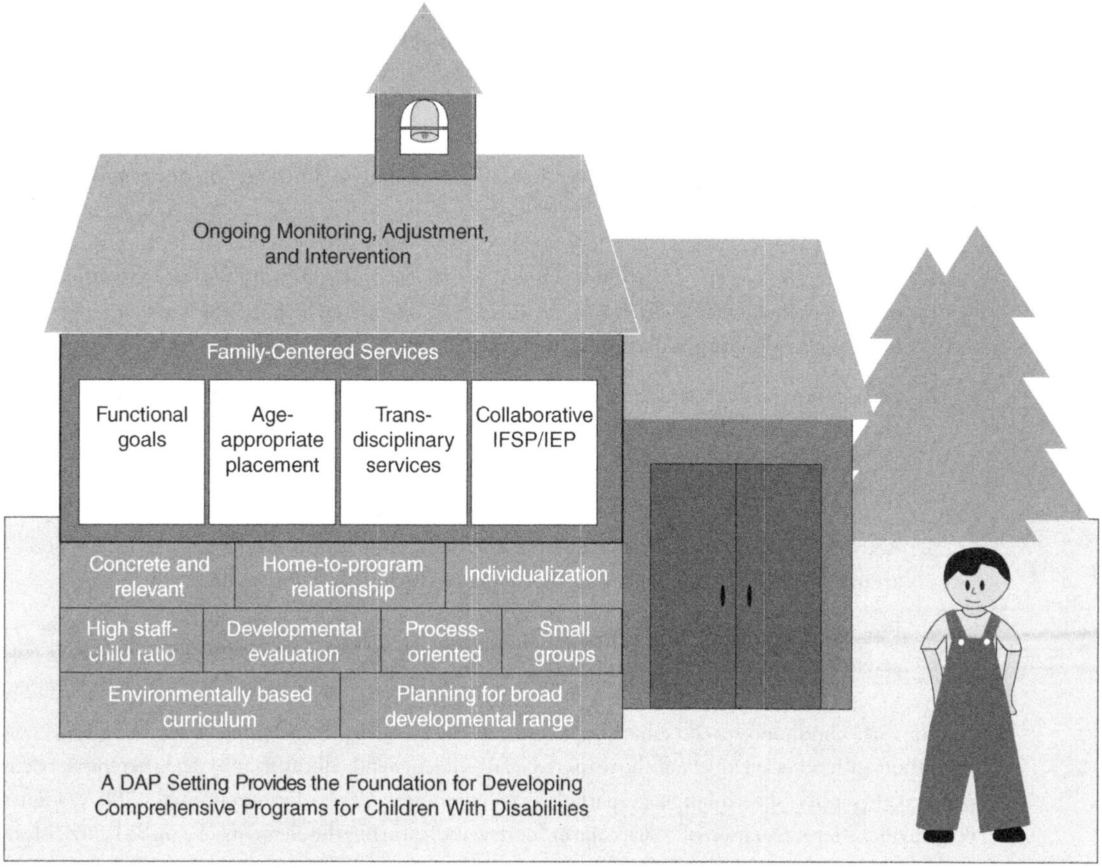

Source: Adapted from T. Udell, J. Peters, and T. Templeman, "From Philosophy to Practice in Inclusive Early Childhood Programs," *Teaching Exceptional Children, 30*(3), p. 48–49. Copyright © 1998 Council for Exceptional Children (CEC). Reprinted by permission.

education and early childhood special education practices are distinctive types of resources to be used appropriately with individual children.

CURRICULUM FRAMEWORK FOR EARLY CHILDHOOD SPECIAL EDUCATION

Early childhood special education is an evolving field. Each decade brings new challenges and new ideas for curriculum development. The purpose of this section is to describe a comprehensive curriculum framework that ensures equitable access to universally designed, developmentally appropriate, and challenging learning experiences for all young children in natural and inclusive environments. A **curriculum framework** is a supportive structure that provides guidance for EI/ECSE professionals to align developmental and content knowledge as well as related pedagogy to plan meaningful learning activities, environments, and individualized supports to ensure all children will make optimal progress in rigorous content and achieve desired learning outcomes. Examples of curriculum frameworks include general early childhood curriculum programs (such as Creative Curriculum, HighScope, Bank Street, Montessori). However, extensive research is needed to regulate the appropriateness and effectiveness of various curriculum frameworks and practices in an ever-changing field.

As described throughout this chapter, curriculum in early childhood special education is influenced by several multifaceted factors. A comprehensive curriculum framework is needed to ensure (a) access to and full participation by all children; (b) that the individual needs of children and families are met; and (c) accountability to federal requirements and state standards. The Division for Early Childhood (2007) recapitulates recommended practices regarding curriculum for children with delays and disabilities as follows: "To benefit all children, including those with disabilities and developmental delays, it is important to implement an integrated, developmentally appropriate, universally designed curriculum framework that is flexible, comprehensive, and linked to assessment and program evaluation activities. Such a curriculum framework can help ensure successful access, which in turn facilitates participation and learning of all children and families regardless of need, ability, or background" (p. 3).

According to Division for Early Childhood (2007) and Grisham-Brown and Hemmeter (2017), a comprehensive curriculum for early intervention, preschool, and early primary programs involves four specific essential elements:

1. Assessment to identify curriculum content, which involves assessing children's strengths, needs, developmental levels in any given area, and interests, which is used as a starting point for program planning and to guide instruction
2. Curriculum content, which includes the scope or what is to be taught (in domains or content areas such as social-emotional, motor, language/literacy, and learner goals/outcomes), and sequence, which refers to the order in which it is taught (usually from simple to difficult skills)
3. Activities and intervention/teaching strategies (e.g., daily routines, schedule, environmental arrangement, child experiences, teacher support, teacher-child interaction)
4. Progress monitoring (or systematic, ongoing assessment) to determine whether planned activities are resulting in identified learning outcomes for children.

For early childhood special educators to address the elements of the curriculum framework, collaboration with other members of the team (e.g., families, general educators, physical therapists, occupational therapists, speech-language pathologists) is required (Pretti-Frontczak et al., 2007). Figure 6.4 provides a representation of a curriculum framework featuring the elements of a linked curriculum process. Each of these elements is described in the subsequent sections.

FIGURE 6.4 ■ Curriculum Framework

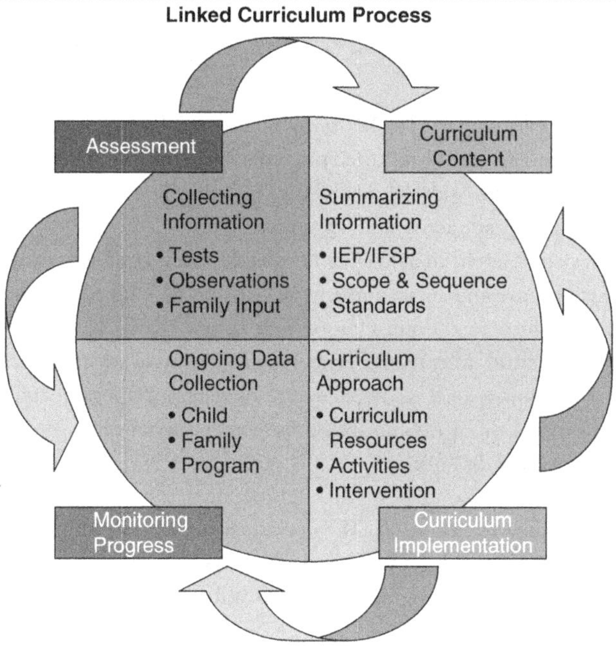

Assessment to Identify Curriculum Content

Ongoing assessment of child performance is a key element of curriculum development. Identifying the content of the curriculum that will be the target of intervention or instruction for each child with a delay or disability is an ongoing process. To determine the targets of intervention or instruction and develop appropriate learning opportunities, the curriculum process must have a mechanism for early childhood special educators, family, and other team members to gain a clear comprehension of children's current skills and abilities (Pretti-Frontczak et al., 2023). As explained in Chapter 5, ongoing assessment can be used to help the team decide the targets of intervention or instruction by observing child characteristics, environmental demands, and the necessary skills to be successful in their environments. Many procedures may be used to identify suitable and meaningful curricula such as curriculum-based tests, observations, family input, and other measures.

Curriculum Content

The content of the curriculum for young children with delays and disabilities includes a broad range of skills that would be relevant and fitting for most young children (DEC, 2007, 2014; Wolery & Sainato, 1996). As portrayed previously, the scope refers to the broad, interrelated areas of developmental and content areas while the sequence refers to the order (e.g., ages, stages, grade levels) in which the content will be taught and learned, which is specified in a developmental progression or by grade level. In the last few years, most states and programs have established standards for early childhood that include the skills that all children are expected to learn. These broad standards often serve as the scope and sequence for all young children in a state or program (Grisham-Brown & Hemmeter, 2017).

Within the broad standards (e.g., scope and sequence) of curriculum, young children with delays and disabilities have individually targeted skills or goals based on the individualized needs of each child, which are stated in their IFSPs or IEPs. Skills on the IFSP or IEP "should not be a restatement of what is being addressed for all learners, but rather the underlying, earlier, or prerequisite skills that are necessary for a child [with a delay or disability] to have access to and participate fully in the curriculum" (Division for Early Childhood, 2007, p. 7). Although these individually targeted skills or goals remain aligned with common standards for all children, team members must work together to adapt the curriculum as needed to address each child's individually targeted skills stated on their IFSPs or IEPs. These standards within the curriculum often necessitate substantial modifications. The scope of early childhood special education services includes information and support for the family in addition to services for the child.

Curriculum Implementation

In addition to collecting information specific to each child and family in designing the curriculum, there are several curriculum resources structured in a sequenced format that are used in early childhood programs serving young children with delays and disabilities. Many of these resources support functional and individually appropriate activities for young children.

Often these guides are referred to as curriculum-based assessment systems because they usually contain an assessment measure and an accompanying curriculum guide. There are many diverse curriculum resources from which to choose. Hanson and Lynch (1995) developed questions for early childhood special educators and other team members to reflect upon when evaluating the quality and appropriateness of curriculum resources. These questions remain important today and can be asked about any curriculum model or curriculum-based assessment system being considered for use with young children with delays and disabilities.

- Is the curriculum organized around a theoretical rationale? Is this philosophical approach clearly stated? And is the philosophical approach consistent with or appropriate to the early childhood special education program's approach and the population served?
- Does the curriculum include a wide range of items/activities (scope), such that the needs of the full range of children in the program will be met?
- Are items appropriate for use with young children with delays and various disabilities (if so, which ones?) and of different ages? Has the curriculum been tested on the populations for which it was designed? Are the validation data available?
- Are the curricular items sequenced in a developmentally appropriate order? Can items be further "branched" or broken down to accommodate children for whom items may be too difficult? Are instructions for this type of branching provided?
- Do items meet the test of being both developmentally and functionally appropriate for young children? Are the curricular items culturally appropriate and nonbiased?
- Is the family a central focus of the curriculum? Are professionals from different disciplines involved? Can families, care providers, and other team members implement the curriculum?
- Is the selection of curricular items integrally linked with assessments and observations of child behavior? Are the goals, objectives, and skills clearly stated so that the child's progress can be monitored?
- Are the goals, outcomes, benchmarks/objectives, and activities written in a jargon-free manner so that they can be easily and consistently used? Are the intervention and instructional techniques and areas of expertise required to implement the curriculum consistent with those of the teacher and other team members? Are the directions for curriculum use clearly and specifically stated?
- Is the amount of time needed to implement the curriculum appropriate to the needs of the program? Can the curriculum be used with various group sizes, and, if so, is it appropriate for the group size(s) of the program? Are the target environments or settings in which the curriculum is to be implemented appropriate to the goals and needs of the program?
- Is the cost of the curriculum reasonable and economically feasible for the program? Are special materials or equipment needed? If so, are these readily available to early childhood special educators and other team members, including family members?
- Can the curriculum be used in formative and summative evaluations of child progress? Can the effectiveness of the curricular approach be evaluated as part of program evaluation?

Most early childhood special educators find curriculum guides, or curriculum-based assessment systems, to be valuable in planning activities in early childhood programs. Selected curriculum-based assessment systems are described in Chapter 5. Some widely used curriculum systems in early intervention and preschool include the following:

- *Assessment, Evaluation, and Programming System (AEPS) for Infants and Children* (3rd ed.) (Bricker et al., 2022)
- *Carolina Curriculum for Infants and Toddlers With Special Needs* (Johnson-Martin, Attermeier et al., 2004) and *Carolina Curriculum for Preschoolers With Special Needs* (Johnson-Martin, Hacker et al., 2004)
- *Hawaii Early Learning Profile (HELP) Strands 0–3* (Parks, 2007) and *Hawaii Early Learning Profile (HELP) Strands 3–6* (formerly titled *HELP for Preschoolers*) (Teaford, 2010)

For the early primary-level children, several curriculum resources are available, including some that are specific to content areas such as literacy, math, and science (Dettmer et al., 2013).

As an example of how various curriculum measures are utilized, the AEPS (Bricker, 2002) contains four volumes. The AEPS permits professionals to match the child's established IFSP or IEP goals/outcomes and objectives/benchmarks and activities with age-appropriate, activity-based interventions that parallel the six areas scored on the AEPS Test. Because the test and curriculum use the same numbering system, users can easily locate activities in the curriculum that correspond to specific goals and objectives identified with the test—a feature that also helps with continuing progress monitoring and evaluation. In both volumes, professionals are provided with instructional sequences, sample intervention or instructional strategies, recommendations for environmental arrangements, and recommendations for incorporating the activities into children's daily routines. To reflect the individual learning styles that children acquire during the preschool years, the AEPS volume for children three to six years old is more adaptable in that it provides general intervention considerations and suggested activities rather than specific instructional sequences.

Activity-based instruction promotes skills from several domains within a routine or planned activity.

Jose Luis Pelaez Inc/DigitalVision/via Getty Images

Curriculum Activities and Intervention

There is increased recognition that the concept of curriculum in early childhood is much broader than the traditional view of a packaged set of goals and activities. As expressed throughout this chapter, curriculum is the entire set of experiences provided in early childhood special education programs, including the degree of structure, types of activities, teacher/adult roles, therapeutic services, physical environment, and peers. We accept a broad view of curriculum to include curriculum planning and the full span of activities experienced by young children receiving early childhood special education services.

In applying the curriculum, the team members must consider each child's individual characteristics and unique needs, the necessary adaptations and modifications to activities, the amount and type of support required, and the therapy services to be offered (e.g., physical therapy, occupational therapy, speech-language pathology) for all children to participate within the environment. A method commonly used to teach targeted skills is activity-based intervention (Johnson et al., 2014), which embeds instruction to speak to each child's individual IFSP or IEP goals and outcomes into the many naturally occurring events and opportunities that exist in the child's daily routine as intervention opportunities in the home, classroom, and other settings. Activity-based intervention and other types of intervention and instructional strategies are described additionally in Chapter 9. This includes **child-initiated routines and activities**, which are those that children initiate themselves, as opposed to routines and activities that are initiated and directed by adults. By following the child's lead, early childhood special educators can support and facilitate the child's learning and development based on their interests, preferences, and strengths.

Curriculum content is addressed by embedding intervention and integrating various types of therapies into activities and routines in the home, child care, and classroom environments (Snyder et al., 2013). Embedded intervention provides chances for early childhood special education professionals and families to address curriculum content at home, in the classroom, and in other environments. In addition to children making progress in achieving desired outcomes, families often profit from this approach as they develop feelings of competence and confidence in their capabilities to provide support for their children's development and learning. More information about embedded interventions is discussed in Chapter 9. Also, readers are referred to the CONNECT Modules to learn more information about embedded interventions (Winton et al., 2010).

Outdoor environments are an important aspect of the curriculum for all young children.

FEATURE 6.1 REPRESENTATIVE WEB RESOURCES

For additional information, please access the following representative websites:

- Division for Early Childhood, https://www.dec-sped.org
- National Association for the Education of Young Children, https://www.naeyc.org/resources/pubs/books/dap-fourth-edition
- Early Childhood Technical Assistance Center, http://ectacenter.org/eco
- RTI Action Network, https://rtinetwork.org
- CONNECT Module 1: Embedded Interventions. Chapel Hill: University of North Carolina, FPG Child Development Institute, CONNECT: The Center to Mobilize Early Childhood Knowledge, http://community.fpg.unc.edu/connect-modules/learners/module-1

Curriculum Progress Monitoring

Early childhood special educators and other team members must frequently monitor child progress to determine how each child is responding to the support provided. This continuing data collection is used to observe progress, which aids in ensuring continuous feedback that is needed to inform and change practice, guide interactions and the selection of materials, and inform decision making regarding all aspects of an early childhood special education program. As discussed in Chapter 5, this necessitates the use of a variety of methods to ensure gathering of reliable, valid, and useful progress monitoring data. Adequate time to review and interpret the data in order to inform and adjust practices also is needed (Dodge, 2004; Grisham-Brown & Pretti-Frontczak, 2003; Helm & Gronlund, 2000; McAfee & Leong, 2011; Pretti-Frontczak et al., 2023).

Curriculum implementation must include documentation regarding the children's progress in relation to the broader curriculum goals, as well as each child's progress in meeting individual goals and outcomes. It is imperative for early childhood special educators and other team members to conduct ongoing monitoring of all children's development and learning. Record keeping and reevaluation are essential for meeting the changing needs of children as well as families. Constant communication about children's progress should be maintained with families using methods families prefer (e.g., daily or weekly notes, email, conferences). When children with delays and disabilities are included in the same environments as their nondisabled peers, the family, along with the general early childhood, early childhood special education, and related service professionals, can discuss ways to coordinate their communication about children's progress. Understanding families from a systems perspective permits professional to approach them as partners in fostering the development and education of their children.

Teacher observes children's interactions to monitor progress and make adjustments to the curriculum.

David Grossman/Alamy Stock Photo

Collaboration in the Curriculum Process

Collaboration, teamwork, and partnerships among early childhood special education professionals and families serve as the foundation of the curriculum framework (Grisham-Brown & Hemmeter, 2017; Hanson & Lynch, 1995). An efficient curriculum process requires that early childhood special educators and other team members work together on several levels. Collaborative efforts or partnerships are created on individual levels among early childhood educators and teaching assistants, home visitors and families/caregivers, child care providers and early childhood special educators, related service personnel and teachers, and many others. These types of partnerships are compulsory routinely for most, if not all, young children with delays and disabilities. In implementing the curriculum, ongoing collaboration is required at another level among team members representing multiple disciplines and family members. Collaboration is essential to the curriculum process to help children with delays and disabilities move toward their desired goals and outcomes.

SUMMARY

In this chapter, we delivered an overview of curriculum in general early childhood and early childhood special education with an emphasis on determining curriculum content to be addressed in programs serving young children with delays and disabilities. Because curriculum focuses holistically on children, the developmental areas cannot actually be separated into isolated skill domains. The developmental domains—cognitive, motor, communication, social-emotional, and adaptive skills—are interdependent and interact in complex ways. The multiple theoretical perspectives, such as developmental, developmental-cognitive, pre-academic/academic, and functional perspectives, form the foundation of numerous curriculum programs. The most recognizable curriculum programs are *The Creative Curriculum, Bank Street, HighScope, Montessori, Reggio Emilia*, and the *Theme-Based or Project Approach*. Each approach has advantages and disadvantages when applied to young children with delays and disabilities.

In addition to the different approaches and programs, organizations that support the education of young children offer guidelines for curriculum development and implementation. There has been much discussion of the DAP guidelines from the NAEYC (2022) regarding the application of these guidelines to curriculum development for young children with delays and disabilities. DEC published guidelines for young children with delays and disabilities, the DEC Recommended Practices (2014). Both sets of guidelines offer input on how to cultivate appropriate curriculum for young children, with NAEYC focused primarily on children without disabilities and DEC highlighting children with disabilities.

Over the last several years, the dialogue that has begun between general early childhood education and early childhood special education has served several important functions in that many misconceptions have been clarified and an augmented understanding of the unique perspectives of both fields has been the outcome. For programs serving young children with delays and disabilities, many professionals suggest a curriculum approach that merges practices from general early childhood education and early childhood special education. DAP laid the foundation for a widely accepted definition of what represents quality early childhood programs for young children. Many professionals suggest that DAP should provide the foundation for all early childhood programs and that strategies and adaptations from early childhood special education should be applied as needed when serving young children with delays and disabilities.

The framework for curriculum development in early childhood special education involves determining the (a) assessment process, (b) curriculum content to be addressed, (c) curriculum implementation process to be followed, and (d) curriculum evaluation procedures to be used. Any evaluation of a particular curriculum guide or approach should consider additional curriculum components when judging effectiveness. Early childhood special education professionals must make decisions concerning curriculum that is based on the unique abilities, needs, backgrounds, and interests of the young children and families they serve.

KEY TERMS

Adaptive behavior
Behavioral approach
Blended practices
Child-initiated routines and activities
Cognitive skills
Communicative intent
Content domains
Culturally and linguistically responsive and affirming
Curriculum
Curriculum framework
Curriculum model
Developmental approach
Developmental-cognitive approach
Developmental domains
Developmentally Appropriate Practice (DAP)
Emotional skills
Expressive language
Fine motor skills
Functional approach
Gross motor skills
Language

Multi-tiered systems of support (MTSS)
Outcomes
Play
Pre-academic/academic approach
Receptive language
Scope
Self-care skills
Sequence
Social-emotional skills
Speech
Universally designed curriculum

CHECK YOUR UNDERSTANDING

1. Define curriculum as it applies to programs serving young children with delays and disabilities.
2. List the theoretical perspectives that have influenced curriculum development in early childhood special education. Discuss the advantages and disadvantages of each perspective when applied to curriculum development for young children with delays and disabilities.
3. List and describe at least three well-known curriculum programs and discuss the advantages and disadvantages of their use with young children with delays and disabilities.
4. Describe important features of commercially available curriculum resources to be used with young children with delays and disabilities.
5. Describe Developmentally Appropriate Practice. Explain how the components of age appropriateness, individual appropriateness, and cultural and social appropriateness influence curriculum in early childhood.
6. Describe the conclusions that have been drawn in the fields of general early childhood education and early childhood special education about the applicability of Developmentally Appropriate Practices to young children with delays and disabilities.
7. Describe a model for blending recommended practices from early childhood education and early childhood special education.
8. Describe a framework for curriculum development in early childhood special education including the four major elements.

REFLECTION AND APPLICATION

1. Observe an early intervention program, an inclusive preschool classroom, and an inclusive early primary classroom where children with delays and disabilities are receiving services. How does the curriculum change depending on the age group—infants and toddlers, preschoolers, or early primary children with delays and disabilities?
2. Examine several commercially available curriculum resources described in this chapter. Evaluate them using the questions developed by Hanson and Lynch that are included in this chapter.
3. Of the curriculum programs described, which one do you think would be most appropriate for Maria, for T. J., and for Cheryl? Explain why.
4. Review the descriptions of the National Association for the Education of Young Children's Developmentally Appropriate Practices and the Division for Early Childhood's Recommended Practices. Why do you think both are important to consider in meeting the needs of Maria, T. J., and Cheryl?

PART III

ORGANIZATION AND INTERVENTION FOR YOUNG CHILDREN WITH DELAYS AND DISABILITIES

iStock.com/kali9

7 DESIGNING LEARNING ENVIRONMENTS FOR YOUNG CHILDREN WITH DELAYS AND DISABILITIES

LEARNING OBJECTIVES

After reading this chapter, you will be able to

7.1 Describe the key characteristics of well-designed indoor and outdoor learning environments for young children with delays and disabilities.

7.2 Outline the types of activity areas or learning centers usually found in learning environments designed for infants, toddlers, preschoolers, and children in the early primary grades.

7.3 List the requirements of accessible learning environments for young children.

7.4 Describe safe and healthy learning environments for young children.

DEC Recommended Practices

The content of this chapter aligns with the following Division for Early Childhood (DEC) Recommended Practices:

Environments

- E1. Practitioners provide services and supports in natural and inclusive environments during daily routines and activities to promote the child's access to and participation in learning experiences.
- E2. Practitioners consider Universal Design for Learning principles to create accessible environments.
- E3. Practitioners work with the family and other adults to modify and adapt the physical, social, and temporal environments to promote each child's access to and participation in learning experiences.
- E4. Practitioners work with families and other adults to identify each child's needs for assistive technology to promote access to and participation in learning experiences.
- E5. Practitioners work with families and other adults to acquire or create appropriate assistive technology to promote each child's access to and participation in learning experiences.
- E6. Practitioners create environments that provide opportunities for movement and regular physical activity to maintain or improve fitness, wellness, and development across domains.

Authors' Note: As you read this chapter, you will find these recommended practices identified throughout the chapter. See Appendix B for a complete list of the DEC Recommended Practices.

Young children with delays and disabilities interact with peers and adults on an ongoing basis within a wide variety of learning environments such as their home, school, and community (e.g., playground, park, church). Therefore, one of the most important responsibilities of an early childhood special educator is to ensure that learning environments facilitate the delivery of effective intervention, instruction, and services.

In center- or school-based programs, the role of the early childhood educator has been equated to that of an architect, and the skills performed are sometimes considered "environmental engineering." Early childhood special educators must be aware of the potential influences of the environment on the behavior and performance of young children with delays and disabilities whether it be the home, classroom, playground, or other natural environments.

This chapter addresses how to effectively arrange physical space, consider environmental practices that maximize learning, and discuss how to present safe and accessible learning environments. The first consideration is the definition of the environment as it applies to early learning settings. According to Gordon and Browne (2024), the **environment** is the sum total of the physical and human qualities that combine to create a space in which children and adults work and play together. Environment is the content teachers arrange, an atmosphere they create, a feeling they communicate. Environment is the total picture (p. 293).

Gordon and Browne (2024) emphasize that environments speak volumes to young children because they have a powerful effect on their behavior, as well as the behavior of adults, and the learning and interactions that occur. Over the past decades, proponents of diverse theoretical learning models, such as behaviorism, constructivism, and social learning, increasingly have stressed the importance of environmental elements in their learning and instructional paradigms (Bredekamp, 2020). Montessori, for example, through her concepts of auto-education and the "prepared classroom," emphasized environmental considerations in the educational process. The focus of her work was based on the premise that, during early development, an enriched learning environment could offset the effects of impoverished living conditions. As described in Chapter 6, the schools of Reggio Emilia in Italy, which have gained popularity in the United States and across the world, have a "beautiful environment" as one of the three major components of their program. In these programs and others, the environment plays a central role and is considered to be the "third teacher" (Bredekamp, 2020; New & Kantor, 2013; Pisha & Spencer, 2016).

Early childhood special educators increasingly have focused on evidence-based environmental practices to be used in designing learning environments to enhance learning for all young children. Environmental practices refer to "aspects of the space, materials (toys, books, etc.), equipment, routines, and activities that practitioners and families can intentionally alter to support each child's learning across developmental domains" (Division for Early Childhood, 2014, p. 9). Through the implementation of these practices, practitioners and families can promote responsive environments to foster children's learning and development.

The focus of this chapter is classroom ecology, which refers to the physical environment (e.g., space, room arrangement, equipment, materials) and the modifications and arrangements of features of classroom environments that can have an impact on learning for young children with delays and disabilities. Modifications and arrangements often must be made to features of the learning environment including, but not limited to, activity areas or learning centers, types of seating and seating arrangements, materials, acoustics, and lighting. Emphasized in this chapter are the principles and practices that can be adapted or modified to ensure success for infants and toddlers, preschoolers, and early primary students with delays and disabilities. The key is to promote learning environments that encourage the growth, development, and learning of children with varying abilities and needs.

In addition to the physical environment, environmental practices focus on the social environment and human aspects of the environment (e.g., interactions with peers, adults, family members) and the temporal environment (e.g., length of routines and activities, sequence of activities, daily schedule; Division for Early Childhood, 2014, 2016; Jalongo & Isenberg, 2012). These practices (social and temporal) are addressed further in Chapters 8 and 9. Early childhood special educators must remember that environmental dimensions (physical, social, temporal) are interconnected for young children with delays and disabilities and their families.

These components collectively set the stage for learning and play a key role in establishing high-quality learning environments for all young children (Catalino & Meyer, 2016). As the Division for Early Childhood (2014) suggests, EI/ECSE practitioners work with families and other adults to design, modify, and adapt these environmental dimensions to support each child's access to and participation in learning activities [DEC Recommend Practices E3]. Environmental practices must not only support each child's access to and participation in learning activities, but also supply appropriate evidence-based classroom interventions to improve the child's outcomes (McLeod et al., 2017). In addition, EI/ECSE professionals must ensure children's safety in the learning environment.

ORGANIZING THE LEARNING ENVIRONMENT

A primary role of the EI/ECSE practitioner is to intentionally create and organize the learning environment. The creation of an engaging and effective early learning environment is an ongoing process that requires careful planning to maximize learning opportunities. They must observe and guide children within the learning environments and then make necessary changes to create more meaningful learning opportunities and extend learning (McDonald, 2018). In home-based services, the EI/ECSE professionals work with and support families in optimizing environments to facilitate learning.

Positive Effects of High-Quality Environments

There are many positive effects of secure, organized, engaging learning environments. By skillfully arranging learning environments, early childhood special educators and families can positively affect a variety of behaviors and interactions in young children, including those with delays and disabilities, such as encouraging learning, enhancing self-confidence, and minimizing disruptive actions. Knowledge of the impact of the environment on young children's learning is used to create environments that maximize, and even magnify, the effectiveness of intervention, instruction, and services. To maximize instructional efficiency, early childhood special educators must ensure that the children experience learning environments that communicate the messages "This is a safe place"; "This is a fun, enjoyable place"; "You are accepted and can be successful here"; and, most importantly, "You can learn here at your individual ability level."

In organizing the classroom environments for young children, a number of factors must be considered.
iStock.com/mgstudyo

According to Jalongo and Isenberg (2012), high-quality environments for young children are constructed around the following five principles of environmental design. They recommend that learning environments should

- Be organized, challenging, and aesthetically pleasing
- Be capable of creating a caring community of learners that affirms diversity
- Have clear goals that reflect a particular instructional emphasis
- Protect the health and safety of the children
- Allow all children equal access to age-appropriate materials and equipment

The design of classroom environments must be based on the EI/ECSE practitioner's fundamental knowledge of learning theory, knowledge about children's growth and development, advice from experts, recommended practice guidelines from professional organizations, and evidence-based practices.

Key Dimensions

Creating an engaging and effective learning environment for young children with delays and disabilities and their typically developing peers is a tremendous undertaking. Building on knowledge of child growth and development coupled with an understanding of the characteristics and needs of children with delays and disabilities, early childhood special educators also must consider several other factors. Effective environmental arrangements are related to issues of

- Available space and room arrangement
- Age of the children
- Population density
- The children's individual characteristics and differences
- Aesthetics and visual appeal
- Accessibility
- Safety and health
- Materials and equipment

- Organization
- Length of day, activities, and schedule
- Child–adult ratios
- Budget

Consideration of these factors and other variables helps determine the appearance and atmosphere of learning environments.

In some instances, various aspects of learning environments, such as room design, are predetermined and established by the location of the learning space (e.g., early intervention program, child care program, public school). Although some variables may not be under the early childhood special educator's control, the structure of the learning environment is often a clear indication of the priorities, goals/outcomes, and expectations for the children. Designing a learning environment is not a onetime event; it is an ongoing process. As the needs of the children change, the classroom environment frequently requires modifications. The purpose here is to briefly review some of the important dimensions of arranging the learning environment. This is an important consideration because the physical environment sets the stage for learning and what is expected of young children within the environment (Bredekamp, 2020).

Physical Space

The ratio of room size or area to the child population (e.g., infants, toddlers, preschoolers, early primary children) is an important factor in designing learning environments. The National Association for the Education of Young Children (NAEYC, 2019) recommends that preschool classrooms maintain a minimum of thirty-five square feet of space per child for indoor settings, although fifty square feet per child is desirable, and seventy-five square feet for outdoor spaces. Many states have adopted these figures for inclusion in their licensing regulations and specifications for early childhood programs. Dimension requirements for infant and toddler environments tend to be slightly lower due to the limited mobility of the children. As stated earlier, the amount of square footage provided per child may not be as significant as the way in which the available space is arranged.

Other Variables

Environmental conditions, such as acoustics, lighting, color, and temperature, strongly influence learning environments and are important for early childhood special educators to consider. The acoustics, of course, are affected by the sounds within a learning environment, which are natural by-products of children's interactions and explorations of the environment. Excessive noise, however, is uncomfortable and may negatively affect children's ability to communicate, interact socially, and concentrate while impeding their ability to learn (Readdick, 2006), which is particularly true for children with hearing impairments, attention disorders, or behavior issues. Appropriate lighting is another important environmental variable and can affect the emotional well-being of children. Classroom and other learning environments must have as much natural light as possible. For example, art and literacy/reading areas must be located near windows. If natural light is insufficient, soft lighting from floor lamps is recommended instead of harsh fluorescent lighting. Appropriate lighting is especially important for children with visual impairments.

Color contributes to the quality of the learning environment. Color selection must be stimulating but not agitating or distracting. Although soft colors often are restful to adults, they may be uninteresting to young children. Because some children spend a large portion of their day in classrooms, classroom environments need to be as aesthetically pleasing as possible. Children with attention disorders or behavior issues may be influenced by color or temperature. If a learning environment is too hot or too cold, children may find it difficult to concentrate and learn. An optimal room temperature is generally between 68 and 72 degrees Fahrenheit, or 20 and 22 degrees Celsius.

Feeney et al. (2023) offer the following suggestions for producing an aesthetically pleasing classroom that is functionally organized, attractive, appealing, and conducive to learning:

- *Choose soft, neutral colors.* Light colors are recommended for walls and ceilings. If color selection is not possible, coordination with the color of the walls is recommended.
- *Display children's artwork.* Mounting and displaying the children's artwork shows its importance and value. Artwork must be displayed at eye level.
- *Incorporate natural objects and materials.* Plants, stones, seeds, and shells can be used as learning materials, as well as to enhance the beauty of the classroom.
- *Pay attention to storage.* Storage must be functional, organized, and attractive. An organized learning environment helps to maintain order, safety, and stability.
- *Avoid clutter; rotate materials.* Crowded shelves and storage areas are unattractive. Materials can be rotated instead of placing all items out for use at once. If a new item is brought out, then another item can be put away.
- *Label shelves.* Children will become more self-sufficient if they know where to put things away. Shelves and containers can be labeled with photos or symbols for young children with delays and disabilities.

CREATING ACTIVITY AREAS OR LEARNING CENTERS

Classroom space often is divided into activity areas or learning centers. Depending on the ages and developmental levels of the children, the activity areas or learning centers will differ. There can be a permanent location in classrooms for the activity areas or learning centers, or they can be temporary or rotating. Activity areas or learning centers provide a sense of order in classrooms and can serve as the focal points of daily scheduling and activity planning. The content of these areas will vary depending on the ages and abilities of the children. Because developmental changes occur so rapidly in the early years, the learning environment must be designed to account for varying levels of ability and needs as the children learn and develop, and have changing interests and needs (Essa & Burnham, 2020). Teachers must consider the purpose of each activity area or learning center and the appropriateness and meaningfulness of what occurs in each space.

Infants and Toddlers

Activity areas or learning centers for infants and toddlers must be safe, secure, aesthetically pleasing, stimulating, and supportive. Safety and cleanliness are of paramount importance. Younger infants (birth to nine months), for example, need a safe and secure environment; mobile infants (eight to eighteen months) need areas to engage in exploration; and toddlers (sixteen to thirty-six months) need expanded space to continue to develop their identities (Copple & Bredekamp, 2009). In creating activity areas, early childhood special educators must consider each of these developmental stages and the characteristics, needs, and interests of the children.

Recall that infants and toddlers are at the sensorimotor stage of cognitive development (Piaget, 1963), learning about their world through touch, taste, sight, smell, and hearing. Accordingly, an appropriate learning environment must be a responsive environment that supports and encourages movement, exploration, and discovery through interactions with peers, adults, materials, routines, and activities (Allen & Cowdery, 2022). Activity areas for infants, for example, may include a toy and a manipulation center, a sensory area, an exercise mat, and an early literacy area, as well as others.

A large part of an infant's or toddler's day is structured around predictable routines—eating, sleeping, toileting, and playing. Therefore, areas must be available that allow for changing, sleeping, and feeding/eating, as well as quiet and active play. Inclusive infant and toddler environments often are structured around activities of daily living such as dressing, eating, and toileting. These tasks are equally as important for young children with delays and disabilities as they are for typically developing children (O'Brien, 2001). Infants and toddlers with delays and disabilities may have much of their program determined by their individual needs based on input from members of their team that includes such professionals as physical therapists, occupational therapists, and speech–language pathologists, as well as families.

Due to the increased mobility and developing cognitive skills of most toddlers, activity areas or learning centers become increasingly complex and varied. Environments for toddlers often include developmentally appropriate activity areas like those suggested for older preschool children (National Association for the Education of Young Children, 2022). Typical areas include music, creative play, literacy, construction and blocks, problem solving, sand and water play, as well as fine and gross motor activities. Spaces for role-playing, outdoor play, and privacy also are available. Figure 7.1 illustrates one example of an infant and toddler classroom arrangement, although infants and toddlers have separate classrooms in most center-based programs.

FIGURE 7.1 ■ Representative Design of an Infant and Toddler Learning Environment

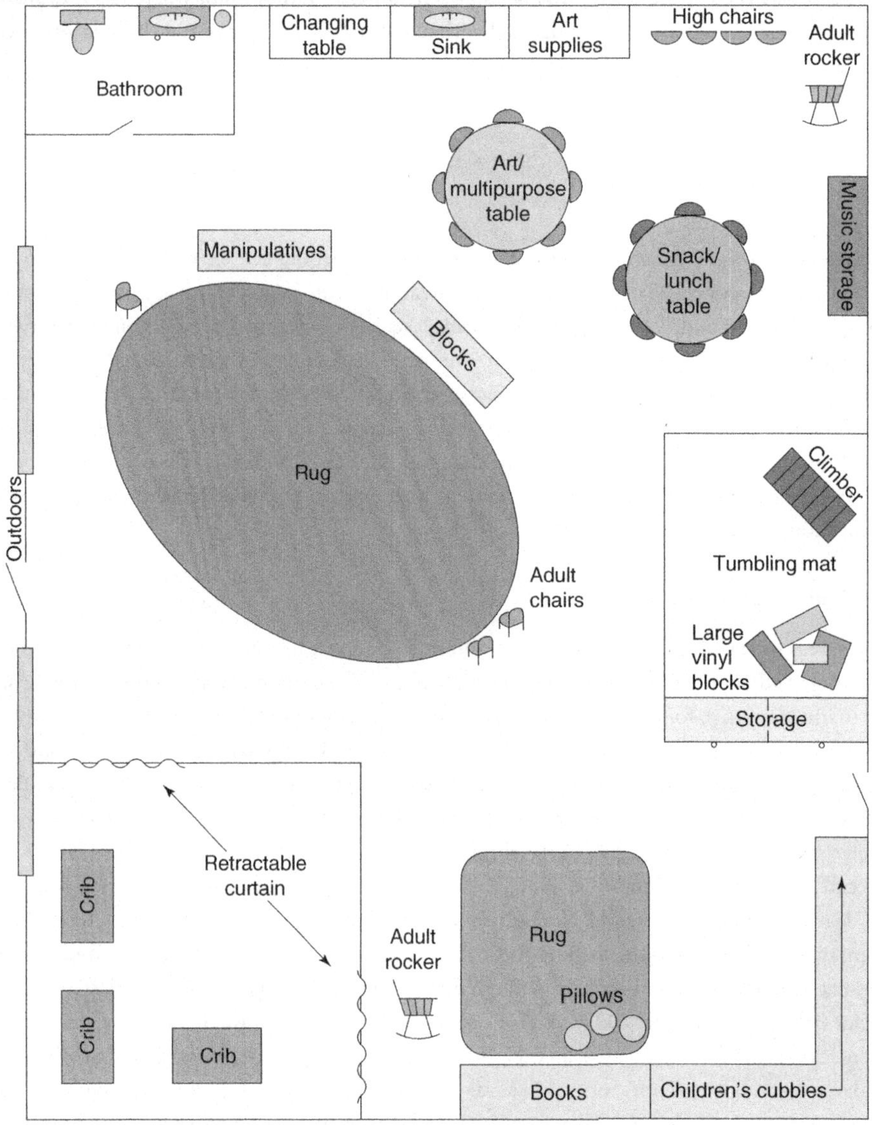

Source: M. Henniger, *Teaching Young Children: An Introduction*, 6th ed. (New York, NY: Pearson Education, 2018), p. 255.

Preschoolers

A question that often arises when planning physical space within learning environments for preschoolers is whether to construct open- or closed-plan facilities. Open plans tend to have undivided internal spaces within a large room, while closed-plan facilities usually entail several self-contained rooms connected by corridors or hallways. Each design has specific advantages and disadvantages. Designers often suggest the use of both large and small activity areas that give young children some protection from distraction while allowing them the ability to view other areas in the room and the activity choices available to them.

Decisions must be made about the boundaries established in classrooms. According to Olds (1987), the use of "fluid boundaries" is recommended for separating areas of the preschool classroom. This recommendation is still appropriate today. Fluid boundaries consist of environmental clues that a change of area has occurred without placing physical barriers to impair mobility. For example, an activity area may be differentiated from other areas by lowering the ceiling with a parachute canopy rather than surrounding the area with bookcases or storage units. Painted lines on the floor, or colored tape if the floor is carpeted, can form effective boundaries, as can distinct, varying carpet colors. Several activity areas or learning centers are present in most preschool classrooms. Typically, these areas are designed to accommodate small groups of young children and a teacher or other professionals, although some areas such as a circle time or group area for introductory, circle time, morning meeting, sharing, or music activities may be designed to accommodate the entire group of children.

Learning activities must be organized to encourage the meaningful participation of children who exhibit a wide range of skills and abilities and represent various social and cultural backgrounds (Bredekamp, 2020; National Association for the Education of Young Children, 2022). Classrooms should include centers that are based on the ages, abilities, and interests of the children while also being linked to individual outcomes and goals as outlined on the student's individualized family service plans (IFSPs) or individualized education programs (IEPs). Additionally, learning centers and materials should be age appropriate, as well as individually appropriate, while reflecting social and cultural appropriateness. A skillful matching of the individual strengths and needs of the children with the organization of the classroom often leads to equitable learning opportunities for all children while ensuring that the children with delays and disabilities are fully included (Winter, 2007).

Activity centers for young children should be attractive and encourage learning.

iStock.com/DGLimages

NAEYC (2019) recommends that the physical space be divided to facilitate a range of small-group and individual activities, including block building, dramatic play, art, music, science, math, and language/literacy. Feeney and her colleagues (2023) recommend the addition of technology, writing, and sensory play/stimulation areas. Within these general areas, an almost endless number of specific activity areas or learning centers can be arranged. The quiet, calm area may include a literacy and language center, private space, listening center, and rest area. During the day, the use of an area may change, taking on dual or triple roles. For example, the quiet area may be used first for language and literacy activities, then as a listening center, and then as the rest area. The discovery area could have rotating centers based on the theme of the week or special projects. This may be an appropriate area for hands-on science activities and to house classroom pets.

The dramatic play area should have activities that promote creative expression and real-life simulations. Materials must be selected to stimulate role-playing such as dress-up clothes, accessories, and mirrors; play kitchen sets, cookware, and utensils; and grocery store items. Also, dolls or human figures representing various ages, cultural backgrounds, and occupations should be available for creative play. Through the careful selection of toys and objects, there is much that early childhood special educators and other professionals can do to promote learning of new language and social behaviors such as tolerance for differences, sharing, and collaboration.

The range of activities provided in the art area must be limited only by the media available through the program's budget; even then, the creative professional often can work around this limitation. If possible, this area must be near the bathroom or a sink to ease cleanup, and the flooring must be slip-proof tile or linoleum. Child-size easels are recommended as well as space for the display of the children's work. Besides traditional coloring and painting projects, other activities may include woodworking projects, Play-Doh or clay pottery, or printmaking. In classrooms with children with physical or sensory differences, it is particularly important to have a variety of media available so that all children can be working on projects appropriate for their skills and specific abilities.

A question that frequently arises is how therapeutic and specialized interventions can be afforded within an inclusive learning environment. A rapidly increasing body of empirical evidence suggests that to be effective, therapy and interventions must be delivered during naturally occurring, ongoing, and routine events and activities (Cook et al., 2020; Noonan & McCormick, 2014). Therapy and intervention are designed specifically to support services in natural and inclusive environments [DEC Recommended Practices E1].

The inclusion of speech–language, physical, and occupational therapy, for example, in the natural and inclusive environment usually can be accomplished with minimal adaptations. Although environmental arrangements are important for certain interventions, major adaptations to the environment are rarely needed. The inclusion of physical or occupational therapy in a classroom setting often requires the addition of adaptive equipment that necessitates additional space for use and storage. Early childhood special educators and related service providers using an integrated therapy approach generally want to limit the number of adaptations necessary to accommodate the needs of the children. There are two reasons for this. One is a social consideration; the amount of undue attention given to young children related to their delay or disability must be limited. The second is functional consideration; children with delays and disabilities must learn to navigate, participate, and communicate in the natural environment during daily routines and activities (Benjamin et al., 2017; Brown et al., 2020; Johnson et al., 2015; Noonan & McCormick, 2014) [DEC Recommended Practices E1]. The motor performance of preschool children was found to increase in group settings, which may be explained by their motivation, modeling, and competition with peers (Fay et al., 2017).

Another consideration is the need to create physical space for individual or private areas. Time and space must be available for individual private areas in terms of both social time, or lack thereof, and privacy in the storage and care of belongings (Brewer, 2007). Children's sense of independence and need for privacy can be managed by providing individual "cubbies" or areas for storage of personal items, which are labeled with their names and/or photographs, and attractive and comfortable areas designed for young children to have private social time as an option. When designing classroom space, it also is important to consider factors related to the needs of the adults. Just as children need appropriate physical space, adults need space as well. Areas for adults to meet, plan, store files and materials, and so on must be available so that they can be as effective as possible in carrying out their roles and responsibilities.

Over time, many early childhood special educators recognize the need to change the environment based on their own observations and experiences and the children's needs and interests. Once again,

EI/ECSE professionals acting as "environmental engineers" must weigh the benefits of a consistent environment against the need for new opportunities for exploration. Figure 7.2 presents a representative diagram of a preschool learning environment.

FIGURE 7.2 ■ Sample Preschool Classroom

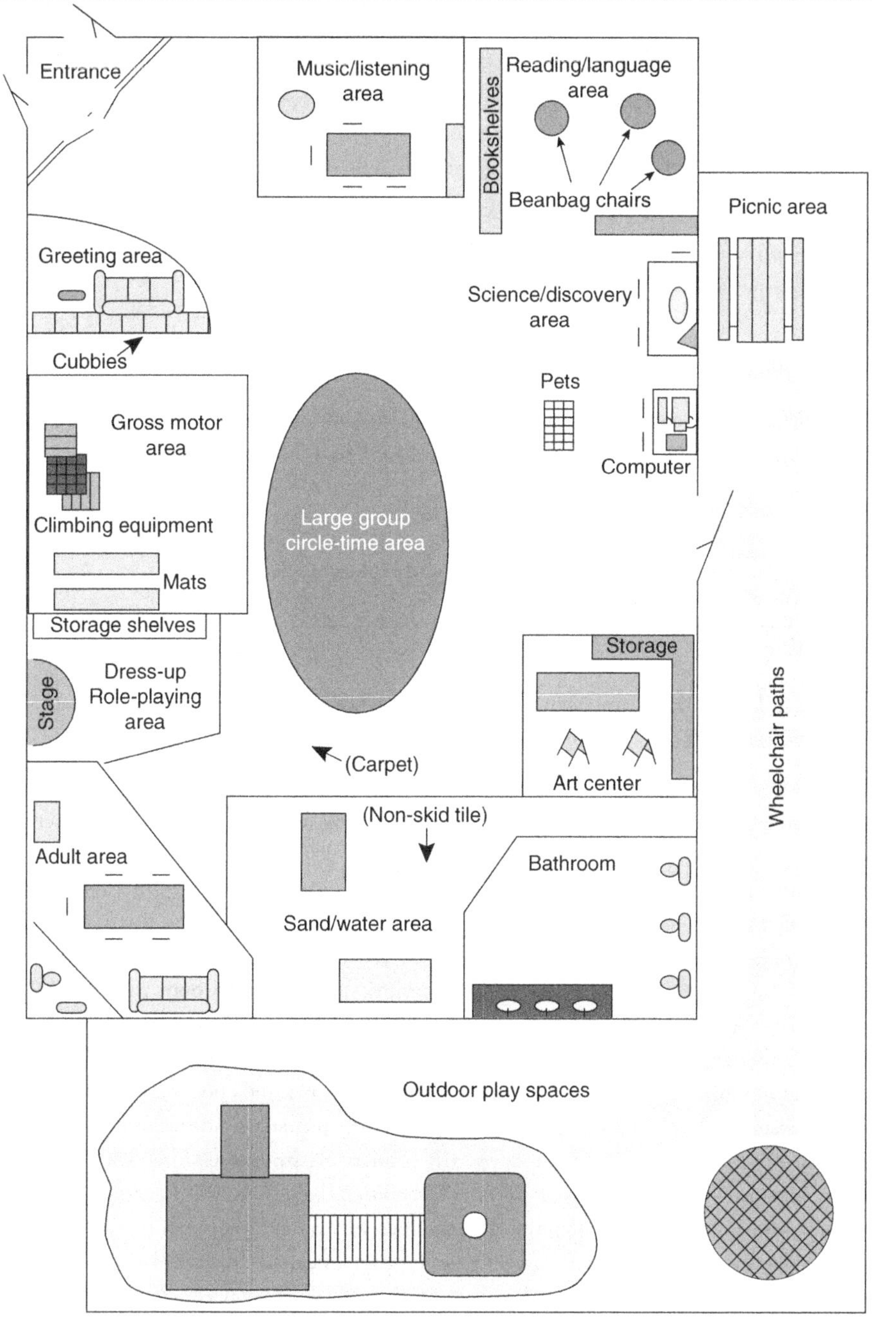

Source: ECE Photo library.

Children in the Early Primary Grades

Classrooms for children in the early primary grades typically are filled with students who are engaged in learning in a different manner than younger children. At this age, according to Tomlinson (2009), children "delight in their new intellectual prowess, social skills, and physical abilities" (p. 257). Developing an enjoyment of learning is a major goal for this age group. At this point in time, children learn best through concrete experiences; therefore, they need to see the relevance of what they are learning and the connections across various learning domains (Tomlinson, 2009). Likewise, early primary students with delays and disabilities learn best when they are fully engaged and involved in their learning by exploring, reasoning, and problem solving. The learning environments for early primary students must encourage self-initiation, personal responsibility, and self-regulation (Raver, 2009). Early childhood educators, therefore, must organize their classrooms carefully to support these various goals.

Based on the recommendations of NAEYC's DAP guidelines (Copple & Bredekamp, 2009), exemplary early primary classrooms in which children with delays and disabilities are included are designed around the following eight practices. In classrooms, early childhood special educators

1. Arrange tables or flexible groupings of desks and tables to enable children to work alone or in small groups.
2. Provide a safe environment and age-appropriate supervision as children are gradually given more responsibility.
3. Anticipate and prevent situations in which children might be hurt, while supporting children's risk-taking behavior within safe boundaries.
4. Foster a learning environment that encourages exploration, initiative, positive peer interaction, and cognitive growth, and choose materials that comfortably challenge children's skills.
5. Provide various types of spaces for silent or shared reading, working on construction projects, writing, playing math or language games, and exploring science.
6. Organize the daily schedule to allow for alternating periods of physical activity and quiet time.
7. Give children advance notice of transitions and, when possible, allow them to complete what they are working on before moving on to the next activity.
8. Plan the curriculum, schedule, and environment so that children can learn through active involvement in various learning experiences with peers, adults, and a variety of materials.

Many early primary classrooms emphasize the use of learning centers with this age group, which is recommended based on the developmental level and learning that occurs at this age. The physical environment of early primary-grade classrooms, however, usually shows fewer activity areas or learning centers. When learning centers are incorporated into the design of the classroom, their focus frequently is on mathematics and literacy centers where students can develop academic skills linked to the curriculum. Also, dramatic play, art, and music centers often are supplied (Henniger, 2018). Desks arranged in clusters and/or tables are available to allow for small-group work and cooperative learning activities. Figure 7.3 presents one type of room arrangement for an early primary-grade classroom.

As stressed throughout this text, in today's early primary classrooms, children with delays and disabilities are included alongside their peers without disabilities, thereby requiring adaptations to inclusive learning environments. Children with physical disabilities, for example, may require wider doorways and clear pathways to successfully maneuver around the classroom. Learning materials may need to be placed on lower shelves so students can independently access them. Desks may need to be raised to accommodate children in wheelchairs. Additional storage areas may be necessary to house specialized equipment or adaptive seating devices. Some children with visual impairments may need preferential seating, clear pathways for movement, different types of lighting, and distinguishable landmarks so they can easily orient themselves in the classroom. Nonprint signs or symbols may be needed for children with cognitive delays and disabilities. In most cases, the adaptations are relatively minor (Gargiulo & Bouck, 2021).

As described by the Division for Early Childhood (2014), environments must provide opportunities for movement and regular physical activity, which is important to maintain or improve fitness, wellness, and development across multiple domains [DEC Recommended Practices E6]. Early childhood professionals have an obligation to be responsive to the individual needs of all children. As stated

FIGURE 7.3 ■ Representative Design of an Early Primary Classroom

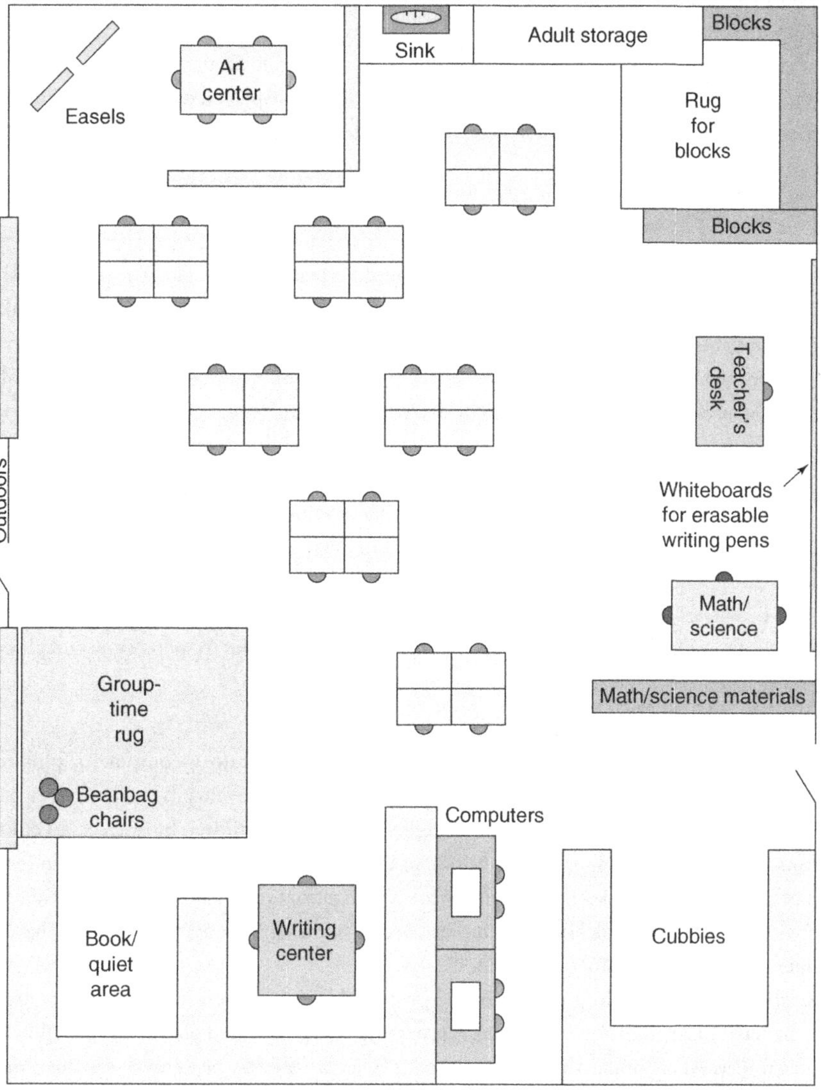

Source: M. Henniger, *Teaching Young Children: An Introduction*, 6th ed. (New York, NY: Pearson Education, 2018), p. 259.

The learning environments for children with delays and disabilities in the early primary grades should be planned carefully to allow them to be fully engaged in their learning.

Klaus Vedfelt/DigitalVision/via Getty Images

earlier in this chapter, environments facilitate learning for young children and should communicate the expectations of the environment (e.g., a large open space invites movement and physical activity while a cozy area with soft chairs, pillows, and books invites reading). Early childhood special educators must consider what the learning environment says to children about what activities and behaviors are expected within that environment (e.g., toys and materials displayed on low shelves invite children to play with them). This applies to both indoor and outdoor learning environments.

OUTDOOR LEARNING ENVIRONMENTS

Most early childhood programs have some form of outdoor play space. In fact, the playground is viewed as an outdoor component of the classroom. "Outdoor environments stimulate children's thinking, ability to solve problems, make decisions, socialize, and try new ideas in ways that are often different from indoor environments" (Jalongo & Isenberg, 2012, pp. 187–188). Outdoor play is an integral part of a child's natural environment, imparts upon children the opportunity to receive the health benefits associated with sunshine and fresh air, and provides breaks for both children and adults from the indoor routines. Properly designed outdoor settings not only benefit young children's physical development but also support their cognitive, language, and social-emotional development (Chang & Shire, 2019). Outdoor play is an essential component emphasized in NAEYC's DAP guidelines for young children (Copple & Bredekamp, 2009; National Association for the Education of Young Children, 2022). The American Academy of Pediatrics (2019), in conjunction with other professional associations, recommends that all children, including infants and toddlers, must have daily opportunities to spend time and play outdoors.

Recommendations for Designing Outdoor Space

Ideally, a large, accessible, grassy area with interactive and exploratory equipment, plus traditional swings and slides, is generally recommended for outdoor areas. Seventy-five square feet per child is generally the norm. Playground designers also suggest that young children have access to climbers, balance beams, a sandbox, and other fixed equipment in addition to a gardening area when feasible. The addition of playhouses provides opportunities for socialization and role-playing activities. For young children with developmental delays and disabilities who are unable to participate, adaptive equipment appropriate to their abilities must be provided.

If possible, space for outdoor eating should be available, and the entire outdoor play area must be fenced in for safety purposes. Paved surfaces connecting equipment and play areas will allow for wheelchair accessibility. Areas under the play equipment lined with bark, pea gravel, sawdust, or sand will cushion any falls. The U.S. Consumer Product Safety Commission (n.d.) recommends that materials be twelve inches deep to prevent serious injury. Safety concerns always must be the major priority when planning playground and other outdoor learning environments.

The number of accidents requiring medical attention that occur on playgrounds is alarming. Emergency rooms report more than two hundred thousand cases of children who are injured on playgrounds annually (U.S. Consumer Product Safety Commission, n.d.). Many of these accidents occur with swings, slides, and climbing equipment. A contributing factor to these numbers may be that young children are engaged in risk-taking behavior involving activities or equipment that are beyond their developmental levels. If the outdoor space involves a mix of toddlers and preschoolers or preschoolers and early primary-age children, the design must incorporate activities and equipment that is developmentally appropriate for each group. Playgrounds often are equated with "equipment"; however, the use of open, natural outdoor spaces must not be undervalued. A natural space with several height levels and simple materials to allow for the development of balance and other gross motor skills can be as effective as more complex designs, especially in terms of safety and cost. Developmentally appropriate outdoor environments provide young children with a variety of natural and commercially produced landscape elements.

Considerations for Young Children With Delays and Disabilities

Most young children, including those with delays and disabilities, enjoy and benefit from playing outdoors. Play can be the vehicle through which young children, regardless of individual differences, grow, develop, and learn; it provides a natural opportunity for interaction with peers and inclusive experiences. Some children with delays and disabilities, however, may have differences in abilities, skills, and behaviors that require encouragement, reinforcement, and modeling to maximize their outdoor experience (Henniger, 2018). In some circumstances, the outdoor environment must be modified to accommodate children with delays and disabilities to address accessibility and safety, which are two of the primary concerns. For example, pathways must be five feet wide for use by children with wheelchairs or walkers; the installation of handrails may be needed; wider gates may be necessary; and playground surfaces must be accessible by children with physical, sensory, or other types of delays and disabilities.

The U.S. Access Board (2021) and the Department of Justice (2010) have developed specific guidelines for playgrounds that are in compliance with the Americans with Disabilities Act. Examples include the following:

1. *Ground-level playground equipment.* One type of each piece of equipment (swings or slides) must be accessible.
2. *Elevated structures.* Fifty percent of elevated play components must be accessible.
3. *Dramatic play equipment.* Structures such as a playhouse can easily be made accessible simply by locating them adjacent to accessible walkways.
4. *Play tables.* Tables used for board games, for sand and water play, or merely as a gathering place must be on an accessible route and meet minimum wheelchair requirements.
5. *Water play, sandboxes, and garden areas.* The recommendation is for these items or areas to be at the edge of pathways and raised to a level that is wheelchair accessible.

Table 7.1 offers an example of the type of outdoor play adaptations often necessary to accommodate young children with delays and disabilities. The intent of these suggestions is to ensure that young children can meaningfully participate with their peers to the maximum extent possible.

TABLE 7.1 ■ Planning Guide for Outdoor Play Adaptations

Activities	For a Child With a Visual Impairment	For a Child With Autism Spectrum Disorder
Transition to playground	Upon entering the playground, give the child verbal directions about where friends and equipment are located; use a sighted guide (peer or teacher) to help the child move to an area of choice.	Prior to entering the playground, tell the child that they are going to the playground next; give them a ball to carry outside and repeat, "We are going outside now."
Gardening	Orient the child to the garden area verbally and physically; describe other children's activities (watering, digging) and offer choices for participating.	Create a physical boundary around the garden area (fence or other physical structure); establish for the child a specific area in which to dig, plant, and water.
Water table	Tell the child which materials are in the water table, where materials are located, which friends are present, and what they are doing.	Model ways to use materials and describe what you are doing or what the child is doing.
Balls	Use an adapted ball with a beeper noise inside; place the ball under the child's hands.	Communicate rules and boundaries clearly when playing with balls and repeat in different ways, as needed.
Climbing equipment	Alert the child to any potential safety concerns (bumping head) and describe the location of possible danger.	No modification necessary; the activity should be monitored for safety.
Sandbox	Tell the child which materials are available and who is playing; be aware of the potential need to facilitate the child's entering and maintaining play with peers.	Limit the number of toys/materials available to those specifically of interest to the child.

Source: Adapted from L. Flynn and J. Kieff, "Including Everyone in Outdoor Play," *Young Children, 57*(3), 2002, p. 23. Copyright © 2002 NAEYC®. Reprinted with permission.

Figure 7.4 is an example of an outdoor playground in an inclusive setting. Feature 7.1 identifies several play resources specific to children with delays and disabilities.

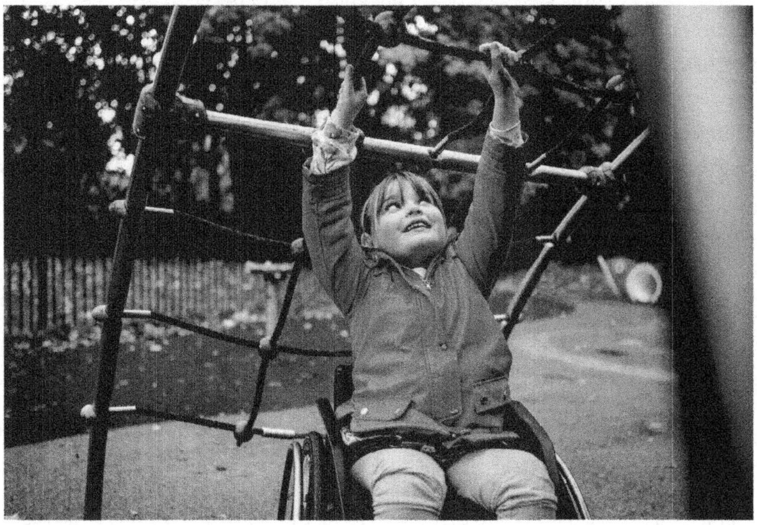

Outdoor play is an important component of developmentally appropriate practices.

iStock.com/SolStock

FIGURE 7.4 ■ Example of an Inclusive Outdoor Playground

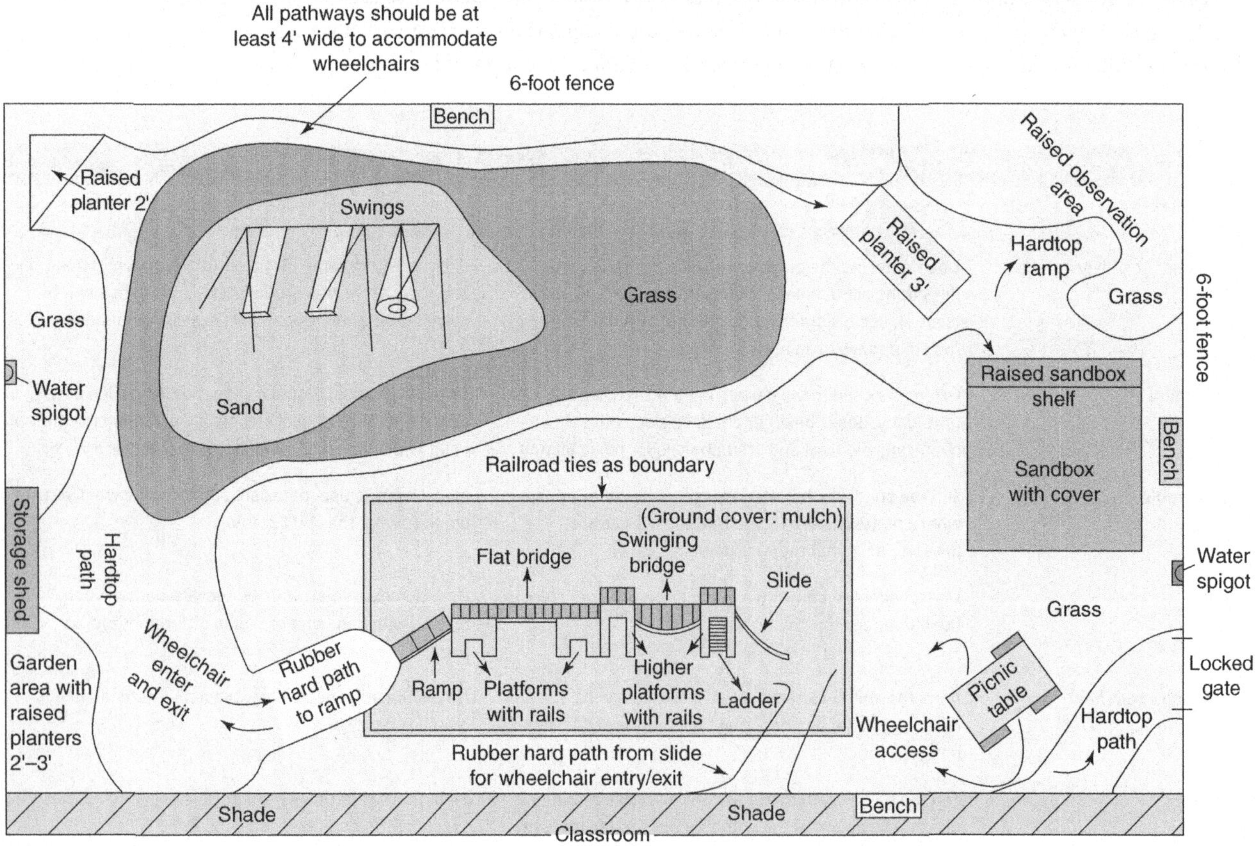

Source: M. Henniger, *Teaching Young Children: An Introduction*, (Upper Saddle River, NJ: Pearson Education, 1999), p. 319.

FEATURE 7.1 REPRESENTATIVE WEB RESOURCES

For additional information about playground safety and play resources for children with delays and disabilities, access the following representative websites:

- **eSpecial Needs**, https://www.especialneeds.com
- **Fat Brain Toys**, www.fatbraintoys.com/special_needs
- **Special Needs Toys**, https://specialneedstoys.com/usa/content
- **National Program for Playground Safety**, https://playgroundsafety.org/

DESIGNING THE LEARNING ENVIRONMENT

When designing learning environments for young children, early childhood special educators must consider multiple factors based on the individual needs of children. In addition to making the environment accessible and safe, early childhood special educators must maintain a healthy environment. They must ensure that children exhibit appropriate behavior when working in various activity areas of a classroom environment. How the learning environment is structured will affect children's involvement with the environment and the learning that occurs therein. What follows is a more specific examination of the various components of effective learning environments.

Environmental Arrangement

An important principle related to environmental arrangement is that of stimulus-control. Stimulus-control refers to the fact that certain behaviors are more likely to occur in the presence of stimuli while the behavior is being reinforced. Thus, physical prompts in the learning environment can be used to cue desired behaviors. Early childhood special educators often manipulate stimulus-control when designing learning environments (Brown et al., 2020). The reading/literacy center, for instance, can include environmental print (e.g., printed words or symbols found in the environment such as McDonald's signs, cereal boxes, juice boxes), posters of children reading, and attractive books/book covers, which serve as prompts for looking at written print, books, and other literacy materials. In this manner, stimulus-control can be used to promote and maintain children's engagement.

Classroom management can be facilitated by color-coding the areas. Brightly colored free play and gross motor areas may encourage louder noise levels. Softer, pastel hues in the reading/literacy areas can serve to prompt quiet behavior. To limit distractions and interference, quiet areas must not be in proximity to noisier areas. Movement within the classroom can be cued by using functional objects. A simulated stop sign or red light can cue children that an area is off-limits for the time being. A green light can signal areas children may visit. By allowing the environment to give cues about the routine and rules, the early childhood special educator can save time and energy. Children often will monitor peer behavior, and there will be less temptation for them to test limits when a visual prompt is present. These strategies can be very helpful for children with delays and disabilities.

Reinforcement and Responsivity

Elements of learning environments also can serve as reinforcers for young children's behavior. Activity areas or learning centers can be manipulated so that young children receive immediate feedback and reinforcement. For example, a child working in the math activity center who successfully completes a task may be rewarded with time to work on the computer or another activity that has high value to the child. Activity areas or learning centers can be designed so that they permit flexible sequencing of child activities.

The Premack principle (Alberto et al., 2022), also known as Grandma's Law, is a method that can be used for scheduling activities so that children move from less desirable to more desirable activities. **Premacking** involves sequencing activities so that less-probable or low-probability activities are followed by high-probability and motivating activities (e.g., "You don't get your dessert until after you eat your broccoli"). If children are uninterested in the reading area and highly motivated by the gross motor area, time in the gross motor area can serve as a reinforcer following participation in the reading/literacy center. Likewise, if children enjoy the dress-up activity area or learning center, they can attend this area contingent on completion of prescribed activities in a less desirable setting such as the listening center.

Related to the idea of reinforcement is the concept of **responsivity**. Researchers have identified responsivity as an environmental factor closely linked to academic gain (Brown et al., 2020). A responsive environment is one that provides the learner with predictable and immediate outcomes from any environmental interaction. Toy manufacturers make great use of responsivity in the production of material for infants. Mobiles, toys, or learning materials that are placed by infants' activity mats or seats can provide them with visual or auditory responses. For instance, pushing a rubber bulb results in a ding or running a hand across a cylinder produces a spinning, jingling response. The infant's verbal and facial reactions to these types of immediate feedback indicate the strength of responsivity to promote engagement. Young children will return again and again to these stimuli because they understand that their actions can influence the environment.

A setting that provides immediate and consistent reinforcement of behaviors will permit young children to acquire a sense of power and security in controlling their environment. This sense of empowerment can be an important motivator for young children with delays and disabilities, and it serves to encourage them to further explore their environment. The antithesis to the concept of empowerment, **learned helplessness**, is typical of some individuals with delays and disabilities. Children develop this sense of helplessness when their interactions with the environment prove to be futile or produce inconsistent results (Gargiulo & Bouck, 2021). Children may shy away from risks and new experiences because they are unsure of the results their actions will bring.

Self-correcting materials provide good examples of intervention or instructional methods that can give immediate feedback. Because self-correcting materials can be completed by a child or a small group of children with or without the teacher or adult being present, children also will develop independence. Montessori preschools have long used self-correcting materials in their curriculum designs. Many computer software programs designed for preschoolers and children in the early primary grades use a self-correcting format. For example, an animated creature will appear on the screen and say "good job" or will provide a soft form of correction and urge young children to try again. Early childhood special educators can make use of the same procedures when constructing their own self-correcting instructional materials. Windows and flaps that conceal the correct response or a picture of the correct response can be incorporated easily into either two-dimensional or three-dimensional manipulative materials constructed from cardboard, poster board, or other materials. Some examples of these materials are presented in Figure 7.5.

Responsivity can be facilitated when working with young children with physical, sensory, or multiple disabilities by using switches and adapted materials (Romski & Sevcik, 2005). Any battery-operated toy can be adapted to operate when pressure is applied to a connected switch. Switches come in a variety of shapes and sizes to fit the specific abilities of the child. They can be placed on the lapboard of a child's wheelchair for hand use, placed on the top side of the wheelchair for response to head movement, or connected to sip-and-puff devices that respond to air pressure.

For children with speech delays or who are nonverbal, **augmentative and alternative communication (AAC)** devices can be used to allow them to activate a switch to scan possible responses within learning center or group activities. For example, during story time, the teacher/adult may be reading a Beatrix Potter story. Beforehand, the paraeducator records the words *Peter, Flopsy,* and *Mopsy* into the device and places corresponding pictures in spaces provided. When the teacher asks comprehension questions, children can scan the device by pressing the switch and, by pressing the switch again, can stop the scan on the answer they wish to give. The answer will then be stated

FIGURE 7.5 ■ Examples of Self-Correcting Manipulatives

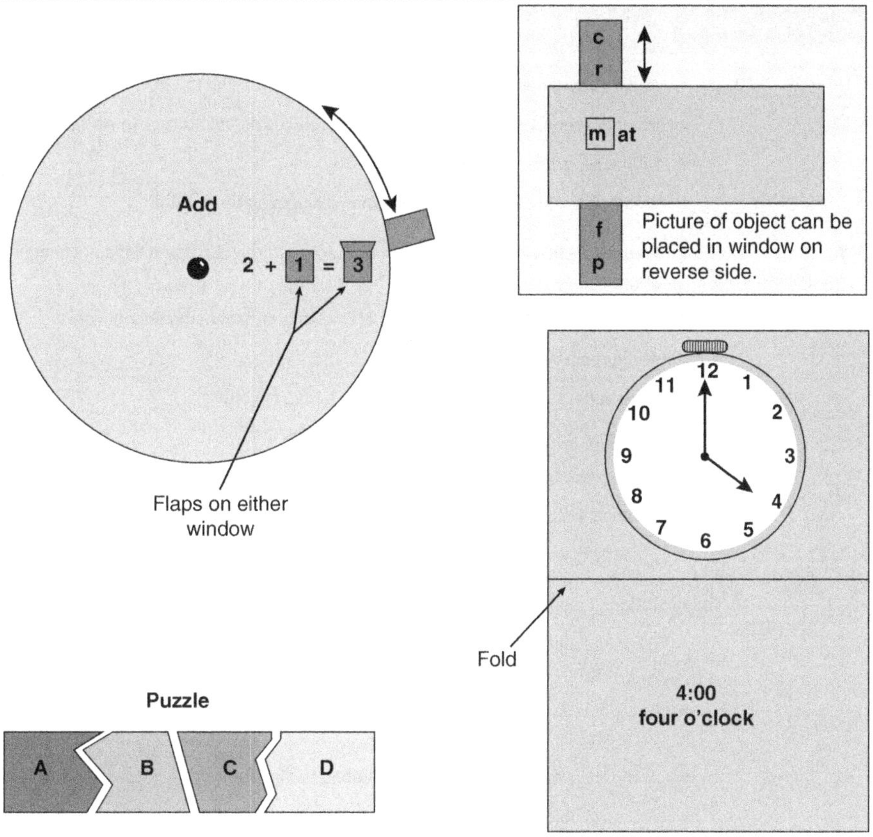

verbally. With the use of adaptive equipment and advanced technology, it is now possible for all young children with delays and disabilities to meaningfully participate and interact within their learning environments.

An Accessible Environment

The Americans with Disabilities Act requires that reasonable accommodations be made to ensure that public facilities, including child care centers, preschool programs, and schools, are accessible to individuals with delays and disabilities. To create accessible environments, practitioners must consider universal design for learning (UDL) principles [DEC Recommended Practices E4]. UDL principles strive to provide all young children with access to learning opportunities in their environments (Chen & Dote-Kwan, 2021; Gargiulo & Metcalf, 2023; Parette & Blum, 2014).). Having access to learning environments is crucial if young children with delays and disabilities are to be successfully included alongside their peers without disabilities in both indoor and outdoor environments (Barton et al., 2016; Gauvreau et al., 2023; Moore et al., 2022; Pisha & Spencer, 2016; Stockall et al., 2012).

Technology is a vital tool for teaching and learning in early childhood environments. It may be used for an entire class or for individual children. Table 7.2 lists examples of the ways various technology tools can be incorporated throughout the curriculum to support learning.

Although the term *accessibility* often is used in the context of providing equal opportunity to enter an environment, it is more encompassing in education circles. Accessibility in educational contexts includes adaptations necessary to ensure physical and cognitive access and successful goal attainment by young children with delays and disabilities. This may require changes in the communication methods and the physical arrangements, as well as the environmental supports and services, to provide greater access to the environment.

TABLE 7.2 ■ Uses for Technology Tools in Curricula

Area	Examples
Circle Time/Morning Meeting	• Audio recordings of songs that children can sing along to • Images aligned with a story or a song displayed on an interactive whiteboard • Digital timers for games • Weather applications on a tablet when discussing the weather
Literacy	• Websites, such as Storyline Online, where children can listen to books being read aloud • Tablet applications, such as Logic of English, for practicing phonograms • Audio recordings of letter sounds • Pen readers, which can read text from books to children • Books on tape • Word processing software for learning spelling words • Reading applications on tablets • E-readers with decodable books for children who are independent readers
Math	• Talking calculators • Websites and tablet applications for practicing mathematics skills, such as counting and basic addition and subtraction • Computer games or activities created or purchased for sorting items or creating patterns • Audio recordings of the teacher counting to one hundred • Videos of objects being counted
Science	• Tablet-based digital observation logs for children to note what they observe in science experiments • Digital cameras or tablets for children to take photographs of science experiments • Computer-based drawing applications for children to create images of what they observe during science experiments • Video

Programs that cater to the individual needs of children will be relatively easy to adapt for young children with sensory or physical disabilities. In these programs, modifications to meet the needs of children are part of daily activities. Early childhood programs often conduct accessibility assessments. As a rule, adaptations to an environment to accommodate young children with delays and disabilities are kept to a minimum. In other words, adaptations must be as subtle and unobtrusive as possible to minimize pointing out the differences in young children with delays and disabilities. As described previously, classroom adaptations may include the following:

- Adjustable shelves containing books, supplies, and learning materials
- Adequate pathways and turnaround space for children using walkers, wheelchairs, or other mobility devices
- Lowered or raised desktops and work tables of varying sizes and shapes
- Lowered sinks and water fountains or the use of a cup dispenser
- Restrooms designed to accommodate individuals with physical or sensory disabilities

Adaptations to the physical environment are arranged to enhance learning, social interactions, communication, and independence. Practitioners modify the learning environment only if children are unable to participate or access an activity without modification (Heller et al., 2009; Noonan & McCormick, 2014). The adaptations required will depend on the child's disability or delay. A child with physical disabilities, for example, most likely will need additional space for maneuvering their mobility device and may require various pieces of adaptive equipment to use in accessing the classroom and other aspects of the school environment. Equipment often used in this context includes wheelchairs, walkers, prone standers, sidelyers, wedges, posture chairs, and support bars. The purpose of a wedge, for example, is to provide lower trunk and torso support so that the arms and hands are free to manipulate objects. A young child using a wedge may freely participate in activities such as block play, art, and role-playing with human or animal figures and dolls. Sidelyers and prone standers serve the same purpose for children with a variety of physical disabilities. Examples of adaptive equipment used to assist children with physical disabilities are presented in Figure 7.6.

FIGURE 7.6 ■ Examples of Adaptive Equipment

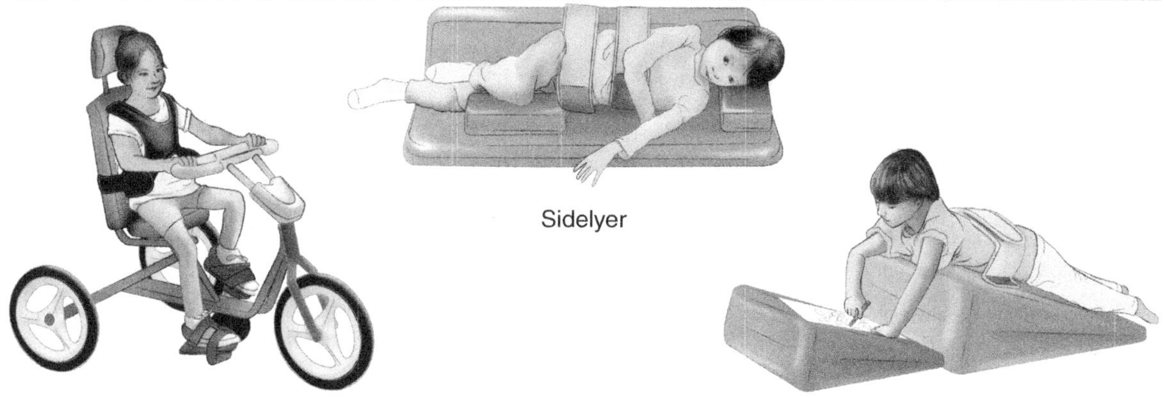

Source: S. Best, K. Heller, and J. Bigge, *Teaching Individuals with Physical or Multiple Disabilities*, 6th ed. (Upper Saddle River, NJ: Pearson Education, 2010). p. 195.

Adaptations to the environment may require the use of educational and assistive technology that reduces the impact of a child's impairment on their capacity to participate in the learning environment. Professionals work with families and other team members to identify, create, or acquire each child's assistive technology needs to maximize learning opportunities [DEC Recommended Practices E4, E5]. Assistive technology may include a range of low-tech materials and strategies (sign language, flip-picture cards); more sophisticated devices (calculators, computers); and high-tech augmentative communication devices (electronic communication boards, switch-operated scanning keyboards). It may be necessary to modify classroom materials to accommodate low-tech alternative forms of communication. Putting signs or symbols along with the printed word on materials may facilitate learning by all class members. Accessibility is improved for children with speech delays or who are nonverbal because they are provided a universal method of communication.

Finally, when considering how to adapt the learning environment to include young children with delays and disabilities, it is helpful to address the following three key concepts: accessibility, usability, and developmental appropriateness. Remember, it is not always necessary for children with delays and disabilities to participate in an activity to the same degree as their typically developing peers for the activity to be beneficial. The concept of "partial participation states that, regardless of [the] severity of disability, individuals can be taught to participate in [a] variety of activities to some degree, or activities can be adapted to allow participation" (Sheldon, 1996, p. 116). Adaptations to activities increase opportunities for interaction and enhance the quality of participation so that the environment is engaging for all children (Brown et al., 2020).

Table 7.3 offers a checklist of environmental adaptations often needed to accommodate young children with diverse abilities. Feature 7.2 provides a list of web resources for obtaining adaptive toys and equipment.

TABLE 7.3 ■ Checklist for an Accessible Environment

Physical Environment

Questions to consider:

- How do different children use the space around them for learning?
- How can early childhood special educators enhance or adapt the physical environment for children who have difficulty moving (or move too much)?
- How can early childhood special educators capitalize on the physical environment for young children who learn by moving?

Accessing the environment safely:

- Are doorway widths in compliance with local building codes?
- Ramps in addition to or instead of stairs?
- Low, wide stairs where possible (including playground equipment)?
- Handrails on *both* sides of stairs?
- Easy handles on doors, drawers, etc.?
- At least some children's chairs with armrests?
    - "Cube" chairs are great!
    - Often a footrest and/or seat strap will provide enough stability for young children to engage in fine motor activities.
- When adapting seating, mobility, and/or gross motor activities for a specific child with physical disabilities, the physical therapist should be consulted.

Learning through the environment:

- Do the environment and equipment reflect variety?
    - Surface, heights (e.g., textured, smooth, low, high)
    - Space for gross motor activity (open spaces, climbing structures, mats)
    - Quiet/comfort spaces (small spaces, carpet, pillows)
    - Social spaces (dramatic play area, groups of chairs or pillows)
- Are toys and equipment physically accessible?
    - Glue magnets to backs of puzzle pieces and attribute blocks.
    - Attach large knobs or levers to toys with lids and movable parts.
    - Attach tabs to book pages for easier turning.
    - Occupational therapists can provide specific suggestions for adapting materials and activities so that children with physical disabilities can participate.

Visual Environment

Questions to consider:

- How do different children use their vision for learning?
- How can early childhood special educators enhance the visual environment for children with vision impairments?
- How can early childhood special educators capitalize on the visual environment for children who learn by seeing?

Accessing the environment safely:

- Are contrasting colors used on edges and when surfaces change (e.g., tile to carpet, beginning of stairs)?
- Can windows be shaded to avoid high glare?
    - Also consider darker nonglossy floors and tabletops.
    - Some children's behavior and learning may improve dramatically once a strong glare is eliminated.
- Is visual clutter avoided on walls, shelves, etc.?
    - Visual clutter can interfere with learning, predictability, and safety.

- Is "spot lighting" (swing arm lamp) in a dimmer room available?
  - Spot lamps help some children pay attention and work better on table tasks.
  - Orientation and mobility specialists can help children with visual impairments learn to navigate the environment.

Learning through the environment:

- Are objects and places in the environment labeled (*door, chair*)?
- Are the size and contrast of pictures and letters adequate for children with visual impairments?
- Are visual displays at the children's eye level?
- Are large-print materials, textured materials, and auditory materials available (big books, sandpaper letters, books on tape)?
- Is the daily schedule represented in words and pictures?
  - A Velcro schedule that allows children to post the schedule and then remove items as activities are completed can help children stay focused and transition more easily from one activity to the next.
- Are children with low vision seated close to the center of the activity and away from high glare?
  - Early childhood special educators can select and adapt materials for children with low vision.
  - Children who are blind may need a running commentary of events, places, etc. Pictures in books and food on plates, for example, should be described.

Auditory Environment

Questions to consider:

- How do different children use their hearing for learning?
- How can teachers enhance the auditory environment for children who are deaf, are hearing impaired, or have poor auditory discrimination skills?
- How can early childhood special educators capitalize on the auditory environment for auditory learners?

Accessing the environment safely:

- Does background noise (from indoor or outdoor sources) filter into the area?
- Is there a way to eliminate or dampen background noise (using carpeting, closing windows and doors)?
  - Some children are unable to automatically filter out background noises that usually are done unconsciously.
- Is "auditory competition" avoided?
  - Raising one's voice to compete with a room of children who are noisy is rarely as effective as "silent signals." For example, the early childhood special educator can hold up a sign or encourage children to raise their hands until the room is full of quiet children holding up signs or raising their hands. Are nonauditory signals needed to alert children with hearing impairments?
  - Turning the lights on and off is a common strategy.
  - Families can be asked about what strategies are used at home.

Learning through the environment:

- Are auditory messages paired with visual ones (simple sign language, flannel boards, picture schedules)?
- Are children with hearing impairments seated so they can see the faces and actions of others?
  - Teachers can determine strategies for modifying activities for children with hearing impairments.

Social Environment

Questions to consider:

- How do different children use social cues for learning?
- How can the early childhood special educator adapt the social environment for children with impulsive behavior or attention issues?
- How can early childhood special educators capitalize on the social environments for children who learn by their interactions with others?

Accessing the environment safely:

- Is the schedule predictable? Are children informed of schedule changes?
- Does the schedule provide a range of activity levels (adequate opportunities for physical activity)?
  - School psychologists and behavior specialists can help address behaviors and modify the environment or schedule to minimize problems for children with attention or behavior issues.

(Continued)

TABLE 7.3 ■ Checklist for an Accessible Environment (*Continued*)

Learning through the environment:

- Does the environment have a positive impact on self-esteem?
- Allow all children to feel safe?
- Invite all children to participate?
- Maximize all children's opportunities for independence?
- Do learning materials and toys include representations of diverse individuals, including children and adults with disabilities and various cultural backgrounds?
  - Individuals with disabilities should be represented in active and leadership roles.
- Does the schedule include opportunities for a variety of groups (pairs, small groups, whole class) as well as quiet time or time alone?
  - Pairing or grouping children with complementary abilities eases the demands on the teacher and enables young children to help one another.
  - When given a chance, peers often develop creative ways for children with delays and disabilities to participate.
  - Creative use of staffing may be needed to provide additional support for some children during certain activities.
- Does the schedule provide both structured and open activity times?
  - Young children who have difficulty with a particular type of activity may need extra support at those times.

Additional Strategies When Adapting the Environment for Individual Children

- Early childhood special educators should make use of the diverse strengths of the various professionals and family members on each child's team.
- Early childhood special educators should be creative when developing multisensory, inclusive activities that take individual children's skills and needs into account.
- Early childhood special educators should look for ways in which children modify environments and activities for themselves and their peers.
- Families should be included when making accommodations for children with delays and disabilities; their knowledge of their children is critical.
- Respect for each child's strengths and needs is the most important ingredient in creating appropriate environments for all young children.

Source: Adapted from K. Haugen, "Using Your Senses to Adapt Environments," *Child Care Information Exchange, 114*, 1997, pp. 50, 55–56.

The learning environment must be arranged so that it is accessible to all children.

iStock.com/Wavebreakmedia

FEATURE 7.2 REPRESENTATIVE WEB RESOURCES

For additional information about adaptive toys and equipment, access the following representative websites:

- **Abilitations**, www.abilitations.com
- **Lekotek**, www.lekotek.org
- **Rifton**, www.rifton.com

A Safe Environment

Keeping young children safe and healthy is the most critical role of the early childhood special educator and other professionals on the team. Regulations governing these two critical areas are found in all licensing and accreditation standards. These standards and recommendations must be applied to home, center, and school environments. Of course, it is imperative that early childhood special educators and other professionals are committed to children's safety and well-being. The responsibility for a safe classroom environment resides with the teacher. EI/ECSE professionals must be vigilant when caring for infants and toddlers, especially those who are particularly vulnerable (Feeney et al., 2023). The task of providing a safe environment for young children with delays and disabilities has been made easier due to the development of safer toys and equipment and the production of safer building materials. Many early childhood programs are now equipped with slip-proof linoleum that has a rubber underlining to help prevent breakage. This product can be essential in making bathrooms, wet areas, and art areas safer for young children.

As matters of safety and efficiency, activity areas or learning centers can be partitioned by using shelving or dividers that are approximately three feet high for preschoolers and older, with a recommendation of two feet for toddlers. This allows the teacher and other adults to have a clear field of vision across the classroom, provides a sense of privacy to the areas, and places storage of materials adjacent to the area where they most likely will be used. Consumer protection groups have worked diligently to ensure that toys and materials are nontoxic and fire retardant. Most young children's toys now carry labels and warnings concerning age appropriateness and possible safety problems experienced by young children. Although these improvements have decreased potential dangers, early childhood special educators must be ever aware of environmental conditions that may put children at risk of injury. For example, a throw rug used in a high-traffic area of a room will invariably lead to stumbles or falls. This arrangement will also tend to limit accessibility for children with visual or motor impairments.

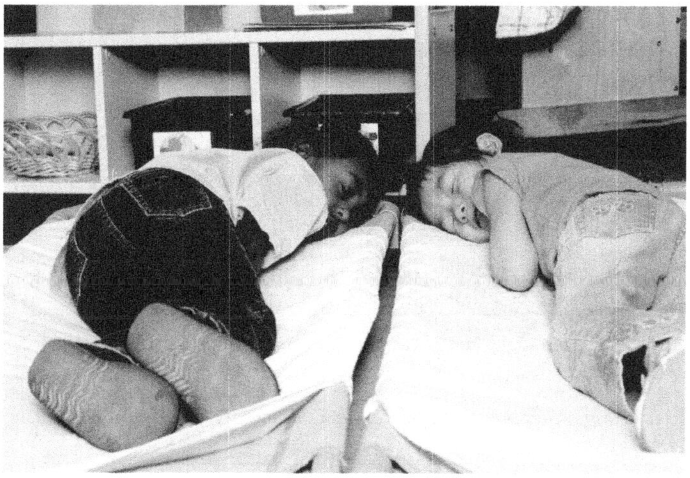

The safety and well-being of children is of vital importance to early childhood special educators.

Another safety consideration is that a source of accidents in environments for young children is electrical shock and resulting burns. Of course, it is much easier to work on preventative measures than to initiate treatment after the accident. In new construction, wall outlets must be teacher/adult height, approximately five to six feet off the floor. Extension cords must be used with extreme caution or be completely excluded from settings for young children (American Academy of Pediatrics, 2019). Young children can separate an extension cord and place the exposed end in their mouth, which can be fatal or cause severe burns to the tongue and other parts of the oral cavity. All teachers and adults working with young children must be trained in first aid and CPR to handle emergencies if they arise. A final topic related to safety is classroom organization. A cluttered room is not safe; thus, cleanup time between and following activities is important. Not only is cleanup desirable for safety reasons, but it also promotes good work habits and responsibility among young children.

Early childhood special educators can consult the following resource manual for guidance on establishing a safe and secure learning environment:

- *Caring for Our Children: National Health and Safety Performance Standards—Guidelines for Early Care and Education Programs* (4th ed., 2019), American Academy of Pediatrics, Itasca, IL.

Table 7.4 details specific suggestions for maintaining a safe classroom, while Table 7.5 offers the "golden rules" for selecting safe learning materials and toys.

TABLE 7.4 ■ Classroom Safety Suggestions

1. Check the environment, both inside and outside, for any hazards. Check electrical outlets and cords; make sure children cannot pull over any equipment (televisions, computers, DVD players); remove dangerous plants; cover sharp edges; make sure fences are sturdy and exit gates are childproof; and eliminate any other hazards to children's safety.
2. Practice emergency procedures on a regular basis. Responses to fire drills (and, in some areas, tornado and earthquake procedures) must become automatic.
3. Make sure that the classroom contains a fire extinguisher and that all staff know how to use it.
4. All early childhood special educators and other adults should be trained in first aid and CPR. At a minimum, one person with such training should be present at all times. For programs that serve infants, adults should be required to have special training in CPR for infants.
5. Post a list of the names of all children and a map of fire exit routes near each exit.
6. Each classroom should be equipped with a well-stocked first aid kit that is kept in a specific location so staff members can quickly find it. A second kit should be available for use on field trips and outdoor outings.
7. Keep cleaning agents, insecticides, medications, and other such items in a locked cabinet out of the reach of children.
8. Maintain an up-to-date list of emergency phone numbers (parents, other family members, doctors, and hospitals) for each child. Children with health impairments may have a health care plan. Take a copy of this information with you when going on field trips or other excursions.
9. Keep the number for the poison control center posted near the telephone.
10. Post a list of children's allergies, including reactions to insects or certain foods, and check it before planning any food experiences or outdoor activities.
11. Keep a list by the door of the adults authorized to pick up each child and, of course, do not release a child to any unauthorized person.
12. Make all posted information readily available to substitute teachers and other professionals.

Source: Adapted from J. Brewer, *Introduction to Early Childhood Education,* 6th ed. (Boston, MA: Pearson Education, 2007), pp. 98–100.

TABLE 7.5 ■ Creating a Safe Learning Environment for Young Children

1. Choose toys and art materials that are labeled nontoxic. Crayons and paints should say "ASTM D4236" on the package. This means that the item has been tested and evaluated by ASTM International (formerly known as the American Society for Testing and Materials).
2. Choose water-based paints, glue, and markers.
3. Avoid battery-operated or electrical toys that may cause shock.
4. Do not use toys with strings or cords longer than 7 inches.
5. Check all toys regularly to ensure that they are in good repair with no cracks, rips, sharp edges, or loose parts.
6. Avoid materials with small removable or loose parts that could easily be swallowed. For children under the age of three, choose toys that are larger than 1.25 inches and balls that are larger than 1.75 inches in diameter.
7. Avoid toy chests or similar storage facilities that might trap children or pinch fingers.

Source: Adapted from S. Feeney, E. Moravcik, and S. Nolte, *Who Am I in the Lives of Children?* 12th ed. (New York, NY: Pearson Education, 2023), p. 205.

A Healthy Environment

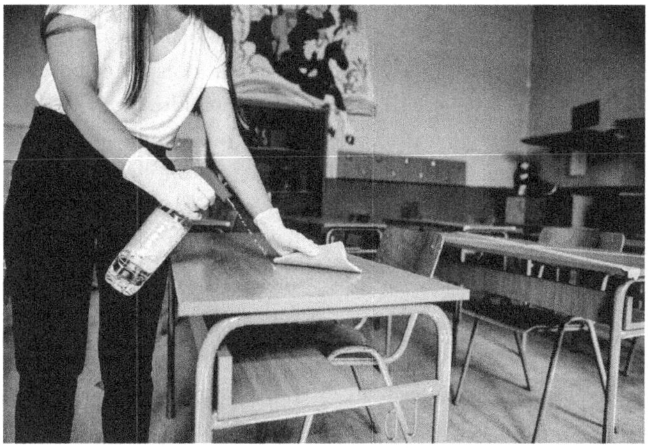

Early childhood special educators should always practice universal precautions.
iStock.com/BjelicaS

To maintain a healthy learning environment, cleanliness is an important factor. Early childhood classrooms must be cleaned daily. Equipment must be sanitized periodically, and dramatic play items (dress-up clothes), personal blankets, and fabric toys all require regular laundering. Several additional precautions must be considered in designing a healthy learning environment. One component is the protection of children from the spread of communicable diseases. Another element is teaching personal hygiene skills to children in early childhood and early primary-level programs.

Some children with delays and disabilities are particularly at risk for certain infections due to related problems with immune systems, heart conditions, or chronic illnesses. Infectious diseases that are of increased concern for infants and young children include hepatitis A and B, cytomegalovirus (CMV), herpes simplex Type 1, and less frequently, AIDS (Aronson & Shope, 2020; Heller et al., 2009). CMV produces only flulike symptoms in children but can be devastating if transmitted to a teacher, parent, or another adult who is pregnant. Both hepatitis B, which is the more virulent form of hepatitis, and herpes simplex are incurable and can be spread through bodily fluids. Herpes simplex Type 1 and CMV are the most infectious of these diseases because they can be spread through airborne effects of coughing and sneezing. AIDS has the least likelihood of transmission because of the need for semen or blood transference (Heller et al., 2009). The spread of these and other communicable diseases can be controlled by applying appropriate health practices such as frequent hand washing, which is considered by many health care professionals to be the most effective way of controlling the spread of disease and illness.

This hygiene practice, commonly referred to as universal precautions, also requires that the cleansing of materials and surfaces with disinfectant become a regular part of an adult's duties in the classroom. Surfaces such as diaper-changing areas, toilet seats, positioning boards, wheelchair trays, and eating areas must receive special attention. Toys and materials must be washed after use, and adults should pay special attention to material handled by children who display signs of illness (e.g., coughing, runny noses) and to toys placed in or near the mouth. A recommended rule to follow in the classroom is that anything that touches the mouth is immediately taken and placed in a tub to be disinfected. Teachers and other adults must always wash their hands following any contact involving bathroom assistance, positioning, feeding, or diaper changing.

Health care professionals recommend that adults working with children must wear disposable latex-free gloves during these duties. Any open cuts or sores noticed on adults or children must be covered with bandages.

Including these hygiene procedures in the daily routine not only helps prevent the spread of disease but also serves as a model of safety behavior for children. Lastly, because it always is better to prevent an illness, early childhood special educators find it beneficial to provide hand sanitizers and tissues throughout their rooms.

Although the preceding health recommendations and suggestions provide valuable guidance for early childhood special educators under normal circumstances, the worldwide pandemic of COVID-19 has presented numerous new challenges with specific implications for young children, families, and communities. How instruction is delivered, and how young children with delays and disabilities are provided with learning opportunities, was completely transformed in 2020 and, most likely, transformation will continue for the foreseeable future. Maintaining a healthy learning environment requires strict adherence to guidelines from local and state health departments and the Centers for Disease Control and Prevention, in addition to the best thinking of professional organizations such as the American Academy of Pediatrics.

Selecting Learning Materials

Effective early childhood special educators must carefully select learning materials and must consider the children's interests regarding the materials they will find most appealing. Often, young children are interested in items within the environment that are not toys. For example, a consistent source of frustration expressed by families is when their child spends hours playing with the cardboard box and wrapping paper and ignores the expensive toy they bought the child as a birthday or holiday present. Early childhood special education professionals must be good consumers and consumer advocates, not always purchasing materials that are widely advertised and neatly packaged. The money that is spent on resources for early childhood special education services must be spent wisely, as the amount of money typically available seems to be limited. An outline of representative considerations for purchasing classroom materials is offered in Table 7.6.

A key consideration when purchasing or creating materials is to focus on durability and cost. Almost all two-dimensional materials can and must be laminated or covered with clear plastic to facilitate cleaning and promote longevity. Young children can be rough on materials, especially materials used frequently. Even materials designed specifically for teacher/adult use (e.g., curricula kits, idea books, thematic units) can receive much wear in a short time. Because most commercially made materials can be costly, it is highly recommended that early childhood special educators accumulate their own teacher-made materials. Not only will this save on expenses, but it is much easier for teachers to create materials geared to the individual needs and interests of children. Many early childhood special educators find the making of materials worthwhile for intrinsic reasons. Having one's own materials

TABLE 7.6 ■ Considerations for Purchasing Instructional Materials

I. General Considerations
1. Safety
2. Cost and durability
3. Target population
4. Skill level(s) required
5. Aesthetics and attractiveness
6. Necessity of adult supervision
7. Children's individual differences
8. Avoiding cultural stereotypes
II. Instructional Considerations
1. Is the item developmentally appropriate?
2. Does the item allow for versatility and flexibility of use (e.g., age and ability levels)?
3. Is corrective feedback provided?
4. Is the item aligned with specific learning goals/outcomes and objectives/benchmarks?
5. Does the item allow for individual and/or group work?

in the classroom may provide a sense of investment and self-fulfillment. The concept of personal pride and investment also can be applied to the activities of young children and their families.

As described in Chapter 6, before the purchase of any materials such as prepackaged curricula, early childhood special educators must examine any available information on the development and field-testing of the learning materials. Information obtained can be helpful in determining whether this material is suitable for a specific group of children and the specific purposes behind its development. The appropriateness of materials in terms of age, ability, and cultural appropriateness is especially relevant when dealing with children with delays or disabilities. Materials field-tested with populations that did not include young children with disabilities may be inappropriate for similar-aged populations with delays and disabilities. Feature 7.3 lists resources for selecting safe materials when designing learning environments for young children.

FEATURE 7.3 REPRESENTATIVE WEB RESOURCES

For additional information, please access the following representative websites:

- **National Resource Center for Health and Safety in Child Care and Early Education**, http://nrckids.org
- **Occupational Safety & Health Administration (OSHA)**, http://www.osha.gov/
- **U.S. Access Board**, www.access-board.gov
- **U.S. Consumer Product Safety Commission**, http://www.cpsc.gov

SUMMARY

Environmental arrangements are critically important in the education of young children with delays and disabilities. Early childhood special educators must take on the roles of environmental engineers, architects, and interior designers in learning environments to maximize the impact of intervention, instruction, and services. They need to be prepared to provide support to families, caregivers, and other professionals who are responsible for the natural environment in which young children with delays and disabilities participate. This ability is dependent on a basic understanding of children's growth and development and how the environment affects the learning process. Variables such as room arrangement and effective use of space, color, lighting, acoustics, and room temperature are all key dimensions of an effective learning environment.

The DEC Recommended Practices provide guidance regarding environments for young children (home, child care, school, neighborhood) that are focused on environmental practices. By applying these environmental practices, practitioners and families can promote engaging learning environments that foster each child's health, development, and learning. Universal design for learning principles are emphasized that focus not only on physical access to learning environments but also on the elimination of barriers to learning for all children.

Early childhood learning environments are organized around activity areas or learning centers. The number and type of areas within an environment are dependent on the children's ages, abilities, developmental needs, and interests. Regardless of the focus of the activity areas or learning centers (literacy, fine motor, dramatic play), these areas must be individually and developmentally appropriate and designed to meet the needs of all children.

Outdoor play is essential to the overall development of young children with delays and disabilities and is an integral component of daily activities. Play is a natural mechanism for facilitating inclusive experiences for young children with delays and disabilities. Two factors of utmost importance for the early childhood special educator are the safety of the children as they interact with the environment and the issue of accessibility; no child ought to be denied meaningful participation because of a lack of appropriate adaptations.

Early childhood special educators must carefully consider how they design learning environments for young children, especially those with delays and disabilities. The physical arrangement of the room and the organization of materials significantly influence children's behavior. The teacher's/adult's primary responsibility is keeping the children safe and healthy. Equally important is the requirement that the learning environment be readily accessible so that young children with different types of delays and disabilities can participate. Instructional materials, whether teacher-made or commercially available, must be developmentally appropriate, durable, and designed to meet the unique needs of all the young children within the learning environment.

KEY TERMS

Accessibility
Activity areas or learning centers
Assistive technology
Augmentative and alternative communication (AAC)
Classroom ecology
Environment
Environmental practices
Learned helplessness
Premacking
Responsivity
Stimulus-control
Universal design for learning (UDL)
Universal precautions

CHECK YOUR UNDERSTANDING

1. Discuss how interactions with the learning environment can help shape young children's learning and development.
2. Explain how the DEC Recommended Practices provide guidance in designing learning environments for young children with delays and disabilities. Provide examples of specific practices.
3. What are some of the key dimensions to consider when designing a classroom environment for young children with delays and disabilities?

4. Identify the various types of activity areas or learning centers typically found in most classrooms for infants and toddlers, preschoolers, and early primary students. Describe the components of each.
5. What steps would you take to ensure that an outdoor learning environment is appropriate and accessible for children with delays and disabilities?
6. How can stimulus-control enhance learning?
7. Describe the concept of Premacking. Provide examples.
8. Why is responsivity important for learning in young children with delays and disabilities? Provide examples.
9. List the steps you would take to ensure an accessible, safe, and healthy learning environment for young children with delays and disabilities.
10. What are some of the factors to consider when selecting instructional materials?

REFLECTION AND APPLICATION

1. You have been asked by a local benefactor of young children to submit a proposal for establishing an inclusive preschool program in your community. She has requested that your proposal include the following points:
    - A sketch of the floor plan, including room design and planned activity areas
    - Supplies and instructional materials, including their cost
    - Plans to make the program accessible
    - An outdoor learning environment, including needed equipment
    - Health and safety requirements
2. What other items would you include in your proposal?
3. Observe an outdoor learning environment at a local area preschool and an elementary school. Prepare a report to present for your class. The issues to address in your presentation include the following:
    - A sketch of the playground
    - The kinds of activities in which the children were engaged
    - The types of equipment available—did you observe a difference in the equipment at each location?
    - Was the equipment being used appropriately by the children?
    - Was the environment accessible for children with delays and disabilities? What types of adaptations did you observe?
    - Were safety standards maintained?
    - What was the role of the teacher during outdoor play?
    - Suggestions for improving the outdoor experience

iStock.com/twinsterphoto

8 ADAPTING LEARNING ENVIRONMENTS FOR YOUNG CHILDREN WITH DELAYS AND DISABILITIES

LEARNING OBJECTIVES

After reading this chapter, you will be able to

8.1 Identify adaptations in the home, educational, and other natural environments for young children with cognitive, social and emotional, communication and language, sensory, and motor delays and disabilities; health impairments; and autism spectrum disorders.

8.2 Identify and adapt appropriate materials and equipment for working with young children with delays and disabilities at home, in educational environments, and in other natural environments.

8.3 Identify, adapt, and apply appropriate interventions and instructional strategies for teaching young children with delays and disabilities in learning environments.

8.4 Indicate strategies and applications to use for young children with delays and disabilities in the areas of communication and language.

8.5 Identify appropriate interventions and instructional strategies for teaching young children with vision impairments in learning environments.

8.6 Describe appropriate interventions and instructional strategies for teaching young children with hearing impairments in learning environments.

8.7 Identify and adapt appropriate materials, equipment, and strategies for working with young children with motor delays and disabilities in school, home, and other natural environments.

EI/ECSE Professional Standards

The content of this chapter aligns with the following EI/ECSE Standards:

Standard 1. Child Development and Early Learning

Candidates understand the impact of different theories and philosophies of early learning and development on assessment, curriculum, instruction, and intervention decisions. Candidates apply knowledge of normative developmental sequences and variations, individual differences within and across the range of abilities, including developmental delays and disabilities, and other direct and indirect contextual features that support or constrain children's development and learning. These contextual factors as well as social, cultural, and linguistic diversity are considered when facilitating meaningful learning experiences and individualizing intervention and instruction across contexts.

Standard 6. Using Responsive and Reciprocal Interactions, Interventions, and Instruction

Candidates plan and implement intentional, systematic, evidence-based, responsive interactions, interventions, and instruction to support all children's learning and development across all developmental and content domains in partnership with families and other professionals. Candidates facilitate equitable access and participation for all children and families within natural and inclusive environments through culturally responsive and affirming practices and relationships. Scholars use data-based decision-making to plan for, adapt, and improve interactions, interventions, and instruction to ensure fidelity of implementation.

DEC Recommended Practices

The content of this chapter aligns with the following Division for Early Childhood (DEC) Recommended Practices:

Environment

- E1. Practitioners provide services and supports in natural and inclusive environments during daily routines and activities to promote the child's access to and participation in learning experiences.
- E3. Practitioners work with the family and other adults to modify and adapt the physical, social, and temporal environments to promote each child's access to and participation in learning environments.

Instruction

- INS1. Practitioners, with the family, identify each child's strengths, preferences, and interests to engage the child in active learning.
- INS2. Practitioners, with the family, identify skills to target for instruction that help a child become adaptive, competent, socially connected, and engaged and that promote learning in natural and inclusive environments.
- INS4. Practitioners plan for and provide the level of support, accommodations, and adaptations needed for the child to access, participate, and learn within and across activities and routines.
- INS5. Practitioners embed instruction within and across routines, activities, and environments to provide contextually relevant learning opportunities.
- INS6. Practitioners use systematic instructional strategies with fidelity to teach skills and to promote child engagement and learning.
- INS13. Practitioners use coaching or consultation strategies with primary caregivers or other adults to facilitate positive adult–child interactions and instruction intentionally designed to promote child learning and development.

Authors' Note: As you read this chapter, you will find the EI/ECSE Standards and DEC Recommended Practices discussed throughout. See Appendix A for a complete list of the EI/ECSE Standards and Appendix B for a complete list of the DEC Recommended Practices.

Over the past few decades, state and federal laws have focused attention on the participation of young children with delays and disabilities in their natural environments or least restrictive educational settings. This model, known as inclusive education, is now widely accepted as an effective way to meet the educational needs of young children with delays and disabilities. Today, children with delays and disabilities are commonly served in child care centers, preschools, Head Start programs, and public schools, learning alongside their typically developing peers. Some children are successful with minimal supports from general education teachers, early childhood special educators, and related service professionals. Most children with delays and disabilities, however, will require some adaptations, accommodations, and modifications to the curriculum and learning environment, and, in most instances, personnel may require specialized training. It is the charge of collaborative teams of families and professionals representing multiple disciplines, therefore, to work together to create a plan and provide supports and services that will meet the individual needs of each child and family.

Research in the field of early childhood special education indicates that high-quality early learning programs result in more positive outcomes for young children with delays and disabilities (Odom et al., 2011). Providing a high-quality learning environment, however, is not enough to address the individual needs of young children with delays and disabilities. The framework for realistic and meaningful outcomes for children with delays and disabilities is the individualized family service plan (IFSP) or the individualized education program (IEP) that guides the intervention, instruction, curriculum modifications, or adaptations for each child. Sandall and her colleagues (Sandall et al., 2019) identify several key components that they believe are necessary to support the individual needs of children with delays and disabilities in an inclusive learning environment. These elements include (1) curriculum modifications and adaptations, (2) embedded learning opportunities, and (3) explicit, child-focused intervention or instructional strategies. We are in agreement with their approach that is aligned with DEC Recommended Practice INS6. Embedded learning opportunities are detailed later in this chapter. Child-focused intervention and instructional learning strategies for young children with delays and disabilities are discussed in Chapter 9.

Practitioners determine and provide the support, accommodations, and adaptations that children need to be able to participate in activities and routines. The terms *modifications, accommodations*, and *adaptations* are often used interchangeably when speaking of individualizing intervention, instruction, materials, and supports for children with delays and disabilities. The terms are similar, but they have some distinct differences. A **modification** indicates a change in what is being taught and the expectations for the student. For example, an individualized curriculum may be required to teach a child with a visual impairment how to read and write in Braille. This modification allows the student to participate yet learn using a different mode, at a different pace, and with specialized materials. An **accommodation**, on the other hand, is a change in the teaching content but *not* student expectations. An example of a classroom accommodation for child with a behavior disorder would be working in a smaller peer group or one to one with an adult in an attempt to model appropriate turn-taking skills. Appropriate responses from the child are expected; however, adult modeling and facilitation with fewer peers are needed in order for the student to participate successfully. Finally, **adaptation** is a broader term often used to describe any adjustment made by the IFSP or IEP team to allow children with delays and disabilities to participate fully in their learning environments. Early childhood special educators and related service providers often use the terms *modifications, accommodations*, and *adaptations* to describe the individual supports outlined in these documents. What is truly important is that the supports are skillfully chosen and carefully implemented to help young children with delays and disabilities learn and achieve meaningful progress.

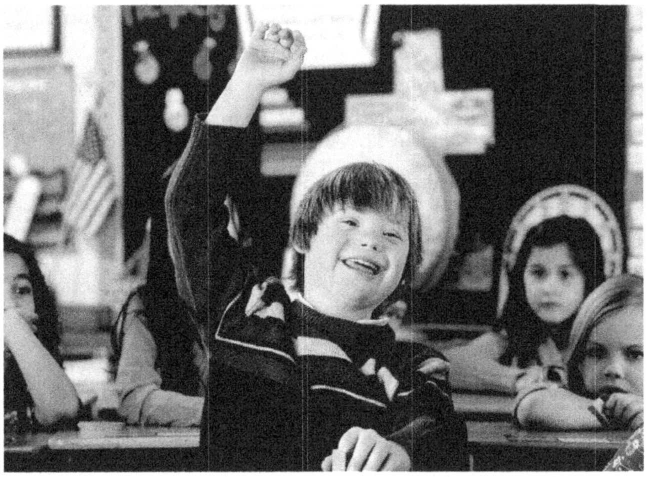

Teachers should capitalize on a child's strengths when planning activities.

Ariel Skelley/Photodisc/via Getty Images

For the purposes of this chapter, and to prevent any confusion in terminology, we use the term *adaptation* or *adapting* when describing supports for young children with delays and disabilities. This chapter provides suggestions for adapting and modifying the learning environment, materials, and instructional delivery for young children with delays and disabilities. For ease of communication, we discuss young children using noncategorical descriptors. Where appropriate, we discuss children using more traditional categorical terminology, as some young children already meet guidelines for specific disabilities (e.g., visual impairment, hearing impairment, or autism spectrum disorders).

YOUNG CHILDREN WITH COGNITIVE DELAYS AND DISABILITIES

Children with cognitive delays and disabilities represent a diverse population. They may learn at a slower rate, experience a high rate of forgetting, or have difficulty regulating their own behavior and transferring (generalizing) learning to new events, situations, or people (Gargiulo & Bouck, 2021). Because these children may not readily understand lengthy verbal instructions, they often require more adult guidance, direct instruction, and concrete activities. These characteristics are variable from one child to the next; therefore, it would be a mistake to assume that all young children with cognitive delays and disabilities exhibit similar characteristics or learning difficulties. To understand the importance of goals applicable to young children with cognitive delays and disabilities, we look to Neitzel (2011) for suggestions. First, early intervention and early childhood special education programs should focus on furthering development in all developmental domains in an integrated manner in order to reduce or minimize the impact of the delay on typical development. Second, professionals should support the family's efforts to achieve desired outcomes and independence levels in all areas of development.

Adapting the Environment

Creating a rich and stimulating environment for children with cognitive delays and disabilities is critical to their development. As with all children, early childhood special educators and families should capitalize on the interests and preferences of each child. Practitioners and families collaboratively identify each young child's individual interests, strengths, and preferences in an effort to engage them in active learning [DEC Recommended Practices INS1]. Children should be observed, and parents should be asked about what toys, foods, or activities their children enjoy or prefer. Focusing on the child's interests will ensure that some aspect of the tasks and activities is reinforcing to the child. For example, Matt, a five-year-old with Down syndrome, enjoys playing with race cars. His teacher incorporated the race cars into the learning center for color, number, and letter identification. Each car was a different color and had a letter or number attached to it. While at the learning center that focused on cars, Matt raced the cars and then identified the winning cars by color and letter/number. The use of a child's interest offers multiple learning opportunities across the child's day.

The Division for Early Childhood (2014) indicates that practitioners should embed instruction within and across routines, activities, and environments [DEC Recommended Practices INS5]. Professionals offer ways in which intervention and instruction can be embedded into typical classroom activities and routines to provide contextually relevant learning opportunities (Division for Early Childhood, 2014; Jennings et al., 2012; Noonan & McCormick, 2014; Snyder et al., 2013).

> Embedding is defined as identifying times and activities when a child's goals and the instructional procedures for those goals can be inserted into children's ongoing activities, routines and transitions in a way that relates to the context.
>
> It involves distributing opportunities to learn goals and apply instructional procedures for those goals across different activities, routines, and transitions of the day. (Wolery, 2005, p. 94)

When teachers and other adults embed effective instruction into activities that are interesting, fun, and motivating for children, learning is likely to occur more readily. Children learn the skills in a natural setting where they use the skills. With embedded objectives, the activities and routines become the structure for supporting the child's learning in the early childhood classroom and other learning environments. For example, Lauren, a second grader with cognitive delays, participates in the writing workshop daily with her peers. Lauren's task is modified by her general education teacher. Lauren works with the teacher initially to verbalize her thoughts using a specified writing prompt such as "My Favorite Food." Lauren's teacher writes down her thoughts in sentence form. Lauren and her teacher review the story. Lauren then copies her story onto her specially lined paper. Lauren does her written work with a peer partner. As can be seen in this example, several goals were embedded in this instruction. The teacher and Lauren worked on her language and sentence formation. They worked on the identification of familiar words and sight words. Lauren practiced fine motor and writing skills. Lauren worked with a peer using appropriate social skills and practiced using her attention skills by staying on task and finishing her writing.

The Division for Early Childhood (2014) points out that practitioners support young children with delays and disabilities during daily routines and activities in natural environments to promote access to and participation in learning experiences [DEC Recommended Practices E1]. As with all young children, consistency in the routine provides the child with security and promotes self-assuredness (e.g., "I know what I am supposed to be doing here"). This is especially important for young learners with cognitive delays and disabilities. A consistent routine facilitates memory for children who may have difficulty remembering items or activities that occur out of sequence. Possible strategies include establishing a routine, remaining consistent with the routine when possible, and preparing children for changes in the routine when necessary. In addition, early childhood special educators should ensure that there is adequate time to finish tasks within the established routine for children who may require more time to complete activities.

Unlike typically developing children, a child with cognitive delays and disabilities does not necessarily acquire many needed cognitive, language, or social skills during social interactions and play with others without support to promote these skills (Fenlon et al., 2010; Hollingsworth & Buysse, 2009). Therefore, it is important for early childhood special educators to examine the schedule to determine whether there are multiple opportunities in the day for socialization and speech/language production at home and in learning environments. Teachers may need to employ active strategies of arranging children and explicitly facilitating their interactions in some situations. For example, structured play with typically developing peers is an excellent strategy for providing models for language development and socialization within the learning environment (Mastrangelo, 2009).

Adapting Materials and Equipment

As much as possible, hands-on, concrete materials should be available for young children with cognitive delays. Especially when teaching abstract concepts (up, down, in, out) or common pre-academic skills (letter recognition, numbers, colors, shapes), it is critical for early childhood special educators to have multiple ways of presenting these abstract concepts in concrete ways. Using predictable activities and games with an infant or toddler is an ideal way to address this issue. During play, a parent lifts the toddler up while saying "Up, up, up!" followed by "Down, down, down!" as the child is lowered. In this way, the abstract concepts of up and down are embedded within an enjoyable, predictable game sequence.

Substituting favorite toys within the same routine extends the play routine with the same concepts, encourages generalization, and sustains interest. With a preschooler or early primary-age child, using real objects when counting, using real food when measuring, or talking about colors of clothing when matching socks are all examples of concrete learning materials and activities. Not only are these more authentic ways to promote skills acquisition; they are also activities that relate learning to the child's real world and increase the likelihood of generalization of skills (Copple & Bredekamp, 2009; National Association for the Education of Young Children, 2022).

A variety of materials may be needed to accommodate the needs of young children with diverse cognitive abilities. Blocks of different sizes or toys with a variety of switches representing different levels of difficulty may enable a toddler to have some challenges and successes. Puzzles with varying degrees of difficulty could be available in the free play area or books with different levels of difficulty in the literacy learning center. Likewise, it is important to select materials or toys that are more likely to increase social interactions (Copple & Bredekamp, 2009; Mastrangelo, 2009; National Association for the Education of Young Children, 2022). Examples include toys that allow for two or more children to engage in activities together (playground equipment, telephones, walkie-talkies). Children with cognitive delays may exhibit memory issues, requiring visual cues to prompt behavior. For example, if their photographs are placed above their cubbies, young children can find their photographs when trying to locate their cubbies. Pictures of the steps for washing hands can be placed by the sink at the children's eye level to support independence in hand washing.

Adapting Intervention and Instruction

All young children have strengths or areas in which they excel, including children with cognitive delays and disabilities. It is critical to capitalize on each child's strengths when planning activities in order to increase the likelihood of success, promote self-esteem, maintain interest, and diminish frustration. For example, Martha, a child with Down syndrome, exhibited cognitive and language delays but excelled in gross motor activities. Her mother reported that as a toddler, she sat independently, crawled, and walked early, but she did not use words until she was three years old. Now, as a preschooler, Martha enjoys outdoor play equipment (e.g., slide, swings) and the obstacle course. Her parents, teachers, and other adults often incorporate language skills within gross motor activities where Martha finds success and enjoyment. When she is on the swing, waiting for someone to push her, the adult waits for Martha to indicate or communicate what she wants. Initially, even an approximation of "pu" for "push" is accepted, and later, the desired vocalization is modeled: "Say 'push'" and, expanded, "Say 'push swing.'" (These examples of modeling are consistent with activity-based intervention and incidental teaching, topics that will be presented in Chapter 9.)

Children with cognitive delays and disabilities may have a smaller vocabulary, use less complex sentence structure, use language less frequently, and sometimes have difficulty making friends (Gargiulo & Bouck, 2021). As mentioned previously, playing with typically developing peers is an excellent context for promoting these skills. However, even within these structured play opportunities, practitioners may need to frequently monitor and support children by using prompts or praise in their interactions to maximize socialization and communication (Barton & Wolery, 2010). Without such supports, children with cognitive delays and disabilities may engage in fewer social interactions and less mature social behavior, be rejected by peers, and ultimately have difficulty developing social relationships (Barton et al., 2011; Gargiulo & Bouck, 2021). In addition, to expand the child's communicative and social attempts, language should be integrated into all aspects of the curriculum, including transition activities ("Where are we going next?"), self-care activities ("Tell me what you are doing"), and play activities ("James, ask Francie to help you cook dinner"). The assistance of a speech–language pathologist is often sought for suggestions on how to insert language goals into daily routines and activities.

Because young children with cognitive delays and disabilities often have memory problems, it is not unusual for them to have difficulty transferring or generalizing knowledge or skills acquired in one context to a new or different setting (Gargiulo & Bouck, 2021). **Generalization** is a phase of learning that refers to learning to use a skill outside of the context in which it was initially acquired. This is often thought of as performing a skill in a different setting, with other people, or with materials different from the ones used in the initial instruction. Suggested strategies for promoting generalization are as follows:

- *A variety of adults can be involved when teaching skills.* For example, periodically, another adult, such as a classroom assistant or a volunteer, can teach a particular skill so that a child becomes accustomed to different people. It is important that the directives and expectations for the child are consistent across people. This implies that communication, collaboration, and coaching should occur among teachers, families, other caregivers, and professionals to ensure consistency across settings [DEC Recommended Practices INS13].
- *Skills can be embedded into naturally occurring activities.* For example, if putting socks on and taking them off is a skill area that the child needs to focus on, instruction should occur during the dressing and undressing routines during the day (before and after naptime). The use of a pincer grasp can be promoted during snack time (eating crackers or cheese cubes), art (picking up tissue squares or pebbles to glue on an art project), and dressing routines (buttoning or zipping). For an example of an activity that is embedded into a naturally occurring activity, see the Making Connections feature about Maria, a young child with cognitive delays.
- *Activities can be created in the learning environment by designing them as similar as possible to the generalization setting.* The greater the similarities between the educational setting and other settings, the more likely the generalization will occur. For example, if the child is learning to drink from a two-handled cup at home, the same type of cup should be used at school.
- *The instructional environment should be varied.* By expanding the settings and activities in which the children utilize targeted skills and the people with whom they utilize the skills, teachers can increase the probability of the generalization of skills.

MAKING CONNECTIONS

IMPLEMENTING AN EMBEDDED LEARNING ACTIVITY FOR MARIA

The implementation of an embedded learning opportunity is one of the strategies that Maria's teachers and other adults use to practice individual goals and objectives that are meaningful and interesting to her. The teachers embed the learning activities using the natural routine across the activities, people, and materials in the inclusive classroom. Using the daily routine at snack time, when Maria's glass is empty, she signs "more." The teacher asks Maria, "More what?" Maria signs "more" again. The teacher uses the opportunity to model for Maria. She signs "more drink" and gives Maria a questioning look. Maria imitates and signs "more drink" and receives more juice. At the block center, Maria needs more blocks for the tower she is building. She asks the teacher for "more blocks" and receives them. This is an example of an embedded objective that crosses activities throughout Maria's day. Later at free play, Maria asks the teacher for "more toys" and receives them. In this example, the embedded learning objective has crossed to other adults in the classroom environment. Maria's objective was practiced within the natural routine, with different activities, with different adults, and with different materials within her classroom setting.

An intervention or instructional strategy often used with children with cognitive delays and disabilities is task analysis. Task analysis involves breaking down a skill, activity, or behavior into smaller, more manageable steps. Alberto et al., (2022) offer the following five guidelines for conducting a task analysis:

1. Identify the long-term goal, outcome, or objective.
2. Break the skill, activity, or behavior into smaller steps.
3. Eliminate unnecessary and redundant behaviors.
4. Sequence the steps for teaching.
5. Specify the prerequisite behaviors that must be acquired before teaching the skill, activity, or behavior.

For some children, pictures of each step can be provided to support the child in independent completion of a particular task. As previously noted, pictures of each step used in washing hands could be placed near the sink area at the child's eye level. In this way, an unobtrusive prompt serves as a reminder for all children. Teaching young children phrases or songs that accompany daily activities is another strategy for providing the steps to a task. It is not only enjoyable but functional because the child can use the phrase or song wherever they go. For example, a phrase or song created to accompany the motions or steps for tying shoes can be used over and over by young children at home, in school, or in other settings. (See Table 8.1 for a sample task analysis.)

Task analysis can also be individualized with some children, particularly those who are younger, using backward chaining. For example, for a toddler who does not assist in dressing or undressing, the parent, teacher, or other adult can complete all of the steps of a task analysis for pulling up pants or taking off a shirt and leave the last step for them to complete, such as pulling pants from mid-thigh to hips or removing the shirt once the arms are out. In this way, the child begins to assist in dressing, successfully completes the new skill, and is then able to participate in an enjoyable and reinforcing activity (e.g., play or snack). Once this step is achieved with consistency, the parent, teacher, or other adult can raise the expectation that the child should pull up his pants from the knees, from the ankles, and so on. This example of backward chaining starts with the last step of a task analysis. It is typically used with younger children or children with lower cognitive skills because they can successfully complete the last steps(s) and are immediately reinforced by moving onto the next enjoyable activity.

TABLE 8.1 ■ Task Analysis for Washing Hands (Sequenced by Order in Which Each Step Is to Be Performed)

Step on the stool to reach the sink.
Place hands on faucet handles.
Turn the water on.
Place hands under the water.
Squeeze the soap on both hands.
Rub hands together with soap.
Rub hands together and over back and front.
Rinse hands in the sink.
Turn the faucets to the off position.
Reach for a paper towel.
Dry hands on the paper towel.
Put the paper towel in the trashcan.
Step down from the stool.

Note: This activity is easily adapted to use picture symbols if needed for visual supports and prompting.

Task analysis is a common instructional strategy.

iStock.com/Narongrit Sritana

One final example of a strategy for children with cognitive delays and disabilities is scaffolding, introduced in Chapter 1. This technique helps children become independent, proficient problem solvers. In this teacher-directed strategy, various forms of support are provided as the child initially engages in learning a new task or skill. As the child becomes competent, the supports or "scaffolds" are gradually removed. This instructional strategy begins with what the child knows and attempts to connect new information with previously learned material. New information is presented in a logical sequence building on the child's knowledge base. Children are given the opportunity to apply and practice the new skill (Gargiulo & Bouck, 2021; Vaughn & Bos, 2020).

We conclude our discussion of young children with cognitive delays and disabilities by recognizing the significance of the many environments that support the learning and development of these children. It is crucial that early childhood special educators are cognizant of the importance of the physical, social, and temporal environments. According to the Division for Early Childhood (DEC, 2014), "it is important for practitioners to remember that these environmental dimensions are inextricably intertwined for young children who have or are at risk for developmental delays/disabilities and their families" (p. 9). Consequently, DEC recommends the following practices:

- Practitioners provide services and supports in natural and inclusive environments during daily routines and activities to promote the child's access to and participation in learning experiences.
- Practitioners consider universal design for learning principles to create accessible environments.
- Practitioners work with the family and other adults to modify and adapt the physical, social, and temporal environments to promote access to and participation in learning experiences.
- Practitioners work with families and other adults to identify each child's needs for assistive technology to promote access to and participation in learning experiences.
- Practitioners work with families and other adults to acquire or create appropriate assistive technology to promote each child's access to and participation in learning experiences.
- Practitioners create environments that provide opportunities for movement and regular physical activity to maintain or improve fitness, wellness, and development across domains. (p. 9)

FEATURE 8.1 REPRESENTATIVE WEB RESOURCES

For additional information about young children with cognitive delays and disabilities, access the following websites:

- **American Association on Intellectual and Developmental Disabilities**, http://aaidd.org
- **Division on Autism and Developmental Disabilities, Council for Exceptional Children**, www.daddcec.com
- **National Down Syndrome Society**, http://ndss.org

YOUNG CHILDREN WITH SOCIAL AND EMOTIONAL DELAYS AND DISABILITIES

The term behavior disorder is frequently used to describe a wide variety of social and emotional challenges that include, but are not limited to, conduct disorders (aggressiveness and disruptive or destructive behaviors), difficulty with interpersonal relationships, depression, and anxiety disorders (overanxiousness, withdrawal). At least four characteristics are common to most definitions of individuals with emotional or behavioral disorders. These dimensions include the following:

1. The frequency or rate of occurrence of the behavior
2. The intensity of the behavior
3. The duration of the behavior (over a period of time)
4. The age appropriateness of the behavior (Smith et al., 2018).

Environmental factors can sometimes contribute to inappropriate behaviors.

iStock.com/patrickheagney

Typically, very young children are not given specific labels but may exhibit some early signs that may later develop into behavioral problems. Because of the diversity of children with delays and disabilities in this area of development, it is critical to individualize strategies used with each child. There are some issues and considerations, however, that may be applicable across children who exhibit problems in social and emotional development when adapting the environment, materials, intervention, and instruction.

Adapting the Environment

Early childhood special educators and other adults should think about several issues when considering environmental modifications for young children with challenging behaviors. Adults should make note of when and where the behavior occurs. Questions that might be asked include the following: Are there aspects of the home or learning environment that trigger inappropriate behavior? For example, is the schedule realistic, or is there too little time to complete activities? Are activities too long, and if so, are there planned activities for the child to move on to when their attention is waning? Is there too little or too much space for each child? It is important to compare the number of children and amount of space to determine whether space is contributing to unwanted behaviors. Are there enough materials, or has the lack of materials led to problems? Are the expectations realistic? It is important to remember that young children often have not yet learned to share. Therefore, it is not uncommon to have some problems when materials are limited. Does the inappropriate behavior always involve the same children or the same activity? Do problems occur at the same time of the day such as when the child is overtired, seated next to a specific peer, or after snack time? Is there something happening in the home setting that is contributing to problems in the educational setting such as the birth of a sibling, a move to a new house, or other transition events?

The IRIS Center (2015) along with Sandall et al. (2019) offer several ways to structure the learning environment for success. Recommend strategies include the following:

- *Provide a balance between child-directed and adult-directed activities.* Provide opportunities for children to make choices throughout their day.
- *Provide a variety of areas within the learning environment that have boundaries and are easily viewed.* The teacher and other adults should be able to view all areas of the classroom easily. Children should learn to recognize the boundaries of their learning areas.
- *Ensure materials are organized and in good working order.* Materials should be engaging and attractive to young children. Organize the materials in a fashion that tells the children where they belong.
- *Offer activities that provide many ways for children to respond.* Consider children's current skills and interests. Plan activities that allow choices and different ways to respond.

For young children with behavior issues, it is critical that they have a predictable, consistent learning environment. Rules should be established and maintained for the classroom with input from the children when possible, and the rules should be consistently applied. A routine should be established and followed consistently, and children should be prepared for changes in the routine.

Transitions within the learning environment can be a difficult time during the day for many young children, particularly those with behavior issues. Transitions are unpredictable and hard for some children to understand. Early childhood special educators should consider preparing children for transitions and should be specific in teaching children what to do during transitions (e.g., "You must wait until your name is called"). For some children, using picture cues or Social Stories may be helpful. Some children may require specific instruction about the routine for the transition to be successful ("When you are finished, please raise your hand"). If children have difficulty leaving one activity for another, the teacher can begin the activity with just a few children. If the new activity is interesting and engaging, the other child may join those children who made the transition quickly. Warning signals such as a bell, music, singing, or a "cleanup song" can be provided to give notice that a transition is about to happen. These are simple environmental strategies that may allow all young children to feel secure, knowing what is happening throughout their day.

Table 8.2 offers educators suggestions that may help young children with emotional delays and disabilities succeed in their classrooms.

TABLE 8.2 ■ Tips for Supporting Preschool Children With Social and Emotional Delays and Disabilities

Work collaboratively with multidisciplinary team members (school psychologists, social workers, administrators, special educators) to identify evidence-based instructional and behavioral strategies.
Establish class schedules, routines, rules, and positive consequences.
Create a learning and social environment that is nurturing for *all* students.
Explicitly teach social behaviors—following directions, raising one's hand, sharing toys or other items, using words to express anger or frustration, and so on.
Ask more socially competent peers to help with social skills training or readiness tasks.
Be sure that paraprofessionals, parent volunteers, and other adults know how to appropriately respond when presented with challenging behaviors.
Teach typically developing children how to respond to classmates who exhibit behavioral challenges—for instance, ignoring the classmate, walking away from the situation, or informing an adult.
Collaborate with parents so similar management strategies for appropriate and inappropriate behaviors are used both in the classroom and at home.
When necessary, ask other professionals for ideas and suggestions as to how to resolve a perplexing situation. Collaboration is often the key to success.

Source: Adapted from M. Hardman, M. Egan, and C. Drew, *Human Exceptionality*, 12th ed. (Boston, MA: Cengage Learning, 2017), p. 196.

Adapting Materials and Equipment

The use of materials can often guide a child's behavior. For instance, are materials available that encourage self-expression (modeling clay, paints, writing supplies, tape recorders)? One kindergarten teacher provided a tape recorder and drawing materials for children who acted out. While they were pulled aside to "sit and watch" others engaging in appropriate play, the children would tell what happened using either the art supplies or the tape recorder before talking with the teacher about the incident. The tape or picture was then passed on to the family members to keep them informed of behaviors in the educational environment. Another early childhood special educator had the child dictate what happened, which was then sent home to the family.

Are learning materials safe, and do they promote the kind of interactions that should be encouraged? Some materials and activities may suggest aggressive themes. Even with toddlers, it may become apparent that a particular toy or activity (such as toy weapons, books, or cartoons with aggressive themes) is involved when disruptive behavior occurs. It is important for adults to observe children at play and remove the objects that are associated with problems or discontinue exposure to books or programs that lead to imitations of aggressive play behavior. It is equally as important for teachers to provide toys and materials in the educational environment that promote appropriate social interaction as it is those that encourage cooperation and opportunities to share (Hollingsworth & Buysse, 2009).

Are there enough materials? Early childhood special educators must judge the amount of materials needed in the educational environment. On the one hand, teachers and other adults need to promote sharing among preschoolers; on the other, they want to avoid conflicts over limited resources. Is recreational equipment available that naturally promotes cooperative play? Seesaws, rocking boats, and wagon rides are all examples of equipment that rewards cooperative play, as they require children to play together. Riding toys, however, such as tricycles or scooters, may be needed for each child in order to avoid possible conflicts. Are the materials and activities reinforcing and of high interest to children?

It is critical that children have choices of materials that are of interest, especially if access to preferred materials or activities is contingent on appropriate or desired behavior.

Adapting Intervention and Instruction

One of the first steps for intervention or instruction is to determine, with the family's help, the cause of a behavior issue, noting when, where, and with whom a particular inappropriate behavior occurs. This process of gathering information and data about the particular behavior is called a **functional behavior analysis** (Alberto et al., 2022). Is the behavior something that can be ignored? Or is it a behavior that warrants attention? In other words, is it interfering with performance, or is it unsafe for the child or others? Are there environmental elements that are contributing to problem behaviors? For example, almost daily, Amy exhibited disruptive behavior when it was time to transition to another activity such as naptime or snack. When she was given a little more time to complete activities, the disruptive behavior subsided.

If it is determined that the behavior warrants attention, an individualized behavior plan with positive behavioral supports can be created to address challenging behaviors. **Positive behavioral support** is a comprehensive approach focusing on facilitating appropriate behaviors while reducing or preventing challenging behaviors (Gargiulo & Metcalf, 2023). Specific strategies can be discussed with the family and other professionals (paraprofessionals, related service providers) to ensure consistency across people in the home and educational setting.

Of critical importance is that all adults address challenging behaviors in positive and instructional ways (Division for Early Childhood, 2017). Strategies can be selected for promoting desired behaviors that include activities, materials, and people that are reinforcing to the child.

Children learn and persist in inappropriate behaviors because they are motivated to do so. Early childhood special educators, families, and other adults using positive behavioral supports are encouraged to look at discovering the function of the behavior. There are several possible reasons or functions of behaviors in young children that may be described as (1) sensory seeking, (2) escape or avoidance, (3) attention seeking, (4) a desire for tangible reinforcers, or (5) power and control (Hott et al., 2017). For example, if adult attention is sought by Micki, a child who exhibits frequent tantrums, the adults should make sure she receives adequate attention for desired behaviors ("That's a great picture; tell me about it"; "I like the way you and Roman are playing together") while withholding attention for undesired behavior. A child whose function for inappropriate behaviors is sensory seeking may be highly motivated by touch, smell, taste, visuals, or hearing. Roman, a first grader with autism, exhibits behaviors such as waving his hands in a flapping manner, rocking, and loud shouts. The teacher and occupational therapist designed a series of sensory activity breaks for Roman to engage in daily. These breaks were embedded within his daily schedule. Among these activities were jumping on a small trampoline, rolling on a therapy ball, and interacting with toys that light up and make repetitive noises.

When possible, the teacher and other service providers should provide choices for children instead of placing demands on them. For example, if T. J. refuses to leave the block area to come to the small group circle time activity, the teacher may give him choices by saying, "T. J., we need to sit for circle time. You may bring a red or blue block to the circle area with you." Or, "You can hop like a bunny or jump like a frog to the circle." In this way, T. J. has the choice of the way he comes to the circle, and the teacher has accomplished the desired behavior.

Multiple opportunities can be provided for choice making throughout the day (learning centers, art supplies, snack, or toys) so that children have a sense of control over some aspects of the environment. Opportunities can be provided for self-expression (art, music, or social dramatic play) that serves as a channel for appropriate behaviors for a child who might have difficulty expressing himself or herself in acceptable ways. When creating small-group activities, peers should be carefully selected who can serve as models for appropriate behavior, socialization, and communication (Hollingsworth & Buysse, 2009; Mastrangelo, 2009).

Teachers and other adults should set clear, consistent, and fair limits for the learning environment. Children will have an easier time meeting expectations if they know what is expected and what behaviors are appropriate.

A limited number of rules are recommended for both preschool and early primary classrooms. Having the rules posted in the classroom and revisiting and reminding children of the rules throughout the day is a positive approach to build in repeated presentations of the expected behaviors. Many preschool and early primary teachers include the children in the creating and discussing classroom rules. In this way, the children have a better understanding of the rules and limits.

Redirection is another strategy that leads young children to more acceptable behaviors. Redirection can often keep a small problem from escalating into a larger one. Sometimes redirection can be embedded into an established behavioral pattern. For example, Kevin is a five-year-old kindergartener who does not separate from his mother at the classroom door without crying and throwing a tantrum. The teacher and parent engaged in many discussions over the first three weeks of the school year to brainstorm ways to make the transition easier for all. During one discussion, the teacher discovered that Kevin had a preference for building with blocks. The next morning, the teacher and two of Kevin's peers were sitting outside the classroom door playing with a new set of colored blocks. Kevin quickly separated from his mother to join in playing with his classmates. His crying and tantrums gradually diminished over the next few days. The teacher had successfully embedded a redirection to a preferred activity for Kevin.

Time out has been used to address a wide range of inappropriate behaviors across a variety of learning environments. Parents and educators have reported using this strategy in their homes, classrooms, and other settings. Providing a young child with a time out when aggressive behavior occurs is often effective when dealing with aggression (Alberto et al., 2022). **Time out** is a strategy that involves removing a child to a location away from reinforcing conditions. The child is briefly removed (one minute for each year of chronological age) from rewarding activities (including attention from peers and other people). Application of appropriate time-out strategies coupled with changing the classroom environment to add areas of personal space have been found to be effective when attempting to change adverse behaviors in young children with delays and disabilities (Guardino & Fullerton, 2010). Table 8.3 offers guidelines for using time out appropriately in the learning environment.

TABLE 8.3 ■ Guidelines for Using Time Out
Time out should only be used to supplement a plan that provides positive behavioral supports.
Remember, time out only teaches the child what not to do; therefore, it is essential to teach positive behaviors and reinforce them.
Always have a plan for how time out will be used, and ensure that all adults are familiar with how the plan will be implemented.
Always keep records to document progress. If the frequency of time outs is not decreasing, then the use of time out is not working.

Time out is often used when confronted with behavioral issues.

Fancy/Veer/Corbis/via Getty Images

There is some concern, however, about the appropriateness of the use of time out with young children, as it has the potential to be overused and misused. Examples of misuse include the following:

- Being placed in time out too frequently and without the child understanding the reasons
- Being placed out of view of teachers and other adults
- Use of time out without other strategies that promote desired behavior (that is, without talking about the behavior with the child)
- Use as the first and only option when dealing with behavior issues
- Use without the knowledge or consent of parents or families
- Placement in time out for long periods of time

When thoughtfully used, time out can be one of many valuable strategies for dealing with behavioral issues. It provides children (and sometimes adults) with a chance to control their own emotions. It separates the aggressor from the victim. It is best applied briefly, immediately, and in a matter-of-fact fashion without anger or reprimands. Explaining to young children which behaviors will result in time out, as well as the reason, will enable them to understand that it is one way to help them learn to change their behavior. Teachers, parents, and other adults can demonstrate time-out procedures, showing children that they are provided a space and time to compose themselves before rejoining the group. One alternative to the traditional time out is to have a child "sit and watch." In this way, the child can step aside briefly, watch other children at play or work, and learn from children who are demonstrating appropriate behaviors (Gargiulo & Metcalf, 2023).

A young child with challenging behaviors may lack the communication skills and/or social competence needed to negotiate the interactions in his or her world (Greenwood et al., 2011; Marsili & Hughes, 2009; Park et al., 2011). For example, some young children may not have the words to express their emotions of anger or anxiety; others may lack the appropriate social skills necessary for asking for a toy from a peer; some may lack self-control in a conflict situation. Some young children may require direct instruction of words and/or social skills, while others may need prompts for appropriate self-expression ("Show me what you want"; "Tell me what you want"; "Tell Jo Ann how you feel"; "Tell him that it's your turn with the truck"). Likewise, a child may benefit from opportunities to interact with children who model appropriate communication and social skills. If a lack of communication skills is contributing to the behavioral issue, teachers and other adults can explore alternative ways of communicating (e.g., use picture cards to express feelings). See the Making Connections feature for an application of using positive behavioral strategies in working with T. J., a child who has behavioral issues, as well as Cheryl, a student with ADHD and a Section 504 plan.

FEATURE 8.2 REPRESENTATIVE WEB RESOURCES

For additional information about young children with delays and disabilities in social and emotional development, access the following websites:

- **American Psychological Association**, www.apa.org
- **Center for Early Childhood Mental Health Consultation**, www.ecmhc.org
- **Center on the Social and Emotional Foundations for Early Learning**, http://csefel.vanderbilt.edu
- **Division for Emotional and Behavioral Health, Council for Exceptional Children**, https://debh.exceptionalchildren.org/
- **DEC Position Paper on Challenging Behavior and Young Children**, https://www.decdocs.org/position-statement-challenging-beha
- **National Center for Pyramid Model Innovations**, https://challengingbehavior.cbcs.usf.edu/about/index.html
- **National Federation of Families for Children's Mental Health**, www.ffcmh.org

MAKING CONNECTIONS

STRATEGIES FOR PROVIDING POSITIVE BEHAVIORAL SUPPORT

A Positive Behavioral Support Plan for T.J.

Based on the information presented in the vignette on T.J. Browning (see Chapter 2) and the information on characteristics of young children with behavioral issues, there are several strategies that can be utilized to address T.J.'s unique needs. For example, because of his aggressive behavior, it would be important to create an individualized plan to address behavioral issues. The parent is very concerned about her son and can provide useful information about him. She can be asked what kind of strategies she has used at home to mediate behavior, including the ones that are successful as well as those that have been unsuccessful. It is important to pay attention to when the aggression typically occurs and whether it is directed at specific individuals or preceded by predictable events. A plan of action can be created with the mother and T.J. so that he understands what is expected of him, understands the consequences of his actions, has opportunities for success and praise throughout his day, and sees that his mother is working closely with the teacher to help him.

T.J. should be provided with alternatives to aggressive behavior such as being encouraged to "use his words"; should be provided with opportunities for choices and self-expression through art, music, and social dramatic play; and should have the option of having peer-mediated social interventions used, whereby appropriate social skills are modeled and taught. In addition, it is important for T.J. to hear praise for the things he is doing well, rather than receiving adult attention in the form of reprimands for inappropriate behavior.

It would be important for an examination of his social network to occur. Does he have friends and social relationships that are rewarding to him? It may be necessary for some of the strategies for promoting acceptance (see Chapter 9) to be utilized if he does not have a social network within the learning environment. Moreover, to address his problems with distractibility, it would be important to determine his interest in materials, toys, and activities to ensure that high-interest items and activities are available for intervention and instruction. Environmental factors (e.g., too much noise, too much visual simulation, close proximity to others) that may be contributing to the distractibility should also be examined.

A Positive Behavioral Support Plan for Cheryl

Cheryl Chinn was introduced in Chapter 2 as a first grader with a diagnosis of attention deficit hyperactivity disorder. In Chapter 4, we learned that Cheryl's teachers and parents collaborated to create a Section 504 plan to address difficulties with concentration. Cheryl is easily distracted, and her classroom assignments are often not completed. In this vignette, Cheryl's parents and classroom teacher, Mrs. Newman, have discussed the use of positive behavioral supports to help Cheryl be successful in the classroom. They have decided to implement a daily contract with Cheryl to increase her time on task without distraction and work to complete her assignments.

Goal 1: Cheryl will increase her time on task in her classroom activities and assignments daily.

Goal 2: Cheryl will complete her class assignments.

Environmental Supports

1. Cheryl will be seated near the teacher (proximity seating) and close to attentive peers. She will have designated space on the carpet marked by tape for small-group activities.
2. Cheryl and a peer will help keep her desk clean and uncluttered. Mrs. Newman will check her desk at dismissal time daily.
3. Cheryl will have the classroom rules printed at the top of her daily checklist. They will be clear and concise. The teacher will alert Cheryl if a change in the daily schedule is going to occur.

Academic Supports

1. Mrs. Newman will make directions to the class in brief statements. Directions will be both oral and visual (see daily checklist).
2. The teacher will break Cheryl's activities and assignments into small parts. She will be given extended time, if needed.

3. Mrs. Newman will model the activities and use Cheryl as the helper as much as possible.
4. Cheryl will be assigned a peer helper, if needed.

Behavioral Supports

1. Mrs. Newman will give Cheryl frequent specific verbal praise and encouragement for desired behaviors.
2. Cheryl will be given verbal and visual reminders of the classroom rules and expectations throughout the day.
3. If needed, Mrs. Newman will repeat and model the desired behaviors for the whole class in a nonthreatening manner.
4. Mrs. Newman will review Cheryl's daily checklist with her (via a private conversation or conference) prior to dismissal.

Cheryl Chinn's Daily Checklist

Classroom Rules

Look at and listen to the teacher.

Stay in my seat or place.

Raise my hand.

Respect others.

Finish my work.

Daily Schedule

Warm-up: journal writing	Reading/language	
Math meeting—calendar time	Lunch	
Math	Library	
Math centers	Science—hands-on activity	
Recess	Cleanup/daily conference	
Spelling	Dismissal	
Did I pay attention to the teacher?	YES	NO
Did I stay in my seat?	YES	NO
Did I finish my work?	YES	NO
Did I earn my reward?	YES	NO
Cheryl's choice reward:		
(as determined by Cheryl and Mrs. Newman)		

YOUNG CHILDREN WITH AUTISM SPECTRUM DISORDERS

The number of young children diagnosed with **autism spectrum disorders (ASD)** has been steadily increasing over the past several years. ASD is considered the fastest-growing childhood disorder (Gonzalez et al., 2017) and a growing concern among educators, related service providers, and, of course, families. Recent estimates from the Centers for Disease Control and Prevention (2021) suggest that one in every forty-four children at age eight is identified with autism spectrum disorders. ASD is four times more common in boys than in girls. It ignores social, economic, ethnic, and racial boundaries. There is no known single cause of autism spectrum disorders; current thinking suggests multiple etiologies (Gargiulo & Bouck, 2021).

Recent data from the U.S. Department of Education (2023) reveal that more than 91,000 three- to five-year-old children were identified with autism (the federal legislative term) during the 2020–2021 school year. This number represents approximately 12 percent of all preschoolers with a disability. Likewise, almost 172,000 six- to eight-year-old students were receiving a special education due to autism during the 2019–2020 school year. This figure represents 12.3 percent of all early primary students ages six to eight with a disability (U.S. Department of Education, 2022). Statistics like this give rise, in some circles, to calling ASD an epidemic.

The Individuals with Disabilities Education Improvement Act of 2004 (PL 108–446) defines autism as a developmental disability significantly affecting verbal and nonverbal communication and social interaction, usually evident before age three, that adversely affects a child's educational performance. Other characteristics often associated with autism are engagement in repetitive activities and stereotyped movements resistive to environmental change or change in daily routines and unusual responses to sensory experiences. Autism does not apply if the child's educational performance is adversely affected primarily because the child has an emotional disturbance. A child who manifests the characteristics of autism after age three could be diagnosed with autism if the criteria in paragraph (c)(1)(i) of this section are satisfied. (34 C.F. R. § 300.8 [c][1])

Most early childhood special education professionals would agree that young children with autism spectrum disorders exhibit a wide range of symptoms and degrees of impairment ranging from mild to severe, hence the term *spectrum disorders.* Although young children with autism spectrum disorders are individuals with their own unique personalities, some common characteristics have been identified, such as delays in communication and social skills. Behaviorally, children with autism spectrum disorders may exhibit restrictive behaviors and interests, short attention span, hyperactivity or impulsivity, aggressiveness, or self-injurious behaviors (Gargiulo & Bouck, 2021; Hughes & Henderson, 2017). Clearly, young children with autism spectrum disorders manifest features with complex medical and educational needs requiring early identification, evaluation, and developmentally appropriate educational services that may result in more positive outcomes (Autism Society of America, 2023b).

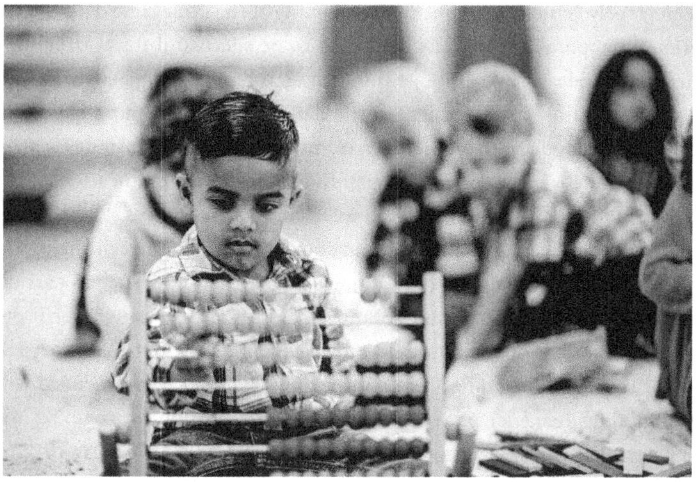

Young children with autism spectrum disorders exhibit a wide range of characteristics.

iStock.com/FatCamera

Families, educators, and other professionals in the field of early childhood special education often struggle with providing comprehensive programs that address the individual needs of children with autism spectrum disorders that may vary from a mild educational impact to a need for an intense, structured special education program. Early diagnosis and access to developmentally appropriate interventions and services may lead to positive outcomes for children with ASD. Due to the wide range and variability of educational and behavioral impact evidenced within the autism spectrum, interventions, educational approaches, and methodologies should be developed by a multidisciplinary team of professionals working with families collaboratively to build effective programs based on the child's individual strengths and developmental levels (Gargiulo & Bouck, 2021).

Adapting the Environment

Parents or caregivers of children with autism spectrum disorders are often the first to notice delays and differences in their child's development. Children with more severe characteristics tend to be recognized sooner than those with less noticeable traits. Families often observe language deficits, hand-flapping and other repetitive behaviors, toe-walking, food aversions or restrictive diets, and short attention spans or distractibility, along with poor social interactions with other children. Given that ASD can reliably be diagnosed by age two (National Institute of Mental Health, 2023), it is vitally important that the family members and multidisciplinary team members carefully select evidence-based strategies and interventions appropriate to the unique needs of the child. Most toddlers diagnosed with autism spectrum disorders before the age of three will receive early intervention services in the home or a center-based setting. Early intervention services typically focus on the areas of communication, adaptive behaviors or self-care skills, behavioral issues, and social skills training (Autism Society of America, 2023a; Gargiulo & Bouck, 2021). The delivery of customized services for young children with ASD is determined by a team of professionals working in conjunction with the family via the IFSP or IEP. (Review Chapter 5 for information about IFSPs and IEPs.)

In adapting the learning environments for young children with autism spectrum disorders and other delays and disabilities, families, early childhood special educators, and other professionals should consider temporal adaptations and environmental arrangements [DEC Recommended Practices E3].

Temporal adaptations are the structure, routine, and predictable activities that occur naturally in the home and educational setting. The National Autism Center (2015) identifies structure and predictability as important adaptations when teaching new skills to children with autism spectrum disorders. Routine activities identified in the home, center, or classroom help children with ASD know what the expectations are and what is coming next. Naturalistic teaching within the environment occurs when a child is taught the routine that is part of a "typical day" (National Autism Center, 2015; Noonan & McCormick, 2014). For example, routines in the home might revolve around outside playtime, mealtime, bath time, and bedtime. An example from the classroom routine might include circle time, snack time, literacy centers, play centers, and lunch, all occurring at the same time daily.

Three additional temporal adaptations identified to be successful for both home and classroom environments are (1) provide "break times," (2) match active and sitting activities, and (3) adjust the schedule, if needed. Providing "break times" in the daily schedule so young children with ASD can engage in preferred activities or go to a quiet area of the room for a few minutes is a good strategy for helping reduce anxiety and overstimulation. Depending on their communication level, many children can identify their need to "take a break" through words or picture choices. Planning the daily routine with appropriate active or movement times with an equal amount of quiet or sitting times is a recommended strategy for children with ASD. An example is to plan activities such as participating in circle time for ten minutes followed by five minutes of movement to songs or dancing that provides children with autism spectrum disorders opportunities to move, which may help with sensory input. Observing patterns of behavior that occur at similar times of the day is another recommended strategy. If a child exhibits crying or anxious behavior prior to lining up in preparation for the next activity, this may indicate that they have difficulty transitioning from one activity to another. Making an adjustment in the schedule or providing a cue or signal to the child five minutes prior to the transition may diminish or alleviate the behavior. ("You have five more minutes at this center. When you hear the bell, you will go to the next center"; "After this song, circle time will be over, and you will line up to go to the playground").

Environmental arrangements or physical adaptations involve making changes to the home or educational environment to increase the likelihood of targeted behavioral, communication, and engagement expectations for young children with ASD. Environmental arrangement or adaptations should be considered after the team members and family have observed or assessed the current level of participation of the child in a certain activity. Adaptations considered should be initially tried in the least intrusive manner before moving to a more intrusive adaptation. As an example, a young child with ASD has trouble sitting with three peers for an early literacy activity. He tends to leave the carpet area and go to the bookshelf to choose a toy or go to another center. After observation, the early childhood special educator decides that the child is distracted. She covers the bookshelf with material that hides the toys when not in use but that can be easily removed. She places the child in a different location on the carpet, closer to her, with the child's back to the covered bookshelf. The book and the daily picture schedule are located in close proximity. She can monitor when the child becomes distracted and quickly redirect him to the early literacy task with the book and visual schedule. The child's attention to the early literacy activity increases with the simple removal of the distraction and closer placement of the child to the activity content and visual routine schedule. These adaptations allow the child to participate more independently in the learning environment. This environmental adaptation was natural and far less intrusive to the activity than requiring an adult to sit behind the child to redirect his behavior.

Environmental arrangements in the home may involve the early childhood special educator and related service personnel, such as an occupational therapist or speech–language pathologist, coming for a home visit in an effort to assist the family in adapting the home environment. Families often report that their child is overly sensitive to noise or light. Some environments may simply be overstimulating for the child with ASD. Reducing the level of noise in the home by turning off the television, lowering the volume on background music, or turning off the sound on the computer may help with auditory sensitivity. Some children with autism spectrum disorders enjoy wearing lightweight, noise-reducing earphones. Lighting can be adjusted with a dimmer switch or by removing one or two light bulbs from a multiple-bulb overhead lighting fixture.

Children with autism spectrum disorders frequently exhibit some type of eating difficulty (Autism Speaks/ Autism Treatment Network, 2014). An occupational therapist or physical therapist can help the family in finding the optimum seating options for mealtimes such as a highchair, booster seat, or appropriate table and chair height. An eating specialist or occupational therapist can plan with the family a feeding program that addresses increasing the child's intake of new and different foods to expand their food choices and preferences.

Additional environmental adaptations for both home and classroom environments include defining "quiet or soft areas" in the room with bean bag chairs, pillows, or blankets where young children with autism spectrum disorders can retreat to when needing a break; covering a table with a sheet or blanket; setting up small tents; or purchasing commercially available fabric tunnels where children with ASD can go when they become anxious, need personal space, or require a less stimulating environment. Finally, when considering learning centers, early childhood special educators can choose those that will create the most opportunities for children with autism spectrum disorders to interact and play with their typically developing peers. Structuring learning centers for dramatic play, games with turn-taking opportunities, or free play with peers can create multiple opportunities for children with autism to engage in active participation (Mastrangelo, 2009).

Review Chapter 7 for additional information about environmental arrangement.

Adapting Materials and Equipment

In adapting materials and equipment for young children with ASD, professionals and families need to consider the functional level of the child. Many young children with autism spectrum disorders often lack the basic communication skills needed to make their wants and needs known (Gargiulo & Bouck, 2021). In planning for communication and behavioral interventions, IFSP/IEP teams should consider the use of **visual supports**. Children with autism spectrum disorders often have difficulty processing spoken language. Using visual supports such as pictures of real objects, picture symbols, and written words incorporated into daily routines and schedules has been found to be an excellent strategy in assisting the child with ASD in comprehending the rules, expectations, and transitions that occur in the home or classroom (Meadan et al., 2011; Travers & Nunes, 2017).

Visual pictures and materials help support the predictability of the routine that children with autism spectrum disorders require in a learning environment. Visual supports can be used to design individual picture schedules where one picture denotes one activity. The schedule is individualized for each child's schedule for that day. Early childhood special educators and other adults may use several cards in a row or vertically to correspond to the classroom daily routine. The child is prompted to

"Check your schedule." The child looks at the card for circle or group time, follows the routine, and goes to be seated on the carpet denoted for the circle or group time activity. Following the end of the circle time or group activity, the child is verbally prompted, "Circle time is finished." The child is taught to remove the circle time picture from the schedule, put it in an attached envelope or box, then "Check your schedule" for the next activity. Picture schedules linked to the routine help children by reinforcing classroom rules, increasing appropriate behaviors, supporting greater independence with instructional activities, and making transitions easier by illustrating clear expectations of "what is coming next" (Cohen & Gerhardt, 2016; National Autistic Society, 2023).

The use of visual supports through pictures and picture schedules can be adapted easily to the functioning levels of each child. Large pictures of real objects or preferred objects can be used to increase the amount of time on task. The early childhood special educator may choose to use single pictures of objects, or they can use pictures of preferred objects or activities (e.g., a picture of a computer or sensory toy) to place on a child's reward schedule. The child's task schedule would be labeled "First" and "Then" at the top. The teacher would place the picture denoting the work activity under the "First" column and the reward picture the child has chosen under the "Then" column. The child is verbally prompted with "First, work box. Then, computer time." Large pictures can be faded to smaller pictures over time. Some teachers may choose to use pictures to illustrate appropriate classroom behaviors quickly, such as "Hands down," "Quiet mouth," "Hands to self," or "Listen."

Picture schedules can be integrated into many daily activities in a learning environment. The task analysis for washing hands illustrated in Table 8.1 could be coupled with pictures to create a schedule to teach a child with autism spectrum disorders using visual supports. Picture schedules can be embedded easily into circle time or group activities used frequently in preschool and primary-grade classrooms. For example, pictures could be used to illustrate the names of favorite songs, alphabet activities, or counting games. Using visual supports to teach language, vocabulary, and comprehension of early literacy skills has been found to be a viable strategy for engagement with stories, books, and building oral language (Cohen & Gerhardt, 2016; Noonan & McCormick, 2014; Whalon et al., 2007). In addition, visual supports can be used to increase comprehension in the areas of simple sequencing ("What came first, next, and last?") and answering simple yes/no, detail, and setting or location questions.

Another visual support strategy that has been used successfully for children with ASD is Social Stories™. Based on the work of Carol Gray, Social Stories describe "a situation, skill, or concept in terms of a relevant social cue, perspectives and common responses in a specifically defined style and format" (The Gray Center, 2012). Social Stories are particularly effective when teaching appropriate social skills to children with ASD. Social Stories are created for a child who may have difficulty understanding an event, transition, or social concept. The Social Story is personalized to teach children options for responding in a more socially appropriate manner or may be used to assist in replacing inappropriate behaviors (Ryan et al., 2011; Vanderbilt Kennedy Center, 2023). Social Stories use both written words and pictures depending on the developmental level of the child.

The Gray Center (2012, 2023) developed guidelines for creating a Social Story. Stories should contain text of approximately five to ten sentences. Gray's guidelines include the following five steps:

1. Define a targeted behavior, skill, or concept to be taught.
2. Identify an appropriate replacement behavior.
3. Write the text from the child's viewpoint.
4. Include pictures or picture symbols relevant to the child.
5. Include a directive sentence for every two to three descriptive or perspective sentences.

See the accompanying feature for an illustration of a Social Story.

When considering the use of visual supports for young children with ASD, team members may want to review a commercially available intervention system widely used to teach communication skills to children with autism spectrum disorders, the Picture Exchange Communication System™ or PECS

(Bondy & Frost, 1994). PECS is a form of augmentative and alternative method for teaching children functional communication skills. Developed in the late 1980s, this method uses photographs, drawings, pictures of objects, or an object that a child prefers. The child is taught to exchange the symbol for the object, person, or activity. The initial instructional phases of this method of visual support include (1) teaching a child to request an item through exchange, (2) generalizing the request by making the exchange with another person in the room, and (3) discriminating between two different symbols to make a generalized request in the room (Bondy & Frost, 1994; Ryan et al., 2011). PECS is viewed as an evidence-based practice for children with ASD (National Autism Center, 2015; Pyramid Educational Consultants, 2023). For more information on PECS, please visit the official website at https://pecsusa.com/pecs/.

Lastly, in reviewing materials to adapt for visual supports, this section would not be complete without mentioning the Boardmaker® Software Family, which includes the Mayer-Johnson Picture Communication Symbols™. This line of computer software is used as a publishing and editing tool to create symbol-based educational activities and materials for children with delays and disabilities. The program allows early childhood educators and other professionals to adapt a wide range of curriculum materials for children who need visual supports. This commercially available software comes with a basic picture communication symbol inventory of more than 4,500 symbols. The large inventory allows professionals to use the symbols to develop a wide range of pictures, schedules, communication boards, and Social Stories. For more information about the Mayer-Johnson Picture Communication Symbols and Boardmaker Software, visit www.mayer-johnson.com/pages/what-is-boardmaker.

Adapting Intervention and Instruction

In choosing intervention and instructional strategies for young children with autism spectrum disorders, families and team members should carefully review the many educational choices currently available. It is the task of the child's team to observe, evaluate, and match intervention and instructional strategies based on each child's strengths and needs. Children with autism spectrum disorders may exhibit needs in all developmental areas. To varying degrees, they may manifest delays in developing communication and language skills, acquiring cognitive and readiness skills, modulating their behavior, and using appropriate social skills for interacting with peers and adults. Indeed, many of the interventions and instructional strategies presented in the first two sections of this chapter regarding children with cognitive and behavioral delays and disabilities may be applicable to children with autism spectrum disorders [DEC Recommended Practices INS2, INS4, INS5].

In 2015, the National Autism Center published a document, *Findings and Conclusions: National Standards Project, Phase 2,* with the goal of providing a review of the then-available research on effective educational and behavioral interventions for individuals with ASD. This report identified several evidence-based practices to help families, educators, and related service providers make informed decisions regarding intervention and instructional strategies. Two of the reported interventions are applicable for discussion when considering how to adapt instruction: the use of naturalistic teaching strategies and peer support.

AN EXAMPLE OF A SOCIAL STORY

Eating in the Lunchroom

I eat my lunch in the lunchroom every day at school.
I walk to the lunchroom with my class and my teachers.
I walk with my class and don't run ahead.
I am quiet in the hall because I don't want to disturb other students in their classes.
When I get to the lunchroom, there will be other students eating lunch too.
The lunchroom may be noisy.

Some noises I hear are people talking, people laughing, lunch trays being thrown in the trash-can, and the bell ringing.
If the noise is too loud, I can put on my headphones or ask the teacher for a break.
I go through the lunch line.
I pick up a tray, a napkin, and silverware.
Silverware is the fork, spoon, and knife I use to eat my lunch.
I choose my lunch, get a drink, and pay for my lunch.
I have a lunch number, which I give to the cashier to pay for my food.
If I forget my lunch number, the lunchroom staff can look it up or my teacher will help me.
Once I have my food, I will sit at my table and talk to my friends.
If I need help with my food, I can ask my teachers or one of the lunchroom workers.
When I finish eating my food, I throw my lunch tray away and walk back to class with my friends.
My teachers are proud of me when I follow the rules for eating in the lunchroom.

Naturalistic teaching strategies or interventions are a broad category of educational methods that are frequently used in an inclusive learning environment. Naturalistic teaching interventions use children's typical daily routine and activities to teach brief discrete skills within the context of the classroom and other natural environments (DiCarlo & Vagianos, 2009). Naturalistic teaching strategies or interventions are applicable for young children with ASD particularly in the area of interaction and play with peers. Children with autism spectrum disorders may need some level of adult support or facilitation to promote successful social interactions with peers (Chang & Shire, 2019; Papacek et al., 2016). Play and peer social interactions for children with disabilities have been studied for well over forty years. Lifter, Mason, and Barton (2011) note that children with autism spectrum disorders display fewer spontaneous play skills in the areas of symbolic and complex play and less variety in their choice of toys. Therefore, teaching play and peer interaction skills in the learning environment provides a wide variety of naturally occurring opportunities. Play skills are a key element of development as they are often associated with gains in cognitive, language, and social competency (Chang & Shire, 2019).

Many different definitions of play exist in the literature. Children with autism spectrum disorders may present a challenge to identifying and assessing their play behaviors. Careful observation by the teachers and related service providers is often helpful in identifying the functioning level of play for children with ASD. Interviewing the parents and other family members may help the team to assess and plan strategies for facilitating play. Reviewing the levels of play in the literature may provide a context to begin defining each child's level of play. Research, largely based on the work of Piaget, reveals common developmental levels of children's play. Object play is exploratory in nature and involves manipulating an object or toy. Children with autism spectrum disorders often show limited variety of toy preference and tend to choose the same object. They may not associate a purpose with the object and use it in a stereotypical manner (Mastrangelo, 2009). In functional play, the child displays the correct use or function of the object, such as the child holding a play phone to his ear. Symbolic play is often difficult for young children with ASD because it involves the use of complex language and social interaction. Peer play is a complex skill for children with autism spectrum disorders as well. Social play with peers involves requesting, greeting, sharing, following directions, turn-taking, and participating in relationships with other peers. Understanding categories of peer play can be useful in conducting play assessment. For additional information about appropriate play with peers, see Table 8.4.

There are several naturalistic strategies for facilitating play in early childhood settings. Child interest or preference is one example. If the early childhood special educator observes a child showing an interest in interacting with a specific toy or activity, the teacher can step in to provide support for the child to enter the activity, participate, or complete the task (DiCarlo & Vagianos, 2009; Noonan & McCormick, 2014). Identifying the child's most and least preferred toys and activities may guide the intervention or instruction. This naturalistic strategy, also referred to as incidental teaching, is discussed in detail in Chapter 9.

TABLE 8.4 ■ Peer Play Categories

Category	Definition	Example
Unoccupied	Target child is not engaged in play.	Target child is wandering around the classroom.
Solitary	Target child is playing separately from others; they are not interested in what others are doing.	Target child plays with cars in the block area. Their peers are building a tower of blocks.
Onlooker	Target child watches other children play but does not engage in their play.	Target child watches their peers build a tower of blocks but does not participate in their play.
Parallel	Target child is playing with similar toys or objects as their peers but does not play with them.	Target child builds a tower of blocks next to a peer building a tower of blocks. The children do not interact with one another.
Associative	Target child is playing with a peer. Their play is not organized. There are some initiations and responses and sharing of toys and materials. No specific play roles are demonstrated.	Target child builds a tower of blocks with peers. Target child and their peers take turns adding blocks to the tower.
Cooperative	Target child is playing with a peer. Their play is organized around roles. Children initiate, respond, and take turns with one another. Toys and materials are shared.	Target child builds a tower of blocks with their peers. The children are pretending to be construction workers. One child takes the lead and tells their peers where to place the blocks.

Source: T. Stanton-Chapman and S. Hadden, "Encouraging Peer Interactions in Preschool Classrooms: The Role of the Teacher," *Young Exceptional Children, 14*(1) p. 20. Copyright © 2011 Sage Publications, Inc. Reprinted by permission.

Another strategy is to provide a child-choice format throughout the child's day. Interest- and theme-based learning centers used in the classroom can provide a variety of activities, use of materials, and small groups of peers (DiCarlo & Vagianos, 2009). The skill-specific areas that the child needs to practice can be easily embedded into a variety of developmental opportunities. For example, dramatic play can provide increased opportunities for verbalizations, learning new vocabulary, turn-taking, cooperation, and shared practice. Block building and manipulative play opportunities also can provide for problem-solving creativity, increased attention span, and cooperative practice activities. Music and movement, physical play, or literacy centers may all provide opportunities to engage with peers. Teachers may want to extend the amount of time for each activity to provide sufficient opportunities for child engagement. Early childhood special educators can mix high-preference choice activities with low-preference activities to promote the introduction of new desired skills.

Early childhood special educators and other adults may need to assist children with autism spectrum disorders by creating opportunities to interact with their peers. In addition to providing social interaction opportunities and child choice, adults can place children with ASD in planned pairs or small peer groupings. Routine classroom activities such as circle or group time, classroom jobs, and snack time or lunchtime can be used to support social interactions with typically developing peers. Early childhood special educators may want to choose specific skills to infuse into daily teaching such as greeting, sharing, helping others, being a friend, maintaining a conversation, and solving conflicts (Sandall et al., 2019). Peers can become a highly effective part of social interventions in the inclusive classroom. Finding a suitable model peer for a child with autism spectrum disorders may be effective for increasing language and reciprocal conversational practice (Marsili & Hughes, 2009). Peers can be coached to use appropriate responses or questions to increase the motivation for children to participate.

Finally, children with autism spectrum disorders may initially require more support in the area of language. One method that is compatible with naturalistic teaching intervention is teacher talk. **Teacher talk** is a set of specific assistance to become better communicators and promote peer interactions. Sharpe (2008) identified five formats of teacher talk that can be effective strategies for extending language, teaching vocabulary, and increasing conversations with peers for children with disabilities, which are applicable for children with autism spectrum disorders. These strategies are

1. *Recasting:* A teacher or another adult changes a child's word into a more appropriate word such as "Want juice or milk" instead of "Want drink."
2. *Repeating:* A teacher/adult restates what a child has said such as "My daddy is at work" to "Your daddy is at work."
3. *Expanding:* A teacher/adult extends or adds onto the statement the child makes such as "I want ball" to "You want the *blue* or *big* ball."
4. *Questioning:* The teacher/adult initiates a turn-taking conversation by asking open-ended questions. For example, the teacher asks, "What did you draw?" to which the child replies, "A house." The teacher then asks, "Who lives in the house?"
5. *Prompting:* A teacher/adult may provide a specific cue or prompt to a child. For example, at a table activity, the teacher/adult directs the child by stating, "Your friend is talking to you."

Prompting as a supportive strategy will be discussed in greater detail in Chapter 9.

FEATURE 8.3 REPRESENTATIVE WEB RESOURCES

For additional information about young children with autism spectrum disorders, access the following websites:

- **Autism Society of America**, www.autism-society.org
- **Autism Speaks**, www.autismspeaks.org
- **Division on Autism and Developmental Disabilities, Council for Exceptional Children**, www.daddcec.com
- **Kennedy Krieger Institute**, www.kennedykrieger.org
- **The National Professional Development Center on Autism Spectrum Disorder**, http://autismpdc.fpg.unc.edu

YOUNG CHILDREN WITH COMMUNICATION AND LANGUAGE DELAYS AND DISABILITIES

Communication refers to the exchange of messages between a speaker and a listener. *Language* refers to the use of symbols (letter sounds that are used in various combinations to form words), syntax (rules that guide sentence structure), and grammar when communicating with another person. Speech is the oral-motor action used to communicate (Gargiulo & Bouck, 2021). The federal definition found in IDEA 2004 refers to children with communication disorders such as stuttering, impaired articulation, a language impairment, or voice impairment that adversely affects their educational performance. In this area of development, a young child could have difficulty with one or more of these aspects of communication. Moreover, there are many potential causes of problems in communication or language development. A language delay could be related to cognitive delays, hearing impairments, emotional problems, autism spectrum disorders, motor impairments (such as cerebral palsy), or linguistic and cultural differences. Because the delay in communication and language development may be tied to a variety of etiologies, the early indicators may vary widely. For example, a young child with a **pervasive developmental disorder** may use **echolalic speech** patterns, wherein they repeat what is said instead of generating original words; a child with a cognitive delay may develop language at a slower pace and may not progress in their use of more complex language structures; or a youngster with a hearing loss may have difficulty following directions or exhibit poor articulation. Because of the interrelated nature of communication or language delays and disabilities with other disorders, the early indicators must be examined very carefully, keeping in mind that all children do not acquire language and communication skills at the same pace and that many young children exhibit difficulty with articulation or fluency during the early years of development.

Adapting the Environment

Adapting the home, school, or other learning environments will depend, in part, on the cause of the communication or language delay. However, general guidelines include the following:

- *Provide a language-rich home or classroom setting.* Children should be exposed early on to music, conversation, and printed language in books and the environmental print (words on a cereal box). A language-rich setting provides models for speech production, language structures, and social exchanges (Dennis & Horn, 2011; Gardner-Neblett & Gallagher, 2013).
- *Children's nonverbal and verbal communication should be responded to by teachers and other adults.* Infants and toddlers communicate often through cries, gestures, eye gaze, and sound and word production. It is critical that infants and toddlers have a responsive caregiver who responds to early communicative efforts (Gardner-Neblett & Gallagher, 2013). The same responsiveness is required of professionals and other adults who work with preschool and early primary children.
- *Turn-taking games should be used to have "conversations" with young children.* Simple games such as peek-a-boo or pat-a-cake can be used to support turn-taking behavior that is a necessary component of communication. The games and interactions become more advanced as children's communication and language skills develop.
- *Actions and objects in the child's surroundings should be labeled.* For example, as a mother is dressing her toddler, she could say, "Now, let's put on your socks and shoes. Socks go on. Shoes go on." In this way, the child is given labels for the actions and the objects in her surroundings. One mom commented that after doing this on a regular basis during dressing routines with her son with Down syndrome, he began bringing the socks and shoes to her in anticipation of the dressing routine. Clearly, the labeling activity had an impact on her child's language development. Again, these labeling activities become more advanced as children's communication and language skills become more advanced.

Interactions with peers and adults are important in developing communication skills.

Tatjana Kaufmann/Moment/via Getty Images

Adapting Materials and Equipment

Materials should spark children's interest and expand their development. Keep the following in mind when choosing materials:

- *Select materials and activities that are appealing to children's unique interests.* For example, the parents of Andrea, who has a language delay, noted her keen interest in animals and, therefore, purchased many toys and books that depicted animals. Many of the toys had a feature that allowed the child to activate the animal sounds. Some of the first sounds Andrea made were imitations of these animals. She later went on to imitate other sounds and words in her environment. Likewise, activities that the child is interested in will be more enjoyable, maintain attention, and have greater potential for language production.

- *Place materials in a location where the child can see them but is unable to access them.* This strategy provides a visual incentive for children to request desired materials. Although it may be easier to place all materials out for children, following this strategy creates a natural opportunity for children with language and communication delays to use their skills.
- *Limit the materials or equipment.* When preparing lunch, an adult can place a child's cup on the table without his favorite juice while the adult fills their own cup with juice. In this way, the child will note something is missing and need to request the missing item. Again, this intentional limitation of materials creates a natural opportunity for the child to use language.
- *Use materials for choice-making opportunities.* If a child is provided with multiple choices throughout their home and classroom routines, they gain more control and autonomy and is supported in communication attempts.

Adapting Intervention and Instruction

Every activity should be viewed as an opportunity for developing language. Routine activities such as going to the grocery store, washing the dishes, playing after breakfast, taking daily walks in the neighborhood, and getting dressed are all opportunities to expose young children to language. Times should be selected across the day at home, in the community, and in school environments where language and communication skills can be addressed. The following illustrations represent strategies that are often useful in promoting the development of communication and language skills.

Imitate the child's actions and sounds. Imitation of early actions and vocalizations is an ideal way to reinforce a young child's motor and verbal movements. For example, Jonathan, who is a toddler, and his mother are playing with sand. His mother drops sand from her hand while saying "ma, ma, ma." Pairing vocal models with physical imitation may encourage children to use more complex and frequent vocalizations during play. When Jonathan pushes his fingers into the sand, his mother can imitate by pushing her fingers into the sand while adding the vocalization "ma." Adults can model conventional gestures, such as pointing to objects out of reach, shrugging one's shoulders, upturning the palms, nodding the head to indicate yes or no, waving, and making the "shhh" gesture. Imitation is a strategy that is effective for teaching turn-taking behaviors and the use of communication to regulate others' behaviors. For example, Susan and her mother are rolling a ball back and forth. One day, instead of rolling the ball back, Susan's mother waits. After Susan looks at her mother and vocalizes "ba," her mother rolls the ball back to her.

Expand the language that a child uses. For example, if Alina says "down" when the ball falls down, the teacher or other adults can say "ball down" or "ball fell down." In this way, adults can capitalize on Alina's initiation and interest, imitate or reinforce her vocalization, and provide a model for expanding her vocalization. Elaborative modeling is an effective procedure used when a child has not yet acquired independent production of communication skills. For example, Stacy is playing with the teacher in the doll center. She says "bottle" while reaching for the baby bottle. The teacher gives her the bottle as she says "Say, 'I want bottle.'" Stacy responds with "Want bottle." The teacher then provides the corrective model by saying "*I* want bottle." Stacy then imitates "I want bottle" and receives the bottle. The teacher follows with feedback and compliance with Stacy's request by expanding the language, saying "Yes, here is the bottle for your baby!"

Couple vocalizations with gestures, if necessary. For example, a teacher could say "no" while shaking her head and "yes" while nodding her head. This provides a visual cue as well as a vocal directive. Another example would be pointing to the door while saying "Go to the door." Again, it provides the child with visual and auditory input while labeling the action as it occurs.

Use pauses (verbally and physically) to provide an opportunity to communicate. This seems like such an obvious strategy, but when trying to communicate with a child who has limited verbal skills, it is easy for caregivers to talk so much that the child does not have an opportunity to verbalize or communicate.

Likewise, it is easy for adults to provide children with all of the materials before they have indicated a need for them. This strategy requires the teacher or adult to make a conscious effort to slow down their own communication or sit back and wait to allow children a chance to communicate what they want or need.

Early childhood special educators should collaborate with related service personnel (such as the speech–language pathologist). It is critical that everyone working with a child use the same strategies and have the same expectations for addressing individualized communication and language goals for the child. Collaboration will ensure consistency across settings and people and increase the likelihood of the generalization of skills (Basu et al., 2010). Moreover, the selection of effective strategies is highly dependent on the unique needs of each child. For example, if the child has a visual impairment, the strategies used to adapt instruction to facilitate communication and language development may be different from those selected for a child with a hearing impairment. Also, the related service personnel who are involved may vary. Therefore, it is important for early childhood special educators to look at each child individually and collaborate with the appropriate related service professional. There are many more ways to adapt instruction that will be discussed in detail in Chapter 9. In particular, early childhood special educators should pay attention to monitoring communicative input, peer initiation intervention, cooperative learning strategies, routine-based strategies, and milieu strategies.

FEATURE 8.4 REPRESENTATIVE WEB RESOURCES

For additional information about young children with delays in communication and language development, access the following websites:

- **American Speech-Language-Hearing Association**, www.asha.org
- **Division for Communication, Language, and Deaf/Hard of Hearing, Council for Exceptional Children**, https://dcdcec.org

YOUNG CHILDREN WITH SENSORY IMPAIRMENTS: VISION

Children with visual impairments are generally identified as partially sighted or blind. The Individuals with Disabilities Education Improvement Act of 2004 defines **visual impairment** as an impairment in vision that, even with correction, adversely affects an individual's educational performance. The impact of a visual impairment depends on the age of onset, the amount of functional vision, its etiology, and the presence of other disabilities. Visual impairments often adversely impact several domains of development including fine and gross motor skills, concept development, and self-help skills, as well as social development and language, to mention a few areas (Gargiulo & Bouck, 2021). It is vitally important, therefore, that early childhood special educators work collaboratively with vision specialists and other professionals in crafting an IFSP/IEP designed to meet the unique needs of the young child with a visual impairment.

Adapting the Environment

First and foremost, children with visual impairments should be encouraged to use their residual vision, if any. The home and educational settings should have good lighting, and the child should be in areas away from glares, shadows, or flickering lights. Making the area brighter or dimmer according to the child's needs should be considered both in the home and in the classroom. Poor lighting or changing lighting may interfere with the limited vision that the child does have. Learning centers or activity areas (literacy area, block area) should have high-quality lighting. The noise level should be monitored to ensure that it does not interfere with individuals' ability to use auditory cues. For example, Tameka, a five-year-old child with a visual impairment, relies heavily on auditory cues to know where to go, what is happening next, and what she is supposed to be doing. Each morning, Lisa, a two-year-old with limited vision, relies on the auditory cues from the kitchen (Mom removing the dishes from the cabinet, refrigerator humming, Dad listening to the morning news on the television) to navigate her way to the kitchen. Refer to Table 8.5 for a list of common environmental adaptations for children with visual impairments.

TABLE 8.5 ■ Environmental Adaptations for Children With Visual Impairments

Lighting	Color and Contrast	Size and Distance	Time
What to Observe			
Variety of lighting situations Lighting at different times of day Low-vision devices used	Contrast between object and background	Placement and size of objects near or far	Time for completion of visual discrimination during tasks Tactile tasks such as cubby or locker for belongings or books
What to Use			
Light sensitivity: shades, visors, tinted glasses Low light: lamp or illuminated low-vision device Room obstructions: preferential seating, furniture placement Glare: nonglare surface on areas such as computer screens, desktop, paper	Bold-line paper Black print on white background Dark markers One-sided writing on paper Dark placemat for contrast during eating Floor contrast for mobility ease Tactile markings for outline discrimination Contrast to define borders on walls	Enlarged materials Preferred seating Electronic devices Magnification Optical character recognition Adjustment of desks, tables, and chairs Additional storage space for Braille, large-print books, low-vision devices near each work station or learning center	Verbal cues for actions in classroom Increase time for task completion Call student by name Announce when entering or leaving room Encourage participation in demonstrations Provide opportunity to observe materials prior to lesson Use authentic manipulative objects Schedule instructional time in early part of day Convenient use and storage of materials Lock-and-key is preferred over combination locker
Desired Results			
Better posture Greater concentration Less fatigue	Better visual efficiency Less fatigue Safer travel	Ease of viewing Appropriate adaptations for specific vision loss	Less fatigue Inclusion in class activities Time efficiency

Source: R. Gargiulo and E. Bouck, *Special Education in Contemporary Society: An Introduction to Exceptionality*, 7th ed. (Thousand Oaks, CA: Sage, 2021), p. 431.

Attention must also be given to the layout and arrangement of the environment. Children need to be able to successfully orient themselves to their home and classroom setting. In both instances, children need to demonstrate that they are capable of accessing the environment. Marking the home or classroom areas with easily identifiable tactile cues is an important adaptation. Early childhood special educators and family members should enlist the assistance of an orientation and mobility specialist who can help children enhance their mobility and level of independent movement about the learning environment including home, classroom, and other settings. Orientation and mobility refer to a related service available to children with visual impairments. **Orientation** is defined as being aware of where you are, where you are going, and the route you will use to get there. **Mobility** is moving from one place

Children with visual impairments can experience success within their learning environment with appropriate adaptations.

Marmaduke St. John / Alamy Stock Photo

to another (Gargiulo & Metcalf, 2023). Orientation and mobility training uses sensory awareness and motor development to help children move independently about the environment. The use of orientation and mobility skills will facilitate movement within current environments and support independence in future settings.

Adapting Materials and Equipment

Adaptations for children with visual impairments fall into several categories: visual aids and the use of hands-on real-life situations; tactile methods and the use of Braille along with auditory strategies and aids. Additionally, children with visual impairments should be taught self-awareness skills as well as mobility and orientation skills (Turnbull et al., 2020). Examples of visual aids include glasses, magnifiers, bookstands, bold-line paper, closed-circuit television, high-intensity lamps, large-print materials, an abacus, beeper balls, and toys with auditory output devices. When using visual aids, the main focus is to create a contrast. For example, when offering children a choice of toys or clothing, dark items should be aligned against lighter backgrounds and vice versa. Or, if a toddler is eating in a highchair that is light colored, dark dishes should be used to assist him in finding the food. When using printed material, dark lines should be placed around pictures or items in the books to guide children using the materials.

Tactile aids allow children to obtain information through the sense of touch. Examples of tactile aids include books in Braille, Braille writers (machines used to produce materials in Braille, such as the Perkins Brailler), raised-line paper, abacuses for math calculations, and tactual maps. Toys with interesting tactile components include fabric balls with different textures and dominoes that require children to match different textures. In addition, the use of Braille readiness materials is recommended.

These would include materials that require children to match raised line patterns, match textures, identify big or small shapes, and so on. Tactual symbols and Braille could be placed throughout the home and educational environment to mark personal belongings or differentiate between similar items (such as different cans of food). Texture changes underfoot assist children in identifying different locations (e.g., the carpeted area is the living room, the tile is in the kitchen). Teachers may also use carpet runners to assist children in following specific paths across an open room (from doorway to play area, from doorway to bathroom).

Auditory aids allow children to obtain information through the sense of hearing. Examples of auditory aids include toys with auditory signals (bells within a ball), talking books, clocks with auditory signals, tapes, or synthetic speech (computerized production of sound). It is important for very young children with visual impairments to learn to reach, move toward, or follow the sound sources. These skills will be critical as they learn to move independently about the home and other environments. For example, as children learn to associate sounds in their surroundings (the kitchen has the refrigerator sound, the television is in the family room), they will begin to understand the direction in which they must move in order to get where they want to go. In addition to sounds that naturally occur in the environment, artificial sounds can be created to facilitate the location of specific objects. Placing a wind chime over the toy box and a music box at the dresser will enable toddlers to learn the location of objects in the room while they are in their cribs. Creating a sound library can help children to learn sounds associated with different places and activities. This involves recording sounds that might be heard in different environments, such as sounds from school, sounds at the grocery store, sounds of a city bus, and so on. The use of auditory aids will support children's understanding of the auditory signals in their environment and ultimately lead to greater engagement and independence.

When developing printed materials or visual media, attention should be given to the edging paperwork, and the use of too much detail should be avoided. Children with partial vision may use tactile cues from the edging of the paper to determine where to begin writing or even from the edging of furniture to determine where to place objects. Using bright or fluorescent colors in activities or to modify toys encourages children to use their vision. For children who are partially sighted, too much detail may clutter printed material, making it more difficult for them to focus on the most critical aspects on the paper or poster board. A vision specialist will be a valuable resource in determining the kind of adapted materials needed and will be able to offer advice on the many recent technological advances that have created products that are advantageous for young children with visual impairments. Equipment is now available that helps children by "reading" printed material (e.g., Kurzweil 1000), providing a Braille printout of what is displayed on a computer monitor, and converting Braille to print. A scanner with optical character recognition (machines that "read") or speech synthesis is a technology that "talks" or speaks (text-to-speech software) aloud anything on a computer disk (Bouck, 2017). Television and video programming is made accessible to viewers with blindness or low vision by video description. Brief, spoken descriptions of on-screen action are inserted into the video when no dialog is occurring, allowing the viewer to follow the story (Hallahan et al., 2022). Adaptations and changes in instructional materials should occur only when necessary and should be based on the individual needs of the student. It would be incorrect to think that all children with visual impairments require similar adaptations. For examples of available technology for children with visual impairments, see the accompanying Teacher Technology Tips feature.

Adapting Intervention and Instruction

Bishop (2004) offers some guidelines for working with young children with visual impairments:

- *Use consistent labels for objects.* Using different words for the same object (*jacket, overcoat*, and *parka* or *cat* and *kitty*) may be confusing for children who cannot see.
- *Actively assist children to explore the environment.* Give children the opportunity to explore new environments with adult help initially. If children bump into/trip over something, go back and allow them to explore the obstacle visually and tactilely. If children are startled by a loud noise, help them investigate the source and cause.

- *Work from behind children, putting them through the movements of what is expected of them while providing verbal feedback.* Children with vision can observe the movements of others, monitor and change their actions, and understand what is expected of them. Because young children with visual impairments do not have this input, it is necessary to demonstrate what is expected using a hand-over-hand approach and to provide feedback about what they are doing correctly and what they need to do differently. When demonstrating, the teacher or other adults should work from behind children. In this way, the teacher provides a sense of security and allows children to feel the natural fluidity of movement. Furthermore, it enables the teacher to be more responsive to the children. However, as with any assistance, it is important that the level of assistance be gradually decreased in order to increase independence in the children.
- *Listen and explain everyday environmental sounds and visual information.* Children with sight take in so much with their vision. Sight enables individuals to connect a sound with a sound source by seeing something happen, understand what sound belongs to what source, and locate the direction from which the sound came. By identifying sounds (e.g., the cabinet doors opening and closing, or the humming of the air conditioner), parents and teachers can provide children with an understanding of the sounds in the environment and enable them to use the auditory cues as landmarks for organizing the environment. In addition, whenever visual information is presented, auditory input must be provided. For example, a teacher may say out loud what he is doing while he is doing it ("I am tying your shoe"; "I am peeling your orange"). In this way, *all* children within the class have access to visual information.
- *Teach self-care skills in the places and at the times where they naturally occur.* For example, a child who is toilet trained on a potty chair in the kitchen and then must transition to toileting in the bathroom may have difficulty when generalizing the skills to the new setting. The two environments have very different olfactory and auditory cues, which may be confusing for children who cannot see. Teaching the skill in the bathroom is consistent with activity-based instruction or intervention that stresses embedding skills within the natural environment or daily routines to promote skill acquisition and generalization (Johnson et al., 2015; Noonan & McCormick, 2014).
- *Present objects before the instruction.* Early childhood special educators using models, manipulative toys, or other equipment should introduce children with visual impairments to the materials before teaching the skills or lessons. If children have the opportunity to explore the materials before the activity begins, they will be more able to concentrate on the concept being taught rather than on the equipment or materials.

TEACHER TECHNOLOGY TIPS

TECHNOLOGY FOR CHILDREN WITH SENSORY IMPAIRMENTS: VISUALLY IMPAIRED AND BLIND

Technology plays a vital role in the lives of young children with visual impairments. Examples of tools are listed below.

Adaptive Hardware	Braille writer Refreshable Braille display Screen enlargement Speech synthesizer Printer Braille embosser Electronic note-taker Voice output device Braille input/output device

Adaptive Software	Braille translation software Screen reader Screen enlargement software Speech recognition software
Use of Adapted Output Systems	Enhanced imaging system Synthesized speech system Braille printer

Teachers should be attentive to the length of time children wear glasses. When children first wear glasses or there is a change in their prescriptions, children may be required to wear the glasses for a specified length of time. In addition, children may have an adjustment period associated with the way the glasses feel or look and may be reluctant to wear their glasses. It may be necessary to provide incentives for wearing glasses. High-preference activities should be provided that require children to wear their new glasses in order to participate. This would be one way of creating a need to see that might be highly reinforcing to young children. For preschoolers or early primary children, it may also be necessary to provide a unit on feelings, providing children with an outlet for talking about self-awareness and feelings related to the way they look in their new glasses.

Another instructional consideration is the modality of input. Young children with a visual impairment may need families, teachers, and peers to provide information that utilizes other senses. For example, Bentley, a six-year-old who is blind, relies on her sense of hearing and smell to navigate her way around the classroom. By noticing olfactory cues (an apple, a bowl of potpourri, or flowers) on the teacher's desk, she is readily able to locate the teacher's desk using her sense of smell. Placing the cage for the pet gerbil by the door to the playground provides an olfactory cue and sometimes audible cue to where the door is located for Jane, who is enrolled in a Head Start program. Coupling a verbal directive, such as "Put your cups here," with auditory cues, such as tapping on the tabletop, enables the child to place an object in the designated location. The unobtrusive nature of these adaptations makes them particularly appealing because they do not single out children with delays and disabilities.

Early childhood special educators and other professionals must recognize that for children with visual impairments, learning may require more adaptations, repeated presentations, and intensive direct instruction. This, of course, is highly dependent on the individual needs of children. But it may require a teacher to find creative ways to reteach skills that were not initially achieved the first time, examine lessons to determine whether a visual element to the lesson interfered with learning, and allow sufficient time for the child to complete a task successfully.

FEATURE 8.5 REPRESENTATIVE WEB RESOURCES

For additional information about young children with visual impairments, access the following websites:

- **American Council for the Blind**, www.acb.org
- **American Foundation for the Blind**, www.afb.org
- **Division on Visual Impairment and Deafblindness, Council for Exceptional Children**, https://dvidb.exceptionalchildren.org/
- **National Federation of the Blind**, www.nfb.org

YOUNG CHILDREN WITH SENSORY IMPAIRMENTS: HEARING

Children with hearing impairments can be classified as having a mild, moderate, severe, or profound hearing loss (Gargiulo & Bouck, 2021). The federal definition found in IDEA 2004 describes **deafness** as a condition that adversely affects educational performance and is so severe that the child is impaired in processing linguistic information or communication through hearing, with or without amplification (e.g., hearing aids). Typically, a young child with a mild (26–40 dB) to moderate (41–55 dB) hearing loss is considered hard of hearing, while a child with a severe (71–90 dB) or profound (91 dB or greater) hearing loss is classified as deaf. Decibels (dB) are units of sound pressure associated with the psychological sensation of loudness (Gargiulo & Metcalf, 2023). Children who are deaf have a hearing loss that is so significant that they are unable to process spoken language without the use of amplified hearing devices (such as hearing aids or auditory trainers).

Children who are hard of hearing have a less significant hearing loss and may be able to process spoken language (hear and speak) with or without the support of amplified hearing devices. Some children have a prelingual hearing loss, which is a hearing loss present at birth or whose onset is prior to the development of speech and language. Other children exhibit a postlingual hearing loss or a hearing impairment that manifests itself after the acquisition of language. Although children with hearing impairments represent a diverse group, there are some common issues and considerations related to adapting the learning environment, materials, intervention, and instruction.

Adapting the Environment

Attention should be given to the light source in the home and educational settings, making sure that there is adequate lighting and that the speaker is not standing in a shadow or location where a glare is present. The child may be using the visual cues of speechreading (lip reading), body language, facial expressions, sign language, or natural gestures to supplement hearing.

Attention should be given to seating and positioning. It may be necessary to seat children with hearing impairments directly in front of the teacher or to the left or right of the teacher, if they are dependent on a preferred ear for auditory input. Early childhood special education teachers and other adults should be encouraged to position themselves at the child's level to allow easy access to visual cues given when speaking. Teachers and other adults should not talk with their backs to children (e.g., while searching for items inside the closet) or obscure their lips with anything (e.g., their hands, a book, a newspaper). Children with hearing impairments may be heavily dependent on the movement of lips as the teacher/adult is speaking. Early childhood special educators also should monitor classroom acoustics including noise levels and background noise. When a child wears a hearing aid, *all* sounds in the environment are amplified.

Adapting Materials and Equipment

There are several considerations related to using hearing aids. It is important to know how to manipulate the controls and how to troubleshoot minor problems—for example, what to do if and when the hearing aid whistles. Parents and other family members are excellent resources and can familiarize teachers and other professionals with their child's hearing device (such as knowing how to determine whether the hearing aid is on or off and how to adjust the volume controls). Even young children may learn quickly how to turn the hearing aid off and go about doing as they desire. In addition, it is important to have a spare set of batteries on hand at home and at school and to frequently check them to ensure that they are working. Teachers and other adults should make note if the hearing aid appears to fit improperly or has a damaged ear mold and notify the parents accordingly. A periodic visual examination of the ear, the cords of the hearing aid, and the hearing aid mold can ensure that children are properly fitted and have working hearing aids.

Current technologies have led to improvements over previously available personal hearing aids. One example of this new technology is the digital programmable hearing aid. This device transmits sound as digital signals and is capable of distinguishing noise from speech (Bouck, 2017). Assistive listening devices are frequently used by children with hearing impairments to enhance the use of auditory input. Many of these children benefit from using an auditory trainer or FM system. Gargiulo and Bouck (2021) note that these systems are often very effective and help manage acoustical problems found in the classroom and other learning environments. Some classrooms employ the use of a sound field system. With this system, the teacher wears a small microphone. The voice is then transmitted to speakers placed strategically around the room. These systems often benefit children with a minimal (16–25 dB) hearing loss as well as those children with a cochlear implant.

Young children with hearing impairments and deafness are sometimes surgically implanted with a cochlear implant. A **cochlear implant** is not a hearing aid but a tiny array of electrodes implanted in the cochlea of the inner ear. It is attached to a tiny transmitter behind the ear. The child wears a microphone and speech processor connected by wiring and held in place by a magnet over the implant site behind the ear. Children with cochlear implants frequently require the services of an audiologist and a speech–language pathologist. The audiologist can provide training for the parent, teacher, and other adults in the usage and maintenance of the external parts of the implant equipment. The speech–language pathologist can provide intensive intervention in speech, language, and communication in order to further enhance the child's developing communication skills.

Technology often plays an important part in developing the auditory and communication skills of young children with hearing impairments or deafness. See the Teacher Technology Tips feature for more information on available technologies for children with hearing impairments and deafness.

Adapting Intervention and Instruction

Young children with hearing impairments have limited auditory input; therefore, they may exhibit delays in communication development as language becomes more intertwined with other areas such as social or cognitive development, and because they have had limited auditory input. For example, a two-year-old with a hearing impairment may not be producing sounds, word approximations, or words as typically developing peers would be at this same age. Young children who are deaf typically have less language interaction during play and appear to prefer groups of two rather than groups of three or more. These patterns may be attributed to the difficulty of dividing their attention, which is visual in nature, and their limited knowledge of language appropriate for play situations. They also engage in less pretend play, possibly because language deficits impede their ability to script elaborate imaginary situations.

Children who are deaf spend less time in cooperative peer play (Gargiulo & Bouck, 2021). The implication for the early childhood special educator is to utilize other modalities, such as tactile or visual methods or materials that include photos, pictures, charts, or gestures, and to provide multiple opportunities for social interaction (Shirin et al., 2011).

Sign language is an instructional approach appropriate for some children with hearing impairments.

BSIP SA / Alamy Stock Photo

TEACHER TECHNOLOGY TIPS

TECHNOLOGY TIPS FOR CHILDREN WITH SENSORY IMPAIRMENTS: HEARING

Technology is an important component in the lives of individuals with disabilities. Nowhere are the effects of technological advances more evident than in the lives of young children with hearing impairments. Examples of technology for children with hearing impairments are listed below.

Amplification of Auditory Information	Personal hearing aids Assistive listening devices Auditory training devices or FM systems Sound field systems Cochlear implants
Computers	Specialized software for speech drill, auditory training, speechreading, and sign language instruction Synthesized speech from keyboards to input and transcribe speech onto a printed display screen
Alerting Devices	Wristwatches with vibratory alarm devices Doorbells, fire alarms, and alarm clocks with vibratory mechanisms or flashing lights
Captioning Devices	Provides captioning for many current television programs, movies, and videos
Telecommunication Devices	A telecommunication device for the deaf (TDD) is a small keyboard with an electronic modem. Messages are typed onto the keyboard and carried as different sets of tones over the telephone to the other party's telephone, which must be linked to another TDD. Amplified telephones

One of the biggest concerns for families, teachers, and other professionals who serve young children with hearing impairments is the communication mode chosen as the means for teaching the child who is hard of hearing or deaf. Three common educational approaches are **auditory–oral**, **bilingual–bicultural**, and **total communication** (Gargiulo & Bouck, 2021).

Auditory–oral is an educational approach that emphasizes the development of speech, speechreading, and listening with appropriate amplification. Neither sign language nor gesture is used with this approach. A bilingual–bicultural approach emphasizes the early use of American Sign Language (ASL) because it is thought to be the natural language of the deaf and it permits children who are deaf to advance through the typical stages of language acquisition. ASL is used as the language of instruction, and English is taught by reading and writing. Both ASL and English are valued as educational tools in this method. Total communication focuses on using individual children's preferred modes of communication. It includes oral, auditory, speechreading, sign language, finger spelling, writing, and gestures as methods for intervention or instruction. For a detailed view of the educational approaches used when working with children with hearing impairments, see Table 8.6.

TABLE 8.6 ■ Educational Approaches Often Used When Working With Children With Hearing Impairments

Bilingual–Bicultural	
Basic position	Considers American Sign Language (ASL) to be the natural language of the Deaf culture and urges recognition of ASL as the primary language of choice with English considered a second language
Objective	Provide a foundation in the use of ASL with its unique vocabulary and syntax rules ASL instruction provided for English vocabulary and syntax rules
Method of communication	ASL
Total Communication	
Basic position	Supports the belief that simultaneous use of multiple communication techniques enhances children's ability to communicate, comprehend, and learn
Objective	Provides a multifaceted approach to communication to facilitate which method(s) works best for each individual

(Continued)

TABLE 8.6 ■ Educational Approaches Often Used When Working With Children With Hearing Impairments (*Continued*)

Bilingual–Bicultural	
Method of communication	Simultaneous combination of sign language (accepts the use of any of the sign language systems), finger spelling, and speechreading
Auditory–Oral	
Basic position	Supports the belief that children with hearing impairments can develop listening/receptive language and oral language expression (English) skills with emphasis placed on using residual hearing (the level of hearing an individual possesses), amplification (hearing aids, auditory training), and speech/language training
Objective	Facilitate the development of spoken or oral English
Method of communication	Spoken or oral English

Source: Adapted from R. Gargiulo and E. Bouck, *Special Education in Contemporary Society: An Introduction to Exceptionality*, 7th ed. (Thousand Oaks, CA: Sage, 2021), p. 390.

Consulting with the speech–language pathologist enables early childhood special educators to learn firsthand about the mode of communication that is supported by the family and therapist. Likewise, peers and adults who interact with children should know how to communicate in children's preferred mode. Professionals recommend that everyone use the same communication mode when interacting with children with hearing impairments.

A normal voice, gestures, and touch should be used in communicating with children with hearing impairments (Heward et al., 2022). For example, a light touch on the shoulder to gain the child's attention or gestural motions are subtle visual cues that allow children to understand what is happening or where to go. See Table 8.7 for a list of intervention or instructional suggestions designed to enhance language development in young children with hearing impairments.

TABLE 8.7 ■ Promoting Language Development in Young Children With Hearing Impairments

Speak using an ordinary tone/volume. Make sure the child's attention is focused on the speaker. Talk naturally and clearly and use simple phrases or simple but complete sentences, depending on the child's language level. Do not shout or exaggerate words or slow down your speech unnaturally. Highlighting lips with lipstick can assist a young child in following speech. A mustache or long hair obscuring the face can cause loss of visual information.

Clarify idioms. Explain idioms in context (e.g., explain "It's raining cats and dogs" when you have used the expression after running inside during a storm). This prevents misunderstandings and enriches the child's language.

Check with the child to ensure comprehension. Sometimes saying "Tell me what I just said" provides information about how much a child understands. However, many children with a hearing loss have difficulty articulating their responses. Therefore, you may need to observe the child's action for a short period to check for understanding. A perplexed look or doing nothing may indicate lack of understanding, and you will need to find additional, preferably visual, methods for getting the message across.

Institute a buddy system to facilitate children's understanding of directions and curriculum content. Many times children understand another child better than they do an adult, so have a child's buddy explain the information again after you have finished. Furthermore, attentive peer modeling of both speech and behavior is an excellent resource for children with hearing deficits.

Show real-life pictures when reading or talking about a topic, and use simple signs, point, or have an example of the object you are explaining. Children with a hearing loss need visual information to learn. Acting out experience-based language lessons or stories is helpful. Using environmental labels around the classroom can start children on the road to learning language through print.

Provide language boards or books for children who have difficulty with intelligible books or manual signs. Try providing a flannel board with pictures, words, or other graphic symbols to help communicate information, such as available learning centers or answers to routine questions. Children can point to the board to indicate a response or choice. Preteach key vocabulary words from a short story that will be read to the class, or send the book home with the child beforehand so that the words can be introduced by the family and reinforced afterward.

Source: Adapted from L. Katz and T. Schery, "Including Children with Hearing Loss in Early Childhood Programs," *Young Children, 61*(1), 2006, p. 94.

FEATURE 8.6 REPRESENTATIVE WEB RESOURCES

For additional information about young children with hearing impairments and deafness, access the following websites:

- **Alexander Graham Bell Association for the Deaf and Hard of Hearing**, www.agbell.org
- **American Speech-Language-Hearing Association**, www.asha.org
- **Division for Communication, Language, and Deaf/Hard of Hearing, Council for Exceptional Children**, https://dcdcec.org/
- **National Association of the Deaf**, www.nad.org

YOUNG CHILDREN WITH PHYSICAL DELAYS AND DISABILITIES AND HEALTH IMPAIRMENTS

Children with physical and/or health impairments represent a diverse group; physical impairments include spina bifida, cerebral palsy, muscular dystrophy, and spinal cord injury, while health impairments may include asthma, cystic fibrosis, leukemia, or diabetes (Gargiulo & Bouck, 2021). (See Appendix C for the federal definitions associated with physical and health impairments.) Because young children with physical and health impairments reflect a wide range of etiologies and delays and disabilities, early signs or indicators vary, as does the age of onset. However, children with physical or health impairments may share some common issues and considerations related to adapting the environment, materials, intervention, and instruction.

Adapting the Environment

Because children may be using adaptive equipment such as wheelchairs, walkers, and adaptive seating, ample space is needed for them to move independently about their educational environment. Prior to children coming to their classrooms, it must be determined how accessible the travel paths are within the classroom and doorways.

As discussed in Chapter 7, it must be determined whether there are any changes needed in the layout of the home, classroom, or other settings to facilitate mobility. All areas (e.g., toy shelves, bookcases, coat racks, sensory tables, activity centers) should be accessible to all children. Railings may be needed, especially in the restroom and along ramps. The match between the height of the work surface and the child's seating should be examined to ensure that children have access to all of the tabletop activities. Materials should be presented at children's eye level and should be stored at child height to promote independence in retrieving and replacing items. Depending on children's abilities and goals/outcomes, location of objects and materials need careful attention. For example, Caleb is a right-handed toddler with cerebral palsy who has limited range of motion in his right hand and arm, but has excellent grasping ability. If a goal for Caleb is to promote independent play or eating, it would be important to place objects such as toys, food, and drink within his reach. Or, if one of his goals is to increase cross-midline reaching, objects should be placed on the left side of his lapboard to encourage cross-midline reaching.

The accessibility and architectural specifications of the home, center, or school setting should be examined to determine whether children will need adaptations (e.g., the use of ramps or railings) to gain access to restrooms, water fountains, and doorways, as well as passageways within classrooms. Table 8.8 offers some suggestions on how to modify learning environments for children with physical or health impairments.

Proper seating and positioning can combat poor circulation, muscle tightness, and pressure sores and contribute to digestion, respiration, and physical development. In addition, proper seating can promote feelings of physical security and safety, positively affect the use of the upper body, and reduce the possibility of developing additional deformities (Gargiulo & Bouck, 2021). Because of the importance of seating and positioning, several aspects of the environment need attention. There should be

TABLE 8.8 ■ Suggested Classroom Checklist of Accommodations for Children With Physical or Health Impairments

Child's Name: Date of Birth:

Disability:

Check any of the following that apply:

- has a difficult time remaining upright
- poor head control
- deformities that limit the child's ability to function
- tires easily
- abnormal reflexes
- abnormal muscle tone on just one side: right left
- abnormal muscle tone in the legs only
- abnormal muscle tone throughout the body
- low muscle tone/appears floppy
- high muscle tone/appears stiff
- problems with coordination and balance
- difficulty keeping lips closed; drooling
- tremors
- seizures
- unable to walk without help
- unable to sit without help
- joint pain
- bones break easily
- difficulty swallowing
- does not use verbal language in communicating

Check any of the following strategies that will help the child with physical and health impairments in your classroom or other learning environments.

- Position the child carefully so that he is sitting with his hips bent and head back in alignment.
- Make sure that tables and chairs are helping the child to stay upright.
- Stabilize learning materials with suction cups, clamps, or Velcro.
- Provide alternative methods of communication such as picture icons.
- Provide electric switches to activate toys, music, voice-activated output device.
- Make items easier to grasp by adding foam tubing.
- Position items on a tabletop easel to help maintain an upright position.
- Provide a chair with sides.
- Watch for signs of fatigue.
- Encourage the child to use two hands in activities.
- Warn the child before picking him up or moving him.
- Make sure the furniture in the room can support the weight of a child pulling to stand.
- Change the child's position frequently unless medically contraindicated.

Source: Material from *The Inclusive Early Childhood Classroom* by Patti Gould and Joyce Sullivan, page 17, ISBN 978-0-87659-203-8, is reprinted with permission from Gryphon House, Inc. P.O. Box 10, 6848 Leon's Way, Lewisville, NC 27023. (800) 638-0928.

many seating options within the home and other learning environments, such as adaptive chairs, corner chairs, or prop sitting with pillows or wedges. See Figure 8.1 for various types of apparatus.

FIGURE 8.1 ■ Alternative Seating Options

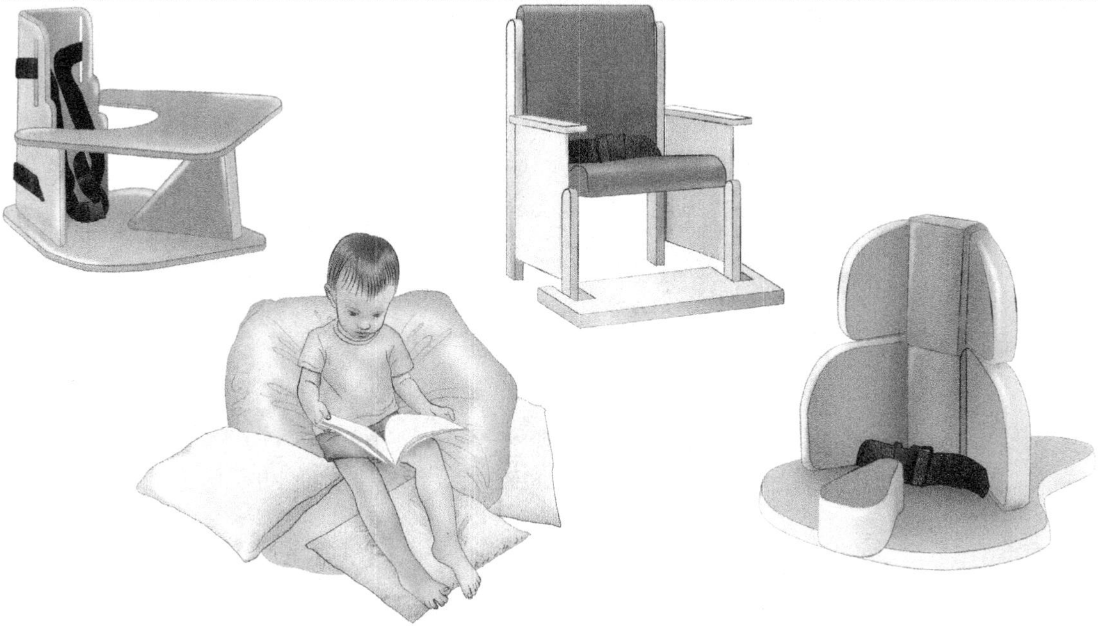

Source: S. Best, K. Heller, and J. Bigge, *Teaching Individuals With Physical or Multiple Disabilities*, 6e. Copyright © 2010. Reprinted by permission of Pearson Education, Inc., Upper Saddle River, NJ. p.198.

If necessary, an abduction block, which is a pummel, block, wedge, or cushion that children's legs can straddle, can be used to prevent children from sliding out of chairs. A seat belt and/or shoulder and chest strap may be necessary to maintain an appropriate upright position. In addition, to ensure maximum trunk control, adding a footstool may be warranted to help the child's feet rest firmly on a flat surface. Prior to any changes in seating or prompting young children to walk or move with or without adaptive equipment, a physical or occupational therapist should be consulted (O'Brien & Kuhaneck, 2020).

Some children may require medication or have specific nutritional needs; therefore, attention is warranted regarding safety precautions and side effects associated with medication or nutrition. Written authorizations from the parents and physicians are required related to the administration of medication or alternative nutritional needs of children (e.g., a child with diabetes). In classroom settings, a determination must be made regarding who will administer the medication, record medication administration, store the medication in a secure locked location, and monitor any changes in children's behavior associated with nutritional or medication needs. It is important for early childhood special educators to be cognizant of their students' medical regimes and any special dietary requirements or issues such as food allergies. For example, medication administered at home could result in side effects (e.g., altered behaviors) during school hours, while food allergies (peanuts) may affect choices at snack time. Therefore, families, teachers, and other professionals need to have ongoing communication about the nutritional and medication needs of the children.

Adapting Materials and Equipment

Physical and occupational therapists should work closely with families, early childhood special educators, and other team members to provide the information and consultation that is necessary for individual children. Specialized equipment for standing, sitting, and ambulation may be necessary due to abnormal muscle tone. Hypotonic muscle tone (floppy muscles) or hypertonic muscle tone (tight muscles) may thwart movement patterns and physical growth. Adaptive equipment and orthotic devices offer a variety of options to optimize learning potential of young children with physical or health impairments. Prosthetic devices support children in the learning environment; however, without careful attention, they can restrict range of motion, cause discomfort and abrasions, or interfere with circulation if not properly fitted. If special equipment such as a wheelchair is used, periodic inspections are necessary to ensure proper fit, comfort, and that the equipment is in good working order (O'Brien & Kuhaneck, 2020). In addition, because of limited physical strength, it may be necessary to examine the weight of materials that the child will be expected to manipulate to determine whether adaptations are warranted.

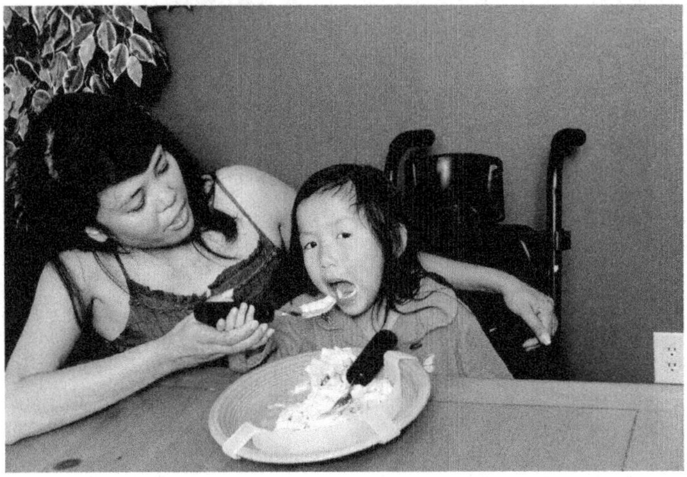

For a young child with physical limitations, adaptations and accommodations are often needed for maximum participation in all aspects of the learning environment.

Early childhood special educators should always enlist the help of therapists and families to adjust and adapt equipment or materials. It is important to remember that simple modifications of everyday materials are preferred, as they are less stigmatizing. For example, if a child cannot use the same materials, such as scissors or a drinking cup, as his peers, adapted scissors or adapted cups can be provided or made from standard materials and equipment. Clothing with Velcro fasteners may increase independent dressing. Velcro straps added to a musical instrument may allow a child who has an unsteady grasp to hold the tambourine while playing it. A spoon handle built up with layers of tape may be enough of an adaptation for a child to grasp the handle and feed himself. Physical therapists and occupational therapists also can support the early childhood special educator by demonstrating effective techniques for using adaptive equipment or for positioning, lifting, carrying, and transfer strategies that can be utilized with confidence and without harming the adult (O'Brien & Kuhaneck, 2020). Assistive technology for children with physical and health impairments can be used to enhance communication, academic tasks, leisure activities, and socialization. For a list of available technologies, see the accompanying Teacher Technology Tips feature.

Adapting Intervention and Instruction

Children with physical and/or health impairments may exhibit fatigue, have limited stamina and vitality, or only be able to participate in limited physical activity. This may require families, teachers, and other professionals to examine the schedule at home and at school, the length of activities, and the pace of the curriculum. Early childhood special educators may need to determine the optimal time to schedule certain activities, adjust the length of activities, or create alternative ways for less active children to participate.

For children who experience problems with fatigue and endurance, it is important for early childhood special educators and other professionals to plan for ambulation when they are setting up activities for the classroom and other learning environments, such as the playground or gym. They must think through the movements that will be needed, as well as equipment and materials necessary to maximize learning. Questions that can be asked include these:

- Does the class really need to transition after this activity?
- How long will the transition take?
- Can the student make this transition within the time allotted, with enough time to move independently, or will the teacher/adult need to always help and thereby be fostering dependence rather than independence?
- Is it better to do two activities at the same table, or do you want to transition to another area to allow an opportunity for the child to use their new walker?
- Is time a factor? Mobilizing several children who are nonambulatory takes time. Therefore, before everyone is moved to new space, it is important that teachers/adults be thoughtful about the transition.
- Is the wait time or transition movement utilized effectively—for example, to address fine motor and gross motor skills, language and listening skills?
- Is the child supported in his own planning related to movement? The child may need assistance with the thinking and reasoning skills related to his independent mobility. For example, when it is time to go outside, Sam, age two, may need a verbal prompt from his caregiver: "Sam, what do you need to get to the door?" He replies, "My walker." She responds, "That's right, go get your walker."

Restrictions in movement, including locomotion and voluntary gross and fine motor actions, can occur and interfere with the mastery of other developmental skills. For example, a young child with physical delays who is able to freely explore his surroundings could exhibit delays in other areas such as speech, language, and social development due to limited exploration of new objects, limited vocabulary, or limited social experiences. The implication is for early childhood special educators and family members to provide a language-rich environment, integrating language into all areas of learning and ensuring that children have as much mobility and accessibility as possible within stimulating home and educational settings.

Within home and educational settings, there are many opportunities for children to take on responsibilities such as assisting with daily events and activities or leadership roles. Allowing children to participate in this capacity promotes independence and positive self-esteem. It is important for children with physical disabilities or health impairments, who are usually on the receiving end of assistance, to be included in the leadership roles available in the home and educational settings. For example, Lee Ann, a five-year-old with spina bifida, was selected to carry books to and from the library using the tray and basket that fit onto her wheelchair. In this way, she was provided with responsibilities and leadership opportunities like her classmates, and the use of the wheelchair tray and basket have become assets for her as opposed to something that separates her from her classmates. Even when she was three years old, she assisted at home by clearing the table and taking folded clothes to the hall closet using a basket attached to her wheelchair. At a very early age, she was participating in family activities that supported her sense of belonging, positive self-esteem, and leadership abilities.

TEACHER TECHNOLOGY TIPS

TECHNOLOGY FOR CHILDREN WITH PHYSICAL DELAYS AND DISABILITIES AND HEALTH IMPAIRMENTS

Children with physical or health disabilities use technology for academic tasks, leisure, and socialization. Computers are widely used. Depending on the type and severity of the delay or disability, many modifications can be made to individualize equipment use to the specific needs of the user. Examples of high- and low-technology solutions are listed below.

Activity	Low Technology	High Technology
Reading	Book stand Turn page with mouth stick Ruler to keep place on page	Electric page-turner Software to scan book into computer or read text aloud
Writing	Pencil with built-up grip Wider-spaced paper Mouth stick with attached pencil	Computer with alternative input (switch or voice recognition)
Math	Counter Abacus Money cards	Graphing calculator Software that positions the cursor for regrouping
Eating	Spoon with built-up handle Hand splint to hold spoon Adaptive cup Scoop dish	Electric feeder Robotic arm
Leisure	Card holder Larger baseball	Sports wheelchair Adapted tricycle/bicycle Computer games

Source: R. Gargiulo, Special Education in Contemporary Society: An Introduction to Exceptionality, 5th ed. (Thousand Oaks, CA: Sage, 2015), p. 525.

Frequent and/or prolonged absences are not uncommon among children with physical or health impairments. For the young child, this may have a negative impact on various areas of development, such as the development of friendships and security in the program or school settings, as well as the parent–child relationship. In addition, some children with significant needs may qualify for homebound or hospital-based educational services depending on a number of factors such as the severity of their condition, fragility, and the status of their immune system.

Adjustments and accommodations for children with physical and/or health impairments may present a unique set of issues for teachers, families, and other professionals. For example, one child may have a physical impairment that does not make significant progress like spina bifida while another may have a physical or health impairment that is progressive in nature (muscular dystrophy) or has episodic recurring medical events (seizures or asthmatic attacks). Still another young child may be sensitive to his own body related to the use of a prosthesis. Other issues relate to stress from repeated hospitalizations, daily or crisis-care events, or the anxiety related to life-threatening illnesses or accidents (e.g., muscular dystrophy, leukemia, or spinal cord injury). Families, teachers, and other professionals alike may be overprotective or have difficulty balancing the amount of attention given to the child with the health problem versus siblings or other children in the class. Likewise, it may be difficult to promote independence in a child who has been sick and becomes dependent on adults and others for support and assistance. Because of these unique stressors, different types of support, such as counseling, may be required for a young child related to their health or physical impairment.

In addition, peers may have a need for counseling related to their friend with a degenerative disability. For example, Joe, a three-year-old child with muscular dystrophy, was progressively losing control of his gross and fine motor abilities, which negatively impacted his ability to walk, play ball, color and paint, carry his belongings, or feed himself. Several of his peers expressed concern and anxiety about how his condition will affect them ("Will I catch what he has?" "My leg hurts today. Does that mean I will be sick like Joe?"). Others expressed concerns about Joe as his illness progressed and resulted in frequent hospitalizations ("I feel sad about Joe. Is he going to ever walk again? Is he going to die?"). Early childhood special educators need to recognize signs of anxiety or stress in young children that may warrant consultation with a school counselor. It is critical that everyone understands the level of anxiety that families and professionals alike may face related to children with severe or life-threatening disabilities (Smith et al., 2011).

FEATURE 8.7 REPRESENTATIVE WEB RESOURCES

For additional information about young children with physical and health disabilities, access the following websites:

- **Centers for Disease Control and Prevention**, www.cdc.gov
- **Complex and Chronic Conditions: The Division for Physical, Health, and Multiple Disabilities, Council for Exceptional Children**, https://ccc.exceptionalchildren.org/
- **Muscular Dystrophy Association**, www.mda.org
- **United Cerebral Palsy**, www.ucp.org

SUMMARY

This chapter focused on adapting, accommodating, and modifying interventions, instruction, materials, and equipment as well as learning environments for young children with diverse abilities. Additionally, brief descriptors of young children with disabilities were provided. It is important to realize that these are only possible characteristics or early indicators of delays and disabilities. A disability may not manifest itself in the same way or at the same time for every child with the same disability. Additionally, the presence of one or more of these early indicators does not always indicate a delay or disability.

Although this chapter delineated several ways to adapt environments, materials, and instruction for children with delays and disabilities, it is important to remember that children with delays and disabilities are first and foremost children who are capable of achieving success with the proper support and guidance from teachers, families, and other professionals. As discussed in this chapter, children with disabilities often learn at different rates, and they may learn through another modality or respond in a variety of different ways. Early childhood special educators, therefore, must be flexible and be willing to use different interventions and instructional strategies.

KEY TERMS

Accommodation
Adaptation
Auditory–oral
Auditory trainer
Autism spectrum disorders (ASD)
Behavior disorder
Bilingual–bicultural
Cochlear implant
Deafness
Echolalic speech
Environmental arrangements
FM system
Functional behavior analysis
Generalization
Hypertonic muscle tone
Hypotonic muscle tone
Mobility
Modification
Naturalistic teaching strategies
Orientation
Orthotic devices
Pervasive developmental disorder
Positive behavioral support
Postlingual
Prelingual
Prosthetic devices
Social Stories
Sound field system
Task analysis
Teacher talk

Temporal adaptations
Time out
Total communication
Visual impairment
Visual supports

CHECK YOUR UNDERSTANDING

1. How can embedded instruction facilitate the learning of young children with delays and disabilities?
2. Define the term *generalization* and provide examples of ways that it can be used to ensure the transfer of skills across environments.
3. Explain how to use task analysis to teach a young child with cognitive delays and disabilities to make a peanut butter and jelly sandwich.
4. What are positive behavioral supports? How would you use these strategies to modify a child's behavior?
5. Identify two types of adaptations to the learning environment that are often used with children with autism spectrum disorders.
6. Communication and language delays are common among young children with delays and disabilities in preschool and early primary classrooms. Identify two strategies that promote language development in an inclusive environment.
7. A second grader with a visual impairment is placed in your classroom. List the adaptations you would use to ensure the social and instructional integration of this child.
8. How would you adapt the learning environment to accommodate a child with a hearing impairment?
9. What are some of the issues that need to be addressed if a child with muscular dystrophy is placed in an inclusive preschool classroom?

REFLECTION AND APPLICATION

1. Observe young children with delays and disabilities and typically developing children between three and eight years of age in their natural environments. Record their conversations with family members, peers, adults, and other significant individuals. In what ways were their language skills the same? Dissimilar? Were any particular strategies used by the adults to enhance the language skills of the children with delays and disabilities? What particular steps could a teacher incorporate in the classroom to develop the language abilities of a child with cognitive delays and disabilities?
2. Visit an inclusive kindergarten or an inclusive early primary classroom in your local school district. If possible, determine which children have delays and disabilities and observe these students for about one hour. Did the individuals exhibit any inappropriate behaviors? How did the teacher respond to these actions? Were the interventions or instructional strategies successful? How did their classmates respond to the children's behavior? If these children were in your classroom, what intervention strategies would you use to guide their behaviors?
3. Choose a preschool or an elementary school known to utilize an inclusive model for providing services to children with delays and disabilities. Schedule two observations in two different classrooms. For your first visit, observe in a general education classroom where the inclusion teacher co-teaches and supports children with delays and disabilities in the classroom. For your second visit, observe an early childhood special educator or related services provider teaching in a one-to-one or small-group setting. Review your notes from both visits. Identify

the instructional strategies used in both settings. How were they similar? How were they different? Decide whether the students' individual needs were addressed in both settings. Which techniques were most effective? Did you observe similar strategies being used in both settings?

4. In your role as an early childhood special educator, you have just been informed that a student with autism spectrum disorders is transferring to your school. You have been assigned as the child's case manager. In preparation for the child's arrival, make a list of questions you will ask when interviewing the family. Which questions are a priority? What strategies will you use to ensure a smooth transition for the child and their family?

iStock.com/SDI Productions

9 INTERVENTION AND INSTRUCTIONAL STRATEGIES FOR SUPPORTING YOUNG CHILDREN WITH DELAYS AND DISABILITIES[1]

[1] Chapter contributed by Jenna M. Weglarz-Ward, University of Nevada, Las Vegas.

LEARNING OBJECTIVES

After reading this chapter, you will be able to

9.1 Define evidence-based practice as it applies to modifying intervention and instructional practices when working with children with delays and disabilities.

9.2 Identify teacher-mediated strategies that focus on active engagement and differing levels of participation of young children with delays and disabilities.

9.3 Identify peer-mediated strategies, including cooperative learning.

9.4 Describe routine-based, play-based, and activity-based strategies used to provide intervention or instruction for young children with delays and disabilities from birth through age eight.

9.5 Describe the specific milieu strategies that facilitate language skills, social interaction, and other developmental skills for young children.

EI/ECSE Professional Standards

The content of this chapter aligns with the following EI/ECSE Standard:

Standard 6. Using Responsive and Reciprocal Interactions, Interventions, and Instruction

Candidates plan and implement intentional, systematic, evidence-based, responsive interactions, interventions, and instruction to support all children's learning and development across all developmental and content domains in partnership with families and other professionals. Candidates facilitate equitable access and participation for all children and families within natural and inclusive environments through culturally responsive and affirming practices and relationships. Candidates use data-based decision-making to plan for, adapt, and improve interactions, interventions, and instruction to ensure fidelity of implementation.

DEC Recommended Practices

The content of this chapter aligns with the following Division for Early Childhood (DEC) Recommended Practices:

Environment

- E2. Practitioners consider Universal Design for Learning principles to create accessible environments.
- E3. Practitioners work with the family and other adults to modify and adapt the physical, social, and temporal environments to promote each child's access to and participation in learning experiences.
- E4. Practitioners work with families and other adults to identify each child's needs for assistive technology to promote access to and participation in learning experiences.
- E5. Practitioners work with families and other adults to acquire or create appropriate assistive technology to promote each child's access to and participation in learning experiences.

Instruction

- INS1. Practitioners, with the family, identify each child's strengths, preferences, and interests to engage the child in active learning.
- INS2. Practitioners, with the family, identify skills to target for instruction that help a child become adaptive, competent, socially connected, and engaged and that promote learning in natural and inclusive environments.
- INS4. Practitioners plan for and provide the level of support, accommodations, and adaptations needed for the child to access, participate, and learn within and across activities and routines.

- INS3. Practitioners gather and use data to inform decisions about individualized instruction.
- INS5. Practitioners embed instruction within and across routines, activities, and environments to provide contextually relevant learning opportunities.
- INS6. Practitioners use systematic instructional strategies with fidelity to teach skills and to promote child engagement and learning.
- INS7. Practitioners use explicit feedback and consequences to increase child engagement, play, and skills.
- INS8. Practitioners use peer-mediated intervention to teach skills and to promote child engagement and learning.
- INS13. Practitioners use coaching or consultation strategies with primary caregivers or other adults to facilitate positive adult-child interactions and instruction intentionally designed to promote child learning and development.

Interaction

- INT3. Practitioners promote the child's communication development by observing, interpreting, responding contingently, and providing natural consequences for the child's verbal and non-verbal communication and by using language to label and expand on the child's requests, needs, preferences, or interests.

Teaming and Collaboration

- TC1. Practitioners representing multiple disciplines and families work together as a team to plan and implement supports and services to meet the unique needs of each child and family.

Authors' Note: As you read this chapter, you will find the EI/ECSE Standard 6 and the aforementioned DEC Recommended Practices discussed throughout. See Appendix A for a complete list of the EI/ECSE Standards and Appendix B for a complete list of the DEC Recommended Practices.

Young children with delays and disabilities are, first and foremost, children who can and do learn. They may learn at a different rate, require the use of different strategies, or learn through different modalities. Their learning may occur through child-initiated activities and exploration with the additional support of peers and/or direction from a teacher or caregiver. The key in creating appropriate educational experiences for any young child is to create a match between the individual strengths, needs, and interests of the child and the intervention or instruction. This may result in early childhood special educators, families, and other team members using a variety or combination of intervention or instructional strategies to facilitate development and learning (Cabell et al., 2013).

Recall from Chapter 4 that the Individuals with Disabilities Education Act (IDEA) and its amendments stress that school-age children should be educated, to the maximum extent appropriate, in the least restrictive environment (LRE) while infants and toddlers are to receive services in the natural environment. In both instances, there is a strong preference for children with delays and disabilities to receive services alongside neurotypical peers and in the environments in which they would be if they did not have a delay or disability. This approach is currently the model of choice for young children with delays and disabilities and their families (DEC & National Association for the Education of Young Children [NAEYC], 2009; NAEYC, 2022). Within inclusive learning communities, young children with delays and disabilities can be functionally and socially included while participating in typical classroom activities with early childhood special educators and other professionals providing an array of services and supports as necessary (Coogle et al., 2022; Love & Horn, 2021; U.S.

Department of Health and Human Services & U.S. Department of Education, 2015). Furthermore, "the purpose of instructional practices is to help children acquire the skills and behaviors that will help them be more independent and successful as young children and through their lives" (Schwartz & Woods, 2015, p. 78).

PRACTICES AND PROCESSES APPROPRIATE FOR YOUNG CHILDREN WITH DELAYS AND DISABILITIES

The Individuals with Disabilities Education Improvement Act of 2004 (PL 108–446) requires that services for young children with delays and disabilities are to be constructed around scientifically based research. In other words, early childhood special educators should incorporate practices and processes that are based on research and recommended practices in their intervention or instruction.

Evidence-Based and Recommended Practices

When determining *how* to provide intervention or instruction for the young child with delays and disabilities, early childhood special educators should partly base their decision on what is commonly known in the field as evidence-based practices (Horn et al., 2019). Simply defined, this means "a decision-making process that integrates the best available research evidence with family and professional wisdom and values" (Buysse & Wesley, 2006, p. 244).

As described in previous chapters, another commonly used term is recommended practices. DEC (2014) offers guidelines for early intervention and early childhood special education through recommended practices based on best-available empirical evidence and wisdom from the field:

> We [DEC] believe that when practitioners and families have the knowledge, skills, and dispositions to implement these practices as intended, children who have or are at risk for developmental delays/disabilities and their families are more likely to achieve positive outcomes, and families and practitioners are more likely to help children achieve their highest potential. (p. 2)

Early childhood special educators should incorporate evidence-based practices in intervention and instruction.

iStock.com/vgajic

Collectively, this thinking suggests that early childhood special educators should attempt to incorporate evidence-based practices whenever possible into their daily instructional routines (Cook et al., 2020). We fully embrace this position. Researchers in the field of early childhood special education have long used evidence-based practices to guide them.

CONNECT Modules: 5-Step Learning Cycle. Although the terminology and terms may have varied throughout the years, researchers at the Center to Mobilize Early Childhood Knowledge located at the University of North Carolina at Chapel Hill have designed learning modules for professionals desiring to incorporate evidence-based practices into their decision-making process. These learning modules provide an informative resource that offers online learning for professionals and families. Currently, modules on embedded interventions, transition, communication for collaboration, family-professional partnerships, assistive technology, dialogical reading, and tiered instruction are available in English and Spanish.

Of note is the 5-Step Learning Cycle framework used in each module that is valuable for implementing evidence-based practices (CONNECT, 2018). This is an approach used to make evidence-based decisions founded on solving realistic dilemmas encountered in early childhood special education.

FEATURE 9.1 REPRESENTATIVE WEB RESOURCE

For additional information about evidence-based practices affecting decision making, access the following website: https://connectmodules.dec-sped.org/

The 5-Step Learning Cycle is anchored in solving problems through the integration of multiple perspectives of professionals and families, as well as other sources of evidence. The five steps of the cycle are as follows:

Step 1. Identify the dilemma or problem. Explore the practitioner's ability to review the dilemma from the perspective of others such as the parents or other professionals familiar with the child.

Step 2. A practitioner uses a practice-focused question that could be answered by utilizing various sources of evidence suggested in current research. This step allows the practitioner to move away from the dilemma to focus on a specific instructional practice, intervention, or behavioral practice. Step 2 establishes the context for solving the dilemma.

Step 3. Gather evidence—the practitioner reviews sources of evidence related to the focused practice identified in Step 2. The key sources of information should include a summary of the best research available on the practice, policies available on the practice, and experience-based knowledge from other professionals, and the family, regarding the practice.

Step 4. The information gathered surrounding the dilemma and its context in relation to the child is integrated in order to make a decision and plan for intervention.

Step 5. Evaluate and refine. The final step involves the monitoring and evaluation of the practice in order to review and refine the practice if needed.

Examples of using this decision-making process can be seen throughout the modules via videos, vignettes, and reflective exercises.

Three evidence-based practices in early childhood special education are *embedded interventions, transition practices*, and *assistive technology interventions.* **Embedded interventions** incorporate the use of intervention or instructional strategies to address a specific learning goal within the context of the child's everyday activities, routines, and transitions occurring at home, at school, or in the community (DEC, 2014; Gulboy et al., 2023; Schwartz & Woods, 2015). A more in-depth view of embedded interventions with child-specific examples will be discussed later in this chapter.

Transition practices are widely identified in the research literature regarding early childhood special education. Defining transition practices is difficult. Most professionals agree that recommended practices in transition should include addressing the skills the child will need in the next environment, coordinating the professionals from the receiving and sending programs, facilitating good communication among the participants, and arranging parent/child visits to the new educational setting (DEC, 2014; Rous et al., 2020). As you may recall, Chapter 4 reviewed the necessary steps for making a successful transition for young children with delays and disabilities. Finally, **assistive technology interventions** refer to the practice of evaluating the child, implementing the use of technology tools, and monitoring the effects of specific technologies in order to increase independence for children with delays and disabilities in all areas of learning. Assistive technology is addressed specifically in Chapter 10.

Engagement in Inclusive Settings

The provision of services to young children with delays and disabilities in the natural environment or inclusive settings is a complex subject that involves many factors in the decision. Some key issues that professionals and families should consider are the quality of the early childhood program, child characteristics, family goals, and experience of the staff (DEC, 2014). Furthermore, inclusion is more than just the physical placement of children with delays and disabilities in educational settings alongside children without disabilities. Inclusion considers intentionally promoting the participation of children with disabilities in all learning activities and environments, using individualized accommodations, and supporting friendships with peers and sense of belonging (U.S. Department of Health and Human Services & U.S. Department of Education, 2015). Barton and Smith (2015) and Guralnick and Bruder (2016), in their work examining the current successes and challenges in early childhood inclusion, state that defining features of inclusive programs for young children with delays and disabilities should include access to high-quality early childhood programs, the child's level of participation, and the individual supports. To support this, practitioners should "use systematic instructional strategies with fidelity to teach skills and promote child engagement and learning" (DEC, 2014, p. 11) [DEC Recommended Practices INS6].

For the purpose of this discussion, **engagement** is defined as a child's sustained attention to and active involvement with people (teachers, family members, other professionals, peers), activities (snack time, play time, group time participation, center selection and participation), and materials (use of toys, art supplies, water play materials) in an age-appropriate manner throughout the child's day that lead to goal achievement (DEC, 2014; Mickelson et al., 2022).

The following sections of this chapter will focus on selected strategies that are organized into the following four categories:

Young children with disabilities need learning environments that are accepting of all children.

iStock.com/SolStock

1. Teacher-mediated strategies
2. Peer-mediated strategies
3. Routine-based strategies
4. Naturalistic (milieu) strategies

Although the discussion focuses primarily on strategies used in inclusive preschool or early primary classrooms, the strategies are appropriate for use with infants and toddlers who receive early intervention services in their homes or inclusive child care settings and other natural environments.

TEACHER-MEDIATED STRATEGIES

The term **teacher-mediated** has typically been used to describe teacher-directed explicit interventions designed to promote social interaction by teaching a specific skill or skill set (DEC & NAEYC, 2009; Gargiulo & Bouck, 2021). We broaden the term *teacher-mediated* to include many techniques that an adult (teacher, parent, other family member, related service professional) can implement before or during activities that promote child engagement with people, materials, or activities. Teacher-mediated strategies include arranging the environment, promoting acceptance, providing prompts and praise, accepting differential levels/types of participation, and monitoring communicative input.

Environmental Arrangements

One of the least intrusive steps that early childhood special educators can take to promote engagement of children within their educational settings is environmental arrangement. Current guidelines are available with suggestions for the organization, structure, and operation of optimal learning environments for children with diverse abilities (Coogle et al., 2022; NAEYC, 2020; Rausch et al., 2021) [DEC Recommended Practices E2]. Three strategies will be discussed that fit within these guidelines: the arrangement of physical space, the selection and use of materials, and the use of structured activities (DEC, 2014; Gargiulo & Bouck, 2021).

As described in Chapter 7, the typical guidelines used when arranging any learning environment include quiet areas that are located away from noisy areas, high-interest materials that are accessible to children, materials that are safe and stimulating, adequate space to provide easy movement throughout the classroom, and an environment that can be easily monitored by adults (DeArment et al., 2016; Sandall et al., 2019). Research has provided evidence to support the use of additional environmental strategies when children with delays and disabilities are included within a setting. The physical environment may be used by early childhood special educators to develop individual goals for children in the classroom and promote children's access to and participation in learning experiences [DEC Recommended Practices E3]. A teacher, for example, may want to promote lunch- or snack-time conversation by placing certain children in proximity to the child working on social communication goals. Another teacher working with a child who is highly distractible may design quiet, isolated play areas for the child away from the large group and assign a friend to explore with him. Even within the designated space, other aspects of the environment warrant attention, which include limiting the amount of materials available to children, attending to the specific considerations related to the individual child with a delay or disability (use of a walker, adaptive seating to maintain trunk control, or a wheelchair for access), and monitoring the number of adults and their behavior (Rausch et al., 2021).

Attention should be given to the selection and use of materials. Materials should be safe, multidimensional, and developmentally appropriate for the children within the learning environment. In addition, early childhood special educators can select toys known to promote high levels of engagement based on the child's preference, monitor the child's access to the materials, and adapt the use of toys or materials (Grisham-Brown & Hemmeter, 2017; Ok et al., 2017).

Some toys or materials result in more isolated play, while others appear to result in more interactive play (Pullum et al., 2022). Toys that are more likely to result in higher social interactions are blocks, dolls, trucks and cars, items that encourage social dramatic play (dress-up, cooking), and games that have multiple parts (Potato Head, farm or zoo animals). Materials that are more likely to result in solitary play include books, puzzles, and art activities (painting, paper-and-pencil drawing). Obviously, how an early childhood special educator structures the use of these more solitary materials will impact the level of interaction. For instance, preschoolers can share a book, each taking turns reading, holding the book, and turning the pages. The selection of the materials should be driven by the goals of the early childhood special educator in the structured play setting. At times the goal may be to promote interactive play, which involves more social and communicative exchanges, while at other times it may be to promote the use of appropriate toy play behavior.

Material selection also should be determined by the level of interest and preferences of the child [DEC Recommended Practices INS1]. Young children with delays and disabilities are more likely to engage with high-interest toys and materials. Preschoolers, for example, are more likely to show high levels of engagement and are less likely to exhibit inappropriate behavior when participating in high-interest activities (Aruz & Yasemin, 2011). Asking family members or the child is an excellent way to ensure that the activities, materials, and toys are preferred by the child.

Although child choice and preference are important, adults may want to provide some guidance to young children who consistently select the same activities, materials, or toys. The teacher or parent could observe the child as they make choices of toys, materials, and activities across a specific period of time. Then the adult could provide suggestions for play or introduce new materials with a high-preference toy as a way of expanding a child's choice to new, and perhaps more challenging, activities. This could be accomplished by coupling the child's choice of materials with that of the adult.

Examples of how child preferences can be combined with adult guidance are as follows. Every day, three-year-old Analise selects blocks during play. One day, the early childhood special educator adds farm animals, suggesting that together they build barns, corrals, and beds for the animals. On another day, she adds zoo animals to the block activity and asks Analise, "What could we do with these animals and blocks?" Peter, age two, chooses to bang together toy objects (blocks, pretend food) on a daily basis and appears to be reinforced by the noise he makes while playing. The early childhood special educator could add to the activity containers with big spoons for stirring and suggest that they cook. Later they can add dolls and bears to the activity for a pretend snack time. In this way, they have extended their play with the materials and still provided an auditory reinforcer as the blocks (or food) are stirred. In both examples, the early childhood special educator still has provided the child with a choice (using the preferred materials), while expanding the activity or the way the child uses the materials. In a home visit, a service provider could show an older sibling how to manipulate preferred materials by giving cues on how to model building a house with blocks. The sibling asks her brother to "build one like mine."

Another environmental strategy that could enhance engagement is the provision of structure within the activity. Planned, structured play activities embedded or integrated in the usual classroom activities or routines result in increased social interactions between children with and without disabilities (Grisham-Brown & Hemmeter, 2017; Sandall et al., 2019). Examples of planned embedded structure include setting rules for a specific activity, identifying children's roles within the activity, asking children to generate ways that they could play within an activity, and identifying a theme for the play ("Let's make pizza with the Play-Doh. What kind of pizza will you make today?"). Another way of structuring the activity is to analyze and monitor the accessibility of the materials. Infants or toddlers who have easy access to every toy may have a decreased need for communicating or socializing within their environments. Alternating the availability of some materials and toys across the day or week may be an effective strategy for promoting engagement. In essence, the novelty of a toy is maintained through the regular rotation of materials. Restricting access to high-interest toys may result in higher levels of communicative attempts. By placing preferred materials within the child's field of vision, but out of reach, the result would be increased child requests for preferred toys and snacks.

Promoting Acceptance

Promoting acceptance is a strategy that can be viewed as creating and preparing the social environment to be more accepting of a child with a delay or disability. It is a strategy that supports engagement with peers and one that is easily overlooked when preparing a class for young children with delays and disabilities.

Although positive attitudes toward children with delays and disabilities and subsequent social relationships among children with and without disabilities are an anticipated benefit of inclusion (Gargiulo & Bouck, 2021; U.S. Department of Health and Human Services & U.S. Department of Education, 2015), empirical evidence is mixed. However, in one synthesis of literature on early childhood inclusion published over the last 25 years, Odom et al. (2011) identified two research points applicable to the benefits of inclusive environments. First, the reviewed research implies that both children with disabilities and peers without disabilities can benefit from an inclusive educational environment. Second, inclusion can be implemented in different forms. Perceptions and attitudes of parents, teachers, other professionals, and members of the community concerning inclusion (children with delays and disabilities learning and developing relationships with peers without disabilities) can be influenced by several factors such as adult beliefs, policies, and the resources available to implement inclusive programs and evaluate outcomes (Barton & Smith, 2015; Coogle et al., 2022; Love & Horn, 2021; U.S. Department of Health and Human Services & U.S. Department of Education, 2015).

Across studies, it is apparent that the placement of children with delays and disabilities alongside peers without disabilities does not automatically ensure acceptance without adult mediation, which means actively promoting understanding and acceptance of children with disabilities. However, children with delays and disabilities placed in inclusive or natural environments make developmental progress at least comparable to children with disabilities in segregated environments (Noonan & McCormick, 2014). In other words, children with delays and disabilities in inclusive environments appear to learn as much as children in segregated environments. Promoting acceptance of children with delays and disabilities may be one of the essential elements for achieving authentic inclusion in later years beyond the preschool setting.

Guidelines are available that provide suggestions for creating accepting environments for young children (Sandall et al., 2019). In addition, teachers can use specific strategies within early childhood settings to actively promote acceptance of children with delays and disabilities. Prior to the transition of a child with a delay or disability into a general early childhood classroom, teachers can prepare children without disabilities by providing information about the child with the delay or disability (Favazza & Ostrosky, 2016). Effective strategies for increasing understanding and promoting acceptance of children with diverse abilities include the use of active and independent involvement in activities for children with delays and disabilities; access to cooperative activities, stories, and guided discussions that highlight similarities as opposed to differences and structured social opportunities; or a combination of these activities (Favazza & Ostrosky, 2016).

Favazza and Ostrosky (2016) found that kindergartners who had contact with children with delays and disabilities expressed low levels of acceptance of children with delays and disabilities. After a six-week intervention, the same kindergartners who were provided with stories and guided discussions about children with disabilities and opportunities for social interaction with children with delays and disabilities had more accepting attitudes than children who did not have these types of experiences. When these same children were assessed two years later, the positive attitudes were maintained. The authors speculate that what contributed to this long-term acceptance was the children's exposure to these components, as well as the fact that the stories and guided discussions about children with disabilities also were provided to the parents of the children without disabilities. In this way, teachers and parents alike were involved in promoting acceptance of children with diverse abilities.

Adults can often facilitate understanding and acceptance of children with delays and disabilities.

iStock.com/lostinbids

In addition to actively promoting acceptance through interventions within a center-based program, early childhood special educators, other professionals, and families can examine the environment to determine whether children without disabilities are exposed to individuals with delays and disabilities (Demetriou, 2022; Morgan et al., 2021). We recommend that teachers examine their classrooms to determine whether children with disabilities are represented in toys, displays, materials, and media, and *how* they are depicted (in ways that highlight similarities? as contributing members of society? in a variety of roles?). In addition, teachers need to be discriminating when selecting materials such as books about children with disabilities. It is important to select books that promote acceptance and emphasize similarities as opposed to differences and disabilities (Yu & Meyer, 2022; see Table 9.1). Research clearly indicates that placement alone will not guarantee acceptance. However, early childhood special educators, families, and other professionals can actively promote acceptance and create more accepting environments by utilizing some of the previously mentioned strategies.

TABLE 9.1 ■ Teacher Resource: Representative Books Portraying Children With Disabilities

Title	Author, Date, Publisher	Description
All the Way to the Top: How One Girl's Fight for Americans with Disabilities Changed Everything	Annette Bay Pimentel, 2020, Sourcebooks Explore	This is a story of a little girl who uses a wheelchair and her advocacy activities to fight for the Americans with Disabilities Act to increase her own access to her school and community.
Be Quiet, Marina!	Kristen DeBear, 2014, Starbright Books	Two young girls, one with cerebral palsy and one with Down syndrome, overcome their frustrations with each other and become friends.
Can You Hear a Rainbow?	Jamee Riggio Heelan, 2002, Rehabilitation Institute of Chicago	Chris is deaf and uses hearing aids. He uses sign language and reads lips to communicate, while also doing all the things other children do.
The Deaf Musicians	Pete Seeger and Paul Dubois Jacobs, 2006, G. P. Putnam's Sons Books for Young Readers	A group of deaf musicians frequently plays in the subway attracting crowds, showing that deaf musicians can make music also.
Don't Call Me Special	Pat Thomas, 2005, Barron's Educational Series	The author explains things children with disabilities can do, describes adaptive equipment, and discusses when to help or avoid helping.
Emmanuel's Dream: The True Story of Emmanuel Ofosu Yeboah	Laurie Ann Thompson and Sean Qualls, 2015, Anne Schwartz Books	Inspired by a true story of Emmanuel Ofosu Yeboah from Ghana who has a physical disability. This book describes his life as a child and eventual cyclist and disability advocate.
Extraordinary Friends	Fred Rogers, 2000, Puffin	The author explains that when children meet people who are different, they should not be afraid to talk to them or to learn more about them.
Ian's Walk	Laurie Lears, 1998, Albert Whitman & Company	Ian, a boy with autism, gets lost at the park. His sister realizes the best way to find him is to see things through his eyes.
Meet ClaraBelle Blue	Adiba Nelson, 2013, Createspace Independent Publishers	This story of about a child who uses a wheelchair going to school, playing in the community, and making new friends highlights how children with and without disabilities are similar.
Moses Goes to a Concert	Isaac Millman, 2002, Square Fish	Moses, who is deaf, goes to a concert where the percussionist is also deaf. He learns that she plays drums by feeling vibrations.
My Brother Charlie	Holly Robinson Peete and Ryan Elizabeth Peete, 2010, Scholastic Press	This story highlights the sibling relationships with a sister and her brother who has autism.
My Friend Has Autism (Friends with Disabilities)	Amanda Doering Tourville, 2010, Picture Window Books	This story focuses on building relationships between children with and without autism and includes child-friendly language to describe autism.

(Continued)

TABLE 9.1 ■ Teacher Resource: Representative Books Portraying Children With Disabilities (*Continued*)

Title	Author, Date, Publisher	Description
My Friend Isabelle	Eliza Woloson, 2003, Woodbine House	Two friends (one with Down syndrome) are very different but still have a lot of fun together and share a great friendship.
My Three Best Friends and Me, Zulay	Cari Best, 2015, Farrar, Straus and Giroux	This story is about four friends in first grade including Zulay, who is blind. They plan for their school's field day, including Zulay running a race with the help of a special aide.
Someone Special, Just Like You	Tricia Brown, 1995, Henry Holt & Co.	The author highlights that children with disabilities such as blindness, deafness, or Down syndrome can do the same things as their peers.
Susan Laughs	Jeanne Willis, 2000, Henry Holt & Co.	A young girl with a physical disability dances, sings, hides, and shows emotions such as happiness and sadness.
We Can Do It!	Laura Dwight, 2005, Starbright Books	Five young children with varying abilities do things differently while also successfully participating in a variety of activities.
We Move Together	Kelly Fritsch and Anne McGuire, 2021, AK Press	This community-focused book follows a group of children with and without disabilities as they interact with their community and disability culture.
We'll Paint the Octopus Red	Stephanie Stuve-Bodeen, 1998, Woodbine House	A boy is born with Down syndrome. His sister worries her brother will be different but learns he will be able to do many things she also enjoys doing.

Source: Adapted from P. Favazza and M. Ostrosky, *The Making Friends Program: Supporting Acceptance in Your K-2 classroom* (Paul H. Brookes, 2016). Adapted from M. Ostrosky, C. Mouzourou, E. Dorsey, P. Favazza, and L. Leboeuf, "Using children's books to support positive attitudes toward peers with disabilities," *Young Exceptional Children, 18*(1), 2013, pp. 30–43. Adapted from P. Morris. (2022). *A quasi-experimental design: Impacts of shared-book reading on young black children's identity formation* [Doctoral dissertation, University of Nevada, Las Vegas].

The Provision of Prompts and Praise

"Practitioners plan for and provide the level of support, accommodations, and adaptations needed for the child to access, participate, and learn within and across activities and routines" (DEC, 2014, p. 11) [DEC Recommended Practices INS4]. Teacher-mediated or direct instruction involves choosing the behavior to be taught. The early childhood special educator selects a specific time to teach a behavior directly to the child. Through discussion, instructions, demonstration, modeling, and the use of concrete examples, the teacher/adult provides direct instruction and practice opportunities. The teacher/adult then follows the instruction with prompts and praise. Prompts and praise are strategies that teachers/adults can employ to promote engagement within the inclusive preschool setting. Praise can be defined as a verbal reinforcement ("I like the way you are sharing those blocks") or a tangible reinforcement (stickers, access to desired activities, or "happy faces"). **Praise** is an effective technique for promoting child engagement among children who have delays and disabilities. **Prompts** are defined as any assistance or help given by another person (teacher/adult) to assist young children in knowing how to make a response or behavior (Brown & Cariveau, 2022; Sandall et al., 2019) [DEC Recommended Practices INS7]. Early childhood special educators can identify a variety of prompts by the type of assistance they provide. Common prompts include direct and indirect verbal prompts, model prompts, partial or full physical prompts, spatial prompts, pictorial prompts, and cued prompts.

- *Direct verbal prompts* are simple statements that provide support for a child in a current task. For example, when a child is trying unsuccessfully to turn on the faucet, the early childhood special educator (or parent, adult, or peer) can say, "Try turning it the other way." This simple statement may be enough for the child to be successful as they attempt to turn on the faucet. Direct verbal prompts or instructions should be short, clear, and focused on the behavior. Instructions and verbal prompts should be stated in positive language such as, "Point to the big car."

- *Model prompts* supply the child with the desired behavior. The model prompt can be verbal or gestural or a combination of the two. For example, an early childhood special educator may Velcro the child's shoe while saying, "I'll do this one, and you do the next one." In this way, the child is supported in the dressing activity by a modeled verbal and gestural prompt.
- *Physical prompts* can provide partial or physical support. Guiding a child's elbow as they lift a spoon, cup, or lunch tray is an example of a partial physical prompt. A full physical prompt for the same behavior might involve hand-over-hand assistance with the early childhood special educator holding the child's hands as they are grasping the object (spoon, cup, or tray).
- *Spatial prompts* involve placing an object in a location that will more than likely increase a desired response. For example, placing paper towels (for wiping paint off of hands) near the sink and placing clips on the clothesline where children will go to hang their completed artwork are examples of spatial prompts.
- *Visual/pictorial prompts* involve providing assistance through the use of pictures (drawings, photographs, Rebus cue cards, picture symbol systems), colors, or graphics. Using different colors for different children or placing a red mark or the letter *C* on Cathy's cup are examples of visual prompts. Placing photographs depicting the steps to hand washing above the sink is a pictorial prompt.
- *Cued prompts* can be verbal and/or gestural and involve drawing direct attention to a specific aspect or dimension of a stimulus or task. Two examples of a cue are "Pick up your paintbrush (or spoon)" and "It's time to paint (or eat)" while pointing to the handle of the brush (or spoon). Cued prompts are used to focus on the most relevant characteristic or dimension of the stimuli.

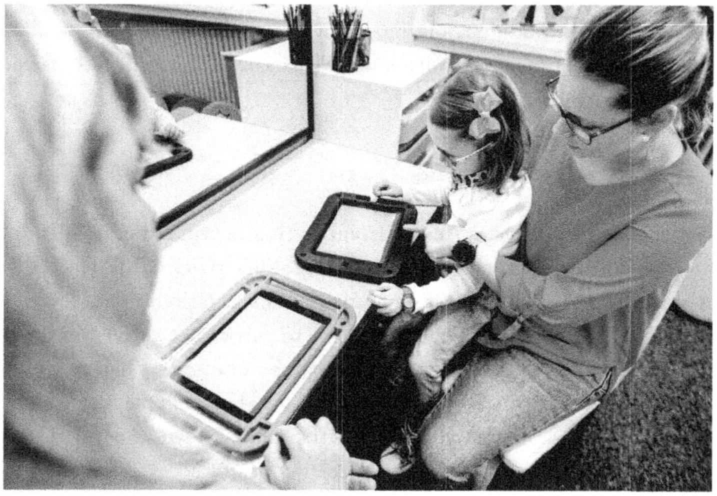

Prompting is a strategy frequently used to teach skills to young children with delays and disabilities.

iStock.com/AndreaObzerova

There are several important points to remember when using praise and/or prompts (Sandall et al., 2019):

1. Early childhood special educators should carefully plan for the provision of praise/prompts. Prompting strategies are effective in a variety of settings for infants, toddlers, preschoolers, and primary-level students. However, teachers and other adults should remember that prompting is a strategy used to teach a skill. As soon as the skill is mastered, a plan to remove the prompting should be incorporated so that the child can work toward independence in

doing the skill. Prompting should not be applied when it is not necessary to support the child's behavior. Providing unnecessary prompts could result in a child becoming overly dependent on the adult and decreasing their own level of independence.

2. Early childhood special educators and other adults should be certain that they have the child's attention when presenting a prompt or praise. The impact or effectiveness of a prompt or praise may be lost unless the child is paying attention and actively engaged in the activity.
3. Prompts should be selected and subsequent praise provided that is the least intrusive while at the same time the most effective for the individual child. For example, a cued prompt (touching the paintbrush) or physical assistance (moving the child's hand to the brush) with a young child with a visual impairment may be less effective and more intrusive than a verbal prompt of "We are going to paint. Everyone, find a paintbrush. Wow! Now we are ready to paint." Not only are the prompt and subsequent praise likely to be successful in assisting the child, but they do not single out the child from the rest of the group at the art table, and a spatial prompt (the paintbrush) has been provided for everyone.
4. The prompts or praise can be changed or faded as the situation warrants. Ideally, a child should perform a task with fewer and fewer prompts and less praise provided. This implies that the teacher or other adults should keep a careful watch on the effectiveness and necessity of prompts and praise to sustain the child's behavior. If a particular strategy is not effective or is not producing the desired results, teachers should shift to another prompt/praise strategy.
5. Early childhood special educators should always consult with the related service personnel (speech-language pathologist, occupational therapist, physical therapist) before applying prompts or changing prompts that they have recommended. Changes in child prompts could be harmful to a child or counterproductive to the objectives that the various therapists have recommended. In addition, it is important to have the same expectation for the use of prompts/praise provided by all adults (teachers, teaching assistants, parents, other professionals).

Accepting Different Levels and Types of Participation

The teacher-mediated strategy of accepting different levels and types of participation allows a child with diverse abilities to become more engaged in a group activity. Children learn best in small groups. The approach requires the teacher to adjust their expectations about levels or ways a child participates in group activities. When a child is unable to participate at the same level as their peers in a group activity, the expectations for participation can be adjusted. When a child uses only a portion of the response, it is referred to as **partial participation**. For example, in a game of Simon Says, the leader says, "Touch your toes." The child extends their hands downward but does not touch their toes. In another situation, the early childhood special educator accepts a single-word response as opposed to a whole- or partial-sentence response in a group discussion. For example, during sharing time, a teacher may have two children come to the front of the group. The early childhood special educator prompts the first child to ask the other child questions about an object brought for sharing time. The prompted questions could be "What do you have?" "What do you do with it?" and "Where did you get it?" The questions for the second child could be shortened to their accepted level of participation with verbalizations like "What have?" or "Have?" "What do?" or "Do?" and "Where get?" or "Get?"

Adapted participation occurs when a child uses an alternative means to participate, such as a child who orients their head or eye gaze instead of pointing or verbalizing, a child with speech delays who uses a communication board, a child with a visual impairment who plays with a sensory ball that emits an auditory signal, or a child with an autism spectrum disorder who uses a structured work system to promote classroom participation in small group activities (Carnahan et al., 2011). These are all examples of adapted participation that enable a child with a delay or disability to fully participate in group activities. For principles to integrate technology in the classroom for young children with delays and disabilities, see the Teacher Technology Tips feature.

Monitoring Communicative Input

Monitoring communicative input is another strategy that enables children with diverse abilities to participate in group activities. The teacher or other adult can have an impact on a child's ability to interact in group activities by adjusting the timing and complexity of their communication, such as using simple vocabulary and shorter sentence length, varying intonation and rate of speech, giving contingent responses, and scaffolding. For example, while young children learn word meanings of objects, people, and actions that are in their immediate surroundings, they usually can understand and attend to input that is gradually introduced at a slightly higher level. Videotaping a group activity is an excellent strategy for examining the level of communication used when speaking to children. Is it understandable by all children? Does the teacher need to alter their communicative input by simplifying the vocabulary or shortening the length of sentences in directives? In this way, the adult matches the receptive and cognitive levels of the child and thus enhances the possibility of every child's participation in group activities. Likewise, videotaping parents or other family members when playing with a child is another way to use this strategy with younger children and provide consistency in communicative input across caregivers.

Varying the speaker's intonation level may provide cuing to certain tasks. For example, an early childhood special educator may state, "We are going outside today," with appropriate intonation and enthusiasm placed on the words *going* and *outside*. Providing verbal input to a child at a slower rate may allow for more processing time and provide more precise cues for relating language to actual events. For example, when giving directions to a child, a pause while the child is moving through the steps enables the child to process each individual step along the way. In a hand-washing activity, an early childhood special educator could say, "Go to the sink." (Pause as the child moves toward the sink.) "Turn on the water." (Pause while the child reaches the sink and turns on the water.) "Wash your hands." (Pause while the child washes her hands.) This strategy could be coupled with task analysis when addressing self-care skills with younger children.

Children learn best in small groups.

iStock.com/Steve Debenport

TEACHER TECHNOLOGY TIPS

PRINCIPLES FOR INTEGRATING TECHNOLOGY

1. Start with the child. Technology should be considered for all children with delays and disabilities. Let the individual needs of the child and the demands of the curriculum drive the selection of the technologies and the ways they are used.
2. Consider all areas of development. Technology applications can be applied to natural learning opportunities and enhance participation in the natural or inclusive environment. Consider the following areas: (a) motor, (b) communication/language, (c) cognitive, (d) social interactions, and (e) adaptive.
3. Consider technology to increase children's ability to participate in less restrictive environments. Use both high-tech and low-tech options such as voice output, picture and word cues, touch screens for tools for prewriting and early literacy, and making choices.
4. Consider age and developmental appropriateness for choosing technology use with young children. Ask for input from other professionals (occupational therapist, physical therapist, speech-language pathologist).
5. Customize the technology. Features such as the ability to control the content and instructional parameters make it easy to adapt activities to the children's needs.
6. Monitor children's work on the computer or with other technologies. Use performance data collected by the technology in making intervention and instructional decisions.
7. Consider the functionality of the technology. Address the level of the children's independence when selecting the technology.
8. Consider the environment in which the technology will be used. Look for available supports, if needed, and address any challenges that might hinder successful use.
9. Teach children to use technology as a tool. Provide opportunities and encouragement for practice. Technology can help children compensate for delays and disabilities and allow for achievement of greater levels of independence.
10. Extend the benefits of technology to teachers, families, and other professionals. Technology is an important tool for adults, as well as children.

Source: Adapted from R. Gargiulo and E. Bouck, *Special Education in Contemporary Society*, 7th ed. (Sage, 2021); R. Gargiulo and D. Metcalf, *Teaching in Today's Inclusive Classrooms: A Universal Design for Learning Approach*, 4th ed. (Cengage Learning, 2023); K. Stremel, Technology Application. In S. Sandall, M. Hemmeter, B. Smith, & M. McLean (Eds.), *DEC Recommended Practices: A Comprehensive Guide for Practical Application* (Sopris West, 2005); NAEYC & the Fred Rogers Center for Early Learning and Children's Media at Saint Vincent College, (2012), *Technology and Interactive Media as Tools in Early Childhood Programs Serving Children From Birth Through Age 8*. Available at https://www.naeyc.org/resources/topics/technology-and-media/resources.

PEER-MEDIATED STRATEGIES

Peer-mediated strategies are a collection of procedures that involve the use of peers to promote the learning and behavior of children with delays and disabilities (Grisham-Brown & Hemmeter, 2017; Martinez et al., 2021) [DEC Recommended Practices INS8]. This may involve having peers model specific behaviors. Peers may be taught how to initiate social interactions with children with delays and disabilities. This may involve teaching peers to respond to social interactions from children with delays and disabilities or to serve as a tutor. Peer-mediated strategies have been effective in promoting social and communication skills and accruing a positive outcome for young children with delays and disabilities (Bohr & Acar, 2021). Peer-mediated strategies involve carefully selecting peers without disabilities, teaching selected peers specific ways to engage their classmates with disabilities, encouraging the peers to persist in their attempts with children with delays and disabilities, providing structured opportunities for the children to interact with one another so as to use the skills taught, and providing support (reinforcement and prompts by adults) during the structured opportunities. Two types of strategies that utilize peers to mediate learning will be discussed: peer-initiation interventions and cooperative learning.

Peer-mediated strategies are often effective in promoting social and communication skills in young children with delays and disabilities.

iStock.com/kate_sept2004

Peer-Initiation Interventions

The interventions that are among the most effective for increasing social behaviors such as initiating, responding, and sharing are peer-mediated strategies (Barton et al., 2011; Bohr & Acar, 2021). An early childhood special educator selects peers without disabilities who are known to be highly social, attend school regularly, have little or no history of negative interactions, have adequate attention spans and the comprehension to participate in the training sessions and have the willingness to participate in the special play groups.

The early childhood special educator instructs the selected peers about ways to interact with children with delays and disabilities, such as how to initiate an exchange ("Ask for a toy" or "Ask Sam to play with you") or suggest a play theme ("Let's play grocery store. You be the clerk"). After practicing the strategies with the teacher and other peers without disabilities, the children are then given brief structured play opportunities (ten to fifteen minutes in length) for using the strategies with classmates with delays and disabilities. When creating structured play sessions, the early childhood special educator or other adults carefully arrange the environment to promote interactions. (See the previous section in this chapter on environmental arrangements.) For example, during an art activity, the teacher/adult provides the supplies and suggests that the children create a picture to hang in the classroom. The teacher then prompts the peers to model cooperative behaviors such as sharing ("Please give T. J. a paintbrush"); requesting materials ("Maria, say, 'Please give me the blue paint'"); complimenting other children ("That's a colorful rainbow"); and making suggestions to the group ("You can add clouds to the sky, Sam").

During the structured play sessions, the teacher/adult remains close by, providing prompts and reinforcement as needed. Instructional resources are available that provide guidelines for promoting social and communication skills such as sharing, initiating, responding, learning alternative ways to initiate, and utilizing persistence in social attempts. The following five suggestions are for early childhood special educators and other adults to use when implementing naturalistic interventions or incidental strategies with peers without disabilities and children with delays and disabilities:

1. *Observe to identify peer models.* Pair a child with a disability with a more skilled partner.
2. *Set up a novel or preferred high-priority activity.* Children are attracted to activities that are new and different in the classroom or other settings. For example, children with autism spectrum disorders may respond positively when a preferred or high-priority activity is offered. Use small, well-defined play areas for activities like building, dramatic play, and computer use.
3. *Invite a peer to join an activity.* Introduce and facilitate the play activity with children without disabilities as well as children with delays and disabilities.
4. *Help children to enter activities.* Children with delays and disabilities often do not know how to enter an activity to begin to engage in play with others. Early childhood special educators may

model social skills, such as obtaining another child's attention, responding to another child, requesting desired items, and negotiating the play process.

5. *Position children to maximize interaction.* Pay attention to where the adults and children are seated. Make sure children are near one another to maximize interaction opportunities. Place a peer with more advanced skills next to a child with disabilities.

Teachers/adults should be encouraged to adapt strategies according to the individual needs of the children in the particular class or setting. For example, children with delays and disabilities may need to be taught alternative means of communication (the use of a communication board) or gestural methods of initiating a response (tapping a peer who has a hearing impairment, waiting until the peer is looking before speaking).

Cooperative Learning

Another strategy that can utilize peers to mediate learning and child engagement is **cooperative learning**, which is defined as an intervention strategy in which small groups of heterogeneous learners are actively involved in jointly accomplishing an activity (Gargiulo & Bouck, 2021). The goals of cooperative learning are to foster cooperative interaction, to teach cooperative learning skills, and to promote positive self-esteem. Research has supported the effectiveness of cooperative learning in promoting positive social interactions between children with and without disabilities. Cooperative learning can be used as a strategy for promoting social and communication skills of preschoolers with disabilities in a typical preschool setting. Preschool and early primary children with delays and disabilities will have more opportunities to practice skills in social and communication behaviors (taking turns, asking/offering assistance) when placed in cooperative learning situations in inclusive classroom environments. Gargiulo and Bouck (2021) emphasize that cooperative learning is an effective strategy for integrating learners with delays and disabilities into the general education classroom.

Cooperative learning can promote social and communication skills.

iStock.com/ SDI Productions

According to Lewis et al. (2017), cooperative learning has been shown to increase opportunities for children with disabilities to experience success in the classroom environment. Cooperative learning uses the social dynamics of the group to support social interactions and friendships, teaches children to encourage one another, and celebrates the success of peers. The four essential elements of cooperative learning are positive interdependence, communication (or face-to-face interactions), accountability of all members, and group process (with emphasis on interpersonal skills) and are described below:

1. *Positive interdependence is promoted.* Members of small groups work together and depend on each other to complete the task.

2. *Communication is required.* To achieve the common goal, the early childhood special educator can encourage or facilitate interactions and communication among the group members as necessary. Materials can be strategically placed to require members to ask for them.

3. *Accountability is expected.* Every member of the group is responsible for contributing to the final product. Within the activity, each child with a disability could have their individual objectives embedded into the activity. Although children may be working on a common project, the objectives may vary according to the needs of the individual child.

4. *Group process is expected.* As two or three children work together, they are expected to follow basic formats such as taking turns, listening, initiating, and responding.

In addition to these strategies, Noonan and McCormick (2014) provide several suggestions for adapting cooperative learning for use with young children with delays and disabilities, including the following:

- A unit with clear objectives should be selected, listing the cooperative skills to be taught.
- A series of lessons or activities can be planned in which the embedded skills will be taught.
- Children can be assigned to dyads or three-member groups that remain intact for the duration of all lessons/activities within the unit (one child with a delay or disability should be within the dyad).
- Cooperation should be encouraged by the way materials are distributed.
- Activities should be prefaced with specific explanations and demonstrations of what it means to be cooperative ("Sit next to your partner" or "Take turns with the glue").
- Children should be assisted and monitored carefully, providing prompts and praise as warranted.
- The child should be evaluated and provided with feedback ("Did you like working together?" "What was the hardest or easiest part?" "How does it feel when you help a friend?" "Who helped you?").

Cooperative learning may be better suited for older preschoolers or early primary-grade students, and the teacher/adult may need to be more involved the first few times that cooperative learning is used to ensure that children understand the nature and process of the activity. Clearly, more research is needed in this area to determine how cooperative learning in early childhood settings could better utilize peers as models, guides, and partners in learning. For an example of the use of cooperative learning strategies within an early primary classroom, see the accompanying Making Connections feature.

ROUTINE-BASED STRATEGIES

Routine-based strategies take advantage of existing events and predictable routine activities such as snack time, diapering, or circle time, play, and transitions (Johnson et al., 2015; Schwartz & Woods, 2015) [DEC Recommended Practices INS5]. Many routine-based strategies are appropriate for use with infants as well as toddlers, preschoolers, and early primary students.

For routine-based strategies to be successful, early childhood special educators and parents need to understand that daily activities that have a specific purpose (snack time is for eating) can also serve as an instructional time. For example, snack time also could be a time for promoting fine motor skills such as reaching or using the neat pincer grasp to eat raisins, Cheerios, or cheese cubes, as well as gross motor skills such as trunk control. The same activity could be used to promote communicative attempts such as verbally or gesturally requesting "more," making a choice when asked, "Do you want an apple or an orange?" and responding by pointing, signing, or saying "Apple." Therefore, before starting routine-based instruction, it would be important that all involved with the child (teachers, assistants, parents, other professionals) are able to recognize the variety of skills that can be promoted within the same routine activity.

Play-Based Intervention (Strategies)

As described in previous chapters, play is a logical and natural activity for incorporating skills of children with disabilities. Play provides an avenue for children to master their thoughts and actions and contributes to children's cognitive, physical, and social/emotional development. Through play, children have opportunities for learning through exploration, self-expression, imitation and imagination, interpretation of situations, negotiation of relationships, and utilization of social and communicative behaviors such as turn-taking, sharing, initiating, and responding (National Association for the Education of Young Children, 2022).

MAKING CONNECTIONS

USING COOPERATIVE LEARNING AND ACCOMMODATIONS IN A PRIMARY CLASSROOM

Cheryl Chinn is a first grader introduced to us in the vignette in Chapter 2. Cheryl is a child with a diagnosis of attention deficit hyperactivity disorder. Her parents, teacher, and school staff team developed a Section 504 plan with accommodations designed to help her remain on task during instruction. Additionally, Cheryl needs extra time and less work per assignment. She has a homework notepad that goes home daily to increase the outcome of completed class work and homework assignments. In class, Mrs. Newman, Cheryl's teacher, has taken advantage of some other accommodations that have been successful for Cheryl. For example, during math meeting or reading circle time, Cheryl is most often seated close to Mrs. Newman. Having this environmental accommodation of proximal seating allows Mrs. Newman to monitor Cheryl's off-task behaviors quickly and quietly to keep her on task more often. Mrs. Newman uses Cheryl as the book holder or page turner to keep her actively involved with the instruction. Throughout the day, Mrs. Newman chooses a peer helper to work with Cheryl. In math centers or quiet reading time, Cheryl and her peer partner often go to a quiet part of the room.

Mrs. Newman is careful when she chooses the peers and has three to five students whom she routinely picks who are good role models for Cheryl. This peer intervention technique has been successful, as Mrs. Newman has noted that Cheryl will follow the peer's model. Also, on the playground at recess, Cheryl has been observed to play consistently with these peer models in an age-appropriate manner. Finally, when working on class projects for science, social studies, or unit time, Mrs. Newman uses cooperative learning activities. She is careful in placing Cheryl in a group where she can contribute her talents and observe good work and study habits. All the above strategies have had a positive effect on Cheryl's classroom performance.

Instructional goals can often be embedded in play activities.

iStock.com/DGLimages

Linder (2008) developed **play-based interventions (strategies)** for incorporating and promoting skill acquisition in the play arena. This approach utilizes a transdisciplinary model (see Chapter 4) whereby all service providers (early childhood special educators, assistant teachers, occupational therapist, speech-language pathologist, physical therapist) and parents or other family members observe and assess the child during play. Each service provider supplies information about the child related to their discipline area while watching the child at play with peers or an adult. The goals for the child are developed based on this transdisciplinary-based assessment and incorporated into the child's playtimes while at school. Using this approach, related service personnel provide support and consultation to teachers for promoting and supporting child goals in regularly occurring playtimes. The transdisciplinary approach is characterized by sharing of expertise through frequent, ongoing communication with all caregivers and training these caregivers to implement interventions. For example, if a toddler exhibits delays in fine motor skills, the occupational therapist would provide information and support to the family, teachers, and other adults on how to address these skill areas during play activities at home and in the program or classroom the child attends [DEC Recommended Practices INS1, INS3, INS13, and TC1].

Embedded child-directed play provides an excellent resource for teachers/adults to integrate concepts and instructional goals of children with diverse abilities into play. For example, using wet and dry sand, fine motor skills (digging, shaking, grasping) and cognitive and communicative skills (vocabulary, concepts such as wet, dry, under, fast, slow, size, texture) are incorporated into sand play (see Figure 9.1). A teacher/adult could examine typical play activities in the preschool setting (Play-Doh, water play, dress-up, transportation toys) and generate a variety of skills that can be addressed within the play setting (Johnson et al., 2015; Snyder et al., 2015). Likewise, the early childhood special educator can assist parents in examining play materials at home, and together they can generate ideas for promoting skill acquisition.

FIGURE 9.1 ■ Play-Based Instruction

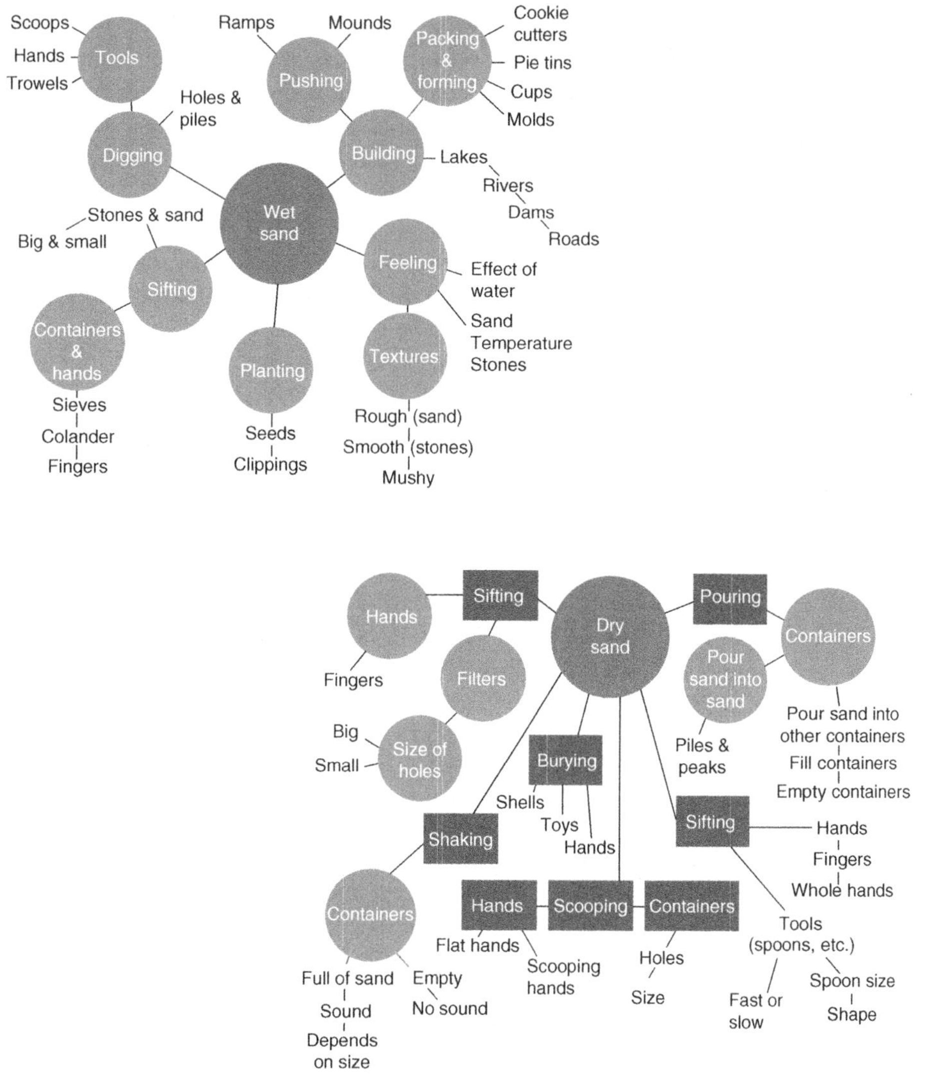

Source: From K. Dolinar, *Learning Through Play* (1e). © 1994 Cengage Learning, Inc. Reproduced by permission.

When setting up activities, it is important to provide a range of difficulty to support active engagement. This strategy enables all children to be successful by participating at their own level with a variety of materials. For example, providing some puzzles with pegs for easy grasp, others without knobs, some with two to three pieces, and others with seven to eight pieces allows many options for children with varying levels of fine motor abilities. During art, a variety of drawing implements (brushes with adaptive grips or of different sizes) can be provided, or within the social-dramatic play area, clothing of different sizes with a variety of fastening devices (snaps, buttons, zippers) and shoes that slip on, buckle, have Velcro straps, and lace up can be provided. In this way, teachers/adults can structure an activity to address the diverse abilities of children that will ultimately challenge and provide success for all.

Activity-Based Instruction or Intervention

Johnson et al. (2015) defined **activity-based instruction or intervention** as "an approach that uses behavioral principles to encourage child interaction and participation in meaningful (authentic) daily activities with the explicit purpose of assisting the child in acquiring, generalizing, and strengthening functional skills" (p. 4). Although it was designed to be used with children with disabilities, it can easily be adapted for use with all children in an inclusive setting. Activity-based instruction uses the child's interest while addressing goals and objectives in routine, planned, or child-initiated activities. Activity-based instruction takes advantage of naturally occurring antecedents and consequences to develop skills that are functional and can be generalized across people and settings.

Two features of this approach are effective when working with young children. First, multiple goals from a variety of the developmental domains can be addressed in one activity. Additionally, the approach provides reinforcement for children for participating in planned activities that are motivating to them. It requires careful planning of the schedule to ensure that activities will occur throughout the child's day in which the child's goals can be addressed. Johnson et al. (2015) demonstrated how a typical preschool classroom schedule can provide multiple opportunities to address a child's targeted goals. (See the accompanying Making Connections feature.)

This is an excellent strategy for infants and toddlers whose objectives can be embedded into daily routine activities at home or in center-based programs. In this way, the likelihood of skill generalization is increased as instruction occurs across settings within activities where the behaviors naturally occur. For example, a parent can address grasping and across-the-midline reaching with an infant or toddler with cerebral palsy by careful placement of a cup of favorite juice during snack time or a favorite toy during bath time. There are many aspects of activity-based instruction that make it appealing to programs as they implement developmentally appropriate practices. Children with motor or communication delays who utilize forms of assistive technology in the home or classroom can benefit from an activity-based approach. Various adapted toys, mobility items, and communication devices can be embedded to be used in naturally occurring situations. In addition, an activity-based approach capitalizes on goals that are individually appropriate, utilizes naturally occurring events and reinforcers as opposed to applying artificial activities or reinforcement, capitalizes on child-initiated transactions, and can be used by early childhood professionals and families alike in addressing child goals. (See the Teacher Technology Tips feature.)

Changing the Content of an Existing Activity

Changing the content of an existing activity is another strategy for embedding child goals into routine activities. For example, appropriate expression of and response to affectionate behavior may be a goal for a young child with an autism spectrum disorder who has difficulty demonstrating and receiving affection (hugs, pats on the back, handshakes). Research suggests that the modification of well-known games or songs is effective in promoting affection activities because children are paired with peers in pleasurable, nonthreatening activities, and there appears to be a desensitization to peer interaction during these activities (Vaiouli & Ogle, 2015). Early childhood special educators can use common group games and songs such as Simon Says and "The Farmer in the Dell" to incorporate affection activities (hugs, pats on the back, handshakes, high fives), and other songs can be used such as "If You're Happy and You Know It" that include such phrases as "Shake a friend's hand, give a friend a hug, pat your friend on the back." As a result of this change in the routine song, children interact more with one another within group activities and during playtime, which often carries over to subsequent activities. At bath time, one dad chose to sing to his toddler, "This is the way we wash our tummy, wash our tummy, wash our tummy [foot, hand] early in the morning." The goal was to increase the child's language. The dad was providing names of body parts and naming the behavior (washing) within an enjoyable routine activity.

Transition-Based Instruction

Transition-based instruction is another example of using daily routine as an opportunity for learning. In using this strategy, the teacher/adult presents an opportunity for participating within the group while children are transitioning to other activities (Johnson et al., 2015; Sandall et al., 2019).

There are several advantages to using routine activities/games/songs to incorporate skills. Examples of regularly occurring transitions include going from free play to the snack table, lining up for outdoor play, and arrival and departure times. During this transition time, the teacher/adult obtains the attention of the children and asks them to respond to questions ("What is this?" or "I spy something yellow; what could it be?") that match their level of functioning. This is an activity that is effective in teaching pre-academic skills such as letter names, shapes, and colors, while utilizing the frequently occurring transitions in children's daily routines. Some children may respond by saying the word, others may respond with a word approximation, and others may use an initial letter sound. Likewise, singing songs during transition times is a strategy that allows for group responding at a variety of levels. In addition, transitions provide an excellent vehicle for using fine motor skills (cleanup activities) or gross motor skills (mobility or ambulation). They do not require using new materials or a change in the existing structure or routine of the day at school or home. They do not require changes in personnel, just informing all personnel of how multiple skills can be incorporated in existing routines. Children with delays and disabilities can receive the attention needed without being singled out from the rest of the group. In addition, transition-based instruction may increase the likelihood of the generalization of skills when the instruction occurs at the place and time when the desired behavior typically occurs. However, to be effective, routine-based instruction does require planning, ongoing monitoring for changes that are needed, and coordination with all personnel involved with the child. Using routine-based instruction, related service personnel can consult with the early childhood special educator and parents, identifying times when child goals can logically be supported and promoted in daily routine activities.

MAKING CONNECTIONS

ACTIVITY-BASED INSTRUCTION OR INTERVENTION

Date: September 12, 2023

Teacher's Name: Miss Linda

Child's Name: T. J. Browning

Write the classroom schedule in the left-hand column. Write the child's learning objectives across the top row. Fill the appropriate cells with a brief version of the plan for embedding the objective into the daily schedule.

	Uses Short Phrases of Four to Five Words	Verbally Sequences Three Events in Sequence (Simple Stories)	Correctly Responds to "What" Questions	Shares or Exchanges Objects With Peers	Follows Adult Instructions	Participates in Activity for Ten Minutes	Prints First and Last Name
Arrival	Greets adults, peers		Responds to "What did you do last night?"				
Planning		Uses unit book for retelling	Uses unit book for questions	Participates in free play with two peers		Attends morning group	
Work	Requests materials			Uses paired activities	Sorts dishes, building toys	Utilizes choice/ preferred materials	Uses raised line paper

	Uses Short Phrases of Four to Five Words	Verbally Sequences Three Events in Sequence (Simple Stories)	Correctly Responds to "What" Questions	Shares or Exchanges Objects With Peers	Follows Adult Instructions	Participates in Activity for Ten Minutes	Prints First and Last Name
Recall				Recalls days of the week and weather			
Snack		Requests preferred snack	Retells steps to make snack		Follows adult directions for manners and cleanup		
Outside				Uses paired activities with two to three peers	Follows adult directions for safety and time to go		
Small-/ large-group play		Facilitates verbal peer interactions		Uses paired activities	Follows center schedule		Puts name on writing center product
Departure		Says appropriate goodbyes					

Source: Adapted from J. Johnson, N. Rahn, and D. Bricker, *An Activity-Based Approach to Early Intervention*, 4th ed. (Paul H. Brookes, 2015).

TEACHER TECHNOLOGY TIPS

USING ASSISTIVE TECHNOLOGY WITH INFANTS, TODDLERS, AND PRESCHOOLERS

Assistive technology devices can be used to increase, maintain, or improve the abilities of all young children with delays and disabilities [DEC Recommended Practices E4 and E5]. Some of the ways in which assistive technology can be used to improve play abilities of young children in early intervention and preschool special education are listed below. For additional illustrations of how assistive technology can benefit young children with delays and disabilities, see Chapter 10.

Adapted commercial toys	• Highlighters—outline or emphasize to help in focusing a child's attention • Extenders—foam or molded plastic that may help children press small buttons or keys • Stabilizers—Velcro or nonslip materials that will hold a toy in place or connect a communication device to a crib • Confinement materials—planter bases, Hula-Hoops, box tops that keep toys from getting out of the child's field of vision
Positioning items	• Sling seats, Boppys®, sidelyers, wedges, floor tables, corner seats, Sassy Seats, rolled towels, and exersaucers all support children so that their hands are free to interact with toys more readily
Mobility items	• Walkers such as toy shopping carts or activity centers with wheels that a child can stand at and push to allow them to explore the environment • Low rocking and riding toys

Switches, adapted battery-operated toys, and interfaces	• Switches that allow for on and off function, battery adapters, timers, latch devices, and series adapters • Adapted computer mouse (for example, BIGmack switch)
Computer hardware	• Built-in touch screens • Enlarged keys • Alphabetical keyboards • Eye gaze systems
Communication items	• Devices that use recorded messages to incorporate language into play or provide a way to use a voice to communicate, such as LITTLE Step-by-Step, Say It Play It, Cheap Talk, and GoTalk

Source: Adapted from S. Lane and S. Mistrett, "Let's Play! Assistive Technology Interventions for Play," *Young Exceptional Children, 5*(2), 2002, pp. 19–27. E. Bouck, *Assistive Technology* (Sage, 2017).

Embedding goals into routine activities is an effective instructional strategy.

iStock.com/kali9

SPECIFIC NATURALISTIC (MILIEU) STRATEGIES

Milieu strategies (or naturalistic strategies) are ideal for being used in early childhood settings because they reflect developmentally appropriate practice by using procedures that are child directed and teacher guided (National Association for the Education of Young Children, 2022). Milieu strategies are used to facilitate language skills, social interaction, and other skills that take advantage of prompting strategies, environmental arrangement, and responsive interactions (Kang & Kim, 2022). These strategies are effective when they are embedded into ongoing activities. These strategies highlight the DEC Recommended Practices on interaction as they focus on children and adults carefully responding contingently to each other. Variations of these naturalistic strategies include the use of incidental teaching, models and expansions, the mand-model procedure, time delay, and interrupted routines.

Incidental Teaching

Incidental teaching is a naturalistic strategy that has been effective in promoting communication and other skills in young children with diverse abilities (Schwartz & Woods, 2015). It involves the use of naturally arising situations to teach skills and is effective when used to encourage peer interactions in the early childhood classroom and other natural settings [DEC Recommended Practices INS2].

Incidental teaching is *always* child-initiated. The environment is structured to increase the probability that the child will initiate an interaction with the teacher or adult [DEC Recommended Practices E3]. When the child initiates, the teacher/adult makes a more elaborate request for a certain behavior. If the more elaborate behavior is forthcoming from the child, the teacher/adult will praise and respond to the child's initiation. If the behavior does not appear to be forthcoming, the teacher/adult can prompt the child, then allow time for the child to respond. Finally, the teacher/adult will respond to the child's initiation. This strategy takes advantage of children's initiations to promote communicative attempts and model more sophisticated language [DEC Recommended Practices INT3]. In addition to providing models, the teacher/adult can incorporate expansions, mands, and time delays within incidental teaching. The four steps for using incidental teaching are as follows:

1. Identify the communication goals of the child and activities or opportune times to address these goals.
2. Arrange the environment to increase the likelihood of initiations from the child. This could involve placing high-interest materials or toys within view, but out of reach; intentionally selecting materials with which the child will need assistance (opening a can of Play-Doh); selecting materials that are new or novel to the child; or intentionally providing materials that have some pieces/parts missing.
3. Within close proximity of the child, watch and wait for their initiation.
4. When the child initiates, follow the steps below:
   a. Focus on precisely what it is the child is requesting.
   b. Ask for more elaborate language by saying, "Use your words," "What about the (ball, swing, Play-Doh, cup)?" or "What do you need?"
   c. Wait expectantly for a more sophisticated response from the child ("Want ball," "Yellow ball," "Push swing," or "Top off").
   d. If the child provides more language, praise them, expand their statement, and provide the desired object or action ("You want the yellow ball"; "Push swing, please"; or "You want the top off").
   e. If the child does not respond adequately, provide a model coupled with an expectant look and wait again for them to respond. Once the child imitates the model, provide what is needed (assistance or the desired object).

The Model and Expansion

The model and expansion techniques involve providing the child with a verbal or gestural model and an expansion with new information. For example, after showing the child the desired object (ball, cup of juice), the teacher/adult says, "Ball" or "Say 'ball.'" The teacher/adult then pauses expectantly, looking at the child. Once the child gives the desired response, the teacher/adult provides the desired object or action and an expansion of what the child said ("OK, you want the *blue* ball").

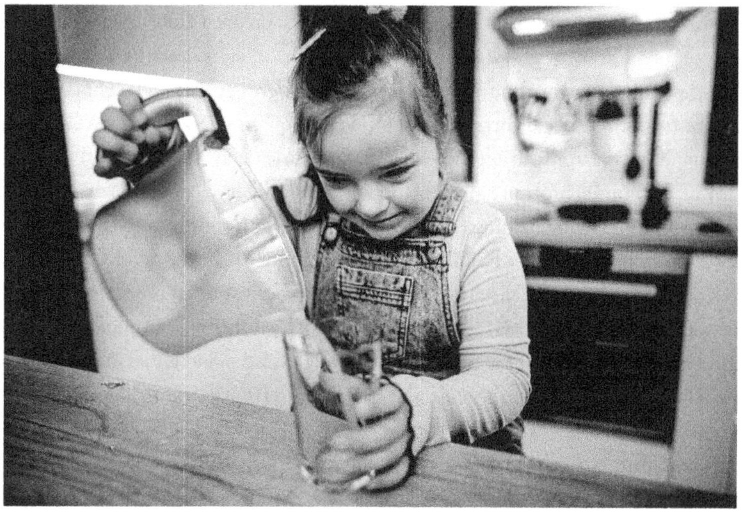

Incidental teaching incorporates naturally occurring events to teach skills.
iStock.com/StefaNikolic

The Mand Model

The mand-model technique differs from the previously mentioned incidental teaching strategies. Mand-model strategies are initiated by the teacher/adult and not the child. The mand-model technique involves the adult observing the child's focus of attention and asking a non-yes/no question (a mand). The question presented is about the focus of the child's attention. The teacher/adult waits for a response. If no response is evident, then a model is provided. The mand model is a directive and, therefore, is a more intrusive technique that can be used successfully in conjunction with and to augment child-initiated activities. The mand model can be embedded easily into children's play or interactions. This model is often used with children with limited verbal or play skills (Grisham-Brown & Hemmeter, 2017). For example, when a child finishes her juice and obviously wants more (begins looking around for juice or looks inside cup), the adult says, "Tell [or show] me what you want." The directive is always related to *exactly* what/where the child's attention is focused at the time. If the child responds, the child is given what they want and is provided with a verbal confirmation and expansion. Using the previous example, if the child responds by saying "Juice," the adult could say, "Oh, you want the *orange* juice," "Oh, you want *more* juice," or "You want the *delicious* juice." In this way, the adult has confirmed their response, given the desired object, and provided an expansion of the response with an additional word or descriptor. If the child does not respond or does not respond correctly, a model of the desired response should be provided for the child immediately followed by the desired object or action. The adult would verbalize, "Say 'swing,'" then push them in the swing.

Time Delay

Time-delay procedures systematically employ a brief waiting period to teach the child to initiate an interaction and can be embedded into routine activities in the home, the classroom, or other environments. Time delay can refer to three different strategies as identified by Grisham-Brown and Hemmeter (2017):

1. Waiting for a child to initiate a behavior
2. Using constant time delay
3. Using progressive time delay

Simple time-delay procedures can occur throughout a child's natural routine. An adult simply waits for the child to initiate a behavior. An example could be a mother opening the refrigerator and waiting for the child to initiate communication by asking for juice. Constant time delay occurs when the adult initially provides a prompt for a child to perform and then on subsequent trials delays the assistance for a fixed period of time (constant number of seconds). Progressive time delay occurs when the adult provides a prompt for a child to perform and then on subsequent trials progressively increases the time before giving help. With the application of both constant time delay and progressive time delay, correct responses (with or without a prompt) are reinforced. Time delay is particularly effective in teaching language and response behavior to preschool children and older children with delays and disabilities (Sandall et al., 2019). For example, a child may be presented with high-preference objects within view but out of reach at the snack table. Once the child shows an interest in an object (juice, food, spoon), the teacher/adult waits briefly for the child to emit a desired behavior (for example, look expectantly at the adult, say "more," say "juice," orient eye gaze, reach). The desired behavior or range of desired behaviors is predetermined based on the child's individual goals. Four steps in a time-delay approach are as follows:

1. The teacher/adult faces the child with an expectant look. The desired object should be within the child's field of vision (favorite toy, snack items, paints, or water play pieces). The adult should encourage eye contact.
2. The teacher/adult should wait a brief period of time (five seconds, ten seconds) for the child to initiate a request.
3. If the child responds, the teacher/adult provides the desired object.
4. If the child does not respond, the teacher/adult provides a verbal prompt ("Want juice") or a physical prompt (hand-over-hand assistance in reaching toward the desired object) and reinforces the response by providing the desired object (Gomez et al., 2007).

For an example of the use of a time-delay approach that is embedded within daily instruction, see the accompanying Making Connections feature.

Interrupted Routine

Interrupting a routine activity is another strategy that can be used to promote child engagement and to teach communication, social, cognitive, motor, and self-care skills (Johnson et al., 2015). Daily routines include caregiving routines (diaper changing, snack time, dressing and undressing), social routines (greeting and departure times, waking up from naptime), and activity routines (specific steps or actions that typically occur with a song or game).

MAKING CONNECTIONS

PLANS TO EMBED AND DISTRIBUTE TIME DELAY FOR MARIA'S GOALS

Steps for Using Time Delay	Using Words to Request	Using Words for Actions	Increasing Muscle Strength and Fine Motor Skills
Step 1: Identify the skills to be taught.	Naming food and drink items. Using "want" or "please" forms. Naming toys when given the choice between two.	Naming actions she is performing (stacking, pushing, drinking, building, drawing, eating).	Using utensils (spoon, fork) and writing tools (crayons, markers).
Step 2: Identify the activities and routines for teaching.	Snack, lunch, and when given a choice of toys during free play.	Free play and during play on the playground.	Breakfast, lunch, or snack time and during art or writing activities.

Steps for Using Time Delay	Using Words to Request	Using Words for Actions	Increasing Muscle Strength and Fine Motor Skills
Step 3: Decide how many and how often trials will be used.	Every time she makes a nonverbal request.	Ten times per day. At least two minutes and no more than ten minutes between trials.	About four times per day; every time she engages in art or writing activities at centers.
Step 4: Select an interval time delay procedure.	Constant time delay—response intervals are all the same length.	Progressive time delay—response time gradually increases over trials or days.	Constant time delay—response intervals are all the same length.
Step 5: Identify a task cue and controlling prompt.	Her nonverbal request (sign or gesture) and any choice she is given; the prompt is the verbal model.	Prompt is the verbal model: "Maria, what are you doing?"	Hand-over-hand at the center or prompt is physical guide.
Step 6: Select a reinforcer.	Receives the item she requested.	Continuing to play; praise for approximation or word Maria used.	Item and activity she enjoys and adult praise.
Step 7: Determine the number of zero-second trials to use.	Four days of zero-second trials.	Four days of zero-second trials.	Four days of zero-second trials.
Step 8: Determine the length of the response interval.	Ten seconds	Increase by one-second increments every two days; stop at fifteen seconds.	Ten seconds
Step 9: Select and use a monitoring system.	Count the number of requests, number of verbal requests using a prompt, and number of nonverbal requests.	Count the number of questions, number of action words using a prompt, and number of no responses.	Count the number of steps before the prompt and number of steps wrong before the prompt.
Step 10: Implement the plan and monitor use and effects.	Record how many requests occur and whether the steps of time delay were completed correctly.	Record how many questions were asked and whether the steps of time delay were completed correctly.	Keep track of the number of opportunities for using utensils and art/writing tools in which she was taught and whether the steps of time delay were completed correctly.

Source: Adapted with permission from M. Wolery, (2001). "Embedding Time Delay Procedures in Classroom Activities." In M. Ostrosky & S. Sandall, (Eds.), Young Exceptional Children Monograph Series 3: *Teaching Strategies: What to do to Support Young Children's Development*, Division for Early Childhood. pp. 84–85. Copyright © Division for Early Childhood.

There are three ways to apply interrupted routines: (a) provide an incomplete set of materials, (b) withhold or delay the provision of expected or high-interest items or events, and (c) make "silly" mistakes. Many routines or activities require a set of materials such as clothing when dressing; food, drink, plates, and cups when having a snack; and paints, brushes, and paper during art. The teacher/adult simply sets up the materials for the activity or routine but does not provide all the needed materials to prompt an initiation by the child. The adult waits until the child says something about the missing item(s). For this procedure to be effective, the routine should be reinforcing, and it must require a known set of materials.

Withholding or delaying an expected action, event, or object is another way of applying interrupted routines. For example, during the finger play "Itsy Bitsy Spider," the adult "forgets" to do the next action in the sequence of hand motions. Or during snack time, the adult passes out the napkins and juice cups but withholds the crackers and tells the children, "Eat your crackers." The omitted action or object will likely result in a protest response from the child or children. Purposefully withholding the object from one child could also prompt their peers to tell the child, "Tell Miss Micki that you did not get crackers."

Making "silly mistakes" involves violating the function of an object or what children know to be the correct action or word. Examples of "silly mistakes" while dressing include putting shoes on hands or hats on feet. Also, the dad who routinely sang as he bathed their toddler changed some of the words once the routine and words were familiar to the child. He would sing, "This is the way we wash our hands," while he was washing the child's tummy. As he made the silly mistake, he looked at the toddler with an expectant gaze (raised eyebrows, mouth and eyes wide open), waiting for the toddler's protest, "Tummy, Daddy! Tummy!" Another example with older children would be to give the wrong response in a counting or color identification activity. These types of exchanges can increase child engagement and communication but require that the children know the correct or expected behavior.

Caregiving routines provide opportunities for developing a wide variety of skills.

Mareen Fischinger/Alamy Stock Photo

When considering routines in which to use the interrupted routine strategy, the following characteristics need attention: (a) The routine should be established so that the child can anticipate the steps in the routine, (b) the routine should involve a variety of high-interest objects, (c) the whole routine should be completed quickly to increase the potential for multiple interactions, and (d) the routine should be functional to increase the probability of generalization. (See the Making Connections feature.)

MAKING CONNECTIONS

STRATEGIES FOR ADDRESSING MARIA'S GOALS/OUTCOMES IN NATURALISTIC SETTINGS

Based on the information presented in the vignette on Maria (see Plans to Embed and Distribute Time Delay for Maria's Goals, above) and the information on young children with cognitive delays, a variety of intervention strategies could be used to address the unique needs of Maria in the home setting. For example, Maria has the following goals/outcomes: (a) verbally request items that she wants, (b) use words for actions she is performing (pushing, running, cooking, drawing), and (c) increase muscle strength and fine motor skills, especially her ability to use utensils (spoon, toothbrush) and writing tools (crayons). Based on these goals/outcomes, Maria's daily schedule could be examined to determine opportunities for addressing these skills in her routine activities. Specifically, during breakfast, lunch, or dinner, Maria could use eating utensils, and during an art activity, she could use a paintbrush, markers, and crayons. In a discussion with the family, they noted that one of her favorite activities is art. Both activities could serve to strengthen her fine motor skills. Also, during each of these activities, materials could be withheld to encourage Maria to request the items she wants and needs. For example, she could be given the art paper without the paint or paintbrushes. The early childhood special educator could request that Maria name the action she is performing during the art activity. If Maria needs a model, the teacher could say, "You are drawing, Maria." Or "You are painting with the paintbrush." During mealtime, she could be given her cup without the juice. In this way, she would be provided with multiple opportunities to use the skills she is developing in a naturalistic setting (home) within routine activities.

SUMMARY

This chapter focuses on current recommended interventions and instructional strategies from the field of early childhood special education. Inclusive service provisions and practices for young children with delays and disabilities are highlighted as the method of choice for meeting individual needs in the child's least restrictive environment for the following reasons. First, inclusive practices meet the IDEA mandate for children with delays and disabilities to be educated with their age-appropriate peers without disabilities. Second, when children with delays and disabilities are included in typical classroom activities with early childhood special educators and other professionals providing individualized services and supports, we increase the likelihood of children generalizing and achieving functional and social goals alongside their age-appropriate peers and thereby their independence in future educational settings. Finally, inclusive practices may provide a multitude of opportunities for children with delays and disabilities to achieve active engagement in their educational environment. As stated earlier in this text, it is the responsibility of the collaborative team to create a plan that balances the individual needs of the child with the strategies and supports that will ensure success in meeting the individual goals and outcomes of each child and family (Ronfeldt et al., 2015).

This chapter began with two themes that continue throughout the text in our discussion of specific teaching strategies. *Evidence-based* and *recommended practices* were defined as methods used to guide early childhood special educators and other practitioners in determining *how* to choose the appropriate intervention or instructional strategy for young children with delays and disabilities. Both methods encourage practitioners to base their decision making on current available research evidence, well-documented recommended practices from the professional literature, and the use of professional judgment when working collaboratively with families. We also provided one example of a method used to guide practitioners when making evidence-based decisions. The 5-Step Learning Cycle presents an outline for solving problems through the integration of multiple perspectives of professionals and families as well as other sources of evidence.

Finally, this chapter devoted much of its content to presenting best practice and general guidelines for creating appropriate educational and instructional environments for young children with delays and disabilities. Research has shaped these guidelines, providing specific strategies in each of four categories that have evidence to support their effectiveness when teaching young children with delays and disabilities. The four strategies are teacher-mediated, peer-mediated, routine-based, and specific naturalistic (milieu). Each section defines the particular strategy and provides examples of their usage in the home as well as the preschool or early primary classroom.

In summary, early childhood special educators and practitioners have the responsibility to make thoughtful choices when designing individualized instruction for young children with delays and disabilities. The key is to be flexible and to create collaborative, supportive teams of families and professionals. We believe that well-informed teams using current research and recommended practices will influence the ways in which we create the best possible educational experiences in the most appropriate environments.

KEY TERMS

Activity-based instruction or intervention
Adapted participation
Assistive technology interventions
Cooperative learning
Embedded interventions
Engagement
Evidence-based practices
Milieu strategies (or naturalistic strategies)
Partial participation
Peer-mediated strategies
Play-based intervention (strategies)
Praise
Prompts
Recommended practices
Routine-based strategies
Teacher-mediated
Transition practices

CHECK YOUR UNDERSTANDING

1. Define evidence-based practices when applied to selecting intervention and instructional practices for supporting young children with delays and disabilities.
2. Define "active engagement" when referring to young children with delays and disabilities in an inclusive learning environment.
3. What factors should early childhood special educators consider when making environmental arrangements to promote engagement of young children with delays and disabilities within educational settings?
4. Describe the differences between the various types of prompts and assistance provided to young children with delays and disabilities.
5. What are some naturalistic interventions for peer-mediated strategies for peers without disabilities and children with delays and disabilities in the natural environment or inclusive settings?
6. Describe the elements of cooperative learning.
7. What is the difference between a time delay and an interrupted routine?
8. Describe the kinds of strategies that can be used to prepare the social environment for young children with delays and disabilities.
9. Provide an example of the model and expansion milieu instructional procedure.

REFLECTION AND APPLICATION

1. Each morning, a particular preschool classroom has circle or group time. Some children rarely or never participate in this activity. Describe two teacher-mediated strategies that could be used to increase the level of child engagement during this group activity.
2. A child with delays in cognitive development is in your preschool classroom. They use sign language to communicate. One of their goals is to indicate when they want items (to request) using the sign "more." Provide an example of how activity-based instruction could be used to address this goal throughout the daily classroom routine.

PART IV

CONTEMPORARY ISSUES AND CHALLENGES IN EARLY CHILDHOOD SPECIAL EDUCATION

iStock.com/monkeybusinessimages

10 EMERGING ISSUES AND CONTEMPORARY CHALLENGES IN EARLY CHILDHOOD SPECIAL EDUCATION

LEARNING OBJECTIVES

After reading this chapter, you will be able to

10.1 Discuss why early childhood special educators should demonstrate cultural and linguistic awareness, sensitivity, and responsiveness.

10.2 Describe what early childhood special educators can do to assist children with delays and disabilities from growing populations.

10.3 Explain how response to intervention, assistive technology devices, and universal design for learning are being used in today's early learning environments.

EI/ECSE Professional Standards

The content of this chapter aligns with the following EI/ECSE Standards, as well as the other standards discussed throughout the previous chapters:

Standard 7: Professionalism and Ethical Practice

Candidates identify and engage with the profession of early intervention and early childhood special education (EI/ECSE) by exhibiting skills in reflective practice, advocacy, and leadership while adhering to ethical and legal guidelines. Evidence-based and recommended practices are promoted and used by candidates.

DEC Recommended Practices

The content of this chapter aligns with the following Division for Early Childhood (DEC) Recommended Practices:

Environment

- E1. Practitioners provide services and supports in natural and inclusive environments during daily routines and activities to promote the child's access to and participation in learning experiences.
- E2. Practitioners consider Universal Design for Learning principles to create accessible environments.
- E4. Practitioners work with families and other adults to identify each child's needs for assistive technology to promote access to and participation in learning experiences.
- E5. Practitioners work with families and other adults to acquire or create appropriate assistive technology to promote each child's access to and participation in learning experiences.

Authors' Note: Discussed throughout this chapter are the standards and recommended practices as they relate to issues and challenges in the field. See Appendix A for a complete list of the EI/ECSE Standards and Appendix B for a complete list of the DEC Recommended Practices.

A number of current and emerging issues in early intervention/early childhood special education (EI/ECSE) have been identified and are being addressed within the field. These issues represent evolving trends, challenges, and areas of focus that are shaping EI/ECSE policies and practices. The Division for Early Childhood (DEC), the primary EI/ECSE professional organization, has an ongoing commitment to respond to issues in the field and the impact they will have on the children and families they serve. As described in EI/ECSE Standard 7, to address these issues EI/ECSE professionals must develop skills in evidence-based practices, advocacy, and leadership and follow ethical and legal guidelines of the profession. EI/ECSE professionals also must demonstrate skills in reflective practice, which is a process by which they are aware of their knowledge base and learn from their experience (Division for Early Childhood, 2020a). Further, they must exhibit professionalism and ethical practices, which calls for engaging with the EI/ECSE profession to be informed of the recent issues and developments in the field. The purpose of this chapter is to consider issues such as these that are relevant to early interventionists and childhood special educators of the twenty-first century.

As described throughout this text, the field of EI/ECSE has evolved and changed dramatically over the years and particularly in recent years. One can only speculate what the years that follow will hold for young children with delays and disabilities and their families. A safe assumption is that change will continue to occur, affecting service providers, families, and the children themselves. The 2020 DEC Priority Issues Agenda calls for the field of EI/ECSE to (a) achieve high-quality inclusion for all young children, (b) address bias, (c) respond appropriately to child behavior, (d) create and maintain strong family partnerships, (e) adequately equip a high quality EI/ECSE workforce, and (f) provide high quality learning experiences for all young children (Division for Early Childhood, 2020b). Throughout this text we have addressed many of the changes that are likely to occur in the field of early childhood special education in several different arenas, such as the inclusion movement (which is discussed in Chapter 4), the response to an increasingly diverse population of children and families, in addition to instructional matters such as universal design for learning and assistive technology for young children with delays and disabilities.

CULTURAL AND LINGUISTIC RESPONSIVENESS

The United States is an immensely diverse society, as discussed in Chapter 3, representing many different people and cultures rich in diversity of national origins, languages, foods, music, folkways, values, religious practices, and traditions. For the nation, there are great benefits from this mix—it is a strength of the country (Gargiulo & Metcalf, 2023). Although diversity is celebrated and, in most instances, this richness of diversity is valued, all too often cultural differences generate stereotypes, biases, discrimination, and unequal educational opportunities. Therefore, in an increasingly culturally pluralistic society, building competence among EI/ECSE practitioners to effectively support the diverse needs of children and families from various cultural and linguistic backgrounds is of paramount importance.

The composition of America's population is rapidly changing, and the number of young children and families from culturally and linguistically diverse backgrounds is increasing at an extraordinary rate. EI/ECSE programs and classrooms in the coming years will become especially heterogeneous and evidence greater diversity than today. Changing demographics will present a multitude of new challenges to early intervention, early childhood, and early primary special education programs, as well as the professionals who work therein. Consider the implications of the following statistics:

- Children of color are expected to constitute more than 50 percent of the school-age population by 2027 (Gollnick & Chinn, 2021).
- Approximately 22 percent of the U.S. population over the age of five speaks a language other than English at home (United States Census, 2020).
- Currently, children of color make up the majority of children in several states and many urban centers (Children's Defense Fund, 2021; Lustig et al., 2018).

The effectiveness of early childhood programs and schools in meeting the needs of an expanding culturally diverse population will largely depend upon early childhood special educators' ability to respond to cultural differences and utilize culturally and linguistically responsive and affirming practices. DEC's position statement on Family Culture, Values, and Language calls for personnel who provide "respectful, responsive, and evidence-based practices...[to] ensure that children and families from culturally and linguistically diverse backgrounds have equal access to educational services and learning opportunities" (DEC, 2010, p. 4), as does their Position Statement on Ethical Practice (DEC, 2022).

Although it is axiomatic that early childhood special educators are sensitive to the individual differences of the children they serve, increasing emphasis is being placed on cultural and linguistic differences. The DEC guidelines on recommended practices (Division for Early Childhood, 2014; Sandall et al., 2005) for young children with delays and disabilities and their families reflect the importance of cultural awareness, sensitivity, and responsiveness as crucial components in the delivery of services. The guidelines call for professionals to acknowledge, honor, respect, and value the culture and language of *all* children and their families (Division for Early Childhood, 2010).

Recognition of and responsiveness to cultural diversity and the use of culturally and linguistically responsive and affirming practices also are important elements of developmentally appropriate practice. One aspect of individual appropriateness is how the professionals respond to the various cultural backgrounds represented by the children in the program or classroom (NAEYC, 2022). The key is to include this diversity in all aspects of the curriculum and to make programs and services culturally relevant for all children (Kostelnik et al., 2019; Lynch & Hanson, 2011).

Culture

Before continuing this discussion, the definition of **culture** is considered. Culture is defined as the attitudes, values, belief systems, norms, and traditions shared by a particular group of people that collectively form their heritage. A culture is transmitted from one generation to another. It is typically reflected in language, religion, dress, diet, social roles, and customs, in addition to other aspects of a particular lifestyle.

Tiedt and Tiedt (2002) support this thinking, which is still relevant today. They write that culture denotes a complex integrated system of values, beliefs, and behaviors common to a large group of people. A culture may include shared history and folklore, ideas about right and wrong, and specific communication styles—the "truths" accepted by members of the group. (p. 23)

These authors further state that every child grows up belonging to a particular culture. The cultural background of the child influences their response to the educational process and must be considered when planning instruction.

"As educators working in increasingly culturally diverse environments, we need to model respect for and sensitivity to the cultural and linguistic characteristics represented by students and their families" (Gargiulo & Bouck, 2021, p. 75). Consequently, it is important to guard against generalizing and stereotyping when working with young children and families from various cultural backgrounds. Even within specific groups, each child (and family) is unique despite many sharing similar group characteristics. Stated another way, early childhood special educators need to be cognizant of children's intra-individual differences regardless of shared cultural backgrounds. Two early primary students from the same racial background will likely perform quite differently in the classroom irrespective of their common background.

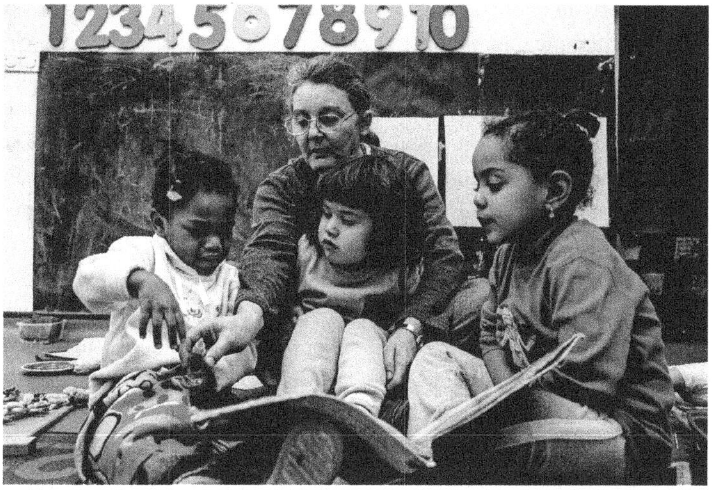

Early childhood special educators need to model respect for and sensitivity to cultural and linguistic differences.

jacky chapman / Alamy Stock Photo

Early Childhood Special Education and Cultural Diversity

For some children with delays and disabilities, entrance into an early intervention or early childhood special education program may be their first exposure to cultural practices and a language that is different from that of their home. The values of the child's home and the values of society typically confront each other for the first time in school (Gallagher et al., 2023). Thus, there is the potential for cultural conflict as roles, relationships, and expectations may clash. Hanson and Zercher (2001) write, if "preschool goals, and values for children's learning, social and behavioral expectations, and demands for interactional and communication abilities differ from those that the children and their families possess, then potential differences [conflict] may arise" (p. 418). Language, race, and ethnicity may potentially influence access to early intervention and early childhood special education services and supports (Sandall et al., 2005). Early childhood special educators must be alert to these possibilities. They must also communicate to the child and their family that they value and respect the child's cultural heritage. Effectiveness in working with children and families representing diverse cultural backgrounds further requires that early childhood professionals understand and are comfortable with their own cultural influences (Gollnick & Chinn, 2021).

One particular challenge confronting early childhood special educators is distinguishing between ethnicity and disability. Professionals who work with young children and their families need to ensure that ethnicity is not mistaken for a disability (Hallahan et al., 2023). This can easily occur when early childhood special educators view their own cultural group as setting the standard against which other groups are to be measured. When this happens, early childhood special educators are guilty of exhibiting **ethnocentric behavior**, whereby they view their own cultural group characteristics as appropriate or superior and the ways of other groups as odd or inferior. Consequently, actions that are considered atypical or deviant by the early childhood special educator may, in fact, be fairly typical and adaptive within the context of the child's cultural environment (Hallahan et al., 2023). It is important to recognize that everyone views other people and the world around them through "culturally tinted lenses." Individuals representing different cultural backgrounds interpret behavior differently—it all depends on one's perspective.

It is vitally important that early childhood special education professionals do not generalize or stereotype based on the child's cultural or linguistic heritage. Likewise, educators should not assume that all individuals within a particular cultural group will perform or react in a predetermined fashion. EI/ECSE professionals must always view the child and their family as individuals with unique characteristics, structures, experiences, and backgrounds (Aldridge et al., 2015, 2016). Remember, differences do *not* equate to deficits.

Cultural differences should not routinely translate into disabilities. Far too often, however, belonging to a particular racial/ethnic group results in an automatic assumption that the child will behave in certain ways. Possible reasons for this situation are that differences are sometimes not valued or are easily misunderstood, while in other instances it may be the direct result of prejudice and stereotyping. This frequently leads to the overrepresentation of children from minority populations in some special education programs (such as those for individuals with intellectual disability) and an underrepresentation in others (such as programs for the gifted and talented). The issue of over- and underrepresentation of children of color has been a long-standing concern among educators. Although there is a myriad of possible reasons for this relationship, it is perhaps best understood as a relationship between family socioeconomic status and disability rather than being an issue of disability and minority group status per se (Gargiulo & Bouck, 2021). Report after report routinely indicates an overrepresentation of children from minority groups living in poverty (Children's Defense Fund, 2019, 2021). Poverty contributes to limited access to health care, poor nutrition, and inadequate living conditions, among other adverse circumstances. All of these variables increase the probability of the young child being at risk for future learning and development difficulties. Cultural and language differences only exacerbate the child's needs and heighten the likelihood of them requiring special education services.

As the number of infants, toddlers, preschoolers, and early primary students with delays and disabilities continues to grow, one can reasonably anticipate a corresponding increase in the number of young children with delays and disabilities from culturally diverse groups. Unfortunately, the diversity of the teaching workforce has failed to keep pace with the increasing number of children representing culturally and linguistically diverse backgrounds. Educators today simply do not reflect the diversity of their students (Gollnick & Chinn, 2021; Pollard, 2016). Over the years, the racial profile of America's teachers has generally remained fairly constant. Federal statistics suggest that the overwhelming majority of teachers (approximately 79 percent) are white, while about 7 percent are African American, and the remaining 12 percent are Hispanic or represent other racial groups (Taie & Goldring, 2020). This means that those working in early intervention and early childhood special education programs, most of whom are white, should exhibit heightened cultural sensitivity as they work with an increasingly culturally diverse population of children. This will present many unique challenges to early childhood special educators. Cultural differences may present themselves in several ways. Examples of some of the issues that may confront professionals include cultural interpretations of the etiology of disability, the family's perception of the child with a delay or disability, the perceived value of early intervention and early childhood special education services, child-rearing practices, family strengths and coping strategies, medical practices and traditions, the role of family members, and the acceptance of "outsiders" who help with the child's care and education (Hanson & Espinosa, 2016; Lynch & Hanson, 2011). It would not be uncommon for the best intentions of professionals to be misinterpreted due to their failure to consider the family's value system and cultural traditions.

Many years ago, Hanson et al. (1990) recognized the difficulty of the task confronting early childhood special educators as they work with families of culturally and linguistically diverse children. Their concerns are still valid today. These experts believe that professionals serving young children with delays and disabilities and their families must not only acknowledge different cultural perspectives but also learn "how to work effectively within the boundaries that are comfortable for the family" (p. 117). This will require that service providers become ethnically competent. It is not necessary, however, for the professional to know everything about a particular culture to provide sensitive and appropriate services (Hanson, 2011). What is often necessary is an attitude of openness and respect for the many beliefs, values, practices, and behaviors presented by the children and their families. Service providers who are open and eager to learn, respectful of and responsive to differences, and willing to conduct honest and reflective self-examinations and make changes when necessary are capable of developing cultural competence (Gollnick & Chinn, 2021; Lustig et al., 2018).

The importance of early childhood special educators demonstrating cultural awareness, sensitivity, and responsiveness cannot be overemphasized. In future years, the success of early intervention and early education efforts may well depend upon the ability of early childhood special educators to exhibit culturally sensitive behavior while providing culturally responsive services.

Table 10.1 offers examples of strategies that may help early childhood special educators work effectively with culturally diverse families. Important to realize, of course, is that no list of ideas can guarantee that services to young children with delays and disabilities and their families will be provided in a culturally responsive fashion.

TABLE 10.1 ■ Recommendations for Providing Families With Culturally Responsive Services

1. Provide information using the family's desired language and preferred means of communication—written notes, calls, informal meetings, etc.
2. When appropriate, recognize that extended family members often play a key role in a child's educational development. Give deference to key decision makers in the family.
3. Use culturally competent interpreters who are not only familiar with the language but also knowledgeable about educational issues and the special education process.
4. Seek cultural informants from the local community who can assist early childhood special educators in understanding culturally relevant variables such as nonverbal communication patterns, child-rearing strategies, gender roles, academic expectations, medical practices, and specific folkways that might affect the family's relationship with professionals.
5. Attend social events and other functions held in the local community.
6. With the help of other parents or volunteers, develop a survival vocabulary of key words and phrases in the family's native language.
7. Address parents and other caregivers as "Mr.," "Ms.," or "Mrs." rather than using first names. Formality and respect are essential, especially when speaking with older members of the family.
8. In arranging meetings, be sensitive to possible barriers such as time conflicts, transportation difficulties, and child care issues.
9. Conduct meetings, if necessary, in family-friendly settings such as local community centers or houses of worship.
10. Invite community volunteers to serve as cultural liaisons between the program or school and the child's family.

Source: R. Gargiulo and E. Bouck, *Special Education in Contemporary Society*, 7th ed. (Thousand Oaks, CA: Sage, 2021), p.118.

Early Childhood Special Education and Linguistic Diversity

As described earlier in this chapter, more than one out of five (22 percent) children older than the age of five speak a language other than English at home. This means that there are approximately 11.7 million children enrolled in schools whose primary language is not English (Kids Count Data Center, 2023a). Of course, the critical question now confronting early childhood special educators and other service providers is how to best meet the educational needs of these children who represent a very heterogeneous group of learners. Children whose first language is not English are typically identified as an English learner (EL). Other professionals, however, prefer the label *limited English proficient*, the term incorporated in IDEA 2004. Because the latter term could be viewed by some as disparaging or derogatory, the more contemporary term, EL (a term codified in federal legislation, PL 114–95, the Every Student Succeeds Act), is used.

Some early childhood programs and school districts have chosen to meet the challenge of serving ELs via an instructional approach known as **bilingual education**. Simply defined, bilingual education is "an educational strategy whereby students whose first language is not English are instructed primarily through their native language while developing their competency and proficiency in English" (Gargiulo & Bouck, 2021, p. 79). Although this may initially appear to be a promising solution, it is not without controversy. Thirty-two states have enacted legislation or passed constitutional amendments establishing English as the "official" language of their state (U.S. English, 2022), while several other states are considering such legislation. Five states prohibit bilingual education in their schools (Baca & Baca, 2004).

Bilingual Education: Concepts and Characteristics[1]

The primary purpose of bilingual education is not to teach English or a second language, per se, but rather to assist children with limited skills in English by delivering instruction using the language the children know best and then reinforcing this information through English. Bilingual education also promotes cognitive as well as affective development and cultural enrichment (Gollnick & Chinn, 2013). Although it is not explicitly stated, another principal goal of bilingual education is to provide increased educational opportunities for students whose native language is not English. It is interesting to note that, contrary to popular belief, the original aim of bilingual education was not to advocate bilingualism but rather to promote the acquisition of English language skills. Bilingual education is believed to be the most effective way for a non-English-speaking person to become literate in English.

Research evidence on the effectiveness of bilingual education strongly suggests that bilingual education is the most appropriate approach for working with children who have limited skills and proficiency with the English language. Greater academic gains and improved language skills can be directly attributed to bilingual education (Gollnick & Chinn, 2021). Of course, the key to effective bilingual education is to match the instructional strategy to the specific needs and background of the individual. Depending on the child's proficiency in their native language and English, different instructional models are used. Table 10.2 summarizes some of the approaches typically used with children who are bilingual.

TABLE 10.2 ■ Instructional Options for Children Who Are Bilingual
Transitional Programs
• Children are taught in pre-academic or academic content areas via their native language only until they are sufficiently competent in English; then they transition to all-English instruction. The primary goal of this program is to move children as quickly as possible to English-only classes. Many children exit after two to three years of instruction. Transitional programs are the most common instructional model; bilingual education legislation favors this approach.
Maintenance (Developmental) Programs
• These programs include a strong native language emphasis, incorporating children's cultural background into the instruction. Children maintain proficiency in their first language while receiving instruction in English. Such programs provide a long-term approach with less emphasis on leaving the program. A solid academic foundation is stressed.
Enrichment Programs
• Typically, these programs are used to introduce new languages and cultures to monolingual children.
Immersion Programs
• Immersion programs follow a "sink-or-swim" philosophy, with English language the exclusive medium of instruction; first language and culture are not incorporated.

[1] Content adapted from R. Gargiulo and D. Metcalf, *Teaching in Today's Inclusive Classrooms,* 4th ed. (Boston, MA: Cengage Learning, 2023).

English as a Second Language (ESL) Programs
• ESL programs, in which children typically receive instruction in English outside the regular classroom, are not a true form of bilingual education. The goal is to quickly develop English proficiency in bilingual students through exclusive emphasis on English for teaching and learning; native language is not used in instruction. ESL programs offer an assimilationist model with multiple variations.
Sheltered English
• Here, children receive instruction in pre-academic or academic subjects exclusively in English; no effort is made to maintain or develop proficiency in their first language. English instruction is continually monitored and modified to ensure child's comprehension. Sheltered English provides simultaneous exposure to English language and subject content matter.

Source: Adapted from R. Gargiulo and E. Bouck, *Special Education in Contemporary Society*, 7th ed. (Thousand Oaks, CA: Sage, 2021), p. 83.

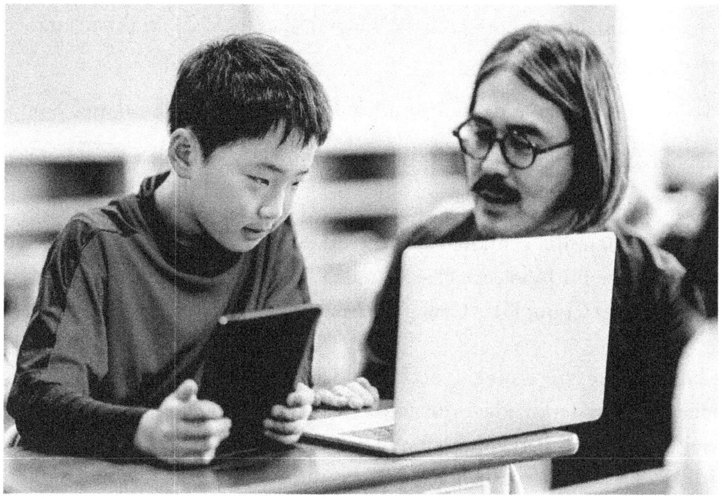

Bilingual education affords increased educational opportunities for children whose first language is not English.

iStock.com/recep-bg

Teachers of young children face the challenge of selecting the most appropriate bilingual instructional approach for young children whose primary language is not English. There is general agreement among experts in the field of bilingual education that the more opportunities young children who are bilingual have to use their newly acquired language skills with peers, family members, and others, the more proficient they will become. In comparison to classroom settings, the natural environment seems to better facilitate language development.

Another often daunting task is to distinguish between exceptionality and language differences. Delays and disabilities are often masked by language differences. Educators sometimes do not acknowledge the possibility that a child has a disability because they incorrectly assume that a child's educational struggles are the result of a lack of proficiency in English. On the other hand, a child may be placed in an early childhood special education program because of a presumed learning problem when in actuality their difficulties are a direct consequence of limited English language skills. This is a difficult issue even for the most experienced of early childhood special educators, and, unfortunately, there is no easy solution to this dilemma.

EMERGING POPULATIONS OF YOUNG CHILDREN WITH DELAYS AND DISABILITIES

The professional issues confronting today's early childhood special educators are many. Although only a select few of these challenges are identified, other issues, which seem to be a product of the times, also are affecting the lives of young children, their families, and the professionals who serve them. It is indeed unfortunate that children are not immune to the myriad of issues that are rampant in society. Homelessness, child maltreatment, and children suffering the effects of parental/caregiver substance abuse are only some of the problems facing early intervention and early childhood special education professionals. Consider the following portrait of contemporary life in the United States:

- One in thirty children in the United States experiences homelessness annually, 51 percent of whom are under five years of age.
- Fetal alcohol spectrum disorder (FASD) is recognized as one of the leading causes of intellectual disability in the United States.
- Every forty-eight seconds a child is a victim of abuse or neglect.
- 3.6 million children under the age of six lived in poverty in 2019.
- More than 675 infants are born each day into families who lack health insurance or one child every two minutes.
- Each day in America, 860 infants are born at low birth weight (less than 5.8 pounds).
- In 2022, only 75 percent of two-year-olds were immunized against preventable childhood illnesses.
- Between 3 and 10 million children are exposed to domestic violence each year (Bassuk et al., 2014; Child Witness to Violence Project, n.d.; Children's Defense Fund, 2021; Gargiulo & Bouck, 2021; Kids Count Data Center, 2023b).

The preceding data are concerning, especially when one considers the implications for early intervention and educational systems. The evidence is clear that young children throughout the U.S. are experiencing trauma at increasingly high rates. These numbers are even higher for children with disabilities. Further, there is clear documentation that trauma can impact all aspects of children's development (Chudzik et al., 2024; Corr et al., 2018). Historically, programs, schools, and services have responded to the needs of society. The challenges that are now upon us dictate, therefore, that early childhood special educators and other professionals have a greater awareness of the magnitude of the crisis and are positioned to deal effectively with changing societal conditions and the resulting changing clientele. ECSE professionals need to be better prepared in providing trauma-informed care that includes working with families, implementing classroom strategies, and supporting young children with disabilities who have experience trauma (Chudzik et al., 2024).

The goal of this section of the chapter is to highlight a few of the areas of concern and recommend strategies to support young children and their families to mitigate the effects of these issues. Selected for brief review are the topics of poverty, homelessness, child abuse and neglect, and young children with complex health care needs.

Childhood Poverty

Poverty is probably one of the most significant factors placing children at risk for developmental delays as well as affecting their success in school. Regrettably, poverty is a fact of life for too many young children in the United States. Despite tremendous national wealth, the child poverty rate in the country is one of the highest among developed countries (Children's Defense Fund, 2019; Statista, 2022). Sadly, a baby is born into poverty in the United States every 60 seconds—that's more than 1,500 infants on a daily basis. More than 15 percent of children under six years of age were poor in 2019, with more than 7 percent considered very poor (Children's Defense Fund, 2021). The 2022 federal poverty threshold for a family of four is $30,000 (U.S. Department of Health and Human Services, 2023b). Unfortunately, young children of color suffer disproportionately from the ravages of poverty. Thirty-two percent of Black children and 25 percent of Hispanic (Latino) children live in poverty. Children from these two groups are two to three times as likely to live in poverty as white or Asian children (Annie E. Casey Foundation, 2022).

Childhood poverty is associated with a multitude of perils, many of which place a child at risk of being unsuccessful in school. These factors, many of which are interrelated, include limited prenatal health care, inadequate nutrition, increased childhood illness, greater stress, substandard housing, lack of health insurance, and greater likelihood of abuse or neglect, as well as fewer school supplies and cognitively stimulating educational materials. Generally speaking, in comparison to their more economically advantaged peers, children of poverty are more likely to exhibit poor academic achievement, drop out of high school, become unemployed later in life and thereby experience economic hardships (Children's Defense Fund, 2020). Additionally, poverty-related factors place young children at higher risk for disabilities and developmental delays while also serving as impediments to securing needed services for the children and their families.

> The research is clear: Children who grow up in low-income families are less likely to successfully navigate life's challenges and achieve future success. The younger they are and the longer they are exposed to economic hardship, the higher the risk of failure. (Annie E. Casey Foundation, 2011, p. 10)

Poverty is one variable frequently associated with learning and developmental delays and disabilities.

Robert Nickelsberg/Contributor/via Getty Images

Each year that a child spends living in persistent poverty further impedes their future potential (Edelman, 2010). Very young children are the most vulnerable to economic adversity. A child's brain develops rapidly in the first three years of life, and the quality of the child's environment often will have lasting and enduring effects on later development. Cognitive, behavioral, and social difficulties are frequently evident early on and will persist without intervention (Annie E. Casey Foundation, 2011). Because the negative impact of economic deprivation on development is cumulative, children with greater exposure to poverty during childhood are less likely to escape the consequences of poverty as adults. Stated another way, young children growing up in a poor family are more likely to be poor in adulthood. Figure 10.1 illustrates some of the pervasive and detrimental effects of poverty.

Few professionals would argue that poverty will significantly affect a child's overall development and educational performance in the classroom and other environments. A growing body of research, however, suggests that poverty does not exclusively account for the academic difficulties experienced by children from low-socioeconomic backgrounds; instead, teachers' perceptions of children who experience poverty play a major role. Because no child rises to low expectations, educators who anticipate mediocre performance from their students will oftentimes not be disappointed. It is imperative, therefore, that early childhood special education professionals (and all teachers) maintain high academic expectations for *all* the students they serve regardless of the child's economic background (Smith et al., 2018).

FIGURE 10.1 ■ Impact of Poverty on Family Life

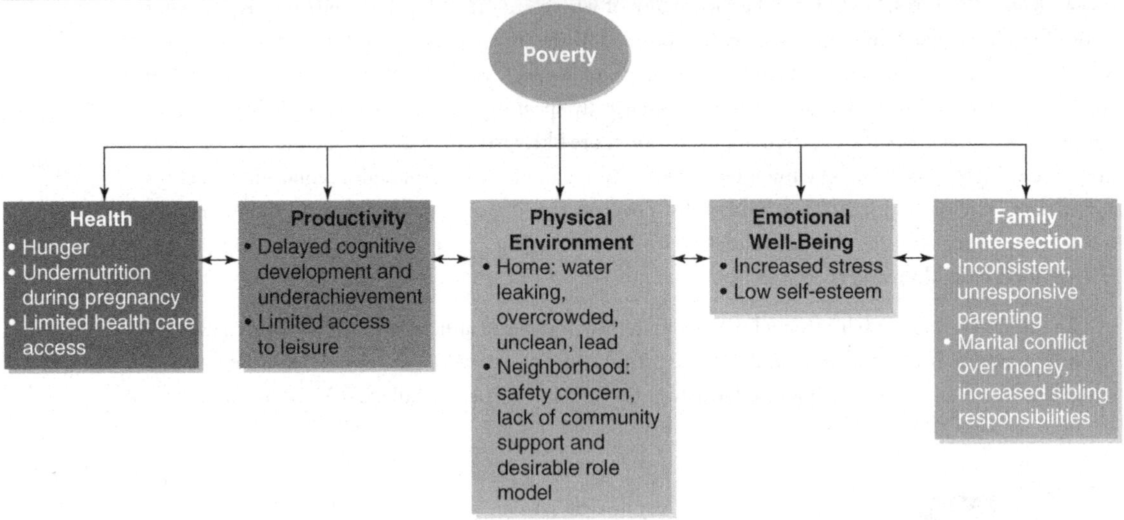

Source: J. Park, A. Turnbull, and H. Turnbull, "Impact of Poverty on Quality of Life in Families of Children with Disabilities," *Exceptional Children, 68*(2), 2002, p. 154.

Homelessness

A frequent social malady associated with the deleterious effects of poverty is homelessness. Obviously, not all children who are poor are homeless, but the link between homelessness and poverty is substantial. Homelessness is a tragic and growing phenomenon in the United States. Over the years, the "face" of homelessness has gradually changed. Historically, adult males were the primary group of citizens without permanent shelter. Today, however, families with children constitute a growing and substantial segment of homeless Americans. Statistics suggest that families account for 37 percent of the homeless population and 50 percent of the population residing in shelters. More families experience homelessness in America than in any other developed nation. One in thirty children in the United States experience homelessness annually. More than 2.5 million children are homeless each year; 51 percent are under the age of five (Doorways, 2022). Of course, the transient status of families who are homeless leads to a significant problem of underreporting the actual incidence of homelessness. Many of the families who are homeless are headed by young, single mothers with two young children. These mothers typically have limited education, few job skills, and minimal work experience (Bassuk et al., 2015).

In its simplest terms, a homeless child is any child who lacks a fixed, regular, and adequate nighttime residence as defined in federal legislation (PL 114–95, Every Student Succeeds Act). Some examples of inadequate living arrangements are individuals and families who reside in abandoned buildings, parks, campgrounds, automobiles, bus/train stations, motels, or emergency/transitional shelters. Essentially, homelessness is a lack of permanent housing resulting from a wide variety of reasons such as a lack of affordable housing, unemployment, poverty, domestic violence, and mental illness (National Coalition for the Homeless, 2023).

The experience of being homeless is especially destructive for children. Due to their homelessness, they are frequently absent from early programs or schools, and when they can attend, many of these children evidence learning problems in addition to social/emotional difficulties. The consequences of homelessness, however, are especially devastating for young children. Homelessness is portrayed as a breeding ground for disabilities. Many young children who are homeless often exhibit inattentiveness, frustration, aggression, and withdrawal, and developmental delays (Gargiulo, 2006; Morrison et al., 2022). Homelessness also extracts a significant toll on the physical and emotional well-being of young children. This profile of characteristics often contributes to many of these children being eligible for early intervention or special education services; however, the transient nature of their families' lifestyles frequently prohibits the delivery of needed services.

Children who are homeless also encounter numerous obstacles to securing educational services. Barriers confronting students who are homeless

> come in many forms, including school policies pertaining to residency requirements, immunization records, transportation issues, availability of school records, guardianship requirements, and in some instances, a disregard for federal mandates coupled with a lack of parental understanding of their child's educational rights. (Gargiulo, 2006, p. 359)

Families with children are the fastest growing group of homeless Americans.

AP Photo/Gregory Bull

Early childhood special educators and other professionals need to be cognizant of the warning signs of possible homelessness. Table 10.3 portrays *potential* indicators of homelessness. Because of the tremendous variability among young children who are homeless, it is essential that early childhood special education professionals remember that individual children may vary greatly from these general characteristics.

TABLE 10.3 ■ Representative Warning Signs of Possible Homelessness

Behavioral and Social Indicators
• Poor self-esteem
• Extreme shyness
• Difficulty trusting people
• Reluctance to establish relationships with peers and teachers
• Fear of abandonment
• Anxiety late in the school day
• "Old" beyond years
• Clinging behavior

(Continued)

TABLE 10.3 ■ Representative Warning Signs of Possible Homelessness (*Continued*)
• Difficulty socializing with others
• Need for immediate gratification
Health and Hygiene Indicators
• Wearing same clothes on consecutive school days
• Poor personal hygiene
• Fatigue
• Chronic hunger
• Unmet dental/medical needs
• Inappropriate attire for season or weather
• Heightened vulnerability to colds, flu, earaches, or respiratory problems
Educational and Learning Indicators
• Short attention span
• Poor organizational skills
• Lack of basic school supplies
• Incomplete or missing homework
• Excessive absences or tardiness
• History of multiple school attendance
• Lack of participation in school trips or after-school activities
• Gaps in academic skills
• Loss of textbooks on a regular basis
• Concern for security of personal belongings and school supplies
• Refusal of social invitations from classmates
• Inability to recall current address

Source: Adapted from the National Center for Homeless Education, *Potential Warning Signs of Homelessness.* https://nche.ed.gov/wp-content/uploads/2019/12/Common-Signs-of-Homelessness.pdf

Educational Rights of Children Who Are Homeless[2]

The Stewart B. McKinney Homeless Assistance Act (PL 100–77) was the first, and remains the only, federal law focused specifically on the educational needs of children who are homeless. Enacted in 1987 as part of the reauthorization of the Elementary and Secondary Education Act, this legislation was intended to ensure that children who are homeless have access to a free appropriate public education, including a preschool education. The McKinney Act did not establish separate educational programs for children who are homeless; rather, it reinforced their right to participate in existing public school programs. In November 1990, the original legislation was amended by PL 101–645, which specifically addressed the obligations of state and local education agencies in ensuring that the educational needs

[2] Adapted from R. Gargiulo, "Homeless and Disabled: Rights, Responsibilities, and Recommendations for Serving Young Children with Special Needs," *Early Childhood Special Education Journal, 33*(5), 2006, pp. 357-362.

of children who are homeless were considered. It is interesting, however, that this legislation is silent regarding children with disabilities who are homeless.

The McKinney Act has been reauthorized and amended several times since 1990: first in 1994 via the Improving America's Schools Act (PL 103–382), second by the enactment of the McKinney-Vento Homeless Education Assistance Improvements Act of 2001 incorporated as part of the No Child Left Behind Act (PL 107–110), and in 2015 by the enactment of PL 114–95 (Every Student Succeeds Act).

Collectively, these amendments provide considerable protection to and ensure the educational rights of children who are homeless. In addition to mandating a public education, children who are homeless are entitled to the same programs and services as their housed peers, including preschool programs (e.g., Head Start, Even Start), early intervention and special education, compensatory education, and after-school and extended-school-year opportunities. These laws further indicate that simply being homeless is not sufficient reason to separate children from the educational environment.

The enactment of IDEA 2004 specifically addresses the needs of children who are homeless. This legislation incorporates the McKinney-Vento definition of homelessness and requires states to locate, identify, and evaluate children with disabilities who are homeless. Additionally, if children who are homeless have an existing individualized education program (IEP), early childhood programs and schools are mandated to provide services as described in the previously developed IEP. Infants and toddlers who are homeless but who have delays and disabilities are also eligible to receive early intervention services, as appropriate (Santos, 2017).

The Role of Early Childhood Programs and Schools

Early childhood special educators and other professionals need to be especially sensitive to the plight of children who are homeless. Eddowes (1994) once described schools as "safe harbors" for these children. Besides offering appropriate educational experiences, the early childhood program or classroom becomes an island of safety; early childhood programs and schools can also provide special services like bathing facilities, clean clothes, and nutritious meals.

The importance of an education for children who are homeless cannot be overstated. It represents one of the most effective strategies available for overcoming the detrimental effects of homelessness. For children who are homeless, attending school might be the most normal activity they will experience. The early childhood program or classroom is more than just a learning environment; it becomes an island of safety and support, a place to make friends, and a place to have personal space (Driver & Spady, 2013). Yet young children without a permanent address need more than just access to an education; they require individually tailored instructional programs designed to compensate for negative life experiences. At this point in time, an appropriate education is probably the most promising intervention tactic available. It is interesting to note that educational programs and schools are the only institutions in the country that are legally responsible for identifying and serving children who are homeless (Bassuk et al., 2014). Table 10.4 offers several suggestions for how early childhood special educators can meet the needs of children who are homeless.

FEATURE 10.1 REPRESENTATIVE WEB RESOURCES

- **National Association for the Education of Homeless Children and Youth,** www.naehcy.org
- **National Center on Family Homelessness,** www.air.org/center/national-center-family-homelessness
- **National Center for Homeless Education,** https://nche.ed.gov
- **National Law Center on Homelessness and Poverty,** www.nlchp.org

TABLE 10.4 ■ What Early Childhood Special Educators Can Do to Support Children Who Are Homeless to Succeed in School

Children Experiencing Homelessness May	Early Childhood Special Educators Can Help By	Early Childhood Special Educators Can Use The Following Strategies
● Need positive peer relationships	● Facilitating a sense of belonging	● Provide cooperative learning activities. ● Assign a welcome buddy to support transition to a new environment. ● Provide activities that promote acceptance of diversity. ● Maintain a relationship when the child/family leaves by providing self-addressed stamped envelopes and paper/postcards.
● Move frequently and lack educational program continuity	● Addressing individual learning needs	● Immediately begin to plan for the next transition. ● Assess present academic levels quickly. ● Provide necessary assistance/tutoring. ● Uphold challenging academic expectations. ● Contact the program or school previously attended to help with placement decisions. ● Expeditiously follow up on any special education referrals or services. ● Remind parents to keep copies of educational records and IFSPs/IEPs to share with a new school upon arrival.
● Come to class/program unprepared	● Meeting basic needs in the classroom	● Provide school supplies if necessary (crayons, pencils, paper, etc.) that can be shared with the child privately. ● Make sure the child has a chance to have a class job/role. ● Avoid the removal of the child's possessions as a disciplinary measure. ● Share books and materials with the local shelter.
● Have high levels of depression, anxiety, and low self-esteem due to the stress of homelessness	● Addressing these needs and related behavioral considerations	● Reinforce positive behaviors. ● Teach and model skills such as problem solving, critical thinking, and cooperative learning. ● Support and recognize individual accomplishments. ● Maintain the privacy of the child. ● Enlist support of community organizations and health and social services agencies. ● Enlist services of program or school personnel (e.g., service coordinator, counselor, school psychologist).
● Live in shelters and homes that house more than one family and are often noisy	● Compensating in the classroom	● Provide quiet time during program or school hours. ● Have a new student packet containing a few school supplies and a welcome card from the class for all new children. ● Allow the child to do homework at school. ● Assign the child a personal space. ● Have a safe place for the child's belongings.
● Have parents who may be embarrassed by their homelessness	● Respecting and supporting parents or other family members	● Make families feel valued as partners in their children's education. ● Provide parents with assessment results and related goals and objectives prior to their next move. ● Provide an informal support system in which they feel it is safe to discuss parenting issues or concerns. ● Allow parents extra time to pay for trips or assist in accessing resources to help pay for special events if assistance is desired. ● Help parents become familiar with services available for homeless children, including outside agencies.

Source: B. Driver and P. Spady, 2013. *What Educators Can Do: Homeless Children and Youth.* Project HOPE—Virginia, College of William and Mary, Williamsburg, VA.

Child Abuse and Neglect

Child abuse and neglect have reached epidemic proportions in the United States. On an almost daily basis, the media expose us to accounts of various acts of cruelty inflicted on children by adult perpetrators. Tragic illustrations of these acts include the following:

- A father [who] poured lighter fluid on his child's arm and lit it
- A 42-month-old child [who] had been beaten and sexually abused by a babysitter
- A small child [who] was kicked in the face for simply making a noise
- A child [who] was left alone in a locked car on a 90° summer day
- A parent [who] failed to regularly send her child to school
- A mother [who] refused to seek medical care for her children (Gargiulo, 1990, p. 1)

EI/ECSE practitioners have a legal and, perhaps more importantly, a moral and ethical obligation to see that such actions do not continue. Abuse flourishes due to secrecy, privacy, and a lack of attention. Greater awareness and active involvement on the part of early childhood special educators can help break the cycle of child abuse and may even save the life of a child.

Definitions

How does one define the terms *abuse* and *neglect?* What might seem to be a simple task is actually quite difficult due to varying accepted practices of childrearing. Societal and community standards generally dictate what is considered abuse. Most people, for example, oppose the beating of children; yet, in some families, parents use physical punishment as a routine means of disciplining their children. Corporal punishment is still a very common disciplinary strategy in schools. In fact, nineteen states permit school authorities to administer corporal punishment to children (Gershoff & Font, 2016).

One simple way of distinguishing between physical abuse and neglect is to view the former as an act of *commission*, while the latter implies an act of *omission*. The four major types of child maltreatment include physical abuse, neglect, emotional abuse, and sexual abuse. Although the definitions of these terms vary according to individual state law, many definitions reflect the following thinking. Physical abuse is an act of commission. It refers to an assault on a child designed to cause physical injury or harm. Examples include hitting, kicking, shaking, stabbing, and other nonaccidental inflictions. Spanking is usually considered a disciplinary action; however, if the child is injured or bruised, it can be classified as abusive.

Neglect is an act of omission and involves a variety of caregiver behaviors that include such things as abandonment, inadequate physical supervision, failure to provide necessities (shelter, adequate nourishment, attention and affection, clothing), and the failure to provide necessary medical treatment or require a child to attend school.

Emotional abuse is a difficult term to define and can be an act of commission or omission. It is generally distinguished by a constellation of interactions instigated by the caregiver and designed to be psychologically destructive for the child. Verbal attacks on the child's self-esteem and self-image by constant screaming, criticizing, and humiliation illustrates one form of emotional maltreatment. Rejection and inadequate nurturance also define emotional abuse, the effect of which is cumulative.

A description of sexual abuse, which is an act of commission, contains two parts: sexual abuse and sexual exploitation. Gargiulo and Metcalf (2023) emphasize that sexual abuse lives in a veil of secrecy and a conspiracy of silence. It represents the most underreported form of abuse. Sexual abuse includes rape, incest, indecent exposure, and inappropriate fondling, along with sexual exploitation via prostitution or pornography.

Federal statutes also define child abuse and neglect (see Public Law 93-247, the Child Abuse Prevention and Treatment Act). Unfortunately, like state law, much of the legislation is ambiguous and lacks precision when describing types of child maltreatment.

Prevalence

The number of cases of child abuse and neglect is increasing at an alarming rate. It is difficult, however, to obtain accurate and reliable data because definitions vary from state to state and because there is a significant problem of underreporting. These problems notwithstanding, national surveys reveal that each day in America 5 children die because of abuse or neglect while more than 651,000 children experienced some type of maltreatment in 2019. (Children's Defense Fund, 2021). An estimated 3.98 million referrals to Child Protective Services alleging child maltreatment were recorded in fiscal year 2021 (U.S. Department of Health and Human Services, 2023a). By way of comparison, only 1.9 million cases of abuse or neglect were filed in 1985, and fewer than 700,000 were recorded in 1976 (National Center on Child Abuse and Neglect, 1986).

Child abuse and neglect can occur in all families—ignoring racial, religious, ethnic, and socioeconomic boundaries. It equally occurs in urban, suburban, and rural communities. Approximately eight out of ten perpetrators are parents acting alone or with someone else. Neglect is the most common form of child maltreatment (76 percent), with approximately 17 percent of children being physically abused and slightly more than 9 percent experiencing sexual abuse. Almost three out of ten victims (28.6 percent) of abuse or neglect are between birth and two years of (U.S. Department of Health and Human Services, 2022a).

Child Characteristics

Child abuse requires three elements—the perpetrator, the victim, and a precipitating crisis, like the loss of employment or severe health problems. All parents have the potential to be abusive, and some children are more vulnerable to abuse and neglect than others. The focus here is on the role that the child plays in the child maltreatment triangle.

Over the years, research (Baladerian et al., 2013; Carr & Santos, 2017; Division for Early Childhood, 2016; Legano et al., 2021; Stalker & McArthur, 2012) has suggested that individuals with disabilities, but especially children, are particularly vulnerable to abuse. According to Gargiulo (1990), some of the specific variables that heighten a child's vulnerability include the following:

- Low birth weight
- Intellectual disability
- Prematurity
- Orthopedic impairments (cerebral palsy, spina bifida)
- Emotional/behavioral disorders
- Developmental delays
- Provocative or unmanageable behavior (colic, hyperactivity)
- Impairment in mother–infant bonding
- Language and speech delays
- Impaired social skills

An intriguing question that frequently arises is whether a particular characteristic, such as intellectual disability or hyperactivity, is the cause or consequence of abuse. A conclusive answer, however, is not currently available. Contemporary thought suggests that some children are part of a reciprocal process whereby specific behaviors provoke abuse, which in turn exacerbates the situation and thus gives rise to additional maltreatment. One must remember, however, that a child's characteristics or actions, in and of themselves, do not cause abuse. Specific individual traits are only one factor in the formula for abuse. Child abuse is the outcome of the interplay of parental/caregiver characteristics, cultural factors, environmental considerations, and a precipitating event. It is rare that the etiology of abuse can be linked to a sole condition (Child Welfare Information Gateway, 2018). The interrelationship among these variables is illustrated in Figure 10.2.

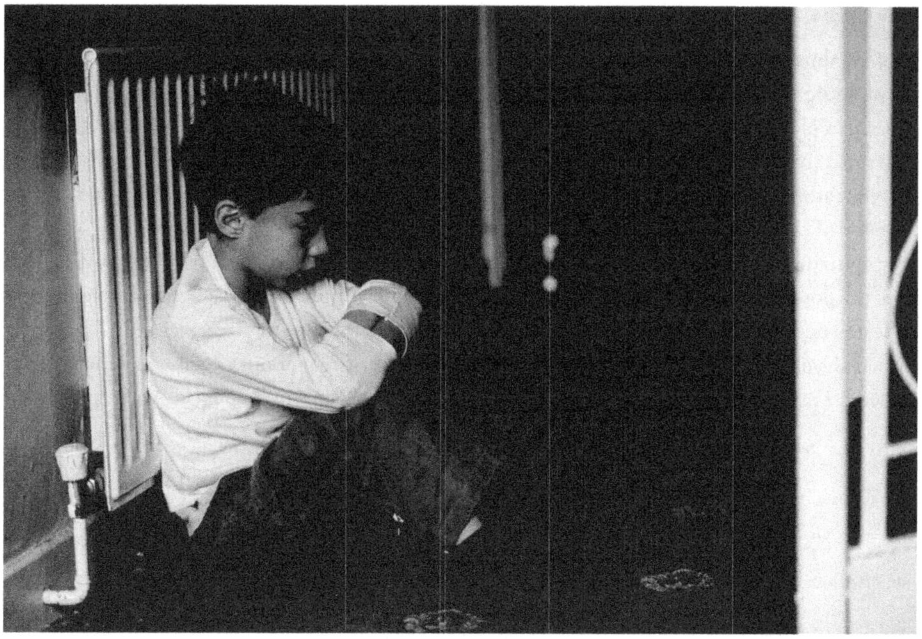

Instances of child abuse and neglect have increased dramatically.

iStock.com/fiorigianluigi

FIGURE 10.2 ■ A Model of the Interaction of Primary Factors Contributing to Parental Physical Child Abuse

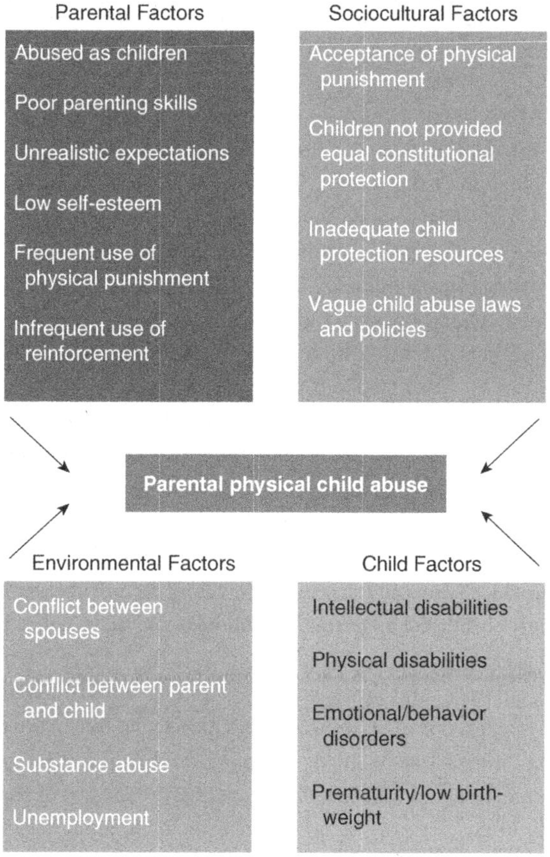

Source: T. Zipoli, "Child Abuse and Children with Handicaps," *Remedial and Special Education*, 7(2), p. 42. Copyright ©, 1986 Sage Publications, Inc. Reprinted with permission.

A Role for Schools and the Early Childhood Special Educator

The toll of abuse and neglect on young children is almost unimaginable. It affects them emotionally, socially, physically, and intellectually (Hooper & Umansky, 2014). Early childhood special educators, however, can play a vital role in the identification and prevention of child abuse and neglect. They may well be the only professionals who have daily and continuous contact with the child. Early childhood special educators are in a unique position, therefore, to intervene and assist in breaking the intergenerational cycle of child abuse and neglect.

Recognizing the signs of abuse and neglect can sometimes be difficult. Table 10.5 provides a list of some of the possible indicators of child abuse and neglect. If a number of these signs are evident or there are repeated occurrences, then you should be alert to the possibility of maltreatment.

What should an EI/ECSE practitioner do if a child tells them about possible instances of abuse or neglect? The following suggestions (Morrison et al., 2022) should help guide the response to the child:

- Remain calm. A child may retract information or stop talking if they sense a strong reaction.
- Believe the child. Children rarely make up stories about abuse.
- Listen without passing judgment. Most children know their abusers and often have conflicted feelings.
- Tell the child that you are glad that they told you.
- Assure the child that the abuse is not their fault.
- Do what you can to ensure that the child is safe from further abuse.
- Do not investigate yourself; instead, call the police or Child Protective Services. The National Child Abuse Hotline is 1–800–4-A-Child (1–800–422–4453).

Every state has child abuse reporting laws. Teachers, in fact, are mandated reporters. They are legally required to report their *suspicion* of instances of abuse and neglect to the appropriate law enforcement agency or child protective service. The purpose of this legislation is to protect abused and neglected children, not to punish the perpetrators. To make a report, proof is not necessary. Reasonable cause to suspect maltreatment is all that is required. Educators who act in good faith and without malice are protected from civil or criminal liability. Failure to report could lead to legal difficulties for the teacher. Fines, misdemeanor charges, and in some instances charges of negligence are possible. Perhaps the greatest tragedy, however, is the child who suffers and possibly dies because of inaction by a teacher or other professional.

Clearly, all early childhood programs and schools should have a written policy outlining the steps to be taken in recording suspected episodes of abuse and neglect. Schools are also logical places for prevention programs to begin. Examples of such efforts include professional development activities for staff and administrators focusing on recognizing child maltreatment and reporting requirements (Carr & Santos, 2017) in addition to offering parent education programs (possibly sponsored by the parent–teacher organization) providing hints and suggestions on child care, behavior management techniques, and parenting skills. Early childhood programs and schools can also spearhead community awareness programs on abuse and neglect.

Obviously, the eradication of child abuse and neglect is not possible. Informed and concerned early childhood special education professionals, however, can play a vital role in attempts to bring this crisis under control. By being informed and vigilant, attempts can be made to improve the quality of life for many young children with delays and disabilities, and maybe the veil of secrecy surrounding child abuse and neglect will be lifted.

TABLE 10.5 ■ Examples of Physical and Behavioral Indicators of Child Abuse and Neglect

Physical Indicators	Behavioral Indicators
Physical Abuse	
• Bruises and cuts • Burn marks • Lacerations and abrasions • Head injuries • Skeletal injuries • Fractures, sprains	• Fearful of physical contact • Overly compliant, passive • Wearing concealing clothing • Unwillingness to go home • Wariness of adults • Behavioral extremes—overly aggressive or very withdrawn • Lacks reasonable explanation for injury • Complains about pain or soreness
Neglect	
• Poor personal hygiene • Inadequate or inappropriate clothing • Lack of needed medical/dental care • Abandonment • Lack of supervision • Complaints of constant hunger • Excessive school absence and/or tardiness	• Hoarding or stealing of food • Lethargic, falls asleep in school • Irregular school attendance • Rejection by classmates due to offensive body odor • Dirty clothes, wears same attire for several days
Emotional Abuse	
• Emotional abuse is rarely manifested via physical signs. It is usually associated with other forms of maltreatment. The individual's behavior is often the best clue.	• Lack of positive self-image • Low self-esteem • Depression • Sleep and/or eating disorder • Overly fearful, vigilant • Behavioral extremes—overly compliant/passive or aggressive/demanding • Poor peer relationships • Suicidal ideation • Temper tantrums • Enuresis

(Continued)

TABLE 10.5 ■ Examples of Physical and Behavioral Indicators of Child Abuse and Neglect (*Continued*)

Sexual Abuse	
Physical Indicators	**Behavioral Indicators**
• Torn, stained, or bloody undergarments	• Sexually sophisticated/mature
• Pain in genital area	• Sexual themes during play
• Presence of sexually transmitted diseases	• Poor peer relationships
• Pregnancy	• Seductive behavior
• Difficulty with urination	• Irregular school attendance
• Presence of semen	• Reluctance to participate in physical activities
• Difficulty walking or sitting	• Infantile behavior
	• Fear of physical contact
	• Statements of sexual abuse

Source: Adapted from R. Gargiulo, "Child Abuse and Neglect: An Overview," in R. Goldman and R. Gargiulo (Eds.), *Children at Risk* (Austin, TX: Pro-Ed, 1990). Pp. 19–23.

FEATURE 10.2 REPRESENTATIVE WEB RESOURCES

For additional information about child maltreatment, access the following representative websites:

- **Child Abuse Prevention Network**, www.child-abuse.com
- **Child Welfare Information Gateway**, www.childwelfare.gov
- **Childhelp**, www.childhelp.org
- **Prevent Child Abuse America**, www.preventchildabuse.org

Young Children With Complex Health Care Needs

There are many health issues that affect the quality of life of young children. Increasingly, early childhood special education professionals are encountering children with a variety of infectious and chronic conditions. Schools and programs, therefore, are playing larger roles in the health care arena. One result of this expanded role is new professional and personal challenges that now confront the early childhood special educator.

Attention here is placed on young children with complex health care needs sometimes identified as "medically fragile." This population is increasing due to rapid medical and technological advances that are saving lives and improving the quality of life for many of these children. As this population continues to grow, early childhood programs and schools will encounter new challenges in service delivery as these children increasingly seek educational services and supports. It is likely, therefore, that EI/ECSE professionals will provide services to children with significant health needs at some point during their careers. The rights of children with complex health care needs to receive an appropriate education in the least restrictive environment is guaranteed by statute (IDEA and Section 504 of the Rehabilitation Act of 1973 [PL 93–112]) and reinforced by substantial legal precedents (e.g., *Irving Independent School District v. Tatro; Timothy W. v. Rochester, New Hampshire, School District;* and *Cedar Rapids School District v. Garret F.*).

Who are these children who will present early childhood special educators with personal and professional challenges? This question defies a simple answer and there are several reasons for this difficulty. The first reason is the absence of a universally accepted definition, the second reason is due to differences in terminology, and the final reason is the complexity of health issues usually found within this population. Early childhood special educators will frequently encounter descriptive labels such as *chronically ill, technologically dependent, medically fragile*, or the IDEA term of *other health impaired*. Contemporary thinking suggests, however, that these labels are often inappropriate as they perpetuate stereotypes and imply inaccurate information about the actual health status of these individuals. The preferred term among professionals, therefore, is **children with complex health care needs** (Turchi & Giardino, 2019), which generally refers to "students who require complex health procedures, special therapy or specialized medical equipment/supplies to enhance or sustain their lives during the school day" (American Federation of Teachers, 2009, p. 1). This thinking keeps the primary focus on the child while their unique health needs are secondary.

Part of the problem in clearly understanding this population is the wide diversity of medical conditions embraced by the concept of young children with complex health care needs. These children do not present a single set of characteristics. Included in this group are children with chronic problems such as asthma and those with physical deformities, congenital defects, infectious conditions, heredity difficulties, and life-threatening illnesses (Deiner, 2013). Due to the great variety of conditions represented, generalizations are difficult to make. Yet, one of the keys to working with this group of children is for early childhood special educators to appreciate the highly individualized nature of each child's condition. Although children might share a similar medical condition—muscular dystrophy, for example—the course and severity of the disease or illness and its impact on the child and their family is uniquely personal. Consequently, educational programming must be determined on an individual basis.

Medical and educational services for young children with complex health care needs reflect the contemporary belief that early childhood experiences should be as inclusive as possible. This philosophy has contributed to the growth of community-based care and the opportunity for these children to attend a variety of early childhood programs in their local communities (Noonan & McCormick, 2014).

As Downing (2008) stated, the inclusion of children with complex health care needs in early childhood settings should be seen as the norm rather than the exception. Yet such a decision requires that families, early childhood special educators, and other professionals thoughtfully weigh medical opinion about possible harm to the child with the desire to have the child participate in typical school activities. Any placement decision obviously has both positive and negative features, and the advantages and disadvantages must be carefully considered (Hallahan et al., 2023).

An integral aspect of providing services for these children, regardless of the educational setting, is the development of a detailed health care plan (see Figure 10.3). This document, which is a critical

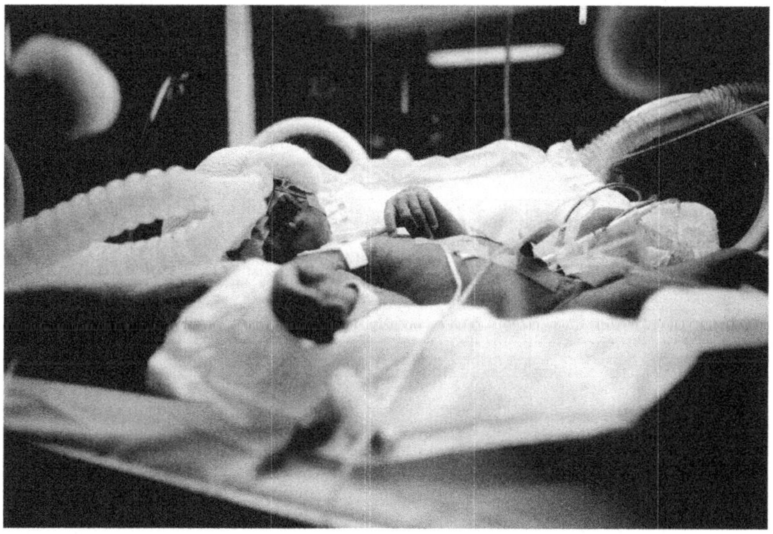

Children with complex health needs often present challenges to programs and schools.

Barbara Alper/Archive Photos/Getty Images

FIGURE 10.3 ■ Sample Individualized Health Care Plan

Student: ______ DOB: ______ Age: ______ Grade/Class: ______

Primary Caregivers: ______ Daytime Phone: ______

______ Daytime Phone: ______

Primary Health Care Provider: ______ Phone: ______

Date Plan Approved: ______ Frequency of Plan Review: ______ Date Plan Last Updated: ______

Team Members

Team Member Signature	*Title*	*Role/Responsibility*	*Phone*	*Mobile Phone*

Alternate Team Members

AlternateTeam Member Name	*Title*	*Role/Responsibility*	*Phone*	*Mobile Phone*

Training Requirements

Team Member	*Health Care Procedure, Assistive Technology, or Medical Equipment Training Required*	*Frequency of Initial and Ongoing Training*	*Date of Last Training*

Brief Medical History

Current Medical Condition

Positioning or handling requirements:
Precautions/possible adverse reactions to health care procedures:
Restricted activities:
Behavior considerations:

Medical Management

Description of Health Care Procedure	*Frequency and Number of Repetitions*	*Location*

Medical Management Log

Description of Health Care Procedure	*Frequency and Number of Repetitions*	*Location*	*Date/Time*	*Authorized Caregiver*	*Signature of Caregiver*

Feeding and Nutritional Needs

Special Feeding Instructions: Amount of Food; Temperature of Food; Number of Feedings, etc.	*Nutrition Of fered*	*Frequency and Time*	*Notable Concerns*

Feeding and Nutritional Needs Log

Nutrition Of fered	*Date*	*Time*	*Notable Concerns*	*Caregiver Signature*

Special Equipment and Devices

Assistive Technology Device or Medical Equipment Required	*Details on the Use and Maintenance of Apparatus*

Transportation Needs

Transportation Needs	*Destination*	*Provider of Transportation*	*Provider Phone*
Transportation to School			
Transportation From School			
Transportation Around School			
Field Trips			
Emergency Transportation			
Other			

Adaptations/Accommodations Req'd: ☐ None ☐ Bus Lift ☐ Seat Belt ☐ Wheel Chair Lockdown ☐ Chest Harness ☐ Booster Seat
☐ Other: ______________ Method of Mobility: ______________

Family/Caregiver Requests

Health Status Profile Leading to Emergency Interventions

Description of Change/Symptoms of Distress	*Interventions*

Source: B. Rueve, M. Robinson, L. Worthington, and R. Gargiulo, "Children with Special Health Needs in Inclusive Settings: Writing Health Care Plans," *Physical Disabilities Education and Related Services, 19*(1), 2000, pp. 17–18.

element of the student's IEP, "should contain all of the information necessary in order to provide complete medical and educational services to the child with special health needs" (Rueve et al., 2000, p. 16). Early childhood special educators must also be prepared for unforeseen circumstances, the "What do I do if" incidents, which hopefully will never materialize. A written plan for potential emergency situations should be created based on the child's particular health needs. (See Figure 10.4 for an example of an emergency medical plan.) Copies of this plan should be in the classroom and other sites frequented by the child (lunch room, school bus, playground).

FIGURE 10.4 ■ Sample Medical Emergency Plan

Student: ______________ DOB: __________ Age: __________ Grade/Class: __________

Date Plan Approved: __________ Frequency of Plan Review: __________ Date Plan Last Updated: __________

Emergency Contact Information

Emergency Contact	*Relation to Student*	*Contact for What Type of Emergency?*	*Daytime Phone*	*Mobile Phone*
	Primary Physician			
	Dentist			
	Ambulance			
	EMT			
	Hospital			
	Fire Department			
	Medical Supplier			

Emergency Procedures

Description of Medical Emergency	*What to Do*	*Location of Medication/ Equipment*	*Transportation Requirement*

Source: B. Rueve, M. Robinson, L. Worthington, and R. Gargiulo, "Children with Special Health Needs in Inclusive Settings: Writing Health Care Plans," *Physical Disabilities Education and Related Services, 19*(1), 2000, p. 22.

Providing an appropriate education to young children with unique health care needs requires collaboration and cooperation with families and the various agencies that provide the necessary services. It also requires open lines of communication with professionals from a variety of disciplines. Providing services for the child with complex health care needs, regardless of where they are delivered, is a shared responsibility. Teamwork, flexibility, and the familiar themes of individualized, inclusive, and family-centered services also apply to these children. Additionally, in-depth training is frequently required, as many early childhood special education professionals are often ill prepared to effectively meet the needs of children with complex health care needs (Mancini & Layton, 2004; Rueve et al., 2000). Several years ago, the Council for Exceptional Children (1988) recommended that personnel preparation and professional development focus on the following components to effectively serve children with significant health care needs, and they are still necessary and important for today's educators.

1. Awareness and understanding of students' health care, emotional, and educational needs
2. Knowledge of common medical and health terms
3. Knowledge of medical characteristics including etiology and implications
4. Knowledge of physical, developmental, and emotional characteristics
5. Knowledge of appropriate curricular and environmental modifications
6. Knowledge of the roles and responsibilities of the health care professional in the classroom
7. Knowledge of the importance and necessity for establishing support systems for personnel, students, and families
8. Knowledge of resources for the family (pp. 5–6)

Regardless of the medical condition presented by the child—be it pediatric AIDS, cancer, or some form of neurological disorder—these children, like all infants, toddlers, preschoolers, and early primary students, have a right to expect high-quality care and beneficial early education experiences from their EI/ECSE service providers.

CONTEMPORARY ISSUES IN EARLY CHILDHOOD SPECIAL EDUCATION

As described throughout this chapter, the children in today's early childhood programs and classrooms represent a very diverse group of learners. Some of these children may be homeless, others might have health issues, and still others may speak a language other than English. Collectively, these children and others, including typically developing peers, present multiple instructional challenges for early childhood special educators. Yet, just as the population of children has changed, so have the instructional practices. To successfully meet the individual needs of *all* the children they serve, early childhood special educators are teaching differently today. It is not unusual at all to see assistive technology (AT) incorporated in the twenty-first-century classroom or teachers redesigning their instruction based on principles of universal design for learning (UDL). In other instances, both general early childhood educators and early childhood special educators are increasingly using a strategy known as **response to intervention (RTI)** to ensure the academic progress of all children, particularly those confronting learning and behavioral challenges. (See Chapter 6 for additional information.) In fact, current thinking views AT, UDL, and RTI as compatible and integrated concepts (Wissick & Gardner, 2011) worthy of consideration by both general educators and special education practitioners. Next is an examination of some of the underlying principles, components, and strategies associated with each of these concepts.

RTI involves providing all children with evidence-based instruction.

iStock.com/kali9

Response to Intervention[3]

RTI originally came to the forefront of education as a result of the reauthorization of IDEA in 2004. It was initially offered as an alternative to a discrepancy model for identifying students who might have a learning disability. Although schools still have the option to use RTI to determine the existence of a learning disability, this procedure is now commonly used as an early intervention system to assess *all* children who may have been exposed to inadequate or ineffective instruction as well as children who lack the necessary preparatory skills for success in school (e.g., children of poverty, learners with few preschool or enrichment experiences, English learners; Gargiulo & Metcalf, 2023; O'Connor et al., 2017)—factors that may place them at risk or impede their academic or social progress in the classroom.

There is no formal definition of RTI, nor is there one widely accepted model or strategy (Gargiulo & Metcalf, 2023; Vaughn & Bos, 2020). Essentially, RTI involves providing *all* students with scientifically validated instruction (also known as evidence-based practices) and then systematically assessing their academic progress through ongoing monitoring frequently referred to as curriculum-based assessment.

RTI has been characterized as a

> systematic decision-making process designed to allow for early and effective responses to children's learning and behavioral difficulties, provide children with a level of instructional intensity matched to their level of need, and then provide a data-based method for evaluating the effectiveness of instructional approaches. RTI relies on evidence-based instructional practices and frequent progress monitoring to provide the data necessary to make decisions about child progress and need for more intensive intervention. (Fox et al., 2010, p. 3)

RTI is a multi-tiered data-driven model in which students are exposed to several levels or tiers of increasingly intensive instructional intervention derived from scientifically validated research (Gargiulo & Bouck, 2021; see Figure 10.5). Initially, a core curriculum is offered to all children; then modification of this curriculum is provided to those learners who fail to show adequate growth, while a more intensive level of support is implemented for those children who do not progress with the modified curriculum (Fox et al., 2010). Bayat et al. (2010) describe this three-prong multi-tiered system approach as follows:

Tier 1. At the first tier, screening of all students occurs followed by exposure to whole-group, high-quality research-based instruction and progress monitoring.

Tier 2. Children who still have difficulty following the implementation of an evidenced-based curriculum receive more intensive support and services.

Tier 3. Children who continue to demonstrate a lack of progress are provided individualized and highly intensive services beyond those offered in Tier 2. Instruction is typically provided by a specialized instructor such as a reading specialist or a special educator. If a child shows little or no progress, a referral for special education normally follows.

Originally designed to assess reading performance, RTI has been expanded to include mathematics (Clarke et al., 2010; VanDerHeyden, 2022) and social behaviors (Sugai, 2017). An RTI framework represents a conceptual shift from a "wait to fail" approach to one that emphasizes early recognition and possible prevention of learning difficulties.

Applying RTI in Early Education

There is a growing recognition of the appropriateness of RTI for young children (Carta et al., 2016; Coleman et al., 2009; Division for Early Childhood, 2021). While the research evidence is growing, this approach is being applied increasingly to prevention and intervention efforts for young children

---

[3] Content adapted from R. Gargiulo and D. Metcalf, *Teaching in Today's Inclusive Classrooms*, 4th ed. (Boston, MA: Cengage Learning, 2023).

FIGURE 10.5 ■ A Representative Response to Intervention Model

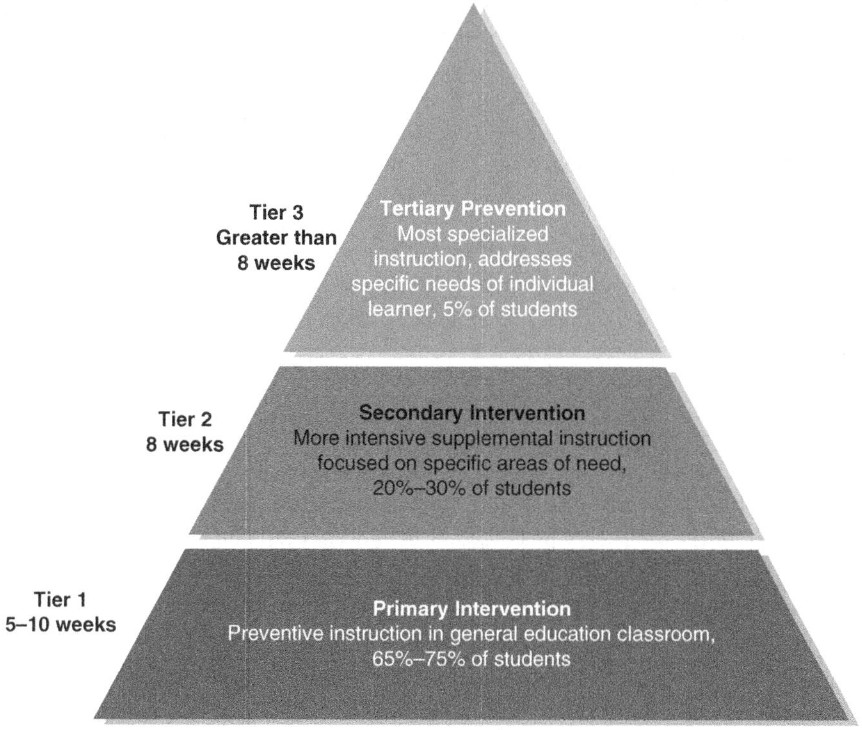

Source: R. Gargiulo and E. Bouck, *Special Education in Contemporary Society*, 7th ed. (Thousand Oaks, CA; Sage, 2021), p. 210.

Note: Percentage of students participating at each level is approximate. Duration of intervention is also approximate. Students may move between tiers as individual needs dictate.

in inclusive early childhood settings (Bayat et al., 2010; Division for Early Childhood et al., 2013; National Professional Development Center on Inclusion, 2012). RTI has pragmatic appeal for early childhood special educators; and according to Fox et al. (2010), "it is consistent with the conceptual and theoretical framework of early childhood special education and the national recognition of the critical importance of high-quality early childhood programs to promote young children's development" (p. 5). The core principles of RTI are also aligned with the recommended practices of early childhood (Division for Early Childhood, 2021, n.p.). A multi-tiered framework is a way to provide high-quality teaching and responsive caregiving through the delivery of differentiated support for all young children. The needs of *every* child regardless of ability, eligibility status, cultural and linguistic background, or socioeconomic status, are addressed by integrating assessment and intervention within a multilevel framework to maximize outcomes.

The goal is to acknowledge that each child has differing needs and to match systems of support to their individual needs.

FEATURE 10.3 REPRESENTATIVE WEB RESOURCES

For additional information about response to intervention and young children, access the following representative websites:

- **Response to Intervention (RTI) in Early Childhood,** https://npdci.fpg.unc.edu/sites/npdci.fpg.unc.edu/files/resources/NPDCI-RTI-Concept-Paper-FINAL-2-2012.pdf
- **Frank Porter Graham Child Development Institute,** www.fpg.unc.edu

- **RTI Action Network**, www.rtinetwork.org
- **National Center on Response to Intervention,** https://files.eric.ed.gov/fulltext/ED526859.pdf

The features of an RTI model at the preschool level are basically no different from the key components of RTI for school-age students (Bayat et al., 2010; Division for Early Childhood et al., 2013; National Professional Development Center on Inclusion, 2012). In fact,

> a tiered intervention model is an excellent fit with the presumption in early childhood and early intervention that young children should be educated within natural environments in inclusive settings and that intervention should be designed to match child and family needs. (Fox et al., 2010, p. 5)

Yet, professionals do acknowledge that conventional testing is not the recommended assessment option for preschoolers. Instead, ongoing authentic assessment coupled with parental observations should be used for data collection and progress monitoring (Bayat et al., 2010).

The role of RTI with preschoolers is often one of preventing academic failure, minimizing challenging behaviors, or the occurrence of a delay or disability via early intervention efforts. Viewed as a recommended practice, RTI holds great promise for supporting the learning and development of young children (National Professional Development Center on Inclusion, 2012). RTI seeks to maximize students' potential for success in the classroom. According to Bruder (2010), RTI "addresses the needs of *all* [italics added] children for a quality early childhood experience that prepares them for school" (p. 351).

Assistive Technology

Technology is a fact of life in today's early childhood programs and classrooms, and it is reflected throughout children's daily lives. Some educators believe that children in twenty-first-century programs and classrooms are vastly different from their peers of just a decade or so ago. Many children, since they were very young, are comfortable and proficient with smartphones, texting, Google, podcasting, iPods, Skype, blogs, iPads, and other such tools and devices. They are surrounded daily by technology, and essentially, they were born into a digital world. Commonly referred to in some circles as members of the Net Generation, these children read, write, think, communicate, and seek information differently—they often think digitally. Children today expect that technology will be an integral part of their learning environment. It's not too surprising, therefore, that almost 98 percent of three- and four-year-old children have access to a computer or smartphone in their homes (de Brey et al., 2022). The question is not whether technology has a place in today's programs and classrooms; it is more a matter of *how* technology is used. The effective use of technology requires that it be integrated into the curriculum in such a fashion that it corresponds to the individual needs of the learner. Technology is not a replacement for direct instruction, nor should it be treated as an add-on to classroom activities (Wissick & Gardner, 2011).

Technology and Young Children With Delays and Disabilities

Technology is a game changer, and for people with disabilities, it is seen as the "great equalizer" (Dell et al., 2017). For children with disabilities, it means that "having a disability no longer has to mean that things cannot be done; it means that we can find new ways to get them done" (Alliance for Technology Access, 2004, p. 3). When considering technology being used with young children with delays and disabilities, the term *assistive technology* (AT) is used, which is codified in various federal laws.

The introduction of assistive technology devices and services first appeared in federal legislation in 1988 with the enactment of PL 100–407, the Technology-Related Assistance for Individuals with Disabilities Act. This law is often referred to as the "Tech Act." Although other pieces of federal legislation also address AT, attention is focused on PL 108–446, or IDEA 2004. Using language similar to the terms found in PL 108–364, the Assistive Technology Act of 2004, IDEA 2004 defines AT devices and services as follows:

1. Assistive Technology Device—
   - **A.** In General—The term *assistive technology device* means any item, piece of equipment, or product system, whether acquired commercially off the shelf, modified, or customized, that is used to increase, maintain, or improve functional capabilities of a child with a disability.
   - **B.** Exception—The term does not include a medical device that is surgically implanted, or the replacement of such device.
2. Assistive Technology Service—
   The term *assistive technology service* means any service that directly assists a child with a disability in the selection, acquisition, or use of an assistive technology device. This service includes:
   - **A.** the evaluation of the needs of such child, including a functional evaluation of the child in the child's customary environment;
   - **B.** purchasing, leasing, or otherwise providing for the acquisition of assistive technology devices by such child;
   - **C.** selecting, designing, fitting, customizing, adapting, applying, maintaining, repairing, or assistive technology devices;
   - **D.** coordinating and using other therapies, interventions, or services with assistive technology devices, such as those associated with existing education and rehabilitation plans and programs;
   - **E.** training or technical assistance for such a child, or, where appropriate, the family of such child; and
   - **F.** training or technical assistance for professionals (including individuals providing education and rehabilitative services), employers, or other individuals who provide services to, employ, or are otherwise substantially involved in the major life functions of such child. (20 U.S.C. § 1401[1][A])

It is important to note the exception contained in IDEA 2004. The law excludes surgically implanted devices (e.g., a cochlear implant) from the definition of AT devices. Yet, there is a long legislative history of addressing the use of AT devices and services for individuals with disabilities going all the way back to PL 94–142 in 1975. More recently, the 1997 reauthorization of IDEA directly speaks to AT devices and services when developing individualized family service plans (IFSPs) for infants and toddlers with disabilities.

What Are Assistive Technology Devices?

Assistive technology devices are generally thought of as those that help alleviate the impact of a disability, essentially minimizing the functional limitations confronting the individual (Desch, 2019). "The primary purpose of assistive technology is to maximize an individual's ability in completing a task by minimizing barriers and unleashing potential to achieve desired outcomes" (Gargiulo & Metcalf, 2023, p. 323). For young children with delays and disabilities, AT can assist them to access natural environments and to develop functional skills across all developmental areas. AT devices, systems, and software also provide an opportunity for young children to connect with learning opportunities within their daily routines (Sadao & Robinson, 2010).

As you can see from the preceding definition, *AT devices* is a very broad term. One way of organizing the multitude of possibilities is to construct a "technology continuum." Basically, there are three categories of AT: (1) low-tech, (2) mid-tech, and (3) high-tech. According to AT experts (Bouck, 2017; Desch, 2019), **low-tech devices** are those that incorporate low-cost materials and do not require batteries or electrical power. **Mid-tech devices** are a bit more sophisticated and require an electrical source or are viewed as more complex to operate. Lastly, **high-tech devices** are more complicated and generally expensive to own and operate. Table 10.6 provides examples of these devices across the AT spectrum. When considering the use of AT, it is important to keep in mind the maxim of "The simpler the better." A low-tech solution always should be considered first before progressing along the AT continuum to other possible solutions (Bouck, 2017; Gargiulo & Metcalf, 2023).

TABLE 10.6 ■ Representative Assistive Technology Devices

Low-Tech	Mid-Tech	High-Tech
• Slanted writing board	• Audiobooks	• Voice recognition software
• Tape recorder	• Digital voice recorder	• Modified keyboard
• Adapted pencil grip	• Talking calculator	• Augmentative communication device
• Raised-line paper	• Electronic dictionary	• Power wheelchair
• Key guard	• Switch (battery-operated) toys	• Touch screen computer monitor
• Visual schedule		• Environmental control unit
• Handheld magnifying device		• Robotic devices
• "Sticky" notes		• PC tablet or iPad
• Large-print books		• "The Cloud"
• Adjustable table		

Source: Adapted from A. Dell, D. Newton, and J. Petroff, *Assistive Technology in the Classroom*, 3rd ed. (Boston, MA: Pearson Education, 2017). p. 5.

Assistive technology is increasingly commonplace in twenty-first century classrooms.

iStock.com/AndreaObzerova

Assistive Technology in the Classroom and Other Environments

When incorporating AT in the classroom and other learning environments, it is important to remember that it must be customized to meet the unique needs of each student; a one-size-fits-all mindset is inappropriate. Early childhood special educators must carefully consider the individual strengths and needs of each child and then decide what type of technology is needed to help the child be successful in the learning environment. It is critical that AT match the learning needs and preferences of the individual user (Gargiulo & Metcalf, 2023). AT compensates for or builds upon the skills and talents that each learner possesses (Desch, 2019); it is a means to an end. Students must be provided with the AT tools that increase their independence and functioning, engage them in learning, and allow for greater participation in school (Dell et al., 2017).

The challenge that confronts professionals is to how to select the appropriate device(s) that will benefit each child. This issue is crucial to the successful implementation of AT. Guidance, fortunately, is provided by the work of Zabala (1995, 2005), who constructed an AT decision-making framework known as SETT—*S*tudent, *E*nvironments, *T*asks, and *T*ools. By using a series of data-gathering questions, early childhood special educators can choose the appropriate AT device that will meet the unique needs of the learner. SETT is not an assessment protocol; rather, it offers an outline for considering AT support (Dell et al., 2017). This student-focused decision-making guide is as follows:

The Student

- What does the student need to do?
- What are the student's needs?
- What are the student's current abilities?

The Environment

- What materials are currently available in the environment?
- What is the physical arrangement? Are there unique concerns?
- What is the instructional arrangement? Are there likely to be changes?
- What supports are available to the student?
- What resources are available to the people supporting the student?

The Tasks

- What activities take place in the environment?
- What activities support the student's curriculum?
- What are the critical elements of the activity?
- How might the activities be modified to accommodate the student's needs?
- How might technology support the student's active participation in those activities?

The Tools

- What no-tech, low-tech, and high-tech options should be considered when developing a system for a student with these abilities doing these tasks in these environments?
- What strategies might be used to invite increased student performance?
- How might these tools be tried out with the student in the customary environments in which they will be used?

The SETT process helps early childhood special educators identify and build on their students' strengths and consequently aids in their success in the classroom.

Young Children With Delays and Disabilities and AT

As noted before, AT is the "great equalizer" for individuals with disabilities. It provides children with delays and disabilities greater opportunities to lead independent lives, learn, and participate fully in school as well as their community (Dell et al., 2017; Desch, 2019). According to Bouck (2017), AT "empowers [young children] and increases their independence in everyday life as well as participation in inclusive environments" (p. 238). Likewise, AT enables young children with delays and disabilities to achieve greater control over their lives and to do things previously thought impossible. AT also can help children with developmental delays and disabilities learn the skills they need to achieve at appropriate levels (Morrison et al., 2022).

One of the most powerful applications of AT in the classroom is to individualize instruction for children with delays and disabilities—it is the vehicle that permits them to access the general education curriculum, master developmental goals, and reach their learning potential. It is important to remember, however, that the use of technology is *not* disability specific; early childhood special educators must focus on the functional learning outcomes rather than technology for a particular delay or disability (Gargiulo & Metcalf, 2023).

IDEA 2004 requires that the IFSP or IEP team consider the AT needs of each student receiving early intervention or a special education. Typically identified as a related service, the IFSP or IEP must stipulate how AT is to be used and how it relates to the child's performance. Provided at no cost to the child's family, AT devices and services offer the individual access to and the ability to participate in the general education curriculum, the opportunity to be educated in the least restrictive or natural environment, and the chance to obtain benefit from a special education (Dell et al., 2017; Gargiulo & Bouck, 2021). AT should be an integral part of the daily activities and routines of young children with delays and disabilities. It offers today's students innumerable opportunities to be part of typical social and learning communities and to learn alongside typically developing peers [DEC Recommended Practices E4, E5].

FEATURE 10.4 REPRESENTATIVE WEB RESOURCES

For additional information about assistive technology devices and services, access the following representative websites:

- **Closing the Gap**, www.closingthegap.com
- **Council for Exceptional Children, Innovations in Special Education Technology,** https://www.isetcec.org/
- **National Assistive Technology in Education Network**, http://natenetwork.org
- **Quality Indicators for Assistive Technology Services,** https://qiat.org/

Universal Design for Learning[4]

With so many young children with delays and disabilities now being served in inclusive learning environments, how are early childhood special educators and other professionals supposed to meet the unique needs of every child? One possible solution to this instructional dilemma is a concept known as **universal design for learning**, more commonly known by its acronym, **UDL**. UDL allows the early childhood special educator to adapt curriculum, customize the delivery of instruction, and assess children in ways that permit them to demonstrate their mastery of the material.

Originally developed for architects and consumer product designers, the principles of UDL have been adapted to the field of education. The following is a concise description of UDL:

> The central practical premise of UDL is that a curriculum should include alternatives to make it accessible and appropriate for individuals with different learning backgrounds, learning styles, abilities, and disabilities in widely varied learning contexts. The "universal" in universal design does not imply one optimal solution for everyone. Rather, it reflects an awareness of the unique nature of each learner and the need to accommodate differences, create learning experiences that suit the learner, and maximize his or her ability to progress. (Rose & Meyer, 2002, p. 70)

Essentially, UDL is an instructional concept or approach to designing instructional methods, materials, activities, and evaluation procedures to assist individuals with "wide differences in their

[4] Adapted from R. Gargiulo and D. Metcalf, *Teaching in Today's Inclusive Classrooms*, 4th ed. (Boston, MA: Cengage Learning, 2023).

abilities to see, hear, speak, move, read, write, understand English, attend, organize, engage, and remember" (Orkwis, 2003, n.p.).

Universal design for learning is accomplished by means of flexible curriculum materials and activities that offer alternatives to children with widely varying abilities and backgrounds. These adaptations are built into instructional design rather than added on later as an afterthought. Universal design for learning provides equal access to learning, not simply equal access to information. UDL assumes that there is no one method of presentation or expression that provides equal access for all children. Learning activities and materials are purposely designed to allow for flexibility and offer various ways to learn (Florian, 2014; Gargiulo & Metcalf, 2023; Meyer et al., 2014). These accommodations are "designed-in" or built "directly into the materials so that all children with varying abilities can use the same material, but in a way tailored to their strengths and instructional needs" (Freund & Rich, 2005, p. 81).

The Division for Early Childhood (2014) specifically addresses the need for early childhood special educators and other practitioners to consider UDL principles in an effort to create learning environments that are accessible for all students [DEC Recommended Practices E2].

Universal design for learning is envisioned as a research-based instructional framework for designing curricula (Sadao & Robinson, 2010), a means for diversifying instruction to deliver the general education curriculum to each student (Orkwis & McLane, 1998). Recall that IDEA 2004 requires that children with disabilities have access to the general education curriculum, and "access to the general curriculum requires accessible curriculum for *all* [italics added] learners" (Sadao & Robinson, 2010, p. 28). UDL does not remove academic challenges; it simply removes barriers to access. The greatest promise of UDL is flexible, equitable, and accessible ways to teach. UDL encourages early childhood special educators to design curriculum, learning environments, and assessments that are "smart from the start" (Pisha & Coyne, 2001). Early childhood special educators are now able to consider the diverse learning needs of their students as part of their initial curriculum planning rather than adapting the curriculum to the needs of the child after the fact.

Three essential qualities of universal design for learning must be considered when developing curriculum for children with diverse learning needs—multiple means of representation, multiple means of action and expression, and multiple means of engagement. These three key components are portrayed in Figure 10.6.

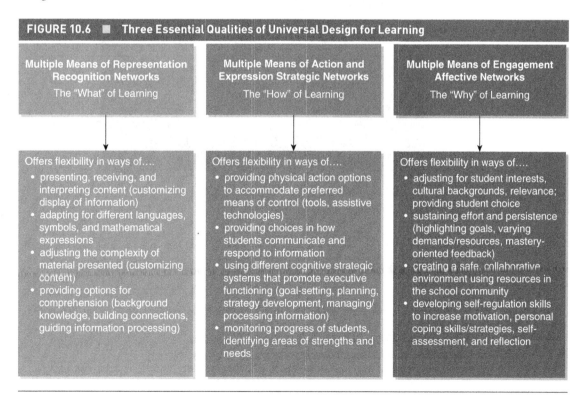

FIGURE 10.6 ■ Three Essential Qualities of Universal Design for Learning

Multiple Means of Representation Recognition Networks The "What" of Learning	**Multiple Means of Action and Expression Strategic Networks** The "How" of Learning	**Multiple Means of Engagement Affective Networks** The "Why" of Learning
Offers flexibility in ways of.... • presenting, receiving, and interpreting content (customizing display of information) • adapting for different languages, symbols, and mathematical expressions • adjusting the complexity of material presented (customizing content) • providing options for comprehension (background knowledge, building connections, guiding information processing)	Offers flexibility in ways of.... • providing physical action options to accommodate preferred means of control (tools, assistive technologies) • providing choices in how students communicate and respond to information • using different cognitive strategic systems that promote executive functioning (goal-setting, planning, strategy development, managing/processing information) • monitoring progress of students, identifying areas of strengths and needs	Offers flexibility in ways of.... • adjusting for student interests, cultural backgrounds, relevance; providing student choice • sustaining effort and persistence (highlighting goals, varying demands/resources, mastery-oriented feedback) • creating a safe, collaborative environment using resources in the school community • developing self-regulation skills to increase motivation, personal coping skills/strategies, self-assessment, and reflection

Source: Adapted from Center for Applied Special Technology. (2018). Universal design for learning guidelines version 2.2. http://udlguidelines.cast.org; R. Gargiulo and D. Metcalf, *Teaching in Today's Inclusive Classrooms*, 4th ed. (Boston, MA: Cengage Learning, 2023). p. 45.

Multiple Means of Representation

The first quality of UDL is multiple means of representation. Students are provided with a variety of ways to receive and interpret information. By offering different ways of presenting information, not only can physical barriers to learning be reduced, but also sensory, perceptual, and other roadblocks that young children with delays and disabilities might confront in their learning environment can be minimized.

Multiple Means of Action and Expression

The second quality of UDL is multiple means of action and expression. This dimension accommodates the various ways that children may respond to the information they receive. When offered alternative approaches to responding, children can reflect on their thinking and organize it (Pisha & Coyne, 2001). There are multiple ways that children might choose to express themselves, for example, oral reports, drawings, demonstrations, or even a puppet performance or a song (Gargiulo & Metcalf, 2023). When children are able to utilize their learning preferences and areas of strength, they are more likely to become engaged in their learning because the material is now interesting and meaningful to them.

Multiple Means of Engagement

The third key aspect of UDL is multiple means of engagement. This principle considers different ways to motivate children, challenge them, and boost their interest in learning. Teaching and learning will only be as effective as its relevance and value to the learner. Material to be learned must be seen as appealing and important to the student. By considering multiple means of engagement, options can be provided to young children with diverse learning needs within their classroom.

By providing young children with delays and disabilities with the flexibility offered by UDL, early childhood special educators are helping their students to become empowered and successful learners.

Universal design for learning provides equal access to learning.

Karl Gehring/Contributor/via Getty Images

FEATURE 10.5 REPRESENTATIVE WEB RESOURCES

For additional information about universal design for learning, access the following representative websites:

- **Center for Applied Special Technology (CAST)**, www.cast.org
- **National Center on Universal Design for Learning**, www.udlcenter.org
- **Center for Universal Design at North Carolina State University,** https://projects.ncsu.edu/ncsu/design/cud/index.htm

SUMMARY

This chapter highlights multiple issues and challenges that confront early childhood special educators and that are likely to continue in the coming years. A growing list of social issues and professional concerns suggests that significant change in early intervention and early childhood special education services is on the horizon. The knowledge and skills needed by EI/ECSE practitioner are addressed in the new standalone EI/ECSE Standards (DEC/CEC, 2020) and are designed to promote excellence in practice and research, shape the future of early childhood special education, and pave the way for more inclusive and equitable services where every child has the opportunity to thrive (Stayton et al., 2023).

Due to our country's rich cultural diversity, early childhood programs and schools serve growing numbers of young children and families representing culturally and linguistically diverse backgrounds. For some children, entrance into an early childhood special education program or a school may be their first exposure to a culture and/or a language that is different from that of their home. Because of this, EI/ECSE practitioners must guard against stereotyping and be certain that cultural and linguistic differences are not misinterpreted. Early childhood special educators must model respect for and sensitivity to the cultural and linguistic backgrounds of the children they serve. For early childhood special education programs to be successful, services must be offered by professionals who demonstrate cultural awareness, sensitivity, and responsiveness.

Additionally, due to a variety of contributing contemporary social issues, early childhood special educators provide services to a growing population of children who face the deleterious consequences of homelessness and child maltreatment and trauma, as well as children with complex health care needs. The causes of these issues are beyond the control of the early childhood special educator; however, they can provide a safe, stable, and nurturing learning environment where children can develop to their maximum potential. Teachers of infants, toddlers, preschoolers, and early primary students have the duty to fulfill roles as purveyors of care and education to all young children, but especially to those most in need.

To meet the educational challenges of an increasingly diverse population, early childhood special educators are incorporating a variety of strategies to ensure that children are successful. Response to intervention (RTI) is just one example. RTI incorporates the use of scientifically validated instruction (evidence-based practices). This model stresses early recognition and possible prevention of learning difficulties. Assistive technology (AT) is yet another illustration of how early childhood special educators are attempting to meet the needs of young children with delays and disabilities in twenty-first-century classrooms. The use of AT must be customized to the individual strengths and preferences of the user. AT offers access to the general education curriculum while also allowing for greater participation in natural or least restrictive learning environments. Equally common in today's classrooms is instruction based on principles of universal design for learning (UDL). UDL permits early childhood special educators to assess, adapt curriculum, and customize instruction for the children they serve in multiple ways. Further, UDL removes barriers to access, provides flexibility, and offers alternatives to children with widely varying abilities.

KEY TERMS

Bilingual education
Children with complex health care needs
Culture
Emotional abuse
Ethnocentric behavior
High-tech devices
Low-tech devices
Mid-tech devices
Multiple means of action and expression
Multiple means of engagement
Multiple means of representation
Neglect
Physical abuse
Response to intervention (RTI)
Sexual abuse
UDL
Universal design for learning

CHECK YOUR UNDERSTANDING

1. Explain the difference between ethnicity and exceptionality.
2. Why is it important for early childhood special educators to understand and respect the cultural heritage of the children and families they serve?
3. Provide examples of the four major types of child maltreatment.
4. What role do early childhood programs and schools play in providing services to young children with complex health care needs?
5. How can response to intervention (RTI) strategies help early childhood special educators identify children who may require academic assistance?
6. Describe the differences between low-tech, mid-tech, and high-tech assistive technology devices. How would you determine which device is most appropriate for a young child with delays and disabilities?
7. Identify the three essential qualities associated with universal design for learning.

REFLECTION AND APPLICATION

1. Visit several early childhood programs and schools in your area. Do these places serve young children who are homeless? What support systems are available to assist these children and their families? How does the teacher address the educational needs of children who are homeless? How does this differ from what is provided for the other children? What would you do if you had a child in your class who was homeless?
2. Interview a school administrator. Does the early childhood program or school have a policy for reporting instances of suspected child abuse or neglect? What is the role of the teacher? Are criminal background checks performed on staff and volunteers?
3. With a group of your classmates, produce a presentation about the characteristics of young children with complex health care needs. Topics may include a child with juvenile rheumatoid arthritis, muscular dystrophy, cystic fibrosis, or epilepsy, among other conditions. Design a health care plan for a young child with one of the preceding examples. How would you explain this child's condition to their classmates? How would you organize your classroom to meet the unique needs of this student? Are there any particular educational strategies you would incorporate in your classroom? How would you involve the student's family?
4. Visit several different early childhood programs or classrooms where assistive technology is being used. Interview the early childhood special educators to learn how they infuse technology in their classrooms. What types of low-tech, mid-tech, and high-tech tools did you observe the children using? Describe these experiences in a blog.
5. Observe an inclusive classroom serving young children with delays and disabilities. Did the teacher and/or therapists incorporate principles of universal design for learning? What types of adaptations or alternatives were used to ensure the children' participation and access to the curriculum? How did the children respond to this instructional approach? Consider the children's home and other learning environments (e.g., the playground) and determine how universal design for learning principles could be applied in these settings.

APPENDIX A

Initial Practice-Based Professional Preparation Standards for Early Interventionists/Early Childhood Special Educators (EI/ECSE) (Initial Birth Through Age 8)

STANDARD 1: CHILD DEVELOPMENT AND EARLY LEARNING

Candidates understand the impact of different theories and philosophies of early learning and development on assessment, curriculum, instruction, and intervention decisions. Candidates apply knowledge of normative developmental sequences and variations, individual differences within and across the range of abilities, including developmental delays and disabilities, and other direct and indirect contextual features that support or constrain children's development and learning. These contextual factors as well as social, cultural, and linguistic diversity are considered when facilitating meaningful learning experiences and individualizing intervention and instruction across contexts.

1.1 Candidates demonstrate an understanding of the impact that different theories and philosophies of early learning and development have on assessment, curriculum, intervention, and instruction decisions.

1.2 Candidates apply knowledge of normative sequences of early development, individual differences, and families' social, cultural, and linguistic diversity to support each child's development and learning across contexts.

1.3 Candidates apply knowledge of biological and environmental factors that may support or constrain children's early development and learning as they plan and implement early intervention and instruction.

1.4 Candidates demonstrate an understanding of characteristics, etiologies, and individual differences within and across the range of abilities, including developmental delays and disabilities, their potential impact on children's early development and learning, and implications for assessment, curriculum, instruction, and intervention.

STANDARD 2: PARTNERING WITH FAMILIES

Candidates use their knowledge of family-centered practices and family systems theory to develop and maintain reciprocal partnerships with families. They apply family capacity-building practices as they support families to make informed decisions and advocate for their young children. They engage families in opportunities that build on their existing strengths, reflect current goals, and foster family competence and confidence to support their children's development and learning.

2.1 Candidates apply their knowledge of family-centered practices, family systems theory, and the changing needs and priorities in families' lives to develop trusting, respectful, affirming, and culturally responsive partnerships with all families that allow for the mutual exchange of knowledge and information.

2.2 Candidates communicate clear, comprehensive, and objective information about resources and supports that help families to make informed decisions and advocate for access, participation, and equity in natural and inclusive environments.

2.3 Candidates engage families in identifying their strengths, priorities, and concerns; support families to achieve the goals they have for their family and their young child's development and learning; and promote families' competence and confidence during assessment, individualized planning, intervention, instruction, and transition processes.

STANDARD 3: COLLABORATION AND TEAMING

Candidates apply models, skills, and processes of teaming when collaborating and communicating with families and professionals, using culturally and linguistically responsive and affirming practices. In partnership with families and other professionals, candidates develop and implement individualized plans and successful transitions that occur across the age span. Candidates use a variety of collaborative strategies while working with and supporting other adults.

3.1 Candidates apply teaming models, skills, and processes, including appropriate uses of technology, when collaborating and communicating with families, professionals representing multiple disciplines, skills, expertise, and roles; and community partners and agencies.

3.2 Candidates use a variety of collaborative strategies when working with other adults that are evidence-based, appropriate to the task, culturally and linguistically responsive, and take into consideration the environment and service delivery approach.

3.3 Candidates partner with families and other professionals to develop individualized plans and support the various transitions that occur for the young child and their family throughout the birth through 8 age span.

STANDARD 4: ASSESSMENT PROCESSES

Candidates know and understand the purposes of assessment in relation to ethical and legal considerations. Candidates choose developmentally, linguistically, and culturally appropriate tools and methods that are responsive to the characteristics of the young child, family, and program. Using evidence-based practices, candidates develop or select as well as administer informal measures, and select and administer formal measures in partnership with families and other professionals. They analyze, interpret, document, and share assessment information using a strengths-based approach with families and other professionals for eligibility determination, outcome/goal development, planning instruction and intervention, monitoring progress, and reporting.

4.1 Candidates understand the purposes of formal and informal assessment, including ethical and legal considerations, and use this information to choose developmentally, culturally and linguistically appropriate, valid, reliable tools and methods that are responsive to the characteristics of the young child, family, and program

4.2 Candidates develop and administer informal assessments and/or select and use valid, reliable formal assessments using evidence-based practices, including technology, in partnership with families and other professionals.

4.3 Candidates analyze, interpret, document, and share assessment information using a strengths-based approach with families and other professionals.

4.4 Candidates, in collaboration with families and other team members, use assessment data to determine eligibility, develop child and family-based outcomes/goals, plan for interventions and instruction, and monitor progress to determine efficacy of programming.

STANDARD 5: APPLICATION OF CURRICULUM FRAMEWORKS IN THE PLANNING OF MEANINGFUL LEARNING EXPERIENCE

Candidates collaborate with families and professionals to use an evidence-based, developmentally appropriate, and culturally responsive early childhood curriculum addressing developmental and content domains. Candidates use curriculum frameworks to create and support universally designed, high quality learning experiences in natural and inclusive environments that provide each child and family with equitable access and opportunities for learning and growth.

5.1 Candidates collaborate with families and other professionals in identifying an evidence-based curriculum addressing developmental and content domains to design and facilitate meaningful and culturally responsive learning experiences that support the unique abilities and needs of all children and families.

5.2 Candidates use their knowledge of early childhood curriculum frameworks, developmental and academic content knowledge, and related pedagogy to plan and ensure equitable access to universally designed, developmentally appropriate, and challenging learning experiences in natural and inclusive environments.

STANDARD 6: USING RESPONSIVE AND RECIPROCAL INTERACTIONS, INTERVENTIONS, AND INSTRUCTION

Candidates plan and implement intentional, systematic, evidence-based, responsive interactions, interventions, and instruction to support all children's learning and development across all developmental and content domains in partnership with families and other professionals. Candidates facilitate equitable access and participation for all children and families within natural and inclusive environments through culturally responsive and affirming practices and relationships. Candidates use data-based decision making to plan for, adapt, and improve interactions, interventions, and instruction to ensure fidelity of implementation.

6.1 Candidates, in partnership with families, identify systematic, responsive, and intentional evidence-based practices and use such practices with fidelity to support young children's learning and development across all developmental and academic content domains.

6.2 Candidates engage in reciprocal partnerships with families and other professionals to facilitate responsive adult-child interactions, interventions, and instruction in support of child learning and development.

6.3 Candidates engage in ongoing planning and use flexible and embedded instructional and environmental arrangements and appropriate materials to support the use of interactions, interventions, and instruction addressing developmental and academic content domains, which are adapted to meet the needs of each and every child and their family.

6.4 Candidates promote young children's social and emotional competence and communication, and proactively plan and implement function-based interventions to prevent and address challenging behaviors.

6.5 Candidates identify and create multiple opportunities for young children to develop and learn play skills and engage in meaningful play experiences independently and with others across contexts.

6.6 Candidates use responsive interactions, interventions, and instruction with sufficient intensity and types of support across activities, routines, and environments to promote child learning and development and facilitate access, participation, and engagement in natural environments and inclusive settings.

6.7 Candidates plan for, adapt, and improve approaches to interactions, interventions, and instruction based on multiple sources of data across a range of natural environments and inclusive settings.

STANDARD 7: PROFESSIONALISM AND ETHICAL PRACTICE

Candidates identify and engage with the profession of early intervention and early childhood special education (EI/ECSE) by exhibiting skills in reflective practice, advocacy, and leadership while adhering to ethical and legal guidelines. Evidence-based and recommended practices are promoted and used by candidates.

7.1 Candidates engage with the profession of EI/ECSE by participating in local, regional, national, and/or international activities and professional organizations.

7.2 Candidates engage in ongoing reflective practice and access evidence-based information to improve their own practices.

7.3 Candidates exhibit leadership skills in advocating for improved outcomes for young children, families, and the profession, including the promotion of and use of evidence-based practices and decision-making.

7.4 Candidates practice within ethical and legal policies and procedures.

STANDARD 8: EI/ECSE FIELD AND CLINICAL EXPERIENCE

Early Interventionist/Early Childhood Special Education candidates progress through a series of planned and developmentally sequenced field experiences for the early childhood age ranges (birth to age 3, 3 through 5 years, 5 through 8 years), range of abilities, and in the variety of collaborative and inclusive early childhood settings that are appropriate to their license and roles. Clinical experiences should take place in the same age ranges covered by the license. If the license covers all three age ranges, the program must provide clinical experiences in at least two of the three age ranges and a field experience in the third age range. These field and clinical experiences are supervised by qualified professionals.

SUPPORTING EXPLANATION

Field and clinical experiences provide opportunities for candidates to apply knowledge and to practice skills in culturally and linguistically diverse classrooms, home-based settings, and other community placements in partnership with families and other professionals. Field and clinical experience sites are developed and enhanced over time through collaborative partnerships among local education agencies and other community stakeholders, including families and university Early Intervention/Early Childhood Special Education (EI/ECSE) faculty. Through collaboration and consultation, placements are selected to provide developmental field experiences that support candidates in using effective practices in a wide array of classrooms, homes, and other community settings.

Field and clinical experiences are designed to link EI/ECSE research and theory to practice and provide rich, scaffolded, developmental, and graduated experiences with increasing responsibilities for prospective early interventionists and early childhood special educators. Thus, field experiences are aligned with coursework and occur early and throughout the Educator Preparation Program beginning with observation and reflection on practices and systematically progressing to implementation of practices with supervision. Examples of these experiences include course-based field work, practica, internships, and student teaching. Field and clinical experiences are connected and sufficiently extensive and intensive that candidates are able to demonstrate through performance assessments that they have mastered the practices required for the professional roles for which they are preparing.

Field and clinical experiences are structured and varied, and ensure that candidates have experiences with infants, toddlers, and young children and their families across the age ranges and range of abilities for which they are preparing. To facilitate this, placements occur in the variety of collaborative, inclusive, and culturally and linguistically diverse early childhood programs in which infants, toddlers, and young children receive services. These include, but are not limited to, public school preschool and K–3 programs; other publicly funded programs such as Early Head Start and Head Start; community preschool and child care programs; and the natural environments of the child and family, for example, home, park, or grocery. All candidates have some field experiences across the complete age range. For example, candidates may observe for a specific child developmental domain across the birth through age 8 age range. Or, as another example, candidates may observe and reflect on the observation in settings that go across the age ranges. Then, as field experiences focus more on application of practices, candidates complete field experiences for the age ranges included in the license and roles for which they are preparing. In addition, all candidates have some field experiences in which they observe and participate in collaborative activities with families and other professionals (e.g., home visits, parent-teacher conferences, cross-disciplinary team meetings).

Clinical practice must take place in the same age ranges covered by the license. For example, if the license covers two of the three age ranges (e.g., birth to age 3 and 3 through 5 years), clinical experiences must be provided for both age ranges. If the license covers all three age ranges, the program must provide clinical experiences in at least two of the three age ranges (e.g., 3 through 5 years and 5 through 8 years) and a field experience specifically focused on the third age range (e.g., birth to age 3).

Site-based professionals are selected for their expertise and experience with infants, toddlers, and young children and for providing the services for which the candidate is preparing. They hold the certification or credential necessary to work in the EI/ECSE program. Site-based professionals demonstrate mentoring and coaching skills in supporting the learning of candidates. In addition, the site-based professionals effectively communicate with and engage the candidate in self-reflection on the interactions and practices utilized with children, families, and other providers. Although university supervisors may not be licensed or certified in the state in which they are employed, they must have substantial formal preparation in the field of EI/ECSE and have expertise and experience with infants, toddlers, and young children and services for which the candidate is preparing.

APPENDIX B

Division for Early Childhood of the Council for Exceptional Children

DEC RECOMMENDED PRACTICES

April 14, 2014

The Division for Early Childhood (DEC) Recommended Practices provide guidance to practitioners and families about the most effective ways to improve the learning outcomes and promote the development of young children, from birth through age five, who have or are at risk for developmental delays or disabilities. Developed by the DEC Recommended Practices Commission.

Division for Early Childhood. (2014). DEC recommended practices in early intervention/early childhood special education 2014. Retrieved from http://www.dec-sped.org/recommendedpractices

INTRODUCTION

The DEC Recommended Practices were developed to provide guidance to practitioners and families about the most effective ways to improve the learning outcomes and promote the development of young children, from birth through five years of age, who have or are at risk for developmental delays or disabilities. The purpose of this document is to help bridge the gap between research and practice by highlighting those practices that have been shown to result in better outcomes for young children with disabilities, their families, and the personnel who serve them. The DEC Recommended Practices support children's access to and participation in inclusive settings and natural environments and address cultural, linguistic, and ability diversity. They also identify key leadership responsibilities associated with the implementation of these practices.

The DEC Recommended Practices are based on the best-available empirical evidence as well as the wisdom and experience of the field. The practices are organized into eight topic areas, but they should be viewed holistically across the topic areas. Family practices, for example, are grouped in one topic area but are fundamental to all of the topic areas. We believe that when practitioners and families have the knowledge, skills, and dispositions to implement these practices as intended, children who have or are at risk for developmental delays/disabilities and their families are more likely to achieve positive outcomes, and families and practitioners are more likely to help children achieve their highest potential.

While developmentally appropriate practices are the foundation of quality programs for all young children and families (Copple & Bredekamp, 2009), we believe that young children who have or are at risk for developmental delays/disabilities often need more specialized practices that allow them to participate and engage meaningfully in their daily living routines and learning activities. While we acknowledge the important role of developmentally appropriate practices in the education and care of all children, we do not include those foundational practices in this document.

The purpose of the DEC Recommended Practices is to highlight those practices specifically known to promote the outcomes of young children who have or are at risk for developmental delays/disabilities and to support their families in accordance with the DEC/NAEYC (2009) position statement on early childhood inclusion. We assume that those who implement the practices

- Have foundational knowledge of developmentally appropriate early childhood practices
- Have a basic understanding of relevant professional, legal, and regulatory guidelines for serving every child
- Act in accordance with the principles of the DEC Code of Ethics and in accordance with the principles of access and participation as described in the DEC/NAEYC (2009) position statement on inclusion
- Engage in ongoing professional development to increase their knowledge, skills, and dispositions for implementing the Recommended Practices as intended

In addition to implementing the DEC Recommended Practices, practitioners working in the field should be guided by their discipline-specific professional standards, competencies, and codes of ethics. All practitioners who work with young children, including those at risk for developmental delays/disabilities, are expected to access professional development and technical assistance systems to build knowledge and skills related to developmentally appropriate practices, the DEC Recommended Practices, and discipline-specific knowledge.

Building on previous efforts to produce DEC Recommended Practices as well as surveys and other opportunities to receive suggestions from the field, we also established the following parameters to guide the production of the current set of DEC Recommended Practices. These parameters include the following:

- *Recommended Practices* are those with the highest expected leverage and impact on outcomes, providing the "biggest bang."
- *Recommended Practices* are supported by research, values, and experience.
- *Recommended Practices* represent the breadth of the topic area.
- *Recommended Practices* are observable.
- *Recommended Practices* are *not* disability-specific.
- *Recommended Practices* can be delivered in all settings including natural/inclusive environments.
- *Recommended Practices* should build on, but not duplicate, standards for typical early childhood settings such as the NAEYC Developmentally Appropriate Practice guidelines.

For the purposes of this document, the definition of young children who have or are at risk for developmental delays/disabilities is not limited to children eligible for services under IDEA. This set of DEC Recommended Practices has eight topic areas. In our presentation of practices that appears below, we begin with the topic area of Leadership, which provides guidance for local and state leaders who support practitioners. We define leaders as those in positions of leadership or authority in providing services to all young children who have or are at risk for developmental delays/disabilities and their families. Examples of such leaders include state, regional, and local administrators; early childhood coordinators; building principals; and assistant directors and coordinators.

The other seven topic areas provide guidance for practitioners:

- Assessment
- Environment
- Family
- Instruction
- Interaction
- Teaming and Collaboration
- Transition

For these Recommended Practices, we define practitioners as those who are responsible for and paid to enhance the optimal development of young children who have or are at risk for developmental delays/disabilities. This includes providing care, education, or therapy to the child as well as support to the child's family.

LEADERSHIP

The work of practitioners on the front line is critical to improving outcomes for young children who have or are at risk for developmental delays/disabilities and their families. But practitioners do not operate in a vacuum. Their ability to implement the DEC Recommended Practices can be supported or constrained by the program, school, agency, or organization for which they work.

State and local leaders establish the conditions that are essential for the successful implementation of the DEC Recommended Practices by, for example, the policies and procedures they develop and implement. Leaders in early intervention and early childhood special education can be program directors and other administrators, practitioners, family members, students, higher education faculty, and others. The set of practices in this section address the responsibilities of those in positions of program authority and leadership related to providing services to young children who have or are at risk for developmental delays/disabilities and their families. Examples of such leaders include state, regional, and local directors and other administrators; early childhood coordinators; building principals; and assistant directors and coordinators.

The provision of these services is a complex undertaking governed by federal and state laws, funded by multiple sources, and structured and administered in different ways. Some of the challenges to implementing the DEC Recommended Practices may be beyond the immediate control of state agency staff or local administrators. These challenges may require sustained advocacy from a variety of groups to create the systems change needed to establish more conducive policies and procedures. Leaders have a professional responsibility to use all the mechanisms within their control to create the conditions needed to support practitioners in implementing the following Recommended Practices.

We recommend the following practices associated with leadership:

L1. Leaders create a culture and a climate in which practitioners feel a sense of belonging and want to support the organization's mission and goals.

L2. Leaders promote adherence to and model the DEC Code of Ethics, DEC Position Statements and Papers, and the DEC Recommended Practices.

L3. Leaders develop and implement policies, structures, and practices that promote shared decision making with practitioners and families.

L4. Leaders belong to professional association(s) and engage in ongoing evidence-based professional development.

L5. Leaders advocate for policies and resources that promote the implementation of the DEC Position Statements and Papers and the DEC Recommended Practices.

L6. Leaders establish partnerships across levels (state to local) and with their counterparts in other systems and agencies to create coordinated and inclusive systems of services and supports.

L7. Leaders develop, refine, and implement policies and procedures that create the conditions for practitioners to implement the DEC Recommended Practices.

L8. Leaders work across levels and sectors to secure fiscal and human resources and maximize the use of these resources to successfully implement the DEC Recommended Practices.

L9. Leaders develop and implement an evidence-based professional development system or approach that provides practitioners a variety of supports to ensure they have the knowledge and skills needed to implement the DEC Recommended Practices.

L10. Leaders ensure practitioners know and follow professional standards and all applicable laws and regulations governing service provision.

L11. Leaders collaborate with higher education, state licensing and certification agencies, practitioners, professional associations, and other stakeholders to develop or revise state competencies that align with DEC, Council for Exceptional Children (CEC), and other national professional standards.

L12. Leaders collaborate with stakeholders to collect and use data for program management and continuous program improvement and to examine the effectiveness of services and supports in improving child and family outcomes.

L13. Leaders promote efficient and coordinated service delivery for children and families by creating the conditions for practitioners from multiple disciplines and the family to work together as a team.

L14. Leaders collaborate with other agencies and programs to develop and implement ongoing community-wide screening procedures to identify and refer children who may need additional evaluation and services.

ASSESSMENT

Assessment is the process of gathering information to make decisions. Assessment informs intervention and, as a result, is a critical component of services for young children who have or are at risk for developmental delays/disabilities and their families. In early intervention and early childhood special education, assessment is conducted for the purposes of screening, determining eligibility for services, individualized planning, monitoring child progress, and measuring child outcomes. Not all of the practices that follow apply to all purposes of assessment. For example, practice A9 focuses on monitoring child progress but does not relate to assessment for eligibility.

We recommend the following assessment practices to guide practitioners:

A1. Practitioners work with the family to identify family preferences for assessment processes.

A2. Practitioners work as a team with the family and other professionals to gather assessment information.

A3. Practitioners use assessment materials and strategies that are appropriate for the child's age and level of development and accommodate the child's sensory, physical, communication, cultural, linguistic, social, and emotional characteristics.

A4. Practitioners conduct assessments that include all areas of development and behavior to learn about the child's strengths, needs, preferences, and interests.

A5. Practitioners conduct assessments in the child's dominant language and in additional languages if the child is learning more than one language.

A6. Practitioners use a variety of methods, including observation and interviews, to gather assessment information from multiple sources, including the child's family and other significant individuals in the child's life.

A7. Practitioners obtain information about the child's skills in daily activities, routines, and environments such as home, center, and community.

A8. Practitioners use clinical reasoning in addition to assessment results to identify the child's current levels of functioning and to determine the child's eligibility and plan for instruction.

A9. Practitioners implement systematic ongoing assessment to identify learning targets, plan activities, and monitor the child's progress to revise instruction as needed.

A10. Practitioners use assessment tools with sufficient sensitivity to detect child progress, especially for the child with significant support needs.

A11. Practitioners report assessment results so that they are understandable and useful to families.

ENVIRONMENT

Young children who have or are at risk for developmental delays/disabilities learn, play, and engage with adults and peers within a multitude of environments such as home, school, child care, and the neighborhood. Environmental practices refer to aspects of the space, materials (toys, books, etc.), equipment, routines, and activities that practitioners and families can intentionally alter to support each child's learning across developmental domains. The environmental practices we address in this section encompass the physical environment (e.g., space, equipment, and materials), the social environment (e.g., interactions with peers, siblings, family members), and the temporal environment (e.g., sequence and length of routines and activities). They relate not only to supporting the child's access to learning opportunities but also ensuring the child's safety. It is important for practitioners to remember that these environmental dimensions are inextricably intertwined for young children who have or are at risk for developmental delays/disabilities and their families. Through implementation of the environmental practices, practitioners and families can promote nurturing and responsive caregiving and learning environments that can foster each child's overall health and development.

We recommend the following practices associated with the child's environment:

E1. Practitioners provide services and supports in natural and inclusive environments during daily routines and activities to promote the child's access to and participation in learning experiences.

E2. Practitioners consider Universal Design for Learning principles to create accessible environments.

E3. Practitioners work with the family and other adults to modify and adapt the physical, social, and temporal environments to promote each child's access to and participation in learning experiences.

E4. Practitioners work with families and other adults to identify each child's needs for assistive technology to promote access to and participation in learning experiences.

E5. Practitioners work with families and other adults to acquire or create appropriate assistive technology to promote each child's access to and participation in learning experiences.

E6. Practitioners create environments that provide opportunities for movement and regular physical activity to maintain or improve fitness, wellness, and development across domains.

FAMILY

Family practices refer to ongoing activities that (1) promote the active participation of families in decision making related to their child (e.g., assessment, planning, intervention); (2) lead to the development of a service plan (e.g., a set of goals for the family and child and the services and supports to achieve those goals); or (3) support families in achieving the goals they hold for their child and the other family members.

Family practices encompass three themes:

1. ***Family-centered practices:*** Practices that treat families with dignity and respect; are individualized, flexible, and responsive to each family's unique circumstances; provide family members complete and unbiased information to make informed decisions; and involve family members in acting on choices to strengthen child, parent, and family functioning.
2. ***Family capacity-building practices:*** Practices that include the participatory opportunities and experiences afforded to families to strengthen existing parenting knowledge and skills and promote the development of new parenting abilities that enhance parenting self-efficacy beliefs and practices.
3. ***Family and professional collaboration:*** Practices that build relationships between families and professionals who work together to achieve mutually agreed-upon outcomes and goals that promote family competencies and support the development of the child.

We recommend the following family practices for practitioners:

F1. Practitioners build trusting and respectful partnerships with the family through interactions that are sensitive and responsive to cultural, linguistic, and socio-economic diversity.

F2. Practitioners provide the family with up-to-date, comprehensive and unbiased information in a way that the family can understand and use to make informed choices and decisions.

F3. Practitioners are responsive to the family's concerns, priorities, and changing life circumstances.

F4. Practitioners and the family work together to create outcomes or goals, develop individualized plans, and implement practices that address the family's priorities and concerns and the child's strengths and needs.

F5. Practitioners support family functioning, promote family confidence and competence, and strengthen family–child relationships by acting in ways that recognize and build on family strengths and capacities.

F6. Practitioners engage the family in opportunities that support and strengthen parenting knowledge and skills and parenting competence and confidence in ways that are flexible, individualized, and tailored to the family's preferences.

F7. Practitioners work with the family to identify, access, and use formal and informal resources and supports to achieve family-identified outcomes or goals.

F8. Practitioners provide the family of a young child who has or is at risk for developmental delay/disability, and who is a dual language learner, with information about the benefits of learning in multiple languages for the child's growth and development.

F9. Practitioners help families know and understand their rights.

F10. Practitioners inform families about leadership and advocacy skill-building opportunities and encourage those who are interested to participate.

INSTRUCTION

Instructional practices are a cornerstone of early intervention and early childhood special education. Teachers, other practitioners, family members, and other caregivers use instructional practices to maximize learning and improve developmental and functional outcomes for young children who have or are at risk for developmental delays/disabilities.

Instructional practices are intentional and systematic strategies to inform what to teach, when to teach, how to evaluate the effects of teaching, and how to support and evaluate the quality of instructional practices implemented by others.

Instructional practices are a subset of intervention activities conducted by practitioners and parents. We use the term *instructional practices* rather than the term *teaching practices* or *intervention* because instruction is the predominant term used in the research literature to refer to intentional and systematic strategies to maximize learning.

The recommended instructional practices below are written from the perspective of the practitioner. They may also be implemented by families or others who interact with the child, often with support of the practitioner.

We recommend the following practices to support instruction:

INS1. Practitioners, with the family, identify each child's strengths, preferences, and interests to engage the child in active learning.

INS2. Practitioners, with the family, identify skills to target for instruction that help a child become adaptive, competent, socially connected, and engaged and that promote learning in natural and inclusive environments.

INS3. Practitioners gather and use data to inform decisions about individualized instruction.

INS4. Practitioners plan for and provide the level of support, accommodations, and adaptations needed for the child to access, participate, and learn within and across activities and routines.

INS5. Practitioners embed instruction within and across routines, activities, and environments to provide contextually relevant learning opportunities.

INS6. Practitioners use systematic instructional strategies with fidelity to teach skills and to promote child engagement and learning.

INS7. Practitioners use explicit feedback and consequences to increase child engagement, play, and skills.

INS8. Practitioners use peer-mediated intervention to teach skills and to promote child engagement and learning.

INS9. Practitioners use functional assessment and related prevention, promotion, and intervention strategies across environments to prevent and address challenging behavior.

INS10. Practitioners implement the frequency, intensity, and duration of instruction needed to address the child's phase and pace of learning or the level of support needed by the family to achieve the child's outcomes or goals.

INS11. Practitioners provide instructional support for young children with disabilities who are dual language learners to assist them in learning English and in continuing to develop skills through the use of their home language.

INS12. Practitioners use and adapt specific instructional strategies that are effective for dual language learners when teaching English to children with disabilities.

INS13. Practitioners use coaching or consultation strategies with primary caregivers or other adults to facilitate positive adult–child interactions and instruction intentionally designed to promote child learning and development.

INTERACTION

Sensitive and responsive interactional practices are the foundation for promoting the development of a child's language and cognitive and emotional competence. These interactional practices are the basis for fostering all children's learning. For children who have or are at risk for developmental delays/disabilities, they represent a critical set of strategies for fostering children's social-emotional competence, communication, cognitive development, problem solving, autonomy, and persistence.

We selected interactional practices to promote specific child outcomes, and these will vary depending on the child's developmental levels and cultural and linguistic background.

Practitioners will plan specific ways to engage in these practices across environments, routines, and activities. In addition, practitioners will assist others in the child's life (family members, other caregivers, siblings, and peers) in learning sensitive and responsive ways to interact with the child and promote the child's development.

We recommend the following practices to support interaction:

INT1. Practitioners promote the child's social-emotional development by observing, interpreting, and responding contingently to the range of the child's emotional expressions.

INT2. Practitioners promote the child's social development by encouraging the child to initiate or sustain positive interactions with other children and adults during routines and activities through modeling, teaching, feedback, or other types of guided support.

INT3. Practitioners promote the child's communication development by observing, interpreting, responding contingently, and providing natural consequences for the child's verbal and non-verbal communication and by using language to label and expand on the child's requests, needs, preferences, or interests.

INT4. Practitioners promote the child's cognitive development by observing, interpreting, and responding intentionally to the child's exploration, play, and social activity by joining in and expanding on the child's focus, actions, and intent.

INT5. Practitioners promote the child's problem-solving behavior by observing, interpreting, and scaffolding in response to the child's growing level of autonomy and self-regulation.

TEAMING AND COLLABORATION

Educational programs and services for young children who have or are at risk for developmental delays or disabilities, by their nature, always involve more than one adult. The quality of the relationships and interactions among these adults affects the success of these programs. Teaming and collaboration practices are those that promote and sustain collaborative adult partnerships, relationships, and ongoing interactions to ensure that programs and services achieve desired child and family outcomes and goals.

It is a given that the family is an essential member of the team and that the team includes practitioners from multiple disciplines as needed. The teaming and collaboration practices we present include strategies for interacting and sharing knowledge and expertise in ways that are respectful, are supportive, enhance capacity, and are culturally sensitive.

We recommend the following practices to support teaming and collaboration:

TC1. Practitioners representing multiple disciplines and families work together as a team to plan and implement supports and services to meet the unique needs of each child and family.

TC2. Practitioners and families work together as a team to systematically and regularly exchange expertise, knowledge, and information to build team capacity and jointly solve problems, plan, and implement interventions.

TC3. Practitioners use communication and group facilitation strategies to enhance team functioning and interpersonal relationships with and among team members.

TC4. Team members assist each other to discover and access community-based services and other informal and formal resources to meet family-identified child or family needs.

TC5. Practitioners and families may collaborate with each other to identify one practitioner from the team who serves as the primary liaison between the family and other team members based on child and family priorities and needs.

TRANSITION

Transition refers to the events, activities, and processes associated with key changes between environments or programs during the early childhood years and the practices that support the adjustment of the child and family to the new setting. These changes occur at the transition from hospital to home, the transition into early intervention (Part C) programs, the transition out of early intervention to community early childhood programs, the transition into Part B/619, and the transition to kindergarten or school-age programs.

Transition is a process that generally involves many activities on the part of the practitioner in collaboration with the family. As with other life transitions or changes, positive relationships—in this case positive teacher–child and practitioner–family relationships—are associated with greater satisfaction, better adjustment, and better child outcomes.

We recommend the following practices associated with transition:

TR1. Practitioners in sending and receiving programs exchange information before, during, and after transition about practices most likely to support the child's successful adjustment and positive outcomes.

TR2. Practitioners use a variety of planned and timely strategies with the child and family before, during, and after the transition to support successful adjustment and positive outcomes for both the child and family.

CITATIONS

Copple, C., & Bredekamp, S. (2009). *Developmentally appropriate practice in early childhood programs serving children from birth through age 8* (3rd ed.). Washington, DC: NAEYC.

DEC/NAEYC. (2009). *Early childhood inclusion: A joint position statement of the Division for Early Childhood (DEC) and the National Association for the Education of Young Children (NAEYC).* Retrieved from DEC website: http://www.dec-sped.org/paper

APPENDIX C

Federal Definitions of Disabilities

Autism means a developmental disability significantly affecting verbal and nonverbal communication and social interaction, generally evident before age three, that adversely affects educational performance. Other characteristics often associated with autism are engagement in repetitive activities and stereotyped movements, resistance to environmental change or change in daily routines, and unusual responses to sensory experiences. The term does not apply if a child's educational performance is adversely affected primarily because the child has an emotional disturbance as defined below.

A child who manifests the characteristics of autism after age three could be diagnosed as having autism if the criteria in this paragraph are satisfied.

Deaf–blindness means concomitant hearing and visual impairments, the combination of which causes such severe communication and other developmental and educational problems that they cannot be accommodated in special education programs solely for children with deafness or children with blindness.

Deafness means a hearing impairment that is so severe that the child is impaired in processing linguistic information through hearing with or without amplification adversely affecting educational performance.

Emotional disturbance is defined as follows:

i. The term means a condition exhibiting one or more of the following characteristics over a long period of time and to a marked degree that adversely affects a child's educational performance:

- **A.** an inability to learn that cannot be explained by intellectual, sensory, or health factors,
- **B.** an inability to build or maintain satisfactory interpersonal relationships with peers and teachers,
- **C.** inappropriate types of behavior or feelings under normal circumstances,
- **D.** a general pervasive mood of unhappiness or depression, or
- **E.** a tendency to develop physical symptoms or fears associated with personal or school problems.

ii. The term includes schizophrenia. The term does not apply to children who are socially maladjusted unless it is determined that they have an emotional disturbance.

Hearing impairment means an impairment in hearing, whether permanent or fluctuating, that adversely affects a child's educational performance but that is not included under the definition of deafness in this section.

Intellectual disability means significantly subaverage general intellectual functioning existing concurrently with deficits in adaptive behavior and manifested during the developmental period that adversely affects a child's educational performance.

Multiple disabilities means concomitant impairments (such as intellectual disability–blindness, intellectual disability–orthopedic impairment, etc.), the combination of which causes such severe educational needs that they cannot be accommodated in special education programs solely for one of the impairments. The term does not include deaf–blindness.

Orthopedic impairment means a severe orthopedic impairment that adversely affects a child's educational performance. The term includes impairments caused by congenital anomaly (e.g., clubfoot, absence of some member, etc.), impairments caused by disease (e.g., poliomyelitis, bone tuberculosis, etc.), and impairments from other causes (e.g., cerebral palsy, amputations, and fractures or burns that cause contractures).

Other health impairments means having limited strength, vitality, or alertness, including a heightened alertness to environmental stimuli that results in limited alertness with respect to the educational environment that

i. is due to chronic or acute health problems such as asthma, attention deficit disorder or attention deficit hyperactivity disorder, diabetes, epilepsy, a heart condition, hemophilia, lead poisoning, leukemia, nephritis, rheumatic fever, and sickle cell anemia; and

ii. adversely affects a child's educational performance.

Specific learning disability is defined as follows:

i. General. The term means a disorder in one or more of the basic psychological processes involved in understanding or in using language, spoken or written, that may manifest itself in an imperfect ability to listen, think, speak, read, write, spell, or to do mathematical calculations, including conditions such as perceptual disabilities, brain injury, minimal brain dysfunction, dyslexia, and developmental aphasia.

ii. Disorders not included. The term does not include learning problems that are primarily the result of visual, hearing, or motor disabilities, of intellectual disability, of emotional disturbance, or of environmental, cultural, or economic disadvantage.

Speech or language impairment means a communication disorder such as stuttering, impaired articulation, a language impairment, or a voice impairment that adversely affects a child's educational performance.

Traumatic brain injury means an acquired injury to the brain caused by an external physical force, resulting in total or partial functional disability or psychosocial impairment or both that adversely affects a child's educational performance. The term applies to open or closed head injuries resulting in impairments in one or more areas, such as cognition; language; memory; attention; reasoning; abstract thinking; judgment; problem solving; sensory, perceptual, and motor abilities; psychosocial behavior; physical function; information processing; and speech. The term does not apply to brain injuries that are congenital or degenerative or brain injuries induced by birth trauma.

Visual impairment including blindness means an impairment in vision that, even with correction, adversely affects a child's educational performance. The term includes both partial sight and blindness.

Source: Individuals with Disabilities Education Improvement Act of 2004, 34 CFR 300.8 (c). August 14, 2006.

APPENDIX D

Sample Individualized Family Service Plan

Sample Individualized Family Service Plan

I. Child and Family Information

Child's Name Maria Ramirez Date of Birth 12-08-20 Age in Months 30 Gender F

Parent(s)/Guardian(s) Bruce & Catherine Ramirez Address 2120 Valley Park Place (Street) Middletown, IN (City) 46810 (Zip Code)

Home Telephone No. (513) 555-0330 Work Telephone No. (513) 555-1819

Preferred Language English Translator Appropriate ___Yes X No

II. Service Coordination

Coordinator's Name Susan Green Agency Indiana Early Intervention Program

Address 105 Data Drive (Street) Burlington, IN (City) 46980 (Zip Code) Telephone No. (513) 555-0214

Appointment Date 6-12-23

III. IFSP Team Members

Name	Agency	Telephone No.	Title/Function
Susan Green	Indiana Early Prevention (EI) Program	513-555-0214	Service Coordinator
Mr. and Mrs. B. Ramirez	N/A	513-555-0330	Parents
Barbara Smith	Indiana EI Program	513-555-0215	Speech-Language Pathologist
Martha King	Indiana EI Program	513-555-0213	Occupational Therapist
Libby Young	Middletown Preschool Program	513-555-3533	Preschool Teacher

IV. Review Dates

Date of IFSP 6-12-23 Six-Month Review 12-12-23 Annual Evaluation N/A

V. Statements of Family Strengths and Resources

Maria's parents are well-educated professionals. They have realistic goals for her educational development. The entire family unit, including her grandparents, is committed and motivated to assist her in any way. Because of the family's geographic location, limited resources are available for service delivery at this time.

VI. Statements of Family Concerns and Priorities

CONCERNS

Due to Maria's medical diagnosis of Down syndrome, her parents are concerned about appropriate early intervention services to assist in ameliorating her developmental delays. Additionally, the parents have stated reluctance about a change in Maria's service delivery from her natural environment (for example, her home) to an inclusive community preschool.

PRIORITIES

The priorities that Maria's parents have for her include improving her communication skills, ability to use utensils, and toileting skills. They desire services to be delivered at home but would like for her to go to a child care/early learning program at least one day a week to interact with other children her age. The eventual goal is placement with typically developing children who attend the local kindergarten. Her parents and grandparents want to learn ways in which they can help to facilitate Maria's development in her natural environment.

VII. Child's Strengths and Present Level of Development

Cognitive Skills (Thinking, reasoning, and learning)

Maria's cognitive abilities are commensurate with a 20-month-old child. She is extremely inquisitive and understands simple object concept skills. Imitative play is consistently observed; however, discrimination of objects, persons, and concepts continues to be an area of need.

Communication Skills (Understanding, communicating with others, and expressing herself with others)

Communication/language competency skills appear to be similar to that of an 18-month-old toddler. Her receptive language is further developed than her expressive abilities. Primitive gestures are her primary mode of communication. She consistently exhibits a desire/interest to interact with others. Verbal responses primarily consist of vocalizations and approximations of single-word utterances (e.g., ma-ma, da-da, ba-ba).

Self-Care/Adaptive Skills (Bathing, feeding, dressing, and toileting)

Eating, in general, such as drinking from a cup and finger feeding, is appropriate at this time. Maria prefers to eat the same foods all the time (for example, SpaghettiOs, Cheetos, Cheerios) and is reluctant to try new foods. A great deal of assistance from caregivers is still required for daily dressing tasks and toileting.

Gross and Fine Motor Skills (Moving, reaching, and grasping)

Maria appears to be quite mobile. She is adept at rambling and walking, but needs to improve muscle strength and endurance. She enjoys movement to music. She can scribble, grasp large objects, and turn pages of books, and she prefers using her right hand while performing tasks. She needs to work on using utensils and writing tools.

Social-Emotional Development (Feelings, coping, and getting along with others)

Maria is a happy, affectionate, and sociable child. She enjoys being the center of attention and engaging in interactive games; however, she also appears content to play alone. Temper tantrums seem to be triggered by frustration from her limited communication skills. Sharing and turn-taking continue to be difficult for Maria.

Health/Physical Development (Hearing, vision, and health)

Maria's general health is good, but she has a history of chronic otitis media and upper respiratory infections. Vision and hearing are monitored frequently.

VIII. Outcome Statements

I. Participate in language activities to increase communication.

Strategies/Activities	Responsible Person/Agency	Begin Date	End Date	Frequency of Service	Location	Evaluation Criteria
1.1 Maria will use sounds combined with consistent gestures (for example, pointing) to show what she wants or needs (for example, for a toy, to be picked up, for a drink).	SLP	6-12-23	12-12-23	Once Weekly	Home	Observation samples
1.2 Maria will use words combined with signs to indicate wants or needs.	Mom and Dad	6-11-18	12-11-18	Once Weekly	Home	Observation samples

II. Maria's daily self-care skills will improve in the areas of dressing, toileting, and eating.

Strategies/Activities	Responsible Person/Agency	Begin Date	End Date	Frequency of Service	Location	Evaluation Criteria
2.1 Maria will push down/pull up undergarments with minimal assistance.	Mom and Dad Service Coord.	6-12-23	12-12-23	Once Weekly	Home	Observation

Strategies/Activities	Responsible Person/ Agency	Begin Date	End Date	Frequency of Service	Location	Evaluation Criteria
2.2 Maria will have a consistent pattern of elimination/toileting.	Mom and Dad Service Coord.	6-12-23	12-12-23	Once Weekly	Home	Recorded data of schedule and frequency of elimination
2.3 Maria will spontaneously indicate by using gestures and vocalizing the need for going to the restroom.	Mom and Dad Service Coord.	6-12-23	12-12-23	Once Weekly	Home	Observation samples
2.4 Maria will eat the same foods as her family members at mealtime.	Mom and Dad Service Coord.	6-12-23	12-12-23	Once Weekly	Home	Observation samples

III. Maria will develop improved abilities to discriminate sounds, movements, colors, and shapes.

Strategies/Activities	Responsible Person/ Agency	Begin Date	End Date	Frequency of Service	Location	Evaluation Criteria
3.1 Sort several colors and shapes consistently	Mom and Dad Service Coord.	6-12-23	12-12-23	Once Weekly	Home	Observation samples

IV. Maria will have opportunities for interaction with other children at a child care/early learning program.

Strategies/Activities	Responsible Person/ Agency	Begin Date	End Date	Frequency of Service	Location	Evaluation Criteria
4.1 After being given options by the Service Coordinator, Mom will visit and select a child care/early learning program for Maria to attend in the fall.	Mom and Dad Service Coord.	6-12-23	12-12-23	Variable		Parent report

IX. Transition Plans

If eligible, the followings steps will be followed to transition Maria Ramirez (CHILDS'S NAME) to preschool services on or about 12-14-23. (PROJECTED TRANSITION DATE)

1. The service coordinator will schedule a meeting with Maria's parents to explain the transition process and rationale, review legal rights, and ascertain their preferences and need for support in addition to their priorities.
2. The service coordinator will arrange for Maria and her parents (and grandparents) to visit the center and meet teachers, staff, and children.
3. The service coordinator will arrange for Maria to visit her classroom on at least three occasions in the month prior to her transition date.
4. At least 90 days prior to Maria's third birthday, the service coordinator will convene a meeting to further develop Maria's transition plan.

X. Identification of Natural Environments

The home environment is considered to be Maria's natural environment at this time.

Justification for not providing services in natural environment: Not applicable.

XI. Family Authorization

We (I) the parent(s)/guardian(s) of Maria Ramirez hereby certify that we (I) have had the opportunity to participate in the development of our (my) son's/daughter's IFSP. This document accurately reflects our (my) concerns and priorities for our (my) child and family.

We (I) therefore give our (my) permission for this plan to be implemented. X Yes ___ No

Catherine Ramirez	6-12-23	Bruce Ramirez	6-12-23
SIGNATURE OF PARENT/GUARDIAN	DATE	SIGNATURE OF PARENT/GUARDIAN	DATE

APPENDIX E

Sample Individualized Education Program

Sample Individualized Education Program

I. Student Information and Instructional Profile

Student Thomas Jefferson (T. J.) Browning Date of Birth March 3, 2019 Student Number 000-60-0361

Parent's/Guardian's Name Angela Browning Address 141 Boulder Ave. Apt. 16-A (Street) Franklin, SC (City) 42698 (Zip Code)

Parent's/Guardian's Phone No. 803-555-1920 Student's Present School Epps Head Start Center Grade Pre-K

Date of IEP Meeting May 8, 2023 Date of Eligibility April 13, 2022 IEP Review Date May 2, 2024

Child's Primary Language English Limited English Proficiency No (Yes/No) Braille Instruction No (Yes/No)

Assistive Technology Needs No (Yes/No) Language/Communication Needs No (Yes/No) BehaviorNeeds No (Yes/No)

II. Present Levels of Academic Achievement and Functional Performance

T. J. is an energetic, creative four-year-old. He loves outdoor play and has age-appropriate gross motor skills. He also demonstrates age-appropriate skills in self-care. Like many of his peers, he still has some difficulty tying his shoes and buttoning smaller-sized buttons.

T. J. communicates his wants and needs to others. Generally, in conveying his message, T. J. uses a lot of gestures to support his verbal language. A language sample collected on May 1, 2023, indicated that, on average, T. J. is using two- to three-word sentences. Within the classroom, T. J. often does not respond to questions asked of him or directives given to him. Classroom observations conducted throughout the school year show that T. J. has the greatest difficulty in answering questions that begin with "Why," "What," and "When." Standardized tests adminis-tered on May 1, 2023, placed T. J. in the age range of a child who is 3 years, 4 months and 3 years, 8 months for auditory comprehension and verbal abilities, respectively. Specific areas of difficulty include vocabulary, recalling details in sequence, language usage, and classification of objects.

T. J. loves to please adults and is responsive to praise. T. J. prefers solitary play. He typically chooses activities in which he demonstrates competence. In four out of five opportunities, these activities involve object assembly such as LEGOs or blocks. T. J. has difficulty playing cooperatively and sharing. Due to his language delays, he tends to display aggressive behavior, rather than interacting verbally, when trying to resolve conflicts with his peers. Although T. J. knows the classroom rules, he requires frequent redirection to task. He has a short attention span, usually staying no more than five minutes with any given activity.

Visual-motor integration is difficult for T. J. when engaged in fine motor activities. He has trouble copying shapes and designs using pencils or crayons. T. J. can cut on a 1/4" straight line, but needs continued practice with cutting other shapes.

Mrs. Browning, T. J.'s mother, is concerned about his ability to communicate and play with children his age at school and at home. She worries about his aggressive behaviors toward his peers at school and church. At home she has noticed that T. J. has difficulty following directions.

The members of the IEP team have identified T. J.'s delayed communication skills, short attention span, poor social interaction, and difficulty with fine motor skills as areas of concern that impact his achievement in the general education classroom.

III. Program Eligibility

Eligible X Not Eligible ______ Area(s) of Disability Language Impairment (Primary) Not applicable (Secondary)

Rationale for Eligibility Delayed receptive and expressive language is significantly below language of same-age peers.

IV. Measurable Annual Goals and Benchmarks

1. Area. Communication/Language: T. J. will improve his receptive and expressive language skills by responding to teacher inquiries using 4- to 5-word sentences 80% of the time given two opportunities to respond.

	Provider	Evaluation Method	Initiation Date	Check Date	Mastery Date
Benchmark #1 T. J. will verbally express his needs using expanded sentences of 4-5 words.	General educator Speech-language pathologist	ⓐ Data collection b. Teacher/Text test c. Work samples ⓓ Classroom observation e. Grades ⓕ Other: Language sample	9/11/23	1/8/24 5/6/24	______
Benchmark #2 T. J. will correctly answer "wh" questions (what, who, where, and when).	General educator Speech-language pathologist	a. Data collection b. Teacher/Text test c. Work samples ⓓ Classroom observation e. Grades f. Other: ______	9/11/23	1/8/24 5/6/24	______

2. Area. Cognitive/Language: T. J. will answer teacher questions using appropriate vocabulary 80% of the time on four out of five occasions.

	Provider	Evaluation Method	Initiation Date	Check Date	Mastery Date
Benchmark #1 T. J. will retell simple stories stating at least 3 events in sequence.	General educator Special educator	ⓐ Data collection b. Teacher/Text test c. Work samples ⓓ Classroom observation e. Grades ⓕ Other: Tape-recorded retellings	9/11/23	1/8/24 5/6/24	______
Benchmark #2 T. J. will appropriately use vocabulary associated with the kindergarten curriculum.	General educator Special educator	ⓐ Data collection b. Teacher/Text test c. Work samples ⓓ Classroom observation e. Grades f. Other: ______	9/11/23	1/8/24 5/6/24	______

	Provider	Evaluation Method	Initiation Date	Check Date	Mastery Date
Benchmark #3					
T. J. will verbally describe objects found in age-appropriate books.	General educator Special educator	ⓐ Data collection b. Teacher/Text test c. Work samples ⓓ Classroom observation e. Grades f. Other:	9/11/24	1/8/24 5/6/24	______

3. Area. Social/Behavioral: T. J. will engage in appropriate social interactions with peers and adults 70% of the time given two verbal or visual prompts.

	Provider	Evaluation Method	Initiation Date	Check Date	Mastery Date
Benchmark #1					
T. J. will respond to conflict with peers without aggression.	General educator Special educator	a. Data collection b. Teacher/Text test c. Work samples ⓓ Classroom observation e. Grades ⓕ Other: Behavior contract	9/11/24	1/8/24 5/6/24	______
Benchmark #2					
T. J. will follow adult instructions and directions with less than two reminders.	General educator Special educator	a. Data collection b. Teacher/Text test c. Work samples ⓓ Classroom observation e. Grades ⓕ Other: Behavior contract	9/11/24	1/8/24 5/6/24	______
Benchmark #3					
T. J. will participate in a group activity for at least 10 minutes.	General educator Special educator	a. Data collection b. Teacher/Text test c. Work samples ⓓ Classroom observation e. Grades f. Other: Behavior contract	9/11/24	1/8/24 5/6/24	______

4. Area. Fine Motor: T. J. will write numbers and letters accurately 75% of the time after teacher modeling.

	Provider	Evaluation Method	Initiation Date	Check Date	Mastery Date
Benchmark #1					
T. J. will recognizably print his first and last name.	General educator	a. Data collection b. Teacher/Text test ⓒ Work samples	9/11/24	1/8/24 5/6/24	______

d. Classroom observation
e. Grades
f. Other: ___________

Benchmark #2

T. J. will print upper- and lowercase letters.	General educator	a. Data collection b. Teacher/Text Test ⓒ Work samples d. Classroom observation e. Grades	9/11/23	1/8/24 5/6/24	___________

V. Supplementary Aids and Related Services

Services/Related Services	Provider	Hours per Week	Location
Instructional support	Special educator	2	General education environment
Speech-language therapy	Speech-language pathologist	2	General education environment

Aids/equipment/program modifications needed to attain annual goals and progress in general education curriculum: Not applicable at this time
Frequency of use: Not applicable.

VI. Special Education Placement

Student to be placed in the following least restrictive environment (LRE):

Location of Services	Duration (Number of hours in location/total number of school hours)	Extent of Participation
General education classroom	35 hours per week/35 hours per week	100%
Special education environments:		
Special day school		
Residential school		
Hospital school		
Homebound services		
Other (e.g., Head Start, preschool program)		
Rationale for placement in setting other than general education class	Not applicable	

VII. Special SERVICES

Physical Education: Regular X Adaptive ___________

Transportation: Regular X Special ___________ Not Applicable ___________

Is student provided an opportunity to participate in extracurricular and nonacademic activities with typical peers? Yes (Yes/No)

Are supports necessary? No (Yes/No) Describe: ___________

Rationale for nonparticipation: Not applicable

VIII. Transition (no later than age 16, earlier if appropriate)

Transition Service Needs Focusing on Course of Study	Not applicable at this time
Employment Outcome	Not applicable at this time
Community Living Outcome	Not applicable at this time
Identify Needed Transition Services	Not applicable at this time
Identify Interagency Responsibilities and Community Linkages	Not applicable at this time

IX. Assessment Modifications

Is student able to participate in state or district-wide assessments? Yes (Yes/No)

Are modifications required? Yes (Yes/No)

Identify type of modifications: Not applicable

Rationale for nonparticipation and alternate assessment plan: Not applicable

X. Progress Report

Parents will be informed of child's progress toward annual goals using same reporting methods used for children without disabilities.

Method		Frequency
Written Progress Report	Yes (Yes/No)	Every 6 weeks
Parent Conference	Yes (Yes/No)	As needed
Other	behavior contact (Identify)	Weekly
Other	(Identify)	

XI. Transferal of Rights

I understand that the rights under the Individuals with Disabilities Education Improvement Act will transfer to me upon reaching my eighteenth birthday.

Student's Signature ____________________ Date ____________________

XII. Recommended Instructional and/or Behavioral Interventions

Behavior contract designed to reduce frequency of aggressive interactions with peers.

XIII. IEP Development Team

Name	Team Member's Signature	Position/Title
Angela Browning	Angela Browning	Parent/Guardian
		Parent/Guardian
Patricia Gwin	Patricia Gwin	LEA Representative
Ann Martin	Ann Martin	Early Childhood Special Education Teacher
Cecelia Watkins	Cecelia Watkins	General Education Teacher Student
Melanie Spangler	Melanie Spangler	Other: Speech-Language Pathologist

GLOSSARY

Accessibility: Adaptations of the environment aimed at equalizing participation opportunities for persons with delays and disabilities. Within educational contexts, this includes adaptations necessary to ensure physical and cognitive access and successful goal attainment by young children with delays and disabilities

Accommodation: According to Piaget, alteration of existing cognitive structures to allow for new information—involves a change in understanding.

Activity areas or learning centers: Organized space within a classroom, typically designed to accommodate small groups of children and a teacher, which are dedicated to activities based on a theme or developmental domain

Activity-based instruction or intervention: A curriculum approach that embeds instruction to address each child's IFSP or IEP goals into naturally occurring events and opportunities in their daily routine in the home, classroom, and other settings

Adaptability: In family systems theory, this is a concept used to describe a family's ability to change its power structure, role relationships, and rules in response to crises or stressful events occurring over a lifetime

Adaptation: Any adjustment that allows a child with delays and disabilities to participate fully with their typically developing peers

Adapted participation: Use of an alternative means of participation (i.e., orienting head or eye gaze instead of pointing; using a communication board instead of speaking)

Adaptive behavior: Primarily center on the areas of eating and personal care (e.g., toileting, grooming, dressing)

Apgar Scale: A screening procedure for newborns given at one minute and again at five minutes following birth to measure heart rate, respiration, reflex response, muscle tone, and color

Arena assessment: Based on a transdisciplinary model in which a group of professionals from various disciplines, along with the child's family, participate in the assessment process

Assessment: The process of gathering information for the purpose of making a decision about children with known or suspected disabilities in the areas of screening, diagnosis, eligibility, program planning, and/or progress monitoring and evaluation

Assimilation: In Piaget's terms, the inclusion of new information and experiences into existing cognitive schemes or structures.

Assistive technology interventions: The evaluation of a student and the implementation of technology tools while monitoring their effects in order to increase the individual's independence

Assistive technology: Any item, piece of equipment, or product system that increases, maintains, or improves functional capabilities of individuals with delays and disabilities

At risk: A child with exposure to certain adverse conditions and circumstances known to have a high probability of resulting in learning and development difficulties.

Auditory trainer: Type of amplification system sometimes used by children with hearing impairments

Auditory-oral: An educational approach for children with hearing impairments that emphasizes the development of speech, speechreading, and listening with appropriate amplification

Augmentative and alternative communication (AAC): For children who are nonverbal or have limited verbal abilities, devices or systems that can be used to allow them to respond within learning activities

Authentic assessment: A type of assessment approach that is based on the premise that the behavior of young children must be observed in natural settings during real-life situations

Autism spectrum disorders (ASD): A developmental disorder characterized by abnormal or impaired development in social interaction and communication and a markedly restricted repertoire of activity and interest

Auto-education: In Montessori terms, the self-teaching that occurs as a result of a child independently interacting with a carefully planned environment.

Behavior disorder: A term used to describe a wide variety of social and emotional problems, such as attention and/or hyperactivity, conduct, and anxiety disorders

Behavioral approach: A model based on learning principles of behavioral psychology that emphasizes direct instruction through a prescribed sequence of instructional activities

Bias: Any characteristic that unfairly discriminates against a child on the basis of gender, socioeconomic status, or cultural or linguistic background

Bilingual education: An educational approach whereby students whose first language is not English are instructed primarily through their native language while developing competency and proficiency in English

Bilingual-bicultural: An educational approach that considers American Sign Language (ASL) to be the natural language of the Deaf culture and urges recognition of ASL as the primary language, with English considered a second language

Biological risk: Young children with a history of pre-, peri-, and postnatal conditions and developmental events that heighten the potential for later atypical development.

Blended practices: A term used in early childhood education and early childhood special education to refer to the integration of knowledge about effective practices for teaching children with and without disabilities into a comprehensive approach to ensure that all children in inclusive settings meet high standards

Center- or school-based programs: Group-oriented service delivery model for young children with delays and disabilities. Intervention and educational services provided in settings other than the child's home

Child Find: System of locating children who may have delays and disabilities and who need further testing to determine whether they are eligible for early intervention/early childhood special education services

Child-initiated routines and activities: Those that children initiate themselves, as opposed to routines and activities that are initiated and directed by adults

Children with complex health care needs: A general term referring to children with a wide variety of serious and often unique health care concerns

Chronosystem: The interaction and influence of historical time on the micro-, meso-, exo-, and macrosystems.

Classroom ecology: Refers to the environmental modifications and arrangements of features of classroom environments that can have an impact on learning for young children with delays and disabilities

Coaching: Working with a child's caregivers (e.g., family, teachers) to explain why specific strategies are selected and how to integrate the strategies into the daily routines; demonstrating, modeling, and practicing the new strategies along with providing encouragement and specific feedback that will help a child make progress toward achieving their goals

Cochlear implant: A surgical procedure capable of restoring hearing in some individuals with a hearing loss

Cognitive skills: Refers to : child's evolving mental and intellectual ability

Cohesion: According to family systems theory, this is a concept used to describe the degree of freedom and independence experienced by each family member within a family unit

Collaboration: The act or process of working together that results in mutual benefits for families and professionals and involves mutual respect and cooperation to reach common goals

Communication: A process used by two or more people to send and receive messages

Communicative intent: Attention is given to what a child is attempting to communicate using a variety of means (e.g., gestures, eye gaze, vocalizations)

Compensatory education: Early experiences and intervention efforts aimed at ameliorating the consequences of living in poverty; the goal is to better prepare young children for school.

Concurrent validity: How well a test correlates with other accepted measures of performance administered close in time

Construct validity: The degree to which a test addresses the constructs on which it is based

Content domains: Areas of knowledge and skills consisting of the body of information on which intervention and instruction are based and that children are expected to learn in academic programs and programs promoting academic readiness

Content validity: How well a test represents the content it purports to measure

Cooperative learning: Instructional process whereby heterogeneous groups of students work together on assignments

Cooperative\Collaborative teaching: An instructional approach in which an early childhood special educator and a general education teacher teach together in a general education classroom to a heterogeneous group of children

Criterion-referenced assessments: A type of measure used to determine whether a child's performance meets established criteria or a certain level of mastery within various developmental domains (e.g., cognitive, motor, self-care) or subject areas (e.g., math, literacy)

Cultural mediator: An individual who helps translate between the culture of a program or school environment and a child's family in order to enhance understanding, share information, and create a relationship that supports children and families

Cultural responsiveness: A complex concept involving the awareness, acknowledgment, and acceptance of each family's culture and cultural values that requires professionals to view each family as a unique unit that is influenced by, but not defined by, its culture

Culturally and linguistically responsive and affirming: A complex concept involving the awareness, acknowledgement, and acceptance of each family's culture and cultural values that requires professionals to view each family as a unique unit that is influenced by, but not defined by, its culture

Culturally biased assessment: A measure that focuses on skills and abilities of the dominant Western culture and places children from non-Western, nondominant cultures at a disadvantage

Culture: The foundational values and beliefs that set the standards for how people perceive, interpret, and behave within their family, school, and community

Curriculum framework: A supportive structure that provides guidance for EI/ECSE professionals to align developmental and content knowledge as well as related pedagogy to plan meaningful learning activities, environments, and individualized supports

Curriculum model: A conceptual framework and organizational structure combining theory with practice, describing what to teach and how to teach

Curriculum-based assessments: A type of assessment measure most relevant for program-planning purposes and used to identify a child's entry point in an educational program, as well as to modify instruction

Curriculum: Viewed as everything that a child should learn in an early childhood setting; it flows from the theoretical or philosophical perspectives on which the program is based

Deafness: A condition that adversely affects educational performance and is so severe that the child is impaired in processing linguistic information or communication through hearing, with or without amplification

Developmental age score: The result from a norm-referenced test for children from birth through age five

Developmental approach: A traditional curriculum model based on theories of typical child development

Developmental delay: A concept defined by individual states when referring to young children with special needs. A delay is usually determined on the basis of various developmental assessments and/or informed clinical opinion.

Developmental domains: The key skill areas addressed in early childhood special education curriculum: cognitive, motor, communication, social, and adaptive skills

Developmental-cognitive approach: A theory-driven model based on the work of Piaget that emphasizes the domain of cognitive skill development

Developmentally Appropriate Practice (DAP): A set of guidelines established by the National Association for the Education of Young Children (NAEYC) to articulate appropriate practices for the early education of young children from birth through age eight

Didactic materials: Instructional items used in Montessori programs.

Disability: An inability to do something; a reduced capacity to perform in a specific way.

Early childhood special education: The provision of customized services uniquely crafted to meet the individual needs of youngsters between three and five years of age with disabilities.

Early Head Start: A federal program providing a variety of services to low-income families with infants and toddlers as well as to women who are pregnant.

Early intervention: The delivery of a coordinated and comprehensive set of specialized services for infants and toddlers (from birth through age two) with developmental delays or at-risk conditions and their families.

Echolalic speech: A condition in which someone repeats what is said rather than generating an original sentence

Eco-map: A drawing or figure that is useful in fostering collaboration among professionals and families and also in depicting and using important information such as family structure, relationships, strengths, and resources

Ecological perspective: A perspective emphasizing that power emerges from the nature and structure of human relationships within environmental contexts

Ecology: The interrelationships and interactions of the various environments or contexts that affect the child and are affected by the child.

Eligibility: A comprehensive assessment process to determine whether a child meets the criteria to be eligible for early intervention or early childhood special education services

Embedded interventions: The process of identifying times and activities when a child's goals *and* the instructional procedures for those goals can be inserted into a child's ongoing activities, routines, and transitions in a way that relates to the context

Emotional abuse: A type of child maltreatment distinguished by caregiver actions that are designed to be psychologically harmful

Emotional skills: Children's abilities to identify and communicate feelings, as well as their capacity to act on their emotions while respecting the rights of others. Skills in this area include how to control one's impulses or temper and how to resolve conflicts

Empowerment: The process of applying strategies whereby individuals and families gain a sense of control over their future as a result of their own efforts and activities

Engagement: Consistent, active involvement with people, activities, and materials throughout the child's day

Environment: The sum total of the physical and human qualities that combine to create a space in which children and adults work and play together

Environmental arrangements: Any changes in the environment that are used to facilitate child engagement, such as altering the physical space, altering the selection and use of materials, and altering the structure of an activity

Environmental practices: "Aspects of the space, materials (toys, books, etc.), equipment, routines, and activities that practitioners and families can intentionally alter to support each child's learning across developmental domains" (Division for Early Childhood, 2014, p. 9)

Environmental risk: Biologically typical children who encounter life experiences or environmental conditions that are so limiting that the possibility of future delayed development exists.

Equilibration: According to Piaget's theorizing, the cognitive process by which a person attempts to balance new information with existing data.

Established risk: Children with a diagnosed medical disorder of known etiology and predictable prognosis or outcome.

Ethnocentric behavior: The viewpoint that the practices and behavior of one particular cultural group are natural and correct while the actions of other groups are inferior or odd

Evidence-based practices: Instructional practices that are based upon empirical research

Exceptional children: Children who differ from society's view of normalcy.

Exosystems: According to Bronfenbrenner, the social systems that exert an influence on the development of the individual.

Expressive language: The ability to communicate thoughts or feelings through vocalizations, words, and other behaviors used to relay information

False negative: Designation of a child who needs special services but was not referred as a result of a screening

False positive: Designation of a child who has been referred as a result of a screening but does not need special services

Family and professional collaboration: Practices that build relationships between families and professionals who work together to achieve mutually agreed upon outcomes and goals that promote family competencies and support the development of the child

Family capacity-building practices: Practices that include the participatory opportunities and experiences afforded to families to strengthen existing parenting knowledge and skills and promote the development of new parenting abilities that enhance parenting self-efficacy beliefs and practices

Family characteristics: According to family systems theory, this is the dimension that makes each family unique (e.g., family size and form, cultural background, geographic location)

Family function: One of the components of family systems theory that refers to one of the eight interrelated activities considered necessary to fulfill the individual and collective needs of a family (e.g., affection, economics, recreation, education)

Family interactions: According to family systems theory, these are the relationships and interactions that occur among and between various family subsystems, like the marital subsystem

Family life cycle: According to family systems theory, this component refers to the changes that occur in families over time that influence their resources, interactions, and functions

Family systems theory: A model that considers the family an interrelated and interdependent unit with unique characteristics and needs. Events and experiences that have an impact on a particular family member (e.g., a child with a delay or disability) also will affect the other members of the family or the entire family unit

Family-centered practices: A philosophy of working with families whereby specific techniques and methods are used that stress family strengths, the enhancement of family skills and competencies, and the development of mutual partnerships between families and professionals

Family: A group of people related by blood or circumstances who rely upon one another for security, sustenance, support, socialization, and/or stimulation

Fine motor skills: The ability to use small muscle groups such as those in the hands, face, and feet

FM system: A wireless communication system available to children with hearing impairments. The teacher wears a transmitter while the child wears the receiver; allows student to adjust the volume of the teacher's voice

Formative assessment: Evaluation of children's learning during program operation for the purpose of improving the quality of teaching and overall learning rather than for evaluating the progress of individual children; often conducted at the beginning of the year and ongoing

Functional approach: A model in which the skills or behaviors are emphasized that have immediate relevance to a child

Functional behavior analysis: A behavioral approach that seeks to determine the purpose or function that a particular behavior serves

Functional behavior assessment: A type of assessment that is used to investigate the environmental variables contributing to and/or maintaining a challenging behavior

Functional skill: A basic skill that is required on a frequent basis (e.g., eating, toileting, requesting assistance, turn-taking) in the natural environment

Generalization: The ability to apply what is learned in one context to different settings, different materials, or different people

Gifts: A Fröbelian term referring to manipulative objects, such as balls and wooden blocks, used as tools for learning in Fröbel's curriculum.

Gross motor skills: The type of skills that involve the movement and control of large muscle groups used to function in the environment

Handicap: The consequences or impact encountered by or imposed on a child with a disability as they attempt to function and interact in the environment.

High-tech devices: A complicated assistive technology device that is expensive to own and operate

Home Start: A derivation of the Head Start program designed to provide comprehensive services to young children and their parents in the home through the utilization of home visitors.

Home visits: Home-based services delivered in the natural environment by professionals to address the development and learning of the child and support the family, which requires coordinated planning and collaboration among families and professionals

Home-based services: A type of service delivery model for young children with delays and disabilities. Intervention is provided in the child's home by the primary caregiver. Professionals make regular visits to work directly with the child and to provide instruction to the caregiver

Hybrid family: A family that redefines itself and produces a family that is different from either family of origin; it consists of a blending of cultural and religious origins

Hypertonic muscle tone: Tight muscles

Hypotonic muscle tone: Floppy muscles that exhibit resistance to being stretched

Inclusion: The process of integrating children with delays and disabilities into educational settings primarily designed to serve children without disabilities

Individualized education program (IEP): Required by federal legislation. A customized educational plan, constructed by a team, for each child with special needs.

Individualized family service plan (IFSP): A written document mandated by federal law. Designed as a guide for services for infants, toddlers, and their families. Developed by a team of professionals and the parent(s).

Informed clinical opinion: The use of professional judgment, based on experience and expertise, and family input to make recommendations for initial and continuing eligibility for EI/ECSE services and to plan services for those children whose developmental status and EI/ECSE needs may be difficult to assess with formal measures

Instructional validity: The extent to which the information gained from an assessment instrument would be useful in planning intervention programs for young children with delays and disabilities

Interdisciplinary team: A type of teaming model utilized in delivering services to young children with delays and disabilities. Team members typically perform their evaluations independently; however, program development and recommendations for services are the results of information sharing and joint planning

Interviews: A form of assessment that can be used to gather information from families or other caregivers about the areas on which to focus during the assessment process; specific information about the child (e.g., how a child responds to various situations); the families' concerns, priorities, and resources; or other types of information that may be relevant to the assessment process

Language: The use of symbols (i.e., letter sounds that are used in various combinations to form words), syntax (i.e., rules that guide sentence structure), or grammar (i.e., the way sentences are constructed) when communicating with one another

Learned helplessness: A sense of helplessness for children when their interactions with the environment prove to be futile or produce inconsistent results or negative feedback. Persons with learned helplessness feel they have little control over elements of their environment

Least restrictive environment (LRE): A concept requiring that children with special needs be educated, to the maximum extent appropriate, with their typical classmates. Settings are individually determined for each pupil.

Low-tech devices: A low-cost assistive technology device that does not require electrical power or batteries to operate

Macrosystems: The ideological, cultural, and institutional contexts that encompass the micro-, meso-, and exosystems.

Mesosystems: The relationships between the various environments of the microsystems.

Meta-analysis: A comprehensive statistical procedure whereby research studies are evaluated in an effort to ascertain global statistical patterns; they yield "effect size," reported as standard deviations.

Microsystems: As proposed by Bronfenbrenner, the immediate environments in which a person develops, such as a child's home and neighborhood.

Mid-tech devices: A sophisticated assistive technology device that requires a power source

Milieu strategies. Estrategias de Milieu. Estrategias para facilitar las habilidades del lenguaje (especialmente la interacción social) que se aprovecha del ambiente natural (personas, materiales, actividades) para apoyar el aprendizaje. Las estrategias incluyen una variedad de procedimientos específicos (retraso de tiempo, modelo de mand, enseñanza incidental).

Mobility: The ability to move around in one's environment

Modification: Changes in the instructional program without altering student expectations

Multi-tiered systems of support (MTSS): Involves consciously creating social interactions to help individuals meet the criteria of academic success, cultural competence, and critical consciousness and includes creating individual-centered learning environments that affirm cultural identities; foster positive learning outcomes; develop children's abilities to connect across lines of difference; elevate historically marginalized voices; empower children as agents of social change; and contribute to individual child engagement, learning, growth, and achievement through the cultivation of critical thinking. These approaches challenge norms (e.g., expectations regarding language, behavior, social interactions) to be responsive to marginalized children and families and work towards greater equity

Multidisciplinary team: A type of teaming model utilized in delivering services to young children with delays and disabilities. This approach refers to the involvement of two or more professionals from different disciplines in early childhood special education activities

Multiple means of action and expression: A dimension of universal design for learning (UDL) that accommodates the various ways that students may respond to learning material

Multiple means of engagement: A dimension of universal design for learning (UDL) in which students are offered a variety of ways of accessing learning material that is viewed as relevant; attempts to motivate the learner

Multiple means of representation: A dimension of universal design for learning (UDL) in which students are provided with a variety of ways to receive and interpret information

Natural environments: A philosophy that emphasizes providing early intervention in settings viewed as typical for young children without disabilities

Naturalistic teaching strategies: Teaching strategies or interventions that incorporate a child's typical daily routine and activities in order to teach discrete skills within the context of an inclusive classroom or other natural environments

Neglect: A form of child maltreatment; characterized by a variety of caregiver actions that may include failure to provide basic necessities, inadequate physical supervision, or failure to render needed medical treatment

No Child Left Behind Act: Federal legislation holding schools accountable for high performance standards of all students.

Nonverbal communication: Any communication other than spoken or written words; involves body language that expresses information

Norm-referenced tests: A type of measure that provides information about how a child is developing in relation to a larger group of children of the same age

Nuclear family: A family group consisting of, most commonly, a father and mother and their children

Observational assessment: A systematic process of gathering recordings and analysis of young children's behavior in real-life situations and familiar settings within their environments

Occupations: A Fröbelian concept describing arts-and-crafts-type activities used to develop eye–hand coordination and fine motor skills.

Orientation: The process of using one's senses to determine one's position in relation to other objects in the environment

Orthotic devices: Devices used to promote body alignment, stabilize joints, or increase motor functioning

Outcomes: The *what* (knowledge, skills, abilities, and understandings) that is to be taught to young children with delays and disabilities

Partial participation: Use of only a portion of the response instead of the full response (e.g., when told to touch the picture of the tree, a child moves their hand in the direction of the correct picture, but does not actually touch the picture)

Peer-mediated strategies: Strategies or approaches that utilize peers (or classmates) to promote learning

Percentile ranks: The percentage of the same-aged population that performed at or below a given score

Performance: A child's behavior that is exhibited while putting specific skills into action and is interpreted in relation to the performance of peers of the same age group who have previously taken the same test

Pervasive developmental disorder: A disorder characterized by severe and pervasive impairment in several areas of development: reciprocal social interaction skills; communication skills; or the presence of stereotyped behavior, interests, and activities

Physical abuse: A type of child maltreatment. An assault on a youngster designed to cause physical injury or harm to the child

PKU screening: A procedure used to detect phenylketonuria (PKU), a metabolic disorder, in infants

Play-based assessment: A systematic observational procedure for observing children during play to determine their level of development

Play-based intervention (strategies): The intentional use of play as the context for implementing interventions

Play: A context for learning and characterized by activities with objects and people that capture a child's attention and interest

Portfolio assessment: A type of authentic assessment system that provides a purposeful and comprehensive overview of a child's accomplishments. It is a systematic and organized collection of children's work and behaviors, which can serve as evidence to be used to monitor their progress

Positive behavioral support: An alternative to punishment; a proactive way of addressing problematic behaviors

Postlingual: A hearing loss or hearing impairment that manifests after acquisition of language

Praise: A technique for promoting child engagement among children who have delays and disabilities

Pre-academic/academic approach: Makes the assumption that the development of nondisabled children is based on a core group of skills that are taught to children during the preschool years—usually referred to as pre-academics, while the early primary years are referred to as academics

Predictive validity: The extent to which a test relates to some future measure of performance

Prelingual: A hearing loss present at birth or whose onset is prior to the development of speech and language

Premacking: Arranging sequences of activities so that less probable or low-probability (less desirable) activities are followed by high-probability and motivating activities (e.g., "you don't get your dessert until after you eat your broccoli")

Prepared environment: An important component in a Montessori classroom; a planned and orderly setting containing specially developed tasks and materials designed to promote children's learning.

Program evaluation: A process that addresses a program's progress in achieving overall outcomes and effectiveness

Program planning and implementation assessment: A type of assessment that is an ongoing process, which focuses on children's skill levels, needs, backgrounds, experiences, and interests, as well as the family's preferences and priorities, as the basis for constructing and maintaining individualized programs

Progress monitoring and program evaluation: A process of collecting information about a child's progress, the family's satisfaction with services, and overall program effectiveness

Progressivism: A school of thought founded by John Dewey. Emphasis placed on interest of children rather than activities chosen by the teacher.

Project Follow-Through: A federal program that attempts to continue the gains developed through Head Start. Funding is available for children in kindergarten through the third grade. Children receive educational, health, and social service benefits.

Project Head Start: A federally funded program aimed at young children in poverty; designed to increase the chances of success in school and opportunity for achievement.

Prompts: Any systematic assistance provided to an individual to enable them to respond, including verbal, pictorial, and physical cues (such as assistance)

Prosthetic devices: Artificial devices used to replace missing body parts

Protocol: A format that can be followed to decide the skill areas on which to focus and the specific skills to be observed during the assessment

Receptive language: Refers to the child's ability to understand and comprehend both verbal and nonverbal information

Recommended practices: Decisions of early childhood special education professionals that are based upon research evidence rather than personal experiences or beliefs

Referral: When a professional comes in contact with a child he or she suspects of having a delay or disability and recommends further assessment

Reliability: The consistency or dependability of an assessment instrument over time and across observers

Response to intervention (RTI): A strategy used for determining whether a student has a learning disability. The student is exposed to increasing levels of validated instruction, responsiveness to instruction is assessed, and a lack of adequate progress typically leads to a referral for possible special education services

Responsivity: The quality of the environment that provides the learner with predictable and immediate outcomes from any environmental interaction or immediate and consistent feedback for child interaction

Routine-based strategies: The intentional use of predictable routine activities (snack time, dressing, etc.), transitions (departure and arrival time, daily transition to the cafeteria, etc.), and routine group activities (e.g., circle time) to implement interventions

Scaffolding: A Vygotskian concept referring to the assistance rendered to the learner by adults or peers, which allows the person to function independently.

Schema: According to Piaget, a cognitive organizational pattern or framework that provides a foundation for the development of cognitive structures used in thinking.

Scope: The developmental skill (e.g., cognitive, motor, communication, adaptive, social) and content areas (e.g., literacy, math, science)

Screening: An assessment procedure designed to determine, from within a large population of children, those who need to be referred for further assessment in one or more areas of development

Section 504 accommodation plan: Found in Public Law 93-112, a customized plan written by a general educator that is designed to meet the unique needs of a child with a disability

Section 504: Section of Public Law 93-112, civil rights legislation aimed at protecting children and adults against discrimination due to their disabilities

Self-care skills: Those skills that allow a child to independently care for themself, are basic for maintaining life, and deal with bodily functions

Sensitive periods: Stages of development early in life during which, according to Montessori, a child is especially capable of learning particular skills or behaviors.

Sensitivity: A screening instrument's ability to identify children who need additional assessment

Sequence: The order in which content is taught (e.g., ages, stages, grade levels); sequence is often specified in a developmental progression—from easier to more difficult

Service coordination: An ongoing process designed to assist families as they access services and assure their rights to services

Sexual abuse: A form of child maltreatment in which developmentally immature individuals engage in sexual activities that they do not fully comprehend or about which they are unable to give informed consent. Sexual abuse may also include sexual exploitation

Social Stories: A visual support strategy used to teach appropriate social skills to children with autism spectrum disorders

Social-emotional skills: A range of behaviors associated with the development of social relationships (how children interact with others, both adults and peers, and how they react in social situations)

Sound field system: An amplification system typically used by students with a hearing impairment. The teacher wears a microphone that transmits a signal to speakers strategically placed around the classroom

Specificity: The capacity of a screening procedure to accurately rule out children who should not be identified

Speech: The oral-motor action used to communicate

Standardized tests: A type of test used during formal assessments in which an individual child's performance is interpreted in relation to the performance of peers from the same age group

Stereotyping: A generalized belief about members of a cultural group

Stimulus-control: A behavioral science concept that states that certain behaviors are more likely to occur in the presence of specific stimuli while the behavior is initially being reinforced

Strengths-based approach: An approach that that concentrates on the inherent strengths of children and families

Summative assessment: Evaluation of children's learning, which is done at the end of the year or at the completion of services, to determine whether the goals and objectives of the program were met

Tabula rasa: Concept attributed to John Locke. Young children seen very much like a blank slate. Learning is not innate but rather the result of experiences and activities.

Task analysis: The process of breaking down a task or skill (brushing teeth, getting a drink of water, putting on a shirt, turning on a computer, etc.) into sequential steps

Teacher talk: A type of assistance offered to children with autism spectrum disorders in an attempt to promote peer interactions and help them become better communicators

Teacher-mediated: Intervention directed by teachers to promote social interactions

Temporal adaptations: The structure, routine, and predictable activities that occur naturally in the home or educational setting

Tests: Predetermined collections of questions or tasks to which predetermined types of responses are sought

Time out: A behavioral intervention approach whereby a child is removed from a reinforcing situation for brief periods of time

Total communication: A method of communication for children with hearing impairments, designed to provide equal emphasis on oral skills and manual skills

Transdisciplinary team: A type of teaming model utilized in delivering services to young children with delays and disabilities. Building on an interdisciplinary model, this approach also includes sharing of roles and interventions delivered by a primary service provider. Support and consultation from other team members is important

Transition practices: The process of moving from one type of educational program or setting to another and the accompanying adjustment period

Universal design for learning (UDL): The design of curriculum materials, instructional activities, and evaluation procedures that meet the individual needs of learners with varying abilities and backgrounds

Universal precautions: Applying good health practices, such as frequent hand washing, to control the spread of communicable diseases and illnesses; also requires that the cleansing of materials and surfaces with disinfectant becomes a regular part of an adult's duties in the classroom

Universally designed curriculum: All aspects of an accessible curriculum (e.g., assessments, outcomes/goals, content, environment, interventions, instructional methods, interactions, materials) that invite active participation of all children regardless of ability

Validity: The extent to which an assessment instrument measures what it was designed to measure

Verbal communication: Strategies and skills, including acute listening and observation skills, that can be practiced and refined over time as early childhood personnel have discussions with families

Visual impairment: Defined in federal legislation as an impairment in vision that, even with correction, adversely affects an individual's educational performance

Visual supports: A support strategy typically used with children with autism spectrum disorders that involves using pictures or picture symbols to assist in the comprehension of rules, expectations, and transitions occurring in the classroom or at home

Zone of proximal development (ZPD): According to Vygotsky, this term refers to the distance between the children's actual development level as determined by independent problem solving and the level of potential development as determined through problem solving under adult guidance or in collaboration with more capable peers.

GLOSARIO

Accessibility. Accesibilidad. Cambios al ambiente hecho con el propósito de igualar los oportunidades de participación de las personas incapacitadas. Dentro de términos educativos, incluye adaptaciones necesarias para garantizar el acceso físico y cognitivo, y la oportunidad de realizar las metas de niños pequeños con retrasos o incapacidades.

Accommodation. Acomodación. Según Piaget, una alteración de la estructura de los cognitivos existentes para poder aceptar nueva información; envuelve un cambio en entender.

Activity areas or learning centers. Áreas de actividades o centros de aprendizaje. Espacio organizado en una sala de clase, usualmente diseñado para enseñar a grupos pequeños, son específicos y basados en una tema o dominación de desarrollo.

Activity-based instruction or intervention. Instrucción o intervención basada en actividades. Un enfoque en currículos que incorporan instrucciones para realizar las metas y el aprendizaje individual del IFSP o el IEP adentro de todos los eventos y oportunidades que existen en la rutina diaria.

Adaptability. Adaptabilidad. En la teoría de sistemas familiares, es un concepto utilizado para describir la habilidad de una familia para cambiar su estructura de poder, relaciones, y reglas de respuesta a crisis o eventos estresantes que ocurren en la vida.

Adaptation. Adaptación. Cualquier cambio que ayude a un niño con necesidades especiales a tener la oportunidad de participar con otros niños de desarrollo típico.

Adapted participation. Participación adaptado. Manera alternativa de participar, por ejemplo cambiando la orientación de la cabeza o el mirar a la posición de la señal; usando una tableta de comunicación en vez de comunicación verbal.

Adaptive behavior. Comportamiento adaptativo. se centran principalmente en las áreas de alimentación y cuidado personal (por ejemplo, ir al baño, asearse, vestirse)

Apgar Scale. Escala de Apgar. Un evaluación de recién nacidos que se administra en un minuto y otra vez en cinco minutos después del nacimiento para evaluar el ritmo cardíaco, la respiración, los reflejos, el tono muscular y el color de la piel.

Arena assessment. Evaluación de la arena. Evaluación basado en un modelo transdisciplinario con un grupo de profesionales de diferentes disciplinas y la familia del niño.

Assessment. Evaluación. El proceso de organizar información con el propósito de tomar una decisión sobre los niños con incapacidades o que puedan tener incapacidades. En esta evaluación se determina el diagnóstico, elegibilidad, programa y/o supervisión de futuro progreso.

Assimilation. Asimilación. Según los términos de Piaget, inclusión de información y experiencias con estructuras cognitivas anteriormente presentes.

Assistive technology interventions. Intervenciones con tecnología de asistencia. La evaluación del estudiante para determinar la implementación de tecnología y supervisar los efectos con la posibilidad de aumentar la independencia del estudiante.

Assistive technology. Tecnología de asistencia. Equipos o sistemas que ayuden y/o mejoren las habilidades funcionables de las personas con incapacidades.

At-risk. En riesgo. Describe a un niño expuesto a ciertas situaciones adversas y circunstancias con mucha probabilidad de terminar dando dificultades de desarrollo y aprendizaje.

Auditory trainer. Entrenador auditivo. Sistema de amplificación para ayudar a estudiantes con incapacidades auditivas.

Auditory-oral. Auditivo-oral. Una aplicación educativa para estudiantes con incapacidades auditivas que se enfoca en el desarrollo del hablar, la lectura, y la audición con la amplificación apropiada.

Augmentative and alternative communication (AAC). Comunicación aumentativa y alternativa (AAC). Sistema para estudiantes con limitaciones verbales. Incluye equipo que les permite responder adentro de actividades de aprendizaje.

Authentic assessment. Evaluación auténtica. Una evaluación basada en la idea que el comportamiento de niños debiera ser observado en el ambiente natural y en situaciones de vida real.

Autism spectrum disorders. Trastorno del espectro autista. Un desorden caracterizado por el desarollo anormal o alterado en la parte social y de comunicación, incluyendo un repertorio muy limitado de actividades e intereses.

Auto-education. Auto-educación. En términos de Montessori, la auto-enseñanza que resulta cuando un estudiante interactúa independientemente en un ambiente planificado.

Behavior disorder. Trastorno de conducta. Un término utilizado para describir una variedad amplia de diferencias sociales y emocionales, por ejemplo atención, hiperactividad, conducta y ansiedad.

Behavioral approach. Enfoque de comportamiento. Un sistema basado en los principios de aprendizaje de la psicología conductista que se enfoca en la instrucción directa por una secuencia prescrita de actividades instructivas.

Bias. Parcialidad. Cualquier situación que discrimina a un niño basada en género, nivel socioeconómico, cultura o conocimientos lingüísticos.

Bilingual education. Educación bilingüe. Un enfoque educativo en que los estudiantes cuyos idioma principal no es inglés reciben instrucción en su idioma principal mientras mientras desarrollan competencia y habilidad en inglés.

Bilingual-bicultural. Bilingüe-bicultural. Expresa que el Lenguaje de Señas Americano (ASL) es el lenguaje natural de la cultura de las personas sordas y es insistido que haya reconocimiento de ASL como el idioma principal y el inglés como idioma secundario.

Biological risk. Riesgo biológico. Niños pequeños con condiciones prenatales, perinatales y postnatales que aumentan la posibilidad para un desarrollo atípico.

Blended practices. Prácticas mezcladas. Un término utilizado en educación especial para referir a la integración de prácticas efectivas para enseñar a los niños con y sin incapacidades enfocadas integralmente para garantizar que todos los niños en ambientes inclusivos cuplan con los máximos estándares.

Center-based programs. Programas basados en centros. Clases de aprendizaje que se basa en centros con grupos de niños pequeños con necesidades especiales. Intervención y servicios educativos dados afuera de la casa del estudiante.

Child Find. Buscar un niño. Sistema que localiza a niños que tengan incapacidades o retardación y que necesitan más determinación de elección para servicios de intervención/educación especial.

Children with complex health care needs. Niños con necesidades especiales de la salud. Término general que se usa para los niños con una amplia variedad de necesidades del salud.

Chronosystem. Chronosistema. La interacción e influencia del tiempo histórico en los micro, meso, exo y macrosistemas.

Classroom ecology. Ecología de clase. Las modificaciones y arreglos en el ambiente que impactan la enseñanza a niños pequeños con retrasos o incapacidades.

Coaching. Entrenamiento. Trabajar con los cuidadores de un niño (por ejemplo, familiares, maestros) para explicar por qué se seleccionan estrategias específicas y cómo integrar las estrategias en las rutinas diarias mediante la demostración, el modelado y la práctica de las nuevas estrategias, además de brindar aliento y retroalimentación específica que ayudará al niño. El niño progresa hacia el logro de sus objetivos.

Cochlear implant. Implante coclear. Un procedimiento de cirugía que puede restaurar la capacidad de la audición en algunas personas con pérdida auditiva.

Cognitive skills. Habilidades cognitivas. La capacidad mental e intelectual en el desarrollo de un niño.

Cohesion. Cohesión. Según la teoría de sistemas familiares, es un concepto que se utiliza para describir el grado de libertad e independencia de cada miembro de la familia.

Collaboration. Colaboración. Trabajo junto con otras personas que resulta en beneficios mutuos para las familias y los profesionales. Este proceso necesita respeto mutuo y cooperación para alcanzar objetivos y metas comunes.

Communication. Comunicación. El proceso utilizado por dos o más personas para enviar y recibir mensajes.

Communicative intent. Intención de la comunicación. Se concentra en lo que un niño está intentando de comunicar utilizando medios diferentes (por ejemplo, gestos, position de ojos, sonidos).

Compensatory education. Educación compensatoria. Experiencias y esfuerzos de intervención que mejorarán las consecuencias y dificultades de vivir en pobreza; el objetivo es preparar a los niños pequeños para la escuela.

Concurrent validity. Validez concurrente. Un tipo de validez/verificación que se enfoca en qué tan bien una prueba/examen correlaciona con otras medidas de rendimiento hechas en el mismo período.

Construct validity. Validez de construcción. Un tipo de validez que se enfoca en el grado a que una prueba/examen representa las construcciones en la cual se basa.

Content domains. Dominios de contenido. áreas de conocimiento y destrezas que constituyen el conjunto de información en el que se basan la intervención y la instrucción y que se espera que los niños aprendan en los programas académicos y en los programas que promueven la preparación académica

Content validity. Validez de contenido. Un tipo de validez que se enfoca en al grado a que una prueba/examen representa el contenido que está dirigido a medir.

Cooperative learning. Aprendizaje cooperativo. Proceso de instrucción en la cual grupos heterogéneos de estudiantes trabajan juntos en las tareas escolares.

Cooperative teaching. Enseñanza cooperativa. Una manera de instrucción en la cual un educador especial y un educador general enseñan juntos en una clase con un grupo heterogéneo de niños.

Criterion-referenced assessments. Evaluaciones basadas en criterios. Un tipo de determinación de ver si el niño cumple con un criterio establecido o el grado de dominio en diferentes partes de desarrollo (cognitivo, motor, cuidado personal) o áreas temáticas (matemáticas, literato).

Cultural mediator. Mediador cultural. Una persona que ayuda a traducir entre la cultura de un programa o ambiente escolar y la familia de un niño para mejorar la comprensión, compartir información y crear una relación que apoye a los niños y las familias.

Cultural responsiveness. Respuesta cultural. Un concepto que incluye la conciencia, el reconocimiento, y la aceptación de la cultura y los valores culturales de cada familia, lo que hace que los profesionales se fijen en cada familia como una unidad única que está influenciada por su cultura, pero no definida por la misma.

Culturally biased assessment. Evaluación cultural. Un tipo de evaluación que se enfoca en las habilidades dominante culturales que pone a los niños de culturas no occidentales, no dominantes, en desventaja.

Culture. Cultura. Los valores y creencias fundamentales que establecen los estándares de cómo las personas perciben, interpretan y se comportan dentro de su familia, escuela y comunidad.

Curriculum model. Modelo curricular. Modelo conceptual y estructura organizacional que mezcla teoría con práctica, describe qué enseñar y cómo enseñar.

Curriculum-based assessments. Evaluaciones basadas en el currículo. Medida de evaluación más enfocado en los propósitos de planificación del programa que se utiliza para identificar el nivel de un niño en un programa de enseñanza, viendo como se puede modificar la instrucción.

Curriculum. Currículo. El plan en el cual se muestra todo lo que el niño debe de aprender elementalmente en la primera infancia; toca las perspectivas teóricas o filosóficas en las que el programa está basado.

Deafness. Sordera. Una condición que afecta negativamente la educación y es tan severa que el niño, lo cual reduce su capacidad de procesar el procedimiento lingüístico o comunicativo con o sin amplificación.

Developmental age scores. Medidas de desarrollo de edad. Los resultados de un examen de desarrollo de niños de infancia a cinco años.

Developmentally appropriate practices. Prácticas apropiadas para el desarrollo. Una combinación de prácticas establecidas por la Asociación Nacional para la Educación de Niños Pequeños (NAEYC) para reconocer prácticas apropiadas para la educación de niños pequeños, desde el nacimiento hasta los ocho años.

Developmental delay. Retraso del desarrollo. Un concepto que se refiere a niños pequeños con necesidades especiales. Un retraso se determina utilizando una variedad de evaluaciones y opiniones clínicas.

Developmental domains. Dominios del desarrollo. Las áreas de habilidades en el currículo de educación especialmente desde infancia: habilidades cognitivas, motrices, de comunicación, sociales y de adaptación.

Developmental-cognitive approach. Enfoque cognitivo de desarrollo. Un modelo basado en la teoría del trabajo de Piaget que implica al desarrollo de habilidades cognitivas.

Developmental or maturational approach. Enfoque de desarollo o maturación. Un modelo de currículo tradicional basado en las teorías del desarollo del niño típico.

Didactic materials. Materiales didácticos. Instrucciónes de enseñanza utilizadas por el programa de Montessori.

Disability. Incapacidad. Una inhabilidad de hacer algo; capacidad reducida que prohíbe realizar metas en maneras específicas.

Early childhood special education. Educación especial para la infancia. La provisión personalizada de servicios para satisfacer las necesidades individuales de niños entre tres y cinco años con incapacidades.

Early Head Start. Inicio Temprano. Una programa federal que provee una variedad de servicios a familias de bajos ingresos con bebés y niños pequeños, por ejemplo, mujeres que están embarazadas.

Early intervention. Intervención primaria. Servicios especiales proveído en coordinación e integral para bebés y niños pequeños (desde el nacimiento hasta los dos años de edad) con retrasos de desarrollo o condiciones de riesgo y a sus familias.

Echolalic speech. Habladuría ecolalia. Una condición en la cual una persona repite lo que se dice en vez de generar una idea original.

Eco-map. Eco-mapa. Un dibujo o figura que ayuda a la colaboración entre profesionales y familias y también para representar y utilizar información importante, como la estructura familiar, las relaciones y los recursos.

Ecological perspective. Perspectiva ecológica. Una perspectiva que se enfoca en el poder de la naturaleza y la estructura de las relaciones humanas dentro de sus ambientales.

Ecology. Ecología. Las interrelaciones e interacciones de los diferentes ambientes que afectan a un niño y se ven afectados en la juventud.

Eligibility. Elegibilidad. Un proceso de evaluación para determinar si un niño cumple con los criterios y requisitos para ser elegible a la intervención temprana o servicios de educación especial.

Embedded interventions. Intervenciones integradas. El proceso de identificar los tiempos y las actividades cuando las metas de un niño y los procedimientos de instrucción para esas metas pueden ser integrados en las actividades normales, rutinas y transiciones del niño de una manera que se relaciona con el contexto.

Emotional abuse. Abuso emocional. Un tipo de maltrato de niños que se distingue por ser psicológicamente dañino para el niño.

Emotional skills. Habilidades emocionales. La capacidad de un niño para identificar y comunicar sus sentimientos, actuar sobre sus emociones con control, respetar a los derechos de otros y resolver los conflictos.

Empowerment. Empoderamiento. El proceso de aplicar estrategias para que los individuos y las familias ganen un sentido de control sobre el futuro como resultado de sus propios esfuerzos y actividades.

Engagement. Obligación. Ser consistente y activo con las personas, actividades y materiales durante el día de un niño.

Environment. Ambiente. La totalidad de las cualidades físicas y humanas que se combina para crear un espacio en el cual niños y adultos trabajan y juegan juntos.

Environmental arrangements. Arreglos ambientales. Cambios en el ambiente utilizado para facilitar la atención y conección de los niños. Por ejemplo, cambiar el espacio físico, cambiar la opción y el uso de materiales, o cambiar la estructura de una actividad.

Environmental practices. Prácticas ambientales. Aspectos del espacio, materiales (juguetes, libros, etc.), equipos, rutinas y actividades que los profesionales y las familias pueden cambiar intencionalmente para apoyar el aprendizaje de cada niño en el desarollo.

Environmental risk. Riesgo ambiental. Un riesgo asociado con niños que son biológicamente típicos que se encuentran con experiencias de vida o condiciones ambientales que son limitantes, creando la posibilidad de un futuro desarrollo retrasado.

Equilibration. Equilibrio. Según la teoría de Piaget, el proceso cognitivo en que una persona intenta equilibrar nueva información con datos existentes.

Established risk. Riesgo establecido. Niños con un trastorno médico diagnosticado de etiología y pronóstico o resultado predicado.

Ethnocentric behavior. Comportamiento etnocéntrico. El punto de vista que describe las prácticas y el comportamiento de un grupo cultural siendo como naturales y correctos mientras se ve las acciones de otros grupos como inferiores o extraños.

Evidence-based practices. Prácticas basadas en evidencia. La utilización de prácticas instruccionales que se basan en la investigación empírica.

Exceptional children. Niños excepcionales. Niños que son diferentes de la percepción de la sociedad sobre la normalidad.

Exosystems. Exosistemas. Según Bronfenbrenner, sistemas sociales que influyen el desarrollo de un individuo.

Expressive language. Lenguaje expresivo. La habilidad de comunicar pensamientos o sentimientos usando vocalizaciones, palabras y otros comportamientos para transmitir información.

False negative. Falso negativo. Designación de un niño que necesita servicios especiales pero no estuvo referido como resultado de una evaluación.

False positive. Falso positivo. Designación de un niño que a sido referido para servicios especiales pero no los necesita.

Family and professional collaboration. Colaboración familiar y professional. Prácticas que construyen relaciones entre familias y profesionales que trabajan juntos para lograr resultados y objetivos mutuamente acordados que promuevan las competencias familiares y apoyen el desarrollo del niño

Family capacity-building practices. Prácticas de capacitación familiar. Prácticas que incluyen las oportunidades y experiencias participativas ofrecidas a las familias para reforzar los conocimientos y habilidades parentales existentes y promover el desarrollo de nuevas habilidades parentales que mejoren las creencias y prácticas de autoeficacia parental

Family characteristics. Características de la familia. Según la teoría de sistemas familiares, los elementos únicos de una familia (por ejemplo, tamaño y forma de la familia, origen cultural, ubicación geográfica).

Family functions. Funciones familiares. Según la teoría de sistemas familiares, se refiere a una de las ocho actividades interrelacionadas que se consideran necesarias para satisfacer las necesidades individuales y colectivas de una familia (por ejemplo, afecto, economía, recreación, educación).

Family interactions. Interaccionales familiares. Según la teoría de sistemas familiares, son las partes de la relación e interacciones que ocurren en la unidad de la familia, como la relación matrimonial.

Family life cycle. Ciclo de vida familiar. Según la teoría de sistemas familiares, se refiere a los cambios que ocurren con el tiempo en las familias y que influyen a sus recursos, interacciones y funciones.

Family systems theory. Teoría de sistemas familiares. Una teoría que considera a la familia como una unidad interdependiente, con características y necesidades únicas. Las experiencias y eventos que han impactado a un miembro de la familia (por ejemplo, un niño con un retraso o incapacitado) también afectarán a los otros miembros de la familia o a la familia en totalidad.

Family-centered practices. Prácticas centradas en la familia. Una filosofía de trabajar con las familias en que se empleas técnicas específicas que dan énfasis a la fortalezas de una familia, el mejoramiento de habilidades familiares, y el desarollo de una colaboración entre la familia y los profesionales.

Family. Familia. Un grupo de personas con relación de sangre o circunstancias quienes necesitan y confían en uno y otro para seguridad, apoyo, socialización y/o la estimulación.

Fine motor skills. Las habilidades motoras finas. La habilidad de usar grupos musculares pequeños como los de las manos, la cara y los pies.

FM system. Sistema FM. Un sistema de comunicación inalámbrico disponible para niños con impedimentos auditivos. El profesor utiliza un transmisor al mismo tiempo que el niño utiliza un receptor; permitiendo que el estudiante ajuste el volumen de la voz del maestro.

Formative assessment. Evaluación formativa. Un tipo de evaluación del aprendizaje de un niño con el propósito de mejorar la calidad de la enseñanza y el aprendizaje en general en vez de evaluar el progreso de los niños individuales; usualmente se hace al principio de año y durante el año.

Functional approach. Enfoque funcional. Un método enfocado en las habilidades o comportamientos que tienen importancia inmediata para el niño.

Functional behavior analysis. Análisis de comportamiento funcional. Un enfoque que busca determinar el propósito o la función de un comportamiento particular.

Functional behavior assessment. Evaluación conductual functional. Un tipo de evaluación que se utiliza para investigar las variables ambientales que contribuyen y/o mantienen un comportamiento desafiante

Functional skill. Habilidad funcional. Una habilidad básica que se requiere con frecuencia (comer, ir al baño, pedir ayuda, turnarse) en el ambiente natural.

Generalization. Generalización. La habilidad de aplicar lo aprendido a diferentes situaciones, diferentes materiales o diferentes personas.

Gifts. Regalos. Un término fröbeliano utilizado para objetos manipuladores, como bolas y bloques de madera, que se usan para el aprendizaje en el plan de estudios de Fröbel.

Gross motor skills. Habilidades motoras gruesas. Habilidades de movimiento y control de grupos musculares grandes que se usa para funcionar en el ambiente.

Handicap. Desventaja. Las consecuencias o impactos encontrados o impuestos a un niño con incapacidad cuando él o ella intenta funcionar e interactuar en el ambiente.

High-tech devices. Dispositivos de alta tecnología. Un objeto de tecnología asistencial complicado que es costoso comprar o utilizar.

Home Start. Hogar Inicio. Una derivación del programa Head Start; diseñado para dar servicios integrales a los niños y sus padres en el hogar a través de visitas.

Home visits. Visitas a domicilio. Servicios a domicilio prestados en el entorno natural por profesionales para abordar el desarrollo y el aprendizaje del niño y apoyar a la familia, lo que requiere una planificación coordinada y la colaboración entre familias y profesionales

Home-based programs. Programas basados en el hogar. Modelo de servicios para niños con necesidades especiales. La intervención es dada por el cuidador principal en el hogar del niño. Los profesionales hacen visitas rutinas para trabajar directamente con el niño y darle instrucciones al cuidador.

Hybrid family. Familia híbrida. Una familia que es diferente de cualquier familia de origen; consiste en una mezcla cultural y religiosa.

Hypertonic muscle tone. Tono muscular hipertónico. Músculos tensos.

Hypotonic muscle tone. Tono muscular hipotónico. Músculos flojos que muestran resistencia cuando son estirado.

Inclusion. Inclusión. El proceso de integración de niños con necesidades especiales en la educación diseñado principalmente para atender a niños sin incapacidades.

Individualized education program (IEP). Programa de educación individualizado (IEP). Un plan educativo individual que es requerido por la legislación federal, construido por un equipo, para cada niño con necesidades especiales.

Individualized family service plan (IFSP). Plan de servicio familiar individualizado (IFSP). Un plan que es requerido por la ley federal. Diseñado como una guía de servicios dados a bebés, niños y sus familias. Construido por un equipo de profesionales y los padres.

Informed clinical opinion. Opinión clínica fundamentada. El uso del juicio profesional, basado en la experiencia y los conocimientos, y la aportación de la familia para hacer recomendaciones sobre la elegibilidad inicial y continua para los servicios de EI/ECSE y para planificar los servicios para aquellos niños cuyo estado de desarrollo y necesidades de EI/ECSE pueden ser difíciles de evaluar con medidas formales

Instructional validity. Validez instruccional. Un tipo de evaluación que se enfoca en la medida en que la información obtenida de un instrumento puede ser útil para planificar programas de intervención para niños con retrasos o incapacidades.

Interdisciplinary team. Equipo interdisciplinario. Un modelo de equipo utilizado para comunicar los servicios a niños con necesidades especiales. Los profesionales generalmente hacen sus evaluaciones independientemente; pero el desarrollo del programa y las recomendaciones para los servicios son el resultado del intercambio de información y la planificación mutual.

Interviews. Entrevistas. Una forma de evaluación que se usa para colectar información de las familias u otros cuidadores sobre las áreas en que se debe enfocar durante el período de evaluación; información específica sobre el niño (por ejemplo, cómo responde un niño en diferentes situaciones); las preocupaciones, prioridades y recursos de las familias; u otros tipos de información que puedan ser relevantes para la evaluación.

Language. Lenguaje. El uso de símbolos (sonidos de letras que se usan en diferentes combinaciones para formar palabras), la sintaxis (reglas que guían la estructura de oraciones) o la gramática (la forma en que se construyen las oraciones) con el propósito de comunicar.

Learned helplessness. Impotencia aprendida. Una sensación de indefensión en los niños cuando sus interacciones con el ambiente son inútiles o producen resultados inconsistentes o comentarios negativos. Las personas con impotencia aprendida se sienten con poco control sobre su ambiente.

Least restrictive environment (LRE). Ambiente menos restrictivo (LRE). Un concepto que se enfoca en los niños con necesidades especiales para que sean educados, en la mejor posibilidad, con sus compañeros de clase típicos. La configuración es determinada individualmente.

Low-tech devices. Dispositivos de baja tecnología. Objetos de tecnología asistencial de bajo costo que no requiere energía eléctrica o pilas para operar.

Macrosystems. Macrosistemas. Los contextos ideológicos, culturales e institucionales que abarcan los micro, meso y ecosistemas.

Mesosystems. Mesosistemas. La relación de diversos ambientes de los microsistemas.

Meta-analysis. Metaanálisis. Procedimiento estadístico en el cual se evalúan los estudios de investigación para determinar patrones estadísticos globales; determina el "tamaño del efecto," comunicado como una desviación estándar.

Microsystems. Microsistemas. Según Bronfenbrenner, son los ambientes inmediatos en los que se desarrolla una persona, como el hogar y el vecindario de un niño.

Mid-tech devices. Dispositivos de tecnología media. Un objeto de tecnología asistencial que necesita energía eléctrica.

Milieu strategies (or naturalistic strategies): Strategies to facilitate language skills (especially social interaction) that take advantage of the naturàl environment (people, materials, activities) to support learning. Milieu strategies include a variety of specific procedures (i.e., time delay, mand model, incidental teaching)

Mobility. Movilidad. La habilidad de moverse en el ambiente

Modification. Modificación del currículo. Cambios en la enseñanza y las expectativas del plan de estudios sin alterar las expectativas del estudiante.

Multi-tiered systems of support (MTSS). Sistemas de apoyo de varios niveles (MTSS). Implica la creación consciente de interacciones sociales para ayudar a los individuos a cumplir los criterios de éxito académico, competencia cultural y conciencia crítica, e incluye la creación de entornos de aprendizaje centrados en el individuo que afirmen las identidades culturales; fomenten resultados de aprendizaje positivos; desarrollen las capacidades de los niños para conectar a través de las líneas de diferencia; eleven las voces históricamente marginadas; empoderen a los niños como agentes de cambio social; y contribuyan al compromiso, el aprendizaje, el crecimiento y los logros individuales de los niños a través del cultivo del pensamiento crítico. Estos enfoques cuestionan las normas (por ejemplo, las expectativas relativas al lenguaje, el comportamiento, las interacciones sociales) para responder a los niños y familias marginados y trabajar por una mayor equidad.

Multidisciplinary team. Grupo multidisciplinario. Modelo de grupo que se utiliza en los servicios a niños con necesidades especiales. Se refiere a la participación de dos o más profesionales de diferentes disciplinas en actividades de educación especial.

Multiple means of action and expression. Múltiples medios de expresión. Una dimensión del diseño universal para el aprendizaje (UDL) que acomoda las varias maneras en quelos alumnos pueden responder al material de aprendizaje.

Multiple means of engagement. Múltiples medios de participación. Una dimensión del diseño universal para el aprendizaje (UDL) en que a los estudiantes se les dan una variedad de formas relevantes de participar con el material de aprendizaje; intentos de motivar al estudiante.

Multiple means of representation. Múltiples medios de representación. Una dimensión del diseño universal para el aprendizaje (UDL) en que los estudiantes reciben una variedad de formas de recibir e interpretar información.

Natural environments. Ambientes naturales. Una filosofía que se enfoca a dedicar la intervención preventiva en el ambiente típico para niños sin incapacidades.

Naturalistic teaching strategies. Estrategias de enseñanza naturalistas. Estrategias de enseñanza o intervenciones que incluyen la rutina y las actividades típicas de un niño para enseñar habilidades dentro de una clase inclusiva u otros ambientes naturales.

Neglect. Negligencia. Una forma de maltrato; caracterizada por una variedad de acciones del guardián que pueden incluir la falta de proveer las necesidades básicas, la supervisión física inadecuada o la falta de tratamiento médico necesario.

No Child Left Behind Act. Ley Que Ningún Niño Se Quede Atrás. Legislación federal que le da responsabilidad a las escuelas por estándares altos de rendimiento de todos los estudiantes.

Nonverbal communication. Comunicación no verbal. Cualquier comunicación distinta de las palabras habladas o escritas; implica un lenguaje corporal que expresa información

Norm-referenced tests. Pruebas basadas en normas. Una evaluación que incluye información sobre cómo se está desarrollando un niño en relación con un grupo más grande de niños de la misma edad.

Nuclear family. Familia nuclear. Un grupo familiar que consiste, usualmente, de un padre, madre y sus hijos.

Observational assessment. Evaluación observacional. Una evaluación sistemática que obtiene grabaciones y análisis del comportamiento de los niños en situaciones de la vida real y ambientes familiares.

Occupations. Ocupaciones. Un concepto fröbeliano que describe las actividades de manualidades que se usa para desarrollar la coordinación ojo-mano y las habilidades motoras finas.

Orientation. Orientación. Proceso de usar los sentidos para determinar la posición de uno en relación con otros objetos en el ambiente.

Orthotic devices. Equipo ortopédicos. Equipo para promover la alineación del cuerpo, estabilizar las articulaciones, o aumentar el funcionamiento del motor del cuerpo.

Outcomes. Resultados. El qué (conocimiento, habilidades y entendimientos) que se debe enseñar a los niños con retrasos o incapacidades.

Partial participation. Participación parcial. Hacer una parte de la respuesta en vez de la respuesta completa (por ejemplo, cuando se le pregunta que toque la imagen del árbol, un niño mueve su mano en la dirección de la imagen correcta, pero no toca la imagen).

Peer-mediated strategies. Estrategias con compañeros. Estrategias o enfoques que utilizan compañeros (o compañeros de clase) para promover la enseñanza.

Percentile ranks. Rangos percentiles. El porcentaje de la población de la misma edad que tuvo un puntaje dado o menor.

Performance. Rendimiento. El comportamiento de un niño que se exhibe poniendo en práctica habilidades específicas y se interpreta en relación con un grupo de compañeros de la misma edad que han hecho la misma prueba.

Pervasive developmental disorder. Trastorno generalizado del desarrollo. Un trastorno caracterizado por un deterioro severo y generalizado en varias áreas del desarrollo: habilidades recíprocas de interacción social; habilidades de comunicación; o la presencia de comportamientos, intereses y actividades estereotipadas.

Physical abuse. Abuso físico. Cualquier maltrato a un niño con el intento de causar daño físico.

PKU screening. Detección de PKU. Un procedimiento utilizado para determinar trastornos metabólicos como la fenilcetonuria (PKU) en bebés.

Play-based assessment. Evaluación basada en el juego. Un procedimiento de observación sistemático para observar a los niños durante el juego y determinar su nivel de desarrollo.

Play-based interventions (strategies). Intervenciones (estrategias) basadas en el juego. El uso intencional del juego para implementar intervenciones.

Play. Juego. Un contexto de aprendizaje caracterizado por actividades con objetos y personas que captan la atención y el interés del niño

Portfolio assessment. Evaluación del portafolio. Sistema de evaluación auténtico que proporciona una visión general e integral de los logros de un niño. Es una colección y organización del trabajo y los comportamientos de los niños que puede servir como evidencia para monitorear el progreso.

Positive behavioral supports. Apoyo de conducta positivo. Una alternativa al castigo; una forma proactiva de cambiar comportamientos problemáticos.

Postlingual. Postlingual. Una pérdida o deficiencia auditiva que occure después de que un niño ha desarrollado el lenguaje.

Praise. Elogio. Una técnica para promover la participación de niños con necesidades especiales.

Pre-academic or academic approach. Enfoque pre-académico o académico. El entendido que el desarrollo de niños sin incapacidades se basan en un grupo reconocido de habilidades que se enseñan a los niños durante los años pre-escolares o pre-académicos, mientras que los primeros años de primaria se conocen como académicos.

Predictive validity. Validez predictiva. Un tipo de validez que se refiere a cómo una evaluación se relaciona a alguna medida futura de habilidades.

Prelingual. Prelingual. Una pérdida o deficiencia auditiva que occure antes de que un niño haya desarrollado el lenguaje.

Premacking. Premacking. Organización de secuencias de actividades en la cual actividades menos probables o de baja probabilidad (menos deseables) se continúa con actividades de alta probabilidad y motivadoras ("No puedes tener tu postre hasta después de comer tu brócoli").

Prepared environment. Ambiente preparado. Un componente importante en una clase de Montessori; un ambiente planificado y ordenado que contiene tareas especialmente desarrolladas y materiales diseñados para ayudar el aprendizaje individual de los niños.

Program evaluation. Evaluación del programa. Un proceso que determina el progreso de un programa en lograr resultados globales y efectivas.

Program-planning and implementation assessment. Evaluación de planificación e implementación de programas. Un tipo de evaluación que es continuante, y se enfoca en los niveles de habilidades, necesidades, antecedentes, experiencias e intereses de los niños, y a la misma vez en las preferencias y prioridades de la familia como base para construir y mantener programas individualizados.

Progress monitoring and program evaluation. Supervisión y evaluación del progreso del programa. Un proceso de obtener información sobre el progreso de un niño, la satisfacción de la familia con los servicios y la eficacia del programa en general.

Progressivism. Progresismo. Una escuela fundada por John Dewey. Basada en el interés de los niños en lugar de las actividades elegidas por el maestro.

Project Follow-Through. Proyecto Seguimiento. Una programa federal que intenta continuar los beneficios desarrollados a través del proyecto Head Start. El financiamiento está disponible para niños de kínder a tercer grado. Los niños reciben beneficios de servicios educativos, de salud y sociales.

Project Head Start. Proyecto Head Start. Una programa federal financiado y dirigido para niños en la pobreza; diseñado para aumentar las posibilidades de éxito en la escuela y la oportunidad de realización.

Prompts. Indicaciones. Cualquier asistencia sistemática dado a una persona para ayudarle a responder, incluyendo señales verbales, pictóricas y físicas (como asistencia).

Prosthetic devices. Equipos protésicos. Equipos artificiales utilizados para reemplazar las partes que faltan en un cuerpo.

Protocol. Protocolo. Un formato para decidir las habilidades y las oportunidades específicas que se observarán durante la evaluación.

Receptive language. Lenguaje receptivo. Se refiere a la capacidad del niño para comprender y entender la información verbal y no verbal.

Recommended practices. Prácticas recomendadas. Decisiones de los profesionales de la educación especial que se basan en la evidencia de investigaciones en vez de experiencias o creencias personales.

Referral. Referencia. Cuando un profesional entra en contacto con un niño, sospecha que tiene un retraso o incapacidad y recomienda una evaluación adicional.

Reliability. Confiabilidad. La consistencia o seguridad de un instrumento de evaluación a lo largo del tiempo y entre diferentes observadores.

Response to intervention (RTI). Reacción a la intervención (RTI). Una estrategia utilizada para determinar si un estudiante tiene una incapacidad de aprendizaje. El estudiante está expuesto a diferentes niveles de instrucción, se evalúa la capacidad de respuesta a la instrucción y, por lo general, la falta de un progreso adecuado indica la necesidad para una referencia para servicios de educación especial.

Responsivity. Responsividad. La calidad del ambiente que proporciona en estudiantes resultados predecibles e inmediatos de cualquier interacción ambiental o reacciones inmediatas y consistentes para la interacción del niño.

Routine-based strategies. Estrategias de rutina. La utilización intencional de actividades rutinarias y predecibles (tiempo de comer, vestimenta, etc.), transiciones (hora de salida y llegada, transición diaria a la cafetería, etc.) y actividades de grupo rutinarias (hora del círculo) para implementar intervenciones.

Scaffolding. Andamio. Un concepto de Vygotsky que se refiere a la asistencia dado al estudiante por adultos o compañeros, para permitir que el estudiante functione independientemente.

Schema. Esquema. Según Piaget, un patrón o guía de organización cognitiva que provee una base para el desarrollo de las estructuras cognitivas utilizadas en pensamiento.

Scope. Alcance. Áreas de desarrollo de habilidades (cognitiva, motora, comunicación, adaptation, social) y áreas de contenido (alfabetización, matemática, ciencia).

Screening. Proceso de control. Un procedimiento de evaluación que determina, dentro de una población grande de niños, los que necesitan ser remitidos para una evaluación adicional en una o más áreas de desarrollo.

Section 504 accommodation plan. Plan de acomodación Sección 504. Un plan individualizado escrito por un educador general diseñado a atender a las necesidades únicas de un niño con descapacidades.

Section 504. Sección 504. Una sección de la Ley Pública 93-112, una legislación de derechos civiles que protege a niños y adultos contra la discriminación debido a sus incapacidades.

Self-care skills. Habilidades de autocuidado. Habilidades que le permiten a un niño cuidarse independientemente; son básicas para mantener la vida y ocuparse de las funciones corporales.

Sensitive periods. Periodos sensitivos. Etapas de desarrollo muy tempranos en la vida durante las cuales, según Montessori, un niño es especialmente capaz de aprender habilidades o comportamientos particulares.

Sensitivity. Sensitividad. La eficacía du un instrumento de exámen en identificar a los niños que necesitan una evaluación adicional.

Sequence. Secuencia. El orden en que se enseña un contenido (edades, etapas o niveles de grado); la secuencia se especifica en una progresión del desarrollo, de más fácil a más difícil.

Service coordination. Coordinación de servicios. Un proceso continuo diseñado para ayudar a las familias a medida que acceden a los servicios y aseguran sus derechos a los servicios

Sexual abuse. Abuso sexual. Una forma de maltrato en cual las personas con desarrollo inmaduro participan en actividades sexuales sin comprender o sin poder dar su consentimiento. El abuso sexual también puede incluir cuestiones de explotación sexual.

Social stories. Historias sociales. Una estrategia de soporte visual para enseñar habilidades sociales apropiadas a niños con trastornos del espectro autista.

Social skills. Habilidades sociales. Una variedad de comportamientos asociados con el desarrollo de las relaciones (cómo los niños interactúan con otros, tanto adultos como compañeros, y cómo reaccionan en situaciones sociales).

Sound field system. Sistema de sonido. Un sistema de aplicación utilizado por estudiantes con impedimentos auditivos. El profesor usa un micrófono que transmite una señal estratégicamente a altavoces alrededor del salón.

Specificity. Especificidad. Un procedimiento de detección para excluir adecuadamente a los niños que no deberían ser identificados.

Speech. Habla. La acción motor-oral utilizada para comunicar.

Standardized tests. Exámenes estandarizados. Un tipo de examen utilizado durante las evaluaciones formales en que los resultados de un nino se interpreta en relación con los de un grupo similar de la misma edad.

Stereotyping. Estereotipos. La creencia generalizada sobre los miembros de un grupo específico.

Stimulus-control. Control del estímulo. Un concepto de la ciencia de comportamiento que establece que ciertas reacciones son más propensas a ocurrir en presencia de estímulos específicos mientras que el comportamiento se refuerza inicialmente.

Strengths-based approach. Enfoque basado en fortalezas. Un enfoque que se centra en los puntos fuertes inherentes a los niños y las familias

Summative assessment. Evaluación sumativa. Una evaluación que se hace al final del año o al finalizar los servicios para determinar si se cumplieron las metas y los objetivos del programa.

Tabula rasa. Tabula rasa. Concepto atribuido a John Locke. Los niños se consideran como una pizarra limpia. El aprendizaje no es innato sino es el resultado de experiencias y actividades.

Task analysis. Análisis de tareas. El proceso de dividir una tarea o habilidad (cepillarse los dientes, tomar un trago de agua, ponerse una camisa, encender una computadora, etc.) en pasos secuenciales.

Teacher talk. Habla del maestro. Un tipo de asistencia que se le ofrece a los niños con trastornos del espectro autista con el intento de promover las interacciones y ayudarlos a ser mejores comunicadores.

Teacher-mediated. Mediado por el maestro. Una intervención dirigida por maestros para promover interacciones sociales.

Temporal adaptations. Adaptaciones temporales. La estructura, rutina y actividades predecibles que ocurren naturalmente en el hogar o en el ambiente educativo.

Tests. Exámenes. Preguntas o tareas a que se busca respuestas predeterminadas.

Time out. Descanso. Un enfoque de intervención de conducta en el cual se quita al niño de una situación durante pequeños períodos de tiempo.

Total communication. Comunicación total. Un método de comunicación para niños con deficiencias auditivas, diseñado para dar igual énfasis a las habilidades orales como manuales.

Transdisciplinary team. Grupo transdisciplinario. Un método de aprendizaje utilizado en los servicios a niños con necesidades especiales. Sobre la base interdisciplinario, este enfoque también incluye el intercambio e intervenciones entregadas por un proveedor de servicios primario. El apoyo y la consulta de otros miembros del equipo es importante.

Transition practices. Prácticas de transición. El proceso de pasar de un tipo de programa educativo o configuración a otro, incluyendo el período de ajuste.

Universal design for learning (UDL). Diseño universal para el aprendizaje (UDL). El diseño de materiales curriculares, actividades de aprendizaje y procedimientos de evaluación que satisface las necesidades individuales de los estudiantes con diferentes habilidades y antecedentes.

Universal precautions. Precauciones universales. Aplicar buenas prácticas de salud, como lavarse las manos frecuentemente, para controlar la propagación de enfermedades y enfermedades transmisibles; también requiere la limpieza de materiales y superficies con desinfectante como una parte regular de los deberes del adulto en la clase.

Universally designed curriculum. Diseño universal de currículo. Todos los aspectos de un plan de estudios accesible (evaluaciones, resultados/metas, contenido, ambiente, intervenciones, métodos de instrucción, interacciones y materiales) que incluyen la participación activa de todos los niños, independientemente de su capacidad.

Validity. Validez. El nivel en que un instrumento de evaluación mide lo que fue diseñado para medir.

Verbal communication. Comunicación verbal. Estrategias y habilidades, como la capacidad de escucha y observación, que pueden practicarse y perfeccionarse con el tiempo a medida que el personal de la primera infancia mantiene conversaciones con las familias

Visual impairment. Incapacidad visual. Definido en la legislación federal como un impedimento en la visión que, incluso con la corrección, afecta negativamente la educación de un individuo.

Visual supports. Soportes visuales. Una estrategia de soporte utilizada para niños con trastornos del espectro autista usando imágenes o símbolos para ayudar a comprender las reglas, las expectativas y las transiciones que ocurren en la clase o en el hogar.

Zone of proximal development (ZPD). Zona de desarrollo próximo (ZPD). Según Vygotsky, es la distancia entre el nivel de desarrollo real de los niños, determinado por la resolución independiente de problemas, y el nivel de desarrollo potencial determinado a través de la resolución de problemas bajo la guía de un adulto o en colaboración con compañeros más capaces.

REFERENCES

CHAPTER 1

Administration for Children and Families. (2017). *Head Start performance standards final rule: General fact sheet*. https://eclkc.ohs.acf.hhs.gov/sites/default/files/docs/pdf/hs-prog-pstandards-final-rule-factsheet_0.pdf

Allen, E., & Cowdery, G. (2022). *The exceptional child*(9th ed.). Cengage Learning.

Bakken, L., Brown, N., & Downing, B. (2017). Early childhood education: The long-term benefits. *Journal of Research in Childhood Education, 31*(2), 255–269.

Ballard, J., Ramirez, B., & Weintraub, F. (1982). *Special education in America: Its legal and governmental foundations*. Council for Exceptional Children.

Berger, K. (2020). *The developing person through the life span*(11th ed.). Worth.

Berk, L., & Winsler, A. (1995). *Scaffolding children's learning: Vygotsky and early childhood education*. National Association for the Education of Young Children.

Berrueta-Clement, J., Schweinhart, L., Barnett, W., Epstein, A., & Weikart, D. (1984). Changed lives: The effects of the Perry Preschool Project on youths through age 19. *Monographs of the High/Scope Education* Research Foundation, 8.

Bloom, B. (1964). *Stability and change in human characteristics*. Wiley.

Brain, G. (1979). The early planners. In E. Zigler & J. Valentine (Eds.), *Project Head Start: A legacy of the war on poverty* (pp. 72–77). Free Press.

Campbell, F., Pungello, E., Burchinal, M., Kainz, K., Pan, Y., Wasik, B., Barbarin, O., Sparling, J., & Ramey, C. (2012). Adult outcomes as a function of an early childhood educational program: An Abecedarian project follow-up. *Developmental Psychology, 48*(4), 1033–1043.

Campbell, F., & Ramey, C. (1994). Effects of early intervention on intellectual and academic achievement: A follow-up study of children from low-income families. *Child Development, 65*, 684–698.

Campbell, F., & Ramey, C. (1995). Cognitive and school outcomes for high risk African-American students at middle adolescence: Positive effects of early intervention. *American Educational Research Journal, 32*, 743–772.

Campbell, F., Ramey, C., Pungello, E., Sparling, J., & Miller-Johnson, S. (2002). Early childhood education: Young adult outcomes from the Abecedarian Project. *Applied Developmental Science, 6*(1), 42–57.

Cicerelli, V., Evans, J., & Schiller, J. (1969). *The impact of Head Start on children's cognitive and affective development: Preliminary report*. Office of Economic Opportunity.

Cook, R., Klein, R., & Chen, D. (2020). *Adapting early childhood curricula for children with special needs*(10th ed.). Pearson Education.

Dewey, J. (1916). *Democracy and education*. Macmillan.

Dunn, L. (1973). *Exceptional children in the schools*(2nd ed.). Holt, Rinehart & Winston.

Dunst, C. J. (2007). Early intervention for infants and toddlers with developmental disabilities. In S. L. Odom, R. H. Horner, M. E. Snell, & J. Blaher (Eds.), *Handbook of developmental disabilities* (pp. 161–180). Guildford Press.

Gargiulo, R., & Bouck, E. (2021). *Special education in contemporary society: An introduction to exceptionality*(7th ed.). SAGE.

Gargiulo, R., & Černá, M. (1992). Special education in Czechoslovakia: Characteristics and issues. *International Journal of Special Education, 7*(1), 60–70.

Gearhart, B., Mullen, R., & Gearhart, C. (1993). *Exceptional individuals*. Brooks/Cole.

Ginsburg, H., & Opper, S. (1969). *Piaget's theory of intellectual development*. Prentice Hall.

Graves, S., Gargiulo, R., & Sluder L. (1996). *Young children: An introduction to early childhood education*. West.

Guralnick, M. (2005). Early intervention for children with intellectual disabilities: Current knowledge and future prospects. *Journal of Applied Research in Intellectual Disabilities, 18*(4), 313–324.

Guralnick, M. J. (2017). Early intervention for young children with developmental delays: Contributions of the developmental systems approach. In H. Sukkar, C. J. Dunst, & J. Kirkby (Eds.), *Early childhood intervention: Working with families of young children with special needs* (pp. 17–34). Routledge.

Halpern, R. (2000). Early childhood intervention for low-income children and families. In J. Shonkoff & S. Meisels (Eds.), *Handbook of early childhood intervention*(2nd ed., pp. 361–386). Cambridge University Press.

Hanson, M., & Lynch, E. (1995). *Early intervention*(2nd ed.). Pro-Ed.

Harkness, S., Super, C. M., Mavridis, C. J., Barry, O., & Zeitlin, M. (2013). Culture and early childhood development: Implications for policy and programs. In P. R. Britto, P. L. Engle, & C. M. Super (Eds.), *Handbook of early childhood development research and its impact on global policy* (pp. 142–160). Oxford University.

Head Start Program Facts. (2019). *Fiscal year 2019*. https://eclkc.ohs.acf.hhs.gov/about-us/article/head-start-program-facts-fiscal-year-2019

Head Start Program Final Rule, 58 F.R. 5492 (January 21, 1993).

Hills, T. (1992). Reaching potentials through appropriate assessment. In S. Bredekamp & T. Rosegrant (Eds.), *Reaching potentials: Appropriate curriculum and assessment for young children*(Vol. 1, pp. 43–63). National Association for the Education of Young Children.

Hunt, J. (1961). *Intelligence and experience*. Ronald Press.

Kilgo, J. (2006). Overview of transdisciplinary teaming in early intervention and early childhood special education. In J. Kilgo (Ed.), *Transdisciplinary teaming in early intervention and early childhood special education* (pp. 9–15). Association for Childhood Education International.

Lawton, J. (1988). *Introduction to child care and early childhood education*. Scott Foresman.

Meisels, S., & Shonkoff, J. (2000). Early childhood intervention: A continuing evolution. In J. Shonkoff & S. Meisels (Eds.), *Handbook of early childhood intervention*(2nd ed., pp. 3–31). Cambridge University Press.

Montessori, M. (1965). *Dr. Montessori's own handbook*. Schocken Books.

Morrison, G. (2009). *Early childhood education today*(11th ed.). Pearson Education.

Morrison, G. (2012). *Early childhood education today*(12th ed.). Pearson Education.

Morrison, G., Breffni, L., & Woika, M. (2022), *Early childhood education today*(15th ed.). Pearson Education.

North American Montessori Center. (2016, July 29). *Montessori and the Circle of Inclusion Project*. http://www.montessoritraining.blogspot.com/2016/07/montessori-and-circle-of-inclusion.html

Odom, S. (2016). The role of theory in early childhood special education and early intervention. In B. Reichow, B. Boyd, E. Barton, & S. Odom (Eds.), *Handbook of early childhood special education* (pp. 21–36). Springer.

Office of Head Start. (2019). *Early Head Start services snapshot, 2018–2019*. https://eclkc.ohs.acf.hhs.gov/sites/default/files/pdf/no-search/service-snapshot-ehs-2018-2019.pdf

Peterson, N. (1987). *Early intervention for handicapped and at-risk children*. Love.

Piaget, J. (1963). *Origins of intelligence in children*. Norton.

Piaget, J. (1970). Piaget's theory. In P. Mussen (Ed.), *Carmichael's manual of child psychology*(3rd ed., Vol. 1, pp. 703–732). Wiley.

Ramey, C., & Campbell, F. (1977). Prevention of developmental retardation in high risk children. In P. Mittler (Ed.), *Research to practice in mental retardation: Care and intervention*(Vol. 1, pp. 157–164). University Park Press.

Ramey, C., & Campbell, F. (1984). Preventive education for high risk children: Cognitive consequences of the Carolina Abecedarian Project. *American Journal of Mental Deficiency, 88*, 515–523.

Ramey, C., & Smith, B. (1977). Assessing the intellectual consequences of early intervention with high-risk infants. *American Journal of Mental Deficiency, 81*, 318–324.

Reynolds, A., & Temple, J. (2005). Priorities for a new century of early childhood programs. *Infants & Young Children, 18*(2), 104–118.

Schweinhart, L., Barnes, H., & Weikart, D. (1993). *Significant benefits: The High/Scope Perry Preschool study through age 27*. High/Scope Press.

Schweinhart, L., Montie, J., Xiang, Z., Barnett, W., Belfield, C., & Nores, M. (2005). *Lifetime effects: The High/Scope Perry Preschool study through age 40*. High/Scope Press.

Shonkoff, J. P., & Richter, L. (2013). The powerful reach of early childhood development. In P. R. Britto, P. L. Engle, & C. M. Super (Eds.), *Handbook of early childhood development research and its impact on global policy* (pp. 24–34). Oxford University.

Spodek, B., Saracho, O., & Davis, M. (1991). *Foundations of early childhood education*(2nd ed.). Prentice Hall.

Temple, J., & Reynolds, A. (2007). Benefits and costs of investments in preschool education: Evidence from the Child-Parent Centers and related programs. *Economics of Education Review, 26*(1), 126–144.

Thurman, S., & Widerstrom, A. (1990). *Infants and young children with special needs*(2nd ed.). Paul H. Brookes.

Tudge, J. (1992). Processes and consequences of peer collaboration: A Vygotskian analysis. *Child Development, 63*, 1364–1379.

U.S. Department of Education. (2022). *Forty-third annual report to Congress on the implementation of the Individuals with Disabilities Education Act, 2021*. U.S. Government Printing Office.

Vygotsky, L. (1978). *Mind in society: The development of higher mental processes*. Harvard University Press.

Vygotsky, L. (1986). *Thought and language*. MIT Press.

Vygotsky, L. (1993). *The collected works of L. S. Vygotsky Vol. 2: The fundamentals of defectology*. Plenum.

Zigler, E., & Valentine, J. (Eds.). (1979). *Project Head Start: A legacy of the War on Poverty*. Free Press.

CHAPTER 2

Allen, K., & Cowdery, G. (2022). *The exceptional child: Inclusion in early education* (9th ed.). Cengage Learning.

Bailey, D. (2000). The federal role in early intervention: Prospects for the future. *Topics in Early Childhood Special Education, 20*(2), 71–78.

Bailey, D., Farel, A., O'Donnell, K., Simeonsson, R., & Miller, C. (1986). Preparing infant interventionists: Interdepartmental training in special education and maternal and child health. *Journal of the Division for Early Childhood, 11*(1), 67–77.

Bailey, D., Hebbler, K., Spiker, D., Scarborough, A., Mallik, S., & Nelson, L. (2005). Thirty-six month outcomes for families of children who have disabilities and participated in early intervention. *Pediatrics, 116*(6), 1346–1352.

Bailey, D., & Wolery, M. (1992). *Teaching infants and preschoolers with disabilities* (2nd ed.). Merrill.

Bowe, F. (2007). *Early childhood special education* (4th ed.). Thomson/Delmar Learning.

Boyd, B., Kucharczyk, S., & Wong, C. (2016). Implementing evidence-based practices in early childhood classroom settings. In B. Reichow, B. Boyd, E. Barton, & S. Odom (Eds.), *Handbook of early childhood special education* (pp. 335–348). Springer.

Bricker, D., Bohjanen, S., Ryan, S., Squires, J., & Xie, H. (2020). *EI/ECSE: A history of early intervention/early childhood special education in the United States*. Division for Early Childhood.

Bronfenbrenner, U. (1977). Toward an experimental ecology of human development. *American Psychologist, 32*(7), 513–531.

Bronfenbrenner, U. (1979). *The ecology of human development: Experiments by nature and design*. Harvard University Press.

Bronfenbrenner, U. (1992). Ecological systems theory. In R. Vasta (Ed.), *Six theories of child development: Revised formulations and current issues* (pp. 187–249). Kingsley.

Bronfenbrenner, U., & Morris, P. (1998). The ecology of developmental processes. In W. Damon & R. Lerner (Eds.), *Handbook of child psychology* (5th ed., Vol. 1, pp. 993–1028). Wiley.

Bruder, M. (2010). Early childhood intervention: A promise to children and families for their future. *Exceptional Children, 76*(3), 339–355.

Bruder, M. B., Dunst, C., Maude, S. P., Schnurr, M., Van Polen, A., Frolek Clark, G., Winslow, A ., & Gethmann, D. (2020). Practitioner appraisals of their desired and current use of the 2014 Division for Early Childhood Recommended Practices. *Journal of Early Intervention, 42*(3), 259–274.

Casto, G., & Mastropieri, M. (1986). The efficacy of early intervention programs: A meta-analysis. *Exceptional Children, 52*(5), 417–424.

Council for Exceptional Children. (2022). *Initial practice-based standards for early interventionist/early childhood special educators.* https://exceptionalchildren.org/standards/initial-practice-based-standards-early-interventionists-early-childhood-special-educators

Danaher, J. (2011). *Eligibility policies and practices for young children under Part B of IDEA* (NECTAC Notes 27). University of North Carolina, FPG Child Development Institute, National Early Childhood Technical Assistance Center.

Division for Early Childhood. (2009, April). *Developmental delay as an eligibility category. (Concept paper). Author.*

Division for Early Childhood. (2014). *DEC recommended practices in early intervention/early childhood special education, 2014.* http://www.dec-sped.org/recommendedpractices

Dunst, C., & Espe-Sherwindt, M. (2016). Family-centered practices in early childhood intervention. In B. Reichow, B. Boyd, E. Barton, & S. Odom (Eds.), *Handbook of early childhood special education* (pp. 37–56). Springer.

Dunst, C., & Snyder, S. (1986). A critique of the Utah State University early intervention meta-analysis. *Exceptional Children, 53*(3), 269–276.

Dunst, C., Trivette, C., & Deal, A. (1988). *Enabling and empowering families: Principles and guidelines for practice.* Brookline Books.

Early Childhood Technical Assistance Center. (2022). *State and jurisdictional eligibility definitions for infants and toddlers with disabilities under IDEA Part C.* https://ectacenter.org/topics/earlyid/state-info.asp

Fallen, H., & Umansky, W. (1985). *Young children with special needs* (2nd ed.). Merrill.

Farran, D. (1990). Effects of intervention with disadvantaged and disabled children: A decade of review. In S. Meisels & J. Shonkoff (Eds.), *Handbook of early childhood intervention* (pp. 501–539). Cambridge University Press.

Farran, D. (2000). Another decade of intervention for children who are low income or disabled: What do we know now? In J. Shonkoff & S. Meisels (Eds.), *Handbook of early childhood intervention* (2nd ed., pp. 510–548). Cambridge University Press.

Gallagher, J., Coleman, M., & Kirk, S. (2023). *Educating exceptional children* (15th ed.). Cengage Learning.

Garcia, J., Heckman, J., Leaf, D., & Prados, M. (2016). *The life-cycle benefits of an influential early childhood program. (Working Paper 2016-035). HECO Working Paper Series, University of Chicago.* https://hceconomics.uchicago.edu/research/papers

Gargiulo, R., & Bouck, E. (2021). *Special education in contemporary society: An introduction to exceptionality* (7th ed.). Sage.

Gargiulo, R., & Metcalf, D. (2023). *Teaching in today's inclusive classroom* (4th ed.). Cengage Learning.

Guralnick, M. (1988). Efficacy research in early childhood intervention programs. In S. Odom & M. Karnes (Eds.), *Early intervention for infants and children with handicaps: An empirical base* (pp. 75–88). Paul H. Brookes.

Guralnick, M. (1991). The next decade of research on the effectiveness of early intervention. *Exceptional Children, 58*(1), 174–183.

Guralnick, M. (1997). *The effectiveness of early intervention.* Paul H. Brookes.

Guralnick, M. (1998). Effectiveness of early intervention for vulnerable children: A developmental perspective. *American Journal on Mental Retardation, 102*(4), 319–345.

Guralnick, M. (2004). Family investments in response to the developmental challenges of young children with disabilities. In A. Kalil & T. Deleire (Eds.), *Family investments in children's potential* (pp. 119–137). Erlbaum.

Guralnick, M. (2005). Early intervention for children with intellectual disabilities: Current knowledge and future prospects. *Journal of Applied Research in Intellectual Disabilities, 18*(4), 313–324.

Guralnick, M., & Bricker, D. (1987). The effectiveness of early intervention for children with cognitive and general developmental delay. In M. Guralnick & F. Bennett (Eds.), *The effectiveness of early intervention for at-risk and handicapped children* (pp. 115–173). Academic Press.

Guralnick, M., & Conlon, C. (2007). Early intervention. In M. Batshaw, L. Pelligrino, & N. Roizen (Eds.), *Children with disabilities* (6th ed., pp. 511–521). Paul H. Brookes.

Hallahan, D., Kauffman, J., & Pullen, P. (2009). *Exceptional learners* (11th ed.). Pearson Education.

Harbin, G., McWilliam, R., & Gallagher, J. (2000). Services for young children with disabilities and their families. In J. Shonkoff & S. Meisels (Eds.), *Handbook of early childhood intervention* (2nd ed., pp. 387–415). Cambridge University Press.

Hardman, M., Egan, M., & Drew, C. (2017). *Human exceptionality* (12th ed.). Cengage Learning.

Hemmeter, M., & Golden, A. (2014). Assessing early childhood environments: Planning high quality learning environments for young children. In M. McLean, M. Hemmeter, & P. Snyder (Eds.), *Essential elements for assessing infants and preschoolers with special needs* (pp. 87–122). Pearson Education.

Howard, V., Williams, B., Miller, D., & Aiken, E. (2014). *Very young children with special needs* (5th ed.). Pearson Education.

Kamerman, S. (2000). Early childhood intervention policies: An international perspective. In J. Shonkoff & S. Meisels (Eds.), *Handbook of early childhood intervention* (2nd ed., pp. 613–629). Cambridge University Press.

Kemp, C. (2003). Investigating the transition of young children with intellectual disabilities to mainstream classes: An Australian perspective. *International Journal of Disability, Development and Education, 50*(4), 403–433.

Kilgo, J. (2022). Our proud heritage. The evolution of family-centered services in early childhood special education. *Young Children, 77*(3).

Kirk, S. (1958). *Early education of the mentally retarded: An experimental study.* University of Illinois Press.

Kirk, S., Gallagher, J., & Coleman, M. (2015). *Education exceptional children* (14th ed.). Cengage Learning.

Kopp, C. (1983). Risk factors in development. In P. Mussen (Ed.), *Handbook of child psychology* (4th ed., Vol. II, pp. 1081–1088). Wiley.

Koppelman, J. (1986). Reagan signs bills expanding services to handicapped preschoolers. *Report to Preschool Programs,* 18, 3–4.

Lazar, I., & Darlington, R. (1979). *Summary report: Lasting effects after preschool* (DHEW Publication No. OHDS 80–30179). U.S. Government Printing Office.

Lazar, I., Darlington, R., Murray, H., Royce, J., & Snipper, A. (1982). Lasting effects of early intervention: A report from the Consortium for Longitudinal Studies. *Monographs of the Society for Research in Child Development, 47*(2–3, Serial No. 195).

Lazara, A., Danaher, J., Kraus, R., Goode, S., Hipps, S., & Festa, C (Eds.). (2010). *Section 619 profile* (17th ed.). University of North Carolina, FPG Child Development Institute, National Early Childhood Technical Assistance Center.

Lipkin, P., & Schertz, M. (2008). Early intervention and its efficacy. In P. Accardo (Ed.), *Capute & Accardo's neurodevelopmental disabilities in infancy and childhood* (3rd ed., Vol. 1, pp. 519–551). Paul H. Brookes.

Long, T. (2019). Early intervention. In M. Batshaw, N. Roizen, & L. Pellegrino (Eds.), *Children with disabilities* (8th ed., pp. 639–648). Paul H. Brookes.

McCormick, M., Brooks-Gunn, J., Buka, S., Goldman, J., Yu, J., Salganik, M., Scott, D., Bennett, F., Kay, L., Bernbaum, J., Bauer, C., Martin, C., Woods, E., Martin, A., & Casey, P. (2006). Early intervention in low birth weight premature infants: Results at 18 years of age for the Infant Health and Development Program. *Pediatrics, 117*(3), 771–780.

McLean, M., Sandall, S., & Smith, B. (2016). A history of early childhood special education. In B. Reichow, B. Boyd, E. Barton, & S. Odom (Eds.), *Handbook of early childhood special education* (pp. 3–20). Springer.

McWilliam, R. (2016). Birth to three: Early intervention. In B. Reichow, B. Boyd, E. Barton, & S. Odom (Eds.), *Handbook of early childhood special education* (pp. 75–88). Springer.

National Early Childhood Technical Assistance Center. (2011a). *The importance of early intervention for infants and toddlers with disabilities and their families*. University of North Carolina, FPG Child Development Institute, Author.

National Early Childhood Technical Assistance Center. (2011b). *The outcomes of early intervention for infants and toddlers with disabilities and their families*. University of North Carolina, FPG Child Development Institute, Author.

National Early Childhood Technical Assistance Center. (2022). *State and jurisdictional eligibility definitions*. University of North Carolina.

Odom, S. (1988). Research in early childhood special education: Methodologies and paradigms. In S. Odom & M. Karnes (Eds.), *Early intervention for infants and children with handicaps* (pp. 1–21). Paul H. Brookes.

Odom, S. (2016). The role of theory in early childhood special education and early intervention. In B. Reichow, B. Boyd, E. Barton, & S. Odom (Eds.), *Handbook of early childhood special education* (pp. 21–36). Springer.

Odom, S., & Wolery, M. (2003). A unified theory of practice in early intervention/early childhood special education: Evidence-based practices. *Journal of Special Education, 37*(3), 164–173.

Peterson, N. (1987). *Early intervention for handicapped and at-risk children*. Love.

Ramey, C., & Ramey, S. (1998). Early intervention and early experience. *American Psychologist, 58*(2), 109–120.

Raver, S. (2009). *Early childhood special education*. Pearson Education.

Reynolds, A., & Temple, J. (2005). Priorities for a new century of early childhood programs. *Infants & Young Children, 18*(2), 104–118.

Rogoff, B., Coppens, A., Alcalá, L., Aceves-Azuara, I., Ruvalcaba, O., López, A., & Dayton, A. (2017). Noticing learners' strengths through cultural research. *Perspectives on Psychological Science, 12*(5), 876–888.

Schweinhart, L., Montie, J., Xiang, Z., Barnett, W., Belfield, C., & Nores, M. (2005). *Lifetime effects: The High/Scope Perry Preschool study through age 40*. High/Scope Press.

Shackelford, J. (2006). *State and jurisdictional eligibility definitions for infants and toddlers with disabilities under IDEA* (NECTAC Notes 21). University of North Carolina, FPG Child Development Institute, National Early Childhood Technical Assistance Center.

Shonkoff, J., & Hauser-Cram, P. (1987). Early intervention for disabled infants and their families: A quantitative analysis. *Pediatrics, 80*(5), 650–658.

Shonkoff, J., & Meisels, S (Eds.). (2000). *Handbook of early childhood intervention* (2nd ed.). Cambridge University Press.

Shonkoff, J., & Phillips, D (Eds.). (2000). *From neurons to neighborhoods: The science of early child development*. National Academy Press.

Skeels, H. (1966). Adult status of children with contrasting early life experiences. *Monographs of the Society for Research in Child Development, 31*(3, Serial No. 105).

Skeels, H., & Dye, H. (1939). A study of the effects of differential stimulation on mentally retarded children. *Proceedings and Addresses of the American Association on Mental Deficiency, 44*, 114–136.

Smiley, L., Richards, S., & Taylor, R. (2022). *Exceptional students* (4th ed.). McGraw-Hill.

Smith, T. (2002). Section 504: Basic requirements for schools. *Intervention in School and Clinic, 37*(5), 259–266.

Smith, T., & Patton, J. (2007). *Section 504 and public schools* (2nd ed.). Pro-Ed.

Sousa, D. (2022). *How the brain learns* (6th ed.). Corwin.

Spicer, P. (2010). Cultural influences on parenting. *Zero to Three, 30*(4), 28–32.

Spodek, B., & Saracho, O. (1994a). *Dealing with individual differences in the early childhood classroom*. Longman.

Spodek, B., & Saracho, O. (1994b). *Right from the start*. Allyn & Bacon.

Strain, P., & Smith, B. (1986). A counter-interpretation of early intervention effects: A response to Casto and Mastropieri. *Exceptional Children, 53*(3), 260–265.

Temple, J., & Reynolds, A. (2007). Benefits and costs of investments in preschool education: Evidence from the Child-Parent Centers and related programs. *Economics of Education Review, 26*(1), 126–144.

Turnbull, A., Turnbull, R., Francis, G., Burke, M., Kyzar, K., Haines, S., Gershwin, T., Shepherd, K., Holdren, N., Singer, G. (2022). *Families and professionals* (8th ed.). Pearson Education.

Turnbull, H., Huerta, N., & Stowe, M. (2004). *The Individuals with Disabilities Education Act as amended in 2004*. Pearson Education.

Trohanis, P. (1989). An introduction to PL 99–457 and the national policy agenda for serving young children with special needs and their families. In J. Gallagher, P. Trohanis, & R. Clifford (Eds.), *Policy implementation and PL 99-457: Planning for young children with special needs* (pp. 1–17). Paul H. Brookes.

U.S. Department of Education. (1997). *Nineteenth annual report to Congress on the implementation of the Individuals with Disabilities Education Act*. U.S. Government Printing Office.

U.S. Department of Education. (2022a). ED *facts data warehouse: IDEA Part B child count and educational environments collection*. https://www2.ed.gov/programs/osepidea/618-data/index.html

U.S. Department of Education. (2022b). *Forty-third annual report to Congress on the implementation of the Individuals with Disabilities Education Act, 2021*. U.S. Government Printing Office.

Vincent, L., Salisbury, C., Strain, P., McCormick, C., & Tessier, A. (1990). A behavioral ecological approach to early intervention: Focus on cultural diversity. In S. Meisels & J. Shonkoff (Eds.), *Handbook of early childhood intervention* (pp. 173–195). Cambridge University Press.

White, K., Bush, D., & Casto, G. (1986). Learning from reviews of early intervention. *Journal of Special Education, 19*(4), 417–428.

Yell, M. (2019). *The law and special education* (5th ed.). Pearson Education.

Yell, M., & Bateman, D. (2020). Defining educational benefit: An update on the U.S. Supreme Court's ruling in Endrew F. v. Douglas County School District (2017). *TEACHING Exceptional Children, 52*(5), 283–290.

Zero to Three. (2014). *When is the brain fully developed?* https://www.zerotothree.org/resources/1371-when-is-the-brain-fully-developed

Zigler, E. (1990). Foreword. In S. Meisels & J. Shonkoff (Eds.), *Handbook of early childhood intervention* (pp. ix–xiv). Cambridge University Press.

Zigler, E. (2000). Foreword. In J. Shonkoff & S. Meisels (Eds.), *Handbook of early childhood intervention* (2nd ed., pp. xi–xv). Cambridge University Press.

Zirkel, P., & Yell, M. (2024). Indicators of progress in the wake of Endrew F.: The distinction between professional recommendations and judicial rulings. *Exceptional Children, 90*(2), 110–125.

CHAPTER 3

Akamoglu, Y., & Dinnebeil, L. (2017). Coaching parents to use naturalistic language and communication strategies. *Young Exceptional Children, 20*(1), 3–15.

Aldridge, J., & Goldman, R. (2007). *Current issues and trends in education*(2nd ed.). Allyn & Bacon.

Aldridge, J., Kilgo, J., & Bruton, A. (2015). Transforming transdisciplinary early intervention and early childhood special education through intercultural education. *International Journal of Early Childhood Special Education, 7*(2), 343–360.

Aldridge, J., Kilgo, J., & Bruton, A. (2016). Beyond the Brady Bunch: Hybrid families and their evolving relationships with early childhood education. *Childhood Education, 92*(2), 140–148.

Aldridge, J., Kilgo, J., & Christensen, L. (2011). How much should we compromise in honoring diversity? *Focus on Inclusive Education, 8*(4), 1–3.

Allen, E., & Cowdery, G. (2022). *The exceptional child: Inclusion in early childhood education*(9th ed.). Cengage Learning.

Banks, R., Santos, R., & Roof, V. (2003). Discovering family concerns, priorities, and resources: Sensitive family information gathering. *Young Exceptional Children, 6*(2), 11–19.

Barrera, I., Corso, R. M., & Macpherson, D. (2003). *Skilled dialogue: Strategies for responding to cultural diversity in early childhood.* Brookes.

Berry, J., & Hardman, M. (2008). *Lifespan perspectives on the family and disability*(2nd ed.). Allyn & Bacon.

Blacher, J., & Hatton, C. (2001). Current perspectives on family research in mental retardation. Current Opinion in Psychiatry, *14*(5), 477–482.

Blue-Banning, M., Summers, J., Frankland, H., Nelson, L., & Beegle, G. (2004). Dimensions of family and professional partnerships: Constructive guidelines for collaboration. *Exceptional Children, 70*(2), 167–184.

Brady, S., Peters, D., Gamel-McCormick, M., & Venuto, N. (2004). Types and patterns of professional-family talk in home-based early intervention. *Journal of Early Intervention, 26*(2), 146–159.

Bronfenbrenner, U. (1979). *The ecology of human development: Experiments by nature and design.* Harvard University Press.

Bronfenbrenner, U., & Morris, P. (2006). The bioecological model of human development. In W. Damon & R. M. Lerner (Eds.), *Handbook of child psychology*: Vol. 1. *Theoretical models of human development*, (6th ed., pp. 793–828). John Wiley & Sons.

Bruder, M. (2010). Early childhood intervention: A promise to children and families for their future. *Exceptional Children, 76*(3), 339–355.

Crnic, K., Neece, C., McIntyre, L., Blacher, J., & Baker, B. (2017). Intellectual disability and developmental risk: Promoting intervention to improve child and family well-being. *Child Development, 88*, 436–445.

Division for Early Childhood. (2014). *DEC recommended practices in early intervention/early childhood special education.* https://www.childrensdefense.org

Division for Early Childhood. (2020). *Initial practice-based standards for early interventionists/early childhood special educators.* Report. https://www.dec-sped.org/ei-ecse-standards

Drotar, D., Baskiewicz, A., Irvin, N., Kennell, J., & Klaus, M. (1975). The adaptation of parents to the birth of an infant with a congenital malformation: A hypothetical model. *Pediatrics, 56*, 710–716.

Dunst, C., Bruder, M., & Espe-Sherwindt, M. (2014). Family capacity-building in early childhood intervention: Do content and setting matter? *School Community Journal, 24*(1), 37–48.

Dunst, C., & Espe-Sherwindt, M. (2016). Family-centered practices in early childhood intervention. In B. Reichow, B. Boyd, E. Barton, & S. Odom (Eds.), *Handbook of early childhood special education* (pp. 37–56). Springer.

Dunst, C., Johanson, C., Trivette, C., & Hamby, D. (1991). Family-oriented early intervention policies and practices: Family-centered or not? *Exceptional Children, 58*(2), 115–126.

Early Childhood Technical Assistance Center. (n.d.) *Service coordination under Part C.* https://ectacenter.org/topics/scoord/scoord.asp

Featherstone, H. (1980). *A difference in the family: Life with a disabled child.* Basic Books.

Ferguson, P. (2002). A place in the family: An historical interpretation of research on parental reactions to having a child with a disability. *Journal of Special Education, 36*(3), 124–131.

Gallagher, P., Fialka, J., Rhodes, C., & Arceneaux, C. (2003). Working with families: Rethinking denial. *Young Exceptional Children, 5*(2), 11–17.

Gargiulo, R., & Bouck, E. (2021). *Special education in contemporary society: An introduction to exceptionality*(7th ed.). SAGE.

Gollnick, D., & Chinn, P. (2017). *Multicultural education in a pluralistic society*(10th ed.). Pearson Education.

Green, B., McAllister, C., & Tarte, J. (2004). The strengths-based practices inventory: A tool for measuring strengths-based service delivery in early childhood and family support programs. *Families in Society, 85*(3), 326–334.

Guralnick, M. (2011). Why early intervention works: A systems perspective. *Infants and Young Children, 24*(1), 6–28.

Hains, A., Rhymer, P., McLean, M., Barnekow, K., Johnson, V., & Kennedy, B. (2005). Interdisciplinary teams and diverse families: Practices in early intervention personnel preparation. *Young Exceptional Children, 8*, 2–10.

Hanson, M., & Espinosa, L. (2016). Culture, ethnicity, and linguistic diversity: Implications for early childhood special education. In B. Reichow, B. Boyd, E. Barton, & S. Odom (Eds.), *Handbook of early childhood special education* (pp. 455–472). Springer.

Hanson, M., & Lynch, E. (1995). *Early intervention: Implementing child and family services for infants and toddlers who are at risk or disabled*. Pro-Ed.

Hanson, M., & Lynch, E. (2013). *Understanding families: Supportive approaches to diversity, disability, and risk* (2nd ed.). Paul H. Brookes.

Kaczmarek, L. (2007). A team approach: Supporting families of children with disabilities in inclusive programs. In D. Koralek (Ed.), *Spotlight on young children and families* (pp. 28–36). National Association for the Education of Young Children.

Kalyanpur, M., & Harry, B. (2012). *Cultural reciprocity with families: Building family-professional relationships*. Paul H. Brookes.

Keilty, B. (2016). *The early intervention guidebook for families and professionals: Partnering for success* (2nd ed.). Teachers College Press.

Kilgo, J. (2022). Our Proud Heritage: The evolution of family-centered services in early childhood special education. *Young Children, 77*(4), 84–89.

Kilgo, J., & Aldridge, J. (2009). Providing family-based and culturally responsive practices for young children with developmental delays and disabilities and their families: Using scenarios for problem solving. *Focus on Inclusive Education, 7*(2), 4–5.

Kilgo, J., & Aldridge, J. (2011). Ten years of transdisciplinary teaming: Lessons learned through a transformational process. *Focus on Teacher Education, 10*(3), 3–6.

Kilgo, J., & Raver, S. (2009). Building partnerships in culturally/linguistically diverse settings. In S. Raver (Ed.), *Early childhood special education—0 to 8 years: Strategies for positive outcomes* (pp. 27–49). Pearson Education.

Levine, K. (2013). Capacity building and empowerment practice. In B. Trute & D. Hiebert-Murphy (Eds.), *Partnering with parents: Family-centered practice in children's services* (pp. 107–129). University of Toronto.

Lynch, E., & Hanson, M. (2011). *Developing cross-cultural competence: A guide for working with children and their families* (4th ed.). Paul H. Brookes.

Mapp, K., & Kuttner, P. J. (2013). *Partners in education: A dual capacity-building framework for family-school partnerships*. Austin, TX: Southwest Educational Development Lab.

Matuszny, R., Banda, D., & Coleman, T. (2007). A progressive plan for building collaborative relationships with parents from diverse backgrounds. *Teaching Exceptional Children, 39*(4), 24–31.

McCormick, K., Stricklin, S., Nowak, T., & Rous, B. (2008). Using eco-mapping to understand family strengths and resources. *Young Exceptional Children, 11*(2), 17–28.

McGoldrick, M., Carter, B., & Garcia-Preto, N. (2015). *Expanding family life cycle: The individual, family, and social perspectives* (5th ed.). Pearson Education.

McWilliam, R. (1999). It's only natural . . . to have early intervention in the environments where it's needed. In S. Sandall & M. Ostrosky (Eds.), *Natural environments and inclusion* (Young Exceptional Children Monograph Series No. 2). Division for Early Childhood.

McWilliam, R. (2012). Implementing and preparing for home visits. *Topics in Early Childhood Special Education, 31*(4), 224–231.

McWilliam, R. (2016). Birth to three: Early intervention. In B. Reichow, B. Boyd, E. Barton, & S. Odom (Eds.), *Handbook of early childhood special education* (pp. 75–88). Springer.

National Association for the Education of Young Children. (2022). Developmentally appropriate practice in early childhood programs serving children from birth through age 8 (4th ed.). NAEYC.

Nichols, M. (2014). *The essentials of family therapy* (6th ed.). Pearson Education.

Odom, S. (2016). The role of theory in early childhood special education and early intervention. In B. Reichow, B. Boyd, E. Barton, & S. Odom (Eds.), *Handbook of early childhood special education* (pp. 21–36). Springer.

Roggman, L. A., Peterson, C. A., Chazan-Cohen, R., Ispa, J., Decker, K. B., Hughes-Belding, K., Cook, G. A., & Vallotoon, C. D. (2016). Preparing home visitors to partner with families of infants and toddlers. *Journal of Early Childhood Teacher Education, 37*(4), 301–313.

Sandall, S., Hemmeter, M., Smith, B., & McLean, M. (Eds.). (2005). *DEC recommended practices: A comprehensive guide for practical application in early intervention/early childhood special education*. Division for Early Childhood.

Seligman, M., & Darling, R. (2007). *Ordinary families, special children: A systems approach to childhood disability* (3rd ed.). Guilford Press.

Summers, J., Hoffman, L., Marquis, J., Turnbull, A., Poston, D., & Nelson, L. (2005). Measuring the quality of family-professional partnerships in special education services. *Exceptional Children, 72*(1), 65–83.

Taibbi, R. (2015). *Doing family therapy* (3rd ed.). Guilford Press.

Tomeny, K., Garcia-Grau, P., & McWilliam, R. (2021). Early interventionists' rating of family-centered practices in natural environments. *Infants & Young Children, 34*(4), 266–283.

Trivette, C., & Banerjee, R. (2015). Using the recommended practices to build parent competence and confidence. In *DEC recommended practices: Enhancing services for young children with disabilities and their families* (DEC Recommended Practices Monograph Series No. 1, pp. 66–75). Division for Early Childhood.

Trivette, C., & Dunst, C. (2004). Evaluating family-focused practices: Parenting Experiences Scale. *Young Exceptional Children, 7*(3), 12–19.

Trivette, C., & Dunst, C. (2005). DEC recommended practices: Family-based practices. In S. Sandall, M. Hemmeter, B. Smith, & M. McLean (Eds.), *DEC recommended practices: A comprehensive guide to practical application in early intervention/early childhood special education* (pp. 107–120). Division for Early Childhood.

Turnbull, A., Turnbull, R., Francis, G., Burke, M., Kyzar, K., Haines, S., Gershwin, T., Shepherd, K., Holdren, N., & Singer, G. (2022). *Families and professionals: Trusting partnerships in general and special education* (8th ed.). Pearson.

Turnbull, A., Winton, P., Rous, B., & Buysse, V. (2010). *CONNECT Module 4: Family-professional partnerships*. University of North Carolina at Chapel Hill, FPG Child Development Institute. https://community.fpg.unc.edu/connect-modules/learners/module-4

Whitbread, K., Bruder, M., Fleming, G., & Park, H. (2007). Collaboration in special education: Parent-professional training. *Teaching Exceptional Children, 39*(4), 6–14.

Winton, P., Buysse, V., Turnbull, A., & Rous, B. (2010). CONNECT Module 3: *Communication for collaboration*. University of North Carolina at Chapel Hill, FPG Child Development Institute. https://community.fpg.unc.edu/connect-modules/learners/module-3

Woods, J., Wilcox, M., Friedman, M., & Murch, T. (2011). Collaborative consultation in natural environments: Strategies to enhance family-centered supports and services. *Language, Speech, and Hearing in Schools, 42*, 379–392.

CHAPTER 4

Allen, K., & Cowdery, G. (2022). *The exceptional child*(9th ed.). Cengage Learning.

Bateman, B., & Linden, M. (2012). *Better IEPs: How to develop legally correct and educationally useful programs*(5th ed.). Attainment Company.

Boyd, B., Kucharczyk, S., & Wong, C. (2016). Implementing evidence-based practices in early childhood classroom settings. In B. Reichow, B. Boyd, E. Barton, & S. Odom (Eds.), *Handbook of early childhood special education* (pp. 335–348). Springer.

Bricker, D. (1978). A rationale for the integration of handicapped and nonhandicapped preschool children. In M. Guralnick (Ed.), *Early intervention and the integration of handicapped and nonhandicapped children* (pp. 3–26). University Park Press.

Bricker, D. (1995). The challenge of inclusion. *Journal of Early Intervention, 19*(3), 179–194.

Bricker, D., Felimban, H., Lin, F., Stegenga, S., & Storie, S. (2022). A proposed framework for enhancing collaboration in early intervention/early childhood special education. *Topics in Early Childhood Special Education, 41*(4), 240–252.

Bronfenbrenner, U. (1977). Toward an experimental ecology of human development. *American Psychologist, 32*(7), 513–531.

Bronfenbrenner, U. (1993). Ecological systems theory. In R. Vasta (Ed.), *Six theories of child development* (pp. 187–249). Kingsley.

Bruder, M. (1994). Working with members of other disciplines: Collaboration for success. In M. Wolery & J. Wilbers (Eds.), *Including children with special needs in early childhood programs* (pp. 45–70). National Association for the Education of Young Children.

Bruder, M. (2001). Inclusion of infants and toddlers. In M. Guralnick (Ed.), *Early childhood inclusion: Focus on change* (pp. 203–228). Paul H. Brookes.

Bruder, M. (2010a). Early childhood intervention: A promise to children and their families for their future. *Exceptional Children, 76*(3), 339–355.

Bruder, M. (2010b). Transitions for children with disabilities. In S. Kagan & K. Tarrant (Eds.), *Transitions for young children* (pp. 67–92). Paul H. Brookes.

Carta, J., Schwartz, I., Atwater, J., & McConnell, S. (1991). Developmentally appropriate practice: Appraising its usefulness for young child with disabilities. *Topics in Early Childhood Special Education, 11*(1), 1–20.

Cook, B., McDuffie-Landrum, K., Oshita, L., & Cook, B. (2017). Co-teaching for students with disabilities. In J. Kauffman, D. Hallahan, & P. Pullen (Eds.), *Handbook of special education*(2nd ed., pp. 233–248). Routledge.

Cook, R., Klein, M., & Chen, D. (2020). *Adapting early childhood curricula for children with special needs*(10th ed.). Pearson Education.

Crais, E., & Woods, J. (2016). The role of speech–language pathologists in providing early childhood special education. In B. Reichow, B. Boyd, E. Barton, & S. Odom (Eds.), *Handbook of early childhood special education* (pp. 363–384). Springer.

Davis, M., Kilgo, J., & Gamel-McCormick, M. (1998). *Young children with special needs: A developmentally appropriate approach*. Allyn & Bacon.

Deiner, P. (2013). *Inclusive early childhood education*(6th ed.). Wadsworth/Cengage Learning.

Dillon, S., Armstrong, E., Goudy, L., Reynolds, H., & Scurry, S. (2021). Improving special education service delivery through interdisciplinary collaboration. *Teaching Exceptional Children, 54*(1), 36–43.

Division for Early Childhood. (2014). *DEC recommended practices in early intervention/early childhood special education, 2014*. http://www.dec-sped.org/recommendedpractices

Division for Early Childhood. (2020). *DEC priority issues agenda*. http://www.dec-sped.org/PriorityIssues

DEC/NAEYC. (2009). *Early childhood inclusion: A joint position statement of the Division for Early Childhood (DEC) and the National Association for the Education of Young Children (NAEYC)*. The University of North Carolina, FPG Child Development Institute.

Downing, J. (2008). *Including students with severe and multiple disabilities in typical classrooms*(3rd ed.). Paul H. Brookes.

Dunst, C., & Espe-Sherwindt, M. (2016). Family-centered practices in early childhood intervention. In B. Reichow, B. Boyd, E. Barton, & S. Odom (Eds.), *Handbook of early childhood special education* (pp. 37–56). Springer.

Friend, M. (2021). *Interactions: Collaboration skills for school professionals*(9th ed.). Pearson Education.

Gargiulo, R., & Bouck, E. (2021). *Special education in contemporary society*(7th ed.). SAGE.

Gargiulo, R., & Metcalf, D. (2023). *Teaching in today's inclusive classrooms*(4th ed.). Cengage Learning.

Graves, S., Gargiulo, R., & Sluder, L. (1996). *Young children: An introduction to early childhood education*. West.

Grisham-Brown, J., & Hemmeter, M. (2017). *Blended practices for teaching young children in inclusive settings*(2nd ed.). Paul H. Brookes.

Guralnick, M. (1990). Major accomplishments and future directions in early childhood mainstreaming. *Topics in Early Childhood Special Education, 10*(2), 1–17.

Guralnick, M. (1994). Mothers' perceptions of the benefits and drawbacks of early childhood mainstreaming. *Journal of Early Intervention, 18*(2), 163–168.

Guralnick, M. (2023). A framework for the design of inclusive community-based early childhood intervention programs. *Infants & Young Children, 36*(4), 270–284.

Hallahan, D., Kauffman, J., & Pullen, P. (2009). *Exceptional learners*(11th ed.). Pearson Education.

Hanson, M. (2011). Diversity in service settings. In E. Lynch & M. Hanson (Eds.), *Developing cross cultural competence*(4th ed., pp. 2–19). Paul H. Brookes.

Hanson, M., & Espinosa, L. (2016). Culture, ethnicity, and linguistic diversity: Implications for early childhood special education. In B. Reichow, B. Boyd, E. Barton, & S. Odom (Eds.), *Handbook of early childhood special education* (pp. 455–472). Springer.

Hanson, M., & Lynch, E. (2013). *Understanding families: Supportive approaches to diversity, disability, and risk*(2nd ed.). Paul H. Brookes.

Harbin, G., McWilliam, R., & Gallagher, J. (2000). Services for young children with disabilities and their families. In J. Shonkoff & S. Meisels (Eds.), *Handbook of early childhood intervention*(2nd ed., pp. 387–415). Cambridge University Press.

Hardman, M., Egan, M., & Drew, C. (2017). *Human exceptionality*(12th ed.). Cengage Learning.

Heward, W., Alber-Morgan, S., & Konrad, M. (2022). *Exceptional children*(12th ed.). Pearson Education.

Hooper, S., & Umansky, W. (2014). *Young children with special needs*(6th ed.). Pearson Education.

Howard, V., Williams, B., Miller, D., & Aiken, E. (2014). *Very young children with special needs*(5th ed.). Pearson Education.

Johnson, J., Rahn, N., & Bricker, D. (2015). *An activity-based approach to early intervention*(4th ed.). Paul H. Brookes.

Kennedy, E., & Effgen, S. (2016). Role of physical therapy within the context of early childhood special education. In B. Reichow, B. Boyd, E. Barton, & S. Odom (Eds.), *Handbook of early childhood special education* (pp. 403–418). Springer.

Kilgo, J. (Ed.). (2006). *Transdisciplinary teaming in early intervention/early childhood special education.* Association for Childhood Education International.

Kilgo, J. (2022). Our Proud Heritage: The evolution of family-centered services in early childhood special education. *Young Children, 77*(4), 84–89.

Kilgo, J., Aldridge, J., Vogtle, L., Ronilo, W., & Bruton, A. (2017). Teaming, collaboration, and case-based learning: A transdisciplinary approach to early intervention/education. *International Journal of Case Studies, 6*(6), 7–12.

Kilgo, J., Aldridge, J., Vogtle, L., & Ronilo, W. (2019). The power of teams: Time to move forward in interprofessional personnel preparation. *Monograph on Teaming and Collaboration of the Division of Early Childhood Education of the Council for Exceptional Children (DEC)*, (pp. 135–143). Division for Early Childhood.

Lazara, A., Danaher, J., Kraus, R., Goode, S., Hipps, C., & Festa, C. (Eds.). (2012). *Section 619 profile*(19th ed.). University of North Carolina, FPG Child Development Institute, National Early Childhood Technical Assistance Center.

Little, M., & Dieker, L. (2009). Coteaching: Two heads are better than one. *Principal Leadership, 9*(8), 42–46.

Love, H., & Horn, E. (2021). Definition, context, quality: Current issues in research examining high-quality inclusive education. *Topics in Early Childhood Special Education, 40*(4), 201–216.

Mahurin-Smith, J. (2022). Transitions out of early intervention: A qualitative investigation of families' experiences. *Infants & Young Children, 35*(2), 150–162.

Malone, D., & Gallagher, P. (2009). Transition to preschool special education: A review of the literature. *Early Education and Development, 20*(4), 584–602.

McDonnell, A., & Hardman, M. (1988). A synthesis of "best practices" guidelines for early childhood services. *Journal of the Division for Early Childhood, 12*, 328–341.

McLean, M., Sandall, S., & Smith, B. (2016). A history of early childhood special education. In B. Reichow, B. Boyd, E. Barton, & S. Odom (Eds.), *Handbook of early childhood special education* (pp. 3–20). Springer.

McWilliam, R. (2016). Birth to three: Early intervention. In B. Reichow, B. Boyd, E. Barton, & S. Odom (Eds.), *Handbook of early childhood special education* (pp. 75–88). Springer.

Mercer, C., Mercer, A., & Pullen, P. (2011). *Teaching students with learning problems*(8th ed.). Pearson Education.

Meyen, E. (1996). *Exceptional children*(3rd ed.). Love.

Miller, L., & Newbill, C. (2006). *Section 504 in the classroom*(2nd ed.). Pro-Ed.

Murawski, W. (2015). Creative co-teaching. In W. Murawski & K. Scott (Eds.), *What really works in secondary education* (pp. 201–215). Corwin.

Noonan, M., & McCormick, L. (1993). *Early intervention in natural environments*. Brooks/Cole.

Noonan, M., & McCormick, L. (2014). *Young children with disabilities in natural environments*(2nd ed.). Paul H. Brookes.

Notari-Syverson, A., & Shuster, S. (1995). Putting real-life skills into IEP/IFSPs for infants and young children. *Teaching Exceptional Children, 27*(2), 29–32.

Office for Civil Rights. (1989). *The civil rights of students with hidden disabilities under Section 504 of the Rehabilitation Act of 1973.* U.S. Department of Education.

Sadler, F. (2003). The itinerant special education teacher in the early childhood classroom. *Teaching Exceptional Children, 35*(3), 8–15.

Salend, S. (2016). *Creating inclusive classrooms*(8th ed.). Pearson Education.

Scruggs, T., & Mastropieri, M. (2017). Making inclusion work with co-teaching. *Teaching Exceptional Children, 49*(4), 284–291.

Scruggs, T., Mastropieri, M., & McDuffie, K. (2007). Co-teaching in inclusive classrooms: A metasynthesis of qualitative research. *Exceptional Children, 73*(4), 392–416.

Sexton, D., Snyder, P., Sharpton, W., & Stricklin, S. (1993). Infants and toddlers with special needs and their families. *Childhood Education, 69*(5), 276–286.

Smith, T. (2002). Section 504: What teachers need to know. *Remedial and Special Education, 37*(5), 259–266.

Stowe, M., & Turnbull, H. (2001). Legal considerations of inclusion for infants and toddlers and preschool-age children. In M. Guralnick (Ed.), *Early childhood inclusion: Focus on change* (pp. 69–100). Paul H. Brookes.

Turnbull, A., Turnbull, R., Francis, G., Burke, M., Kyzar, K., Haines, S., Gershwin, T., Shepherd, K., Holdren, N., Singer, G. (2022). *Families and professionals*(8th ed.). Pearson Education.

U.S. Department of Education. (2011). *IDEA data*. Available at https://www.ideadata.org/

U.S. Department of Education. (2022). *Forty-third annual report to Congress on the implementation of the Individuals with Disabilities Education Act, 2021.* http://www.ed.gov/about/reports/annual/osep

U.S. Department of Health and Human Services & U.S. Department of Education. (2015). *Policy statement on inclusion of children with disabilities in early childhood programs.* https://www2.ed.gov/policy/speced/guid/earlylearning/joint-statement-full-text.pdf

Villa, R., Thousand, J., & Nevin, A. (2013). *A guide to co-teaching: New lessons and strategies to facilitate student learning*(3rd ed.). Corwin.

Wakeford, L. (2016). Occupational therapy in early intervention and early childhood special education. In B. Reichow, B. Boyd, E. Barton, & S. Odom (Eds.), *Handbook of early childhood special education* (pp. 385–402). Springer.

Walther-Thomas, C., Korinek, L., McLaughlin, V., & Williams, B. (2000). *Collaboration for inclusive education.* Allyn & Bacon.

Winter, S. (2007). *Inclusive early childhood education.* Pearson Education.

Winton, P. (2016). Taking stock and moving forward: Implementing quality early childhood inclusive practices. In B. Reichow, B. Boyd, E. Barton, & S. Odom (Eds.), *Handbook of early childhood special education* (pp. 57–74). Springer.

Yell, M. (2019). *The law and special education*(5th ed.). Pearson Education.

Yell, M., & Bateman, D. (2020). Defining educational benefit: An update on the U.S. Supreme Court ruling in *Endrew F. v. Douglas County School District*(2017). *Teaching Exceptional Children, 52*(5), 283–290.

Yell, M., Crockett, J., Shriner, J., & Rozalski, M. (2017). Free appropriate public education. In J. Kauffman, D. Hallahan, & P. Pullen (Eds.), *Handbook of special education*(2nd ed., pp. 71–87). Routledge.

Yell, M., Katsiyannis, A., & Bradley, M. (2017). The Individuals with Disabilities Education Act. In J. Kauffman, D. Hallahan, & P. Pullen (Eds.), *Handbook of special education*(2nd ed., pp. 55–71). Routledge.

Zigmond, N. (2003). Where should students with disabilities receive special education services? Is one place better than another? *Journal of Special Education, 37*(3), 193–199.

Zigmond, N. (2007). Delivering special education is a two-person job: A call for unconventional thinking. In J. Crockett, M. Gerber, & T. Landrum (Eds.), *Achieving the radical reform of special education: Essays in honor of James M. Kauffman* (pp. 115–137). Erlbaum.

CHAPTER 5

Albritton, K., Chen, C. I., Bauer, S. G., Johnson, A., & Mathews, R. E. (2021). Collaborating with school psychologists: Moving beyond traditional assessment practices. *Young Exceptional Children, 24*(1), 28–38.

Andersson, L. (2004). Appropriate and inappropriate interpretation and use of test scores in early intervention. *Journal of Early Intervention, 27*(1), 55–68.

Apgar, V., & James, L. (1962). Further observation on the Newborn Scoring System. *American Journal of Diseases of Children, 104*, 419–428.

Bagnato, S. (2005). The authentic alternative for assessment in early intervention: An emerging evidence-based practice. *Journal of Early Intervention, 28*(1), 17–22.

Bagnato, S. (2007). *Authentic assessment for early childhood intervention: Best practices.* Guilford Press.

Bailey, D., Wolery, M., & McLean, M. (1996). *Teaching infants and preschoolers with disabilities*(2nd ed.). Pearson.

Batshaw, M., Roizen, N., & Pellegrino, L. (2019). *Children with disabilities*(8th ed.). Paul H. Brookes.

Branscombe, A., Castle, K., Dorsey, A., Surbeck, E., & Taylor, J. (2014). *Early childhood curriculum: A constructivist perspective*(2nd ed.). Routledge.

Bricker, D., Dionne, C., Grisham, J., Johnson, J. J., Macy, M., Slentz, K., & Waddell, M. (2022). *Assessment, evaluation, and programming system for infants and children* (AEPS®-3; 3rd ed.). Paul H. Brookes.

Bricker, D. D., Felimban, H. S., Lin, F. Y., Stegenga, S. M., & Storie, S. O. (2022). A proposed framework for enhancing collaboration in early intervention/early childhood special education. *Topics in Early Childhood Special Education, 41*(4), 240–252.

Cohen, L., & Spenciner, L. (2020). *Assessment of children and youth with special needs*(5th ed.). Pearson Education.

Cook, R., Klein, M., & Chen, D. (2020). *Adapting early childhood curricula for children in inclusive settings*(10th ed.). Pearson Education.

Division for Early Childhood. (2007). *Promoting positive outcomes for children with disabilities: Recommendations for curriculum, assessment, and program evaluation.*

Division for Early Childhood. (2014). *DEC recommended practices in early intervention/early childhood special education.* http://www.dec-sped.org/recommendedpractices

Dunlap, G., & Fox, L. (2011). Function-based interventions for children with challenging behavior. *Journal of Early Intervention, 33*(4), 333–343.

Grisham-Brown, J., & Hemmeter, M. (2017). *Blended practices for teaching young children in inclusive settings*(2nd ed.). Paul H. Brookes.

Hanson, M., & Espinosa, L. (2016). Culture, ethnicity, and linguistic diversity: Implications for early childhood special education. In B. Reichow, B. Boyd, E. Barton, & S. Odom (Eds.), *Handbook of early childhood special education* (pp. 455–472). Springer.

Harvey, H., & Wennerstrom, E. K. (2023). Hearing their voices: Parents' perceptions of preschool special education evaluations with dual-language learners. *Topics in Early Childhood Special Education, 43*(1), 46–59.

Hendricks, M., & McCracken, T. (2009). Screening, evaluation, and assessment in early childhood special education. In J. Taylor, J. McGowan, & T. Linder (Eds.), *The program administrator's guide to early childhood special education: Leadership, development, & supervision* (pp. 63–80). Paul H. Brookes.

Hojnoski, R., Gischlar, K., & Missall, K. (2009). Improving child outcomes with data-based decision making: Collecting data. *Young Exceptional Children, 12*(3), 39.

IDEA Child Find Project. (2004). https://www.childfind-idea-il.us/

Johnson-Martin, N., Attermeier, S., & Hacker, B. (2004a). *The Carolina curriculum for infants and toddlers with special needs*(3rd ed.). Paul H. Brookes.

Johnson-Martin, N., Hacker, B., & Attermeier, S. (2004b). *The Carolina curriculum for preschoolers with special needs*(3rd ed.). Paul H. Brookes.

Keilty, B., LaRocco, D., & Casell, F. (2009). Early interventionists' reports of authentic assessment methods through focus group research. *Topics in Early Childhood Special Education, 28*(4), 244–256.

Kilgo, J., & Aldridge, J. (2011). Ten years of transdisciplinary teaming: Lessons learned through a transformational process. *Focus on Teacher Education, 10*(3), 3–6.

Kritikos, E., LeDosquet, P., & Melton, M. (2012). *Foundations of assessment in early childhood special education.* Pearson Education.

Kritikos, E., McLoughlin, J., & Lewis, J. (2018). *Assessing students with special needs.* Pearson Education.

Losardo, A., & Notari-Syverson, A. (2011). *Alternative approaches to assessing young children*(2nd ed.). Paul H. Brookes.

Lynch, E., & Hanson, M. (2011). *Developing cross-cultural competence: A guide for working with children and their families*(4th ed.). Paul H. Brookes.

Macy, M. G., Bagnato S. J., Macy R. S., Salaway J. (2015). Conventional tests and testing for early intervention eligibility: Is there an evidence base? *Infants & Young Children, 28*, 182–204.

McAfee, O., & Leong, D. (2011). *Assessing and guiding young children's development and learning*(5th ed.). Pearson Education.

McConnell, S., & Rahn, N. (2016). Assessment in early childhood special education. In B. Reichow, B. Boyd, E. Barton, & S. Odom (Eds.), *Handbook of early childhood special education* (pp. 89–106). Springer.

McCormick, L. (1997). Ecological assessment and planning. In L. McCormick, D. Loeb, & R. Schiefelbusch (Eds.), *Supporting children with communication difficulties in inclusive settings: School-based language intervention* (pp. 223–256). Allyn & Bacon.

McLean, M. (2005). Using curriculum-based assessment to determine eligibility: Time for a paradigm shift? *Journal of Early Intervention, 28*(1), 23–27.

McLean, M., Hemmeter, M., & Snyder, P. (Eds.). (2014). *Essential elements for assessing infants and preschoolers with special needs*(4th ed.). Pearson Education.

McWilliam, R. (2010). *Routines-based early intervention: Supporting young children and their families.* Paul H. Brookes.

Nagle, R. J., Gagnon, S. G., & Kidder-Ashley, P. (2020). Issues in preschool assessment. In *Psychoeducational assessment of preschool children* (pp. 3–31). Routledge.

Neisworth, J., & Bagnato, S. (2005). DEC recommended practices: Assessment. In S. Sandall, M. Hemmeter, B. Smith, & M. McLean (Eds.), *DEC recommended practices: A comprehensive guide to practical application in early intervention/early childhood special education* (pp. 45–69). Division for Early Childhood.

Noonan, M., & McCormick, L. (2014). *Young children with disabilities in natural environments*(2nd ed.). Paul H. Brookes.

Parks, S. (2007). *Hawaii early learning profile (HELP) strands 0–3*. VORT Corporation.

Pretti-Krontczak, K., Grisham, J., & Sullivan, L. (2023). *Assessing young children in inclusive settings: The blended practices approach*(2nd ed.). Paul H. Brookes.

Sandall, S., Schwartz, I. S., Joseph, G., & Gauvreau, A. N. (2019). *Building blocks for teaching preschoolers with special needs*(3rd ed.). Paul H. Brookes.

Sattler, J. (2020). *Assessment of children: Cognitive foundations and applications*(6th ed.).

Shackelford, J. (2002, May). *Informed clinical opinion*. Early Childhood Technical Assistance Center. https://ectacenter.org/~pdfs/pubs/nnotes10.pdf

Slade, N., Eisenhower, A., Carter, S., & Blacher, J. (2018). Satisfaction with individualized education programs among parents of young children with ASD. *Exceptional Children, 84*(3), 242–260.

Steed, E. A., Stein, R., Burke, H., & Charlifue-Smith, R. (2023). Early childhood professionals' reported use of culturally and linguistically responsive practices during initial evaluations: A mixed methods study. *Topics in Early Childhood Special Education, 43*(3), 214–226.

Teaford, P. (2010). *Hawaii early learning profile (HELP) 3–6*(2nd ed.). VORT Corporation.

Turnbull, A., Turnbull, R., Francis, G., Burke, M., Kyzar, K., Haines, S., Gershwin, T., Shepherd, K., Holdren, N., & Singer, G. (2022). *Families and professionals: Trusting partnerships in general and special education*(8th ed.). Pearson.

Vanderheyden, A. (2005). Intervention-driven assessment practices in early childhood/early intervention: Measuring what is possible rather than what is present. *Journal of Early Intervention, 28*(1), 28–33.

CHAPTER 6

Aldridge, J., Kilgo, J., & Bruton, A. (2015). Transforming transdisciplinary early intervention and early childhood special education through intercultural education. *International Journal of Early Childhood Special Education, 7*(2), 343–360.

Aldridge, J., Kilgo, J., & Bruton, A. (2016). Beyond the Brady Bunch: Hybrid families and their evolving relationships with early childhood education. *Childhood Education, 92*(2), 140–148.

Allen, E., & Cowdery, G. (2022). *The exceptional child*(9th ed.). Cengage Learning.

Aloi, A. (2009). Program planning in preschool. In J. Taylor, J. McGowan, & T. Linder (Eds.), *The program administrator's guide to early childhood special education: Leadership, development, & supervision* (pp. 117–146). Paul H. Brookes.

Bailey, D. (1997). Curriculum alternatives for infants and preschoolers. In M. Guralnick (Ed.), *The effectiveness of early intervention* (pp. 227–247). Paul H. Brookes.

Barton, E., & Smith, B. (2015). *The preschool inclusion toolbox*. Paul H. Brookes.

Barton, E. E., & Wolery, M. (2008). Teaching pretend play to children with disabilities: A review of the literature. *Topics in Early Childhood Special Education, 28*(2), 109–125.

Bernstein, D., & Levy, S. (2009). Language development: A review. In D. Bernstein & E. Tiegerman-Farber (Eds.), *Language and communication disorders in children* (pp. 28–100). Pearson Education.

Best, S., Heller, K., & Bigge, J. (2005). *Teaching individuals with physical and multiple disabilities*(5th ed.). Merrill/Prentice Hall.

Bowe, F. (2008). *Early childhood special education: Birth to eight*(4th ed.). Delmar Learning.

Boyd, B., Kucharczyk, S., & Wong, C. (2016). Implementing evidence-based practices in early childhood classroom settings. In B. Reichow, B. Boyd, E. Barton, & S. Odom (Eds.), *Handbook of early childhood special education* (pp. 335–348). Springer.

Bredekamp, S. (Ed.). (1987). *Developmentally appropriate practice in early childhood programs serving children from birth to age 8*(Exp. ed.). National Association for the Education of Young Children.

Bredekamp, S. (1993a). Myths about developmentally appropriate practice: A response to Fowell and Lawton. *Early Childhood Research Quarterly, 8*(1), 177–120.

Bredekamp, S. (1993b). The relationship between early childhood education and early childhood special education: Healthy marriage or family feud? *Topics in Early Childhood Special Education, 13*, 258–273.

Bredekamp, S., & Copple, C. (1997). *Developmentally appropriate practice in early childhood programs: Serving children from birth through age 8*. National Association for the Education of Young Children.

Bredekamp, S., & Rosegrant, T. (1992). *Reaching potentials: Appropriate curriculum and assessment for young children*(Vol. 1). National Association for the Education of Young Children.

Bricker, D., Dionne, C., Grisham, J., Johnson, J. J., Macy, M., Slentz, K., & Waddell, M. (2022). *Assessment, evaluation, and programming system for infants and children*(3rd ed.). (AEPS®-3). Paul H. Brookes.

Brown, S. L. (2009). *Play: How it shapes the brain, opens the imagination, and invigorates the soul*. Penguin.

Brown, W., Odom, S., & McConnell, S. (2008). *Social competence of young children: Risk, disability, and intervention*. Paul H. Brookes.

Bruder, M. (1997). Curriculum for children with disabilities. In M. Guralnick (Ed.), *The effectiveness of early intervention* (pp. 523–548). Paul H. Brookes.

Burton, C., Hains, A., Hanline, M., McClean, M., & McCormick, K. (1992). Early childhood policy, practice, and personnel: The urgency of professional unification. *Topics in Early Childhood Special Education, 11*, 53–69.

Buysse, V., Wesley, P., Snyder, P., & Winton, P. (2006). Evidence-based practice: What does it really mean for the early childhood field? *Young Exceptional Children, 9*(4), 2–11.

Carta, J. (1994). Developmentally appropriate practices: Shifting the emphasis to individual appropriateness. *Journal of Early Intervention, 18*(4), 342–343.

Carta, J., & Kong, N. (2007). Trends and issues in interventions affecting preschoolers with developmental disabilities. In S. Odom, R. Horner, M. Snell, & J. Blacher (Eds.), *Handbook of developmental disabilities* (pp. 181–198). Guilford Press.

Carta, J., McElhattan, T., & Guerrero, G. (2016). The application of response to intervention to young children with identified disabilities. In B. Reichow, B. Boyd, E.

Barton, & S. Odom (Eds.), *Handbook of early special education* (pp. 163–178). Springer.

Carta, J., Schwartz, I., Atwater, J., & McConnell, S. (1991). Developmentally appropriate practice: Appraising its usefulness for young children with disabilities. *Topics in Early Childhood Special Education, 11*, 11–20.

Cook, R., Klein, M., & Chen, D. (2020). *Adapting early childhood curricula for children with special needs*(10th ed.). Pearson Education.

Copple, C., & Bredekamp, S. (Eds.). (2009). *Developmentally appropriate practice in early childhood programs: Serving children from birth through age 8*. National Association for the Education of Young Children.

Council for Exceptional Children & Division for Early Childhood. (2020). *Initial practice-based professional standards for early interventionists/early childhood special educators*. Division for Early Childhood. https://www.dec-sped.org/ei-ecse-standards

Cufarro, H., Nager, N., & Shapiro, E. (2005). The developmental interaction approach at Bank Street College of Education. In J. Roopnarine & J. Johnson (Eds.), *Approaches to early childhood education*(4th ed.). Pearson Education.

Davis, M., Kilgo, J., & Gamel-McCormick, M. (1998). *Young children with special needs: A developmentally appropriate approach*. Allyn & Bacon.

Dettmer, P., Knackendoffel, A., & Thurston, L. (2013). *Collaboration, consultation, and teamwork for students with special needs*(7th ed.). Pearson.

Division for Early Childhood. (2007). *Promoting positive outcomes for children with disabilities: Recommendations for curriculum, assessment, and program evaluation*.

Division for Early Childhood. (2014). *DEC recommended practices in early intervention/early childhood special education*. https://www.dec-sped.org/recommendedpractices

Division for Early Childhood. (2021). *Multi-tiered system of support framework for early childhood: Description and implications*.

Division for Early Childhood & National Association for the Education of Young Children. (2009). *Early childhood inclusion: A joint position statement of the Division for Early Childhood (DEC) and the National Association for the Education of Young Children (NAEYC)*. University of North Carolina, FPG Child Development Institute.

Division for Early Childhood Task Force on Recommended Practices. (1993). *DEC recommended practices: Indicators of quality in programs for infants and young children with special needs and their families*. Council for Exceptional Children.

Dodge, D. (2004). Early childhood curriculum models: Why, what, and how programs use them? *Child Care in InformationExchange* (January/February), 71–75.

Dodge, D., Berke, K., Bickart, T., Colker, L., & Heroman, C. (2010). *The creative curriculum for preschool*(5th ed.). Teaching Strategies.

Dodge, D., Rudick, S., & Berke, K. (2006). *The creative curriculum for infants, toddlers and twos*(2nd ed.). Teaching Strategies.

Drew, C., Logan, D., & Hardman, M. (1992). *Mental retardation*(5th ed.). Merrill/Macmillan.

Dunst, C. (1981). *Infant learning: A cognitive-linguistic intervention strategy*. Teaching Resources Corp.

Edwards, C., Gandini, L., & Forman, G. (1993). *The hundred languages of children: The Reggio Emilia approach to early childhood education*. Ablex.

Favazza, P., & Siperstein, G. (2016). Motor acquisition for young children with disabilities. In B. Reichow, B. Boyd, E. Barton, & S. Odom (Eds.), *Handbook of early childhood special education* (pp. 225–246). Springer.

Forman, S. G., & Crystal, C. D. (2015). Systems consultation for multitiered systems of supports (MTSS): Implementation issues. *Journal of Educational and Psychological Consultation, 25*(2–3), 276–285.

Fox, L., & Hanline, M. (1993). A preliminary evaluation of learning within developmentally appropriate early childhood settings. *Topics in Early Childhood Special Education, 13*(3), 308–327.

Fox, L., Hanline, M., Vail, C., & Galant, K. (1994). Developmentally appropriate practices: Applications for young children with disabilities. *Journal of Early Intervention, 18*(3), 243–257.

Freeman, R., Miller, D., & Newcomer, L. (2015). Integration of academic and behavioral MTSS at the district level using implementation science. *Learning Disabilities: A Contemporary Journal, 13*(1), 59–72.

Gargiulo, R., & Metcalf, D. (2023). *Teaching in today's inclusive classrooms*(4th ed.). Cengage Learning.

Gesell, A., & Amatruda, C. (1947). *Developmental diagnosis*(2nd ed.). Harper & Row.

Goffin, S., & Wilson, C. (2001). *Curriculum models and early childhood education: Appraising the relationship*(2nd ed.). Merrill/Prentice Hall.

Goldstein, H., Kaczmarek, L., & English, K. (2001). *Promoting social communication: Children with developmental disabilities from birth to adolescence*. Paul H. Brookes.

Goswami, U. (Ed.). (2011). *Cognitive development in early childhood*(2nd ed.). Wiley and Blackwell.

Gregg, K. (2011). A document analysis of the National Association for the Education of Young Children's Developmentally Appropriate Practice Position Statement: What does it tell us about supporting children with disabilities? *Contemporary Issues in Early Childhood, 12*(2), 175–186.

Grisham-Brown, J., & Hemmeter, M. (2017). *Blended practices for teaching young children in inclusive settings*(2nd ed.). Paul H. Brookes.

Grisham-Brown, J., & Pretti-Frontczak, K. (2003). Preschool teachers' use of planning time for the purpose of individualizing instruction for young children with special needs. *Journal of Early Intervention, 26*(1), 31–46.

Guralnick, M. (1990). Major accomplishments and future directions in early childhood mainstreaming. *Topics in Early Childhood Special Education, 10*(2), 1–17.

Guralnick, M. (1993). Developmentally appropriate practice in the assessment and intervention of children's peer relations. *Topics in Early Childhood Special Education, 13*(3), 344–371.

Guralnick, M. (2001). *Early childhood inclusion: Focus on change*. Paul H. Brookes.

Hanson, J., & Lynch, E. (1995). *Early intervention: Implementing child and family services for infants and toddlers who are at risk or disabled*(2nd ed.). Pro-Ed.

Hanson, M., & Espinosa, L. (2016). Culture, ethnicity, and linguistic diversity: Implications for early childhood special education. In B. Reichow, B. Boyd, E. Barton, & S. Odom (Eds.), *Handbook of early childhood special education* (pp. 455–472). Springer.

Harte, H. (2010). The Project Approach: A strategy for inclusive classrooms. *Young Exceptional Children, 13*(3), 15–27.

Helm, J., & Beneke, S. (Eds.). (2003). *The power of projects: Meeting contemporary challenges in early childhood classrooms: Strategies and solutions*. Teachers College Press.

Helm, J., & Gronlund, G. (2000). Linking standards and engaged learning in the early years. *Early Childhood Research &*

Practice, 2(1). https://ecrp.uiuc.edu/v2n1/helm.html

Hemmeter, M. L., Fox, L., & Hardy, J. (2016). Supporting the implementation of tiered models of behavior support in early childhood settings. In B. Reichow, B. Boyd, E. Barton, & S. Odom (Eds.), *Handbook of early childhood special education* (pp. 247–266). Springer.

Hohmann, M., & Weikart, D. (2002). *Educating young children: Active learning practices for preschool and child care programs*(2nd ed.). High/Scope Press.

Hohmann, M., Weikart, D., & Epstein, A. (2008). *Educating young children: Active learning practices for preschool and child care programs*(3rd ed.). High/Scope Press.

Horn, E., Palmer, S., Butera, G., & Lieber, J. (2016). *Six steps to inclusive preschool curriculum: A UDL-based framework for children's school success*. Paul H. Brookes.

Janney, R., & Snell, M. (2008). *Teachers' guides to inclusive practices: Behavioral support*. Paul H. Brookes.

Jenkins, R. (2005). Interdisciplinary instruction in the inclusionary classroom. *Teaching Exceptional Children, 37*(5), 42–48.

Johnson, C. (1993). Developmental issues: Children infected with human immunodeficiency virus. *Infants and Young Children, 6*(1), 1–10.

Johnson, J., Rahn, N., & Bricker, D. (2014). *An activity-based approach to early intervention*(4th ed.). Paul H. Brookes.

Johnson-Martin, N., Hacker, B., & Attermeier, S. (2004). *The Carolina curriculum for preschoolers with special needs*(3rd ed.). Paul H. Brookes.

Joseph, J., Strain, P., Olskewski, A., & Goldstein, H. (2016). A *Consumer Reports*-like review of the empirical literature specific to preschool children's peer-related social skills. In B. Reichow, B. Boyd, E. Barton, & S. Odom (Eds.), *Handbook of early childhood special education* (pp. 179–198). Springer.

Kilgo, J. (2014). Assessing motor skills in young children. In M. McLean, M. Hemmeter, & P. Snyder (Eds.), *Essential elements for assessing infants and preschoolers with special needs*(4th ed., pp. 356–382). Pearson Education.

Kilgo, J., & Aldridge, J. (2009). Providing family-based and culturally responsive practices for young children with developmental delays or disabilities and their families: Using scenarios for problem solving. *Focus on Inclusive Education, 7*(2), 4–5.

Kilgo, J., & Aldridge, J. (2011). Ten years of transdisciplinary teaming: Lessons learned through a transformational process. *Focus on Teacher Education, 10*(3), 3–6.

Kostelnik, M. (Ed.). (1991). *Teaching young children using themes*. Scott Foresman.

Kostelnik, M., Soderman, A., & Whiren, A. (2010). *Developmentally appropriate curriculum: Best practices in early childhood education*(5th ed.). Prentice Hall.

Lane, J., & Brown, J. (2016). Promoting communication development in young children with or at risk for disabilities. In B. Reichow, B. Boyd, E. Barton, & S. Odom (Eds.), *Handbook of early childhood special education* (pp. 199–224). Springer.

Lifter, K., Mason, E. J., & Barton, E. E. (2011). Children's play: Where we have been and where we could go. *Journal of Early Intervention, 33*(4), 281–297.

Linder, T. (2008). *Transdisciplinary play-based assessment* (TPBA2) (2nd ed.). Paul H. Brookes.

Lynch, E., & Hanson, M. (2011). *Developing cross-cultural competence: A guide for working with children and their families*(4th ed.). Paul H. Brookes.

McAfee, O., & Leong, D. (2011). *Assessing and guiding young children's development and learning*(5th ed.). Pearson Education.

McCormick, L. (1997). Ecological assessment and planning. In L. McCormick, D. Loeb, & R. Schiefelbusch (Eds.), *Supporting children with communication difficulties* (pp. 223–256). Allyn & Bacon.

McLean, M., & Odom, S. (1993). Practices of young children with and without disabilities: A comparison of DEC and NAEYC identified practices. *Topics in Early Childhood Special Education, 13*(3), 274–292.

McLean, M., Sandall, S., & Smith, B. (2016). A history of early childhood special education. In B. Reichow, B. Boyd, E. Barton, & S. Odom (Eds.), *Handbook of early childhood special education* (pp. 3–20). Springer.

Morrison, G., Breffni, L., & M. J. Woika(2022). *Early childhood education today*(15th ed.). Pearson Education.

National Association for the Education of Young Children. (2022). *Developmentally appropriate practice in early childhood programs serving children from birth through age 8*. (4th ed.).

Nirje, B. (1976). The normalization principle. In R. Kugel & A. Shearer (Eds.), *Changing patterns in residential services for the mentally retarded*. President's Committee on Mental Retardation.

Noonan, M., & McCormick, L. (2014). *Teaching young children with disabilities in natural environments*(2nd ed.). Paul H. Brookes.

Odom, S. (2016). The role of theory in early childhood special education and early intervention. In B. Reichow, B. Boyd, E. Barton, & S. Odom (Eds.), *Handbook of early childhood special education* (pp. 21–36). Springer.

Odom, S., Horner, R., Snell, M., & Blacher, J. (2009). *Handbook of developmental disabilities*. Guilford Press.

Odom, S., & Wolery, M. (2003). A unified theory of practice in early intervention/early childhood special education. *Journal of Special Education, 37*(3), 164–173.

Owens, R. (2010). *Language disorders: A functional approach to assessment and intervention*(5th ed.). Allyn & Bacon.

Parks, S. (2007). *Hawaii early learning profile (HELP) strands 0–3*. VORT Corporation.

Peterson, N. (1987). *Early intervention for handicapped and at risk children*. Love.

Piaget, J. (1952). *The origins of intelligence in children*. Norton.

Pretti-Frontczak, K., Grisham, J., & Sullivan, L. (2023). *Assessing young children in inclusive settings: The blended practices approach*(2nd ed.). Paul H. Brookes.

Pretti-Frontczak, K., Jackson, S., Gross, S., Grisham-Brown, J., Horn, E., Harjusola-Webb, S., (2007). A curriculum framework that supports quality early childhood education for all young children. In E. Horn, C. Peterson, & L. Fox (Eds.), *Young Exceptional Children Monograph Series No. 9: Linking curriculum to child and family outcomes* (pp. 16–28). Division for Early Childhood.

Rainforth, B., York, J., & MacDonald, C. (1997). *Collaborative teams for students with severe disabilities: Integrating therapy and educational services*(2nd ed.). Paul H. Brookes.

Reichow, B. (2016). Evidence-based practice in the context of early childhood special education. In B. Reichow, B. Boyd, E. Barton, & S. Odom (Eds.), *Handbook of early childhood special education* (pp. 107–121). Springer.

Sameroff, A., & Chandler, M. (1975). Reproductive risk and the continuum of care-taking casualty. In F. Horowitz, M. Hetherington, S. Scarr-Salapatek, & G. Siegel (Eds.), *Review of child development* research(Vol. 4, pp. 187–244). University of Chicago Press.

Sandall, S., Hemmeter, M., Smith, B., & McLean, M. (Eds.). (2005). *DEC recommended practices: A comprehensive guide for practical application in early intervention/early childhood special education*. Division for Early Childhood.

Sandall, S., McLean, M., & Smith, B. (Eds.). (2000). *DEC recommended practices in early intervention/early childhood special education*. Council for Exceptional Children and Division for Early Childhood.

Sandall, S., Schwartz, I. S., Joseph, G., & Gauvreau, A. N. (2019). *Building blocks for teaching preschoolers with special needs*(3rd ed.) Paul H. Brookes.

Sandall, S., Schwartz, I., & Gauvreau, A. (2016). Using modifications and accommodations to enhance learning of young children with disabilities: Little changes that yield big impacts. In B. Reichow, B. Boyd, E. Barton, & S. Odom (Eds.), *Handbook of early childhood special education* (pp. 349–362). Springer.

Snell, M., & Brown, F. (Eds.). (2011). *Instruction of students with severe disabilities*(7th ed.). Pearson Education.

Snyder, P. (2006). Impacts of evidence-based practices on research in early childhood. In V. Buysse & P. Wesley (Eds.), *Evidence-based practice in the early childhood field* (pp. 35–70). Zero to Three Press.

Snyder, P., Hemmeter, M., McLean, M., Sandall, S., & McLaughlin, T. (2013). Embedded instruction to support early learning in response to intervention frameworks. In V. Buysse & E. Peisner-Feinberg (Eds.), *Handbook of response to intervention in early childhood* (pp. 283–298). Paul H. Brookes.

Strain, P., & Hemmeter, M. (1997). Keys to being successful when confronted with challenging behaviors. *Young Exceptional Children, 1*(1), 2–8.

Strain, P., McConnell, S., Carta, J., Fowler, S., Neisworth, J., & Wolery, M. (1992). Behaviorism in early intervention. *Topics in Early Childhood Special Education, 12*(1), 121–141.

Teaford, P. (2010). *Hawaii early learning profile (HELP)* 3–6 (2nd ed.). VORT Corporation.

Turnbull, A., Turnbull, R., Francis, G., Burke, M., Kyzar, K., Haines, S., Gershwin, T., Shepherd, K., Holdren, N., & Singer, G. (2022). *Families and professionals: Trusting partnerships in general and special education*(8th ed.). Pearson.

Udell, T., Peters, J., & Templeman, T. (1998). From philosophy to practice in inclusive early childhood programs. *Teaching Exceptional Children*(January/February), 44–49.

Winton, P., Buysse, V., Turnbull, A., Rous, B., & Hollingsworth, H. (2010). *CONNECT Module 1: Embedded interventions*. Chapel Hill: University of North Carolina, FPG Child Development Institute. https://community.fpg.unc.edu/connect-modules/learners/module-1

Wolery, M. (2004). Monitoring child progress. In M. McLean, M. Wolery, & D. Bailey (Eds.), *Assessing infants and preschoolers with special needs*(3rd ed., pp. 545–584). Prentice Hall.

Wolery, M., Ault, M., & Doyle, P. (1992). *Teaching students with moderate to severe disabilities*. Longman.

Wolery, M., & Bredekamp, S. (1994). Developmentally appropriate practices and young children with disabilities: Contextual issues in the discussion. *Journal of Early Intervention, 18*(4), 331–341.

Wolery, M., & Sainato, D. (1993). General curriculum and intervention strategies. In Division for Early Childhood, Council for Exceptional Children (Ed.), *DEC recommended practices: Indicators of quality in programs for infants and young children with special needs and their families* (pp. 50–57). Council for Exceptional Children.

Wolery, M., & Sainato, D. (1996). General curriculum and intervention strategies. In S. Odom & M. McLean (Eds.), *Early intervention/early childhood special education: Recommended practices* (pp. 125–158). Pro-Ed.

CHAPTER 7

Alberto, P., Troutman, A., & Axe, J. (2022). *Applied behavior analysis for teachers*(10th ed.). Pearson Education.

Allen, E., & Cowdery, G. (2022). *The exceptional child*(9th ed.). Cengage Learning.

American Academy of Pediatrics, American Public Health Association, National Resource Center for Health and Safety in Child Care. (2019). *Caring for our children: National health and safety performance standards—Guidelines for early care and education programs*(4th ed.). American Academy of Pediatrics.

Aronson, S., & Shope, T. (Eds.). (2020). *Managing infectious diseases in child care and schools*(5th ed.). American Academy of Pediatrics.

Barton, E., Steed, E., & Smith, B. (2016). Solutions and strategies to support access to natural and inclusive environments for all children. In T. Catalino & L. Meyer (Eds.), *DEC recommended practices monograph series No. 2: Environment* (pp. 1–18). Division for Early Childhood.

Benjamin, T., Lucas-Thompson, R., Little, L., Davies, P., & Khetani, M. (2017). Participation in early childhood educational environments for young children with and without developmental disabilities and delays: A mixed methods study. *Physical & Occupational Therapy in Pediatrics, 37*(1), 87–107.

Bredekamp, S. (2020). *Effective practices in early childhood education*(4th ed.). Pearson Education.

Brewer, J. (2007). *Introduction to early childhood education*(6th ed.). Pearson Education.

Brown, F., McDonnell, J., & Snell, M. (Eds.). (2020). *Instruction of students with severe disabilities*(9th ed.). Pearson Education.

Catalino, T., & Meyer, L. (Eds.). (2016). *DEC recommended practices monograph series No. 2: Environment*. Division for Early Childhood.

Chen, D., & Dote-Kwan, J. (2021). Preschoolers with visual impairments and additional disabilities: Using universal design for learning and differentiation. *Young Exceptional Children, 24*(2), 70–81. https://doi.org/10.1177/1096250620922205

Copple, C., & Bredekamp, S. (2009). *Developmentally appropriate practice in early childhood programs*(3rd ed.). National Association for the Education of Young Children.

Department of Justice. (2010, September 15). *2010 ADA standards for accessible design*. https://www.ada.gov/regs2010/2010ADAStandards/2010ADAStandards_prt.pdf

Division for Early Childhood. (2014). *DEC recommended practices for early intervention/early childhood special education*. http://www.dec-sped.org/recommendedpractices

Division for Early Childhood. (2016). *DEC recommended practices with embedded examples*. http://www.dec-sped.org/recommendedpractices

Downing, J. (2008). *Including students with severe and multiple disabilities in typical classrooms*(3rd ed.). Paul H. Brookes.

Essa, E., & Burnham, M. (2020). *Introduction to early childhood education*(8th ed.). SAGE.

Fay, D., Wilkinson, T., Wagoner, M., Brooks, D., Quinn, L., & Turnell, A. (2017). Effect of group setting on gross motor performance in children 3–5 years old with motor delays. *Physical & Occupational Therapy in Pediatrics*, *37*(1), 74–86.

Feeney, S., Moravcik, E., & Nolte, S. (2023). *Who am I in the lives of children?* (12th ed.). Pearson Education.

Gargiulo, R., & Bouck, E. (2021). *Special education in contemporary society*(7th ed.). SAGE.

Gargiulo, R., & Metcalf, D. (2023). *Teaching in today's inclusive classroom: A universal design for learning approach*(4th ed.) Cengage.

Gauvreau, A. N., Lohmann, M. J., & Hovey, K. A. (2023). Circle is for everyone: Using UDL to promote inclusion during circle times. *Young Exceptional Children*, *26*(1), 3–15. https://doi.org/10.1177/1096250621 1028576

Gordon, A., & Browne, K. (2024). *Beginnings and beyond*(11th ed.). Cengage Learning.

Heller, K., Forney, P., Alberto, P., Best, S., & Schwartzman, M. (2009). *Understanding physical, health, and multiple disabilities*(2nd ed.). Pearson Education.

Henniger, M. (2018). *Teaching young children: An introduction*(6th ed.). Pearson Education.

Jalongo, M., & Isenberg, J. (2012). *Exploring your role in early childhood education*(4th ed.). Pearson Education.

Johnson, J., Rahn, N., & Bricker, D. (2015). *An activity-based approach to early intervention*(4th ed.). Paul H. Brookes.

McDonald, P. (2018). Observing, planning, guiding: How an intentional teacher meets standards through play. *Young Children*, *73*(1), 16–27.

McLeod, B., Sutherland, K., Martinez, R., Conroy, M., & Snyder, P. (2017). Identifying common practice elements to improve social, emotional, and behavioral outcomes of young children in early childhood classrooms. *Prevention Science*, *18*(2), 204–213.

National Association for the Education of Young Children. (2019). *NAEYC early learning program accreditation standards and assessment items*.

National Association for the Education of Young Children. (2022). *Developmentally appropriate practices in early childhood programs serving children from birth through age 8*. (4th ed).

New, R., & Kantor, R. (2013). Reggio Emilia in the 21st century. In J. Roopnarine & J. Johnson (Eds.), *Approaches to early childhood education*(6th ed., pp. 331–353). Pearson Education.

Noonan, M., & McCormick, L. (2014). *Young children with disabilities in natural environments*(2nd ed.). Paul H. Brookes.

O'Brien, M. (2001). Inclusive child care for infants and toddlers. In M. Guralnick (Ed.), *Early childhood inclusion: Focus on change* (pp. 229–251). Paul H. Brookes.

Olds, A. (1987). Designing settings for infants and toddlers. In C. Weinstein & T. David (Eds.), *Spaces for children: The built environment and child development* (pp. 117–138). Plenum Press.

Parette, H. P., & Blum, C. (2014). Using flexible participation in technology-supported, universally designed preschool activities. *TEACHING Exceptional Children*, *46*(3), 60–67. https://doi.org/10.1177/00400 5991404600307

Piaget, J. (1963). *Origins of intelligence in children*. Norton.

Pisha, L., & Spencer, K. (2016). Practitioners as architects: Constructing high-quality environments for physical activity in inclusive early childhood settings. In T. Catalino & L. Meyer (Eds.), *DEC recommended practices monograph series No. 2: Environment* (pp. 67–85). Division for Early Childhood.

Raver, S. (2009). *Early childhood special education—0–8 years*. Pearson Education.

Readdick, C. (2006). Managing noise in early childhood settings. *Dimensions of Early Childhood*, *34*(1), 17–22.

Romski, M., & Sevcik, R. A. (2005). Augmentative communication and early intervention: Myths and realities. *Infants & Young Children*, *18*(3), 174–185.

Sheldon, K. (1996). "Can I play too?" Adapting common classroom activities for young children with limited motor abilities. *Early Childhood Education Journal*, *24*(2), 115–120.

Stockall, N. S., Dennis, L., & Miller, M. (2012). Right from the start: Universal design for preschool. *TEACHING Exceptional Children*, *45*(1), 10–17. https://doi.org/ 10.1177/004005991204500103

Tomlinson, H. (2009). Developmentally appropriate practice in the primary grades—ages 6–8. In C. Copple & S. Bredekamp (Eds.), *Developmentally appropriate practice in early childhood programs*(3rd ed., pp. 257–326). National Association for the Education of Young Children.

U.S. Access Board. (2021, May 6). *Accessible play areas*. https://www.accessibilityonline.org/ao/archives/110914

U.S. Consumer Product Safety Commission. (n.d.). *Public playground safety checklist*. https://www.cpsc.gov/safety-education/safety-guides/playgrounds/public-playground-safety-checklist

Winter, S. (2007). *Inclusive early childhood education*. Pearson Education.

CHAPTER 8

Alberto, P., Troutman, A., & Axe, J. (2022). *Applied behavior analysis for teachers*(10th ed.). Pearson Education.

Autism Society of America. (2023a). *Early intervention*. https://www.autism-society.org/living-with-autism/autism-through-the-lifespan/infants-and-toddlers/early-intervention/

Autism Society of America. (2023b). *Understanding autism*. https://autismsociety.org/the-autism-experience/

Autism Speaks/Autism Treatment Network. (2014). *Exploring feeding behavior in autism*. www.autismspeaks.org/sites/default/files/docs/sciencedocs/atn/feeding_guide.pdf

Barton, E., Reichow, B., Wolery, M., & Chen, C. (2011). We can all participate! Circle time for children with autism. *Young Exceptional Children*, *14*(2), 2–21.

Barton, E., & Wolery, M. (2010). Training teachers to promote pretend play in young children with disabilities. *Exceptional Children*, *77*(1), 85–106.

Basu, S., Salisbury, C., & Thorkildsen, T. (2010). Measuring collaborative consultation practices in natural environments. *Journal of Early Intervention*, *33*(2), 127–150.

Bishop, V. (2004). *Teaching visually impaired children*(3rd ed.). Charles C Thomas.

Bondy, A., & Frost, L. (1994). The picture exchange communication system. *Focus on Autistic Behavior*, *9*(3), 1–19.

Bouck, E. (2017). *Assistive technology*. SAGE.

Centers for Disease Control and Prevention. (2021). Prevalence and characteristics of autism spectrum disorder among children aged 8 years—Autism and Developmental Disabilities Monitoring Network, 11 sites, United States, 2018. *Morbidity and Mortality Weekly Report*, *70*(11), 1–16.

Chang, Y., & Shire, S. (2019). Promoting play in early childhood programs for children with ASD: Strategies for educators and practitioners. *Teaching Exceptional Children, 52*(2), 66–76.

Cohen, M., & Gerhardt, P. (2016). *Visual supports for people with autism*(2nd ed.). Woodbine House.

Copple, C., & Bredekamp, S. (Eds.). (2009). *Developmentally appropriate practice in early childhood programs: Serving students from birth through age 8*(3rd ed.). National Association for the Education of Young Children.

Dennis, L., & Horn, E. (2011). Strategies for supporting early literacy development. *Young Exceptional Children, 14*(3), 29–40.

DiCarlo, C., & Vagianos, L. (2009). Using child preference to increase play across interest centers in inclusive early childhood classroom. *Young Exceptional Children, 12*(4), 31–39.

Division for Early Childhood. (2014). *DEC recommended practices in early intervention/early childhood special education, 2014.* http://www.dec-sped.org/recommended practices

Division for Early Childhood. (2017). *Position statement on challenging behavior and young children.* https://www.decdocs.org/position-statement-challenging-beha

Fenlon, A., McNabb, J., & Pidlypchak, H. (2010). "So much potential in reading!" Developing meaningful literacy routines for students with multiple disabilities. *Teaching Exceptional Children, 43*(1), 42–48.

Gardner-Neblett, N., & Gallagher, K. (2013). *More than baby talk: 10 ways to promote the language and communications skills of infants and toddlers.* University of North Carolina, Frank Porter Graham Child Development Institute.

Gargiulo, R., & Bouck, E. (2018). Foundational concepts: Etiology of intellectual disability and characteristics of students with intellectual disability. In R. Gargiulo & E. Bouck (Eds.), *Instructional strategies for students with mild, moderate, and severe intellectual disability* (pp. 29–48). SAGE.

Gargiulo, R., & Bouck, E. (2021). *Special education in contemporary society: An introduction to exceptionality*(7th ed.). SAGE.

Gargiulo, R., & Metcalf, D. (2023). *Teaching in today's inclusive classrooms*(4th ed.). Cengage Learning.

Gonzalez, K., Cassel, T., Durocher, J., & Lee, A. (2017). Overview of autism spectrum disorders. In A. Boutot (Ed.), *Autism spectrum disorders*(2nd ed., pp. 1–20). Pearson Education.

The Gray Center. (2012). *What are social stories?* http://www.thegraycenter.org/social-stories/what-are-social-stories [Currently offline].

The Gray Center. (2023). *What is a social story?* https://carolgraysocialstories.com/social-stories/what-is-it/

Greenwood, C., Buzhardt, J., Walker, D., Howard, W., & Anderson, R. (2011). Program-level influences on the measurement of early communication for infants and toddlers in Head Start. *Journal of Early Intervention, 33*(2), 110–134.

Guardino, C., & Fullerton, E. (2010). Changing behaviors by changing the classroom environment. *Teaching Exceptional Children, 42*(6), 8–13.

Hallahan, D., Kauffman, J., & Pullen, P. (2022). *Exceptional learners*(15th ed.). Pearson Education.

Heward, W., Alber-Morgan, S., & Konrad, M. (2022). *Exceptional children*(12th ed.). Pearson Education.

Hollingsworth, H., & Buysse, V. (2009). Establishing friendships in early childhood inclusive settings: What roles do parents and teachers play? *Journal of Early Intervention, 31*(4), 287–305.

Hott, B., Walker, J., Robinson, A., & Raymond, L. (2017). Search for the miracle cure. In W. Murawski & K. Scott (Eds.), *What really works with exceptional learners* (pp. 207–224). Corwin.

Hughes, C., & Henderson, L. (2017). Addressing the autism spectrum disorder "epidemic" in education. In W. Murawski & K. Scott (Eds.), *What really works with exceptional learners* (pp. 225–243). Corwin.

IRIS Center. (2015). *Early childhood environments: Designing effective classrooms.* https://iris.peabody.vanderbilt.edu/modules/env/

Jennings, D., Hanline, M., & Woods, J. (2012). Using routines-based interventions in early childhood special education. *Dimensions of Early Childhood, 40*(2), 13–22.

Johnson, J., Rahn, N., & Bricker, D. (2015). *An activity-based approach to early intervention*(4th ed.). Paul H. Brookes.

Lifter, K., Mason, E., & Barton, E. (2011). Children's play: Where we have been and where we could go. *Journal of Early Intervention, 33*(4), 281–297.

Marsili, A., & Hughes, M. (2009). Finding Kirk's words: An infant mental health approach to preschool intervention. *Young Exceptional Children, 12*(2), 2–15.

Mastrangelo, S. (2009). Harnessing the power of play: Opportunities for children with autism spectrum disorders. *Teaching Exceptional Children, 42*(1), 34–44.

Meadan, H., Ostrosky, M., Triplett, B., Michna, A., & Fettig, A. (2011). Using visual supports with young children with autism spectrum disorder. *Teaching Exceptional Children, 43*(6), 28–35.

National Association for the Education of Young Children. (2022). *Developmentally appropriate practice in early childhood programs serving children from birth through age 8.* (4th ed.).

National Autism Center. (2015). *Findings and conclusions: National standards project, phase 2.*

National Autistic Society. (2023). *Visual supports.* https://www.autism.org.uk/advice-and-guidance/topics/communication/communication-tools/visual-supports

National Institute of Mental Health. (2023). *Autism spectrum disorder.* https://www.nimh.nih.gov/health/topics/autism-spectrum-disorders-asd#part_2282

Neitzel, J. (2011). Early indicators of developmental delays in infants and toddlers. *Perspectives on Language and Literacy, 37*(3), 25–27.

Noonan, M., & McCormick, L. (2014). *Young children with disabilities in natural environments*(2nd ed.). Paul H. Brookes.

O'Brien, J., & Kuhaneck, H. (2020). *Occupational therapy for children and adolescents*(8th ed.). Elsevier Mosby.

Odom, S., Buyesse, V., & Soukakou, E. (2011). Inclusion for young children with disabilities: A quarter century of research perspectives. *Journal of Early Intervention, 33*(4), 344–356.

Papacek, A., Chai, Z., & Green, K. (2016). Play and social interaction strategies for young children with autism spectrum disorder in inclusive preschool settings. *Teaching Young Children, 19*(3), 3–17.

Park, J., Alber-Morgan, S., & Fleming, C. (2011). Collaborating with parents to implement behavioral interventions for children with challenging behaviors. *Teaching Exceptional Children, 43*(3), 22–30.

Pyramid Educational Consultants. (2023). *Evidenced-based practices.* https://pecsusa.com/evidence-based-practices/

Ryan, J., Hughes, E., Katsiyannis, A., McDaniel, M., & Sprinkle, C. (2011). Research-based educational practices for students with autism spectrum disorders. *Teaching Exceptional Children, 43*(3), 56–64.

Sandall, S., Schwartz, I., Joseph, G., & Gauvreau, A. (2019). *Building blocks for teaching preschoolers with special needs*(3rd ed.). Paul H. Brookes.

Sharpe, T. (2008). How can teacher talk support learning? *Linguistics and Education, 19*(2), 132–148.

Shirin, D., Jones, P., Luckner, J., & Reed, S. (2011). Social outcomes of students who are deaf and hard of hearing in general education classrooms. *Exceptional Children, 77*(4), 489–504.

Smith, A., Romski, M., Sevcik, R., Adamson, L., & Bakeman, R. (2011). Parent stress and its relation to parent perceptions of communication following parent-coached language intervention. *Journal of Early Intervention, 33*(2), 135–150.

Smith, D., Tyler, N., & Skow, K. (2018). *Introduction to contemporary special education*(2nd ed.). Pearson Education.

Snyder, P., Hemmeter, M., McLean, M., Sandall, S., & McLaughlin, T. (2013). Embedded instruction to support early learning in response to intervention frameworks. In V. Buysse & E. Peisner-Feinberg (Eds.), *Handbook of response to intervention in early childhood* (pp. 283–298). Paul H. Brookes.

Travers, J., & Nunes, L. (2017). Environmental arrangement to prevent contextually inappropriate behavior. In A. Boutot (Ed.), *Autism spectrum disorders*(2nd ed., pp. 59–78). Pearson Education.

Turnbull, A., Turnbull, R., Wehmeyer, M., & Shogren, K. (2020). *Exceptional lives: Special education in today's schools*(9th ed.). Pearson Education.

U.S. Department of Education. (2022). *EDFacts data warehouse, IDEA part B child count and educational environments collection, 2020–2021.* https://data.ed.gov/dataset/idea-section-618-data-products-static-tables-part-b-count-environ-tables20/resources

U.S. Department of Education. (2023). *Forty-fourth annual report to Congress on the implementation of the Individuals with Disabilities Education Act, 2022.* U.S. Government Printing Office.

Vanderbilt Kennedy Center. (2023). *How to write a Social Story™.* https://vkc.vumc.org/assets/files/tipsheets/socialstoriestips.pdf

Vaughn, S., & Bos, C. (2020). *Strategies for teaching students with learning and behavior problems*(10th ed.). Pearson Education.

Whalon, K., Hanline, M., & Woods, J. (2007). Using interactive storybook reading to increase language and literacy skills of children with autism spectrum disorders. *Young Exceptional Children, 11*(1), 16–26.

Wolery, M. (2005). DEC recommended practices: Child-focused practices. In S. Sandall, M. Hemmeter, B. Smith, & M. McLean (Eds.), *DEC recommended practices: A comprehensive guide for practical application in early intervention/early childhood special education* (pp. 71–106). Division for Early Childhood.

CHAPTER 9

Arzu, Ö., & Yasemin, E. (2011). Activity-based intervention practices in special education. *Educational Sciences: Theory & Practice, 11*(1), 359–362.

Barton, E., Reichow, B., Wolery, M., & Chen, C. (2011). We can all participate! Circle time for children with autism, *Young Exceptional Children, 14*(2), 2–21.

Barton, E., & Smith, B. (2015). Advancing high-quality preschool inclusion: A discussion and recommendations for the field. *Topics in Early Childhood Special Education, 35*(2), 69–78.

Brown, A., & Cariveau, T. (2022). A systematic review of simultaneous prompting and prompt delay procedures. *Journal of Behavioral Education.* https://doi.org/10.1007/s10864-022-09481-6

Buysse, V., & Wesley, P. (2006). Making sense of evidence-based practice: Reflections and recommendations. In V. Buysse & P. Wesley (Eds.), *Evidence-based practice in the early childhood field* (pp. 225–244). Zero to Three Press.

Cabell, S. Q., DeCosteor, J., LoCasale-Crouch, J., Hamre, B. K., & Pianta, R. C. (2013). Variation in the effectiveness of instructional interactions across preschool classroom settings and learning activities. *Early Childhood Research Quarterly, 28*(4), 820–830.

Carnahan, C., Harte, H., Schumacher-Dyke, K., Hume, K., & Borders, C. (2011). Structured work systems: Supporting meaningful engagement in preschool settings for children with autism spectrum disorders. *Young Exceptional Children, 14*(1), 2–16.

Collier, M., Keefe, E. B., & Hirrel, L. A. (2015). Preparing special education teachers to collaborate with families. *School Community Journal, 25*(1), 117–136.

CONNECT. (2018). *5-step learning cycle.* https://connectmodules.dec-sped.org/connect-modules/5-step-learning-cycle/

Coogle, C., Storie, S., & Rahn, N. (2022). A framework for promoting access, increasing participation, and providing support in early childhood classrooms. *Early Childhood Education Journal, 50*, 867–877.

Cook, R., Klein, D., & Chen, D. (2020). *Adapting early childhood curricula for children with special needs*(10th ed.). Pearson Education.

DeArment, S., Xu, Y., & Coleman, S. (2016). Optimizing accessibility through universal design for learning. In T. Catalino & L. Meyer (Eds.), *DEC recommended practices monograph no. 2: Environment: Promoting meaningful access, participation, and inclusion* (pp. 33–50). Division for Early Childhood.

Division for Early Childhood. (2014). *DEC recommended practices for early intervention/early childhood special education.* http://www.dec-sped.org/recommendedpractices

Division for Early Childhood & National Association for the Education of Young Children. (2009). *Early childhood inclusion: A joint position statement of the Division for Early Childhood (DEC) and the National Association for the Education of Young Children (NAEYC).* University of North Carolina, FPG Child Development Institute.

Favazza, P., & Ostrosky, M. (2016). *The Making Friends Program: Supporting acceptance in your K–2 classroom.* Paul H. Brookes.

Favazza, P., Ostrosky, M., de Boer, A., & Rademaker, F. (2022). How do we support the peer acceptance of children with disabilities? In M. Jones (Ed.) *Peer relationships in classroom management* (pp. 72–90). Routledge.

Gargiulo, R., & Bouck, E. (2021). *Special education in contemporary society: An introduction to exceptionality*(7th ed.). SAGE.

Gomez, C., Walls, S., & Baird, S. (2007). On the same page: Seeking fidelity of intervention. *Young Exceptional Children, 10*(4), 20–29.

Grisham-Brown, J., & Hemmeter, M. (2017). *Blended practices for teaching young children in inclusive settings*(2nd ed.). Paul H. Brookes.

Gulboy, E., Yucesoy-Ozkah, S., & Rakap, S. (2023). Embedded instruction for young children with disabilities: A systematic review and meta-analysis of single-case experimental research studies. *Early Childhood Research Quarterly, 63*, 181–193.

Guralnick, M., & Bruder, M. (2016). Early childhood inclusion in the United States. *Infants & Young Children, 29*(3), 166–177.

Horn, E., Parks, S., & An, Z. (2019). Inclusive special education for young learners with severe and multiple disabilities. In F. Obiakor & J. Bakken (Eds.) *Special education for young learners with disabilities: Advances in special education.* (Vol. 34, pp. 119–137). Emerald.

Johnson, J., Rahn, N., & Bricker, D. (2015). *An activity-based approach to early intervention*(4th ed.). Paul H. Brookes.

Kang, V., & Kim, S. (2022). Effects of enhanced milieu teaching and book reading on the target word approximations of young children with language delay. *Journal of Early Intervention.* https://doi.org/10.1177/10538151221092406

Lane, L., Stanton-Chapman, T., Jamison, K., & Phillips, A. (2007). Teacher and parent expectations of preschoolers' behaviors: Social skills necessary for success. *Topics in Early Childhood Special Education, 27*(1), 86–97.

Lewis, R., Wheeler, J., & Carter, S. (2017). *Teaching special education students in general education classrooms*(9th ed.). Pearson Education.

Linder, T. (2008). *Transdisciplinary play-based intervention*(2nd ed.). Paul H. Brookes.

Love, H., & Horn, E. (2021). Definition, context, quality: Current issues in research examining high-quality inclusive education. *Topics in Early Childhood Education, 40*(4), 204–216.

Martinez, J., Waters, C., Conroy, M., & Reinchow, B. (2021). Peer-mediated interventions to address social competence needs of young children with ASD: Systematic review of single-case research design studies. *Topics in Early Childhood Special Education, 40*(4), 217–228.

Mickelson, A., Correa, V., & Stayton, V. (2022). Early childhood and early intervention/early childhood special education: Reflecting on the past, paving a path forward. *Teacher Education and Special Education, 45*(2), 101–122.

Morgan, C., Du, K., & Friesen, A. (2021). Responding to difference: Enacting inclusive early education through the social relations approach. *Young Exceptional Children, 24*(3), 170–187.

Morris, P. (2022). *A quasi-experimental design: Impacts of shared-book reading on young black children's identity formation*[Doctoral dissertation, University of Nevada, Las Vegas].

National Association for the Education of Young Children. (2022). *Developmentally appropriate practice in early childhood programs serving children from birth through age 8*(4th ed.). NAEYC.

Noonan, M., & McCormick, L. (2014). *Young children with disabilities in natural environments*(2nd ed.). Paul H, Brookes.

Odom, S., Buysse, V., & Soukakou, E. (2011). Inclusion for young children with disabilities: A quarter century of research perspectives. *Journal of Early Intervention, 33*(4), 344–356.

Ok, M., Rao, K., Bryant, B., & McDougall, D. (2017). Universal design for learning in pre-k to grade 12 classrooms: A systematic review of research. *Exceptionality, 25*(2), 116–138.

Ostrosky, M., Mouzourou, C., Dorsey, E., Favazza, P., & Leboeuf, L. (2013). Using children's books to support positive attitudes toward peers with disabilities. *Young Exceptional Children, 18*(1), 30–43.

Pullum, M., King, S., & Kennedy, K. (2022). Structured teaching and the play of preschoolers with developmental disabilities: An evaluation. *Topics in Early Childhood Special Education, 42*(1), 105–117.

Rausch, A., Joseph, J., Strain, P., & Steed, E. (2021). Fostering engagement within inclusive settings: The role of the physical-social-temporal environment in early childhood settings. *Young Children, 76*(4), 16–21.

Ronfeldt, M., Farmer, S., McQueen, K., & Grissom, J. (2015). Teacher collaboration in instructional teams and student achievement. *American Educational Research Journal, 52*(3), 475–514.

Rous, B., McLaughlin, T., & Sandall, S. (2020). Transition: Introduction and overview. In B. Rous, T. McLaughlin, & S. Sandall (Eds.). *Division for Early Childhood recommended practices monograph no. 8: Transition practices* (pp. v–viii). Division for Early Childhood.

Sandall, S., Schwartz, I., Joseph, G., Gaurvreau, A., & Hemmeter, M. (2019). *Building blocks for teaching preschoolers with special needs*(3rd ed.). Paul H. Brookes.

Schwartz, I., & Woods, J. (2015). Making the most of learning opportunities. In Division for Early Childhood (Ed.), *DEC recommended practices monograph no. 1: Enhancing services for young children with disabilities and their families.* Division for Early Childhood.

U.S. Department of Health and Human Services & U.S. Department of Education. (2015). *Policy statement on inclusion of children with disabilities in early childhood programs.* http://www2.ed.gov/policy/speced/guid/earlylearning/joint-statement-full-text.pdf

Vaiouli, P., & Ogle, L. (2015). Music strategies to promote engage and academic growth of young children with ASD in the inclusive classroom. *Young Exceptional Children, 18*(2), 19–28.

CHAPTER 10

Aldridge, J., Kilgo, J., & Bruton, A. (2015). Transforming transdisciplinary early intervention and early childhood special education through intercultural education. *International Journal of Early Childhood Special Education, 7*(2), 343–360.

Aldridge, J., Kilgo, J., & Bruton, A. (2016). Beyond the Brady Bunch: Hybrid families and their evolving relationships with early childhood education. *Childhood Education, 92*(2), 140–148.

Alliance for Technology Access. (2004). *Computer resources for people with disabilities*(4th ed.). Hunter House.

American Federation of Teachers. (2009). *The medically fragile child.*

Annie E. Casey Foundation. (2011). *2011 kids count data book.*

Annie E. Casey Foundation. (2022). *2022 kids count data book.*

Baca, L., & Baca, E. (2004). Bilingual special education: A judicial perspective. In L. Baca & H. Cervantes (Eds.), *The bilingual special education interface*(4th ed., pp. 76–99). Pearson Education.

Baladerian, N., Coleman, T., & Stream, J. (2013). *Abuse of people with disabilities: Victims and their families speak out.* Spectrum Institute.

Bassuk, E., DeCandia, C., Beach, C., & Berman, F. (2014). *America's youngest outcasts: A report card on child homelessness.* National Center on Family Homelessness at the American Institutes for Research.

Bassuk, E., DeCandia, C., & Richard, M. (2015). *Services matter: How housing and services can end family homelessness.* https://www.bassukcenter.org/wpcontent/uploads/2015/11/Services-Matter.pdf

Bayat, M., Mindes, G., & Covitt. S. (2010). What does RTI (response to intervention) look like in preschool? *Early Childhood Education Journal, 37*(6), 493–500.

Bouck, E. (2017). *Assistive technology.* SAGE.

Bruder, M. (2010). Early childhood intervention: A promise to children and families for their future. *Exceptional Children, 76*(3), 339–355.

Busby, J., Ernst, J. V., Kelly, D. P., & DeLuca, V. W. (2019). Professional organizations. *Technology and Engineering Teacher, 78*(6), 18–20.

Carr, C., & Santos, R. (2017). Abuse and young children with disabilities: A review of the literature. *Journal of Early Intervention, 39*(1), 3–17.

Chudzik, M., Corr, C., & Fisher, K. W. (2024). Trauma-informed care: The professional development needs of early childhood special education teachers. *Journal of Early Intervention, 46*(1), 113–129.

Corr, C., Miller, D., & Spence, C. (2018). "... Something is going on": Defining maltreatment and trauma-informed care. In C. Corr, & D. Miller (Eds.), *Maltreatment and toxic stress* (pp. 1–8). (Young Exceptional Children Monograph; No. 17). Division for Early Childhood of the Council for Exceptional Children.

Carta, J., McElhattan, T., & Guerrero, G. (2016). The application of response to intervention to young children with identified disabilities. In B. Reichow, B. Boyd, E. Barton, & S. Odom (Eds.), *Handbook of early childhood special education* (pp. 163–178). Springer.

Child Welfare Information Gateway. (2018). *The risk and prevention of maltreatment of children with disabilities.* https://www.childwelfare.gov/pubPDFs/focus.pdf

Child Witness to Violence Project. (n.d.). *Facts & myths: How many children are exposed to violence*? https://www.childwitnesstoviolence.org/facts--myths.html

Children's Defense Fund. (2019). *Ending child poverty now.*

Children's Defense Fund. (2020). *The state of America's children 2020.*

Children's Defense Fund. (2021). The state of America's children 2021.

Clarke, B., Gersten, R., & Newman-Gonchar, R. (2010). RTI in mathematics. In T. Glover & S. Vaughn (Eds.), *The promise of response to intervention* (pp. 187–203). Guilford Press.

Coleman, M., Roth, R., & West, T. (2009). *Roadmap to pre-K RTI: Applying response to intervention in preschool settings.* http://www.rtinetwork.org/images/roadmaptoprekrti.pdf

Council for Exceptional Children. (1988). *Report to the Council for Exceptional Children ad hoc committee on medically fragile students.*

de Brey, C., Zhang, A., & Duffy, S. (2022). *Digest of education statistics 2020.* https://nces.ed.gov/programs/digest/d20/tables/dt20_702.10.asp

Deiner, P. (2013). *Inclusive early childhood education*(6th ed.). Wadsworth/Cengage Learning.

Dell, A., Newton, D., & Petroff, J. (2017). *Assistive technology in the classroom*(3rd ed.). Pearson Education.

Desch, L. (2019). Assistive technology. In M. Batshaw, N. Roizen, & L. Pellegrino (Eds.), *Children with disabilities*(8th ed., pp. 719–734). Paul H. Brookes.

Division for Early Childhood. (2010). *Position statement on family, culture, values, and language.*https://www.decdocs.org/position-statement-family-culture

Division for Early Childhood. (2014). *DEC recommended practices in early intervention/early childhood special education.* http://www.dec-sped.org/recommendedpractices

Division for Early Childhood. (2016). *Child maltreatment: A position statement of the Division for Early Childhood.*

Division for Early Childhood. (2020a). *Initial Practice-Based Standards for Early Interventionists/Early Childhood Special Educators.* Report. https://www.dec-sped.org/ei-ecse-standards

Division for Early Childhood. (2020b). *DEC priority issues agenda.* http://www.dec-sped.org/PriorityIssues

Division for Early Childhood. (2021). *Multitiered system of support framework in early childhood: Description and implications.* https://www.decdocs.org/position-statement-mtss

Division for Early Childhood. (2022). *Position statement on ethical practice.* https://www.dec-sped.org/single-post/new-position-statement-position-statement-on-ethical-practice

Division for Early Childhood, National Association for the Education of Young Children, & National Head Start Association. (2013). *Framework for response to intervention in early childhood: Description and implications.* https://www.dec-sped.org/position-statements

Doorways. (2022). *The facts about family homelessness.* https://www.doorwaysva.org/our-work/education-advocacy/the-facts-about-family-homelessness/

Downing, J. (2008). *Including students with severe and multiple disabilities in typical classrooms*(3rd ed.). Paul H. Brookes.

Driver, B., & Spady, P. (2013). *What educators can do: Homeless children and youth.* Project HOPE–Virginia. College of William and Mary.

Eddowes, E. (1994). Schools providing safer environments for homeless children. *Childhood Education, 70*, 271–273.

Edelman, M. (2010, November 10). *Marian Wright Edelman's child watch column: The threat of persistent poverty.* https://www.childrensdefense.org/child-watch-columns/health/2010/the-threat-of-persistent-poverty/

Florian, L. (2014). Reimagining special education: Why new approaches are needed. In L. Florian (Ed.), *The Sage handbook of special education*(2nd ed., Vol. 1, pp. 9–22). SAGE.

Fox, L., Carta, J., Strain, P., Dunlap, G., & Hemmeter, M. (2010). Response to intervention and the pyramid model. *Infants & Young Children, 23*(1), 3–13.

Freund, L., & Rich, R. (2005). *Teaching students with learning problems in the inclusive classroom.* Pearson Education.

Gallagher, J., Coleman, M., & Kirk, S. (2023). *Educating exceptional children*(15th ed.). Cengage Learning.

Gargiulo, R. (1990). Child abuse and neglect: An overview. In R. Goldman & R. Gargiulo (Eds.), *Children at risk* (pp. 1–36). Pro-Ed.

Gargiulo, R. (2006). Homeless and disabled: Rights, responsibilities, and recommendations for serving young children with special needs. *Early Childhood Education Journal, 33*(5), 357–362.

Gargiulo, R., & Bouck, E. (2021). *Special education in contemporary society: An introduction to exceptionality*(7th ed.). SAGE.

Gargiulo, R., & Metcalf, D. (2023). *Teaching in today's inclusive classrooms*(4th ed.). Cengage Learning.

Gershoff, E., & Font, S. (2016). Corporal punishment in U.S. public schools: Prevalence, disparities in use, and status in state and federal policy. *Social Policy Report, 30*(1), 1–26.

Gollnick, D., & Chinn, P. (2013). *Multicultural education in a pluralistic society*(9th ed.). Pearson Education.

Gollnick, D., & Chinn, P. (2021). *Multicultural education in a pluralistic society*(11th ed.). Pearson Education.

Hallahan, D., Kauffman, J., & Pullen, P. (2023). *Exceptional learners*(15th ed.). Pearson Education.

Hanson, M. (2011). Diversity in service settings. In E. Lynch & M. Hanson (Eds.), *Developing cross-cultural competence*(4th ed., pp. 2–19). Paul H. Brookes.

Hanson, M., & Espinosa, L. (2016). Culture, ethnicity, and linguistic diversity: Implications for early childhood special education. In B. Reichow, B. Boyd, E. Barton, & S. Odom (Eds.), *Handbook of early childhood special education* (pp. 455–472). Springer.

Hanson, M., Lynch, E., & Wayman, K. (1990). Honoring the cultural diversity of families when gathering data. *Topics in Early Childhood Special Education*, *10*(1), 112–131.

Hanson, M., & Zercher, C. (2001). The impact of cultural and linguistic diversity in inclusive preschool environments. In M. Guralnick (Ed.), *Early childhood inclusion: Focus on change* (pp. 413–431). Paul H. Brookes.

Hooper, S., & Umansky, W. (2014). *Young children with special needs*(6th ed.). Pearson Education.

Howard, V., Williams, B., Miller, D., & Aiken, E. (2014). *Very young children with special needs*(5th ed.). Pearson Education.

Hunter, W., Taylor, J. C., Bester, M., Nichols, S., & Panlilo, C. (2021). Considerations for incorporating trauma-informed care content within special education teacher preparation and professional development programs. *Journal of Special Education Preparation*, *1*(2), 48–55. https://doi.org/10.33043/JOSEP.1.2.48-55

Kids Count Data Center. (2023a). *Children who speak a language other than English at home*. https://datacenter.kidscount.org/data/tables/81-children-who-speak-a-language-other-than-english-at-home#detailed/1/any/false/2048,1729,37,871,870,573,869,36,868,867/any/396,397

Kids Count Data Center. (2023b). *2-year-olds who were immunized in the United States*. https://datacenter.kidscount.org/data/tables/8001-2-year-olds-who-were-immunized? loc=1&loct=1#detailed/1/any/false/1729,37,871,870,573,869,36,868,867,133/any/15387

Kilgo, J. (2022). Our proud heritage: The evolution of family-centered services in early childhood special education. *Young Children*, *77*(4), 84–89.

Kostelnik, M., Soderman, A., Whiren, A., & Rupiper, M. (2019). *Developmentally appropriate curriculum*(7th ed.). Pearson Education.

Legano, L., Desch, L., Messner, S., Idzerda, S., Flaherty, E., Council on Child Abuse and Neglect, Council on Children with Disabilities, Haney, S., Sirotnak, A., Gavril, A., Girardet, R., Gilmartin, A., Laskey, A., Mohr, B., Nienow, S., Rosado, N., Kuo, D., Apkon, S., Davidson, L., Ellerbeck, K., Foster, J., Hyman, S., ... Yin, L. (2021). Maltreatment of children with disabilities. *Pediatrics*, *147*(5), e20221050920. doi:10.1542/peds.2021-050920

Leverson, M., Smith, K., McIntosh, K., Rose, J., & Pinkelman, S. (2021). *PBIS cultural responsiveness field guide: Resources for trainers and coaches*. Center on Positive Behavioral Interventions & Supports. https://www.pbis.org

Lindo, E. J. (2021). View from the CEC Division for Culturally and Linguistically Diverse Exceptional Learners (DDEL): Committed to advancing cultural competence and culturally sustaining pedagogy. *Teaching Exceptional Children*, *53*(1), 10–11. https://doi.org/jz4g

Lindo, E. J., & Lim, O. J. (2020, Spring). Becoming more culturally competent educators. *Perspectives on Language and Literacy*, *46*, 33–38. https://dyslexiaida.org/perspectives/

Lindo, E. J., & Lim, O. J. (Spring, 2020). Becoming more culturally competent educators. *Perspectives on Language and Literacy*, *46*, 33–38. https://dyslexiaida.org/perspectives/

Lustig, M., Koester, J., & Halualani, R. (2018). *Intercultural competence: Interpersonal communication across cultures*(8th ed.). Pearson Education.

Lynch, E., & Hanson, M. (2011). *Developing cross-cultural competence*(4th ed.). Paul H. Brookes.

Mancini, K., & Layton, C. (2004). Meeting fears and concerns effectively: The inclusion of early childhood students who are medically fragile. *Physical Disabilities: Education and Related Services*, *22*(2), 29–48.

Meyer, A., Rose, D., & Gordon, D. (2014). *Universal design for learning: Theory and practice*. CAST Professional Publishing.

Morrison, G., Breffni, L., & Woika, M. (2022). *Early childhood education today*(15th ed.). Pearson Education.

National Association for the Education of Young Children. (2022). *Developmentally appropriate practice in early childhood programs serving children from birth through age 8*. (4th ed.).

National Center on Child Abuse and Neglect. (1986). *Child abuse and neglect: An informed approach to a shared concern*(No. 20–01016).

National Coalition for the Homeless. (2023). *Homelessness in America*. https://nationalhomeless.org/about-homelessness/

National Professional Development Center on Inclusion. (2012). *Response to intervention (RTI) in early childhood*. University of North Carolina, FPG Child Development Institute.

Noonan, M., & McCormick, L. (2014). *Teaching young children with disabilities in natural environments*(2nd ed.). Paul H. Brookes.

O'Connor, R., Sanchez, V., & Kim, J. (2017). Responsiveness to intervention and multi-tiered systems of support for reducing reading difficulties and identifying learning disability. In J. Kauffman, D. Hallahan, & P. Pullen (Eds.), *Handbook of special education*(2nd ed., pp. 189–202). Routledge.

Orkwis, R. (2003). *Universally designed instruction*. https://eric.ed.gov/?id=ED475386

Orkwis, R., & McLane, K. (1998, Fall). *A curriculum every student can use: Design principles for student access*. ERIC/OSEP Topical Brief, ERIC Clearinghouse on Disabilities and Gifted. (ERIC Document Reproduction Service No. ED 423 654)

Pisha, B., & Coyne, P. (2001). Smart from the start: The promise of universal design for learning. *Remedial and Special Education*, *22*(4), 197–203.

Pollard, D. (2016). Understanding and supporting gender equity in schools. In J. Banks & C. Banks (Eds.), *Multicultural education issues and perspectives*(9th ed., pp. 115–131). Wiley.

Rose, D., & Meyer, A. (2002). *Teaching every student in the digital age: Universal design for learning*. Association for Supervision and Curriculum Development.

Rueve, B., Robinson, M., Worthington, L., & Gargiulo, R. (2000). Children with special health needs in inclusive settings: Writing health care plans. *Physical Disabilities Education and Related Services*, *19*(1), 11–24.

Sadao, K., & Robinson, N. (2010). *Assistive technology for young children*. Paul H. Brookes.

Sandall, S., Hemmeter, L., Smith, B., & McLean, B. (2005). *DEC recommended practices*. Sopris West.

Santos, M. (2017). *The most frequently asked questions on the educational rights of children and youth in homeless situations*. National Association for the Education of Homeless Children and Youth & National Law Center on Homelessness and Poverty.

https://naehcy.org/wp-content/uploads/2018/02/2017-10-16_NAEHCY-FAQs.pdf

Smith, D., Tyler, N., & Skow, K. (2018). *Introduction to contemporary special education*(2nd ed.). Pearson Education.

Stalker, K., McArthur, K. (2012). Child abuse, child protection and disabled children: A review of recent research. *Child Abuse Review, 21*(1), 24–40.

Stayton, V., Kilgo, J., Horn, E., Kemp, P., & Bruder, M. B. (2023). Standards for early intervention/early childhood special education: The development, uses, and vision for the future. *Topics in Early Childhood Special Education, 0*(0). https://doi.org/10.1177/02711214231165192

Sugai, G. (2022). *School-wide positive behavior support and response to intervention.* RTI Action Network. http://www.rtinetwork.org/learn/behavior-supports/schoolwide behavior

Taie, S., & Goldring, R. (2020). *Characteristics of public and private elementary and secondary school teachers in the United States.* https://nces.ed.gov/pubs2020/2020142.pdf

Tiedt, P., & Tiedt, I. (2002). *Multicultural teaching: A handbook of activities, information, and resources*(6th ed.). Allyn & Bacon.

Turchi, R., & Giardino, A. (2019). Medical home and health care systems. In M. Batshaw, N. Roizen, & L. Pellegrino (Eds.), *Children with disabilities*(8th ed., pp. 799–821). Paul H. Brookes.

United States Census. (2020). *Selected characteristics of the total and native populations in the United States.* https://data.census.gov/cedsci/table? tid=ACSST5Y2020.S0601

U.S. Department of Health and Human Services. (2023a). *Child maltreatment 2021.* https://www.acf.hhs.gov/cb/data-research/child-maltreatment

U.S. Department of Health and Human Services. (2023b). *HHS poverty guidelines for 2023.* https://aspe.hhs.gov/topics/poverty-economic-mobility/poverty-guidelines

U.S. English. (2022). *About U.S. English.* https://www.usenglish.org/us-states-official-english-laws/

VanDerHeyden, A. (2023). *Using RTI to improve learning in mathematics.* RTI Action Network. http://www.rtinetwork.org/learn/what/rtiandmath

Vaughn, S., & Bos, C. (2020). *Strategies for teaching students with learning or behavior problems*(10th ed.). Pearson Education.

Wissick, C., & Gardner, J. (2011). Technology and academic instruction. In J. Kauffman & D. Hallahan (Eds.), *Handbook of special education* (pp. 484–500). Routledge.

Zabala, J. (1995, March). *The SETT framework: Critical areas to consider when making informed assistive technology decisions.* Paper presented to the Florida Assistive Technology Impact Conference, Orlando. (ERIC Document Reproduction Service No. ED381962)

Zabala, J. (2005). Ready, SETT, go! Getting started with the SETT framework. *Closing the Gap, 23*(6), 1–3.

INDEX

Made in the USA
Las Vegas, NV
10 January 2025

16152568R00260